ALGEBRA I

Isidore Dressler

Author of
  Current Mathematics: A Work-Text, Book 1
  Preliminary Mathematics
  Geometry
  Algebra Two
  Algebra Two and Trigonometry
  Trigonometry
  Integrated Mathematics: Course I
  Integrated Mathematics: Course II

Dedicated to serving

AMSCO

our nation's youth

When ordering this book, you may specify:

either R 27 H *or* ALGEBRA I, HARDBOUND EDITION

AMSCO SCHOOL PUBLICATIONS, INC.
315 Hudson Street   New York, N.Y. 10013

ISBN   0-87720-208-7

PRINTED IN THE UNITED STATES OF AMERICA

PREFACE

Today, groups of professional mathematicians, as well as teachers of mathematics, are suggesting that significant changes be made in the elementary algebra course. These changes concern themselves not only with the content of the course, but also with its organization and the methods to be used in teaching it.

Algebra I was written to meet the changing needs of both the student and the teacher of elementary algebra. The book, therefore, is modern in concept, includes topics not previously included in a traditional elementary algebra course: the basic concepts and language of sets, the properties of numbers, absolute value, the function concept, inequalities, a broader role of the coordinate plane, and deductive proof of algebraic theorems.

The major purpose of the book is twofold: (1) to aid the student in understanding the basic concepts of elementary algebra, and (2) to help him acquire the important manipulative algebraic skills. Although the text presents a modern structural approach, the author has avoided an extremely rigorous treatment of the subject matter. The topics are developed on a level appropriate to the mathematical maturity and sophistication of the average student.

Algebra I, which treats fully the topics included in a modern elementary algebra course, is organized so that it can be used by the teacher in conjunction with the various textbooks now in use. The methods used in presenting the subject matter will help the student to understand and master the material that he studies. The book makes available to both the student and the teacher an abundance of exercises, model problems, and instructional materials. These may be used as a supplement to the class textbook, and may also be used as a source book for remedial and review work.

An unusual feature of the book is its method of organization. Each chapter contains a series of learning units which, with proper application, the student can master by himself. The basic concepts of the unit are carefully developed with the use of simple language and symbolism. New words are clearly defined. Explanations and teaching problems lead to the statement of important general principles and procedures. These principles and procedures are then stated clearly and concisely. Model problems, whose solutions are accompanied by detailed, step-by-step explanations, teach the student how to apply the principles and follow the procedures. The student completes his mastery of the unit by doing a series of carefully graded exercises. The exercises cover almost every type of difficulty and test the student's understanding of basic concepts as well as his mastery of manipulative skills.

—I. D.

CONTENTS

CHAPTER I

SYMBOLS, NUMBERS, AND NUMERALS

1. Symbols and Numerals

SYMBOLS FOR OBJECTS, PERSONS, AND IDEAS

A *symbol* may be a picture or a written word that is used to represent an object, a person, or an idea. For example, represents a glass, "George Washington" represents a person, and "democracy" represents an idea.

We generally use quotation marks, " ", when we refer to the symbol for an object, a person, or an idea rather than to the thing itself. For example, a bird has a head, whereas "bird" has four letters. However, when there can be no confusion as to whether we are talking about the object itself or about the symbol for the object, we omit the quotation marks. Thus, when George Washington is written on a blackboard, it is obvious that the name of a person, not the person himself, appears there.

It may be possible to represent the same object, person, or idea by several different symbols. For example, "George Washington" and "the father of our country" are different symbols for the same person.

SYMBOLS FOR NUMBERS

In your study of arithmetic, you used symbols to represent numbers. In algebra, we will work with the numbers of arithmetic and we will use their customary names and symbols. Number names or number symbols are called *numerals* or *numerical expressions.*

Remember that a numeral and the number it represents are not the same thing. A number is an idea that we can talk about and think about; a numeral is the name or symbol for a number. We know, for example, that the number 8 is larger than the number 6. In the figure, however, the numeral "6" is larger than the numeral "8."

SYMBOLS FOR OPERATIONS

The symbol "+" is used to indicate the operation of *addition*. The numeral "6 + 2" represents the result obtained when 2 is added to 6. The result, 8, is called the **sum.**

The symbol "×" is used to indicate the operation of *multiplication*. The numeral "6 × 2" represents the result obtained when 2 is multiplied by 6. The result, 12, is called the **product.**

The symbol "−" is used to indicate the operation of *subtraction*. The numeral "6 − 2" represents the result obtained when 2 is subtracted from 6. The result, 4, is called the **difference.**

The symbol "÷" is used to indicate the operation of *division*. The numeral "6 ÷ 2" represents the result obtained when 6 is divided by 2. The result, 3, is called the **quotient.** The fraction "$\frac{6}{2}$" also indicates a quotient which is the result of dividing 6 by 2.

Since addition, multiplication, subtraction, and division are operations which are performed on two numbers, each of these operations is called a **binary operation.**

A number may be represented by many numerals. For example, each of the following numerals may be used as a number name for a collection of eight objects:

"8"	"eight"	"VIII"	"ocho"
"6 + 2"	"18 − 10"	"4 × 2"	"6400 ÷ 800"

Note that "8" is probably the simplest looking of all the preceding numerals, each of which represents the number eight.

Exercises

1. Select three different objects and give a symbol for each object.
2. Select three different persons and give a symbol for each person.
3. Select three different ideas and give a symbol for each idea.

In 4–19, each sentence contains an underlined symbol. State whether the sentence refers to the object, person, or idea, or whether the sentence refers only to the symbol itself.

4. A house has a roof.
5. House ends with an *e*.
6. Buffalo is a word which has two *f*'s.
7. A buffalo is an animal.

8. <u>Pen</u> is used to represent two different things.

9. He wrote with the <u>pen</u>.

10. <u>Franklin D. Roosevelt</u> was a President of the United States.

11. <u>Franklin D. Roosevelt</u> appears in many books.

12. <u>Ruth</u> is a short girl.

13. <u>Ruth</u> is a short name.

14. Mr. Crane selected <u>Tom</u> as his companion.

15. Mr. Crane selected <u>Tom</u> as his son's name.

16. <u>Honesty</u> is the best policy.

17. He wrote <u>honesty</u> in his notebook.

18. Robert spelled <u>beauty</u> incorrectly.

19. She walks in <u>beauty</u> like the night.

20. Give two different symbols for the same   (a) object   (b) person   (c) idea.

In 21–24, tell which number every numeral in each exercise represents.

21. $3 + 1$ $6 - 2$ 4×1 $12 \div 3$ IV

22. $12 - 3$ $36 \div 4$ $8\frac{1}{2} + \frac{1}{2}$ $36 \times \frac{1}{4}$ IX

23. $5 - 5$ 7×0 $\frac{1}{2} - \frac{1}{2}$ $.7 - .7$ 0×1

24. $.5$ $\frac{1}{4} + \frac{1}{4}$ $1\frac{1}{2} - 1$ $\frac{25}{50}$ 50%

25. Write five different numerals for each of the following numbers:

    a. 6   b. 20   c. 100   d. 1   e. 0   f. $\frac{1}{4}$

In 26–33, state whether the two numerals represent the same number.

26. $5 + 3$, $16 \div 2$ 27. 8×1, 12×1 28. 8×0, 4×0 29. $\frac{1}{3} + \frac{1}{3}$, $\frac{1}{2} + \frac{1}{4}$

30. $6 + 4$, $4 + 6$ 31. 5×7, 7×5 32. $8 \div 2$, $2 \div 8$ 33. 7×0, $7 - 0$

In 34–37, four of the five numerals in each exercise represent the same number. Select the numeral which represents a number different from this number.

34. $8 + 4$ $36 - 24$ 12×0 $24 \div 2$ $6 \div \frac{1}{2}$

35. 8×1 $8 - 0$ $1.5 + 6.5$ $80 \div 100$ 800%

36. $5 \times \frac{1}{5}$ $\frac{1}{2} + \frac{1}{2}$ $3\frac{2}{3} - 2\frac{2}{3}$ $1.25 \div 1.25$ 1%

37. $2 \times .15$ $\frac{1}{10} + \frac{1}{5}$ $.03 \times 10$ $\frac{4}{15} - \frac{1}{5}$ 30%

In 38–53, write a simpler looking numeral for each given numeral.

38. $\frac{3}{5} + \frac{7}{5}$ 39. $75 + 1.25$ 40. $\frac{3}{4} + \frac{5}{8}$ 41. $35 + 1.05$

42. $\frac{12}{7} - \frac{5}{7}$ 43. $4.65 - 2.25$ 44. $\frac{7}{8} - \frac{2}{8}$ 45. $\frac{15}{3} - \frac{1}{2}$

46. $12 \times \frac{1}{3}$ 47. $\frac{21}{2} \times \frac{1}{7}$ 48. $\frac{1}{4} \times 4$ 49. $2.5 \times .64$

50. $6 - .35$ 51. 1.25×4 52. $6.28 \div 4$ 53. $60 \div 1.25$

2. The Numbers of Arithmetic

Let us recall the numbers with which you became familiar when you studied arithmetic. We shall refer to these numbers as the *numbers of arithmetic.*

COUNTING NUMBERS OR NATURAL NUMBERS

In your study of arithmetic, you learned how to count. You know that when we count, we start with a first number which is named "one," or "1." The number which follows 1 is named "two," or "2." The number 2 is called the *successor* of the number 1. The number 2 in turn has a successor which is named "three," or "3." Each counting number has a successor which is 1 more than the number. Because of this, the process of counting is endless; there is no last counting number.

The *counting numbers,* which are also called *natural numbers,* are represented by the symbols:

$$1, 2, 3, 4, 5, 6, 7, 8, 9, 10, 11, 12, \ldots$$

The three dots after the 12 indicate that the numbers continue in the same pattern without end.

The first ten natural numbers may be represented by the symbols:

$$1, 2, 3, 4, \ldots, 10$$

The three dots after the 4 indicate that the numbers continue in the same pattern until 10 is reached.

WHOLE NUMBERS

The number zero is not one of the counting numbers. Therefore, 0 is not a natural number. The number zero, together with all the natural numbers, forms a new collection of numbers called *whole numbers.* The whole numbers are represented by the symbols:

$$0, 1, 2, 3, 4, 5, 6, 7, 8, 9, 10, 11, 12, \ldots$$

FRACTIONS

In arithmetic you learned several meanings of a *fraction.* We shall say that *a fraction is a symbol which indicates the quotient of two numbers.* You are familiar with fractions like $\frac{1}{2}$, $\frac{3}{4}$, $\frac{12}{5}$, $\frac{8}{8}$, and $\frac{20}{10}$.

There are many different fractions which name the same number. For example, each of the different symbols $\frac{6}{2}$, $\frac{9}{3}$, $\frac{12}{4}$, and $\frac{36}{12}$ is a fraction which names the number 3.

Mixed numbers are numbers that are named by symbols such as $1\frac{1}{4}$, $4\frac{2}{3}$, $5\frac{3}{8}$. Note that a mixed number is the sum of a whole number and a proper fraction. A mixed number may be named by many different fractions. For example, the number named by $1\frac{1}{4}$ can be represented by the fractions $\frac{5}{4}$, $\frac{10}{8}$, $\frac{15}{12}$, etc.

Decimal fractions are numbers which are named by symbols such as .4, .23, .035, 2.5. They can also be represented by quotients. For example, the number named by .4 can be represented by $\frac{4}{10}$, $\frac{2}{5}$, $\frac{8}{20}$, etc.

RATIONAL NUMBERS

If a number can be represented by a fraction which indicates the quotient of a whole number divided by a natural number, the number is called a *rational number.*

For example, $\frac{1}{2}$, $\frac{2}{3}$, $1\frac{1}{4}$, .4, 3, and 0 are rational numbers.

The whole numbers are included among the rational numbers because any whole number can be represented as a fraction which indicates the quotient of that number and 1. For example:

$$0 = \frac{0}{1} \qquad 1 = \frac{1}{1} \qquad 2 = \frac{2}{1} \qquad 3 = \frac{3}{1} \qquad 5 = \frac{5}{1} \qquad 10 = \frac{10}{1}$$

Therefore, we see that all the numbers of arithmetic which we have discussed are rational numbers.

For reasons that we shall learn later, we may not divide a number by zero. For example, $\frac{5}{0}$ has no value because it does not name any number. We say that division by zero is meaningless.

We shall learn later that not all fractions represent rational numbers. We shall also learn to work with additional rational numbers which are not among the numbers of arithmetic we have studied.

Exercises

1. Name the first counting number.
2. Name the successor of each of the following natural numbers:
   - *a.* 75   *b.* 120   *c.* 999   *d.* 514,621   *e.* 64,499,999
3. State a rule for finding the successor of a given natural number.
4. Name a number which is a whole number but is not a natural number.
5. Write four fractions that are different names for each of the following numbers:
   - *a.* 4   *b.* 9   *c.* 12   *d.* 50   *e.* 0
6. Write four fractions that are different names for each of the following fractions:
   - *a.* $\frac{1}{2}$ *b.* $\frac{3}{4}$ *c.* $\frac{4}{6}$ *d.* $\frac{8}{5}$ *e.* $\frac{7}{1}$

7. Write four fractions that are different names for each of the following decimal fractions:

   a. .6   *b.* .25   *c.* .80   *d.* 1.5   *e.* 2.75

8. Write four fractions that are different names for each of the following mixed numbers:

   a. $1\frac{1}{4}$ *b.* $2\frac{1}{2}$ *c.* $4\frac{3}{4}$ *d.* $10\frac{1}{5}$ *e.* $12\frac{2}{3}$

9. State which of the numbers 0, 3, 5, $\frac{1}{5}$, $1\frac{1}{4}$ are   (*a*) natural numbers (*b*) whole numbers   (*c*) rational numbers.

10. State which of the symbols 0, 1, $\frac{0}{1}$, $\frac{1}{0}$ represent   (*a*) natural numbers (*b*) whole numbers   (*c*) rational numbers.

In 11–22, state whether the sentence is true or false.

11. Every counting number is a natural number.
12. Every natural number is a whole number.
13. Every whole number is a natural number.
14. Every natural number has a successor.
15. There is a first counting number.
16. There is a last natural number.
17. A whole number may be represented by many different fractions.
18. Every fraction names a whole number.
19. Every whole number is a rational number.
20. Every rational number is a whole number.
21. Every rational number may be represented as a fraction.
22. Every fraction represents a rational number.

3. The Number Line

If we think of a straight line as a collection or set of points, we can **associate** (make correspond) all the numbers of arithmetic (rational numbers) with points on the line. Such a line is called a **number line.**

To construct a number line, we choose two points on a straight line. We label the one at the left "0" and the one at the right "1." We use the length of the segment from 0 to 1 as a unit of measure to mark off equally spaced points to the right of 1. The numbers 2, 3, 4, etc. are assigned to these points as shown.

The arrowhead indicates that the number line extends without end to the right. Therefore, it is possible to associate every whole number with a point on the line. Note that every point that we have located on the line is associated with a whole number.

Consider a number line on which points have been associated with whole numbers. If we divide the intervals between whole numbers into halves, thirds, quarters, etc., we can label additional points as shown.

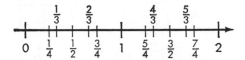

On the number line, each point that has been located is associated with a rational number. The number which is associated with a point on the number line is called the **coordinate** of that point. The point on the number line which is associated with a number is called the **graph** of that number.

Notice that on a number line the point which is associated with the smaller of two numbers is to the left of the point which is associated with the larger of the two numbers. For example, the number 1 is less than the number 2; the point labeled 1 lies to the left of the point labeled 2. Any number less than 1 corresponds to a point to the left of 1. On the other hand, any number greater than 1 corresponds to a point to the right of 1.

When we say that 1 is **between** 0 and 2, we mean that 1 is greater than 0 but less than 2; also, the graph of 1 is to the right of the graph of 0 but to the left of the graph of 2.

No matter how close two points may be on a number line, there are always an endless number of points between them. These points can be graphed (determined) by dividing the interval between the points which are associated with the whole numbers into more and more equal parts. For example, the interval between the points which are associated with the numbers 0 and 1 can be divided first into halves, then into thirds, then into fourths, etc., thus obtaining an infinite number of points. Therefore, there are infinitely many numbers that can be named between any two given numbers, no matter how close together they may be. For example, since $\frac{1}{2}$ may also be named $\frac{12}{24}$, and $\frac{2}{3}$ may also be named $\frac{16}{24}$, the numbers $\frac{13}{24}$, $\frac{14}{24}$, and $\frac{15}{24}$ are between $\frac{1}{2}$ and $\frac{2}{3}$. Similarly, since $\frac{1}{2}$ may also be named $\frac{24}{48}$, and $\frac{2}{3}$ may also be named $\frac{32}{48}$, the numbers $\frac{25}{48}$, $\frac{26}{48}$, . . . , $\frac{31}{48}$ are between $\frac{1}{2}$ and $\frac{2}{3}$. You can see that this process is endless.

From our previous discussion, we see that every rational number can be associated with a point on a number line. It might also appear that every point on a number line has been associated with some rational number. However, this is not true. Later we will learn that there are infinitely many points on a number line which cannot be associated with rational numbers. We will associate these points with other collections of numbers which we will study.

～～～～～～～～ MODEL PROBLEMS ～～～～～～～～

Use the number line in the figure to answer questions 1–10.

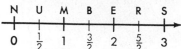

1. Name the number assigned to point S.   *Ans.* 3

2. Name the coordinate of point M.   *Ans.* 1

3. Name the point which is the graph of $\frac{1}{2}$.   *Ans.* U

4. Name the point which is the graph of $1\frac{1}{2}$.   *Ans.* B

5. Name the points which are associated with natural numbers.   *Ans.* M, E, S

6. Name the points which are the graphs of whole numbers.   *Ans.* N, M, E, S

7. Name the points which are the graphs of fractions.   *Ans.* U, B, R

8. Name the points which are the graphs of rational numbers.   *Ans.* N, U, M, B, E, R, S

9. Name the point which is the graph of a whole number that is not a natural number.   *Ans.* N

10. Give three additional numerals which can be used to represent the coordinate of point M.   *Ans.* $\frac{2}{2}, \frac{3}{3}, \frac{4}{4}$

11. On the number line shown at the right, locate the points that can be associated with the numbers   (a) $\frac{1}{3}$ (b) .5   (c) $\frac{20}{20}$ (d) $1\frac{2}{3}$ (e) 1.8.

Answer:

a. Point G, which is $\frac{1}{3}$ of the way from M to A.

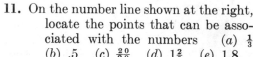

b. Point R, which is $\frac{1}{2}$ of the way from M to A. (Remember that .5 names the same number as $\frac{1}{2}$.)

c. Point A. (Remember that $\frac{20}{20}$ names the same number as 1.)

  d. Point *P*, which is $\frac{2}{3}$ of the way from *A* to *T*. (Remember that $1\frac{2}{3}$ names the same number as $\frac{5}{3}$.)

  e. Point *H*, which is $\frac{4}{5}$ of the way from *A* to *T*. (Remember that 1.8 names the same number as $\frac{18}{10}$ or $\frac{9}{5}$.)

12. *a.* How many whole numbers are there be-   *Ans.* Two
tween 3 and 6?

  b. List these numbers.   *Ans.* 4, 5

13. *a.* How many numbers are there between 3
and 6?   *Ans.* Infinitely many

  b. List four numbers between 3 and 6.   *Ans.* 3.5, $\frac{13}{3}$, 5, $5\frac{1}{2}$

Exercises

In 1–4, name the number which can be associated with each of the labeled points on the number line.

1.

2.
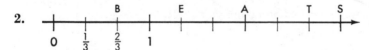

3.
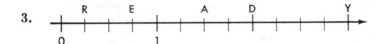

4.

5. Draw a number line and on it locate the points whose coordinates are:

  a. $\frac{1}{2}, \frac{3}{2}, \frac{6}{2}, \frac{9}{2}, \frac{11}{2}$ *b.* $\frac{1}{3}, \frac{2}{3}, \frac{5}{3}, \frac{6}{3}, \frac{13}{3}, \frac{15}{3}$

  c. $\frac{1}{4}, \frac{3}{4}, \frac{6}{4}, \frac{8}{4}, \frac{13}{4}, \frac{16}{4}$ *d.* $\frac{1}{10}, \frac{5}{10}, \frac{9}{10}, \frac{13}{10}, \frac{25}{10}, \frac{30}{10}$

  e. $\frac{1}{5}, \frac{3}{5}, \frac{9}{5}, \frac{10}{5}, 2\frac{1}{5}, 3\frac{2}{5}$ *f.* .1, .3, .7, 1.0, 2.7, 3.4

  g. $\frac{1}{4}, \frac{1}{2}, \frac{3}{8}, 1\frac{1}{4}, 2.25, \frac{25}{8}$ *h.* $\frac{1}{4}, \frac{1}{3}, \frac{5}{12}, \frac{9}{6}, 2\frac{1}{2}, 3.75$

  i. rational numbers represented by fractions whose denominators are 3, beginning with $\frac{1}{3}$ and ending with $\frac{15}{3}$

In 6–11, use the following number line:

6. Name the point which is the graph of the number:

    a. 1   *b.* $\frac{8}{4}$ *c.* $1\frac{3}{4}$ *d.* $2\frac{1}{2}$ *e.* .5   *f.* 1.25   *g.* 2.75

7. Give three different names for the coordinate of each of the following points:

    a. E   *b. C*   *c. D*   *d. G*   *e. L*

8. Name the points which are associated with natural numbers.

9. Name the points which are the graphs of whole numbers.

10. Name the points which are the graphs of rational numbers.

11. Name the point which is the graph of a whole number that is not a natural number.

12. State the number of natural numbers there are between:

    a. 0 and 1   *b.* 2 and 3   *c.* 2 and 6   *d.* 1 and 10

13. List the natural numbers between:

    a. 2 and 6   *b.* 3 and 8   *c.* 1 and 10   *d.* 12 and 17

In 14–17: (*a*) State the number of rational numbers there are between the given numbers. (*b*) List three numbers between the given numbers.

14. 5, 6   **15.** $\frac{5}{100}$, $\frac{6}{100}$ **16.** .4, .5   **17.** .24, .25

In 18–29: (*a*) State whether on a number line the graph of the first number lies to the left or to the right of the graph of the second number. (*b*) State whether the first number is smaller or greater than the second number.

18. 12, 18	**19.** 29, 23	**20.** $\frac{9}{2}$, $\frac{4}{2}$	**21.** $\frac{1}{4}$, $\frac{1}{8}$
22. $3\frac{2}{3}$, $5\frac{1}{3}$	**23.** 3.9, 1.3	**24.** 3.1, 9.3	**25.** .5, .05
26. 11, 110	**27.** .47, 4.7	**28.** 6.4, 6.45	**29.** .95, .905

30. Name a number which is between:

    a. 8 and 9   *b.* .8 and .9   *c.* 3.21 and 3.22   *d.* 4.666 and 4.667

4. Comparing Numbers

SYMBOL OF EQUALITY

The equal sign, =, is read "equals" or "is equal to." When the symbol = is placed between two numerals, it indicates that the numerals represent the same number. To indicate that the numerals "7 + 2" and "5 + 4" both represent the same number, 9, we write "7 + 2 = 5 + 4" which is read "seven plus two equals five plus four."

A statement that two numerals represent the same number is called an **equality**. Such a statement may be a true statement or it may be a false statement. For example, 7 + 2 = 5 + 4 is a true statement because 7 + 2 represents the number 9 and 5 + 4 also represents the number 9. But 7 − 2 = 5 − 4 is a false statement because 7 − 2 represents the number 5, whereas 5 − 4 represents the number 1.

Exercises

In 1–12, state whether the statement is true or false. Give a reason for your answer.

1. 5 + 4 = 4 + 5   **2.** 12 × 4 = 4 × 12   **3.** 5 − 3 = 3 − 5
4. 12 ÷ 4 = 4 ÷ 12   **5.** 6 + 0 = 6   **6.** 6 × 0 = 6
7. 6 − 0 = 6   **8.** 0 ÷ 6 = 0   **9.** 6 ÷ 0 = 6
10. .5 + .4 = .09   **11.** 5 × .4 = 10 × .2   **12.** $5 \times \frac{1}{5} = 2 \div 2$

In 13–18, replace the question mark with a numeral which will make the resulting statement true.

13. 8 + ? = 4 + 6   **14.** 8 − ? = 5 × 1   **15.** 7 − ? = 7 × 1
16. $\frac{1}{4}$ + ? = 1 − $\frac{1}{4}$ **17.** .8 + .2 = 4 × ?   **18.** 4 × .5 = 12 ÷ ?

SYMBOLS OF INEQUALITY

The false statement 3 + 6 = 5 may be changed to a true statement by replacing the symbol = with the symbol ≠, read "is not equal to." Thus, 3 + 6 ≠ 5 is a true statement. A statement that one number is not equal to another number is called an **inequality**.

For any two numbers of arithmetic, we can say that one must be greater than the other, equal to the other, or less than the other. To compare unequal numbers, we use the following symbols:

> is read "is greater than." Thus, 4 > 2 is read "4 is greater than 2."

< is read "is less than." Thus, 1 < 3 is read "1 is less than 3."

≯ is read "is not greater than." Thus, 2 ≯ 7 is read "2 is not greater than 7."

≮ is read "is not less than." Thus, 5 ≮ 4 is read "5 is not less than 4."

Notice that in an inequality which is a true sentence involving the symbol $>$ or $<$, for example, $4 > 2$ or $1 < 3$, the symbol points to the *smaller* number.

An inequality, just like an equality, may be a true sentence or may be a false sentence.

⟜⟜⟜⟜⟜⟜⟜⟜ MODEL PROBLEMS ⟜⟜⟜⟜⟜⟜⟜

In 1–6, tell whether the statement is true or false.

1. $6 + 7 \neq 15$ *Ans.* True

2. $0 \neq 8 - 8$ *Ans.* False

3. $8 + 6 > 10$ *Ans.* True

4. $3 \times 6 \not> 10$ *Ans.* False

5. $20 \div 5 < 8$ *Ans.* True

6. $15 - 13 \not< 7$ *Ans.* False

Exercises

In 1–5, state whether the inequality is true or false.

1. $8 + 5 \neq 6 + 4$ **2.** $9 + 2 \neq 2 + 9$ **3.** $6 \times 0 \neq 4 \times 0$
4. The sum of 8 and 12 is not equal to the product of 24 and 4.
5. The product of 5 and 4 is not equal to 5 divided by 4.

In 6–11, write the inequality using the symbol $>$ or the symbol $<$.

6. 25 is greater than 20.   **7.** $12 + 3$ is less than 20.
8. $6 - 3$ is less than $5 + 4$.   **9.** $80 \div 4$ is greater than $6 + 3$.
10. The sum of 9 and 4 is less than the product of 10 and 5.
11. The sum of 8 and 7 is greater than the quotient 20 divided by 5.

In 12–14, express each inequality in words.

12. $9 + 8 > 16$ **13.** $12 - 2 < 4 \times 7$ **14.** $5 + 24 \not< 90 \div 3$

In 15–23, state whether the inequality is true or false.

15. $20 - 4 < 5 + 8$ **16.** $6 \times 0 > 3 + 5$ **17.** $18 + 0 > 4 + 0$
18. $2.05 < 20.5$ **19.** $\frac{1}{2} + \frac{1}{8} < .8$ **20.** $3 - .25 > 2\frac{1}{2}$
21. $4.6 - 2.1 > 1.5 + .9$ **22.** $8 \times .5 \not< 6 \div \frac{1}{2}$ **23.** $\frac{1}{2} + \frac{1}{3} \not> 1 - \frac{1}{4}$

In 24–29, replace the question mark with a numeral which will make the resulting statement true.

24. $5 + \,? \neq 11$ **25.** $? - 7 > 3$ **26.** $15 \div 5 < \,? \div 2$
27. $8 \times \frac{1}{2} \neq 6 - ?$ **28.** $10 \div \,? \not> 10$ **29.** $4 - .7 \not< 1 \times ?$

In 30–35, state which of the symbols $+$, $-$, $\times$, $\div$ can replace the question mark and make the resulting statement true.

30. $4 ? 2 \neq 6$ **31.** $20 ? 5 > 10$ **32.** $12 ? 6 < 10$

33. $\frac{1}{2} < 1 ? \frac{1}{4}$ **34.** $6 - 4 > 6 ? 4$ **35.** $3 + 1.5 > 3 ? 2$

ORDERING NUMBERS ON A NUMBER LINE

On a number line, the smaller of two num-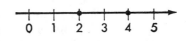
bers appears to the left of the larger, and the
larger of the two numbers appears to the right
of the smaller. Thus, the true statement $2 < 4$ tells us that on a number line the graph of 2 is to the left of the graph of 4. Also, the true statement $4 > 2$ tells us that the graph of 4 is to the right of the graph of 2. We say that the phrases "less than" and "greater than" express an **order relation** as is illustrated by the order in which the numbers appear on a number line.

We know that the statement "4 is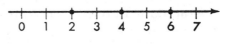
between 2 and 6" means that 4 is
greater than 2 ($4 > 2$) and also 4 is less
than 6 ($4 < 6$). On a number line, 2 is to the left of 4 and also 4 is to the left of 6. Hence, we can combine the symbols $4 > 2$ and $4 < 6$ into a single symbol "$2 < 4 < 6$." This symbol is read "2 is less than 4 and 4 is less than 6" or "4 is between 2 and 6."

Exercises

In 1–5, state how you can tell from a number line that the statement is true.

1. $1 < 7$ **2.** $10 > 5$ **3.** $0 < 6$ **4.** $\frac{3}{4} < 1$ **5.** $2\frac{1}{2} > 1.5$

In 6–15, arrange the numbers in proper order so that they will appear from left to right on a number line.

6. $5, 8$ **7.** $16, 4$ **8.** $\frac{1}{2}, \frac{1}{4}$ **9.** $2.5, 3.2$ **10.** $2\frac{3}{5}, 2.8$

11. $2, 3, 9$ **12.** $9, 6, 11$ **13.** $\frac{1}{4}, \frac{7}{8}, \frac{2}{3}$ **14.** $3.2, 2.6, 4.3$ **15.** $3\frac{1}{3}, 3.75, 3\frac{1}{4}$

In 16–20, arrange the numbers in proper order so that they will appear from right to left on a number line.

16. $11, 7$ **17.** $5\frac{1}{2}, 5\frac{5}{8}$ **18.** $5, 11, 14$ **19.** $5.4, 4.9, 6.2$ **20.** $2\frac{1}{2}, 3.3, 1.2$

In 21–24, select the number that is between the other two numbers and use the symbol $<$ to write that the selected number is between the other two.

21. $13, 17, 9$ **22.** $5\frac{1}{3}, 4\frac{1}{2}, 6\frac{1}{4}$ **23.** $4.7, 6.6, 5.3$ **24.** $4\frac{7}{8}, 4.5, 5\frac{1}{4}$

5. Order of Operations

Sometimes a numeral is enclosed in parentheses to indicate clearly that it is a numeral. For example, "(5 + 3)" is another numeral for 8.

A **numerical phrase,** sometimes called a **numerical expression,** is any numeral written as an expression that involves other numerals together with signs of operation. For example, "4 + 3," "5 × 7," "(8 + 6) − 3," and "(9 + 7) − (3 + 6)" are numerical phrases. Since a numerical phrase must name a number, the symbol "(5⁺) × (3₋)" is not a numerical phrase.

The symbol "5 + 3 × 2" does not name a definite number. "5 + 3 × 2" might mean 5 + 6, or 11; or it might mean 8 × 2, or 16. To give a single meaning to this symbol and others like it, mathematicians have agreed to follow a procedure which gives the order of operations in such expressions.

Procedure. In numerical expressions involving numerals along with signs of operation:
1. **Do all multiplications and divisions first, performing them in order from left to right.**
2. **Then do all additions and subtractions, performing them in order from left to right.**

By following the above procedure, expressions such as "5 + 3 × 2" may be used as numerical phrases.

MODEL PROBLEMS

1. Give the meaning of the numerical phrase 15 − 12 ÷ 2.

Solution: 15 − 12 ÷ 2 means the quotient of 12 and 2 is to be subtracted from 15.

2. Find a simpler name for the numerical phrase 28 − 4 × 2.

How To Proceed	*Solution*
1. Write the numerical phrase.	28 − 4 × 2
2. Do the multiplication first.	= 28 − 8
3. Then do the subtraction.	= 20 *Ans.*

3. Simplify the numerical phrase $30 - 10 \div 5 + 6 \times 2$.

How To Proceed	*Solution*
1. Write the numerical phrase.	$30 - 10 \div 5 + 6 \times 2$
2. First do the multiplication and division from left to right.	$= 30 - 2 + 12$
3. Then do the addition and subtraction.	$= 40$ *Ans.*

Exercises

In 1–9: (*a*) Give the meaning of the numerical phrase. (*b*) Find a simpler name for the numerical phrase.

1. $5 + 3 \times 7$ **2.** $6 + 8 \times 2$ **3.** $15 - 6 \times 2$
4. $14 - 2 \times 5$ **5.** $10 + 8 \div 2$ **6.** $16 \div 4 + 4$
7. $26 - 14 \div 2$ **8.** $72 \div 8 - 2$ **9.** $9 \times 2 + 3 \times 4$

In 10–15, simplify the numerical phrase.

10. $6 \times 5 - 8 \times 2$ **11.** $20 + 20 \div 5 + 5$ **12.** $36 - 12 \div 4 - 1$
13. $36 + \frac{1}{2} \times 10$ **14.** $24 - 4 \div \frac{1}{2}$ **15.** $28 + 0 \div 4 - 10 \times .2$

6. Using Grouping Symbols

In mathematics, parentheses are used to indicate the meaning of an expression. For example, if we wish "$4 \times 6 + 7$" to mean that the number represented by "4×6" and 7 are to be added, we write "$(4 \times 6) + 7$." However, if we wish "$4 \times 6 + 7$" to mean 4 times the number represented by "$6 + 7$," we write "$4 \times (6 + 7)$," or merely "$4(6 + 7)$." Notice that the part of the expression which is to be considered as a numeral is enclosed in the parentheses.

Thus, $30 - (6 + 5)$ means $30 - 11$, or 19.

Also, $6(4 + 1)$ means $6(5)$, which means 6×5, or 30.

To simplify a numerical phrase which involves parentheses, first perform the operations indicated on the numbers within the parentheses.

Observe that the use of a grouping symbol makes it possible to give a numerical phrase a meaning other than the meaning it would have according to the agreement on the order of operations. For example, we have agreed that $4 \times 6 + 7$ means $24 + 7$, or 31. However, $4 \times (6 + 7)$ means 4×13, or 52.

In addition to the parentheses, several other symbols of grouping are used to show that a given expression is to be considered as a numeral. These symbols are brackets, [ ], and bar $\overline{}$.

The expressions $2(5 + 9)$, $2[5 + 9]$, and $2\,\overline{5 + 9}$ all mean that the sum of 5 and 9 is to be multiplied by 2.

The bar may also be used below the expression that is to be considered as a numeral. In the fraction $\dfrac{20 - 8}{3}$, the bar, or fraction line, indicates that the number $(20 - 8)$ is to be divided by 3. Therefore, $\dfrac{20 - 8}{3} = \dfrac{12}{3} = 4$.

When there are two or more grouping symbols in an expression, we perform the operations on the numbers in the innermost symbol first. For example:

$$5 + 2[6 + (3 - 1) \times 4]$$
$$= 5 + 2[6 + 2 \times 4]$$
$$= 5 + 2[6 + 8]$$
$$= 5 + 2 \times 14$$
$$= 5 + 28$$
$$= 33$$

MODEL PROBLEM

Simplify the numerical expression $80 - 4(6 - 4)$.

How To Proceed	Solution
1. Write the expression.	$80 - 4(6 - 4)$
2. Simplify the expression within the parentheses.	$= 80 - 4(2)$
3. Do the multiplication.	$= 80 - 8$
4. Do the subtraction.	$= 72$ *Ans.*

Exercises

In 1–8, state the meaning of the symbol in part (*a*) and the meaning of the symbol in part (*b*) and give the most common (the simplest) name for each symbol.

1. *a.* $20 + (6 + 1)$ *b.* $20 + 6 + 1$

2. *a.* $18 - (4 + 3)$ *b.* $18 - 4 + 3$

3. *a.* $17 + (6 - 4)$ *b.* $17 + 6 - 4$
4. *a.* $12 - (3 - \frac{1}{2})$ *b.* $12 - 3 - \frac{1}{2}$
5. *a.* $15 \times (2 + 1)$ *b.* $15 \times 2 + 1$
6. *a.* $.4 \times (8 + 2)$ *b.* $.4 \times 8 + 2$
7. *a.* $(12 + 8) \div 4$ *b.* $12 + 8 \div 4$
8. *a.* $48 \div (8 - 4)$ *b.* $48 \div 8 - 4$

In 9–14, give the most common name for the numerals in the parentheses and then perform the indicated operation.

9. $6 \times (8 + 4)$ **10.** $12 + (7 - 2)$ **11.** $34 - (7 + 8)$
12. $36 \div (9 + 3)$ **13.** $(12 + 7) - (6 - 2)$ **14.** $(12 \times 6) \div (9 - 3)$

In 15–20, use parentheses to express the sentence in symbols.

15. The sum of 10 and 8 is to be found and then 5 is to be subtracted from this sum.
16. 15 is to be subtracted from 25 and 7 is to be added to the difference.
17. 8 is to be multiplied by the difference of 6 and 2.
18. 12 is to be subtracted from the product of 10 and 5.
19. The difference of 12 and 2 is to be multiplied by the sum of 3 and 4.
20. The quotient of 20 and 5 is to be subtracted from the product of 16 and 3.

In 21–44, simplify the number expression.

21. $10 + (1 + 4)$ **22.** $13 - (9 + 1)$ **23.** $36 - (10 - 8)$
24. $7(5 + 2)$ **25.** $(6 - 1)10$ **26.** $20 \div (7 + 3)$
27. $48 \div (15 - 3)$ **28.** $(24 - 8) \div 2$ **29.** $(17 + 13) \div 10$
30. $15 - (15 \div 5)$ **31.** $3(6 + 3) - 4$ **32.** $25 + 3(10 - 4)$
33. $26 - 4(7 - 5)$ **34.** $25 \div (6 - 1) + 3$ **35.** $3(6 + 4)(6 - 4)$

36. $\dfrac{12 - 5 + 14}{3}$ **37.** $\dfrac{39}{8 + 7 - 2}$ **38.** $\dfrac{10 + 14}{10 - 2}$

39. $\dfrac{7(6 + 14)}{2}$ **40.** $\dfrac{3}{2}(6 + 9)$ **41.** $\dfrac{1}{2}(8)(12 + 14)$

42. $10[4 + (7 - 1) \times 5]$
43. $75 - [6(8 - 6) + 3]$
44. $36 + 4[1 + (12 - 8) \times 2]$

7. Simplifying Numerical Expressions Containing Powers

We know that 3^2 means 3×3 and that 3^2 is called the second power of 3.
   Since $40 - 3^2$ means $40 - (3 \times 3)$, then $40 - 3^2 = 40 - 9 = 31$. Therefore, the most simple (common) name for the numeral $40 - 3^2$ is 31.

Since $2(3)^2$ means $2(3 \times 3)$, then $2(3)^2 = 2(9) = 18$.

Since $40 - 2(3)^2$ means $40 - 2(3 \times 3)$, $40 - 2(3)^2 = 40 - 2(9) = 40 - 18 = 22$.

The preceding examples illustrate the fact that in simplifying numerical expressions which contain powers, we first evaluate the powers and then follow the usual order for the other operations.

To evaluate $40 - 2(2 + 1)^2$, we first represent the numeral within the parentheses, "$2 + 1$," as "3." Then we simplify $40 - 2(3)^2$ as we did before, and get 22.

Procedure. To simplify a numerical expression:
1. **Simplify any numerical expressions that are within parentheses or within other symbols of grouping.**
2. **Simplify any powers and roots. (Roots will be studied later.)**
3. **Do all multiplications and divisions, performing them in order from left to right.**
4. **Do all additions and subtractions, performing them in order from left to right.**

～～～～～～～ MODEL PROBLEMS ～～～～～～～

1. Evaluate $6^2 + 8^2$.

How To Proceed	*Solution*
1. Write the expression.	$6^2 + 8^2$
2. Simplify the powers.	$= 36 + 64$
3. Do the addition.	$= 100$ *Ans.*

2. Evaluate $5(6 - 4)^3 - 5$.

How To Proceed	*Solution*
1. Write the expression.	$5(6 - 4)^3 - 5$
2. Simplify the expression within the parentheses.	$= 5(2)^3 - 5$
3. Evaluate the power.	$= 5(8) - 5$
4. Do the multiplication.	$= 40 - 5$
5. Do the subtraction.	$= 35$ *Ans.*

Exercises

In 1–18, give the most common name for the numeral.

1. 9^2 **2.** 12^2 **3.** 10^3 **4.** 2^5 **5.** 1^3 **6.** 0^4

7. $(\frac{1}{2})^2$ **8.** $(\frac{3}{5})^2$ **9.** $(\frac{1}{4})^3$ **10.** $(.4)^2$ **11.** $(.5)^3$ **12.** $(.1)^4$

13. $(1.3)^2$ **14.** $(7.5)^2$ **15.** $(6.4)^2$ **16.** $(1\frac{1}{2})^2$ **17.** $(8\frac{1}{3})^2$ **18.** $(2\frac{1}{4})^3$

In 19–50, simplify the numerical expression.

19. 2×3^2 **20.** 4×5^2 **21.** $81 \times (\frac{1}{3})^3$

22. $64 \times (.5)^2$ **23.** $2^3 \times 1^2$ **24.** $10^2 \times 3^3$

25. $1^4 \times 9^2$ **26.** $(2^5)(\frac{1}{2})^3$ **27.** $5^2 + 12^2$

28. $16^2 + 9^2$ **29.** $13^2 - 5^2$ **30.** $20^2 - 12$

31. $6 + 4(5)^2$ **32.** $3(2)^2 + 6$ **33.** $120 - 6(2)^4$

34. $100(6)^2 - 75$ **35.** $(4 + 6)^2$ **36.** $(5 + 12)^2$

37. $(20 - 15)^2$ **38.** $(7 - 2 \times 3)^3$ **39.** $2(4 + 6)^2 - 10$

40. $200 - 3(5 - 1)^3$ **41.** $12(5^2 \cdot - 4^2)$ **42.** $(7^2 - 6^2)(1^2 + 2^2)$

43. $\dfrac{8^2 + 6^2}{2}$ **44.** $\dfrac{12^2 + 9^2 + 7^2}{4}$ **45.** $\dfrac{15^2 + 25^2}{2(4 + 1)}$

46. $\dfrac{16^2 + 12^2}{5^2 - 3^2}$ **47.** $6 + (\frac{1}{2})^2$ **48.** $(\frac{3}{2})^3 - \frac{1}{8}$

49. $(\frac{3}{5})^2 + (\frac{4}{5})^2$ **50.** $(\frac{12}{13})^2 - (\frac{5}{13})^2$

8. Expressing Verbal Phrases and Sentences by Using Mathematical Symbols

Study the following model problems to learn how to express verbal phrases and number relationships by using mathematical symbols:

⌁⌁⌁⌁⌁⌁ MODEL PROBLEMS ⌁⌁⌁⌁⌁⌁

Use mathematical symbols to express each of the following:

1. Four increased by the product of two and
one.   *Ans.* $4 + 2 \times 1$

2. Twelve decreased by the quotient of six
and three.   *Ans.* $12 - 6 \div 3$

3. The product of nine and five decreased by
the sum of eight and seven.   *Ans.* $9 \times 5 - (8 + 7)$

4. When nine is added to the quotient of eight and four, the result is eleven.   *Ans.* $8 \div 4 + 9 = 11$

5. When twice the difference between sixteen and four is decreased by three, the result is greater than zero.   *Ans.* $2(16 - 4) - 3 > 0$

~~~~~~

Exercises

In 1–15, express the phrase or sentence by using mathematical symbols.

1. Five increased by the product of six and seven.
2. Ten decreased by the product of eight and four.
3. The sum of one and eight, added to ten.
4. Eighteen decreased by twice the sum of three and four.
5. When eight is added to four times six, the result is thirty-two.
6. When twenty-seven is decreased by the sum of seven and three, the result is seventeen.
7. When fourteen is increased by twice the sum of four-tenths and six-tenths, the result is sixteen.
8. The sum of six and twelve is not equal to twenty.
9. Sixteen diminished by fourteen is greater than one.
10. The quotient of thirty and two, decreased by the product of two and four, is less than twenty-five.
11. The difference between eighteen and ten, divided by five, is not equal to nine.
12. When twice the sum of seven and four is decreased by the product of ten and zero, the result is twenty-two.
13. When the product of fifty and ten is added to twice the sum of eight and fifteen, the result is less than one thousand.
14. The difference between sixteen and one, divided by the sum of two and three, is not equal to seven.
15. When five-tenths of three hundred is added to three-tenths of the difference between eight hundred and three hundred, the sum equals three hundred.

In 16–27, express the symbol as a verbal phrase or a verbal sentence.

16. $5 \times 6 - 4$
17. $(5 + 3) - 4$
18. $20 \div 5 - (2 + 1)$
19. $30 \div 5 - (2 + 4)$
20. $(15 + 5) - (15 - 5)$
21. $2 \times (7 + 3) - 10$
22. $8 + 4 = 17 - 5$
23. $20 - (5 + 1) \neq 4 \times 3$
24. $(28 + 12) \div 5 = 8(6 - 1)$
25. $2 \times (6 + 5) \neq 20$
26. $20 - 2(3 + 1) > 9$
27. $(5 - 1) \div (4 + 3) < 10$

CHAPTER II

SETS

1. The Meaning of a Set

When a collection of distinct objects is so clearly described that it is always possible to tell whether or not an object belongs to it, we call the collection a **well-defined set,** or a **set.** For example, a girl's parents form a set. Her father belongs to this set. However, her uncle does not belong to it. Also, the odd counting numbers less than 10 form a set. The numbers 1, 3, 5, 7, and 9 belong to this set. But the numbers 2, 4, and 6 do not belong to it.

Every object that belongs to a set is called a **member,** or an **element,** of the set. For example, a trumpet is a member of the set of wind instruments; the number 5 is an element of the set of counting numbers.

HOW TO INDICATE A SET

One way of indicating a set is to list the names of its elements between braces, $\{\ \}$. For example, to indicate the set whose elements are 2, 4, 6, 8, we can write $\{2, 4, 6, 8\}$. This method of representation is called **tabulating** the set, or giving a **list,** or **roster,** of the set.

By using a capital letter to represent the set, we can write $A = \{2, 4, 6, 8\}$. This is read "A is the set whose elements are 2, 4, 6, and 8." To indicate that the number 4 is an element of set A, we use the symbol $\in$ and write $4 \in A$. To indicate that the number 5 is not an element of set A, we use the symbol $\notin$ and write $5 \notin A$.

The elements of a set may be tabulated in any order. For example, $\{2, 4, 6, 8\}$ and $\{8, 6, 4, 2\}$ represent the same set whose elements are tabulated differently.

It is not necessary for the elements of a set to be related to one another in any way other than that they are listed together. If we wish certain objects to be the elements of a set, we simply list them as members of the set. For example, in the set $\{$golf, Saturday, cow, football$\}$ the elements of the set are related to each other in no way other than that they are tabulated as the members of a set.

Sometimes it is inconvenient to tabulate the elements of a set. For example, if we wish to indicate the set of even whole numbers between 1 and 999, we would have to tabulate $\{2, 4, 6, \ldots, 998\}$, a total of 499 numbers. In such a case we can **describe** the set, that is, state the rule which describes the elements of the set. We write {even whole numbers between 1 and 999}, which is read "the set of even whole numbers between 1 and 999."

To write the word "keep," four symbols are used. However, the set of letters to which these symbols refer has only three elements, the letters k, e, and p. Therefore, we say that the word "keep" is composed of the letters of the set $\{k, e, p\}$. Observe that when we use the roster method of describing a set, the same element is listed only once.

MODEL PROBLEM

Indicate the set of letters a, b, c, d, e by (a) tabulating the elements and (b) describing the set.

Solution:

$a.$ $\{a, b, c, d, e\}$
$b.$ {first 5 letters in the English alphabet}

Exercises

In 1–12, describe two sets whose elements are:

1. men	**2.** women	**3.** fish	**4.** tools
5. lakes	**6.** buildings	**7.** ships	**8.** teachers
9. numbers	**10.** angles	**11.** quadrilaterals	**12.** solid figures

In 13–21, tell whether the collection may be regarded as a set.

13. Mary, Sue	**14.** hat, top, day	**15.** 1, 2, 3, 5, 6
16. some even numbers	**17.** all pretty girls	**18.** all odd natural numbers
19. all honest men	**20.** 2, 4, 6, 8, 10	**21.** all small numbers

In 22–27, the elements of a set are given. Indicate the set by tabulating its members.

22. Bill, Saul, Ted	**23.** June, Tuesday, Easter	**24.** 11, 13, 15, 17
25. violin, piano, drum	**26.** cat, cow, deer	**27.** chair, bench, sofa

In 28–34, tell whether the sentence is true or false.

28. Paul is an element of the set {Cary, Paul, Harold}.

29. 4 is an element of the set {14, 24, 34, 44}.

30. 8 is not an element of the set of odd natural numbers.

31. $12 \in \{10, 12, 14, 16, 18, 20\}$.

32. $\triangle \in \{\bigcirc, \square, \square, \square\}$.

33. bat $\notin$ {base, glove, bat, ball}.

34. Claire $\notin$ {Sue, Sally, Bess, Helen}.

35. Select from the following those that are elements of the set of the months of the year:

    a. June   *b.* May   *c.* Sunday   *d.* December   *e.* Tuesday

36. Select from the following those that are elements of the set of counting numbers:

    a. 7   *b.* $\frac{2}{3}$ *c.* 22   *d.* 0   *e.* 1

37. Select from the following those that are elements of the set of United States coins:

    a. nickel   *b.* lira   *c.* peso   *d.* dime   *e.* pound

In 38–45, tabulate the elements of the set that is described.

38. The set of the months of the year beginning with the letter *J*.

39. The set of United States Presidents since Franklin D. Roosevelt.

40. The set of letters in the word "prevail."

41. The set of different letters in the word "Missouri."

42. The set of months that have 31 days.

43. The set of odd natural numbers greater than 70 and less than 80.

44. The set of even natural numbers between 11 and 19.

45. The set of odd numbers by which 36 is exactly divisible.

46. How many elements are there in the set of states of the United States?

47. Write the set whose elements are the letters used in spelling the word:

    a. "street"   *b.* "pump"   *c.* "happiness"   *d.* "Mississippi"

48. Write the set whose elements are the digits used in writing the number:

    a. 100   *b.* 1000   *c.* 5756   *d.* 9999

In 49–55, describe the set that is indicated by tabulation.

49. {Tuesday, Thursday}

50. {November, June, April, September}

51. {21, 23, 25, 27, 29}

52. {3, 6, 9, 12, 15, 18}

53. {Huron, Ontario, Superior, Michigan, Erie}

54. {*a, e, i, o, u*}

55. {Alaska, Arizona, Alabama, Arkansas}

In 56–58, tell whether the sentence is true or false.

56. {horse, mule, pony} is the same set as {mule, pony, horse}.
57. {trout, salmon, bass} is the same set as {pike, bass, salmon}.
58. {6, 12, 18} is the same set as {all counting numbers between 1 and 20 that are exactly divisible by 6}.

2. Kinds of Sets

FINITE SETS

We have learned that the set of odd natural numbers less than 10,000, a set which has a large number of elements, may be indicated as follows:

$$\{1, 3, 5, 7, 9, 11, \ldots, 9999\}$$

Since there is an end to the tabulation of the elements of this set, the number of elements in the set can be counted. We call a set whose elements can be counted a *finite set.* Some examples of finite sets are:

1. the set of pupils in your mathematics class
2. the set of natural numbers less than 100

INFINITE SETS

Sometimes the tabulation of the elements of a set is an endless process. For example, it is impossible to tabulate all the elements of the set of odd numbers. In this case, we indicate the set as follows:

$$\{1, 3, 5, 7, 9, \ldots\}$$

Since there is no end to tabulating the members of this set, there is no end to counting its members. We call such a set an *infinite set.* Some examples of an infinite set are:

1. the set of natural numbers
2. the set of circles
3. the set of numbers between 1 and 2

THE EMPTY SET

It is possible for a set to have no elements. For example, the set of women more than 10 feet tall has no members. Such a set is called the *empty set,* or **null set.** It is usually designated by the symbol $\emptyset$. The empty set may also be expressed by a pair of empty braces { }. Other examples of the empty set are:

1. the set of months that begin with the letter B
2. the set of odd numbers exactly divisible by 4

Note that {0} is not the null set because it is a set that has one element, the number 0.

Exercises

In 1–4, tabulate the elements of the set that is described. Use three dots when convenient or necessary.

1. {odd numbers between 300 and 310}
2. {multiples of 5 between 1 and 49}
3. {even natural numbers less than 500 that are exactly divisible by 4}
4. {whole numbers exactly divisible by 3}

In 5–25, state whether the set is a finite set, an infinite set, or an empty set.

5. the set of all people who live in the United States today
6. the set of all animals in the world
7. the set of men who weigh a ton
8. the set of all natural numbers greater than 1 million
9. the set of all natural numbers less than 1 million
10. the set of numerals that represent the number 5
11. the set of angles whose vertex is a given point
12. the set of numbers less than 2
13. the set of natural numbers between 8 and 9
14. the set of homes in your city
15. {1, 3, 5, 7, 9, . . . , 49}
16. {10, 20, 30, 40, 50, 60, . . .}
17. {vowels in the English language}
18. {0}
19. {rectangles}
20. {triangles having 2 and only 2 sides}
21. {months of the year having 40 days}
22. {2-digit numbers between 1 and 100}
23. {whole numbers which are multiples of 9}
24. {all the grains of sand on the beaches of Coney Island}
25. {all fractions whose numerator is 1}

EQUAL SETS

We have seen that a number may be represented by different numerals. Similarly, a set may be represented by different names. For example, $A = \{3, 5\}$ and $B = \{$odd numbers between 2 and 6$\}$ are different names for the same set. When we tabulate the elements of set B, we find that $B = \{3, 5\}$. Since both set A and set B have the same elements, we say that A and B are equal sets and write $A = B$. Another way of saying this is:

Set A is equal to set B if every element of A is an element of B and every element of B is an element of A.

If $R = \{3, 4\}$ and $S = \{2, 3\}$, set R does not equal set S because set R and set S do not have the same elements. In this case, we write $R \neq S$, which is read "R does not equal S."

Exercises

In 1–9, use either the symbol $=$ or $\neq$ to write a true sentence about the two sets.

1. $A = \{5, 7, 9, 10\}$ and $B = \{9, 7, 5, 10\}$
2. $C = \{6, 8, 4, 3\}$ and $D = \{6, 8, 4, 2\}$
3. $E = \{4, 6, 8\}$ and $F = \{4, 6, 8, 10\}$
4. $G = \{$spring, summer, autumn, winter$\}$ and $H = \{$four seasons of the year$\}$
5. $I = \{a, e, i, o, u\}$ and $J = \{$consonants in the English language$\}$
6. $K = \{4, 8, 12, 16\}$ and $L = \{$counting numbers less than 20 that are exactly divisible by 4$\}$
7. $M = \{0, 1, 2, 3, 4, 5, 6, 7, 8, 9\}$ and $N = \{$all one-digit counting numbers$\}$
8. $R = \{$all birds that have fins$\}$ and $S = \varnothing$
9. $X = \varnothing$ and $Y = \{0\}$
10. Define two sets A and B which are equal.
11. Define two sets C and D which are not equal.

EQUIVALENT SETS

Let us consider the two sets $A = \{1, 3, 5\}$ and $B = \{2, 4, 6\}$. Since their elements are different, set A does not equal set B. However, both sets have the same number of elements. We can see this when we pair, in different ways, the elements of set A (1, 3, 5) with the elements of set B (2, 4, 6) as follows:

$$A = \{1, 3, 5\} \qquad A = \{5, 3, 1\} \qquad A = \{1, 5, 3\}$$

OR   OR

$$B = \{2, 4, 6\} \qquad B = \{2, 6, 4\} \qquad B = \{6, 4, 2\}$$

Notice that in each of the pairings, every element of set A has been matched with an element of set B; every element of set B has been matched with an element of set A; and there is no element of either set A or set B that has not been matched with an element of the other set. When two sets can be matched in this way, we say that there is a **one-to-one correspondence** between the two sets; and the sets are called **matching sets,** or **equivalent sets.** The symbol $A \sim B$ means "set A is equivalent to set B."

A simple way to determine whether or not two finite sets are equivalent sets is to count the number of elements in each set. If both sets have the same number of elements, they are equivalent sets.

Note that two equal sets must always be equivalent sets. However, two equivalent sets must not always be equal sets.

It may also be possible to match two infinite sets, for example, the set of *all odd natural numbers* and the set of *all natural numbers*.

Let $A = \{1, 3, 5, 7, 9, 11, 13, 15, 17, 19, \ldots\}$ and $B = \{1, 2, 3, 4, 5, 6, 7, 8, 9, 10, \ldots\}$. Then we can match the elements of set A and set B as follows, and we could continue the process endlessly:

$$A = \{1, 3, 5, 7, 9, 11, 13, 15, 17, 19, \ldots\}$$

$$B = \{1, 2, 3, 4, 5, 6, 7, 8, 9, 10, \ldots\}$$

We see that there is a one-to-one correspondence between the set of all odd natural numbers and the set of all natural numbers. Therefore, we can say that {all odd natural numbers} $\sim$ {all natural numbers}.

Exercises

In 1–6, tell whether or not there is a one-to-one correspondence between the two sets.

1. $\{5, 6, 9, 4, 8\}$ and $\{1, 3, 5, 6, 7\}$ **2.** $\{a, b, c, d\}$ and $\{x, y, z\}$
3. $\{M, E, A, T\}$ and $\{T, E, A, M\}$ **4.** $\{5, 6, 7, 8\}$ and $\{\frac{1}{8}, \frac{1}{7}, \frac{1}{6}, \frac{1}{5}\}$
5. {odd numbers between 50 and 60} and {odd numbers between 60 and 70}
6. {all even natural numbers} and {all natural numbers}

In 7–12, tell whether or not the given sets are equivalent sets.

7. {Bill, Carl, Ted, Jim} and {Sue, Tess, Rose, Hilda}
8. {a, e, i, o, u} and {c, d, r, s, t}
9. {△, ○, □} and {1, 2, 3, 4, 5}
10. {2, 4, 6, 8, 10, 12} and {12, 14, 16, 18, 20}
11. {counting numbers between 30 and 40} and {odd counting numbers between 30 and 40}
12. {even counting numbers} and {odd counting numbers}

In 13–15, state whether the two sets are (a) equivalent and (b) equal.

13. {1, 2, 3, 4} and {a, b, c, d}
14. {B, A, T} and {T, A, B}
15. {even natural numbers between 1 and 10} and {odd natural numbers between 1 and 10}

16. Describe two finite sets that are equivalent sets but not equal sets.
17. Describe two finite sets that are not equivalent sets.
18. Describe two infinite sets that are equivalent sets.

SUBSETS

Let U be a set of students who are members of a committee.

$$U = \{\text{Harry, Marie, Susan, Ted, William}\}$$

Let B be the set of boys who are members of this committee.

$$B = \{\text{Harry, William, Ted}\}$$

Notice that every element of set B is also an element of set U. In such a case, we say: "Set B is a **subset** of set U" (and "set U is a **superset** of set B") and we write: "$B \subset U$."

The set $U = \{\text{Harry, Marie, Susan, Ted, William}\}$ from which we chose elements to form a new set is called the **universe,** or **universal set.**

The universal set $U = \{1, 2, 3\}$ has several subsets. Every subset of U which does not contain all the elements of U is called a **proper subset** of U. For example, the sets $\{1\}$ and $\{2, 3\}$ are proper subsets of U. We can write $\{1\} \subset \{1, 2, 3\}$ and $\{2, 3\} \subset \{1, 2, 3\}$.

The subset $\{1, 2, 3\}$ which contains every element of U is called an **improper subset** of U. We can write $\{1, 2, 3\} \subset \{1, 2, 3\}$. This example illustrates that **every set is a subset of itself.**

Although the empty set $\varnothing$ does not contain any elements of U, mathematicians have agreed to call $\varnothing$ a subset of U. In fact, **the empty set is considered a subset of every set.**

Exercises

In 1–16, tell whether the sentence is true or false. Justify the answer given.

1. {Paul, Harry} is a subset of {Sam, Harry, Paul}.
2. {10, 11, 12, 13} is a subset of {10, 11, 12}.
3. {5, 8, 7} is a subset of {7, 8, 9, 10}.
4. {10, 20, 30} is a subset of {30, 20, 10}.
5. ∅ is a subset of {tent, cabin, house}.
6. {mathematics teachers in your school} is a subset of {teachers in your school}.
7. {athletes in your school} is a subset of {baseball players in your school}.
8. $\{a, b, c\} \subset \{a, b, c, d, e\}$.
9. $\{10, 11, 12, 13\} \subset \{13, 12, 11, 10\}$.
10. {horses} $\subset$ {animals}.
11. {fish} $\subset$ {birds}.
12. {ships} $\subset$ {submarines}.
13. $\varnothing \subset \{a\}$.
14. $\{a\} \subset \varnothing$.
15. $\varnothing \subset \{0\}$.
16. $A \subset A$.

In 17–20, state whether the first set is a proper or improper subset of the second set.

17. $\{10, 15, 20\} \subset \{10, 15, 20, 25\}$.
18. $\{r, s, t\} \subset \{t, s, r\}$.
19. $\{6, 8, 10\} \subset \{6, 8, 10, 12\}$.
20. {natural numbers exactly divisible by 4} $\subset$ {even natural numbers}.

In 21–28, list all the subsets (including the empty set) of the given set.

21. {5}   22. {5, 6}   23. {5, 6, 7}   24. {5, 6, 7, 8}
25. {a}   26. {Ted, Sid}   27. {Sue, Ann, Kit}   28. $\{w, x, y, z\}$

29. Find the number of subsets (including the empty set) of set A if the number of elements in set A is:

    a. 1   b. 2   c. 3   d. 4

OVERLAPPING SETS

Consider the sets $A = \{1, 2, 3, 4\}$ and $B = \{3, 4, 5\}$. Since A and B do not have the same elements, A does not equal B. A is not a subset of B because 2 is an element of A and is not an element of B. Also, B is not a subset of A

because 5 is an element of B and is not an element of A. Yet A and B have in common the elements 3 and 4. In such a situation, we say that A and B are *overlapping sets.*

Set A and set B are overlapping sets if there are elements of set A which are also elements of set B but neither set is a subset of the other.

Exercises

In 1–7, state whether or not set A and set B are overlapping sets. Justify your answer.

1. $A = \{a, e, i, o, u\}$, $B = \{a, b, c, d, e\}$
2. $A = \{5, 6, 7, 8, 9\}$, $B = \{9, 7, 5, 6, 8\}$
3. $A = \{rose, lily, tulip\}$, $B = \{lily, tulip\}$
4. $A = \{June, July, August\}$, $B = \{months of the year\}$
5. $A = \varnothing$, $B = \{counting numbers\}$
6. $A = \{set of men older than 25 years\}$, $B = \{professional baseball players\}$
7. $A = \{even numbers\}$, $B = \{counting numbers\}$

8. Describe two sets that are overlapping sets.

DISJOINT SETS

Consider the sets $A = \{1, 3, 5, 7, 9\}$ and $B = \{2, 4, 6, 8\}$. Notice that A and B have no elements in common. In this event, we say that A and B are *disjoint sets.*

Set A and set B are disjoint sets if no element of set A is also an element of set B.

Exercises

In 1–5, state whether or not set A and set B are disjoint sets. Justify your answer.

1. $A = \{William, John, Robert\}$, $B = \{Marion, Ruth, Martha\}$
2. $A = \{even counting numbers\}$, $B = \{odd counting numbers\}$
3. $A = \{animals that walk\}$, $B = \{animals that swim\}$
4. $A = \{vowels in the English language\}$, $B = \{consonants in the English language\}$
5. $A = \{blond girls\}$, $B = \{legal secretaries\}$

6. Describe two sets that are disjoint sets.

3. Picturing a Universal Set and Its Subsets

We have learned that the set from which we choose elements to form a new set is called the universal set, or the universe. For example, if we are considering the set of members of the United Nations, we can write the universal set, represented by U, as $U = \{$members of the United Nations$\}$. If we are considering the set of even numbers between 1 and 17, we can write $U = \{2, 4, 6, 8, 10, 12, 14, 16\}$. We can represent the universal set pictorially by a rectangle and its interior.

The Universal Set U

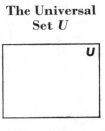

Set A Is a Subset of Universal Set U

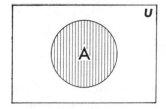

Let us see how we can picture a subset of a universal set.

If from the universal set $U = \{2, 4, 6, 8, 10, 12, 14, 16\}$ we select the set of numbers, A, each of whose elements is exactly divisible by 4, we get $A = \{4, 8, 12, 16\}$. Set A is a subset of set U. We can picture this fact by representing U by a rectangle and its interior, and by representing the subset A by a circle and its interior. Notice that the circle is placed within the rectangle. Such a picture is called a *Venn diagram.*

Exercises

1. *a.* If the set of objects under consideration is the collection of American coins of different denomination in use, list the elements of the universal set U.
   b. If set A is a set each of whose elements is an American coin worth less than 25 cents, list the elements of set A.
   c. Make a Venn diagram to show pictorially that set A is a subset of the universal set U.
2. *a.* If the set of objects under consideration is the months of the year, tabulate the elements of the universal set U.
   b. If set B is a set each of whose elements is a month beginning with J, list the elements of set B.
   c. Make a Venn diagram to show pictorially that set B is a subset of set U.
3. *a.* If the set of objects under consideration is the set of odd counting numbers less than 20, tabulate the elements of the universal set U.

    b. If set C is a set each of whose elements is an odd number less than 20 that is divisible by 5, list the elements of set C.

    c. Make a Venn diagram to show pictorially that set C is a subset of set U.

4. If the universal set U is the set of all quadrilaterals and set D is the set of all rectangles, make a Venn diagram to show pictorially that set D is a subset of set U.

5. *a.* If the universal set U is the set of all triangles, describe a set E that is a proper subset of set U.

    b. Make a Venn diagram to show pictorially that set E is a subset of set U.

6. Two sets under consideration are the set of even natural numbers less than 5 and the set of natural numbers less than 5. One of these sets is the universal set; the other is a subset of the universal set.

    a. Tabulate the elements of the universal set U.

    b. Tabulate the elements of the subset A.

    c. Make a Venn diagram to show pictorially that set A is a subset of set U.

4. Intersection of Sets

    Let us suppose that the universal set is the set of natural numbers, $U = \{\text{natural numbers}\}$. If A is the set of natural numbers greater than 4 and less than 12, then $A = \{5, 6, 7, 8, 9, 10, 11\}$. If B is the set of natural numbers greater than 8 and less than 15, then $B = \{9, 10, 11, 12, 13, 14\}$. Notice that set A and set B are overlapping sets, and that the numbers 9, 10, 11 are elements of both set A and set B. The set whose elements belong to both set A and set B, $\{9, 10, 11\}$, is called the ***intersection*** of set A and set B.

    The intersection of two sets, A and B, is the set containing those and only those elements of set A that are also elements of set B.

    The intersection of set A and set B is represented by the symbol $A \cap B$, read "A intersection B," or "A cap B." Thus, if $A = \{5, 6, 7, 8, 9, 10, 11\}$ and $B = \{9, 10, 11, 12, 13, 14\}$, then $A \cap B = \{9, 10, 11\}$. The intersection of set A and set B, $A \cap B$, can be shown pictorially by a Venn diagram. The crosshatched part of the circles represents $A \cap B$.

$A \cap B$ When A and B Intersect

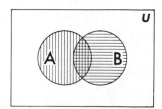

Suppose U = {natural numbers}. If A is the set of even natural numbers less than 10, then A = {2, 4, 6, 8}. If B is the set of odd natural numbers less than 10, then B = {1, 3, 5, 7, 9}. Notice that set A and set B have no common elements. Therefore, the intersection of set A and set B is the empty set, or null set, $\varnothing$ or { }. We know that two sets such as set A and set B, which have no common elements, are called disjoint sets.

$A \cap B$ When A and B Are Disjoint Sets

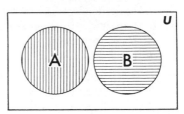

The intersection of set A and set B, $A \cap B$, when A and B are disjoint sets, can be shown pictorially by a Venn diagram. Since A and B have no common elements, no part of the circles is crosshatched.

$A \cap B$ When B Is a Subset of A

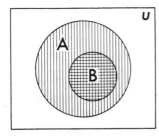

Suppose U = {natural numbers}. If A is the set of natural numbers less than 10, then A = {1, 2, 3, 4, 5, 6, 7, 8, 9}. If B is the set of odd natural numbers less than 10, then B = {1, 3, 5, 7, 9}. Notice that set B is a subset of set A. The intersection of set A and set B, $A \cap B$, when set B is a subset of set A, can be shown pictorially by a Venn diagram. The crosshatched part of the circles represents $A \cap B$. When B is a subset of A, then $A \cap B = B$.

Exercises

1. If A = {1, 3, 5} and B = {0, 1, 2, 3}, find $A \cap B$.
2. If R = {6, 7, 8} and S = {3, 4, 5, 6, 7}, find $R \cap S$.
3. If C = {5, 10, 15, 20} and D = {5, 6, 7, 8, 9, 10}, find $C \cap D$.
4. U = {natural numbers}, A = {10, 11, 12, 13, 14, 15}, and B = {13, 14, 15, 16, 17}.
   a. Tabulate the elements of $A \cap B$.
   b. Picture $A \cap B$ with a Venn diagram.
5. U = {natural numbers}, A = {even natural numbers less than 20}, and B = {natural numbers less than 20 that are divisible by 4}.
   a. List the elements of set A and set B.
   b. List the elements of $A \cap B$.
   c. Picture $A \cap B$ with a Venn diagram.

6. $U = $ {natural numbers less than 20}, $A = $ {natural numbers less than 10}, and $B = $ {natural numbers greater than 10 and less than 20}.
   a. List the elements of the universal set U, set A, and set B.
   b. How many elements are common to set A and set B?
   c. Describe the set $A \cap B$.
   d. Picture $A \cap B$ with a Venn diagram.

7. $U = $ {people who have hair}, $A = $ {people who have blond hair}, and $B = $ {women who have blond hair}. Picture $A \cap B$ with a Venn diagram.

8. $U = $ {people who have hair}, $A = $ {women who have hair}, and $B = $ {women who have blond hair}. Picture $A \cap B$ with a Venn diagram.

9. $U = $ {people who have hair}, $A = $ {women who have blond hair}, and $B = $ {men who have blond hair}. Picture $A \cap B$ with a Venn diagram.

10. $U = $ {triangles}, $A = $ {isosceles triangles}, and $B = $ {right triangles}. Picture $A \cap B$ with a Venn diagram.

11. $U = $ {triangles}, $A = $ {scalene triangles}, and $B = $ {isosceles triangles}. Picture $A \cap B$ with a Venn diagram.

12. $U = $ {triangles}, $A = $ {isosceles triangles}, and $B = $ {isosceles right triangles}. Picture $A \cap B$ with a Venn diagram.

13. $U = $ {geometric polygons}, $A = $ {quadrilaterals}, and $B = $ {rectangles}. Picture $A \cap B$ with a Venn diagram.

14. $U = $ {geometric polygons}, $A = $ {triangles}, and $B = $ {squares}. Picture $A \cap B$ with a Venn diagram.

15. $U = $ {geometric polygons}, $A = $ {parallelograms}, and $B = $ {rectangles}. Picture $A \cap B$ with a Venn diagram.

16. The universe is the set of men who are members of the Best College athletic teams. A is the set of men on the Best College football team. B is the set of men on the Best College basketball team. C is the set of men on the Best College tennis team. D is the set of men on the Best College baseball team.
   a. Make a Venn diagram for $A \cap B$ when some of the Best College men who are on the football team are also part of the basketball team.
   b. Make a Venn diagram for $B \cap D$ when none of the Best College men who are on the basketball team are also on the baseball team.
   c. Make a Venn diagram for $B \cap C$ when every man on the 10-man tennis team is also a member of the 15-man basketball team.

17. Set U represents the universe and set A and set B are subsets of set U. In a Venn diagram that pictures $A \cap B$, the circle representing set A coincides with the circle representing set B. What relationship must exist between set A and set B?

18. If U = {all pupils in a school}, A = {all pupils in the school who are on the honor roll}, and B = {all pupils in the school who are presidents of their official classes}, tell what each of the following Venn diagrams means:

a.
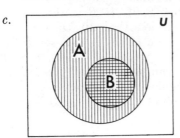

b.
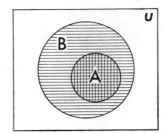

c.
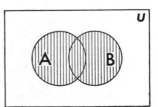

d.

19. If U is the universe, set A is a subset of U, and $\emptyset$ is the null set, represent with a Venn diagram:

   a. $A \cap U$ b. $A \cap A$ c. $A \cap \emptyset$

5. Union of Sets

The *union* of two sets A and B is the set containing all the elements of both set A and set B, any elements present in both set A and set B being listed only once.

The union of set A and set B is represented by the symbol $A \cup B$, read "A union B," or "A cup B." Thus, if A = {5, 6, 7, 8, 9, 10, 11} and B = {9, 10, 11, 12, 13, 14}, then $A \cup B$ = {5, 6, 7, 8, 9, 10, 11, 12, 13, 14}. Note that both set A and set B are subsets of the set $A \cup B$. The union of set A and set B, $A \cup B$, can be shown pictorially by a Venn diagram in which U is the set of natural numbers. The shaded region represents $A \cup B$.

$A \cup B$ When A and B Intersect

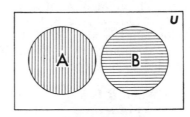

Suppose U = {natural numbers}. If A is the set of even natural numbers less than 10, then A = {2, 4, 6, 8}. If B is the set of odd natural numbers less than 10, then B = {1, 3, 5, 7, 9}. The union of set A and set B can be written $A \cup B$ = {1, 2, 3, 4, 5, 6, 7, 8, 9}. The union of set A and set B, $A \cup B$, can be shown pictorially by a Venn diagram. Both shaded regions represent $A \cup B$.

$A \cup B$ When A and B Are Disjoint Sets

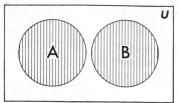

$A \cup B$ When B Is a Subset of A

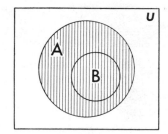

Suppose U = {natural numbers}. If A is the set of natural numbers less than 10, then A = {1, 2, 3, 4, 5, 6, 7, 8, 9}. If B is the set of odd natural numbers less than 10, then B = {1, 3, 5, 7, 9}. The union of set A and set B can be written $A \cup B$ = {1, 2, 3, 4, 5, 6, 7, 8, 9}. A Venn diagram can be used to represent $A \cup B$ pictorially. The shaded region represents $A \cup B$. When B is a subset of A, then $A \cup B = A$.

Exercises

1. If A = {0, 2, 4} and B = {1, 2, 3, 4}, find $A \cup B$.
2. If C = {1, 2, 3, 4, 5} and D = {2, 4, 6, 8, 10}, find $C \cup D$.
3. If R = {1, 3, 5} and S = {0, 2, 4, 6}, find $R \cup S$.
4. U = {natural numbers}, A = {10, 11, 12, 13}, B = {11, 12, 13, 14}.
   a. Tabulate the elements of $A \cup B$.
   b. Picture $A \cup B$ with a Venn diagram.
5. U = {letters of the English alphabet}, A = {a, e, i, o, u}, B = {r, s, t}.
   a. Tabulate the elements of $A \cup B$.
   b. Picture $A \cup B$ with a Venn diagram.
6. U = {natural numbers}, A = {natural numbers less than 30 that are divisible by 5}, B = {natural numbers less than 30 that are divisible by 10}.
   a. List the elements of set A, set B, and $A \cup B$.
   b. Picture $A \cup B$ with a Venn diagram.
7. U = {pupils in your school}, A = {boys in your class}, B = {girls in your class}. Picture $A \cup B$ with a Venn diagram.
8. U = {pupils in a class}, A = {girls in the class}, B = {blue-eyed girls in the class}. Picture $A \cup B$ with a Venn diagram.
9. U = {pupils in a class}, A = {blond girls in the class}, B = {blue-eyed, blond girls in the class}. Represent $A \cup B$ with a Venn diagram.

10. If U is the universe, set A is a subset of U, and $\emptyset$ is the null set, represent with a Venn diagram: *a.* $A \cup U$ *b.* $A \cup A$ *c.* $A \cup \emptyset$

6. Graphing Sets of Numbers

The **graph of a set of numbers** is the set of points on a number line which are associated with the numbers in the set. When we make such a graph, we use:

1. a darkened circle ● to represent a point on the number line which is associated with the number in the set
2. a non-darkened circle ○ to represent a point which does not belong to the graph
3. a darkened line ▬▬▬ to indicate that every point on the line is associated with a number in the set

~~~~~~~~~~ **MODEL PROBLEMS** ~~~~~~~~~~

1. Draw the graph of each set.

a. $\{2, 4, 6\}$

Answer:

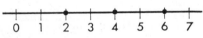

b. {numbers between 2 and 5}

Answer:

c. $\{3\frac{1}{2}$ and numbers greater than $3\frac{1}{2}\}$

Answer:

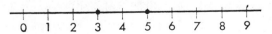

2. If set $A = \{1, 3, 5, 7\}$ and set $B = \{0, 2, 3, 4, 5, 6, 8\}$, *(a)* write and graph the intersection of set A and set B, $A \cap B$; *(b)* write and graph the union of set A and set B, $A \cup B$.

Solution:

a. Since the intersection of set A and set B is a set whose elements are numbers that are elements of both set A and set B, $A \cap B = \{3, 5\}$.

b. Since the union of set A and set B is a set whose elements are numbers that are elements of set A, of set B, or of both set A and set B, $A \cup B = \{0, 1, 2, 3, 4, 5, 6, 7, 8\}$.

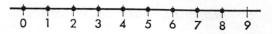

Exercises

In 1–12, name the points on the line pictured which are the graph of the given set of numbers.

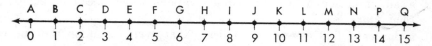

1. $\{1, 3, 5, 7\}$ 2. $\{10, 0, 6\}$ 3. $\{11, 12\}$ 4. $\{0\}$ 5. $\varnothing$
6. {whole numbers between 1 and 10}
7. {even whole numbers between 1 and 10}
8. {whole numbers between 7 and 8}
9. {multiples of 3 between 1 and 15}
10. {whole numbers greater than 10 but less than 15}
11. {odd whole numbers between 3 and 13, and including 3 and 13}
12. {multiples of 2 between 14 and 15}

In 13–23, draw the graph of the given set of numbers.
13. $\{0, 2, 4\}$ 14. $\{1, 2\frac{1}{2}, 3.5\}$ 15. $\{1, 2, 3, \ldots, 10\}$ 16. $\{0\}$
17. {whole numbers between 3 and 10}
18. {even whole numbers greater than 4 but less than 12}
19. {odd whole numbers less than 14 and greater than 9 or equal to 9}
20. a. {whole numbers less than 7}   b. {numbers less than 7}
21. a. {numbers greater than 4}   b. {numbers greater than $1\frac{1}{2}$}
22. {numbers less than 3 and including 3}
23. {numbers between 4 and 6}

24. If set $U = \{1, 2, 3, \ldots, 20\}$, write and graph a subset of U whose elements are:

   a. odd numbers   b. even numbers   c. numbers exactly divisible by 4

In 25 and 26:   (a) Write and graph the set which is the intersection of set P and set Q, $P \cap Q$.   (b) Write and graph the set which is the union of set P and set Q, $P \cup Q$.
25. $P = \{1, 3, 4, 6, 7, 8\}$, $Q = \{2, 4, 5, 6, 8, 9\}$
26. $P = \{0, 1, 4, 6, 8, 9, 10\}$, $Q = \{0, 1, 3, 4, 5, 6\}$

CHAPTER III

OPEN PHRASES, OPEN SENTENCES, AND TRUTH SETS

1. Open Sentences and Truth Sets

Consider the following sentence: It is the capital of New York State.

We cannot tell whether this sentence is true or false until more information, the name of the particular city that is to replace "It," is known. Such a sentence is called an **open sentence.** Let us assume that "It" can be replaced by an element of the set {New York, Rochester, Albany, Buffalo}. If "It" is replaced by Albany, the resulting sentence, "Albany is the capital of New York State," is a true sentence. Suppose "It" is replaced by any other element of the given set of cities, for example, Rochester. Now the resulting sentence, "Rochester is the capital of New York State," is a false sentence.

In the sentence "It is the capital of New York State," "It" does not refer to a definite city, but to any one of a set of cities. "It" is a symbol which holds a place for, or represents, any one of a given set of cities. Such a symbol is called a **variable.**

The set from which the replacements for the variable are selected is called the **replacement set,** or **domain** of the variable. In the previous discussion, {New York, Rochester, Albany, Buffalo} is the replacement set.

The subset of the domain of the variable consisting of those elements of the domain which make the open sentence true is called the **truth set,** or the **solution set,** of the open sentence. In our previous discussion, {Albany} is the truth set of the open sentence.

In mathematics, we often use a letter such as n or x to represent a variable. For example, the open sentence "A number $+ 3 = 7$" may be written "$n + 3 = 7$" if we use the letter n to represent "A number." If the domain of the variable n is {1, 2, 3, 4, 5}, then 4 is the only element of the domain which makes the open sentence a true sentence.

$$n + 3 = 7$$
If $n = 1$, then $1 + 3 = 7$ is a false sentence.
If $n = 2$, then $2 + 3 = 7$ is a false sentence.
If $n = 3$, then $3 + 3 = 7$ is a false sentence.
If $n = 4$, then $4 + 3 = 7$ is a *true* sentence.
If $n = 5$, then $5 + 3 = 7$ is a false sentence.

Therefore, the truth set of the sentence $n + 3 = 7$ is $\{4\}$.

This is sometimes written as $\{n \mid n + 3 = 7\} = \{4\}$, and is read "the set of all numbers n such that $n + 3 = 7$ is the set consisting of the number 4." We must remember that $n \in \{1, 2, 3, 4, 5\}$.

The elements of the domain of a variable are called the **values** of the variable. Thus, in the previous problem the values of the variable n were 1, 2, 3, 4, and 5. If a variable has only one value it is called a **constant.**

If no member of a replacement set will make a sentence a true sentence, we say that the truth set is the **empty set,** or **null set,** represented by the symbol $\varnothing$.

~~~~~~~~~~ MODEL PROBLEMS ~~~~~~~~~~

1. Using the replacement set {Japan, France, Greece, Canada, India}, find the replacement or replacements for x that will change the open sentence "x is in North America" into a true sentence.

   Solution: In the open sentence "x is in North America," replace the variable x by each member of the replacement set.

   x is in North America.
   Japan is in North America is a false sentence.
   France is in North America is a false sentence.
   Greece is in North America is a false sentence.
   Canada is in North America is a *true* sentence.
   India is in North America is a false sentence.

   Answer: Canada

   > [*Note:* Since Canada is the replacement that changes the open sentence to a true sentence, the set {Canada} is the truth set of the open sentence.]

2. Using the domain $\{0, 1, 2, 3\}$, find the truth set for the open sentence $2n > 3$.

   Solution: Replace the variable n in the open sentence $2n > 3$ by each member of the replacement set.

   $2n > 3$
   If $n = 0$, then $2 \times 0 > 3$, or $0 > 3$, is a false sentence.
   If $n = 1$, then $2 \times 1 > 3$, or $2 > 3$, is a false sentence.
   If $n = 2$, then $2 \times 2 > 3$, or $4 > 3$, is a *true* sentence.
   If $n = 3$, then $2 \times 3 > 3$, or $6 > 3$, is a *true* sentence.

Answer: Since $n = 2$ and $n = 3$ are replacements that make $2n > 3$ a true sentence, the truth set is $\{2, 3\}$.

The answer may also be written as follows:
$$\{n \mid 2n > 3\} = \{2, 3\} \text{ when } n \in \{0, 1, 2, 3\}$$

3. Using the domain $\{1, 2, 3\}$, find the solution set for the open sentence $y + 5 = 9$.

Solution: Replace the variable y in the open sentence $y + 5 = 9$ by each member of the replacement set.

$$y + 5 = 9$$
If $y = 1$, then $1 + 5 = 9$ is a false sentence.
If $y = 2$, then $2 + 5 = 9$ is a false sentence.
If $y = 3$, then $3 + 5 = 9$ is a false sentence.

Answer: Since no member of the replacement set changes the open sentence $y + 5 = 9$ into a true statement, we say that the solution set has no members. In other words, the solution set is the empty set, or null set, symbolized $\varnothing$.

4. If $x \in \{1, 2, 3\}$, determine the elements of $\{x \mid 3x - 1 < 8\}$.

Solution: Replace the variable x in the open sentence $3x - 1 < 8$ by each member of the domain.

$$3x - 1 < 8$$
If $x = 1$, then $3 \times 1 - 1 < 8$, or $2 < 8$ is a *true* sentence.
If $x = 2$, then $3 \times 2 - 1 < 8$, or $5 < 8$ is a *true* sentence.
If $x = 3$, then $3 \times 3 - 1 < 8$, or $8 < 8$ is a false sentence.

Answer: $\{x \mid 3x - 1 < 8\} = \{1, 2\}$ when $x \in \{1, 2, 3\}$

Exercises

In 1–16, tell whether or not the sentences are open sentences.

1. Franklin D. Roosevelt was a President of the United States.
2. She is pretty.
3. Mercury is the smallest planet.
4. X is a member of the United Nations.
5. Columbus discovered Alaska.
6. He hit the most home runs in a season.
7. Y is the world's heavyweight champion.

8. $2 + 3 = 5 + 0$ **9.** $6 - 3 = 5 + 1$ **10.** $x + 10 = 14$
11. $y - 4 = 12$ **12.** $6 + 5 > 10$ **13.** $3 + 2 < 10 \times 0$
14. $n > 7$ **15.** $r < 5 + 2$ **16.** $2t > 5$

In 17–31, tell what is the variable.

17. He is the tallest boy in our class.
18. She has blue eyes.
19. It is the longest river in the United States.
20. He is our principal.
21. X is a senator.
22. The population of New York City is N people.
23. The highest mountain in the world is R.
24. $x + 5 = 9$ **25.** $4y = 20$ **26.** $r - 6 = 12$ **27.** $.5x = 30$
28. $n > 6$ **29.** $n + 1 < 3$ **30.** $2d > 7$ **31.** $14 < h + 9$

32. Using the replacement set {New York, California, Colorado, Rhode Island, Maine}, find the replacement or replacements for Y that will change the open sentence "Y is east of Ohio" to a true sentence.
33. Using the domain {Russia, China, United States, France, Argentina}, find the replacement or replacements for X that will change the open sentence "X has the greatest population in the world" to a true sentence.
34. Using the replacement set {baseball, bridge, football, basketball, checkers, chess}, find the replacement or replacements for G that will change the open sentence "In playing a game of G, a ball is used" to a true sentence.

In 35–50, use the domain {0, 1, 2, 3, 4, 5} to find all the replacements that will change the open sentence to a true sentence. If no replacement will make a true sentence, write *None*.

35. $n + 3 = 7$ **36.** $5 - n = 2$ **37.** $2x = 4$ **38.** $5z = 0$
39. $y + 7 = 15$ **40.** $2m = 7$ **41.** $2x + 1 = 5$ **42.** $x - x = 0$
43. $n > 2$ **44.** $2n < 6$ **45.** $n + 3 > 9$ **46.** $2n + 1 < 8$
47. $\dfrac{n + 1}{2} = 2$ **48.** $\dfrac{2n + 1}{3} = 4$ **49.** $\dfrac{n}{4} > 1$ **50.** $\dfrac{3x}{2} < x$

In 51–58, using the replacement set {1, 2, 3, 4, 5, 6, 7, 8, 9, 10}, find the truth set.

51. $x + 6 = 9$ **52.** $8 - x = 5$ **53.** $2x + 1 = 24$ **54.** $16 = 18 - x$
55. $y > 9$ **56.** $4 < m$ **57.** $2m > 17$ **58.** $2x - 1 > 50$

In 59–66, using the domain {2, $2\frac{1}{2}$, 3, $3\frac{1}{2}$, 4, $4\frac{1}{2}$}, find the solution set.

59. $x + 2 = 4\frac{1}{2}$ **60.** $2x = 7$ **61.** $5 - r = \frac{1}{2}$ **62.** $\dfrac{x}{2} = 2.25$

63. $y > 4$ **64.** $m < 3$ **65.** $2x > 8$ **66.** $3a < 4.5$

In 67–74, using the domain $\{1, 2, 3, 4, 5\}$, find the truth set.

67. $y + 2 = 6$ **68.** $7 - t = 2$ **69.** $5n + 1 = 1$ **70.** $3x - 1 = 7$

71. $q < 2$ **72.** $2s + 1 > 8$ **73.** $4 < n + 1$ **74.** $2t + 3 > 15$

In 75–82, using the domain $\{3, 3\frac{1}{2}, 4, 4\frac{1}{2}, 5, 5\frac{1}{2}\}$, find the truth set.

75. $x + 2 = 6\frac{1}{2}$ **76.** $y - 2 = 3.5$ **77.** $2x - 1 = 5$ **78.** $5\frac{1}{2} = x + \frac{1}{2}$

79. $m > 5$ **80.** $m < 4\frac{1}{2}$ **81.** $2n > 8$ **82.** $2n < 7$

In 83–90, using the domain $\{2.1, 2.2, 2.3, 2.4, 2.5\}$, find the solution set.

83. $4n = 10$ **84.** $x + .1 = 2.4$ **85.** $3x - 4 = 2.3$ **86.** $\dfrac{y}{2} = 3.6$

87. $n > 2.0$ **88.** $y > 2\frac{1}{4}$ **89.** $z < 2\frac{1}{3}$ **90.** $2x + 3 < 6.5$

In 91–98, determine the elements of the set if the domain of the variable is the one indicated.

91. $\{n \mid n + 2 = 5\}$, $n \in \{0, 1, 2, 3, 4, 5\}$

92. $\{x \mid x - 4 = 6\}$, $x \in \{7, 8, 9, 10\}$

93. $\{r \mid r > 4\}$, $r \in \{3, 4, 5, 6\}$

94. $\{y \mid y - 1 < 8\}$, $y \in \{7, 8, 9, 10\}$

95. $\{x \mid 2x + 1 = 8\}$, $x \in \{0, 2, 4, 6\}$

96. $\{r \mid 2r - 1 > 4\}$, $r \in \{1, 2, 3, 4\}$

97. $\{d \mid 9 - d = 5\}$, $d \in \{0, 1, 2, 3, 4, 5\}$

98. $\{x \mid 3x + 1 < 12\}$, $x \in \{0, 1, 2, 3, 4, 5\}$

2. Graphing the Truth Set of an Open Sentence Containing One Variable

After we have found the truth set of an open sentence, we can graph the truth set by using the procedure we have already learned for graphing sets on a number line.

―――――――― **MODEL PROBLEMS** ――――――――

1. Using the replacement set $\{0, 1, 2, 3, 4\}$, find and graph the truth set for $2x + 1 = 5$.

Solution:

Step 1. Replace the variable x in the open sentence $2x + 1 = 5$ by each element of the replacement set.

$$2x + 1 = 5$$
If $x = 0$, then $2 \times 0 + 1 = 5$ is a false sentence.
If $x = 1$, then $2 \times 1 + 1 = 5$ is a false sentence.
If $x = 2$, then $2 \times 2 + 1 = 5$ is a *true* sentence.
If $x = 3$, then $2 \times 3 + 1 = 5$ is a false sentence.
If $x = 4$, then $2 \times 4 + 1 = 5$ is a false sentence.

Step 2. Since 2 is the only element of the replacement set that changes the open sentence to a true sentence, the truth set is {2}.

Step 3. Graph the truth set {2}.

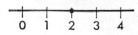

2. Find and graph the solution set of $n + 1 > 2$ when the domain is {0, 1, 2, 3, 4}.

Solution:

Step 1. Replace the variable n in the open sentence $n + 1 > 2$ by each element of the domain.

$$n + 1 > 2$$
If $n = 0$, then $0 + 1 > 2$ is a false sentence.
If $n = 1$, then $1 + 1 > 2$ is a false sentence.
If $n = 2$, then $2 + 1 > 2$ is a *true* sentence.
If $n = 3$, then $3 + 1 > 2$ is a *true* sentence.
If $n = 4$, then $4 + 1 > 2$ is a *true* sentence.

Step 2. Since the values 2, 3, and 4 are the elements of the domain that change the open sentence to a true sentence, the solution set is {2, 3, 4}.

Step 3. Graph the solution set {2, 3, 4}.

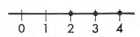

3. If the domain is {numbers of arithmetic}, graph the truth set of $x > 2$ or $x = 2$ (meaning x is greater than 2 or x is equal to 2). $x > 2$ or $x = 2$ may be written more compactly $x \geq 2$.

Solution:

Step 1. We see that 2 or any number greater than 2 are elements of the domain that change the open sentence to a true sentence. Therefore, the truth set is {2 and the numbers greater than 2}.

Step 2. Graph the truth set {2 and the numbers greater than 2}.

4. Graph the truth set of $1 < x \le 4$; $x \in$ {numbers of arithmetic}.

Solution:

Step 1. We see that 4 and any number that is greater than 1 and also less than 4 are elements of the domain that change the open sentence to a true sentence. Therefore, the truth set is {4 and the numbers between 1 and 4}.

Step 2. Graph the truth set {4 and the numbers between 1 and 4}. Note that the non-darkened circle at 1 indicates that 1 is not an element of the truth set.

Exercises

In 1–8, find and graph the truth set when the replacement set is {0, 1, 2, 3, 4, 5}.

1. $2n = 4$ **2.** $n + 3 = 6$ **3.** $2x - 1 = 7$ **4.** $5x = 0$

5. $y > 4$ **6.** $t \le 1$ **7.** $t - 3 > 1$ **8.** $3t + 1 \le 7$

In 9–16, find and graph the solution set when the domain is {0, 1, 2, 3, 4, 5, 6, 7, 8, 9, 10}.

9. $4x = 12$ **10.** $y - 6 = 4$ **11.** $2z + 8 = 8$ **12.** $3a - 1 = 26$

13. $t \ge 5$ **14.** $s + 2 < 11$ **15.** $19 < 3x + 2$ **16.** $14 > 5x + 1$

In 17–36, if $x \in$ {coordinates of points on the number line}, graph the truth set.

17. $x = 5$ **18.** $x + 7 = 10$ **19.** $x - 3 = 5$ **20.** $2x = 14$

21. $2x + 1 = 13$ **22.** $3x - 1 = 8$ **23.** $x > 4$ **24.** $x < 6$

25. $2x > 6$ **26.** $3x < 8$ **27.** $x \ge 5$ **28.** $x \le 8$

29. $1 < x < 5$ **30.** $2 \le x < 6$ **31.** $4 < x \le 8$ **32.** $0 \le x \le 7$

33. $x + 3 = x + 3$ **34.** $x + 3x = 4x$ **35.** $x + 4 = 4 + x$ **36.** $x - 1 = x + 4$

3. Translating Verbal Phrases Into Algebraic Language

An expression or mathematical phrase that contains one or more variables is called an ***open expression***, or an ***open phrase***. For example, $2n$ is an open phrase because we do not know what number $2n$ represents until we know what number n represents, that is, the value of n. An open phrase such as $2n$ is also called an ***algebraic expression***.

In Chapter I on pages 19 and 20, we saw how number relationships could be expressed with mathematical symbols. Now let us learn how to translate verbal phrases into the language of algebra. In algebra, we use letters to represent variables and we use symbols to represent operations on numbers.

VERBAL PHRASES INVOLVING ADDITION

$5 + 4$ means that 5 and 4 are to be added.

$a + b$ means that a and b are to be added.

All of the verbal phrases "a plus b," "the sum of a and b," "a and b are added," "a increased by b," "b more than a" are written $a + b$ in algebraic language. Notice that many different verbal phrases can be expressed by a single algebraic expression.

When we say "7 exceeds 5 by 2," we mean that 7 is 2 more than 5, $7 = 5 + 2$. If we wish to write a number which exceeds 10 by 4, we write a number that is 4 more than 10: $10 + 4$, or 14. To write a number which exceeds a by b, we write a number that is b more than a, or $a + b$.

VERBAL PHRASES INVOLVING SUBTRACTION

$5 - 4$ means from 5 subtract 4.

$a - b$ means from a subtract b.

All of the verbal phrases "the difference between a and b," "a minus b," "b subtracted from a," "a decreased by b," "a diminished by b," "b less than a," "a reduced by b" are written $a - b$ in algebraic language.

VERBAL PHRASES INVOLVING MULTIPLICATION

5×4 means that 5 and 4 are to be multiplied.

$a \times b$ means that a and b are to be multiplied.

Phrases such as "the product of a and b" and "a times b" mean that a and b are to be multiplied.

In algebra, multiplication may be indicated in several ways. For example, to write in symbols that 7 and t are to be multiplied, we can use the following methods:

1. $7 \times t$, using the symbol $\times$ between 7 and t.
2. $7 \cdot t$, using a raised center dot between 7 and t. (Be careful not to confuse the dot with a decimal point.)

3. $7t$, omitting the multiplication symbol and placing 7 and t next to each other. Note that this cannot be done with numbers of arithmetic. If we wish to multiply 5 and 4, we *may not* place the 5 next to the 4 and write 54. We know that 54 means the number fifty-four, whereas 5×4 is a numeral which names the same number as twenty.

4. $7(t)$, $(7)t$, $(7)(t)$, placing the 7 and t next to each other and enclosing one or both in parentheses.

Similarly, there are four ways in which we may write in symbols that a and b are to be multiplied: $a \times b$, $a \cdot b$, ab, $(a)(b)$.

VERBAL PHRASES INVOLVING DIVISION

$5 \div 4$ and $\dfrac{5}{4}$ mean that 5 is to be divided by 4.

$a \div b$ and $\dfrac{a}{b}$ mean that a is to be divided by b.

In some verbal phrases, we can use a comma to prevent misreading. For example, in "the product of x and y, decreased by 2," the comma after y tells us that the phrase means $(xy) - 2$ and not $x(y - 2)$.

～～～～～～～～～ MODEL PROBLEMS ～～～～～～～～～

1. Use mathematical symbols to translate each of the following verbal phrases into algebraic language:

   a. w more than 3   *Ans.* $3 + w$

   b. r decreased by 2   *Ans.* $r - 2$

   c. the product of $5r$ and s *Ans.* $5rs$

   d. 4 divided by x *Ans.* $4 \div x$

   e. twice x decreased by 10   *Ans.* $2x - 10$

   f. 25, diminished by 4 times n *Ans.* $25 - 4n$

   g. the sum of t and u, divided by 6   *Ans.* $\dfrac{t + u}{6}$

   h. 100 decreased by twice $(x + 5)$ *Ans.* $100 - 2(x + 5)$

2. Represent in algebraic language:

   a. a number which exceeds 5 by m *Ans.* $5 + m$

   b. a number which x exceeds by 5   *Ans.* $x - 5$

    c. twice the sum of x and y *Ans.* $2(x + y)$
    d. a weight which is 40 lb. heavier than p lb.   *Ans.* $p + 40$ lb.
    e. a distance which is 20 ft. shorter than f ft.   *Ans.* $f - 20$ ft.
    f. a sum of money which is twice d dollars   *Ans.* $2d$ dollars

    g. the number of yards in x ft.   *Ans.* $\dfrac{x}{3}$ ft.

Exercises

In 1–22, use mathematical symbols to translate the verbal phrase into algebraic language.

1. the sum of b and 8   **2.** x diminished by y
3. the product of x and y **4.** the quotient of s and t
5. 12 increased by a **6.** 5 less than d
7. 8 divided by y **8.** y multiplied by 10
9. the product of $2c$ and $3d$ **10.** t more than w
11. d less than c **12.** twice the difference of p and q
13. one-third of z **14.** x subtracted from 5
15. a number that exceeds m by 4   **16.** one half of the sum of $L + W$
17. 5 times x, increased by 2   **18.** 10 decreased by twice a
19. 36 divided by the sum of t and u **20.** 7 less than one-half d
21. the product of x and y decreased by one-half the sum of x and y
22. 4 less than twice the sum of a and 5

In 23–40, using the letter n to represent the variable "a number," write the verbal phrase in algebraic language.

23. a number increased by 2
24. 20 more than a number
25. 8 increased by a number
26. a number decreased by 6
27. 2 less than a number
28. 12 decreased by a number
29. 3 times a number
30. three-fourths of a number
31. 4 times a number, increased by 3
32. 10 times a number, decreased by 2
33. 30 increased by 4 times a number
34. 8 more than the product of 3 times a number
35. 3 less than twice a number
36. 30 decreased by a number

37. one-third of the product of 5 times a number
38. one-half of, 10 more than a number
39. the product of 5 more than a number, and 4
40. twice the sum of, one-half a number and 1

In 41–52, represent the answer in algebraic language, using the variable mentioned in the problem.

41. The number of miles traveled by Warren is represented by m. If Bill traveled 100 miles farther than Warren, represent the number of miles Bill traveled.
42. Mary's age in years is represented by y. If Tom is 5 years older than Mary, represent his age in years.
43. Betty weighed w pounds. Represent her weight after she reduced 10 pounds.
44. Mr. Gold invested $1000 in stocks. If he lost d dollars when he sold them, represent the amount he received for them.
45. The cost of a fur coat is 5 times the cost of a cloth coat. If the cloth coat costs x dollars, represent the cost of the fur coat.
46. Sally weighs 2.5 times as much as Helen. If Helen weighs m pounds, represent Sally's weight.
47. The length of a rectangle is represented by L. If the width of the rectangle is one-half of its length, represent its width.
48. Robert is 4 times as tall as Perry. If Robert is y inches tall, represent Perry's height.
49. Harry weighs 90 pounds. If Charles's weight exceeds Harry's weight by w pounds, represent Charles's weight.
50. After 2 feet had been cut from a piece of lumber, there were f feet left. Represent the length of the original piece of lumber.
51. Saul is 25 years old. Represent his age x years ago.
52. Paul and Martha saved 100 dollars. If the amount saved by Paul is represented by x, represent the amount saved by Martha.

In 53–56, translate the verbal phrase into algebraic language, representing the two numbers by L and W, with L being the larger.

53. the sum of twice the larger number and twice the smaller number
54. the sum of the larger number and the smaller number, doubled
55. 10 times the smaller number, decreased by 6 times the larger number
56. 1 less than 5 times the larger number, this result divided by 3 times the smaller number

In 57–72, write a verbal phrase which gives a meaning of the symbol, if n in the symbol represents "a number."

57. $3n$ **58.** $n + 4$ **59.** $n - 3$ **60.** $\frac{1}{2}n$
61. $2n + 1$ **62.** $3n - 1$ **63.** $5 - n$ **64.** $10 + n$

65. $\dfrac{n}{4}$ **66.** $\dfrac{n+2}{2}$ **67.** $\dfrac{n-8}{3}$ **68.** $\dfrac{20-2n}{5}$

69. $2(n+1)$ **70.** $4(3n-1)$ **71.** $\frac{1}{2}(2n+1)$ **72.** $4+2(n-1)$

In 73–78, state the difference in meaning between the two symbols.

73. $x-10;\ 10-x$ **74.** $2(x+3);\ 2x+3$ **75.** $a-b;\ b-a$

76. $3(a+b);\ 3a+b$ **77.** $\dfrac{x}{4};\ \dfrac{4}{x}$ **78.** $\frac{1}{2}(x-6);\ \frac{1}{2}x-6$

4. Problems Involving Variables Represented by Letters

Procedure. To solve problems in which letters represent variables:

1. **Write a similar problem involving numbers of arithmetic.**
2. **Solve this arithmetic problem.**
3. **Use the same method to solve the problem involving the letters.**

~~~~~~~~~~ **MODEL PROBLEMS** ~~~~~~~~~~

1. Represent the value of n hats, each worth d dollars.

   Solution: First write a similar problem. Represent the value of 5 hats, each worth 10 dollars. We can solve this problem by multiplying the number of hats, 5, by the value of each hat, 10 dollars, giving 5×10, or 50 dollars. Similarly, in the original problem, the value of all the hats will be the number of hats, n, times the value of each hat, d, which is $n \times d$, or nd dollars.

   Answer: nd dollars

2. Express the number of yards in d feet.

   Solution: First find the number of yards in 15 feet. Since each yard contains 3 feet, find the number of yards in 15 feet by dividing 15 by 3, giving $\frac{15}{3}$ or 5 yards. Similarly, to represent the number of yards in d feet, divide d by 3, giving $\dfrac{d}{3}$.

   Answer: $\dfrac{d}{3}$

Exercises

1. A suit costs $65. Represent the cost of n suits.
2. A ballpoint pen sells for 39 cents. Represent the cost of x pens.
3. Represent the cost of t feet of lumber which sells for g cents a foot.
4. If Sam started on a trip with w dollars and spent $50 on the trip, represent the amount he had left at the end of the trip.
5. If Helen weighs p pounds, represent her weight after she has gained 8 pounds.
6. If Hilda weighed 90 pounds, represent her weight after she had lost x pounds.
7. Ronald, who weighs c pounds, is d pounds overweight. Represent the number of pounds Ronald should weigh.
8. Toby is n years old now. Represent his age 4 years from now.
9. Saul is b years old now. Represent his age x years from now.
10. Pauline is x years old. Represent her age 10 years ago.
11. A man is x years old. Represent his age b years ago.
12. Helen is 35 years of age. If Sue is x years younger than Helen, represent Sue's age.
13. The sum of the length and the width of a rectangle is 20 feet. If the length is represented by x feet, represent the width.
14. A man spent $150 for a suit and a coat. If he spent y dollars for the coat, represent the amount he spent for the suit.
15. A car travels r miles per hour. The rate of a train exceeds the rate of the car by 50 miles per hour. Represent the rate of the train.
16. The cost of a sofa exceeds the cost of a chair by $200. If the sofa costs x dollars, represent the cost of the chair.
17. A man bought an article for c dollars and sold it at a profit of $25. Represent the amount for which he sold it.
18. A man gave a total of w dollars to his son and to his daughter. If the boy received m dollars, represent the amount the girl received.
19. The length of a rectangle is represented by L feet. Represent the width of the rectangle if it is 5 feet less than the length.
20. The width of a rectangle is represented by W feet. Represent the length of the rectangle if it exceeds the width by 8 feet.
21. The width of a rectangle is x feet. Represent the length of the rectangle if it exceeds twice the width by 3 feet.
22. Represent the number of cents in n nickels.
23. Represent the number of cents in q quarters.
24. Represent the number of cents in d dimes and h half-dollars.
25. Represent the number of cents in x nickels and $(25 - x)$ dimes.
26. If a plane travels 350 miles per hour, represent the distance it will travel in h hours.

27. If an auto traveled for 5 hours at an average rate of r miles per hour, represent the distance it has traveled.
28. A ship sailed for t hours at an average rate of r miles per hour. Represent the number of miles it sailed.
29. Represent the diameter of a circle whose radius is r inches.
30. Represent algebraically the number of:
    a. inches in f feet   b. feet in i inches   c. days in w weeks
    d. weeks in d days   e. hours in d days   f. days in h hours
31. Represent the cost of a foot of lumber if a yard of lumber costs m dollars.
32. A boy weighs p pounds. Represent the number of pounds he must gain to weigh 90 pounds.
33. Represent the number of toys you can buy with c dollars if each toy costs m dollars.
34. Represent the number of pieces of candy you can buy with n nickels and d dimes if each piece of candy is worth 5 cents.

5. Understanding the Meaning of Some Vocabulary Used in Algebra

TERM

A **term** is a numeral, a variable, or both numerals and variables which are connected by multiplication or division signs. For example, 5, x, $4y$, $5(x - 4)$, and $\frac{2x}{3y}$ are terms. In an algebraic expression such as $4a + 2b - 5c$, which has more than one term, the terms $4a$, $2b$, and $5c$ are separated by $+$ and $-$ signs.

FACTORS OF A PRODUCT

If two or more numbers are to be multiplied, each of the numbers, as well as the product of any of them, is a **factor** of the product. For example, in the product $3xy$, the factors are 1, 3, x, y, $3x$, $3y$, xy, and $3xy$. Note that when we factor whole numbers, we usually concern ourselves only with factors that are whole numbers.

COEFFICIENT

In a product, any factor or group of factors is the **coefficient** of the remaining factor or factors. In the product $4ab$, 4 is the coefficient of ab, $4a$ is the coefficient of b, and $4b$ is the coefficient of a.

When a constant and variables are factors of a product, the constant is called the **numerical coefficient** of the product. For example, in $4ab$, the numerical coefficient is 4.

Since x names the same number as $1 \cdot x$, we sometimes say that the coefficient of x is understood to be 1. Likewise, we may say that the coefficient of ab is understood to be 1.

BASE, EXPONENT, POWER

We know that 4×4 may be written 4^2, which is read "4 square," "four squared," or "4 to the second power." The product $s \times s$ may be written s^2, which is read "s square," "s squared," or "s to the second power."

In 4^2, the small ^{2} above and to the right of 4 tells us that 4 is to be used as a factor 2 times. Similarly, in s^2, the small ^{2} above and to the right of s tells us that s is to be used as a factor 2 times.

The product $4 \times 4 \times 4$ may be written 4^3, which is read "4 cube," "4 cubed," or "4 to the third power." The product $e \times e \times e$ may be written e^3, which is read "e cube," "e cubed," or "e to the third power."

In 4^3, the small ^{3} above and to the right of 4 tells us that 4 is to be used as a factor 3 times. Similarly, in e^3, the small ^{3} above and to the right of e tells us that e is to be used as a factor 3 times.

The product $3 \times 3 \times 3 \times 3$ may be written 3^4, which is read "3 to the fourth power." Since $3 \times 3 \times 3 \times 3 = 81$, 3^4 names the same number as 81. We say that the value of 3^4 is 81. We can also say that 81 is the fourth power of 3.

The Fourth Power of 3

$$3^4 = 3 \times 3 \times 3 \times 3 = 81$$

base $\longrightarrow 3 = 81 \longleftarrow$ power, with $4 \longleftarrow$ exponent

In $3^4 = 81$, the 3 is called a base, the 4 is called an exponent, and the 81 is called a power. A **base** is a number which is used as a factor two or more times. An **exponent** is a number which tells how many times the base is to be used as a factor. A **power** is a number which can be expressed as a product in which all the factors are the same.

We will agree that 4 means 4^1 and that a means a^1.

Note that an exponent refers only to the base which is directly to the left of it. Thus:

$$c^3d^4 \text{ means } cccdddd \qquad cd^4 \text{ means } cdddd \qquad 5d^2 \text{ means } 5dd$$

If we wish to use $5d$ as a factor 2 times, that is $(5d)(5d)$, we write $(5d)^2$. Notice how the meanings of $5d^2$ and $(5d)^2$ differ: $5d^2$ means $5dd$, whereas $(5d)^2$ means $(5d)(5d)$.

MODEL PROBLEM

Name the coefficient, base, and exponent in the term $4x^5$.

Answer: The coefficient is 4, the base is x, and the exponent is 5.

Exercises

In 1–6, name the factors (other than 1) of each product.

1. xy **2.** $3a$ **3.** $5n$ **4.** $7mn$ **5.** $13xy$ **6.** $11st$

In 7–12, name the numerical coefficient of x.

7. $8x$ **8.** $(5+2)x$ **9.** $\frac{1}{2}x$ **10.** x **11.** $1.4x$ **12.** $2+7x$

In 13–18, name the base and exponent in the term.

13. m^2 **14.** s^3 **15.** t **16.** 10^6 **17.** $(5y)^4$ **18.** $(x+y)^5$

In 19–27, write each product using exponents.

19. $m \cdot m \cdot m$ **20.** $b \cdot b \cdot b \cdot b \cdot b$ **21.** $10 \cdot 10 \cdot 10 \cdot 10$
22. $2 \cdot 2 \cdot 2 \cdot 2 \cdot 2 \cdot 2$ **23.** $4 \cdot x \cdot x \cdot x \cdot x \cdot x$ **24.** $a \cdot a \cdot a \cdot a \cdot b \cdot b$
25. $7 \cdot r \cdot r \cdot r \cdot s \cdot s$ **26.** $9 \cdot c \cdot c \cdot c \cdot d$ **27.** $(6a)(6a)(6a)$

In 28–33, write the term without using exponents.
28. r^6 **29.** $5x^4$ **30.** x^3y^5 **31.** $4a^4b^2$ **32.** $3c^2d^3e$ **33.** $(3y)^5$

6. Evaluating Algebraic Expressions

The algebraic expression $3n + 1$ represents an unspecified number. It is only when we replace the variable n by a specific number that $3n + 1$ represents a specific number. For example, suppose that the domain of n is $\{1, 2, 3\}$. The specific numbers that $3n + 1$ represents (the values of $3n + 1$) can be found as shown on the next page.

If $n = 1$, $3n + 1 = 3(1) + 1 = 3 + 1 = 4$.
If $n = 2$, $3n + 1 = 3(2) + 1 = 6 + 1 = 7$.
If $n = 3$, $3n + 1 = 3(3) + 1 = 9 + 1 = 10$.

When we determine the number which an algebraic expression represents for specified values of its variables, we are *evaluating the algebraic expression*; that is, we are finding its value or values.

Procedure. To evaluate an algebraic expression:
1. Replace the variables by their specific values.
2. Simplify any number expressions that may be included within symbols of grouping such as parentheses.
3. Simplify any powers and roots. (Roots will be studied later.)
4. Do all multiplications and divisions, performing them in order from left to right.
5. Do all additions and subtractions, performing them in order from left to right.

7. Evaluating Algebraic Expressions Involving Addition, Subtraction, Multiplication, and Division

~~~~~~~ MODEL PROBLEMS ~~~~~~~

1. Evaluate $50 - 3x$ when $x = 7$.

How To Proceed	*Solution*
1. Write the expression.	$50 - 3x$
2. Replace the variable by its given value.	$= 50 - 3 \times 7$
3. Do the multiplication.	$= 50 - 21$
4. Do the subtraction.	$= 29 \quad Ans.$

2. Evaluate $\dfrac{5r}{3} + \dfrac{7s}{2} - \dfrac{t}{5}$ when $r = 6$, $s = 4$, and $t = 15$.

How To Proceed	*Solution*
1. Write the expression.	$\dfrac{5r}{3} + \dfrac{7s}{2} - \dfrac{t}{5}$
2. Replace the variables by the given values.	$= \dfrac{5 \times 6}{3} + \dfrac{7 \times 4}{2} - \dfrac{15}{5}$

3. Do the multiplications.

$$= \frac{30}{3} + \frac{28}{2} - \frac{15}{5}$$

4. Do the divisions.

$$= 10 + 14 - 3$$

5. Do the addition and subtraction.

$$= 21 \quad Ans.$$

Exercises

In 1–18, find the numerical value of the expression. Use $a = 8$, $b = 6$, $d = 3$, $x = 4$, $y = 5$, and $z = 1$.

1. $5a$

2. $\frac{1}{2}x$

3. $.3y$

4. ax

5. $3xy$

6. $\frac{2b}{3}$

7. $\frac{3bd}{9}$

8. $2x + 9$

9. $3y - b$

10. $20 - 4z$

11. $5x + 2y$

12. $ab - dx$

13. $a + 5d + 3x$

14. $9y + 6b - d$

15. $ab - d - xy$

16. $\frac{7y}{5} + \frac{b}{2}$

17. $\frac{dy}{3z} - \frac{z}{d}$

18. $\frac{xy}{z} - \frac{y}{x} - \frac{dy}{xz}$

8. Evaluating Algebraic Expressions Involving Powers

MODEL PROBLEMS

1. Evaluate $4x^3y^2$ when $x = 2$ and $y = 3$.

How To Proceed	*Solution*
1. Write the expression.	$4x^3y^2$
2. Replace the variables by their given values.	$= 4(2)^3(3)^2$
3. Evaluate the powers.	$= 4(2 \times 2 \times 2)(3 \times 3) = 4(8)(9)$
4. Do the multiplication.	$= 288 \quad Ans.$

2. Evaluate $x^2 - 5x + 4$ when $x = 7$.

How To Proceed	*Solution*
1. Write the expression.	$x^2 - 5x + 4$
2. Replace the variable by its given value.	$= (7)^2 - 5(7) + 4$
3. Evaluate the power.	$= 49 - 5(7) + 4$
4. Do the multiplication.	$= 49 - 35 + 4$
5. Do the addition and subtraction.	$= 18 \quad Ans.$

3. Evaluate $4x^2 + 9y^2$ when $x = 1$ and $y = 4$.

How To Proceed	*Solution*
1. Write the expression.	$4x^2 + 9y^2$
2. Replace the variables by their given values.	$= 4(1)^2 + 9(4)^2$
3. Evaluate the powers.	$= 4(1) + 9(16)$
4. Do the multiplications.	$= 4 + 144$
5. Do the addition.	$= 148 \quad Ans.$

Exercises

In 1–27, find the numerical value of the expression. Use $a = 8$, $b = 6$, $d = 3$, $x = 4$, $y = 5$, and $z = 1$.

1. a^2

2. b^3

3. d^4

4. $4d^3$

5. $6z^5$

6. $\dfrac{b^2}{9}$

7. $\frac{3}{4}x^3$

8. xy^2

9. $2a^2b^3$

10. $\frac{1}{5}x^2y^3z^3$

11. $a^2 + b^2$

12. $b^2 - y^2$

13. $a^2 + b^2 - d^2$

14. $x^2 + x$

15. $b^2 + 2b$

16. $y^2 - 4y$

17. $2b^2 + b$

18. $2y^2 - y$

19. $9a - a^2$

20. $5z - 3z^2$

21. $x^2 + 4y^2$

22. $x^2 + 3x + 5$

23. $y^2 + 2y - 7$

24. $2a^2 - 4a + 6$

25. $2b^2 - 5b - 10$

26. $15 + 5z - z^2$

27. $36 + 5y - 2y^2$

9. Evaluating Expressions Containing Parentheses or Other Symbols of Grouping

~~~~~~~~~~~~~~~~~~~~ **MODEL PROBLEMS** ~~~~~~~~~~~~~~~~~~~~

1. Evaluate $a + (n - 1)d$ when $a = 40$, $n = 10$, and $d = 3$.

How To Proceed	*Solution*
1. Write the expression.	$a + (n - 1)d$
2. Replace the variables by their given values.	$= 40 + (10 - 1)(3)$
3. Simplify the expression within the parentheses.	$= 40 + (9)(3)$
4. Do the multiplication.	$= 40 + 27$
5. Do the addition.	$= 67$ *Ans.*

2. Evaluate $(2x)^2 - 2x^2$ when $x = 4$.

How To Proceed	*Solution*
1. Write the expression.	$(2x)^2 - 2x^2$
2. Replace the variable by its given value.	$= (2 \times 4)^2 - 2(4)^2$
3. Simplify the expression within the parentheses.	$= (8)^2 - 2(4)^2$
4. Evaluate the powers.	$= 64 - 2(16)$
5. Do the multiplication.	$= 64 - 32$
6. Do the subtraction.	$= 32$ *Ans.*

3. Evaluate $\dfrac{b^2 + c^2 - a^2}{2bc}$ when $a = 5$, $b = 4$, and $c = 3$.

How To Proceed	*Solution*
1. Write the expression.	$\dfrac{b^2 + c^2 - a^2}{2bc}$
2. Replace the variables by their given values.	$= \dfrac{(4)^2 + (3)^2 - (5)^2}{2 \times 4 \times 3}$
3. Since the fraction line is a symbol of grouping, evaluate the numerator and denominator separately.	$= \dfrac{16 + 9 - 25}{24}$ $= \dfrac{0}{24}$
4. Do the division.	$= 0$ *Ans.*

Exercises

In 1–24, find the value of the expression. Use $w = 10$, $x = 8$, $y = 5$, and $z = 2$.

1. $2(x + 5)$ **2.** $x(y - 2)$ **3.** $3(2x + z)$

4. $4(2x - 3y)$ **5.** $\dfrac{x}{2}(y + z)$ **6.** $\frac{1}{2}x(y + z)$

7. $\frac{5}{9}(4x - 5)$ **8.** $\frac{5}{9}(4y - z)$ **9.** $4x + (y + z)$

10. $3y - (x - z)$ **11.** $2x + 5(y - 1)$ **12.** $2(x + z) - 5$

13. $30 - 4(x - y)$ **14.** $(w + x)(y + z)$ **15.** $(w - z)x - y$

16. $3x^2$ **17.** $(3x)^2$ **18.** $y^2 + z^2$

19. $(y + z)^2$ **20.** $w^3 - x^3$ **21.** $(w - x)^3$

22. $3w^2 - 2x^2$ **23.** $(3w - 2x)^2$ **24.** $(3w)^2 - (2x)^2$

In 25–37, find the value of the expression. Use $a = 8$, $b = 6$, $d = 3$, $x = 4$, $y = 5$, and $z = 1$.

25. $\dfrac{x + 2a}{4}$ **26.** $\dfrac{3a - 2x}{3x - a}$ **27.** $\dfrac{a + b + x}{y - d + z}$

28. $\dfrac{dx - yz + a}{bx - ad + dy}$ **29.** $\dfrac{a^2 + b^2}{y^2}$ **30.** $\dfrac{x^2}{y^2 - d^2}$

31. $\dfrac{d^2 + x^2 - y^2}{2dx}$ **32.** $\dfrac{b^3 - d^3}{(b - d)^3}$ **33.** $\dfrac{(4y)^2 - (3x)^2}{4y^2 - 3x^2}$

34. $4y^2 - 3(2y + 1)(3y - 12)$ **35.** $4(2a^2 + b^2) - 6(4a - 3b)$

36. $\dfrac{x^2 + 2xy + y^2 - z^2}{(x + y + z)(x + y - z)}$ **37.** $\dfrac{x^4 - 2x^2 + 1}{(x - 1)^2(x + 1)^2}$

CHAPTER IV

POSTULATES AND PROPERTIES OF OPERATIONS

During your study of arithmetic, you have probably noticed that numbers have various properties. For example, after many experiences with adding two even numbers, you have concluded that their sum is always an even number. Actually, you have only assumed the truth of this conclusion. You do not know that it is always true. No matter how many times you test the conclusion, there is always the possibility that there is some instance where the sum of two even numbers is not an even number.

Mathematicians have agreed to accept, or have assumed to be true, many properties of numbers. In mathematics, any statement which we accept as being true without proof is called an *assumption,* an *axiom,* or a *postulate.*

Now, we will study some important properties of numbers in the following postulates:

1. Postulates of Equality

THE REFLEXIVE PROPERTY OF EQUALITY

The *reflexive property of equality* states that any number is equal to itself. For example, $5 = 5$, or $7 = 7$.

In general, we assume that for every number a:

$$a = a$$

THE SYMMETRIC PROPERTY OF EQUALITY

The *symmetric property of equality* states that an equality may be reversed. For example, if $4 + 3 = 5 + 2$, then $5 + 2 = 4 + 3$.

In general, we assume that for every number a and every number b:

$$\text{if } a = b, \text{ then } b = a$$

THE TRANSITIVE PROPERTY OF EQUALITY

The *transitive property of equality* states that if one number is equal to a second number, and the second number is equal to a third number, then the first number is equal to the third number. For example, if $5 + 4 = 6 + 3$, and $6 + 3 = 7 + 2$, then $5 + 4 = 7 + 2$.

In general, we assume that for every number a, every number b, and every number c:

$$\text{if } a = b, \text{ and } b = c, \text{ then } a = c$$

The transitive property of equality is useful in the following ways:

If (1) $a = b$ and (2) $b = c$, the transitive property of equality makes it possible for us to replace b in (2) by a and to obtain $a = c$.

Also, we may replace b in (1) by c and obtain $a = c$. We call this replacement process **substitution**, or the **substitution principle.**

Finally, the transitive property of equality allows us to state that two numbers are equal if each of them is equal to a third number.

Exercises

In 1–6, name the property of equality which the sentence illustrates.

1. $5 + 2 = 5 + 2$

2. If $6 + 2 = 5 + 3$, and $5 + 3 = 7 + 1$, then $6 + 2 = 7 + 1$.

3. If $4 + 3 = 6 + 1$, then $6 + 1 = 4 + 3$.

4. $x + y = x + y$

5. If $x = y$, then $y = x$.

6. If $m + n = r + s$, and $r + s = x + y$, then $m + n = x + y$.

In 7–12, name the property of equality which is illustrated in each part.

7. If $10 + 8 = 18$ and $8 + 10 = 18$, then:

    a. $18 = 8 + 10$ *b.* $10 + 8 = 8 + 10$

8. If $2 \times 3 = 6$ and $3 \times 2 = 6$, then:

    a. $6 = 3 \times 2$ *b.* $2 \times 3 = 3 \times 2$

9. If $(2 + 3) + 4 = 9$ and $2 + (3 + 4) = 9$, then:

    a. $9 = 2 + (3 + 4)$ *b.* $(2 + 3) + 4 = 2 + (3 + 4)$

10. If $(2 \times 3) \times 4 = 24$ and $2 \times (3 \times 4) = 24$, then:

    a. $24 = 2 \times (3 \times 4)$ *b.* $(2 \times 3) \times 4 = 2 \times (3 \times 4)$

11. If $3 \times (4 + 1) = 15$, and $3 \times 4 + 3 \times 1 = 15$, then:

    a. $15 = 3 \times 4 + 3 \times 1$ *b.* $3 \times (4 + 1) = 3 \times 4 + 3 \times 1$

12. If $5 \times (3 + 1) = 5 \times 4$, and $5 \times 4 = 20$, and also $20 = 15 + 5$, then:

    a. $5 \times (3 + 1) = 20$ *b.* $5 \times (3 + 1) = 15 + 5$

2. Understanding the Meaning of Closure Under an Operation

From your experience in arithmetic, you have discovered that if two elements of the set of natural numbers are added, the result is always another natural number. Further, the result is always unique; there is one—and only one—natural number which represents the result when two natural numbers are added. For example, $6 + 2 = 8$, and only 8. We say that *the set of natural numbers is closed under addition.*

In general, for all a and b which are elements of the set of natural numbers, there is a unique natural number c such that:

$$a + b = c$$

If two elements of the set of natural numbers are multiplied, the result is always a unique natural number. For example, $6 \times 4 = 24$, and only 24. We say that *the set of natural numbers is closed under multiplication.*

In general, for all a and b which are elements of the set of natural numbers, there is a unique natural number c such that:

$$ab = c$$

However, when one element of the set of natural numbers is subtracted from another element of the set, the result does not always represent a natural number. For example, $4 - 6$ does not represent a natural number. Hence, we say that *the set of natural numbers is not closed under subtraction.*

Likewise, since $6 \div 4$ does not represent a natural number, we say that *the set of natural numbers is not closed under division.*

A set is closed under an operation when the number that results from performing the operation on two elements of the set is always a member of the set.

Closure under an operation depends on two things: the operation and the domain of numbers being used. We have seen that the set of natural numbers is closed under multiplication but is not closed under division. Thus, closure depends on the operation.

When the operation is addition, the set of even numbers is closed, but the set of odd numbers is not closed. Thus, closure depends on the domain.

Remember that when a set is closed under an operation, it is possible to perform the operation on any two elements of the set and get a result that is also an element of the set.

THE SUBSTITUTION PRINCIPLE

An indicated sum or product of numbers is not dependent upon the numerals that are used to represent the numbers. For example:

$$88(65 + 35) = 88(100) \text{ because } 65 + 35 = 100$$
$$37(24 - 14) = 37(10) \text{ because } 24 - 14 = 10$$

These examples illustrate the substitution principle:

For every number a and every number b, if $a = b$, then b may be substituted for a, and a may be substituted for b in any expression or open sentence.

~~~~~~~~~~~~~ MODEL PROBLEM ~~~~~~~~~~~~~

State whether or not {natural numbers which are multiples of 4} is closed under   (a) addition   (b) subtraction   (c) multiplication   (d) division. Give a reason for your answer in each part.

Solution: The set {natural numbers which are multiples of 4} is the same as the set {4, 8, 12, . . .}.

a. Closed under addition—because the sum of any two elements in the set is also an element of the set.

b. Not closed under subtraction—because $4 - 8$ does not name a number which is an element of the set.

c. Closed under multiplication—because the product of any two elements of the set is also an element of the set.

d. Not closed under division—because $12 \div 4$ does not name a number which is an element of the set.

Exercises

In 1–8, state whether the numerical phrase names a natural number.

1. $8 + 2$ 2. $2 + 8$ 3. $8 - 4$ 4. $4 - 8$
5. 8×4 6. 4×8 7. $8 \div 4$ 8. $4 \div 8$

9. If x and y represent natural numbers, select the phrases that always represent natural numbers.

   a. $x + y$ b. $x - y$ c. xy d. $x \div y$

In 10–19, state whether the set is closed under the indicated operation.

10. {1}; multiplication   **11.** {4}; subtraction
12. {0}; addition   **13.** {1}; division
14. {0, 1}; multiplication   **15.** {0, 2, 4}; subtraction
16. {2, 4, 8}; division   **17.** {0, 1, 2}; multiplication
18. {2, 4, 6, 8, . . .}; addition   **19.** {1, 3, 5, . . .}; multiplication

In 20–28, state whether the set is closed under   (a) addition   (b) subtraction   (c) multiplication   (d) division. Give a reason for your answer in each part.

20. {0}   **21.** {1}   **22.** {10}
23. {0, 1}   **24.** {1, 3, 5}   **25.** {2, 4, 6}
26. {all even numbers}   **27.** {all odd numbers}   **28.** {all multiples of 3}

29. Describe a set which is closed under:
   a. addition   b. subtraction   c. multiplication   d. division

3. Properties of Addition

COMMUTATIVE PROPERTY OF ADDITION

In arithmetic, we assume that we may change the order in which two numbers are added without changing the sum. For example, $4 + 5 = 5 + 4$, and $\frac{1}{2} + \frac{1}{4} = \frac{1}{4} + \frac{1}{2}$. These examples illustrate the **commutative property of addition**.

In general, we assume that for every number a and every number b:

$$a + b = b + a$$

Notice that subtraction does not have the commutative property because $5 - 4 \neq 4 - 5$.

ASSOCIATIVE PROPERTY OF ADDITION

When adding three numbers, we assume that we may group the numbers in different ways without changing the sum. For example, $2 + 5 + 8$ can be found by first adding 2 and 5, getting 7, and then adding 7 to 8, getting 15. In the symbols of mathematics, this is written $(2 + 5) + 8 = 15$. Or, we may add 5 and 8, getting 13, and then add 13 to 2, getting 15. This is written $2 + (5 + 8) = 15$. Therefore, we see that $(2 + 5) + 8 = 2 + (5 + 8)$. This example illustrates the **associative property of addition**.

In general, we assume that for every number a, every number b, and every number c:

$$(a + b) + c = a + (b + c)$$

Notice that subtraction is not associative because $(10 - 8) - 2 \neq 10 - (8 - 2)$.

USES OF PROPERTIES OF ADDITION

When we check addition by adding in the opposite direction, we are using the commutative property.

Adding	Checking
3489 ↓	3489 ↑
1546	1546
5035	5035

The commutative and associative properties may be used to find an indicated sum quickly and easily. Study the following steps that make it simple to add $78 + 64 + 22$ mentally:

Step	Reason
1. $(78 + 64) + 22 = (64 + 78) + 22$	1. Commutative property of addition.
2. $\quad\quad = 64 + (78 + 22)$	2. Associative property of addition.
3. $\quad\quad = 64 + 100$	3. Substitution principle, $(78 + 22) = 100$.
4. $\quad\quad = 164$	4. Substitution principle, $64 + 100 = 164$.

Since the commutative and associative properties of addition make it possible to add numbers in any order, grouped in any way, parentheses may be omitted in indicated sums. For example, $(78 + 64) + 22$, or $78 + (64 + 22)$ may be written $78 + 64 + 22$.

In general, $(a + b) + c$, or $a + (b + c)$ may be written:

$$a + b + c$$

~~~~~~~~~ **MODEL PROBLEMS** ~~~~~~~~~

1. Name the property illustrated in each true sentence.

a. $5 + 13 = 13 + 5$

Ans. Commutative property of addition.

b. $(5 + x) + y = 5 + (x + y)$

Ans. Associative property of addition.

2. State the reason that justifies each step in the following set of related equalities:

Step		Reason
a. $3 + (x + 9) = 3 + (9 + x)$		*Ans.* Commutative property of addition.
b. $= (3 + 9) + x$		*Ans.* Associative property of addition.
c. $= 12 + x$		*Ans.* Substitution principle.

Exercises

In 1–6, name the property illustrated in each true sentence.

1. $7 + 2 = 2 + 7$ **2.** $(9 + 3) + 7 = 9 + (3 + 7)$
3. $8 + (6 + t) = (8 + 6) + t$ **4.** $m + 2n = 2n + m$
5. $(r + s) + t = t + (r + s)$ **6.** $(x + y) + 2z = x + (y + 2z)$

In 7–10:   (*a*) Give a replacement for the question mark which makes the sentence true for all values of the variable.   (*b*) Name the property illustrated in the sentence that is formed when the replacement is made.

7. $2 + x = x + ?$ **8.** $(4 + a) + 7 = 4 + (a + ?)$
9. $23 + ? = x + 23$ **10.** $(8 + ?) + 2 = 8 + (x + 2)$

In 11–16, use properties of addition and the substitution principle to perform the indicated addition mentally in the simplest way.

11. $275 + 83 + 125$ **12.** $398 + 124 + 102 + 376$
13. $.79 + .63 + .21$ **14.** $1.41 + .49 + 2.59 + .26$
15. $2\frac{3}{4} + 1\frac{1}{3} + 4\frac{1}{4}$ **16.** $1\frac{1}{6} + 2\frac{1}{8} + 2\frac{5}{8} + 3\frac{3}{8}$

In 17–20, state the reason that justifies each step in the set of related equalities.

17. *a.* $(31 + 89) + 69 = (89 + 31) + 69$
    b. $= 89 + (31 + 69)$
    c. $= 89 + 100$
    d. $= 189$

18. *a.* $7 + (78 + 13) = 7 + (13 + 78)$
    b. $= (7 + 13) + 78$
    c. $= 20 + 78$
    d. $= 98$

19. $a.$ $5 + (x + 1) = 5 + (1 + x)$
     $b.$ $\qquad\qquad = (5 + 1) + x$
     $c.$ $\qquad\qquad = 6 + x$

20. $a.$ $(x + z) + y = x + (z + y)$
     $b.$ $\qquad\qquad = x + (y + z)$
     $c.$ $\qquad\qquad = (x + y) + z$

In 21–24:   (*a*) Develop the steps of a set of related equalities which show that the sentence is true.   (*b*) Name the property or principle used in each step.

21. $(592 + 649) + 408 = 649 + (592 + 408)$
22. For every y, $12 + (y + 6) = (12 + 6) + y$.
23. For every t, $(10 + t) + 13 = t + 23$.
24. For every a, every b, and every c, $(a + c) + b = c + (b + a)$.

4. Properties of Multiplication

COMMUTATIVE PROPERTY OF MULTIPLICATION

When we multiply numbers of arithmetic, we assume that we may change the order of the factors without changing the product. For example, $5 \times 4 = 4 \times 5$, and $\frac{1}{2} \times \frac{1}{4} = \frac{1}{4} \times \frac{1}{2}$. These examples illustrate the ***commutative property of multiplication.***

In general, we assume that for every number a and every number b:

$$a \times b = b \times a$$

Notice that division does not have the commutative property because $8 \div 4 \neq 4 \div 8$.

ASSOCIATIVE PROPERTY OF MULTIPLICATION

To find a product which involves three factors, we first multiply any two factors and then multiply this result by the third factor. We assume that we do not change the product when we group the numbers differently. For example, to find the product $5 \times 4 \times 2$, we can multiply as follows:

$$5 \times 4 \times 2 = (5 \times 4) \times 2 = 20 \times 2 = 40$$

We can also multiply in a different way as follows:

$$5 \times 4 \times 2 = 5 \times (4 \times 2) = 5 \times 8 = 40$$

Therefore, $(5 \times 4) \times 2 = 5 \times (4 \times 2)$.

This example illustrates the ***associative property of multiplication.***

In general, we assume that for every number a, every number b, and every number c:

$$(a \times b) \times c = a \times (b \times c)$$

Notice that division is not associative because $(8 \div 4) \div 2 = 2 \div 2 = 1$, whereas $8 \div (4 \div 2) = 8 \div 2 = 4$. Therefore, $(8 \div 4) \div 2 \neq 8 \div (4 \div 2)$.

USES OF PROPERTIES OF MULTIPLICATION

When we check multiplication by changing the order of the factors, we are using the commutative property.

Multiplying	Checking
57	23
$\times\,23$	$\times\,57$
171	161
114	115
1311	1311

The commutative and associative properties may be used to find an indicated product quickly and easily. Study the following steps that make it simple to find the product $4 \times 89 \times 25$ mentally:

Step	Reason
1. $(4 \times 89) \times 25 = (89 \times 4) \times 25$	1. Commutative property of multiplication.
2. $= 89 \times (4 \times 25)$	2. Associative property of multiplication.
3. $= 89 \times 100$	3. Substitution principle.
4. $= 8900$	4. Substitution principle.

MODEL PROBLEMS

1. Name the property illustrated in each true sentence.

   a. $6 \times 13 = 13 \times 6$

   Ans. Commutative property of multiplication.

   b. $(4 \times a) \times b = 4 \times (a \times b)$

   Ans. Associative property of multiplication.

2. Give a set of related equalities which show that $(4a) \times 5 = 20a$ is a true sentence, and name the property or principle used in each step.

Solution:

Step	*Reason*
1. $(4a) \times 5 = 4 \times (a \times 5)$	1. Associative property of multiplication.
2. $\quad\quad = 4 \times (5 \times a)$	2. Commutative property of multiplication.
3. $\quad\quad = (4 \times 5) \times a$	3. Associative property of multiplication.
4. $\quad\quad = 20a$	4. Substitution principle.

~~~~~~

Exercises

In 1–6, name the property illustrated in each true sentence.

1. $8 \times 12 = 12 \times 8$
3. $y \times 5 = 5 \times y$
5. $4 \times (\frac{1}{4} \times d) = (4 \times \frac{1}{4}) \times d$

2. $\frac{1}{2} \times (2 \times 4) = (\frac{1}{2} \times 2) \times 4$
4. $(y + 6) \times 3 = 3 \times (y + 6)$
6. $(r \times s) \times t = r \times (s \times t)$

In 7–10: (*a*) State a replacement for the question mark which makes the sentence true for all values of the variable. (*b*) Name the property illustrated in the sentence that is formed when the replacement is made.

7. $z \times 4 = 4 \times ?$
9. $5 \times ? = g \times 5$

8. $(9 \times b) \times 7 = 9 \times (b \times ?)$
10. $? \times (10 \times c) = (\frac{1}{10} \times 10) \times c$

In 11–19, use properties of multiplication and the substitution principle to perform the indicated multiplication mentally in the simplest way.

11. $50 \times 93 \times 2$
14. $12\frac{1}{2} \times 87 \times 8$
17. $2.5 \times 6.9 \times 4$

12. $4 \times 876 \times 250$
15. $2\frac{1}{2} \times 49 \times 40$
18. $5 \times 63 \times 1.2$

13. $125 \times 798 \times 8$
16. $3 \times 73 \times 33\frac{1}{3}$
19. $125 \times 7.66 \times 8$

In 20–23, state the reason that justifies each step in the set of related equalities.

20. *a.* $250 \times (9.6 \times 4) = 250 \times (4 \times 9.6)$
    b. $\quad\quad\quad\quad\quad = (250 \times 4) \times 9.6$
    c. $\quad\quad\quad\quad\quad = 1000 \times 9.6$
    d. $\quad\quad\quad\quad\quad = 9600$

21. *a.* $\frac{3}{4} \times (86 \times \frac{4}{3}) = \frac{3}{4} \times (\frac{4}{3} \times 86)$
    b. $\quad\quad\quad\quad\quad = (\frac{3}{4} \times \frac{4}{3}) \times 86$
    c. $\quad\quad\quad\quad\quad = 1 \times 86$
    d. $\quad\quad\quad\quad\quad = 86$

22. *a.* $8d \times 7 = 8 \times (d \times 7)$
   b. $= 8 \times (7 \times d)$
   c. $= (8 \times 7) \times d$
   d. $= 56d$

23. *a.* $(f \times g) \times h = f \times (g \times h)$
   b. $= (g \times h) \times f$
   c. $= (h \times g) \times f$
   d. $= h \times (g \times f)$

In 24–27:   (*a*) Develop the steps of a set of related equalities which show that the sentence is true.   (*b*) Name the property or principle used in each step.

24. $8 \times (736 \times 125) = 1000 \times 736$
25. $\frac{5}{9} \times (731 \times \frac{9}{5}) = 1 \times 731$
26. For every r, $25r \times 4 = 100r$.
27. For every c and every d, $dc \times 8 = 8 \times cd$.

In 28–35, name the properties of addition and multiplication that are illustrated or involved in the true sentence. Include the substitution principle when necessary.

28. $18 + 2e = 2e + 18$
30. $17 + (23 + x) = (17 + 23) + x$
32. $12.25 + (x + 37.75) = 50 + x$
34. $p \times (q + 7) = (7 + q) \times p$

29. $4 \times (9 \times r) = (4 \times 9) \times r$
31. $2 \times (t + 8) = (t + 8) \times 2$
33. $\frac{1}{3} \times (y \times 3) = 1 \times y$
35. $(ba + c) + d = d + (ab + c)$

5. The Distributive Property

We know that $2(20 + 3) = 2(23) = 46$ and that $2 \times 20 + 2 \times 3 = 40 + 6 = 46$. Therefore, we see that $2(20 + 3) = 2 \times 20 + 2 \times 3$.

This example illustrates the **distributive property of multiplication over addition,** also called the **distributive property.** This means that the product of one number times the sum of a second and a third number equals the product of the first and second numbers plus the product of the first and third numbers.

Thus, $5(6 + 4) = 5 \times 6 + 5 \times 4$.

In general, we assume that for every number a, every number b, and every number c:

$$a(b + c) = ab + ac \ \ \text{OR} \ \ ab + ac = a(b + c)$$

Since multiplication is commutative, the distributive property can be written in other forms:

$$(b + c)a = ba + ca \ \ \text{AND} \ \ (b + c)a = ab + ac$$

The distributive property is assumed to be true for more than three numbers:

$$a(b + c + d + \ldots + x) = ab + ac + ad + \ldots + ax$$

The distributive property is also assumed to be true for subtraction:

$$a(b - c) = ab - ac \quad \text{OR} \quad ab - ac = a(b - c)$$

USING THE DISTRIBUTIVE PROPERTY

See how the distributive property may be used to find the following indicated products:

1. $6 \times 23 = 6(20 + 3) = 6 \times 20 + 6 \times 3 = 120 + 18 = 138$
2. $20(\frac{1}{4} + \frac{1}{5}) = 20 \times \frac{1}{4} + 20 \times \frac{1}{5} = 5 + 4 = 9$
3. $9 \times 3\frac{1}{3} = 9(3 + \frac{1}{3}) = 9 \times 3 + 9 \times \frac{1}{3} = 27 + 3 = 30$
4. $6.5 \times 8 = (6 + .5)8 = 6 \times 8 + .5 \times 8 = 48 + 4 = 52$

The distributive property can be used to **transform,** or change, the form of an algebraic expression. When a given expression is an indicated product, see how it may be transformed to an equal expression which is an indicated sum:

1. $5(a + b) = 5a + 5b$
2. $r(m + n + t) = rm + rn + rt$
3. $6(3x + 5) = 6 \cdot 3x + 6 \cdot 5 = 18x + 30$
4. $(x + y)(m + n) = (x + y)m + (x + y)n = xm + ym + xn + yn$

In 4, notice that in the first transformation $(x + y)$ is considered as one number, whereas $(m + n)$ is considered as the sum of two numbers. If we wish, we may consider $(m + n)$ to be one number and $(x + y)$ to be the sum of two numbers. The result will be the same.

The use of the distributive property also makes it possible to transform an algebraic expression which is an indicated sum to an equal expression which is an indicated product. Study the following examples:

1. $3c + 3d = 3(c + d)$
2. $xa + xb + xc = x(a + b + c)$
3. $5L + 3L = (5 + 3)L = 8L$
4. $9y - 4y = (9 - 4)y = 5y$

Exercises

In 1–18, state whether the sentence is a correct application of the distributive property. If you believe that it is not, state your reason.

1. $6(5 + 8) = 6 \times 5 + 6 \times 8$ **2.** $10(\frac{1}{2} + \frac{1}{5}) = 10 \times \frac{1}{2} + \frac{1}{5}$

3. $(7 + 9)5 = 7 + 9 \times 5$ **4.** $(4 + 2)7 = 7 \times 4 + 7 \times 2$

5. $3(x + 5) = 3x + 3 \times 5$ **6.** $2(y + 6) = 2y + 6$

7. $(b + 2)a = ba + 2a$ **8.** $(x - 7)4 = x - 28$

9. $4a(b + c) = 4ab + 4ac$ **10.** $4b(c - 2) = 4bc - 2$

11. $8m + 6m = (8 + 6)m$ **12.** $14x - 4x = (14 - 4)x$

13. $2.7a + 5.3a = 8a$ **14.** $7\frac{1}{2}r - 2\frac{1}{2}r = 5r$

15. $7r + 7s = 7(r + s)$ **16.** $6a + 12 = 6(a + 2)$

17. $2(L + W) = 2L + 2W$ **18.** $\frac{1}{2}hb + \frac{1}{2}hc = \frac{1}{2}h(b + c)$

In 19–24, complete the sentence so that it is an application of the distributive property.

19. $9(7 + 3) = $ _____   **20.** _____ $= 12 \times \frac{1}{2} + 12 \times \frac{1}{3}$

21. $4(p + q) = $ _____   **22.** _____ $= 2x - 2y$

23. $8t + 13t = $ _____   **24.** _____ $= (15 - 7)m$

In 25–32, find the value of the numerical phrase by using the distributive property to simplify the computation.

25. $15 \times 36 + 15 \times 64$ **26.** $3 \times 89 + 5 \times 89 + 2 \times 89$

27. $128 \times 615 - 28 \times 615$ **28.** $1\frac{3}{4} \times 576 + 8\frac{1}{4} \times 576$

29. $937 \times .8 + 937 \times .2$ **30.** $36(\frac{1}{3} + \frac{1}{4})$

31. $50 \times 8\frac{3}{5}$ **32.** $73 \times 632 + 47 \times 632 - 20 \times 632$

In 33–41, use the distributive property to transform the expression to an equal expression without parentheses.

33. $4(m + n)$ **34.** $(x - y)8$ **35.** $7(2x + 1)$

36. $a(x - 4)$ **37.** $12(\frac{2}{3}x + 2)$ **38.** $(\frac{1}{3}m - \frac{3}{5}n)30$

39. $2r(8 + s)$ **40.** $3a(7 - b)$ **41.** $(a + b)(s + t)$

In 42–50, use the distributive property to express each indicated sum as a product.

42. $2p + 2q$ **43.** $8p - 8m$ **44.** $at + ar$

45. $4g + 7g$ **46.** $12y - 4y$ **47.** $4a + 5a + 3a$

48. $8x + 16$ **49.** $2bc + 4b$ **50.** $9r + 6d$

In 51 and 52, name the property that justifies each step in the set of related equations. Use the substitution principle if necessary.

51. $a.$ $s(m + n) = s(n + m)$
  $b.$ $= sn + sm$
  $c.$ $= ns + ms$

52. $a.$ $5x + (3x + 4) = (5x + 3x) + 4$
  $b.$ $= (5 + 3)x + 4$
  $c.$ $= 8x + 4$

6. Properties of Zero and One

ADDITION PROPERTY OF ZERO

The true sentences $5 + 0 = 5$ and $0 + 8 = 8$ illustrate that the sum of any number and zero is that number itself. These examples illustrate the ***addition property of zero.***

In general, we assume that for every number a:

$$a + 0 = a \text{ AND } 0 + a = a$$

We call 0 the ***identity element of addition,*** or the ***additive identity element.***

MULTIPLICATION PROPERTY OF ZERO

The true sentences $4 \times 0 = 0$ and $0 \times 3 = 0$ illustrate that the product of any number and zero is zero. These examples illustrate the ***multiplication property of zero.***

In general, we assume that for every number a:

$$a \times 0 = 0 \text{ AND } 0 \times a = 0$$

MULTIPLICATION PROPERTY OF ONE

The true sentences $5 \times 1 = 5$ and $1 \times 9 = 9$ illustrate that the product of any number and one is that number itself. These examples illustrate the ***multiplication property of one.***

In general, we assume that for every number a:

$$a \times 1 = a \text{ AND } 1 \times a = a$$

We call 1 the ***identity element of multiplication,*** or the ***multiplicative identity element.***

～～～～～～～～ MODEL PROBLEMS ～～～～～～～～

1. Evaluate the number expression $3 \times 1 + (8 + 0)$ and give the reason for each step of the procedure.

   Solution:

Step	*Reason*
1. $3 \times 1 + (8 + 0) = 3 \times 1 + 8$	1. Addition property of 0.
2. $\qquad\qquad\qquad = 3 + 8$	2. Multiplication property of 1.
3. $\qquad\qquad\qquad = 11$	3. Substitution principle.

   Answer: 11

2. Express $6t + t$ as a product and give the reason for each step of the procedure.

   Solution:

Step	*Reason*
1. $6t + t = 6t + 1t$	1. Multiplication property of 1.
2. $\qquad = (6 + 1)t$	2. Distributive property.
3. $\qquad = 7t$	3. Substitution principle.

   Answer: $7t$

～～～～～～～～～～～～～～～～～～～～～～～～～～～～～～

Exercises

In 1–6, evaluate the number expression and give the reason for each step in the procedure.

1. $10 \times 0 + 6 \times 1$ **2.** $(7 + 0) + 7 \times 0$ **3.** $(0 + 6) + 1 \times 8$
4. $6(\frac{1}{2} + 0) - 5 \times 0$ **5.** $4 \times 1 - (0 + 2)$ **6.** $12(8 - 7) + 6 \times 0 - (1 + 0)$

In 7–11, write the algebraic expression as a product and give the reason for each step in the procedure.

7. $10x + x$ **8.** $3b + b$ **9.** $8y - y$ **10.** $7ab + ab$ **11.** $8x^2 - x^2$

12. The following chain of equations can be used to show that $y \cdot 0 = 0$. State the reason for each of the steps from 1 through 5.

   1. $y(1 + 0) \quad = y \cdot 1$
   2. $y(1 + 0) \quad = y \cdot 1 + y \cdot 0$
   3. $y \cdot 1 + y \cdot 0 = y \cdot 1$
   4. $y + y \cdot 0 \quad = y$
   5. $y \cdot 0 \qquad\quad = 0$

7. Combining Like Terms

Similar terms having the same variables as factors, with corresponding variables having the same exponent, are called **like terms.** For example, $3L$ and $5L$, $5x^2$ and $7x^2$, $9ab$ and $2ab$, $4(x + y)$ and $6(x + y)$ are pairs of like terms. On the other hand, $2x$ and $3y$, $3ab$ and $4cd$, $3x^2$ and $5x^3$ are examples of **unlike terms.**

We have learned that the distributive property enables us to transform an indicated sum or difference to an indicated product:

1. $9x + 2x = (9 + 2)x = 11x$
2. $16cd + 3cd = (16 + 3)cd = 19cd$
3. $18y - y = 18y - 1y = (18 - 1)y = 17y$

When we express the indicated sum or the indicated difference of like terms as a single term, we **combine like terms.**

Notice that in each of the preceding examples when two like terms are combined:

1. The result has the same variable factors as the original terms.
2. The numerical coefficient of the result is:
   (*a*) the sum of the numerical coefficients of the terms when the terms are to be added

OR

   (*b*) the difference of the numerical coefficients of the terms when the terms are to be subtracted.

The indicated sum or difference of two unlike terms cannot be expressed as a single term. For example, $2x + 3y$ and $4ac - 5bd$ cannot be simplified.

～～～～～～ MODEL PROBLEMS ～～～～～～

1. Show that $4x + 5x = 9x$ is a true sentence when $x = 10$.

How To Proceed	*Solution*
1. Write the sentence.	$4x + 5x = 9x$
2. Replace the variable by its value.	$4 \times 10 + 5 \times 10 \overset{?}{=} 9 \times 10$
3. Do the multiplication.	$40 + 50 \overset{?}{=} 90$
4. Do the addition. The result is a true sentence.	$90 = 90$ (true)

In 2–6, simplify the expression by combining like terms.

2. $8a + 3a$

    Solution: $8a + 3a = (8 + 3)a = 11a$ *Ans.* $11a$

3. $3.9c - 3.9c$

    Solution: $3.9c - 3.9c = (3.9 - 3.9)c = 0 \cdot c = 0$ *Ans.* 0

4. $3\frac{1}{2}xy + 4\frac{1}{4}xy$

    Solution: $3\frac{1}{2}xy + 4\frac{1}{4}xy = (3\frac{1}{2} + 4\frac{1}{4})xy = 7\frac{3}{4}xy$ *Ans.* $7\frac{3}{4}xy$

5. $9t + 4t - t$

    Solution: $9t + 4t - t = (9 + 4 - 1)t = 12t$ *Ans.* $12t$

6. $7a + 6b + 5a - 2b$

    Solution:

$7a + 6b + 5a - 2b = 7a + 5a + 6b - 2b$	Commutative property.
$= (7a + 5a) + (6b - 2b)$	Associative property.
$= 12a + 4b$	Distributive property.

    Answer: $12a + 4b$

Exercises

1. Show that $3x + 5x = 8x$ is a true sentence when x equals:

    a. 7   *b.* 10   *c.* .4   *d.* $\frac{1}{2}$ *e.* 0

2. Show that $5y^2 - 2y^2 = 3y^2$ is a true sentence when y equals:

    a. 3   *b.* 12   *c.* .2   *d.* $\frac{1}{3}$ *e.* 0

3. Show that $6c + 9d + c + 2d = 7c + 11d$ is a true sentence when:

    a. $c = 10,\ d = 7$ *b.* $c = 1.2,\ d = .1$ *c.* $c = \frac{3}{4},\ d = \frac{2}{3}$

In 4–18, simplify the expression by combining like terms.

4. $7x + 3x$	**5.** $9t - 5t$	**6.** $10c + c$
7. $2\frac{1}{2}d + 1\frac{1}{2}d$	**8.** $13n - 6\frac{2}{3}n$	**9.** $3.4y + 1.3y$
10. $6.2r - r$	**11.** $9ab + 2ab$	**12.** $8z^2 + z^2$
13. $8m + 5m + m$	**14.** $9w + 8w - 3w$	**15.** $8s + 5\frac{1}{2}s + 6\frac{3}{4}s$
16. $8.2b + 3.8b - 12b$	**17.** $2\frac{3}{4}xy - 2xy + \frac{1}{2}xy$	**18.** $9d^2 - 6d^2 - d^2$

In 19 and 20, simplify the sentence by combining like terms.

19. $P = 5x + 5x + 5x$ **20.** $P = x + \frac{3}{2}x + x + \frac{3}{2}x$

21. Express the perimeter of each of the following figures and simplify the result by combining like terms:

(a)   (b)   (c)   (d)

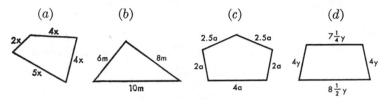

In 22–35, simplify the expression by combining like terms.

22. $8m + 5m + 7n + 6n$ **23.** $5c + 9c + 12d + d$

24. $a + 5m + 2a - 4m$ **25.** $1.5a + 7.2b + 5.1a + 8.6b$

26. $5a + 3m + a + m$ **27.** $5a + b + 3c + 1\frac{1}{3}a + b + \frac{3}{4}c$

28. $8x + 10 + 4x + 5$ **29.** $2x + 9 + 3x + 1 + 5x - 8$

30. $5y^2 + 25 + 2y^2 - 10$ **31.** $6ab + 5ac + 3ac - ab$

32. $2(x + y) + 3(x + y)$ **33.** $6(2x + y) + 4(x - y)$

34. $7(m + 5) + 4(2m + 1)$ **35.** $5(2c + 9) + 3(4c - 7)$

In 36 and 37, simplify the sentence by combining like terms.

36. $P = 4r + 5s + 4r + s$ **37.** $S = 6a + 2\frac{1}{2}b + 3\frac{1}{4}a + \frac{3}{4}b$

38. Express the perimeter of each of the following figures and simplify the result by combining like terms:

(a)   (b)   (c)   (d)

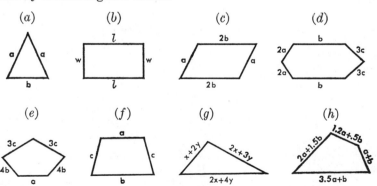

(e)   (f)   (g)   (h)

CHAPTER V

SIMPLE EQUATIONS AND PROBLEMS

1. Understanding the Meaning of Solving an Equation

An *equation* is a sentence which uses the symbol $=$ to state that two algebraic expressions are equal. For example, $x + 3 = 9$ is an equation in which $x + 3$ is called the *left side*, or *left member*, and 9 is called the *right side*, or *right member*.

An equation may be a true sentence such as $5 + 2 = 7$ or a false sentence such as $6 - 3 = 4$. Also, an equation may be an open sentence such as $x + 3 = 9$. We cannot determine whether this sentence is true or false until the value of the variable is known.

Consider the equation $x + 3 = 9$. When x is replaced by an element of {numbers of arithmetic}, the sentence may become either a true sentence or a false sentence. Only when x is replaced by 6 does $x + 3 = 9$ become a true sentence: $6 + 3 = 9$. The number 6, which satisfies the equation $x + 3 = 9$, is called a *root,* or a *solution,* of the equation. The set consisting of all the solutions of an equation is called its *solution set,* or *truth set.*

The solution set of an equation is a subset of the replacement set (the domain) of the variable. This subset consists of the elements of the replacement set which make the open sentence true. Therefore, if the replacement set of x is {numbers of arithmetic}, then the solution set of $x + 3 = 9$ is {6}. Observe that {6} is a subset of {numbers of arithmetic}.

Notice that what we learned about open sentences and truth sets (pages 39 and 40) is true for algebraic equations.

To *solve an equation* means to find its solution set.

If only some elements of the domain satisfy an equation, the equation is called a *conditional equation,* or simply an "equation." Therefore, $x + 3 = 9$ is a conditional equation.

If every element of the domain satisfies an equation, the equation is called an *identity.* Thus, $5 + x = x + 5$ is an identity when the domain of x is {numbers of arithmetic} because every element of the domain makes the sentence true.

Procedure. To verify, or check, whether a number is a root of an equation:
 1. **Replace the variable in the equation by the number.**
 2. **Perform the indicated operations to determine whether the resulting statement is true.**

MODEL PROBLEMS

1. Is 7 a root of the equation $5x - 10 = 25$?

How To Proceed	Solution
1. Write the equation.	$5x - 10 = 25$
2. Replace the variable x by 7.	$5 \times 7 - 10 \overset{?}{=} 25$
3. Do the multiplication.	$35 - 10 \overset{?}{=} 25$
4. Do the subtraction. A true statement results.	$25 = 25$ (true)

Answer: Yes

2. Is 4 a root of the equation $3x + 9 = 27$?

How To Proceed	Solution
1. Write the equation.	$3x + 9 = 27$
2. Replace the variable x by 4.	$3 \times 4 + 9 \overset{?}{=} 27$
3. Do the multiplication.	$12 + 9 \overset{?}{=} 27$
4. Do the addition. A false statement results.	$21 = 27$ (false)

Answer: No

Exercises

In 1–12, find the number of arithmetic which can replace the question mark and make the resulting equation a true statement.

1. $10 - 3 = ?$
2. $? - 5 = 3\frac{1}{2}$
3. $10 + ? = 18$
4. $7 + ? = 9\frac{2}{3}$
5. $12 \times 4 = ?$
6. $4 \times ? = 10$
7. $16 \div 8 = ?$
8. $? \div 2 = 3.5$
9. $3 \times 8 + 4 = ?$
10. $2 \times ? + 6 = 14$
11. $5 \times ? - 1 = 34$
12. $\frac{1}{3} \times ? - 1 = 2$

In 13–24, "guess" a value (a number of arithmetic) which can replace the variable and make the resulting equation a true statement.

13. $4x = 20$ **14.** $36 = 9r$ **15.** $\frac{1}{2}x = 7$
16. $8 = \frac{1}{2}d$ **17.** $x + 7 = 13$ **18.** $18 = c + 5$
19. $r - 4 = 1$ **20.** $15 = m - 4$ **21.** $2x + 1 = 19$
22. $3y + 8 = 17$ **23.** $2x - 3 = 17$ **24.** $4m - 10 = 50$

In 25–33, tell whether the number in the parentheses is a root of the given equation.

25. $5x = 50$ (10)   **26.** $\frac{1}{2}x = 18$ (36)   **27.** $\frac{1}{3}y = 12$ (4)
28. $x + 5 = 11$ (6)   **29.** $y + 8 = 14$ (22)   **30.** $x - 5 = 13$ (8)
31. $m - 4\frac{1}{2} = 9$ ($4\frac{1}{2}$)   **32.** $2x + 7 = 21$ (14)   **33.** $19 = 4x - 1$ (5)

In 34–41, using the domain $\{1, 2, 3, 4, 5, 6, 7, 8, 9, 10\}$, find the solution set of the equation. If the equation has no roots, indicate the solution set as the null set, $\varnothing$.

34. $x + 5 = 7$ **35.** $y - 3 = 4$ **36.** $2x + 1 = 9$
37. $6 = 3x - 18$ **38.** $\frac{1}{2}x + 4 = 50$ **39.** $14 - 2x = 2$

40. $\dfrac{x + 8}{4} = 3$ **41.** $3x - 2 = 28$

In 42–47, using the domain $\{5, 6, 7, 8, 9, 10\}$, tell whether the equation is a conditional equation or an identity.

42. $x + 3 = 3 + x$ **43.** $x + 3 = 10$ **44.** $y + 3 + 4 = 7 + y$
45. $5a = a \times 5$ **46.** $5a = 40$ **47.** $5 \times 2 \times a = a \times 2 \times 5$

2. Writing Verbal Sentences as Equations

In algebra, many verbal problems involving number relations are solved by using equations. Therefore, we must be able to express verbal sentences as equations. In Chapter I on pages 19 and 20, we saw how the symbols of mathematics were used to express number relationships; and in Chapter III on pages 45–47, we saw how verbal phrases were translated into algebraic language. Study the following examples to see how verbal sentences may be expressed as equations:

Verbal Sentence	*Equation*
Four times a number s equals 20.	$4s = 20$
A number y increased by 6 equals 8.	$y + 6 = 8$
A number x decreased by 3 equals 5.	$x - 3 = 5$
A number n divided by 2 equals 4.	$\dfrac{n}{2} = 4$

Procedure. To write a verbal sentence as an equation, choose a letter to represent the variable. Then use this letter to express the verbal sentence as an equation.

MODEL PROBLEM

Write the following sentence as an equation: "5 times a number decreased by 7 equals 13."

Solution: Let x represent the number.

5 times a number decreased by 7 equals 13.

$5x \qquad\qquad - \qquad 7 \quad = \quad 13$

Answer: $5x - 7 = 13$

Exercises

In 1–8, write a verbal sentence which gives a meaning of the equation.

1. $8x = 56$ **2.** $x + 7 = 12$ **3.** $s - 5 = 15$

4. $12 = x - 3$ **5.** $\dfrac{x}{4} = 8$ **6.** $2c + 4 = 12$

7. $5y - 7 = 28$ **8.** $\frac{3}{4}c - 8 = 4$

In 9–16, select the equation which represents, in terms of the given variable, the numerical relationship expressed in the sentence.

9. Three times Harold's height is 108 inches. Let h = Harold's height.
    a. $h + 3 = 108$ *b.* $3h = 108$ *c.* $h - 3 = 108$ *d.* $\frac{1}{3}h = 108$

10. One-half of Mary's weight is 40 pounds. Let w = Mary's weight.
    a. $\frac{1}{2}w = 40$ *b.* $2w = 40$ *c.* $w - 2 = 40$ *d.* $w + 2 = 40$

11. A number increased by 7 equals 28. Let n = the number.
    a. $7n = 28$ *b.* $n + 7 = 28$ *c.* $n - 7 = 28$ *d.* $\frac{1}{7}n = 28$

12. A number decreased by 5 equals 15. Let x = the number.
    a. $x + 5 = 15$ *b.* $5x = 15$ *c.* $\frac{1}{5}x = 15$ *d.* $x - 5 = 15$

13. If 7 is subtracted from a number, the result is 8. Let x = the number.
    a. $7 - x = 8$ *b.* $x - 7 = 8$ *c.* $8 - x = 7$ *d.* $x - 8 = 7$

14. Jim bought $6 worth of toys that cost $2 each. Let t = the number of toys which Jim bought.
    a. $t + 2 = 6$ *b.* $t - 2 = 6$ *c.* $2t = 6$ *d.* $\frac{1}{2}t = 6$

15. Tom, who is 15 years old, is one-third as old as his father. Let $f =$ the father's age.

  a. $3f = 15$ *b.* $f + 3 = 15$ *c.* $\frac{1}{3}f = 15$ *d.* $f - 3 = 15$

16. A merchant bought 15 suits and now has 75 suits. Let $s =$ the number of suits the merchant had originally.

  a. $s + 15 = 75$ *b.* $s - 15 = 75$ *c.* $15s = 75$ *d.* $\dfrac{s}{15} = 75$

In 17–28, write the sentence as an equation. Use n to represent the number.

17. The product of 7 and a number equals 70.
18. Four less than a number equals 32.
19. Twice a number, increased by 7, equals 27.
20. Twice a number, decreased by 5, equals 25.
21. The sum of three times a number and 7 is 22.
22. When 9 is subtracted from 5 times a number, the result is 31.
23. The sum of 100 and a number is equal to three times that number.
24. If 3 times a number is increased by 12, the result is the same as when twice the number is increased by 24.
25. If 8 times a number is decreased by 20, the result is the same as when 3 times the number is increased by 80.
26. The sum of a number and twice that number equals 45.
27. Three times a number decreased by one-half of that number equals 40.
28. The sum of one-half of a number and 8 is the same as the difference between the number and 4.

29. Match the items in column A with those in column B.

Column A	*Column B*
1. Eight times a number is 32.	*a.* $3 - 2n = 1$
2. A number divided by 5 is 35.	*b.* $n + 8 = 32$
3. A number increased by 8 is 32.	*c.* $n - \frac{1}{6}n = 70$
4. The product of 5 and a number is 35.	*d.* $4n + 6 = 30$
5. Four times a number increased by 6 is 30.	*e.* $5n = 35$
6. One-fourth of a number decreased by 6 is 30.	*f.* $n + 6n = 70$
7. When 3 is subtracted from twice a number, the result is 1.	*g.* $8n = 32$
	h. $2n - 3 = 1$
8. One number is 6 times another and their sum is 70.	*i.* $\frac{n}{5} = 35$
	j. $\frac{1}{4}n - 6 = 30$
9. When twice a number is subtracted from 3, the result is 1.	
10. One number is one-sixth of another, and their difference is 70.	

3. Preparing To Solve Equations by Using Inverse Operations

Consider the expression $8 - 2$. Since 2 has been subtracted from 8, it is obvious that if we add 2 to the indicated difference, we will get a result of 8. Thus, $8 - 2 + 2 = 8$. Similarly, if n represents a number, then $n - 2 + 2 = n$.

Consider the expression $x - a$. What operation can we perform to obtain a result of x? Since a has been *subtracted* from x, we *add* a to the indicated difference: $x - a + a = x$. That is, a is the number that must be added to $x - a$ to obtain x.

Consider the expression $8 + 2$. Since 2 has been added to 8, it is obvious that if we subtract 2 from the indicated sum, we will get a result of 8. Thus, $8 + 2 - 2 = 8$. Similarly, if n represents a number, then $n + 2 - 2 = n$.

Consider the expression $x + a$. What operation can we perform to obtain a result of x? Since a has been *added* to x, we *subtract* a from the indicated sum: $x + a - a = x$. That is, a is the number that must be subtracted from $x + a$ to obtain x.

Since subtracting a number undoes the effect of having added that number, and adding a number undoes the effect of having subtracted that number, *__addition and subtraction are inverse operations.__*

Consider the expression 8×2. Since 8 has been multiplied by 2, it is obvious that if we divide the indicated product by 2, we will get a result of 8. Thus, $\dfrac{8 \times 2}{2} = 8$. Similarly, if n represents a number, then $\dfrac{2n}{2} = n$.

Consider the expression ax. What operation can we perform to obtain a result of x? Since x has been *multiplied* by a, we *divide* the indicated product by a: $\dfrac{ax}{a} = x$. That is, a is the number by which ax must be divided to obtain x.

Consider the expression $8 \div 2$, or $\frac{8}{2}$. Since 8 has been divided by 2, it is obvious that if we multiply the indicated quotient by 2, we will get a result of 8. Thus, $2 \times \frac{8}{2} = 8$. Similarly, if n represents a number, then $2 \times \dfrac{n}{2} = n$.

Consider the expression $\dfrac{x}{a}$. What operation can we perform to obtain a result of x? Since x has been *divided* by a, we *multiply* the indicated quotient by a: $a \times \dfrac{x}{a} = x$. That is, a is the number by which $\dfrac{x}{a}$ must be multiplied to obtain x.

Since dividing by a number undoes the effect of having multiplied by that number, and multiplying by a number undoes the effect of having divided by that number, **multiplication and division are inverse operations.**

Whenever a variable and a number of arithmetic are related by the operation of addition, subtraction, multiplication, or division, we can use the inverse operation to obtain the variable itself.

~~~~~~~~ MODEL PROBLEMS ~~~~~~~~

In each of the following: (a) State the operation which involves the variable and the number of arithmetic. (b) State the operation you will use to obtain the variable itself. (c) Give the number you will use when adding, subtracting, multiplying, or dividing to obtain the variable itself. (d) Perform the operation.

1. $5x$ **2.** $\dfrac{d}{6}$ **3.** $t + 4$ **4.** $y - 8$

Solution	*Solution*	*Solution*	*Solution*
a. multiplication	a. division	a. addition	a. subtraction
b. division	b. multiplication	b. subtraction	b. addition
c. 5	c. 6	c. 4	c. 8
d. $\dfrac{5x}{5} = x$	d. $\dfrac{6 \times d}{6} = d$	d. $t + 4 - 4 = t$	d. $y - 8 + 8 = y$

Exercises

In 1–25: (a) State the operation which involves the variable and the number of arithmetic. (b) State the operation you will use to obtain the variable itself. (c) Give the number you will use when adding, subtracting, multiplying, or dividing to obtain the variable itself. (d) Perform the operation.

1. $7x$ **2.** $\dfrac{w}{5}$ **3.** $x + 1$ **4.** $x - 4$ **5.** $20z$

6. $8y$ **7.** $\dfrac{m}{4}$ **8.** $d + 3$ **9.** $x - 6$ **10.** $\dfrac{m}{5}$

11. $\frac{1}{5}w$ **12.** $\frac{1}{3}y$ **13.** $c + 7$ **14.** $t - 1$ **15.** $d + 14$

16. $1\frac{1}{4}m$ **17.** $\dfrac{m}{10}$ **18.** $d + 1\frac{1}{2}$ **19.** $r - \frac{2}{3}$ **20.** $c + 2\frac{1}{2}$

21. $.5c$ **22.** $\dfrac{r}{100}$ **23.** $n + .7$ **24.** $s - .8$ **25.** $x - 1.5$

4. Solving Simple Equations by Using Addition or Subtraction

ADDITION PROPERTY OF EQUALITY

If the same number is added to two equal numbers, the sums are equal.

$$\text{if } 500 + 200 = 700$$
$$\text{then } 500 + 200 + 100 = 700 + 100$$

This is an example of the **addition property of equality**.

In general, for all numbers a, b, and c, we assume:

$$\textbf{if } a = b, \textbf{ then } a + c = b + c$$

Therefore, we can say: **If the same number is added to both members of an equality, the equality is retained.** Study the following examples:

In Arithmetic	*In Algebra*		
if $8 = 8$	if $x - 2 = 8$		
then $8 + 2 = 8 + 2$	then $x - 2 + 2 = 8 + 2$	A_2	(Add 2 to both members of the previous equation.)
and $10 = 10$	and $x = 10$		

In the preceding algebraic example, let us use the substitution principle and replace x with 10 in the first equation.

$$x - 2 = 8$$
$$10 - 2 \stackrel{?}{=} 8$$
$$8 = 8$$

We see that replacing x with 10 results in a true sentence.

If we replace x with 10 in the second equation, $x - 2 + 2 = 8 + 2$, we likewise obtain a true sentence. In fact, the number 10 is the only number that can replace x in each of the equations and make the resulting sentence true. Therefore, 10 is the root and $\{10\}$ is the solution set of each of these equations. Equations that have the same solution set are called **equivalent equations**. Notice that when the addition property is applied in an equation, we obtain an equivalent equation.

When we solve an equation, we transform it into a simpler equivalent equation that reveals the value which can replace the variable and make the resulting sentence true (the truth value of the variable). Now we will use the addition property of equality in solving equations.

---------------------- **MODEL PROBLEMS** ----------------------

1. Solve and check: $x - 5 = 4$

Solution

$$x - 5 = 4$$
$$x - 5 + 5 = 4 + 5 \quad \text{A}_5$$
$$x = 9$$

Check

$$x - 5 = 4$$
$$9 - 5 \overset{?}{=} 4$$
$$4 = 4$$

(Notice that when the variable x is replaced by 9, the resulting sentence is true.)

Answer: $x = 9$, or solution set is $\{9\}$.

2. Solve and check: $5 = y - 3\frac{1}{2}$

Solution

$$5 = y - 3\frac{1}{2}$$
$$5 + 3\frac{1}{2} = y - 3\frac{1}{2} + 3\frac{1}{2} \quad \text{A}_{3\frac{1}{2}}$$
$$8\frac{1}{2} = y$$

Check

$$5 = y - 3\frac{1}{2}$$
$$5 \overset{?}{=} 8\frac{1}{2} - 3\frac{1}{2}$$
$$5 = 5 \quad \text{(true)}$$

Answer: $y = 8\frac{1}{2}$, or solution set is $\{8\frac{1}{2}\}$.

SUBTRACTION PROPERTY OF EQUALITY

If the same number is subtracted from two equal numbers, the differences are equal. This describes the **subtraction property of equality.**

In general, for all numbers a, b, and c, we assume:

$$\textbf{if } a = b, \textbf{ then } a - c = b - c$$

Therefore, we can say: **If the same number is subtracted from both members of an equality, the equality is retained.**

Study the following examples:

In Arithmetic	In Algebra		
if $8 = 8$	if $x + 3 = 8$		
then $8 - 3 = 8 - 3$	then $x + 3 - 3 = 8 - 3$	S_3	(Subtract 3 from both members of the previous equation.)
and $5 = 5$	and $x = 5$		

Notice that the application of the subtraction property in the equation $x + 3 = 8$ resulted in the equivalent equations $x + 3 - 3 = 8 - 3$ and $x = 5$. All three equations have the same solution set $\{5\}$.

Now we will use the subtraction property of equality in solving equations.

～～～～～～～ MODEL PROBLEMS ～～～～～～～

1. Solve and check: $n + 7 = 9$

Solution

$$n + 7 = 9$$
$$n + 7 - 7 = 9 - 7 \quad S_7$$
$$n = 2$$

Check

$$n + 7 = 9$$
$$2 + 7 \overset{?}{=} 9$$
$$9 = 9 \quad \text{(true)}$$

Answer: $n = 2$, or solution set is $\{2\}$.

2. Solve and check: $.8 = .3 + t$

Solution

$$.8 = .3 + t$$
$$.8 = t + .3 \quad \text{(commutative property)}$$
$$.8 - .3 = t + .3 - .3 \quad S_{.3}$$
$$.5 = t$$

Check

$$.8 = .3 + t$$
$$.8 \overset{?}{=} .3 + .5$$
$$.8 = .8 \quad \text{(true)}$$

Answer: $t = .5$, or solution set is $\{.5\}$.

Procedure. To solve an equation in which a variable and a constant are related by the operation of addition or subtraction:
1. **Use the inverse operation, subtracting or adding (as the case may be) the constant to both members of the equation. Perform the indicated operation(s) to obtain an equivalent equation in which only the variable itself is one member of the equation.**
2. **Check by determining that when the value obtained for the variable replaces it in the given equation, the resulting statement is true.**

Exercises

In 1–42, solve and check the equation.

1. $a - 4 = 9$ **2.** $x - 1 = 7$ **3.** $a + 5 = 17$

4. $b + 4 = 13$ **5.** $c - 8 = 12$ **6.** $d + 1 = 12$

7. $18 = a - 3$ **8.** $26 = x - 4$ **9.** $16 = r + 2$

10. $25 = s + 11$ **11.** $60 = y - 15$ **12.** $54 = t + 39$

13. $y - 13 = 14$ **14.** $0 = t - 8$ **15.** $m + 15 = 15$

16. $n - 7 = 3\frac{1}{3}$ **17.** $x - \frac{1}{4} = 5\frac{3}{4}$ **18.** $y + 5 = 8\frac{1}{4}$

19. $x + \frac{1}{2} = 14\frac{1}{2}$ **20.** $6\frac{2}{3} = x + 4$ **21.** $3\frac{2}{3} = m - \frac{1}{3}$

22. $b - 2\frac{3}{4} = 9$ **23.** $8\frac{1}{8} = r - \frac{1}{8}$ **24.** $\frac{7}{8} = y + \frac{3}{8}$

25. $c - 1\frac{1}{4} = 6\frac{1}{2}$ **26.** $d + 1\frac{2}{3} = 5\frac{1}{3}$ **27.** $9\frac{1}{4} = d + 3\frac{1}{2}$

28. $d - 5 = 2.3$ **29.** $z - 6 = 3.7$ **30.** $m + .7 = 2.9$

31. $8.6 = c - .2$ **32.** $n + 3.5 = 4.5$ **33.** $12 = p + 1.8$

34. $15 = x + 1.5$ **35.** $r - 3.5 = 8$ **36.** $3.1 = z - .8$

37. $4 + x = 50$ **38.** $12 + y = 38$ **39.** $19 = 7 + y$

40. $1 + x = 7\frac{1}{2}$ **41.** $3\frac{1}{4} = 2\frac{1}{2} + c$ **42.** $.15 + y = 2.25$

43. If $g + 9 = 11$, find the value of $7g$.

44. If $t - .5 = 2.5$, find the value of $t + 7$.

45. If $22 = y + 8$, find the value of $\frac{1}{2}y$.

46. If $c - 1\frac{1}{4} = 2\frac{1}{2}$, find the value of $8c - 2$.

47. If $1.8 + b = 2.7$, find the value of $\frac{1}{3}b - .3$.

In 48–50, determine the element(s) of the set if $x \in$ {natural numbers}.

48. $\{x \mid x + 5 = 17\}$ **49.** $\{x \mid x - 12 = 48\}$ **50.** $\{x \mid 25 = x - 2\}$

5. Solving Problems by Using Variables and Equations

Now we are ready to solve verbal problems algebraically.

Procedure. To solve a verbal problem by using an equation involving one variable:

1. **Read the problem carefully until you understand it.**
2. **Determine what is given in the problem and what is to be found.**
3. **Select a variable that can be used in representing every number described in the problem.**
4. **Write an equation which symbolizes the information and relationships stated in the problem.**
5. **Find the root, or solution set, of the equation.**
6. **Check the answer by testing it in the word statement of the original problem to see that it satisfies all the required conditions.**

MODEL PROBLEMS

1. When a number is decreased by 7, the result is 9. Find the number.

How To Proceed	*Solution*
1. Represent the number by a variable.	Let x = the number.
2. Write the word statement as an equation.	$x - 7 = 9$
3. Solve the equation. A$_7$ (mentally)	$x = 16$
4. Check in the original problem.	Is 16 decreased by 7 equal to 9? Yes.

Answer: The number is 16.

2. Bill is 10 years older than Sam. If Bill is 28 years old, how old is Sam?

How To Proceed	*Solution*
1. Represent Sam's age by a variable.	Let x = Sam's age.
2. Represent Bill's age using the same variable.	Then $x + 10$ = Bill's age.
3. Write the word statement as an equation.	$x + 10 = 28$ (Bill is 28 years old.)
4. Solve the equation. S$_{10}$ (mentally)	$x = 18$
5. Check in the original problem.	Sam is 18 years old and Bill is 28 years old. Is Bill 10 years older than Sam? Yes.

Answer: Sam is 18 years old.

Exercises

In 1–20, solve the problem using a variable and an equation.

1. A number decreased by 20 equals 36. Find the number.
2. If 7 is subtracted from a number, the result is 46. Find the number.
3. What number increased by 25 equals 40?
4. If 18 is added to a number, the result is 32. Find the number.
5. Ten less than a number is 42. Find the number.
6. The sum of 42 and a number is 96. Find the number.
7. After Henry spent $.25, he had $.85 left. How much money did he have originally?

8. Eight years ago, Ruth was 7 years old. How old is she now?
9. Twelve years from now, Paul will be 30 years old. How old is Paul now?
10. After the price of a car rose $225, it was sold for $2670. What was the original price?
11. After he lost 22 pounds, Ben weighed $187\frac{3}{4}$ pounds. Find Ben's original weight.
12. After $2\frac{1}{2}$ feet were cut from a piece of lumber, there were $9\frac{1}{2}$ feet left. What was the original length of the piece of lumber?
13. After a car increased its rate of speed by 15 miles per hour, it was traveling 48 miles per hour. What was its original rate of speed?
14. During a charity drive, the boys in a class contributed $3.75 more than the girls. If the boys contributed $8.25, how much did the girls contribute?
15. The width of a rectangle is 8 feet less than its length. If the width is 9.5 feet, find the length of the rectangle.
16. A high school admitted 1125 sophomores, which was 78 less than the number admitted last year. How many sophomores were admitted last year?
17. After Marie had gained $7\frac{1}{2}$ pounds, she weighed 97 pounds. What was Marie's original weight?
18. A dealer sold an electric broiler for $39.98. This sum was $12.50 more than the broiler cost him. How much did the broiler cost the dealer?
19. After using his baseball glove for some time, Charles sold it for $7.25 less than he paid for it. If Charles sold the glove for $3.50, how much did he pay for it originally?
20. Sid wishes to buy a radio which costs $38. If he has already saved $26 for this purpose, how much must he still save to buy the radio?

6. Solving Equations by Using Division or Multiplication

DIVISION PROPERTY OF EQUALITY

If two equal numbers are divided by the same non-zero number, the quotients are equal. This describes the *division property of equality*.

In general for all numbers, a, b, and c ($c \neq 0$), we assume:

$$\text{if } a = b, \text{ then } \frac{a}{c} = \frac{b}{c}$$

Therefore, we can say: **If both members of an equality are divided by the same non-zero number, the equality is retained.**

Study the following examples:

In Arithmetic	In Algebra	
if $8 = 8$	if $4w = 8$	
then $\dfrac{8}{4} = \dfrac{8}{4}$	then $\dfrac{4w}{4} = \dfrac{8}{4}$ D_4	(Divide both members of the previous equation by 4.)
and $2 = 2$	and $w = 2$	

Notice that the application of the division property in the equation $4w = 8$ resulted in the equivalent equations $\dfrac{4w}{4} = \dfrac{8}{4}$ and $w = 2$. All three equations have the same solution set $\{2\}$.

Now we will use the division property of equality in solving equations.

~~~~~~~~ MODEL PROBLEMS ~~~~~~~~

Solve and check:

1. $8y = 56$

Solution

$8y = 56$

$\dfrac{8y}{8} = \dfrac{56}{8}$ D_8

$y = 7$

Check

$8y = 56$

$8(7) \overset{?}{=} 56$

$56 = 56$ (true)

Answer: $y = 7$, or solution set is $\{7\}$.

2. $22 = 4x$

Solution

$22 = 4x$

$\dfrac{22}{4} = \dfrac{4x}{4}$ D_4

$5\frac{1}{2} = x$

Check

$22 = 4x$

$22 \overset{?}{=} 4(5\frac{1}{2})$

$22 = 22$ (true)

Answer: $x = 5\frac{1}{2}$, or solution set is $\{5\frac{1}{2}\}$.

3. $.3x = 9$

Solution

$.3x = 9$

$\dfrac{.3x}{.3} = \dfrac{9}{.3}$ $D_{.3}$ $\left[\begin{array}{c} 3\ 0. \\ .3)\overline{9\ .0} \end{array}\right]$

$x = 30$

Check

$.3x = 9$

$.3(30) \overset{?}{=} 9$

$9 = 9$ (true)

Answer: $x = 30$, or solution set is $\{30\}$.

4. Sam weighs 3 times as much as Tim. If Sam weighs 180 pounds, how much does Tim weigh?

How To Proceed	Solution
1. Represent Tim's weight by a variable.	Let $y =$ Tim's weight.
2. Using the same variable, represent Sam's weight.	Then $3y =$ Sam's weight.

3. Write the word statement as an equation.

$3y = 180$ (Sam weighs 180 pounds.)

4. Solve the equation. D_3 (mentally)

$y = 60$

5. Check in the original problem.

Tim weighs 60 pounds and Sam weighs 180 pounds. Does Sam weigh 3 times as much as Tim? Yes.

Answer: Tim weighs 60 pounds.

MULTIPLICATION PROPERTY OF EQUALITY

If two equal numbers are multiplied by the same number, the products are equal. This describes the ***multiplication property of equality.***

In general, for all numbers, a, b, and c, we assume:

$$\text{if } a = b, \text{ then } ac = bc$$

Therefore, we can say: **If both members of an equality are multiplied by the same number, the equality is retained.**

Study the following examples:

In Arithmetic	*In Algebra*		
if $8 = 8$	if $\dfrac{x}{4} = 8$		
then $4 \times 8 = 4 \times 8$	then $4 \times \dfrac{x}{4} = 4 \times 8$	M_4	(Multiply both members of the previous equation by 4.)
and $32 = 32$	and $x = 32$		

Notice that the application of the multiplication property in the equation $\dfrac{x}{4} = 8$ resulted in the equivalent equations $4 \times \dfrac{x}{4} = 4 \times 8$ and $x = 32$. All three equations have the same solution set $\{32\}$.

Now we will use the multiplication property of equality in solving equations.

~~~~~~~~~~~~~~~~~~~~~ **MODEL PROBLEMS** ~~~~~~~~~~~~~~~~~~~~~

Solve and check:

1. $\dfrac{n}{3} = 12$ **2.** $8 = \dfrac{1}{2}x$ **3.** $\dfrac{x}{9} = \dfrac{4}{3}$

Solution *Solution* *Solution*

$$\dfrac{n}{3} = 12$$

$$3 \times \dfrac{n}{3} = 3 \times 12 \quad M_3$$

$$n = 36$$

$$8 = \dfrac{1}{2}x \left(\dfrac{1}{2}x \text{ is } \atop \text{the same} \atop \text{as } \dfrac{x}{2}. \right)$$

$$2 \times 8 = 2 \times \dfrac{1}{2}x \quad M_2$$

$$16 = x$$

$$\dfrac{x}{9} = \dfrac{4}{3}$$

$$9 \times \dfrac{x}{9} = 9 \times \dfrac{4}{3} \quad M_9$$

$$x = 12$$

Check *Check* *Check*

$$\dfrac{n}{3} = 12$$

$$\dfrac{36}{3} \overset{?}{=} 12$$

$$12 = 12 \quad \text{(true)}$$

$$8 = \dfrac{1}{2}x$$

$$8 \overset{?}{=} \dfrac{1}{2} \times 16$$

$$8 = 8 \quad \text{(true)}$$

$$\dfrac{x}{9} = \dfrac{4}{3}$$

$$\dfrac{12}{9} \overset{?}{=} \dfrac{4}{3}$$

$$\dfrac{4}{3} = \dfrac{4}{3} \quad \text{(true)}$$

Answer: $n = 36$, or solution set is $\{36\}$.

Answer: $x = 16$, or solution set is $\{16\}$.

Answer: $x = 12$, or solution set is $\{12\}$.

4. Ned traveled $\frac{1}{4}$ of the distance that Ben traveled. If Ned traveled 12 miles, how far did Ben travel?

How To Proceed	*Solution*
1. Represent the distance Ben traveled by a variable.	Let d = distance Ben traveled.
2. Using the same variable, represent the distance Ned traveled.	Then $\frac{1}{4}d$ = distance Ned traveled.
3. Write the word statement as an equation.	$\frac{1}{4}d = 12$ (Ned traveled 12 miles.)
4. Solve the equation. M_4 (mentally)	$d = 48$

5. Check in the original problem.   Ben traveled 48 miles and Ned traveled 12 miles. Did Ned travel $\frac{1}{4}$ of the distance that Ben traveled? Yes.

Answer: Ben traveled 48 miles.

~~~~~~

Procedure. To solve an equation in which a variable and a constant are related by the operation of multiplication or division:
1. **Use the inverse operation, multiplying or dividing (as the case may be) both members of the equation by the constant. Perform the indicated operation(s) to obtain an equivalent equation in which only the variable itself is one member of the equation.**
2. **Check by determining that when the value obtained for the variable replaces it in the given equation, the resulting statement is true.**

Exercises

In 1–44, solve and check the equation.

1. $5x = 50$ **2.** $10b = 70$ **3.** $\dfrac{a}{2} = 3$ **4.** $\dfrac{x}{7} = 5$

5. $3y = 3$ **6.** $\dfrac{t}{3} = 6$ **7.** $2b = 0$ **8.** $\dfrac{m}{5} = 4$

9. $81 = 27q$ **10.** $16 = \dfrac{t}{4}$ **11.** $15 = 2y$ **12.** $1 = \dfrac{r}{8}$

13. $6c = 44$ **14.** $\frac{1}{2}n = 9$ **15.** $6w = 3$ **16.** $\frac{1}{3}m = 4$
17. $\frac{1}{10}x = 0$ **18.** $21z = 14$ **19.** $2a = .6$ **20.** $\frac{1}{4}y = .25$
21. $.4x = 3.2$ **22.** $9 = .3x$ **23.** $1.4x = 5.6$ **24.** $.04x = 2$
25. $.06y = 12$ **26.** $7.2 = .09x$ **27.** $.15c = 300$ **28.** $1.25d = 10$

29. $\frac{1}{8}x = \frac{1}{4}$ **30.** $\frac{1}{5}x = \frac{1}{2}$ **31.** $\dfrac{1}{3} = \dfrac{m}{4}$ **32.** $\dfrac{c}{8} = \dfrac{3}{2}$

33. $\frac{2}{3}b = 8$ **34.** $30 = \frac{5}{3}m$ **35.** $3\frac{1}{2}x = 7$ **36.** $5x = 8\frac{1}{3}$
37. $7x = 12\frac{1}{4}$ **38.** $\frac{1}{9} = 3x$ **39.** $\frac{1}{3}y = \frac{5}{9}$ **40.** $1\frac{1}{2}d = 5$

41. $\dfrac{x}{.5} = 4$ **42.** $10 = \dfrac{y}{1.2}$ **43.** $\dfrac{t}{1.4} = 1$ **44.** $\dfrac{c}{.01} = .75$

45. If $9x = 36$, find the value of $2x$.
46. If $2x = 64$, find the value of $\frac{1}{4}x$.

47. If $\dfrac{t}{2} = 12$, find the value of $5t$.

48. If $\frac{2}{3}y = 16$, find the value of $3y + 7$.

49. If $.08y = .96$, find the value of $\frac{1}{2}y - 3$.

In 50–52, determine the element(s) of the set if $y \in \{\text{natural numbers}\}$.

50. $\{y \mid 3y = 27\}$ **51.** $\{y \mid \frac{1}{2}y = 8\}$ **52.** $\{y \mid 35 = 5y\}$

In 53–87, solve the problem using a variable and an equation.

53. Seven times a number is 63. Find the number.

54. Five times a number is 50. Find the number.

55. When a number is doubled, the result is 36. Find the number.

56. A number divided by 5 equals 17. Find the number.

57. A number divided by 4 is $3\frac{1}{2}$. Find the number.

58. One-half of a number is 12. Find the number.

59. Three-fifths of a number is 30. Find the number.

60. A number multiplied by .3 is 6. Find the number.

61. Four-hundredths of a number is 16. Find the number.

62. 4% of a number is 8. Find the number.

63. 15% of a number is 4.5. Find the number.

64. One-eighth of a number is $4\frac{1}{2}$. Find the number.

65. $33\frac{1}{3}\%$ of a number is $3\frac{2}{3}$. Find the number.

66. Bill traveled 5 times as far as Harold. Bill traveled 150 miles. How far did Harold travel?

67. Ray is twice as old as Jane. Ray is 46 years old. How old is Jane?

68. A man earned $600 in 4 weeks. What was his weekly salary?

69. One-fifth of Kurt's age is 3 years. Find Kurt's age.

70. Marvin saved 25% of his allowance. If he saved $.50, how much was his allowance?

71. John gained 12 pounds during the last year. If this represents one-tenth of his present weight, find his present weight.

72. A newspaper costs $.05. How many newspapers can be bought for $1.25?

73. Baseballs cost $1.50 each. How many baseballs can be bought for $6.00?

74. The width of a rectangle is $\frac{1}{5}$ of its length. If the width of the rectangle is 6 feet, what is its length?

75. Find Ted's weight if $\frac{3}{4}$ of his weight is 60 pounds.

76. On a trip, Mr. Stanley traveled 75% of the total distance by plane. If he traveled 1500 miles by plane, what was the total distance he traveled?

77. A team won 24 games, which was 60% of all the games it played. How many games did it play?

78. Find Jerry's height if 80% of his height is 40 inches.

79. Pearl bought a coat at a "40% off" sale. If she saved $24, what was the original price of the coat?

80. William deposited $90 in the bank last year. This was $2\frac{1}{2}$ times as much as Robert deposited. How much did Robert deposit?

81. Sandy cut a piece of lumber into 6 equal pieces. If each piece was $1\frac{1}{2}$ feet long, what was the length of the original piece of lumber?

82. Six months after Mr. Doyle bought a car, he sold it, taking a loss of $\frac{1}{5}$ of the original price of the car. If he lost $550, what was the original price of the car?

83. At a sale, a radio sold for $20. This amount was 80% of the original price. What was the original price?

84. George has walked one-fourth of the distance from his home to school. If he has walked $\frac{1}{2}$ mile, find the distance from his home to school.

85. A dealer sold a suit for 150% of the amount he paid for it. If the dealer sold the suit for $90, how much did it cost him?

86. The selling price of an article is 175% of the dealer's cost price. If the dealer sold the article for $28, how much did he pay for it?

87. The amount of money that Harry has in a savings bank is 200% of the amount he had there four years ago. If Harry now has $400 in this bank, find the amount he had in the bank four years ago.

7. Solving Equations by Using Several Operations

In the equation $2x + 3 = 15$, there are two operations indicated in the left member: *multiplication and addition*. To solve the equation we use the inverse operations: *division and subtraction*. In method 1, we first perform subtraction to undo the addition and then perform division to undo the multiplication. In method 2, we first perform division to undo the multiplication and then perform subtraction to undo the addition. Notice that both methods result in the same root.

Method 1	*Method 2*
$2x + 3 = 15$	$2x + 3 = 15$
$2x + 3 - 3 = 15 - 3$ S$_3$	$\dfrac{2x + 3}{2} = \dfrac{15}{2}$ D$_2$
$2x = 12$	$\dfrac{2x}{2} + \dfrac{3}{2} = \dfrac{15}{2}$ $\left(\dfrac{2x}{2} = x\right)$
$x = 6$ D$_2$	$x = \dfrac{12}{2}$ S$_{\frac{3}{2}}$
	$x = 6$

Check

$$2x + 3 = 15$$
$$2 \times 6 + 3 \overset{?}{=} 15$$
$$12 + 3 \overset{?}{=} 15$$
$$15 = 15 \quad \text{(true)}$$

Answer: $x = 6$, or solution set is $\{6\}$.

While both method 1 and method 2 yield the correct answer, method 1 usually avoids awkward fractions. In general, it is preferable to perform addition or subtraction first and then to perform multiplication or division.

Procedure. To solve an equation in which several operations are indicated, perform their inverse operations.

~~~~~ MODEL PROBLEMS ~~~~~

1. Solve and check: $\dfrac{3x}{2} = 30$

Solution

$$\frac{3x}{2} = 30$$
$$2 \times \frac{3x}{2} = 2 \times 30 \quad \text{M}_2$$
$$3x = 60$$
$$x = 20 \quad \text{D}_3$$

Check

$$\frac{3x}{2} = 30$$
$$\frac{3 \times 20}{2} \overset{?}{=} 30$$
$$\frac{60}{2} \overset{?}{=} 30$$
$$30 = 30 \quad \text{(true)}$$

Answer: $x = 20$, or solution set is $\{20\}$.

2. Solve and check: $12 = 2x - 3$

Solution

$$12 = 2x - 3$$
$$12 + 3 = 2x - 3 + 3 \quad \text{A}_3$$
$$15 = 2x$$
$$7.5 = x \quad \text{D}_2$$

Check

$$12 = 2x - 3$$
$$12 \overset{?}{=} 2 \times 7.5 - 3$$
$$12 \overset{?}{=} 15 - 3$$
$$12 = 12 \quad \text{(true)}$$

Answer: $x = 7.5$, or solution set is $\{7.5\}$.

3. Solve and check: $\dfrac{3x}{5} + 6 = 24$

<table>
<tr><td>Solution</td><td>Check</td></tr>
</table>

Solution	*Check*
$\dfrac{3x}{5} + 6 = 24$	$\dfrac{3x}{5} + 6 = 24$
$\dfrac{3x}{5} = 18 \qquad$ S$_6$ (mentally)	$\dfrac{3 \times 30}{5} + 6 \overset{?}{=} 24$
$5 \times \dfrac{3x}{5} = 5 \times 18 \quad$ M$_5$	$\dfrac{90}{5} + 6 \overset{?}{=} 24$
$3x = 90$	$18 + 6 \overset{?}{=} 24$
$x = 30 \qquad$ D$_3$	$24 = 24 \quad$ (true)

Answer: $x = 30$, or solution set is $\{30\}$.

4. If 4 times a number is increased by 7, the result is 43. Find the number.

How To Proceed	*Solution*
1. Represent the number by a letter.	Let $x =$ the number.
2. Write the word statement as an equation.	$4x + 7 = 43$
3. Solve the equation.	$4x = 36 \quad$ S$_7$ (mentally)
	$x = 9 \qquad$ D$_4$

Check: Does 4×9, increased by 7, give a result of 43? Yes.

Answer: The number is 9.

Exercises

In 1–36, solve and check the equation.

1. $3x + 5 = 35$	**2.** $5a + 17 = 47$	**3.** $4x - 1 = 15$
4. $3y - 5 = 16$	**5.** $55 = 6a + 7$	**6.** $17 = 8c - 4$
7. $15x + 14 = 19$	**8.** $75 = 11 + 2x$	**9.** $14 = 12b + 8$
10. $8 = 18c - 1$	**11.** $11 = 15t + 1$	**12.** $11 = 16d - 1$
13. $\dfrac{3a}{8} = 12$	**14.** $\dfrac{4c}{9} = 20$	**15.** $42 = \dfrac{7d}{8}$
16. $\tfrac{2}{3}x = 18$	**17.** $12 = \tfrac{3}{4}y$	**18.** $\tfrac{3}{5}m = 30$
19. $\dfrac{5t}{4} = \dfrac{45}{2}$	**20.** $\dfrac{7t}{3} = \dfrac{14}{3}$	**21.** $1.2 = \dfrac{4m}{5}$

22. $\dfrac{x}{3} + 4 = 13$ **23.** $\dfrac{a}{4} - 9 = 51$ **24.** $15 = \dfrac{b}{7} - 8$

25. $12 = \dfrac{y}{5} + 3$ **26.** $.6m + \frac{1}{3} = 18\frac{1}{3}$ **27.** $9d - \frac{1}{2} = 17\frac{1}{2}$

28. $4a + .2 = 5$ **29.** $4 = 3t - .2$ **30.** $\frac{1}{4}x - 5 = 11$

31. $\frac{1}{9}x + 4 = 13$ **32.** $13 = \frac{1}{3}y - 5$ **33.** $47 = \frac{4}{5}t + 7$

34. $\dfrac{3c}{2} - 7 = 65$ **35.** $\dfrac{5d}{6} - 1\frac{1}{2} = 8\frac{1}{2}$ **36.** $8\frac{2}{3} = \dfrac{b}{6} + 2\frac{2}{3}$

In 37–39, determine the element(s) of the set if $x \in$ {natural numbers}.

37. $\{x \mid 2x + 1 = 37\}$ **38.** $\{x \mid 8x - 1 = 23\}$ **39.** $\{x \mid 19 = 2x + 3\}$

In 40–54, use an algebraic equation to solve the problem.

40. Ten times a number, increased by 9, is 59. Find the number.
41. The sum of 8 times a number and 5 is 37. Find the number.
42. If six times a number is decreased by 4, the result is 68. Find the number.
43. If twelve times a number is diminished by 6, the result is 90. Find the number.
44. The difference between 4 times a number and 3 is 25. Find the number.
45. If a number is multiplied by 7, and the product is increased by 2, the result is 100. Find the number.
46. When 12 is subtracted from 3 times a number, the result is 24. Find the number.
47. A number is multiplied by 15. When the product is increased by 13, the result is 73. Find the number.
48. Two-thirds of a number is 40. Find the number.
49. Five-ninths of a number is 45. Find the number.
50. If 9 is added to one-half of a number, the result is 29. Find the number.
51. If one-third of a number is decreased by 7, the result is 23. Find the number.
52. If two-thirds of a number is decreased by 4, the result is 56. Find the number.
53. If 38 is added to $\frac{5}{9}$ of a number, the result is 128. Find the number.
54. The sum of $\frac{3}{5}$ of a number and 2.3 is 14.6. Find the number.

8. Solving Equations by Combining Like Terms

Procedure. To solve an equation in which like terms appear in either member of the equation:

1. **Use the distributive property of multiplication to combine the like terms.**
2. **Solve the resulting equation by using inverse operations.**

MODEL PROBLEMS

1. Solve and check: $6x + 3x = 36$

How To Proceed	*Solution*	*Check*
1. Write the equation.	$6x + 3x = 36$	$6x + 3x = 36$
		$6 \times 4 + 3 \times 4 \overset{?}{=} 36$
2. Use the distributive property to combine like terms.	$(6 + 3)x = 36$	$24 + 12 \overset{?}{=} 36$
	$9x = 36$	$36 = 36$
		(true)
3. Use the division property, D_9.	$x = 4$	

Answer: $x = 4$, or solution set is $\{4\}$.

2. Solve and check: $5x + 15 + 2x = 71$

How To Proceed	*Solution*	*Check*
1. Write the equation.	$5x + 15 + 2x = 71$	$5x + 15 + 2x = 71$
		$5 \times 8 + 15 + 2 \times 8 \overset{?}{=} 71$
2. Use the commutative property.	$5x + 2x + 15 = 71$	$40 + 15 + 16 \overset{?}{=} 71$
		$71 = 71$
3. Use the distributive property to combine like terms.	$(5 + 2)x + 15 = 71$	(true)
	$7x + 15 = 71$	
4. Use the subtraction property, S_{15}.	$7x = 56$	
5. Use the division property, D_7.	$x = 8$	

Answer: $x = 8$, or solution set is $\{8\}$.

3. The larger of two numbers is 4 times the smaller. If the sum of the two numbers is 55, find the numbers.

How To Proceed	*Solution*
1. Represent the smaller number by a letter.	Let x = the smaller number.
2. Represent "the larger of two numbers is 4 times the smaller."	Then $4x$ = the larger number.

3. Write as an equation "the sum of the two numbers is 55." $x + 4x = 55$

4. Solve the equation. First, combine like terms. Then, D$_5$. $5x = 55$

$x = 11$

5. Find the larger number. $4x = 44$

Check: Is the larger number 4 times the smaller? $44 \stackrel{?}{=} 4 \times 11$. Yes.
Is the sum of the two numbers 55? $11 + 44 \stackrel{?}{=} 55$. Yes.

Answer: The smaller number is 11 and the larger number is 44.

Exercises

In 1–21, solve and check the equation.

1. $2a + 2a = 50$
2. $8x + x = 72$
3. $144 = 9b + 3b$
4. $12x - 4x = 108$
5. $5x - 3x = 22$
6. $18 = 7x - x$
7. $3\frac{1}{2}c + 2\frac{1}{2}c = 54$
8. $3.6d - 2.4d = 24$
9. $8x + 3x + 4x = 60$
10. $7y + 4y - y = 70$
11. $3e - e + 4e = 90$
12. $39 = 8c + 6c - c$
13. $6y + 2y - 3 = 21$
14. $5y + 7 + y = 37$
15. $26 = 3y + 2y - 9$
16. $8y - 3y + 7 = 87$
17. $6x - x + 12 = 52$
18. $95 = 8c - 3c + 15$
19. $\frac{1}{4}x + \frac{1}{2}x = 18$
20. $\frac{2}{3}x - \frac{1}{3}x = 17$
21. $\frac{2}{3}c + \frac{5}{3}c - 8 = 6$

In 22–35, use an algebraic equation to solve the problem.

22. The larger of two numbers is twice the smaller. If the sum of the two numbers is 96, find the numbers.

23. One number is 5 times another. If their difference is 96, find the numbers.

24. A number is one-half of another number. Find the numbers if their difference is 28.

25. A number is $\frac{2}{3}$ of another number. The sum of the two numbers is 50. Find the numbers.

26. Herbert is 5 times as old as Mike. If the sum of their ages is 18 years, find the age of each boy.

27. Bob and Dan earned a total of $24 shoveling snow. If Bob earned 3 times as much as Dan, how much did each boy earn?

28. Lily spent 4 times as much as her sister Sue. If the girls spent $24, how much did each girl spend?

29. Carl and Richard earned $10.50 delivering packages. If they agreed that Carl should get 1.5 times as much as Richard gets, how much did each boy receive?

30. A house and a lot are worth $30,000. If the house is worth 6.5 times as much as the lot, find how much each is worth.

31. Cindy's height is $\frac{3}{4}$ of Sylvia's height. If the difference between their heights is 15 inches, find the height of each girl.

32. The larger of two numbers is 12 more than the smaller. The sum of the numbers is 36. Find the numbers.

33. The larger of two numbers exceeds the smaller by 10. If the sum of the numbers is 76, find the numbers.

34. The number of boys registered in a school is 235 more than the number of girls registered. If there are 885 pupils registered in the school, find the number of boys and the number of girls.

35. Jeff and Marion sold 89 magazines. If Jeff sold 1 more than 3 times the number Marion sold, find the number sold by each.

9. More Practice in Solving Equations

In 1–60, solve and check the equation.

1. $9x = 108$

2. $9b + 8 = 8$

3. $4y + 2y = 39$

4. $.15x = .06$

5. $79 = 5x - 6$

6. $5y + 19 = 27$

7. $18 = 4a + 10$

8. $14 = n - 5.6$

9. $.6m - 4 = .8$

10. $\frac{5}{7}b = 35$

11. $39 = x + 5x$

12. $4y - 46 = 42$

13. $7x - 3x = 68$

14. $48 = 7m - 1$

15. $45 = 6x - 3$

16. $48 = 5.7b - 4.5b$

17. $\dfrac{2x}{5} + 15 = 37$

18. $8t - t = 21$

19. $3x - \frac{1}{3} = 5\frac{2}{3}$

20. $87 = 2x - 13$

21. $41 = \dfrac{3x}{2} - 10$

22. $.11a = 44$

23. $x - 3\frac{1}{8} = 7\frac{1}{4}$

24. $3y + 19 = 94$

25. $\dfrac{3t}{4} = 84$

26. $6x + 3x - x = 60$

27. $.2c - .8 = 3$

28. $10r = 2$

29. $\dfrac{s}{4} - 5 = 7$

30. $\dfrac{3m}{2} = 45\frac{1}{2}$

31. $.8c - 4 = 3.2$

32. $9y - 4 = 68$

33. $7c - 3c - 5 = 15$

34. $.01x = 5$

35. $.9b = .18$

36. $4z + 18 = 56$

37. $p + 11 = 12$

38. $\dfrac{2d}{3} = 16$

39. $5n + 2n - 5 = 30$

40. $8m + 3 = 91$

41. $.3x + .2x = 8$

42. $7c - c - 2 = 2$

43. $\dfrac{n}{6} + 5\frac{2}{3} = 12\frac{1}{3}$

44. $\dfrac{4e}{5} - 32 = 28$

45. $6 = 14a$

46. $29 = \frac{1}{3}a + 12$

47. $5 = 5 + m$

48. $9x - 3x - x = 95$

49. $\dfrac{15}{4} = \dfrac{r}{8}$

50. $\frac{7}{10}x = 35$

51. $19 = \frac{1}{3}m + 5$

52. $\frac{1}{2}t + \frac{1}{4}t = 12$ **53.** $\frac{x}{14} = \frac{5}{7}$ **54.** $6r + 3r - 4 = 32$

55. $x + \frac{1}{8} = \frac{7}{8}$ **56.** $\frac{1}{3}c - 1 = 14$ **57.** $4x - x + 5 = 21$

58. $3m - 6\frac{1}{2} = 8\frac{1}{2}$ **59.** $\frac{y}{8} = \frac{9}{2}$ **60.** $18 = 8c - 2c + 3$

10. Graphing the Solution Set of a Simple Equation

MODEL PROBLEMS

In 1–3, using {numbers of arithmetic} as the domain:
a. Find the solution set of the equation.
b. Graph the solution set of the equation.

1. $\frac{x}{3} = 2$

Solution   *Check*

a. $\frac{x}{3} = 2$ $\frac{x}{3} = 2$

$3 \times \frac{x}{3} = 3 \times 2$ M_3 $\frac{6}{3} \stackrel{?}{=} 2$

$x = 6$ $2 = 2$ (true)

Answer: The solution set of $\frac{x}{3} = 2$ is $\{6\}$.

b. Graph the solution set $\{6\}$.

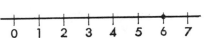

2. $x - 1\frac{1}{2} = 1$

Solution   *Check*

a. $x - 1\frac{1}{2} = 1$ $x - 1\frac{1}{2} = 1$

$x - 1\frac{1}{2} + 1\frac{1}{2} = 1 + 1\frac{1}{2}$ $A_{1\frac{1}{2}}$ $2\frac{1}{2} - 1\frac{1}{2} \stackrel{?}{=} 1$

$x = 2\frac{1}{2}$ $1 = 1$ (true)

Answer: The solution set of $x - 1\frac{1}{2} = 1$ is $\{2\frac{1}{2}\}$.

b. Graph the solution set $\{2\frac{1}{2}\}$.

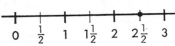

3. $8x - 2x + 5 = 17$

	Solution		*Check*

a. $8x - 2x + 5 = 17$

$\qquad 6x + 5 = 17$ (distributive property)

$\qquad\qquad 6x = 12$ S_5

$\qquad\qquad\quad x = 2$ D_6

$8x - 2x + 5 = 17$

$8 \times 2 - 2 \times 2 + 5 \overset{?}{=} 17$

$16 - 4 + 5 \overset{?}{=} 17$

$17 = 17$ (true)

Answer: The solution set of $8x - 2x + 5 = 17$ is $\{2\}$.

b. Graph the solution set $\{2\}$.

$$\overset{}{\underset{\displaystyle 0 \quad 1 \quad 2 \quad 3 \quad 4}{\rule{0pt}{0pt}}}$$

Exercises

In 1–45, find and graph the solution set. Use {numbers of arithmetic} as the domain.

1. $3x = 15$

2. $2a = 5$

3. $2 = 4r$

4. $1.5x = 6$

5. $\frac{2}{3}x = 4$

6. $\frac{x}{2} = 5$

7. $\frac{y}{4} = \frac{1}{2}$

8. $10 = \frac{r}{.4}$

9. $a + 7 = 10$

10. $a - 3 = 4$

11. $y + 1\frac{1}{2} = 2\frac{3}{4}$

12. $y - 7 = 1$

13. $b + 2 = 2$

14. $x - \frac{1}{2} = 3\frac{1}{2}$

15. $1.8 = z - .7$

16. $4 = 1.5 + y$

17. $2x + 1 = 13$

18. $3x - 6 = 9$

19. $6x + 2 = 5$

20. $4y - 2 = 4$

21. $21 = 7r$

22. $12 = x + 6$

23. $4 = \frac{y}{2}$

24. $5 = y - 3$

25. $13 = 3x + 4$

26. $19 = 5x - 1$

27. $4x + 6 = 20$

28. $5 = 8x - 1$

29. $3x + 2x = 15$

30. $y + 2y = 18$

31. $4a - 2a = 8$

32. $12 = 5x - 2x$

33. $2m + m = 12$

34. $3m - m = 20$

35. $14 = 6x + x$

36. $24 = 9y - y$

37. $5t + 2t + t = 40$

38. $6m + 3m - 2m = 21$

39. $7 = 8y - 5y - y$

40. $4r + 3r + 8 = 50$

41. $8d - 4d + 6 = 26$

42. $3m + 2m - 4 = 6$

43. $12c + 9 + c = 139$

44. $10 = 4z + 8 + 2z$

45. $8 = 9t - t - 4$

46. Graph $\{x \mid 3x = 15\}$ if $x \in$ {natural numbers}.

47. Graph $\{y \mid y - 8 = 2\}$ if $y \in$ {natural numbers}.

48. Graph $\{c \mid 3c + 2 = 17\}$ if $c \in$ {natural numbers}.

49. Graph $\{m \mid 3m + 2m = 35\}$ if $m \in$ {natural numbers}.

CHAPTER VI

SIGNED NUMBERS

Using only the numbers of arithmetic, we can represent a temperature of 50° above zero by 50, but we have no symbol for representing the opposite, a temperature of 50° below zero. We can find a value for the indicated difference $10 - 7$, the number 3; but we cannot find a number to represent $7 - 10$. In order to deal with situations such as these, we will develop a new set of numbers.

1. Extending the Number Line

Until now, we have dealt only with a number line like the one shown. It starts at zero and extends indefinitely to the right.

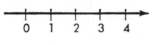

Since a line extends indefinitely in both directions, we can begin at zero and mark off unit intervals to the left as well as to the right. We label successive points to the right of zero $^+1$, $^+2$, $^+3$, etc.; we label successive points in the opposite direction, to the left of zero, $^-1$, $^-2$, $^-3$, etc.

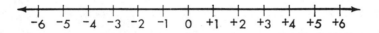

The entire number line which extends both to the right of zero (in a positive direction) and to the left of zero (in a negative direction) is called the *real number line*. The coordinate of each point on the line is called a *real number*. Those numbers which are coordinates of points to the right of zero are called *real positive numbers*; those to the left are called *real negative numbers*. Since signs which indicate direction are used to distinguish between numerals which represent positive and negative numbers, these numbers are called *signed numbers*, or *directed numbers*. Although 0 is not written with a sign, we include it in the set of signed numbers.

We will make frequent use of the set of signed numbers

$$\{\ldots, {}^-4, {}^-3, {}^-2, {}^-1, 0, {}^+1, {}^+2, {}^+3, {}^+4, \ldots\}$$

called the set of **integers.** The numbers $^+1, {}^+2, {}^+3, \ldots$ are called **positive integers;** the numbers $^-1, {}^-2, {}^-3, \ldots$ are called **negative integers.**

Observe that $^+1$ and 1 are considered as numerals which represent the same number, because they are associated with the same point on a number line. Likewise, 2 is another name for $^+2$, and $^+3$ is another name for 3. Actually, the positive numbers do not represent new numbers; only the negative numbers do.

We must be careful not to confuse the "$^+$" and "$^-$" with the "$+$" and "$-$." The "$^+$" and "$^-$" are used in signed numbers to indicate direction; the "$+$" and "$-$" are used to indicate addition and subtraction.

Exercises

In 1–3, draw a real number line. Then locate the points whose coordinates are given.

1. $^+4, {}^-2, 0, {}^-5, {}^+3$ 2. $^+\frac{1}{2}, 0, {}^-1\frac{1}{2}, {}^+3\frac{1}{2}, {}^-\frac{3}{4}$ 3. $^+1, {}^-\frac{1}{3}, 0, {}^+1\frac{2}{3}, {}^-\frac{5}{6}$

In 4–6, graph the set of numbers on a real number line.

4. $\{2, {}^-1, 0, 3, {}^-4\}$ 5. $\{{}^-\frac{1}{2}, \frac{3}{4}, 0, 1\frac{1}{2}, {}^-1\frac{3}{4}\}$ 6. $\{3, {}^-\frac{2}{3}, \frac{5}{6}, {}^-2\frac{1}{3}, 0\}$

In 7–14, state whether the signed numbers are on the same or opposite sides of the zero on a number line.

7. $^+9, {}^+4$ 8. $^-9, {}^-4$ 9. $^+9, {}^-4$ 10. $^-9, {}^+4$
11. $^+3, {}^+6$ 12. $^-5, {}^-4$ 13. $^+10, {}^-3$ 14. $^-8, {}^+7$

15. Which part of the numeral for a signed number reveals whether the number is to the right or to the left of zero on a number line?

In 16–23, select the number which is farther from 0 on a number line.

16. $^+10, {}^+4$ 17. $^-10, {}^-4$ 18. $^+10, {}^-4$ 19. $^-10, {}^-4$
20. $^+9, {}^+3$ 21. $^-6, {}^-8$ 22. $^-7, {}^+5$ 23. $^+8, {}^-1$

24. What part of the numeral for a signed number reveals its distance from 0 on a number line?

In 25–30, graph the numbers on a number line. Then tell which point is to the right of the other.

25. $^+5, {}^-2$ 26. $^-5, {}^+2$ 27. $^+7, {}^+3$ 28. $^-7, {}^-3$ 29. $0, {}^-4$ 30. $^+4, 0$

In 31–37:   (a) Graph the number on a number line.   (b) Locate a point on the number line which is the same distance from 0 as the given point but on the opposite side of 0.   (c) Name the number located in (b).

31. $^+4$ 32. $^-5$ 33. 7 34. $^-3$ 35. $1\frac{1}{2}$ 36. $^-3\frac{1}{4}$ 37. $^+2.5$

In 38–42, use a real number line which extends from ⁻10 to ⁺10 to answer the question.

38. Start at 0 and move a distance represented by ⁺3. From that point, move a distance represented by ⁺5. At what point on the number line have you arrived?

39. Start at 0 and move a distance represented by ⁻3. From that point, move a distance represented by ⁻6. At what point on the number line have you arrived?

40. Start at 0 and move a distance represented by ⁺9. From that point, move a distance represented by ⁻3. At what point on the number line have you arrived?

41. Start at 0 and move a distance represented by ⁺4. From that point, move a distance represented by ⁻9. At what point on the number line have you arrived?

42. Start at 0 and move a distance represented by ⁺8. From that point, move a distance represented by ⁻8. At what point on the number line have you arrived?

2. Using Signed Numbers To Represent Opposite Situations

In daily life, we frequently talk about "opposite situations." For example, we talk about traveling east and traveling west, gaining weight and losing weight, latitudes north of the equator and latitudes south of the equator, etc. The following examples illustrate the use of signed numbers in such situations:

1. If traveling 10 miles east is indicated by ⁺10, then traveling 10 miles west is indicated by ⁻10.

2. If winning $5 is represented by ⁺5, then losing $5 is represented by ⁻5.

3. If a temperature reading of ⁺8° means 8° above zero, then a temperature reading of ⁻8° means 8° below zero.

～～～～～～ MODEL PROBLEM ～～～～～～

If the temperature changes from 2° below zero to 4° above zero, represent the change as a signed number.

Solution: If the temperature changes from 2° below zero to 4° above zero, it rose 6°, which is represented by ⁺6°.

Answer: ⁺6°

Exercises

In 1–8, describe the opposite of each situation.

1. a rise in price
2. above sea level
3. south of the equator
4. traveling west
5. below average
6. a gain in weight
7. depositing money in a bank
8. making a profit

9. If $^+8$ means a profit of \$8, what does $^-8$ mean?
10. If $^+12$ means a gain of 12 pounds, what does $^-12$ mean?
11. If $^+40$ means 40° north of the equator, what does $^-40$ mean?
12. If $^+75$ means depositing \$75 in a bank, what does $^-75$ mean?
13. If $^+90$ means 90 miles east, what does $^-90$ mean?

In 14–21, represent each situation by a positive number, a negative number, or zero.

14. 75° above zero
15. 12° below zero
16. sea level
17. 1200 feet above sea level
18. a gain of \$100
19. a fall of 200 feet
20. the latitude of the equator
21. a withdrawal of \$25 from a bank

22. If sea level is represented by 0, by what signed number would 500 feet below sea level be represented?
23. What is meant by the statement that the altitude of the Dead Sea is $^-1290$ feet?
24. What is meant by the statement that the net change in the value of a stock is $^+2$ dollars?
25. If the temperature changes from 15° above zero to 28° above zero, represent the change as a signed number.
26. If the temperature changes from 3° below zero to 12° below zero, represent the change as a signed number.
27. If the temperature changes from 10° above zero to 2° below zero, represent the change as a signed number.
28. If the temperature changes from 8° below zero to 5° above zero, represent the change as a signed number.
29. On a certain day, the following temperatures were reported:

Time, P.M.	1	2	3	4	5	6	7	8	9
Temperature	$-5°$	$-3°$	$-2°$	0°	$+3°$	$+1°$	$-2°$	$-4°$	$-7°$

a. Give the meaning of the temperature at each hour.
b. What was the highest temperature reported?
c. What was the lowest temperature reported?
d. Between what hours was the temperature rising?
e. Between what hours was the temperature falling?

30. By means of a signed number, indicate for each child the difference between the actual weight and the normal weight:

	Tom	Bill	John	Sam	Mary	Sue	Bess	Ann
Actual weight	23	28	36	50	39	46	42	43
Normal weight	21	29	39	43	35	46	37	49
Difference	+2							

3. Ordering Signed Numbers on a Number Line

A temperature of +4° is higher than a temperature of +2°. That is, +4 is greater than +2, written +4 > +2. On a number line, +4 is to the right of +2.

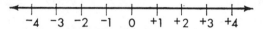

A temperature of −3° is lower than a temperature of −1°. That is, −3 is less than −1, written −3 < −1. On a number line, −3 is to the left of −1.

These examples illustrate the fact that *all signed numbers are ordered on the real number line.* Any number is greater than every number to its left and is less than every number to its right.

If we wish to indicate that −3 is between −4 and −2, we write −4 < −3 < −2.

———————— **MODEL PROBLEMS** ————————

1. State whether each of the following sentences is true or false and give the reason for your answer:

   a. +7 > −2   *Ans.* True because +7 is to the right of −2 on a number line.

   b. −5 > −3   *Ans.* False because −5 is to the left of −3 on a number line.

   c. −4 < +1   *Ans.* True because −4 is to the left of +1 on a number line.

2. If the domain of x is {−3, −2, −1, 0, +1, +2, +3}, graph the solution set for the sentence $x \geq -2$.

Solution: When any element of the domain except −3 replaces x in the sentence $x \geq -2$ (which means $x > -2$ or $x = -2$), the resulting statement is true. Therefore, the solution set of $x \geq -2$ is {−2, −1, 0, +1, +2, +3}.

3. Using the set of signed numbers as the replacement set, graph the solution set of each of the following sentences:

    a. $y > {}^-4$ *b.* $m \leq {}^-2$ *c.* ${}^-3 \leq t < {}^+2$

Solution:

  a. The graph of $y > {}^-4$ consists of all points to the right of ${}^-4$. The non-darkened circle shows that ${}^-4$ is not included.

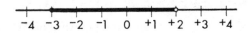

  b. The graph of $m \leq {}^-2$ consists of the point ${}^-2$ and all points to the left of ${}^-2$. The darkened circle shows that ${}^-2$ is included.

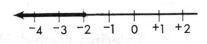

  c. The graph of ${}^-3 \leq t < {}^+2$ consists of the point ${}^-3$ and all points between ${}^-3$ and ${}^+2$. The point ${}^+2$ is not included.

Exercises

In 1–8, state whether the sentence is true or false. Give the reason for your answer.

  1. ${}^+5 > {}^+2$ **2.** ${}^-3 < 0$ **3.** ${}^+2 < 0$ **4.** ${}^+8 > {}^-2$

  5. ${}^-7 > {}^-1$ **6.** ${}^-4 > {}^+2.5$ **7.** ${}^-1\frac{3}{4} > {}^-1\frac{7}{8}$ **8.** $0 < {}^-\frac{1}{4}$

In 9–14, use the symbol $<$ to order the numbers.

  9. ${}^-4, {}^+8$ **10.** ${}^-3, {}^-6$ **11.** ${}^+1\frac{1}{2}, {}^-1\frac{1}{2}$

  12. ${}^+3, {}^-2, {}^-4$ **13.** ${}^-2, {}^+8, 0$ **14.** ${}^-3\frac{1}{2}, {}^+6, {}^+2\frac{1}{2}$

In 15–20, use the symbol $>$ to order the numbers.

  15. ${}^+7, {}^-4$ **16.** ${}^-12, {}^+12$ **17.** ${}^-1\frac{1}{2}, 0$

  18. ${}^+3, {}^-3, {}^+5$ **19.** ${}^-5, {}^-1, 0$ **20.** ${}^-1.5, {}^+3\frac{1}{2}, {}^-2\frac{1}{2}$

In 21–23, state which number is between the other two.

  21. ${}^+8, {}^-2, {}^+2$ **22.** ${}^+9, {}^-9, {}^-4$ **23.** ${}^+.6, {}^+1.1, {}^-.8$

In 24–27, state whether the sentence is true or false.

  24. ${}^+5 \geq {}^+2$ **25.** ${}^-2 \leq {}^+5$ **26.** ${}^-9 \leq {}^-12$ **27.** ${}^-3 \geq {}^+3$

28. If x is a positive number and y is a negative number ($x > 0$ and $y < 0$), tell whether each statement is true or false.

    a. $x = y$ *b.* $x > y$ *c.* $y > x$ *d.* $x < 0$ *e.* $y < 0 < x$

In 29–40, if the replacement set is $\{^-4, ^-3, ^-2, ^-1, 0, ^+1, ^+2, ^+3, ^+4\}$, graph the truth set of the open sentence.

29. $x > 0$ **30.** $x < 0$ **31.** $x \geq 0$ **32.** $x \leq 0$

33. $y > ^-1$ **34.** $t < ^+2$ **35.** $m \geq ^+1$ **36.** $c \leq ^-1$

37. $^-1 < d < ^+3$ **38.** $^-1 \leq x < ^+2$ **39.** $^-1 < y \leq ^+2$ **40.** $^-3 \leq t \leq ^+3$

In 41–52, if the domain is the set of signed numbers, graph the solution set of the sentence.

41. $x > ^+6$ **42.** $y < ^-3$ **43.** $r > 0$ **44.** $s \leq 0$

45. $m \geq ^-1$ **46.** $m \leq ^-4$ **47.** $x \neq ^+2$ **48.** $z \geq ^+2\frac{1}{2}$

49. $^-3 < x < ^+2$ **50.** $^-2 \leq x < ^+4$ **51.** $^-1 < y \leq ^+3$ **52.** $^-3 \leq m \leq 3$

4. The Opposite of a Directed Number

On a real number line, any number can be paired with another number which is the same distance from 0 and on the opposite side of 0. We call such a pair of numbers **opposites**. For example, $^-1$ is the opposite of

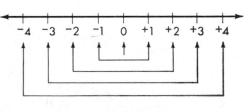

$^+1$, and $^+2$ is the opposite of $^-2$. We say that the opposite of 0 is 0. A centered dash "$-$" placed before a numeral is used as a symbol for "the opposite of."

    $-(^+1) = ^-1$ is read, "the opposite of $^+1$ is $^-1$"

    $-(^-2) = ^+2$ is read, "the opposite of $^-2$ is $^+2$"

We know that $^+4$ and 4 name the same number. Hence, the opposite of $^+4$, written $-(^+4)$, and the opposite of 4, written -4, both name the same number. Since $-(^+4) = ^-4$, then $-4 = ^-4$. Notice that -4 and $^-4$ are really two different names for the same number. Therefore, we will use only one symbol, -4, to represent that number.

In the future, we will simplify our mathematical notation by not using the symbols "$^+$" and "$^-$". The number represented by the symbol $^+4$ will be written 4 or $+4$. The number represented by the symbols $^-4$ and $-(^+4)$ will be written -4. The equation $-(^+4) = ^-4$ will be written $-(+4) = -4$ or, even more simply, $-4 = -4$.

If y is a real number, the opposite of y is written $-y$. The symbol $-y$ is also frequently read "negative y." However, this does not mean that $-y$ is always a negative number. When y is a positive number, its opposite, $-y$, is a negative number; when y is a negative number, $-y$ is a positive number; when y is 0, $-y$ is also 0.

The opposite of the opposite of a number is always the number itself. For example, the opposite of the opposite of 5, $-(-5)$, is 5. The opposite of the opposite of -6, $-[-(-6)]$ is -6.

In general, if y is a real number, then:

$$-(-y) = y$$

~~~~~~~~~~~~~~ MODEL PROBLEMS ~~~~~~~~~~~~~~

In 1–4, write the simplest symbol which represents the opposite of the number.

1. 15   *Ans.* -15 **2.** -10 *Ans.* 10 or $+10$

3. $(4 + 8)$ *Ans.* -12 **4.** $-[-(9 - 3)]$ *Ans.* -6

5. Graph the solution set of $-c > 1$ if the domain is $\{-2, -1, 0, 1, 2\}$.

Solution:

Step 1. In the open sentence $-c > 1$, replace c by the elements of the domain.

$$-(-2) > 1, \text{ or } 2 > 1 \text{ is a } true \text{ sentence.}$$
$$-(-1) > 1, \text{ or } 1 > 1 \text{ is a false sentence.}$$
$$-(0) > 1, \text{ or } 0 > 1 \text{ is a false sentence.}$$
$$-(1) > 1, \text{ or } -1 > 1 \text{ is a false sentence.}$$
$$-(2) > 1, \text{ or } -2 > 1 \text{ is a false sentence.}$$

Therefore, the solution set of $-c > 1$ is $\{-2\}$.

Step 2. Graph the solution set $\{-2\}$.

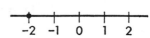

Exercises

In 1–12, write the simplest symbol which represents the opposite of the number.

1. 8   **2.** -8 **3.** $+3\frac{1}{2}$ **4.** -6.5
5. $(10 + 9)$ **6.** $(24 - 10)$ **7.** $(9 - 9)$ **8.** 8×0
9. $-(-7)$ **10.** $-(-\frac{3}{4})$ **11.** $-[-(+5)]$ **12.** $-[-(6 + 8)]$

In 13–16, select the greater of the two numbers.

13. 10, −5   **14.** −1, 7   **15.** −8, −4   **16.** −12, 0

In 17–28, graph the solution set of the open sentence if the domain of the variable is $\{-4, -3, -2, -1, 0, 1, 2, 3, 4\}$.

17. $-w > 2$ **18.** $-t < 1$ **19.** $-m > 0$ **20.** $-y \leq 0$

21. $-x \geq 1$ **22.** $-x > -1$ **23.** $-x < -3$ **24.** $-y > -1$

25. $-c \geq -2$ **26.** $-d \leq -1\frac{1}{2}$ **27.** $-4 < x < 4$ **28.** $-2 < -x < 1$

In 29–40, graph the solution set of the open sentence if the domain of the variable is the set of real numbers.

29. $x < -3$ **30.** $y > -6$ **31.** $m \geq -1$ **32.** $y \leq -2$

33. $-t \geq 4$ **34.** $-s \leq 0$ **35.** $-c < -2$ **36.** $-d > -3$

37. $-m \geq -2\frac{1}{2}$ **38.** $-r \leq -4$ **39.** $-8 < s < 3$ **40.** $-3 < -y < 1$

In 41–46, tell whether the statement is true or false.

41. If a is a real number, then $-a$ is always a negative number.

42. If a is a negative number, then $-a$ is always a positive number.

43. The opposite of a number is always a different number.

44. On a number line, the opposite of a positive number is to the left of the number.

45. On a number line, the opposite of any number is always to the left of the number.

46. The opposite of the opposite of a number is that number itself.

5. The Absolute Value of a Number

In every pair of opposite numbers, other than 0 and 0, the positive number is the greater. On a real number line, the positive number is always to the right of the negative number which is its opposite. For example, 10 is greater than its opposite -10; on a number line, 10 is to the right of -10. The greater of a non-zero number and its opposite is called the **absolute value** of the number. Since 10 is the greater of the two opposite numbers 10 and -10, the absolute value of 10 is 10, written $|10| = 10$. Also, the absolute value of -10 is 10, written $|-10| = 10$. We use the symbol "$|x|$" to represent the absolute value of the number x. The absolute value of 0 is 0, written $|0| = 0$.

Since $|10| = 10$ and $|-10| = 10$, then $|-10| = |10| = 10$. Also, $|-8| = |+8| = 8$. These examples illustrate that, for a pair of opposite numbers, the absolute value of one member of the pair is the same number as the absolute value of the second member. Notice that the absolute value of a positive number is the number itself; the absolute value of a negative number is always its opposite.

The absolute value of a number can also be considered as the distance between 0 and that number on a real number line. For example, $|-9|$ is 9, the distance between 0 and -9 on a real number line: $|-9| = 9$.

~~~~~~~~~~~~~~~~~~ **MODEL PROBLEMS** ~~~~~~~~~~~~~~~~~~

1. Find the value of the number expression $|12| + |-3|$.

Solution: $|12| + |-3| = 12 + 3 = 15$ *Ans.* 15

2. Find the solution set of $|x| = 4$, if the domain is the set of signed numbers.

Solution: If x is replaced by 4, $|x| = 4$ becomes $|4| = 4$, a true sentence. If x is replaced by -4, $|x| = 4$ becomes $|-4| = 4$, a true sentence. No other signed number can replace x and result in a true sentence. Therefore, the solution set of $|x| = 4$ is $\{4, -4\}$.   *Ans.* $\{4, -4\}$

Exercises

In 1–10:   (a) Give the absolute value of the given number.   (b) Give another number which has the same absolute value.

1. 3   **2.** -5 **3.** $+18$ **4.** -13 **5.** -20
6. $1\frac{1}{2}$ **7.** $-3\frac{3}{4}$ **8.** $-1\frac{1}{2}$ **9.** $+2.7$ **10.** -1.4

In 11–18, state whether the sentence is true or false.

11. $|20| = 20$ **12.** $|-13| = 13$ **13.** $|-15| = -15$ **14.** $|-9| = |9|$
15. $|-7| < |7|$ **16.** $|-10| > |3|$ **17.** $|8| < |-19|$ **18.** $|-21| > 21$

In 19–27, find the value of the number expression.

19. $|9| + |3|$ **20.** $|+8| - |+2|$ **21.** $|-6| + |4|$
22. $|-10| - |-5|$ **23.** $|4.5| - |-4.5|$ **24.** $|+6| \times |-4|$
25. $|(8 - 4)| + |-3|$ **26.** $|+12| - |-8| - |+4|$ **27.** $-(|-9| - |7|)$

In 28–35, state whether the sentence is true or false.

28. $|+5| - |-5| = 0$ **29.** $|+9| + |-9| = 0$
30. $|3| \times |-3| = -9$ **31.** $2 \times |-4| = |-2| \times |-4|$
32. $\dfrac{|-8|}{|-4|} = -|+2|$ **33.** $|4| \times |-2| - \dfrac{|-16|}{|2|} = 0$
34. $|-6| \times |4| > 0$ **35.** $|6| + |-4| < 6 - 4$

In 36–43, find the solution set of the open sentence if the domain is the set of signed numbers.

36. $|x| = 5$ **37.** $|m| = 6$ **38.** $|t| = 0$ **39.** $|-x| = 8$
40. $|x| + 2 = 12$ **41.** $|y| + |7| = 13$ **42.** $|x| - 5 = 10$ **43.** $|t| - |4| = 2$

In 44–47, graph the solution set of the open sentence if the domain is the set of signed numbers.

44. $|x| = 2$ **45.** $|x| > 2$ **46.** $|x| < 2$ **47.** $-1 < |x| < 2$

6. Adding Signed Numbers on a Number Line

Addition of signed numbers may be interpreted on a number line as a sequence of directed moves. We will represent "moving to the right" by a positive number and "moving to the left" by a negative number.

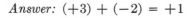

MODEL PROBLEMS

1. Add $+3$ and $+2$.

Solution: Start at 0 and move 3 units to the right to $+3$; then move 2 more units to the right, arriving at $+5$.

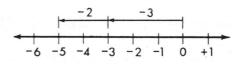

Answer: $(+3) + (+2) = +5$

2. Add -3 and -2.

Solution: Start at 0 and move 3 units to the left to -3; then move 2 more units to the left, arriving at -5.

Answer: $(-3) + (-2) = -5$

3. Add $+3$ and -2.

Solution: Start at 0 and move 3 units to the right to $+3$; then move 2 units to the left, arriving at $+1$.

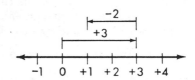

Answer: $(+3) + (-2) = +1$

4. Add −3 and +2.

Solution: Start at 0 and move 3 units to the left to −3; then move 2 units to the right, arriving at −1.

Answer: (−3) + (+2) = −1

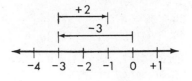

5. Add +3 and −3.

Solution: Start at 0 and move 3 units to the right to +3; then move 3 units to the left, arriving at 0.

Answer: (+3) + (−3) = 0

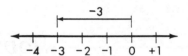

6. Add 0 and −3.

Solution: Start at 0 and move neither to the right nor to the left; then move 3 units to the left, arriving at −3.

Answer: (0) + (−3) = −3

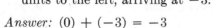

Procedure. To add two signed numbers on a number line:

1. Graph the first number.

2. From this point, move to the right a number of units equal to the absolute value of the second number if the second number is positive; move to the left if the second number is negative; do not move if the second number is 0. The number at the point that is reached is the sum of the two signed numbers.

MODEL PROBLEM

Use positive and negative numbers to do the following problem:

Helen gained 6 pounds during one month and lost 4 pounds during the next month. What was the net change over the two-month period?

Solution: A gain of 6 pounds can be represented by +6, a loss of 4 pounds by −4. The net change can be represented by (+6) + (−4). Using a number line, or adding mentally, (+6) + (−4) = +2.

Answer: The net change was a gain of 2 pounds.

Exercises

In 1–19, use a number line to find the sum of the signed numbers.

1. $(+3) + (+4)$ **2.** $(+6) + (+8)$ **3.** $(-2) + (-4)$

4. $(-5) + (-3)$ **5.** $(+7) + (-4)$ **6.** $(+4) + (-1)$

7. $(-6) + (+5)$ **8.** $(-8) + (+10)$ **9.** $(+4) + (-4)$

10. $(-7) + (+7)$ **11.** $(-2) + (+2)$ **12.** $(0) + (+4)$

13. $(0) + (-6)$ **14.** $(+6) + (0)$ **15.** $(-8) + (0)$

16. $[(+3) + (+4)] + (+2)$ **17.** $[(+8) + (-4)] + (-6)$

18. $[(-7) + (-3)] + (+6)$ **19.** $[(-5) + (+2)] + (+3)$

In 20–22, find the sum in both parts and state the relationship between the two results.

20. *a.* $(+1) + (+6)$ *b.* $(+6) + (+1)$

21. *a.* $(-5) + (-4)$ *b.* $(-4) + (-5)$

22. *a.* $(-7) + (+3)$ *b.* $(+3) + (-7)$

23. Judging from the answers obtained in exercises 20–22, what property of addition seems to hold true for signed numbers?

In 24–26, find the sum in both parts and state the relationship between the two results.

24. *a.* $[(+3) + (+2)] + (+4)$ *b.* $(+3) + [(+2) + (+4)]$

25. *a.* $[(-1) + (-2)] + (-4)$ *b.* $(-1) + [(-2) + (-4)]$

26. *a.* $[(-5) + (+6)] + (-3)$ *b.* $(-5) + [(+6) + (-3)]$

27. Judging from the answers obtained in exercises 24–26, what property of addition seems to hold true for signed numbers?

In 28–30, find the sum of the signed numbers.

28. $(+8) + (-8)$ **29.** $(-6) + (+6)$ **30.** $(-20) + (+20)$

31. Judging from the answers obtained in exercises 28–30, what seems to be the sum of any two signed numbers which are opposites?

In 32–35, find the sum of the signed numbers.

32. $(0) + (+3)$ **33.** $(0) + (-8)$ **34.** $(+7) + (0)$ **35.** $(-5) + (0)$

36. Judging from the answers obtained in exercises 32–35, if a signed number and 0 are added, what seems to be true of the sum?

In 37–43, use signed numbers to solve the problem.

37. In one hour the temperature rose 4° and in the next hour the temperature rose 3°. What was the net change in temperature during the two-hour period?

38. Sid earned $15 one day and spent $4 that day. What was the net change in his financial condition that day?

39. An elevator started on the ground floor and rose 30 floors. Then it came down 12 floors. At which floor was it at that time?

40. A plane started in New York and flew 600 miles south in one hour. During the next hour, it flew 575 miles farther south. At the end of two hours, where is the plane with reference to New York?

41. A football team gained 7 yards on the first play, lost 2 yards on the second, and lost 8 yards on the third. What was the net result of the three plays?

42. Fred deposited $250 in a bank. During the next month, he made a deposit of $60 and a withdrawal of $80. How much money did Fred have in the bank at that time?

43. During a four-day period, the value of a share of stock rose 1\frac{1}{2}$ on the first day, dropped $$\frac{5}{8}$ on the second day, rose $$\frac{1}{8}$ on the third day, and dropped 1\frac{3}{4}$ on the fourth day. What was the net change in the stock during this period?

44. What type of number does the sum of two positive numbers always appear to be?

45. What type of number does the sum of two negative numbers always appear to be?

46. Is it possible for the sum of a positive and a negative number to be (*a*) a positive number? (*b*) a negative number?

47. If two given signed numbers (not opposites) are to be added, how can you tell whether the sum is a positive number or a negative number?

48. Is it possible for the sum of two numbers of arithmetic to be smaller than each of the numbers?

49. *a.* Is it possible for the sum of two signed numbers to be smaller than each of the numbers?

b. If your answer in part *a* is yes, give an example.

50. What appears to be the sum of any signed number and its opposite?

51. What appears to be true of the sum when 0 and any signed number are added?

7. Addition of Signed Numbers

In Chapter IV, we learned that the numbers of arithmetic have various properties of addition. Now we will define the operation of addition so that these properties are also true for signed numbers. Thus, we will be able to add signed numbers without the use of a number line.

ADDITION OF TWO POSITIVE NUMBERS

If $+2$ and $+4$ are added on a number line, the sum is $+6$. We write $(+2) + (+4) = +6$, or $2 + 4 = 6$. Likewise, using a number line, we obtain $0 + 4 = 4$ and $5 + 0 = 5$. Since positive numbers and 0 correspond to the numbers of arithmetic, we can add such numbers in the same manner that we added the numbers of arithmetic.

The sum $(+2) + (+4)$ can also be written vertically as shown at the right.

$+2$	The absolute value of $+2$ is 2.
$+4$	The absolute value of $+4$ is 4.
$+6$	The sum of the absolute values is 6.

Observe that the sum $+6$ is a positive number whose absolute value 6 is the sum of 2 and 4, the absolute values of $+2$ and $+4$.

Rule 1. The sum of two positive numbers is a positive number whose absolute value is found by adding the absolute values of the numbers.

In general, if both a and b are positive numbers:

$$a + b = |a| + |b|$$

―――――――― MODEL PROBLEMS ――――――――

In 1–5, add the two numbers.

1.	$+ 8$	2.	0	3.	$+ 9.1$	4. $6 + 0 = 6$	5. $1\frac{1}{3} + 8\frac{1}{3} = 9\frac{2}{3}$
	$\underline{+10}$		$\underline{+7}$		$\underline{+ 7.5}$		
	$+18$		$+7$		$+16.6$		

ADDITION OF TWO NEGATIVE NUMBERS

If -2 and -4 are added on a number line, the sum is -6. We can write $(-2) + (-4) = -6$, or we can arrange the addition vertically as shown at the right.

-2	The absolute value of -2 is 2.
-4	The absolute value of -4 is 4.
-6	The sum of the absolute values is 6.

Observe that the sum -6 is a negative number whose absolute value 6 is the sum of 2 and 4, the absolute values of -2 and -4.

Rule 2. The sum of two negative numbers is a negative number whose absolute value is found by adding the absolute values of the numbers.

In general, if both a and b are negative numbers:

$$a + b = -(|a| + |b|)$$

MODEL PROBLEMS

Add:

1. $\begin{array}{r} -4 \\ \underline{-3} \\ -7 \end{array}$

2. $\begin{array}{r} -10 \\ \underline{-\ 8} \\ -18 \end{array}$

3. $\begin{array}{r} -\ 7.4 \\ \underline{-\ 8.7} \\ -16.1 \end{array}$

4. $(-5\frac{1}{2}) + (-3\frac{1}{4}) = -8\frac{3}{4}$

ADDITION OF A POSITIVE NUMBER AND A NEGATIVE NUMBER

If $+5$ and -3 are added on a number line, the sum is $+2$. We can write

$(+5) + (-3) = +2,$

or we can arrange the addition vertically as shown at the right.

$+5$	The absolute value of $+5$ is 5.
-3	The absolute value of -3 is 3.
$+2$	The difference of the absolute values is 2.

Observe that the sum $+2$ is a positive number; and $+5$, the number with the larger absolute value, is also a positive number. Observe that 2, the absolute value of the sum $+2$, is the difference of 5 and 3, the absolute values of $+5$ and -3. The difference of two absolute values (unsigned numbers) is simply the larger minus the smaller.

If -5 and $+3$ are added on a number line, the sum is -2. We can write

$(-5) + (+3) = -2,$

or we can arrange the addition vertically as shown at the right.

-5	The absolute value of -5 is 5.
$+3$	The absolute value of $+3$ is 3.
-2	The difference of the absolute values is 2.

Observe that the sum -2 is a negative number; and -5, the number with the larger absolute value, is also a negative number. Observe that 2, the absolute value of the sum -2, is the difference of 5 and 3, the absolute values of -5 and $+3$.

If $+6$ and -6 are added on a number line, the sum is 0. We write $(+6) + (-6) = 0$.

Rule 3. To find the sum of two numbers, one of which is positive or 0 and the other negative, find a number whose absolute value is the difference of the absolute values of the numbers. The sum is positive when the positive number has the greater absolute value; the sum is negative when the negative number has the greater absolute value; the sum is 0 if both numbers have the same absolute value.

In general, if a is a positive number or 0, that is, $a \geq 0$; and if b is a negative number, that is, $b < 0$, then:

$$\text{if } |a| \geq |b|, \text{ then } a + b = |a| - |b|$$

$$\text{AND}$$

$$\text{if } |b| > |a|, \text{ then } a + b = -(|b| - |a|)$$

If b is a positive number or 0, that is, $b \geq 0$; and if a is a negative number, that is, $a < 0$, then:

$$\text{if } |b| \geq |a|, \text{ then } a + b = |b| - |a|$$

$$\text{AND}$$

$$\text{if } |a| > |b|, \text{ then } a + b = -(|a| - |b|)$$

～～～～～～～ MODEL PROBLEMS ～～～～～～～

In 1–6, add the numbers.

1. $+9$	2. -8	3. -6	4. -12	5. $-7\frac{3}{4}$	6. -1.8
$\underline{-2}$	$\underline{+3}$	$\underline{+8}$	$\underline{0}$	$\underline{5\frac{1}{4}}$	$\underline{7.2}$
$+7$	-5	$+2$	-12	$-2\frac{1}{2}$	5.4

In Chapter IV, we studied the addition properties of the numbers of arithmetic. Now let us apply these properties to signed numbers also.

CLOSURE PROPERTY OF ADDITION

The sum of two signed numbers is always a unique member of the set of signed numbers. For example, the sum of -7 and $+2$ is -5, a signed number.

In general, for every signed number a and every signed number b:

$$a + b \text{ is a unique signed number}$$

COMMUTATIVE PROPERTY OF ADDITION

We know that $(-8) + (+6) = -2$, and $(+6) + (-8) = -2$. Therefore, $(-8) + (+6) = (+6) + (-8)$. This example illustrates that the commutative property of addition holds for signed numbers. That is, signed numbers may be added in any order.

In general, for every signed number a and every signed number b:

$$a + b = b + a$$

ASSOCIATIVE PROPERTY OF ADDITION

We know that $[(+3) + (-1)] + (-4) = -2$ and $(+3) + [(-1) + (-4)]$ $= -2$. Therefore, $[(+3) + (-1)] + (-4) = (+3) + [(-1) + (-4)]$. This example illustrates that the associative property of addition holds for signed numbers. That is, in adding signed numbers, we may group them as we please.

In general, for every signed number a, every signed number b, and every signed number c:

$$(a + b) + c = a + (b + c)$$

ADDITION PROPERTY OF ZERO

The true sentences $(-5) + 0 = -5$ and $0 + (+8) = +8$ illustrate that the sum of 0 and a signed number is that number itself. For this reason, 0 is called the **identity element of addition,** or the **additive identity.**

In general, for every signed number a:

$$a + 0 = a \text{ AND } 0 + a = a$$

ADDITION PROPERTY OF OPPOSITES

The true sentence $(+7) + (-7) = 0$ illustrates that the number $+7$ has an opposite number -7 such that their sum is 0.

In general, every signed number a has an opposite $-a$ such that:

$$a + (-a) = 0$$

Note that if a is positive, then $-a$ is negative; if a is negative, then $-a$ is positive; if a is 0, then $-a$ is also 0.

The opposite of a number is also called the **additive inverse** of the number. The additive inverse of $+7$ is -7; the additive inverse of -7 is $+7$. Every signed number x has a unique additive inverse $-x$. The sum of a number and its additive inverse is 0.

PROPERTY OF THE OPPOSITE OF A SUM

We know that $-[(+5) + (-2)] = -[+3] = -3$. We also know that $(-5) + (+2) = -3$. Therefore, $-[(+5) + (-2)] = (-5) + (+2)$. This example illustrates that the opposite of the sum of two signed numbers is equal to the sum of their opposites.

In general, for every signed number a and every signed number b:

$$-(a + b) = (-a) + (-b)$$

ADDING MORE THAN TWO NUMBERS

Since the commutative and associative properties of addition hold for signed numbers, these numbers may be arranged in any order and grouped in any way when we are adding them. It may be helpful to add all the positive numbers first, all the negative numbers second, and then add the two results.

~~~~~~~~ MODEL PROBLEMS ~~~~~~~~

1. Add: $(+5) + (+2) + (-4)$

How To Proceed	*Solution*
1. Write the expression.	$(+5) + (+2) + (-4)$
2. Use the associative property.	$[(+5) + (+2)] + (-4)$
3. Add the positive numbers.	$(+7) + (-4)$
4. Add the positive number and the negative number.	$+3$ *Ans.*

2. Add: $(+6) + (-2) + (+7) + (-4)$

How To Proceed

1. Write the expression.
2. Use the commutative and associative properties and add the positive and negative numbers separately.

3. Add the positive and negative sums.

Solution

$(+6) + (-2) + (+7) + (-4)$

$[(+6) + (+7)] + [(-2) + (-4)]$

$$\begin{array}{r} +\,6 \\ +\,7 \\ \hline +13 \end{array} \qquad \begin{array}{r} -2 \\ -4 \\ \hline -6 \end{array}$$

$(+13) + (-6) = +7$ *Ans.*

USING ADDITION PROPERTIES IN PROOFS

~~~~~~~~~~~~~~~~~~~~~~ *MODEL PROBLEMS* ~~~~~~~~~~~~~~~~~~~~~~

1. Using only the associative and commutative properties of addition, show that:

$$[(+5) + (-7)] + (+8) = [(+5) + (+8)] + (-7)$$

Solution:

	Step	*Reason*
1.	$[(+5) + (-7)] + (+8) = (+5) + [(-7) + (+8)]$	1. Associative property.
2.	$= (+5) + [(+8) + (-7)]$	2. Commutative property.
3.	$= [(+5) + (+8)] + (-7)$	3. Associative property.

2. To show that $[(-3) + x] + 3 = x$, the following chain of equations can be used. State the reason for each of the steps from 1 through 5.

Solution:

	Step	*Reason*
1.	$[(-3) + x] + 3 = -3 + [x + 3]$	1. Associative property.
2.	$= -3 + [3 + x]$	2. Commutative property.
3.	$= [(-3) + 3] + x$	3. Associative property.
•4.	$= 0 + x$	4. Property of opposites (additive inverse).
5.	$= x$	5. Property of 0 (additive identity).

~~~~~~

Exercises

In 1–77, add:

1. $+15$ $+\ 9$	2. -17 $-\ 8$	3. -28 -38	4. $+\ 8$ $+17$	5. -15 -15	6. 34 66
7. $+6\frac{2}{3}$ $+1\frac{1}{3}$	8. $-5\frac{1}{2}$ $-3\frac{1}{2}$	9. $+3\frac{1}{4}$ $+7\frac{1}{4}$	10. $-8\frac{2}{3}$ $-4\frac{2}{3}$	11. $9\frac{1}{2}$ $8\frac{3}{4}$	12. $-6\frac{5}{6}$ $-1\frac{2}{3}$
13. -5.6 -2.2	14. $+6.8$ $+3.2$	15. $+5.4$ $+2.9$	16. -8.8 -7.5	17. 5.7 8.3	18. -5.4 -2.6

19. $+70$	20. -55	21. -15	22. 18	23. $+10$	24. -30
$\underline{-20}$	$\underline{+20}$	$\underline{+42}$	$\underline{-32}$	$\underline{-10}$	$\underline{0}$
25. $+9\frac{1}{2}$	26. $23\frac{5}{6}$	27. $-10\frac{1}{2}$	28. $+7$	29. $-33\frac{1}{3}$	30. $-5\frac{3}{4}$
$\underline{-3}$	$\underline{-9\frac{1}{6}}$	$\underline{8\frac{1}{2}}$	$\underline{-8\frac{3}{4}}$	$\underline{+19\frac{2}{3}}$	$\underline{8\frac{1}{2}}$
31. 7.9	32. -8.7	33. -6.9	34. -8.5	35. 8.3	36. $+7.1$
$\underline{-5.6}$	$\underline{+3.7}$	$\underline{9.4}$	$\underline{+6.1}$	$\underline{-8.3}$	$\underline{-9.4}$

37. $(+15) + (+19)$ 38. $(+13) + (-32)$ 39. $(-41) + (-9)$

40. $(+8) + (-14)$ 41. $(-12) + (+37)$ 42. $(+40) + (-17)$

43. $(-18) + (0)$ 44. $(0) + (-28)$ 45. $(+15) + (-15)$

46. $(-15) + 34$ 47. $14 + 17$ 48. $(-19) + 7$

49. $|-34| + |+20|$ 50. $-|7| + (-10)$ 51. $|15| + (-|-15|)$

52. $+27$	53. -45	54. 15	55. $+20$	56. -1.5	57. $8\frac{1}{2}$
-9	$+12$	-28	-12	$+3.7$	$-4\frac{1}{4}$
$\underline{-12}$	$\underline{+13}$	$\underline{13}$	$\underline{-8}$	$\underline{-8.3}$	$\underline{7\frac{3}{4}}$

58. $+9$	59. -21	60. 14	61. -24	62. $-.7$	63. $8\frac{1}{6}$
$+7$	-13	-9	15	$+3.1$	$-13\frac{1}{6}$
-3	$+17$	-13	19	-9.6	$-3\frac{1}{3}$
$\underline{-5}$	$\underline{+10}$	$\underline{+8}$	$\underline{-12}$	$\underline{+.5}$	$\underline{-9\frac{5}{6}}$

64. $(+18) + (-15) + (+9)$ 65. $30 + (-18) + (-12)$

66. $(-19) + (+8) + (-15)$ 67. $(-17) + (-19) + 40$

68. $(+12) + (-18) + (-4) + (+7)$ 69. $(-19) + 8 + (-5) + 16$

70. $(+36) + (-49) + (-31) + (+20)$ 71. $48 + (-32) + 19 + (-41)$

72. $(-1.5) + (+3.1) + (+6.8) + (-3.4)$

73. $9.6 + (-7.7) + (-5.6) + 2.2$

74. $(+5\frac{1}{4}) + (-8) + (+6\frac{3}{4}) + (-1\frac{1}{2})$

75. $(-4\frac{1}{3}) + 7 + 8\frac{1}{3} - 11$

76. $|+7| + |-8| + |0|$

77. $|-13| + |7| + (-|-20|)$

In 78–86, name the signed number which represents the sum of the quantities.

78. a rise of 4 feet and a rise of 6 feet

79. a gain of $5 and a gain of $3

80. a loss of 6 yards and a loss of 2 yards

81. a rise of 7 feet and a fall of 5 feet

82. a loss of $10 and a profit of $8

83. a deposit of $8 in a bank and a withdrawal of $8

84. a loss of $20 and a profit of $20

85. a gain of 8 pounds, a gain of 4 pounds, and a loss of 7 pounds

86. a rise of 4°, a drop of 3°, and a drop of 5°

In 87–92, give the additive inverse of the given expression.

87. $+10$ **88.** -8 **89.** 15 **90.** -2.5 **91.** C **92.** $-d$

In 93–104, give a replacement for the question mark which will make the resulting sentence true.

93. $(+4) + (?) = 0$ **94.** $(-2) + (?) = 0$
95. $(0) + (?) = 0$ **96.** $(12) + (?) = 0$
97. $(b) + (?) = 0$ **98.** $(-y) + (?) = 0$
99. $(+8) + (?) = (+12)$ **100.** $(+10) + (?) = 7$
101. $(6) + (?) = -4$ **102.** $(-4) + (?) = -9$
103. $(-6) + (?) = (+2)$ **104.** $(-3) + (?) = -3$

In 105–110, give a replacement for the variable which will make the resulting sentence true.

105. $9 + y = 0$ **106.** $x + (-12) = 0$ **107.** $5 + c = 1$
108. $x + 4 = -2$ **109.** $x + (-6) = 8$ **110.** $d + (-5) = -3$

In 111–115, name the addition property which makes each sentence true.

111. $(-3) + (+8) = (+8) + (-3)$ **112.** $(+50) + (-50) = 0$
113. $(-8) + 0 = -8$ **114.** $-[8 + 9] = (-8) + (-9)$
115. $(-6) + [(-4) + (+2)] = [(-6) + (-4)] + (+2)$

116. The following chain of equations can be used to show that $9 + (-5) = 4$. State the reason for each of the steps from 1 through 4.

1. $9 + (-5) = (4 + 5) + (-5)$
2. $\qquad = 4 + [5 + (-5)]$
3. $\qquad = 4 + 0$
4. $\qquad = 4$

In 117–120, use a chain of equations like the one used in exercise 116 to show that the statement is true. Give the reason for each of your steps.

117. $15 + (-8) = 7$ **118.** $12 + (-3) = 9$
119. $(-3) + 9 = 6$ **120.** $(-8) + 5 = -3$

In 121–132, use only the properties of addition to prove that the sentence is true. Give the reason for each step of the proof.

121. $(8 + 9) + 5 = (8 + 5) + 9$
122. $[(-3) + (-4)] + 6 = [(-3 + 6)] + (-4)$
123. $(7 + 9) + 3 = (3 + 7) + 9$
124. $[(-5) + (-6)] + (-2) = [(-2) + (-5)] + (-6)$
125. $(x + 5) + (-5) = x$ **126.** $[y + (-4)] + 4 = y$
127. $(7 + c) + (-7) = c$ **128.** $[(-8) + 2d] + 8 = 2d$
129. $(x + y) + z = (x + z) + y$ **130.** $r + [x + (-r)] = x$
131. $(-c) + (y + c) = y$ **132.** $(x + y) + [(-x) + (-y)] = 0$

In 133–136, state whether the sentence is true or false.

133. $|x| + |-x| = 0$ $(x \neq 0)$

134. $(-c) + (-d) = -(c+d)$

135. $-(-b) = b$

136. $(a+b) + [-(a+b)] = 0$

8. Multiplication of Signed Numbers

We will define multiplication of signed numbers in such a way that the properties of multiplication of numbers of arithmetic will still hold. Our own experiences will be used to illustrate the various situations that arise in the multiplication of signed numbers. We will represent a gain of weight by a positive number and a loss of weight by a negative number, a number of weeks in the future by a positive number and a number of weeks in the past by a negative number.

Case 1. Multiplying a Positive Number by a Positive Number
If a girl gains 2 pounds each week, 4 weeks from now she will be 8 pounds heavier. Using signed numbers, we may write:

$$(+4) \times (+2) = +8$$

Notice that the product of the two positive numbers is a positive number.

Case 2. Multiplying a Negative Number by a Positive Number
If a girl loses 2 pounds each week, 4 weeks from now she will be 8 pounds lighter than she is now. Using signed numbers, we may write:

$$(+4) \times (-2) = -8$$

Notice that the product of the negative number and the positive number is a negative number.

Case 3. Multiplying a Positive Number by a Negative Number
If a girl has gained 2 pounds each week, 4 weeks ago she was 8 pounds lighter than she is now. Using signed numbers, we may write:

$$(-4) \times (+2) = -8$$

Notice that the product of the negative number and the positive number is a negative number.

Case 4. Multiplying a Negative Number by a Negative Number
If a girl has lost 2 pounds each week, 4 weeks ago she was 8 pounds heavier than she is now. Using signed numbers, we may write:

$$(-4) \times (-2) = +8$$

Notice that the product of the two negative numbers is a positive number.

Observe that in all four cases the absolute value of the product, 8, is equal to the product of the absolute values of the factors, 4 and 2.

These four examples illustrate the reasonableness of the following rules:

RULES FOR MULTIPLYING SIGNED NUMBERS

Rule 1. The product of two positive numbers or of two negative numbers is a positive number whose absolute value is the product of the absolute values of the numbers.

Rule 2. The product of a positive number and a negative number is a negative number whose absolute value is the product of the absolute values of the numbers.

In general, if a and b are both non-negative or are both negative, then:

$$ab = |a| \cdot |b|$$

If one of the numbers a and b is non-negative and the other is negative, then:

$$ab = -(|a| \cdot |b|)$$

MODEL PROBLEMS

In 1–6, multiply the two numbers.

1. $+12$	2. -13	3. $+18$	4. -15	5. 0	6. -7
$+4$	-5	-3	6	-8	1
$+48$	$+65$	-54	-90	0	-7

In Chapter IV, we studied the multiplication properties of the numbers of arithmetic. Now let us apply these properties to signed numbers also.

CLOSURE PROPERTY OF MULTIPLICATION

The product of two signed numbers is always a member of the set of signed numbers. For example, the product of -7 and $+3$ is -21, a signed number.

In general, for every signed number a and every signed number b:

ab is a unique signed number

COMMUTATIVE PROPERTY OF MULTIPLICATION

We know that $(+5) \times (-2) = -10$ and $(-2) \times (+5) = -10$.

Therefore, $(+5) \times (-2) = (-2) \times (+5)$.

This example illustrates that the commutative property of multiplication holds for signed numbers. That is, signed numbers may be multiplied in any order.

In general, for every signed number a and every signed number b:

$$ab = ba$$

ASSOCIATIVE PROPERTY OF MULTIPLICATION

We know that $[(-5) \times (+2)] \times (+4) = -40$ and $(-5) \times [(+2) \times (+4)] = -40$.

Therefore, $[(-5) \times (+2)] \times (+4) = (-5) \times [(+2) \times (+4)]$.

This example illustrates that the associative property of multiplication holds for signed numbers. That is, in multiplying signed numbers, we may group them as we please.

In general, for every signed number a, every signed number b, and every signed number c:

$$(ab)c = a(bc)$$

DISTRIBUTIVE PROPERTY OF MULTIPLICATION

We know that $(-5)[(-4) + (+6)] = (-5)(+2) = -10$ and $(-5)(-4) + (-5)(+6) = (+20) + (-30) = -10$.

Therefore, $(-5)[(-4) + (+6)] = (-5)(-4) + (-5)(+6)$.

This example illustrates that the distributive property of multiplication over addition holds for signed numbers. This means that the product of one signed number times the sum of a second and a third signed number equals the product of the first and second numbers plus the product of the first and third numbers.

In general, for every signed number a, every signed number b, and every signed number c:

$$a(b + c) = ab + ac \quad \text{OR} \quad ab + ac = a(b + c)$$

MULTIPLICATION PROPERTY OF ZERO

The examples $(+8)(0) = 0$ and $(0)(-6) = 0$ illustrate that the multiplication property of 0 holds for signed numbers. That is, the product of any number and 0 is 0.

In general, for every signed number a:

$$a \times 0 = 0 \text{ AND } 0 \times a = 0$$

MULTIPLICATION PROPERTY OF ONE

The true sentences $(+5) \times 1 = +5$ and $1 \times (-4) = -4$ illustrate that the multiplication property of 1 holds for signed numbers. That is, the product of 1 and any signed number is that number itself. For this reason, 1 is called the *identity element of multiplication,* or the *multiplicative identity.*

In general, for every signed number a:

$$a \times 1 = a \text{ AND } 1 \times a = a$$

Also, for every signed number a:

$$(a) \times (-1) = -a \text{ AND } (-1) \times (a) = -a$$

For example, $(-1) \times (+5) = -5$ and $(-1) \times (-5) = +5$.

～～～～～ MODEL PROBLEM ～～～～～

Use only the properties of multiplication to show that:

$$5 \times [(-4) + 9] = (-4) \times (5) + (9) \times (5)$$

Solution:

Step	Reason
1. $5 \times [(-4) + 9] = (5) \times (-4) + (5) \times (9)$	1. Distributive property.
2. $ = (-4) \times (5) + (9) \times 5$	2. Commutative property.

MULTIPLYING MORE THAN TWO SIGNED NUMBERS

Since the commutative and associative laws of multiplication hold for signed numbers, signed numbers may be arranged and multiplied in any order we choose. If more than two numbers are to be multiplied, we first multiply any two of them, then multiply this product by one of the remaining factors. We continue this until all factors have been used. See how the product of -2, $+3$, and -4 can be found in several ways:

$$(-2)(+3)(-4) = [(-2)(+3)](-4) = (-6)(-4) = +24$$

$$(-2)(+3)(-4) = (-2)[(+3)(-4)] = (-2)(-12) = +24$$

$$(-2)(+3)(-4) = (+3)[(-2)(-4)] = (+3)(+8) = +24$$

Study the following examples:

$$(+3)(-1)(+3) = -9 \qquad \text{(1 negative factor)}$$
$$(-1)(+3)(-3) = +9 \qquad \text{(2 negative factors)}$$
$$(+3)(-1)(-3)(-1) = -9 \qquad \text{(3 negative factors)}$$
$$(+3)(+1)(-1)(-3)(-1)(-1) = +9 \qquad \text{(4 negative factors)}$$

The preceding examples illustrate the following rules:

Rule 1. When a product contains an *odd* number of negative factors (1, 3, 5, etc.), the product is *negative.*

Rule 2. When a product contains an *even* number of negative factors (2, 4, 6, etc.), the product is *positive.*

~~~~~~~~~~ MODEL PROBLEMS ~~~~~~~~~~

1. Find the value of $(-2)^3$.

   Solution: $(-2)^3 = (-2)(-2)(-2) = -8$ *Ans.*

   [*Note:* The answer is negative because there is an odd number of negative factors (3 negative factors).]

2. Find the value of $(-3)^4$.

   Solution: $(-3)^4 = (-3)(-3)(-3)(-3) = +81$ *Ans.*

   [*Note:* The answer is positive because there is an even number of negative factors (4 negative factors).]

Exercises

In 1–36, find the product of the numbers.

1. $+9$ $+8$	**2.** -11 -7	**3.** -17 $+3$	**4.** 23 5	**5.** $+36$ -2	**6.** -15 -8
7. -25 -4	**8.** -24 $+8$	**9.** 0 -5	**10.** -75 -3	**11.** 15 -9	**12.** $+9$ 0
13. $+1.5$ -2.4	**14.** $-.25$ 80	**15.** $+8$ $+\frac{1}{2}$	**16.** -15 $+\frac{3}{5}$	**17.** $-\frac{1}{2}$ $-\frac{1}{3}$	**18.** $+16$ $-2\frac{1}{4}$

19. $(+8)$ by $(+6)$ **20.** (-12) by (-5) **21.** $(+11)$ by (-7)
22. (-10) by $(+9)$ **23.** (0) by (-3) **24.** (15) by $(-.6)$
25. $(+8)(+\frac{1}{4})$ **26.** $(-\frac{3}{5})(-20)$ **27.** $(2)(\frac{1}{2})$
28. $(+\frac{3}{8})(-\frac{32}{27})$ **29.** $(-4\frac{1}{2})(+\frac{2}{3})$ **30.** $|-15| \cdot (-3\frac{1}{5})$
31. $(+4)(+3)(+2)$ **32.** $(-1)(-7)(-8)$ **33.** $(-3)(-5)(+4)(-1)$
34. $(-7)(+2)(0)$ **35.** $|+10| \cdot |-3| \cdot (-4)$ **36.** $(+8)(-9)(0)(-10)$

37. Multiply each of the following numbers by $+5$:
    a. $+7$ *b.* -3 *c.* -9 *d.* 8 *e.* -15 *f.* 0
38. Multiply each of the following numbers by -8:
    a. $+9$ *b.* -12 *c.* -15 *d.* $+50$ *e.* 100 *f.* 0

In 39–50, find the value of the expression.

39. $(+4)^2$ **40.** $(-3)^2$ **41.** $(+5)^3$ **42.** $(-4)^3$ **43.** $(-5)^3$ **44.** $(-1)^4$
45. $(+\frac{1}{2})^2$ **46.** $(-\frac{1}{2})^2$ **47.** $(+\frac{2}{3})^3$ **48.** $(-\frac{3}{5})^3$ **49.** $(-\frac{1}{4})^3$ **50.** $(-\frac{1}{5})^4$

In 51–56, fill in the blanks so that the resulting sentence is an illustration of the distributive property.

51. $5 \cdot (9 + 7) = $ _____   **52.** $-4(x + y) = $ _____
53. _____ $= (6) \cdot (-3) + 6 \cdot (-5)$ **54.** _____ $= 7a + 7b$
55. $8 \cdot ($_____$) = ($_____$) \cdot 5 + ($_____$) \cdot (-3)$
56. $3 \cdot ($_____$) = ($_____$) \cdot r + ($_____$) \cdot (-s)$

In 57–60, use the distributive property to find the value of the expression.

57. $15 \times 87 + 15 \times 13$
58. $34 \times 26 + 34 \times (-6)$
59. $93 \times (-\frac{3}{4}) + 93 \times (-\frac{1}{4})$
60. $(-5) \cdot (-13) + (-5) \cdot (+4) + (-5) \cdot (+9)$

In 61–64, name the multiplication property illustrated.

61. $(-6) \times (-5) = (-5) \times (-6)$

62. $[(-3) \cdot 4] \cdot 7 = (-3) \cdot [4 \cdot 7]$

63. $-8 \cdot [4 + (-1)] = (-8) \cdot (4) + (-8) \cdot (-1)$

64. $5x + 5 \cdot (-y) = 5 \cdot [x + (-y)]$

65. If we know that $(5)(6) = 30$, the following chain of equations can be used to show that $(5)(-6) = -30$. State the reason for each of the steps from 1 through 5.

1. $\qquad\qquad 5(0) = 0$
2. $\qquad 5[6 + (-6)] = 0$
3. $(5)(6) + (5)(-6) = 0$
4. $\qquad 30 + 5(-6) = 0$
5. $\qquad\quad (5)(-6) = -30$

66. Use a chain of equations like the one used in exercise 65 to show that each of the following equalities is true. Give the reason for each of your steps. Assume that $(a) \cdot (b) = ab$ when a and b are both positive.

   a. $(8)(-3) = -24$ b. $(7) \cdot (-6) = -42$

   c. $(-4)(3) = -12$ d. $(a) \cdot (-b) = -ab$

67. If we know that $(-5)(6) = -30$, the following chain of equations can be used to show that $(-5)(-6) = +30$. State the reason for each of the steps from 1 through 5.

1. $\qquad\qquad (-5)(0) = 0$
2. $\qquad -5[6 + (-6)] = 0$
3. $(-5)(6) + (-5)(-6) = 0$
4. $\qquad -30 + (-5)(-6) = 0$
5. $\qquad\quad (-5)(-6) = +30$

68. Use a chain of equations like the one used in exercise 67 to show that each of the following equalities is true. Give the reason for each of your steps. Assume that $(-a) \cdot (b) = -ab$.

   a. $(-6)(-2) = +12$ b. $(-9)(-3) = +27$

   c. $(-4)(-8) = 32$ d. $(-a)(-b) = ab$

9. Subtraction of Signed Numbers

When we were dealing with the numbers of arithmetic, we were able to subtract 3 from 7. The result was 4. We wrote $7 - 3 = 4$. However, we were not able to subtract 7 from 3 because we had no number to represent $3 - 7$. The set of numbers of arithmetic was not closed with respect to subtraction.

Now, we will learn that we can always subtract one number from another when we are dealing with the set of signed numbers.

In arithmetic, to subtract 3 from 7, we find a number which, when added to 3, will give 7. That number is 4. We know that $7 - 3 = 4$ because $3 + 4 = 7$.

Subtraction in the set of numbers of arithmetic is defined as the inverse operation of addition.

In general, for every number c and every number b, the expression $c - b$ means to find a number a such that $b + a = c$.

We use the same definition of subtraction in the set of signed numbers. To subtract (-2) from $(+3)$, written $(+3) - (-2)$, we must find a number which, when added to -2, will give $+3$. We write $(-2) + (?) = +3$.

We can use a number line to help us find the answer to $(-2) + (?) = +3$. Think as follows: From a point 2 units to the left of 0, what motion must be made to arrive at a point 3

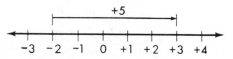

units to the right of 0? We must move 5 units to the right. This motion is represented by $+5$.

Therefore, $(+3) - (-2) = +5$ because $(-2) + (+5) = +3$. We can write $(+3) - (-2) = +5$ vertically as follows:

$$\begin{array}{cc} (+3) \\ -\ (-2) \\ \hline +5 \end{array} \qquad OR \qquad Subtract: \begin{array}{ll} (+3) & \text{minuend} \\ (-2) & \text{subtrahend} \\ \hline +5 & \text{difference} \end{array}$$

Check each of the following examples by using a number line to answer the related question: subtrahend $+ (?) =$ minuend.

Subtract:	$+9$	-7	$+5$	-3
	$+6$	-2	-2	$+1$
	$+3$	-5	$+7$	-4

Now we will consider another way in which addition and subtraction are related. In each of the following examples, compare the result obtained when subtracting the signed number with the result obtained when adding the opposite of that signed number:

Subtract	Add		Subtract	Add		Subtract	Add		Subtract	Add
$+9$	$+9$		-7	-7		$+5$	$+5$		-3	-3
$+6$	-6		-2	$+2$		-2	$+2$		$+1$	-1
$+3$	$+3$		-5	-5		$+7$	$+7$		-4	-4

Observe that in each example adding the opposite of a signed number gives the same result as subtracting that signed number. It therefore seems reasonable to define subtraction as follows:

If a is any signed number and b is any signed number, then:

$$a - b = a + (-b)$$

Procedure. To subtract one signed number from another, add the opposite (additive inverse) of the subtrahend to the minuend.

Notice that it is always possible to subtract one signed number from another. Therefore, the set of signed numbers is closed with respect to subtraction.

USES OF THE SYMBOL "−"

In the expression $7 - (-5)$, the symbol "−" is used in two different ways. The first "−" which stands between the two numerals 7 and (-5) indicates the operation of subtraction. The second "−" which is part of the numeral (-5) indicates the opposite of 5.

Since $7 - 4 = 7 + (-4)$, the symbol $7 + (-4)$ is sometimes written $7 - 4$. Similarly, $(+9) + (-2) + (-4)$ is sometimes written $9 - 2 - 4$.

Likewise, $-3 - 4 - 2$ can mean the sum of -3, -4, and -2; this may be written $(-3) + (-4) + (-2)$.

⎯⎯⎯⎯⎯ MODEL PROBLEMS ⎯⎯⎯⎯⎯

In 1–4, perform the indicated subtraction.

1. $(+30) - (+12) = (+30) + (-12) = +18$

2. $(-19) - (-7) = (-19) + (+7) = -12$

3. $(-4) - (0) = (-4) + (0) = -4$

4. $0 - 8 = 0 + (-8) = -8$

In 5–7, subtract the lower number from the upper number.

5. $+45$	**6.** -19	**7.** -5
-20	17	-5
$+65$	-36	0

[*Note:* In each problem the signed number is subtracted by adding its opposite to the minuend.]

Exercises

In 1–6, use a number line to do the subtraction.

1. $(+6) - (+2)$ **2.** $(+5) - (-3)$ **3.** $(-1) - (+2)$
4. $(-3) - (-4)$ **5.** $(-3) - (+3)$ **6.** $(-3) - (-3)$

In 7–30, subtract the lower number from the upper number.

7. $+50$	**8.** $+18$	**9.** $+15$	**10.** $+36$	**11.** -39	**12.** -26
$+30$	$+29$	$+15$	-15	$+15$	-18
13. $+27$	**14.** -45	**15.** -6	**16.** -8	**17.** 0	**18.** $+7$
$-\ 8$	$+17$	$+6$	-8	-15	0
19. $+8.7$	**20.** $+8.3$	**21.** -6.9	**22.** 6.9	**23.** -3.6	**24.** 5.9
$+6.5$	-6.2	$+3.7$	9.5	-5.2	7.2
25. $+9\frac{1}{2}$	**26.** $-3\frac{1}{4}$	**27.** $-3\frac{1}{6}$	**28.** $7\frac{3}{4}$	**29.** $-6\frac{5}{8}$	**30.** $-8\frac{7}{8}$
$+6\frac{1}{2}$	$-7\frac{3}{4}$	$8\frac{5}{8}$	$-2\frac{1}{4}$	$+3\frac{1}{3}$	$-3\frac{1}{4}$

In 31–39, perform the indicated subtraction.

31. $(+19) - (+30)$ **32.** $(-12) - (-25)$ **33.** $22 - (-8)$
34. $(+6.4) - (+8.1)$ **35.** $(-3.7) - (-5.2)$ **36.** $(-9.2) - 8.3$
37. $(+5\frac{1}{3}) - (+3\frac{1}{3})$ **38.** $6\frac{1}{2} - (-2\frac{1}{4})$ **39.** $(-8\frac{1}{6}) - (-5\frac{2}{3})$

40. Subtract $+5$ from:

    a. $+15$ *b.* -15 *c.* $+3$ *d.* -2 *e.* $+5$ *f.* 0

41. Subtract -9 from:

    a. $+20$ *b.* -30 *c.* $+5$ *d.* -6 *e.* -9 *f.* 0

42. How much is 18 decreased by -7?
43. How much greater than -15 is 12?
44. How much greater than -4 is -1?
45. How much less than 6 is -3?
46. What number is 6 less than -6?
47. From the sum of 25 and -10, subtract -4.
48. Subtract 8 from the sum of -6 and -12.

In 49–54, state the number that must be added to the given number to make the result equal to 0.

49. $+5$ **50.** -3 **51.** $+8.5$ **52.** -3.7 **53.** $+1\frac{7}{8}$ **54.** $-\frac{9}{2}$

In 55–64, find the value of the given expression.

55. $(+7) + (+9) - (-4)$ **56.** $(-12) - (+9) + (-20)$
57. $(+8.9) - (+5.2) + (+6.7)$ **58.** $(-5.1) - (-8.4) - (-1.7)$
59. $(+6\frac{1}{4}) + (+9\frac{1}{2}) - (+7\frac{3}{4})$ **60.** $(-8\frac{5}{8}) - (+2\frac{1}{3}) - (-5\frac{2}{3})$
61. $32 - 49 - 21 + 10$ **62.** $-15 + 8 - 5 + 12$
63. $6\frac{1}{4} - 5 + 7\frac{3}{4} - 1\frac{1}{2}$ **64.** $-5\frac{1}{3} + 8 + 9\frac{1}{3} - 12$

In 65–68, use signed numbers to do the problem.

65. Find the change when the temperature changes from:

    a. $+5°$ to $+8°$ *b.* $-10°$ to $+18°$ *c.* $-6°$ to $-18°$ *d.* $+12°$ to $-4°$

66. Find the change in altitude when you go from a place which is 15 feet below sea level to a place which is 95 feet above sea level.

67. In a game, Sid was 35 points "in the hole." How many points must he make in order to have a score of 150 points?

68. Fred had $12 at the beginning of the week. At the end of the week, he was $5 in debt. How much did Fred spend during the week?

69. State whether the following sentences are true or false:

    a. $(+5) - (-3) = (-3) - (+5)$

    b. $(-7) - (-4) = (-4) - (-7)$

70. If x and y represent numbers:

    a. Does $x - y = y - x$ for all replacements of x and y?

    b. Does $x - y = y - x$ for any replacements of x and y? For which values of x and y?

    c. What is the relation between $x - y$ and $y - x$ for all replacements of x and y?

    d. Is the operation of subtraction commutative? That is, does $x - y = y - x$ for all signed numbers x and y?

71. State whether the following sentences are true or false:

    a. $(15 - 9) - 6 = 15 - (9 - 6)$

    b. $[(-10) - (+4)] - (+8) = (-10) - [(+4) - (+8)]$

72. Is the operation of subtraction associative? That is, does $(x - y) - z = x - (y - z)$ for all signed numbers x, y, and z?

73. State whether the following sentences are true or false:

    a. $5(7 - 3) = 5 \cdot 7 - 5 \cdot 3$

    b. $8[(+4) - (-2)] = 8 \cdot (+4) - 8 \cdot (-2)$

74. Is the operation of multiplication distributive over subtraction? That is, does $x(y - z) = xy - xz$ for all signed numbers x, y, and z?

10. Division of Signed Numbers

USING THE INVERSE OPERATION IN DIVIDING SIGNED NUMBERS

Division may be defined as the inverse operation of multiplication, just as subtraction is defined as the inverse operation of addition. To divide 6 by 2 means to find a number which, when multiplied by 2, gives 6. The number is 3 because $3 \times 2 = 6$. We write $\frac{6}{2} = 3$, or $6 \div 2 = 3$. The number 6 is the **dividend**, 2 is the **divisor**, and 3 is the **quotient**.

It is impossible to divide a signed number by 0. That is, division by 0 is undefined. For example, to solve $(-9) \div 0 = ?$, we would have to find a number which, when multiplied by 0, would give -9. There is no such number since the product of any signed number and 0 is 0.

In general, for every signed number a and every signed number b $(b \neq 0)$:

$$a \div b, \text{ or } \frac{a}{b}, \text{ means to find a number } c \text{ such that } cb = a$$

In dividing non-zero signed numbers, there are four possible cases. Consider the following examples:

Case 1. $\frac{+6}{+3}$ means $(?)(+3) = +6$. Since ? is $+2$, $\frac{+6}{+3} = +2$.

Case 2. $\frac{-6}{-3}$ means $(?)(-3) = -6$. Since ? is $+2$, $\frac{-6}{-3} = +2$.

Case 3. $\frac{-6}{+3}$ means $(?)(+3) = -6$. Since ? is -2, $\frac{-6}{+3} = -2$.

Case 4. $\frac{+6}{-3}$ means $(?)(-3) = +6$. Since ? is -2, $\frac{+6}{-3} = -2$.

In the preceding examples, observe:

1. When the dividend and divisor are both positive, the quotient is positive; when the dividend and divisor are both negative, the quotient is positive.
2. When the dividend is positive and the divisor is negative, or when the dividend is negative and the divisor is positive, the quotient is negative.
3. In all cases, the absolute value of the quotient is the absolute value of the dividend divided by the absolute value of the divisor.

The previous examples illustrate the following rules of division:

RULES FOR DIVIDING SIGNED NUMBERS

Rule 1. The quotient of two positive numbers, or of two negative numbers, is a positive number whose absolute value is the absolute value of the dividend divided by the absolute value of the divisor.

Rule 2. The quotient of a positive number and a negative number is a negative number whose absolute value is the absolute value of the dividend divided by the absolute value of the divisor.

In general:

For every signed number a and every signed number b such that $a > 0$ and $b > 0$, or $a < 0$ and $b < 0$:

$$\frac{a}{b} = \frac{|a|}{|b|}$$

For every signed number a and every signed number b such that $a > 0$ and $b < 0$, or $a < 0$ and $b > 0$:

$$\frac{a}{b} = -\left(\frac{|a|}{|b|}\right)$$

RULE FOR DIVIDING ZERO BY A NON-ZERO NUMBER

The expression $\dfrac{0}{-5}$ means $(?)(-5) = 0$. Since ? is 0, $\dfrac{0}{-5} = 0$. This illustrates that zero divided by any non-zero number is zero.

In general, if a is a non-zero number $(a \neq 0)$:

$$\frac{0}{a} = 0$$

~~~~ MODEL PROBLEMS ~~~~

In 1–5, perform the indicated division.

1. $\dfrac{+60}{+15} = +\left(\dfrac{60}{15}\right) = +4$ **2.** $\dfrac{+90}{-10} = -\left(\dfrac{90}{10}\right) = -9$

3. $\dfrac{-27}{-3} = +\left(\dfrac{27}{3}\right) = +9$ **4.** $(-45) \div 9 = -(45 \div 9) = -5$

5. $0 \div (-3) = 0$

USING THE RECIPROCAL IN DIVIDING SIGNED NUMBERS

When the product of two numbers is 1, one number is called the **reciprocal**, or **multiplicative inverse**, of the other. For example, since $(+8) \cdot (+\frac{1}{8}) = 1$, we say $+\frac{1}{8}$ is the reciprocal, or multiplicative inverse, of $+8$.

Since $(\frac{3}{5}) \cdot (\frac{5}{3}) = 1$, we say $\frac{5}{3}$ is the reciprocal, or multiplicative inverse, of $\frac{3}{5}$.

Since $(-\frac{1}{2}) \cdot (-2) = 1$, we say -2 is the reciprocal, or multiplicative inverse, of $-\frac{1}{2}$.

Since there is no number which, when multiplied by 0, gives 1, the number 0 has no reciprocal.

In general, for every non-zero signed number a $(a \neq 0)$, there is a unique signed number such that:

$$a \cdot \frac{1}{a} = 1$$

Notice that if a number is positive, its reciprocal is positive; if a number is negative, its reciprocal is negative.

The reciprocal of the reciprocal of a number is that number itself. For example, the reciprocal of the reciprocal of 8 is 8 because the reciprocal of 8 is $\frac{1}{8}$ and the reciprocal of $\frac{1}{8}$ is 8.

For non-zero numbers, the reciprocal of the product of two numbers is equal to the product of their reciprocals. For example, consider the numbers 5 and 3.

The product of 5 and 3 is $5 \cdot 3$ or 15; the reciprocal of the product is $\frac{1}{5 \cdot 3}$ or $\frac{1}{15}$.

The reciprocals of 5 and 3 are $\frac{1}{5}$ and $\frac{1}{3}$. The product of the reciprocals is $\frac{1}{5} \cdot \frac{1}{3}$ or $\frac{1}{15}$.

We see that $\frac{1}{5 \cdot 3} = \frac{1}{5} \cdot \frac{1}{3}$.

Using the reciprocal of a number, we can define division in terms of multiplication as follows:

For every signed number a and every non-zero signed number b $(b \neq 0)$, "a (the dividend) divided by b (the divisor)" means "a multiplied by the reciprocal of b," or:

$$\frac{a}{b} = a \cdot \frac{1}{b} \quad (b \neq 0)$$

Procedure. To perform a division, multiply the dividend by the reciprocal of the divisor.

Notice that if we exclude division by 0, the set of signed numbers is closed with respect to division because every signed number has a reciprocal and multiplication is always possible.

MODEL PROBLEMS

In 1–5, perform the indicated division.

1. $\dfrac{+10}{+2} = (+10)\left(+\dfrac{1}{2}\right) = +(10)\left(\dfrac{1}{2}\right) = +5$

2. $\dfrac{-12}{+6} = (-12)\left(+\dfrac{1}{6}\right) = -(12)\left(\dfrac{1}{6}\right) = -2$

3. $\dfrac{-28}{-7} = (-28)\left(-\dfrac{1}{7}\right) = +(28)\left(\dfrac{1}{7}\right) = +4$

4. $\dfrac{0}{-3} = (0)\left(-\dfrac{1}{3}\right) = 0$

5. $(+18) \div \left(-\dfrac{1}{2}\right) = (+18)(-2) = -(18)(2) = -36$

Exercises

In 1–12, name the reciprocal of the given number.

1. 6   **2.** -5 **3.** 9   **4.** -7 **5.** 1   **6.** -1
7. $\frac{1}{5}$ **8.** $-\frac{1}{10}$ **9.** $\frac{3}{4}$ **10.** $-\frac{2}{3}$ **11.** $x\ (x \neq 0)$ **12.** $-x\ (x \neq 0)$

In 13–51, find the indicated quotients.

13. $\dfrac{+18}{+6}$ **14.** $\dfrac{-36}{-3}$ **15.** $\dfrac{+52}{-4}$ **16.** $\dfrac{+84}{-12}$ **17.** $\dfrac{-30}{-6}$ **18.** $\dfrac{+100}{-25}$

19. $\dfrac{55}{-11}$ **20.** $\dfrac{-84}{-12}$ **21.** $\dfrac{-144}{9}$ **22.** $\dfrac{75}{15}$ **23.** $\dfrac{-100}{-20}$ **24.** $\dfrac{144}{-8}$

25. $\dfrac{-108}{+9}$ **26.** $\dfrac{-65}{+5}$ **27.** $\dfrac{0}{3}$ **28.** $\dfrac{+4}{-8}$ **29.** $\dfrac{-6}{-9}$ **30.** $\dfrac{-15}{-12}$

31. $\dfrac{+18}{-4}$ **32.** $\dfrac{-16}{+6}$ **33.** $\dfrac{-34}{4}$ **34.** $\dfrac{+100}{-8}$ **35.** $\dfrac{-36}{-8}$ **36.** $\dfrac{0}{-4}$

37. $\dfrac{-5}{-9}$ **38.** $\dfrac{3}{-7}$ **39.** $\dfrac{20}{-8}$ **40.** $\dfrac{8.4}{-4}$ **41.** $\dfrac{-9.6}{-.3}$ **42.** $\dfrac{-3.6}{1.2}$

43. $(+48) \div (-6)$ **44.** $(-75) \div (-15)$ **45.** $(-50) \div (+10)$
46. $(+12) \div (-\frac{1}{3})$ **47.** $(-\frac{3}{4}) \div (+6)$ **48.** $(-\frac{3}{4}) \div (-\frac{2}{3})$
49. $(-4.8) \div (-4)$ **50.** $(+9.6) \div (-3)$ **51.** $(-1.8) \div (+.9)$

52. Divide each of the following numbers by $+5$:

  a. $+20$ *b.* -15 *c.* -75 *d.* 100 *e.* -120 *f.* 0

53. Divide each of the following numbers by -4:

  a. -48 *b.* $+32$ *c.* $+20$ *d.* -144 *e.* 400 *f.* 0

54. *a.* Find the value of x for which the denominator of the fraction $\dfrac{1}{x-2}$ has a value of 0.

  b. State the value of x for which the multiplicative inverse of $(x-2)$ is not defined.

In 55–58, give the multiplicative inverse of the expression and state the value of x for which the multiplicative inverse is not defined.

55. $x-5$ **56.** $x+3$ **57.** $2x-1$ **58.** $3x+1$

59. State whether the following sentences are true or false:

  a. $(+10) \div (-5) = (-5) \div (+10)$

  b. $(-16) \div (-2) = (-2) \div (-16)$

60. If x and y represent signed numbers:

  a. Does $x \div y = y \div x$ for all replacements of x and y?

  b. Does $x \div y = y \div x$ for any replacements of x and y? If your answer is yes, give an example.

  c. What is the relation between $x \div y$ and $y \div x$ when $x \neq 0$ and $y \neq 0$?

  d. Is the operation of division commutative? That is, does $x \div y = y \div x$ for every non-zero signed number x and every non-zero signed number y?

61. State whether the following sentences are true or false:

  a. $[(+16) \div (+4)] \div (+2) = (+16) \div [(+4) \div (+2)]$

  b. $[(-36) \div (+6)] \div (-2) = (-36) \div [(+6) \div (-2)]$

62. Is the operation of division associative? That is, does $(x \div y) \div z = x \div (y \div z)$ for every signed number x, y, and z, when $y \neq 0$ and $z \neq 0$?

63. State whether the following sentences are true or false:

  a. $(12+6) \div 2 = 12 \div 2 + 6 \div 2$

  b. $[(+25) - (-10)] \div (+5) = (+25) \div (+5) - (-10) \div (+5)$

64. Is the operation of division distributive over addition? That is, does $(x+y) \div z = x \div z + y \div z$ for every signed number x, y, and z when $z \neq 0$?

65. Is the operation of division distributive over subtraction? That is, does $(x-y) \div z = x \div z - y \div z$ for every signed number x, y, and z when $z \neq 0$?

11. Evaluating Algebraic Expressions by Using Signed Numbers

When we evaluate an algebraic expression by using signed numbers, we follow the same procedure that we used when we evaluated algebraic expressions by using the numbers of arithmetic.

~~~~~~~~~~~~~~ **MODEL PROBLEMS** ~~~~~~~~~~~~~~

1. Find the value of $-3x^2y^3$ when $x = +2$ and $y = -1$.

How To Proceed	*Solution*
1. Write the expression.	$-3x^2y^3$
2. Replace the variables by the given values.	$= -3(+2)^2(-1)^3$
3. Evaluate the powers.	$= -3(+4)(-1)$
4. Multiply the signed numbers.	$= +12$ *Ans.*

2. Find the value of $x^2 - 3x - 54$ when $x = -5$.

How To Proceed	*Solution*
1. Write the expression.	$x^2 - 3x - 54$
2. Replace the variable by its given value.	$= (-5)^2 - 3(-5) - 54$
3. Evaluate the power.	$= 25 - 3(-5) - 54$
4. Do the multiplication.	$= 25 + 15 - 54$
5. Do the addition and subtraction.	$= -14$ *Ans.*

~~~~~~

Exercises

In 1–52, find the numerical value of the expression. Use $a = -8$, $b = +6$, $d = -3$, $x = -4$, $y = 5$, and $z = -1$.

1. $6a$	**2.** $-5b$	**3.** ab	**4.** $2xy$
5. $-4bz$	**6.** $\frac{1}{3}d$	**7.** $-\frac{2}{3}b$	**8.** $\frac{3}{8}a$
9. $\frac{1}{2}xy$	**10.** $-\frac{3}{4}ab$	**11.** a^2	**12.** d^3
13. $-y^2$	**14.** $-d^2$	**15.** $-z^3$	**16.** $2x^2$
17. $-3y^2$	**18.** $-3b^2$	**19.** $4d^2$	**20.** $-2z^3$

21. xy^2 **22.** a^2b **23.** $2d^2y^2$ **24.** $\frac{1}{2}db^2$

25. $-2d^3z^2$ **26.** $a + b$ **27.** $a - x$ **28.** $2x + z$

29. $3y - b$ **30.** $a - 2d$ **31.** $b - 4d$ **32.** $5x + 2y$

33. $7b - 5x$ **34.** $x^2 + x$ **35.** $2b^2 + b$ **36.** $y^2 - y$

37. $2d^2 - d$ **38.** $2a + 5d + 3x$ **39.** $8y + 5b - 6d$ **40.** $9b - 3z - 2x$

41. $x^2 + 3x + 5$ **42.** $z^2 + 2z - 7$ **43.** $a^2 - 5a - 6$

44. $d^2 - 4d + 6$ **45.** $2x^2 - 3x + 5$ **46.** $15 + 5z - z^2$

47. $2(a + b)$ **48.** $3(2x - 1) + 6$ **49.** $10 - 3(x - 4)$

50. $(x + 2)(x - 1)$ **51.** $(a - b)(a + b)$ **52.** $(x + d)(x - 4z)$

In 53–60, find the value of the expression. Use $a = -12$, $b = +6$, and $c = -1$.

53. $\dfrac{a}{6}$ **54.** $\dfrac{b}{-2}$ **55.** $\dfrac{2a}{b}$ **56.** $\dfrac{ac}{-3b}$

57. $\dfrac{b^2c}{a}$ **58.** $\dfrac{3a^2c^3}{b^3}$ **59.** $\dfrac{a - b^2}{-2c^2}$ **60.** $\dfrac{b^2 - a^2}{b^2 + a^2}$

CHAPTER VII

OPERATIONS WITH MONOMIALS

1. Adding Like Monomials

A numeral or variable or an expression written as a product or quotient of numerals or variables or both is called a **term.** For example, each of the expressions 5, x, $-7b$, $4y^2$, $\frac{2}{3}abc$, and $\dfrac{x}{x+2}$ is called a term.

The expression $x^2 + 4x - 4$ has three terms: x^2, $4x$, and 4. Notice that $+$ and $-$ signs separate the terms of an algebraic expression which has more than one term.

An algebraic expression which has one term is called a **monomial.** For example, 3, y, $8z$, $-4y^2$, and $\frac{1}{2}xy$ are called monomials.

We have already learned how to add like monomials whose numerical coefficients were numbers of arithmetic. We applied the distributive property of multiplication; for example, $5x + 4x = (5 + 4)x = 9x$.

Now we will use a similar procedure to add like monomials whose numerical coefficients are signed numbers:

$$(+9t) + (-3t) = [(+9) + (-3)]t = +6t$$
$$-3ab + 7ab - 2ab = (-3 + 7 - 2)ab = +2ab$$

In the preceding examples, the middle step may be done mentally.

Procedure. To add like monomials, use the distributive property of multiplication; or find the sum of the numerical coefficients and multiply this sum by the common variable factors.

~~~~~~~~ MODEL PROBLEMS ~~~~~~~~

In 1–6, add:

1.	2.	3.	4.	5.	6.
$+7x$	$-3y^2$	$-15abc$	$+8x^2y$	$-9y$	$+2(a+b)$
$-3x$	$-5y^2$	$+\ 6abc$	$-\ x^2y$	$+9y$	$+6(a+b)$
$+4x$	$-8y^2$	$-\ 9abc$	$+7x^2y$	0	$+8(a+b)$

Exercises

In 1–6, simplify the expression by adding the monomials.

1. $(+8c) + (+7c)$ **2.** $(+10t) + (-3t)$ **3.** $(-4a) + (-6a)$

4. $(-20r) + (5r)$ **5.** $(-7w) + (+7w)$ **6.** $(5ab) + (-9ab)$

In 7–36, add:

7. $+7c$ **8.** $-39r$ **9.** $-19t$ **10.** $+14c$ **11.** $-1.5m$
$\ +8c$ $\ -22r$ $\ +\ 6t$ $\ -\ c$ $\ +1.2m$

12. $+3e$ **13.** $+2x^2$ **14.** $-48y^2$ **15.** $-\ d^2$ **16.** $.5y^3$
$\ -3e$ $\ +9x^2$ $\ -13y^2$ $\ +7d^2$ $\ .8y^3$

17. $+\frac{5}{3}c^4$ **18.** $-10r^3$ **19.** $8rs$ **20.** $-6mn$ **21.** $-4xyz$
$\ -\frac{7}{3}c^4$ $\ 10r^3$ $\ 6rs$ $\ -\ mn$ $\ +5xyz$

22. $+.4cd$ **23.** $-8xy$ **24.** $+3(x+y)$ **25.** $+6a^2b$ **26.** $-\ xy^2$
$\ -.8cd$ $\ +8xy$ $\ +9(x+y)$ $\ +7a^2b$ $\ -3xy^2$

27. $-8c^2d^2$ **28.** $+\frac{3}{4}x^2y^2$ **29.** $+.5r^2s^2$ **30.** $-4(c+d)$ **31.** $+8a$
$\ 9c^2d^2$ $\ -2x^2y^2$ $\ -.5r^2s^2$ $\ +2(c+d)$ $\ -6a$
$\ +7a$

32. $-16x^2$ **33.** $-4rst$ **34.** $-6xy^2$ **35.** $9c^2d^2$ **36.** $+5(r+s)$
$\ -\ x^2$ $\ +8rst$ $\ +9xy^2$ $\ 3c^2d^2$ $\ -6(r+s)$
$\ +15x^2$ $\ +9rst$ $\ -3xy^2$ $\ -7c^2d^2$ $\ +\ (r+s)$

In 37–40, tell whether the sentence is true or false.

37. $5^3 + 5^3 = 2(5)^3$ **38.** $2^3 + 2^5 = 2^8$ **39.** $3^2 + 3^2 = 6^2$ **40.** $2^2 + 2^3 = 4^5$

In 41–52, simplify the expression by combining like terms.

41. $(+6x) + (-4x) + (-5x) + (+10x)$

42. $-5y + 6y + 9y - 14y$

43. $(+7c) + (-15c) + (+2c) + (+12c)$

44. $4m + 9m - 12m - m$

45. $(+8x^2) + (-x^2) + (-12x^2) + (+2x^2)$

46. $13y^2 - 15y^2 - y^2 + 8y^2$

47. $(-9c^2) + (-5c^2) + (+8c^2) + (+2c^2)$

48. $d^2 - 9d^2 - 5d^2 + 13d^2$

49. $(+10ab) + (-15ab) + (+18ab) + (-6ab)$

50. $-7cd - 5cd + 4cd - 2cd$

51. $(-13x^2y^2) + (+6x^2y^2) + (-2x^2y^2) + (+7x^2y^2)$

52. $-10rs^2 + 3rs^2 + 8rs^2 - rs^2$

2. Subtracting Like Monomials

We can subtract like monomials by using the same method that we used to subtract signed numbers:

$$(+7) - (-3) = (+7) + (+3) = +10$$
$$(+7x) - (-3x) = (+7x) + (+3x) = +10x$$

Procedure. To subtract one monomial from another like monomial, add the opposite (additive inverse) of the subtrahend to the minuend.

―――――――――――― **MODEL PROBLEMS** ――――――――――――

In 1–6, subtract:

1. $+8y$	2. $-5x^2$	3. $+15rst$	4. 0	5. $-8m$	6. $+4(m+n)$
$+3y$	$-3x^2$	$-8rst$	$-5t$	$-8m$	$-5(m+n)$
$+5y$	$-2x^2$	$+23rst$	$+5t$	0	$+9(m+n)$

Exercises

In 1–6, simplify the expression by subtracting the monomials.

1. $(+9r) - (+2r)$ 2. $(+15s) - (-5s)$ 3. $(-5q) - (-7q)$

4. $(-17n) - (11n)$ 5. $(-15t) - (-15t)$ 6. $(0) - (-30c)$

In 7–42, subtract:

7. $+9a$	8. $-9b$	9. $-8c$	10. $+7d$	11. $-5.1x$
$+7a$	$-3b$	$+2c$	$-d$	$+2.3x$

12. $-7r$	13. $3x^2$	14. $-9y^2$	15. $7d^2$	16. $-8t^3$
$-7r$	$5x^2$	$-6y^2$	$-3d^2$	$+t^3$

17. $-1.5y^3$	18. $+9(m+n)$	19. $+7cd$	20. $-8mn$	21. $-6rs$
$+.7y^3$	$+5(m+n)$	$+9cd$	$-9mn$	$+5rs$

22. $-3ab$	23. $.4cd$	24. $-5(x+y)$	25. $+3y^2z^2$	26. $-5xy^2$
$7ab$	$-.9cd$	$-3(x+y)$	$+2y^2z^2$	$+2xy^2$

27. $-5a^2b^2$	28. $+8c^2d^2$	29. $+.1x^2y^2$	30. $+3(a+b)$
$-a^2b^2$	$-8c^2d^2$	$+.9x^2y^2$	$-7(a+b)$

31. $(+8x) - (0)$ **32.** $(0) - (+8x)$ **33.** $(0) - (-8x)$
34. $(+9x^2) - (-3x^2)$ **35.** $(-3y^2) - (+7y^2)$ **36.** $(-7c^2) - (-7c^2)$
37. $(+5ab) - (+2ab)$ **38.** $(-12xy) - (+3xy)$ **39.** $(-5mn) - (-9mn)$
40. $(-4rs^2) - (2rs^2)$ **41.** $(+7x^2y) - (9x^2y)$ **42.** $(+3a^2b^2) - (+6a^2b^2)$

43. How much larger is $+15xy$ than $+7xy$?
44. How much larger is $+9x^2$ than $-3x^2$?
45. Subtract $-2x$ from $-8x$.
46. What must be added to $+6x$ to give the result $+10x$?
47. What must be added to $-3y$ to give the result $+7y$?
48. What must be subtracted from $+9d$ to give the result $+5d$?
49. What must be subtracted from $-8z$ to give the result $+3z$?
50. From the sum of $-5xy$ and $+12xy$, subtract the sum of $+9xy$ and $-15xy$.

3. Multiplying Powers of the Same Base

We know that y^2 means $y \cdot y$ and y^3 means $y \cdot y \cdot y$. Therefore:

$$y^2 \cdot y^3 = \overbrace{(y \cdot y)}^{2} \cdot \overbrace{(y \cdot y \cdot y)}^{3} = \overbrace{y \cdot y \cdot y \cdot y \cdot y}^{5} = y^5$$

Similarly, $c^2 \cdot c^4 = \overbrace{(c \cdot c)}^{2} \cdot \overbrace{(c \cdot c \cdot c \cdot c)}^{4} = \overbrace{c \cdot c \cdot c \cdot c \cdot c \cdot c}^{6} = c^6$, and

$$x \cdot x^3 = \overbrace{(x)}^{1} \cdot \overbrace{(x \cdot x \cdot x)}^{3} = x^4 \text{ (Remember that } x \text{ means } x^1.)$$

Observe that the exponent in each product is the sum of the exponents in the factors. These examples illustrate how the exponent of a product is obtained from the exponents of the factors.

In general, when x is a signed number and a and b are positive integers:

$$x^a \cdot x^b = x^{a+b}$$

Procedure. In multiplying powers of the same base, find the exponent of the product by adding the exponents of the factors. The base of the power which is the product is the same as the base of the factors.

Note that this procedure does not apply to the product of powers which have different bases. For example, $c^2 \cdot d^3$ cannot be simplified because $c^2 \cdot d^3 = c \cdot c \cdot d \cdot d \cdot d$, an expression which does not have 5 identical factors.

FINDING A POWER OF A POWER

Since $(x^3)^4 = x^3 \cdot x^3 \cdot x^3 \cdot x^3$, then $(x^3)^4 = x^{12}$. Observe that the exponent 12 can be obtained by addition, $3 + 3 + 3 + 3 = 12$, or by multiplication, $4 \times 3 = 12$. Likewise, we can show that $(x^3y^2)^4 = x^{12}y^8$.

In general, when x and y are signed numbers and a, b, and c are positive integers:

$$(x^a)^c = x^{ac} \text{ AND } (x^a \cdot y^b)^c = x^{ac} \cdot y^{bc}$$

—————— **MODEL PROBLEMS** ——————

In 1–5, simplify the expression by multiplying the powers.

1. $x^5 \cdot x^4 = x^{5+4} = x^9$ **2.** $m^6 \cdot m = m^{6+1} = m^7$

3. $10^3 \cdot 10^2 = 10^{3+2} = 10^5$ **4.** $m^{4a} \cdot m^{3a} = m^{4a+3a} = m^{7a}$

5. $(a^2)^3 = a^2 \cdot a^2 \cdot a^2 = a^{2+2+2} = a^6$ or $(a^2)^3 = a^{2 \cdot 3} = a^6$

Exercises

In 1–35, multiply:

1. $a^2 \cdot a^3$ **2.** $b^3 \cdot b^4$ **3.** $c^2 \cdot c^5$ **4.** $d^4 \cdot d^6$ **5.** $r^2 \cdot r^4 \cdot r^5$

6. $t^2 \cdot t^2$ **7.** $r^3 \cdot r^3$ **8.** $s^4 \cdot s^4$ **9.** $e^5 \cdot e^5$ **10.** $z^3 \cdot z^3 \cdot z^5$

11. $x^3 \cdot x^2$ **12.** $a^5 \cdot a^2$ **13.** $s^6 \cdot s^3$ **14.** $y^4 \cdot y^2$ **15.** $t^8 \cdot t^4 \cdot t^2$

16. $x \cdot x$ **17.** $a^2 \cdot a$ **18.** $b^4 \cdot b$ **19.** $c \cdot c^5$ **20.** $e^4 \cdot e \cdot e^5$

21. $2^3 \cdot 2^2$ **22.** $3^4 \cdot 3^3$ **23.** $5^2 \cdot 5^4$ **24.** $4^3 \cdot 4$ **25.** $2^4 \cdot 2^5 \cdot 2$

26. $(x^3)^2$ **27.** $(a^4)^2$ **28.** $(y^3)^2$ **29.** $(y^5)^2$ **30.** $(z^3)^2 \cdot (z^4)^2$

31. $(x^2y^3)^2$ **32.** $(ab^2)^4$ **33.** $(rs)^3$ **34.** $(2^2 \cdot 3^2)^3$ **35.** $(5 \cdot 2^3)^4$

In 36–40, multiply. (The exponents in each exercise are positive integers.)

36. $x^a \cdot x^{2a}$ **37.** $y^c \cdot y^2$ **38.** $c^r \cdot c^2$ **39.** $x^m \cdot x$ **40.** $(3y)^a \cdot (3y)^b$

In 41–48, state whether the sentence is true or false.

41. $10^4 \cdot 10^3 = 10^7$ **42.** $2^4 \cdot 2^2 = 2^8$ **43.** $3^3 \cdot 2^2 = 6^5$ **44.** $3^3 \cdot 2^2 = 6^6$

45. $5^4 \cdot 5 = 5^5$ **46.** $2^2 + 2^2 = 2^3$ **47.** $(2^2)^3 = 2^5$ **48.** $(2^3)^5 = 2^{15}$

4. Multiplying a Monomial by a Monomial

We know that the commutative property of multiplication makes it possible to rearrange the factors of a product and that the associative property of multiplication makes it possible to multiply the factors in any order. Therefore:

$$(5x)(6y) = (5)(6)(x)(y) = (5 \cdot 6)(x \cdot y) = 30xy$$
$$(-2x^2)(+5x^4) = (-2)(x^2)(+5)(x^4) = [(-2) \cdot (+5)][(x^2) \cdot (x^4)] = -10x^6$$
$$(-3a^2b^3)(-4a^4b) = (-3)(a^2)(b^3)(-4)(a^4)(b)$$
$$= [(-3) \cdot (-4)][(a^2) \cdot (a^4)][(b^3) \cdot (b)] = +12a^6b^4$$

In the preceding examples, the factors may be rearranged and grouped mentally.

Procedure. To multiply monomials:
1. **Use the commutative and associative properties to rearrange and group the factors. This may be done mentally.**
2. **Multiply the numerical coefficients.**
3. **Multiply the variable factors that are powers having the same base.**
4. **Multiply the products previously obtained.**

~~~~~~~~~~~~~ **MODEL PROBLEMS** ~~~~~~~~~~~~~

In 1–6, multiply:

1. $(+8xy)(-3z) = -24xyz$

2. $(-4a^3)(-5a^5) = +20a^8$

3. $(+3a^2b^3)(+4a^3b^4) = +12a^5b^7$

4. $(-5x^2y^3)(-2xy^2) = +10x^3y^5$

5. $(+6c^2d^3)(- \frac{1}{2}d) = -3c^2d^4$

6. $(-3x^2)^3 = (-3x^2)(-3x^2)(-3x^2) = -27x^6$ or
$(-3x^2)^3 = (-3)^3(x^2)^3 = -27x^6$

Exercises

In 1–48, multiply:

1. $(+6)(-2a)$ **2.** $(-4)(-6b)$ **3.** $(+5)(-2)(-3y)$
4. $(4a)(5b)$ **5.** $(-8r)(-2s)$ **6.** $(+7x)(-2y)(3z)$
7. $(+6x)(-\frac{1}{2}y)$ **8.** $(-\frac{3}{4}a)(+8b)$ **9.** $(-6x)(\frac{1}{2}y)(-\frac{1}{3}z)$
10. $(+5ab)(-3c)$ **11.** $(-7r)(5st)$ **12.** $(-2)(+6cd)(-e)$

13. $(+9xy)(-2cd)$ 14. $(-ab)(3mn)$ 15. $(3s)(-4m)(5cd)$
16. $(+5a^2)(-4a^2)$ 17. $(-6x^4)(-3x^3)$ 18. $(-7y^2)(5y^5)(-2y^3)$
19. $(20y^3)(-7y^2)$ 20. $(18r^5)(-5r^2)$ 21. $(-\frac{1}{2}s^4)(-\frac{1}{4}s^2)(8s^3)$
22. $(+3z^2)(+4z)$ 23. $(-8y^5)(+5y)$ 24. $(-9z)(8z^4)(z^3)$
25. $(+6x^2y^3)(-4x^4y^2)$ 26. $(-7a^3b)(+5a^2b^2)$ 27. $(2r^2s^3)(3r^3s^2)(-r^5s^5)$
28. $(+4ab^2)(-2a^2b^3)$ 29. $(-2r^4s)(+8rs)$ 30. $(3ab^3)(-4a^4b)(8ab)$
31. $(-6m^2n)(+5m^2)$ 32. $(-9c)(+8cd^2)$ 33. $(-3y)(5xy)(15xy^2)$
34. $(+\frac{2}{3}x^2)(-6x)$ 35. $(-15ab^2)(-\frac{3}{5}a^2b)$ 36. $(\frac{1}{3}xy)(\frac{1}{2}x)(-12x^2y^2)$
37. $(+7a)^2$ 38. $(-3a)^2$ 39. $(-.5x)^2$
40. $(+5a^2)^3$ 41. $(-4c^2d)^3$ 42. $(-\frac{2}{5}r^2s^2)^2$
43. $(+2x)^2(+3y)^2$ 44. $(-4x)^2(-y)^2$ 45. $(\frac{1}{2}x^2)^3(-4y^3)^2$
46. $5(-2x)^2$ 47. $-5(-3y)^3$ 48. $10(2x)^2(-y^2)^3$

49. Express the area of a rectangle whose length is $5w$ and whose width is $3w$.
50. Express the area of a rectangle whose width is x and whose length is $6x$.
51. Express the area of a square each of whose sides is $5x$ feet.
52. Express the volume of a cube each of whose edges is $2x$ inches.

5. Dividing Powers of the Same Base

We know that division and multiplication are inverse operations.

Since $x^2 \cdot x^3 = x^5$, then $x^5 \div x^3 = x^2$.
Since $y^5 \cdot y^4 = y^9$, then $y^9 \div y^4 = y^5$.
Since $c^4 \cdot c = c^5$, then $c^5 \div c = c^4$. (Remember that c means c^1.)

Observe that the exponent in each quotient is the difference between the exponent of the dividend and the exponent of the divisor.

In general, when $x \neq 0$ and a and b are positive integers with $a > b$:

$$x^a \div x^b = x^{a-b}$$

Procedure. In dividing powers of the same base, find the exponent of the quotient by subtracting the exponent of the divisor from the exponent of the dividend. The base of the power which is the quotient is the same as the base of the dividend and the base of the divisor.

We know that any non-zero number divided by itself is 1. Therefore, $x \div x = 1$ and $y^3 \div y^3 = 1$.

In general, when $x \neq 0$ and a is a positive integer:

$$x^a \div x^a = 1$$

MODEL PROBLEMS

In 1–5, simplify by performing the indicated division.

1. $x^9 \div x^5 = x^{9-5} = x^4$ **2.** $y^5 \div y = y^{5-1} = y^4$ **3.** $c^5 \div c^5 = 1$

4. $10^5 \div 10^3 = 10^{5-3} = 10^2$ **5.** $y^{6b} \div y^{4b} = y^{6b-4b} = y^{2b}$

ANOTHER LOOK AT DIVIDING POWERS OF THE SAME BASE

We know from our experience in arithmetic that $7 \cdot \dfrac{2}{3} = \dfrac{7 \cdot 2}{3}$ and that $\dfrac{3}{4} \cdot \dfrac{1}{2} = \dfrac{3 \cdot 1}{4 \cdot 2}$.

In general, if a, b, x, and y are signed numbers with $b \neq 0$ and $y \neq 0$, then:

$$\frac{a}{b} \cdot \frac{x}{y} = \frac{a \cdot x}{b \cdot y}$$

Now let us study another explanation for $\dfrac{x^5}{x^3} = x^2$:

Step	Reason
1. Since $x^5 = x^3 \cdot x^2$, then $\dfrac{x^5}{x^3} = \dfrac{x^3 \cdot x^2}{x^3}$	1. Substitution principle.
2. $\qquad\qquad = \left(\dfrac{x^3}{x^3}\right) \cdot x^2$	2. Meaning of multiplication.
3. $\qquad\qquad = 1 \cdot x^2$	3. Any non-zero number divided by itself is 1.
4. $\qquad\qquad = x^2$	4. Multiplication property of 1.

We can use a similar approach to solve model problems 1–5 above:

1. $\dfrac{x^9}{x^5} = \dfrac{x^5 \cdot x^4}{x^5} = \dfrac{x^5}{x^5} \cdot x^4 = 1 \cdot x^4 = x^4$ **2.** $\dfrac{y^5}{y} = \dfrac{y}{y} \cdot y^4 = 1 \cdot y^4 = y^4$

3. $\dfrac{c^5}{c^5} = 1$ **4.** $\dfrac{10^5}{10^3} = \dfrac{10^3}{10^3} \cdot 10^2 = 1 \cdot 10^2 = 10^2$

5. $\dfrac{y^{6b}}{y^{4b}} = \dfrac{y^{4b}}{y^{4b}} \cdot y^{2b} = 1 \cdot y^{2b} = y^{2b}$

Exercises

In 1–20, divide:

1. $x^8 \div x^2$ **2.** $a^{10} \div a^5$ **3.** $b^7 \div b^3$ **4.** $c^5 \div c^4$

5. $d^7 \div d^7$ **6.** $\dfrac{d^4}{d^2}$ **7.** $\dfrac{e^9}{e^3}$ **8.** $\dfrac{m^{12}}{m^4}$

9. $\dfrac{n^{10}}{n^9}$ **10.** $\dfrac{r^6}{r^6}$ **11.** $x^8 \div x$ **12.** $y^7 \div y$

13. $z^{10} \div z$ **14.** $t^5 \div t$ **15.** $m \div m$ **16.** $2^5 \div 2^2$
17. $10^6 \div 10^4$ **18.** $3^4 \div 3^2$ **19.** $5^3 \div 5$ **20.** $10^4 \div 10$

In 21–25, divide. (The exponents in each exercise are positive integers.)
21. $x^{5a} \div x^{2a}$ **22.** $y^{10b} \div y^{2b}$ **23.** $r^c \div r^d$ **24.** $s^x \div s^2$ **25.** $a^b \div a^b$

In 26–30, simplify the expression.

26. $\dfrac{2^3 \cdot 2^4}{2^2}$ **27.** $\dfrac{5^8}{5^4 \cdot 5}$ **28.** $\dfrac{10^2 \cdot 10^3}{10^4}$ **29.** $\dfrac{10^6}{10^2 \cdot 10^4}$ **30.** $\dfrac{10^8 \cdot 10^2}{(10^5)^2}$

In 31–34, tell whether the sentence is true or false.
31. $4^5 \div 2^3 = 2^2$ **32.** $5^6 \div 5^2 = 5^4$ **33.** $5^6 \div 5^2 = 5^3$ **34.** $3^8 \div 3^4 = 1^4$

6. Dividing a Monomial by a Monomial

We know that division and multiplication are inverse operations.

Since $(-5x^2)(+4x^4) = -20x^6$, then $(-20x^6) \div (+4x^4) = -5x^2$. Observe that -20 divided by $+4$ equals -5 and that x^6 divided by x^4 equals x^2.

Since $(+7a^2b^3)(-3a^3b) = -21a^5b^4$, then $\dfrac{-21a^5b^4}{-3a^3b} = +7a^2b^3$. Observe that $(-21) \div (-3) = +7$, that $a^5 \div a^3 = a^2$, and that $b^4 \div b = b^3$.

Procedure. To divide monomials:
1. Divide their numerical coefficients.
2. Divide variable factors that are powers having the same base.
3. Multiply the quotients previously obtained.

MODEL PROBLEMS

In 1–4, divide:

1. $(+24a^5) \div (+3a^2) = +8a^3$ **2.** $(-15x^6y^5) \div (-3x^3y^2) = +5x^3y^3$

3. $\dfrac{-18x^3y^2}{+6x^2y} = -3xy$ **4.** $\dfrac{+20a^3c^4d^2}{-5a^3c^3} = -4cd^2$

ANOTHER LOOK AT DIVIDING A MONOMIAL BY A MONOMIAL

Now let us examine another method that may be used to do the preceding model problems:

1. $\dfrac{+24a^5}{+3a^2} = \dfrac{+24}{+3} \cdot \dfrac{a^5}{a^2} = +8a^3$ **2.** $\dfrac{-15x^6y^5}{-3x^3y^2} = \dfrac{-15}{-3} \cdot \dfrac{x^6}{x^3} \cdot \dfrac{y^5}{y^2} = +5x^3y^3$

3. $\dfrac{-18x^3y^2}{+6x^2y} = \dfrac{-18}{+6} \cdot \dfrac{x^3}{x^2} \cdot \dfrac{y^2}{y} = -3xy$

4. $\dfrac{+20a^3c^4d^2}{-5a^3c^3} = \dfrac{+20}{-5} \cdot \dfrac{a^3}{a^3} \cdot \dfrac{c^4}{c^3} \cdot d^2 = (-4) \cdot 1 \cdot c \cdot d^2 = -4cd^2$

Exercises

In 1–37, divide:

1. $18x$ by 2
2. $24y$ by -6
3. $14x^2y^2$ by -7
4. $-35x^3$ by $+7x^2$
5. $-36y^5$ by $+6y^2$
6. $40a^4$ by $-4a$
7. $-12ab$ by $+6a$
8. $-22c^2d$ by $-2c^2$
9. $24a^2b^2$ by $-8b^2$
10. $36a^4b^3$ by $9a^2b^2$
11. $-16a^3b^2$ by $-2a^2b$
12. $15c^4d$ by $-5c^3d$
13. $7r^4c$ by $7rc$
14. $-28c^2d$ by $7cd$
15. $30de^3$ by $5de^2$
16. $(+8cd) \div (-4c)$
17. $(+50x^2y) \div (-5x^2)$
18. $(-14xy^3) \div (-7xy^3)$
19. $(-6a^3b^4) \div (+2a^2b^2)$
20. $(+18m^3n^2) \div (+6m^2n^2)$
21. $(-10a^4b) \div (-5ab)$

22. $\dfrac{18x^6}{2x^2}$
23. $\dfrac{-8c^3}{2c}$
24. $\dfrac{5x^2y^3}{-5y^3}$
25. $\dfrac{-49c^4b^3}{7c^2b^2}$

26. $\dfrac{-24x^2y}{-3xy}$
27. $\dfrac{21r^2s^2}{-7rs^2}$
28. $\dfrac{-27xyz}{9xz}$
29. $\dfrac{-56abc}{8abc}$

30. $\dfrac{-57a^{10}b^8}{+3a^4b^2}$
31. $\dfrac{+81c^9d^7}{-3c^5d^7}$
32. $\dfrac{-63x^9y^2z^3}{+7x^3y}$
33. $\dfrac{-9.5r^{12}s^{10}t^5}{.5rst^5}$

34. $\dfrac{8(a+b)^5}{2(a+b)^2}$
35. $\dfrac{15(x+y)^3}{3(x+y)^2}$
36. $\dfrac{15(c-d)}{5(c-d)}$
37. $\dfrac{18(x-3y)^3}{3(x-3y)^2}$

38. If 10 hats cost $50x$ cents, represent the cost of a hat.
39. If 7 oranges cost $14y$ cents, represent the cost of an orange.
40. If $3y$ pens cost $12y^3$ dollars, represent the cost of a pen.
41. If the area of a rectangle is $35x^4$ and the length is $7x^2$, represent the width.

CHAPTER VIII

OPERATIONS WITH POLYNOMIALS

1. Adding Polynomials

Each of the open phrases $5x$, $6x + 5$, and $3x^2 - 4x + 1$ is called a *polynomial* in x. A polynomial in x is an expression that can be formed from the variable x and numerical coefficients, using only the operations of addition, subtraction, and multiplication. The variable is never in the denominator of a fraction. All exponents of the variable must be positive integers. The polynomial $5x$, which has one term, is called a *monomial;* $6x + 5$, a polynomial of two terms, is called a *binomial;* and $3x^2 - 4x + 1$, a polynomial of three terms, is called a *trinomial.* The expression $\frac{2}{x} + 5$ is *not* a polynomial because the variable x is in the denominator of a fraction.

The *degree of a polynomial* in one variable is the same as the greatest exponent that appears in it. For example, $5x^3 - 4x^2 + 3x - 2$ is a polynomial in x of degree 3. Also, $4x^2 - 6x + 1$ is of degree 2, and $3x + 5$ is of degree 1. The variable in a polynomial need not be x; it may be any other letter. For example, $5a^3 - 6a + 4$ is a third degree polynomial in a.

A polynomial may involve more than one variable. For example, $2L + 2W$ and $x^2 + 2xy + y^2$ are polynomials that involve two variables.

The polynomials $5x^3 - 4x^2 + 3x - 2$, $4x^2 - 6x + 1$, and $3x + 5$ are written in *standard form.* That is, the term with the greatest exponent of the variable is written first and the other terms appear in descending order.

A polynomial is arranged in *descending powers* when the exponents of a particular variable decrease as we move from left to right. Thus, $x^3 - 3x^2 + 5x - 7$ is arranged in descending powers of x because the exponents of x decrease as we move from left to right.

A polynomial is arranged in *ascending powers* when the exponents of a particular variable increase as we move from left to right. Thus, $x^2 + 2xy + y^2$ is arranged in ascending powers of y because the exponents of y increase as we move from left to right.

To simplify a polynomial that has several terms, we collect like terms, making use of the commutative, associative, and distributive properties:

Step	Reason
$4x + 3y - 9x + 6y$	
1. $= 4x - 9x + 3y + 6y$	1. Commutative property of addition.
2. $= (4x - 9x) + (3y + 6y)$	2. Associative property of addition.
3. $= (4 - 9)x + (3 + 6)y$	3. Distributive property of multiplication.
4. $= -5x + 9y$	4. Substitution principle.

To add two polynomials, we use the commutative, associative, and distributive properties to combine like terms. For example:

Step	Reason
1. $(3x + 5) + (6x + 8) = (3x + 6x) + (5 + 8)$	1. Commutative and associative properties.
2. $ = (3 + 6)x + (5 + 8)$	2. Distributive property.
3. $ = 9x + 13$	3. Substitution principle.

To find the sum of the polynomials $4x^2 + 3x - 5$, $3x^2 - 6 - 5x$, and $-x + 3 - 2x^2$, we can write the polynomials vertically, first arranging them in descending (or ascending) powers of x. Then we can add the like terms in each column. As shown at the right, the sum is $5x^2 - 3x - 8$.

$$\begin{array}{r} 4x^2 + 3x - 5 \\ 3x^2 - 5x - 6 \\ -2x^2 - x + 3 \\ \hline 5x^2 - 3x - 8 \end{array}$$

Procedure. To add polynomials, combine like terms by adding their numerical coefficients. For convenience, arrange the polynomials in descending or ascending powers of a particular variable so that like terms are in vertical columns. Then add each column separately.

Addition can be checked by adding again in the opposite direction. Addition can also be checked by substituting convenient values for the variables and evaluating the polynomials and the sum. The sum of the values of the polynomials should be equal to the value of the polynomial which is the sum of the polynomials.

Do not use 0 or 1 as values for checking the addition of polynomials.

~~~~~~~~~~~~~~~ *MODEL PROBLEMS* ~~~~~~~~~~~~~~~

1. Add and check: $4x + 3y - 5z,\ 3x - 5y - 6z,\ -2x - y + 3z$

Solution: *Check:* Let $x = 4,\ y = 3,\ z = 2.$

$$\begin{array}{r} 4x + 3y - 5z \\ 3x - 5y - 6z \\ -2x - y + 3z \\ \hline 5x - 3y - 8z \end{array}$$

$$\begin{array}{rl} 16 + 9 - 10 & = 15 \\ 12 - 15 - 12 & = -15 \\ -8 - 3 + 6 & = -5 \\ \hline 20 - 9 - 16 = -5 \longleftrightarrow & -5 \end{array}$$

Answer: $5x - 3y - 8z$

2. Add: $+7x^2 - 5xy + 4y^2,\ +3xy - x^2,\ -9y^2 + 2xy$

How To Proceed	*Solution*

1. Arrange in descending powers of x.
2. Arrange like terms in the same column.
3. Add like terms in each column.

$$\begin{array}{r} +7x^2 - 5xy + 4y^2 \\ -x^2 + 3xy \\ +2xy - 9y^2 \\ \hline +6x^2 + 0 - 5y^2 \end{array}$$

Answer: $6x^2 - 5y^2$. Check by adding in the opposite direction.

3. Simplify: $6a + [5a + (6 - 3a)]$

Solution: When one grouping symbol appears within another grouping symbol, first perform the operation involving the algebraic expression within the innermost grouping symbol.

$$\begin{aligned} 6a + [5a + (6 - 3a)] &= 6a + [5a + 6 - 3a] \\ &= 6a + [2a + 6] \\ &= 6a + 2a + 6 \\ &= 8a + 6 \end{aligned}$$

Answer: $8a + 6$

~~~~~~

Exercises

In 1–10, simplify the polynomials.

1. $5c + 3d + 2c + 8d$ **2.** $9y + 6w + 3w + y$

3. $8x + 9y - 3x - 6y$ **4.** $-4a + 6b + 3a - b$

5. $3r + 2s + 9t + 4r - 5s + t$ **6.** $-5m + 6n + 8p - 6n + 3m$

7. $-5xy + 7wz - xy - 5wz$ **8.** $7ab - bc - 4ab - 5bc$

9. $3x^2 - 5x + 7 + 2x^2 + 3x - 9$ **10.** $2x + 4x^2 - 7 - x^2 + 7 - 8x$

In 11–24, add and check the result.

11. $5x + 3y$
$6x + 9y$

12. $4a - 6b$
$9a + 3b$

13. $-6m + n$
$-4m - 5n$

14. $-9ab + 8cd$
$3ab - 8cd$

15. $8r - 3t$
$-2r + 3t$
$-6r + 5t$

16. $y + 8z$
$5y - z$
$-8y - 5z$

17. $9x^2 + 5$
$-2x^2 - 8$
$+ x^2 - 3$

18. $-4x^2y^2 + 2r^2s^2$
$-6x^2y^2 - 5r^2s^2$
$+8x^2y^2 + 3r^2s^2$

19. $15x - 26y + 8z$
$3x - 14y - 3z$

20. $x^2 - 33x + 15$
$-4x^2 + 18x - 36$

21. $-5a^2 - 6ab - 4b^2$
$+7a^2 + 6ab - 3b^2$

22. $x^2 + 3x + 5$
$2x^2 - 4x - 1$
$-5x^2 + 2x + 4$

23. $5c^2 - 4cd + 6d^2$
$-c^2 + 3cd + 2d^2$
$-3c^2 + cd - 8d^2$

24. $2.1 + .9z + z^2$
$-.7z - .2z^2$
$-.9 + .2z$

In 25–46, simplify the expression.

25. $4a + (9a + 3)$

26. $7b + (4b - 6)$

27. $8c + (7 - 9c)$

28. $(-6x - 4) + 6x$

29. $r + (s + 2r)$

30. $8d^2 + (6d^2 - 4d)$

31. $(-4m^2 + 9) + 5m^2$

32. $-5x^3 + (4 - x^3)$

33. $6xy + (5xy + 7)$

34. $(5x + 3) + (6x - 5)$

35. $(-6y + 7) + (+6y - 7)$

36. $(5 - 6y) + (-9y + 2)$

37. $(5a + 3b) + (-2a + 4d)$

38. $(5x^2 + 4) + (-3x^2 - 4)$

39. $(3y^2 - 6y) + (3y - 4)$

40. $(x^3 + 3x^2) + (-2x^2 - 9)$

41. $(d^2 + 9d + 2) + (-4d - d^2)$

42. $8 + [5 + (6 + x)]$

43. $[-4x + (10 - 5x)] + 5x$

44. $(x^2 + 5x - 24) + (-x^2 - 4x + 9)$

45. $(-r^3 + 5r^2 + 6r + 8) + (4r^3 - 6r + 2)$

46. $(x^3 + 9x - 5) + (-4x^2 - 12x + 5)$

47. Add: $6c - 3d$, $d - 2c$, $2d - c$

48. Add: $3x - 5$, $-2x + 3$, $2 - x$

49. Add: $9a - 4b + c$ and $-5a + 3c + 4b$

50. Add: $-3a$, $+7a$, $+b$, $+6b$, $-5a$, $-7b$

51. Find the sum of $3c - 7d$, $-2c + 5d$, $-c + 8d$, and $4c - 6d$.

52. Find the sum of $3a + 8b - 5c$, $6a - 9b + 4c$, and $-7a + b + 2c$.

53. Find the sum of $6p - 3q + z$, $-3p + 2q - z$, and $-p + q$.

54. Find the sum of $4x^2 - 6x - 3$ and $3x^2 - 5x + 7$.

55. Add: $3y^2 + 7 - 5y$ and $9 + 4y - 5y^2$

56. Add: $2c^2 + 5c - 3$, $4c^2 - 5$, $6 - 5c$

57. Add: $x^2 - 7xy + 3y^2$, $-2y^2 + 3x^2 - 4xy$, $xy - 2x^2 - 4y^2$

58. Add: $6ab - 3a^2 + 5b^2$, $-4b^2 - 4ab$, $-6a^2 + 3b^2$

59. Add: $x^3 - 4x^2 + 5x$, $3x^2 - 5 + 2x^3$, $-2x + x^2$, $-4x^3 + 3$

60. Add: $7b - 3b^3 + 5b^2$, $-8 + 2b^2 - 4b^3$, $7 - 5b^3 - 9b$, $-6b^2 + b^3 - 7$

61. Add: $x^3 - 4x^2y + 5xy^2 - 4y^3$, $-2xy^2 - 4x^3 + x^2y$, $-3y^3 + 7xy^2 - 9x^2y$

In 62–66, represent the perimeter of a figure whose sides are represented by:

62. $6x - 4, 5x - 5, 8x + 3$

63. $3p - 2q, 4p + q, 4p - 2q, q$

64. $5x - y, 4x + 3y, 3x + y, 5y$

65. $x + 4y, 3y - x, 5x - y, 8x - 2y$

66. $8a + 3b, 9b - 2a, 3a - 2b, 2a - b$

67. Represent the perimeter of a square each of whose sides is

    a. $3x + 5$ *b.* $4x - 1$ *c.* $x^2 + 4x - 3$ *d.* $x^2 + 2xy + y^2$

68. Represent the perimeter of a rectangle whose width is represented by x and whose length is represented by:

    a. $2x + 1$ *b.* $3x - 1$ *c.* $4x + 5$ *d.* $6x - 4$ *e.* $5 - 2x$

69. $3q - 7d, 8q + d, -2q + d$, and $q + 5d$ represent a boy's savings for four weeks. Represent the total.

2. Subtracting Polynomials

To subtract one polynomial from another, we use a procedure similar to that used to subtract like terms; we add the opposite (additive inverse) of the subtrahend to the minuend.

We can write the opposite of a polynomial using the symbol "$-$." For example, the opposite of $2x^2 - 5x - 3$ can be written $-(2x^2 - 5x - 3)$.

We can also write the opposite of a polynomial by forming a polynomial each of whose terms is the opposite of the corresponding terms of the original polynomial. For example, the opposite of $2x^2 - 5x - 3$ is $-2x^2 + 5x + 3$. Thus:

$$\begin{aligned}(5x^2 + 8x - 7) - (2x^2 - 5x - 3) &= (5x^2 + 8x - 7) + (-2x^2 + 5x + 3)\\ &= 5x^2 + 8x - 7 - 2x^2 + 5x + 3\\ &= (5 - 2)x^2 + (8 + 5)x + (-7 + 3)\\ &= 3x^2 + 13x - 4\end{aligned}$$

The solution of a subtraction example can also be arranged vertically as shown at the right. We mentally add the opposite of each term of the subtrahend to the corresponding term of the minuend.

$$\begin{array}{r} 5x^2 + 8x - 7 \\ 2x^2 - 5x - 3 \\ \hline 3x^2 + 13x - 4 \end{array}$$

Procedure. To subtract polynomials, add the opposite of the subtrahend to the minuend. For convenience, place the subtrahend under the minuend, arranging the polynomials so that like terms are in vertical columns. Then subtract the like terms in each column separately.

Subtraction can be checked by adding the subtrahend and the difference. The result should equal the minuend. Subtraction can also be checked by substituting convenient values (not 0 or 1) for the variables. The value of the minuend polynomial minus the value of the subtrahend polynomial should be equal to the value of the difference polynomial.

MODEL PROBLEMS

1. Subtract and check: $(5x^2 - 6x + 3) - (2x^2 - 9x - 6)$

Solution: *Check:*

$5x^2 - 6x + 3$	minuend	$2x^2 - 9x - 6$	subtrahend
$2x^2 - 9x - 6$	subtrahend	$3x^2 + 3x + 9$	difference
$3x^2 + 3x + 9$	difference	$5x^2 - 6x + 3$	minuend

Answer: $3x^2 + 3x + 9$

2. Simplify the expression $9x - [7 - (4 - 2x)]$

Solution:

$$
\begin{aligned}
9x - [7 - (4 - 2x)] &= 9x - [7 + (-4 + 2x)] \\
&= 9x - [7 - 4 + 2x] \\
&= 9x - [3 + 2x] \\
&= 9x + [-3 - 2x] \\
&= 9x - 3 - 2x \\
&= 7x - 3
\end{aligned}
$$

(First perform the subtraction involving the expression within the innermost grouping symbol.)

Answer: $7x - 3$

Exercises

In 1–6, write the opposite (additive inverse) of the expression.

1. $9x + 6$ **2.** $-5x + 3$ **3.** $-6x - 6y$

4. $2x^2 - 3x + 2$ **5.** $-y^2 + 5y - 4$ **6.** $7ab - 3bc$

In 7–20, subtract and check the result.

| **7.** $10a + 8b$ | **8.** $5b + 3c$ | **9.** $6d + 6e$ | **10.** $8x - 3y$ |
| $4a + 5b$ | $4b + c$ | $9d - 8e$ | $-4x + 8y$ |

| **11.** $4r - 7s$ | **12.** 0 | **13.** $6rs - 7bc$ | **14.** $5xy - 9cd$ |
| $5r - 7s$ | $8a - 6b$ | $9rs - 7bc$ | $-3xy + cd$ |

15. $x^2 - 6x + 5$
    $3x^2 - 2x - 2$

16. $3y^2 - 2y - 1$
    $-5y^2 - 2y + 6$

17. $3a^2 - 2ab + 3b^2$
    $- a^2 - 5ab + 3b^2$

18. $7a + 6b - 9c$
    $3a \qquad - 6c$

19. $x^2 \qquad - 9$
    $-2x^2 + 5x - 3$

20. $5 - 6d - d^2$
    $- 4d - d^2$

In 21–46, simplify the expression.

21. $5x - (2x + 5)$

22. $3y - (5y - 4)$

23. $4z - (6z - 2)$

24. $9m - (6 + 6m)$

25. $m - (m - n)$

26. $4d - (5c + 4d)$

27. $5c - (4c - 6c^2)$

28. $8r - (-6s - 8r)$

29. $-(5x + 8) - 2x$

30. $(3y - 6) - (8 - 9y)$

31. $(-4x + 7) - (3x - 7)$

32. $(4a - 3b) - (5a - 2b)$

33. $(2c + 3d) - (-6d - 5c)$

34. $(5x^2 + 6x - 9) - (x^2 - 3x + 7)$

35. $(2x^2 - 3x - 1) - (2x^2 + 5x)$

36. $-9d - (2c - 4d) + 4c$

37. $(3y + z) + (z - 5y) - (2z - 2y)$

38. $(a - b) - (a + b) - (-a - b)$

39. $(x^2 - 3x) + (5 - 9x) - (5x^2 - 7)$

40. $5c - [8c - (6 - 3c)]$

41. $12 - [-3 + (6x - 9)]$

42. $10x + [3x - (5x - 4)]$

43. $x^2 - [-3x + (4 - 7x)]$

44. $3x^2 - [7x - (4x - x^2) + 3]$

45. $9a - [5a^2 - (7 + 9a - 2a^2)]$

46. $4y^2 - \{4y + [3y^2 - (6y + 2) + 6]\}$

47. From $m^2 + 5m - 7$, subtract $m^2 - 3m - 4$.
48. From $12x - 6y + 9z$, subtract $-x - 3z + 6y$.
49. Subtract $2x^2 - 3x + 7$ from $x^2 + 6x - 12$.
50. Subtract $2y + 5y^2 - 8$ from $4y^2 - 5y + 1$.
51. Subtract $9x^2 - 4xy + 3y^2$ from $3xy - 5x^2 - 7y^2$.
52. Subtract $2c^2 + 3c - 4$ from 0.
53. How much greater than $a^2 + 3ab + b^2$ is $4a^2 + 9ab - 2b^2$?
54. a. How much less than 25 is 15?
    b. How much less than $5x + 3y$ is $2x + y$?
55. How much less than $4x^2 - 5$ is $3x^2 + 2$?
56. a. By how much does 13 exceed 10?
    b. By how much does $7x + 5$ exceed $4x - 3$?
57. By how much does $a + b + c$ exceed $a + b - c$?
58. What algebraic expression must be added to $2x^2 + 5x + 7$ to give $8x^2 - 4x - 5$ as the result?
59. What algebraic expression must be added to $4x^2 - 8$ to make the result equal to 0?
60. What algebraic expression must be added to $-3x^2 + 7x - 5$ to give 0 as the result?
61. From the sum of $y^2 + 2y - 7$ and $2y^2 - 4y + 3$, subtract $3y^2 - 8y - 10$.
62. Subtract the sum of $c^2 - 5$ and $-2c^2 + 3c$ from $4c^2 - 6c + 7$.

In 63–68, use grouping symbols to write an algebraic expression which represents the verbal phrase. Then simplify the expression.

63. the sum of $4x - 9$ and $5 - x$ **64.** $9x + 2y$ decreased by $-3x + 5y$

65. 50 decreased by $20 - 2x$ **66.** $3x^2 - 1$ less than $5x^2 + 7$

67. $5x - 7y$ more than $9y - 7x$ **68.** the excess of $3x - 4$ over $9x + 5$

3. Multiplying a Polynomial by a Monomial

We know that the distributive property of multiplication states:

$$a(b + c) = ab + ac$$

Therefore, $x(4x + 3) = (x)(4x) + (x)(3) = 4x^2 + 3x$.

This result can be illustrated geometrically. Remember that the area of a rectangle is equal to the product of its length and width.

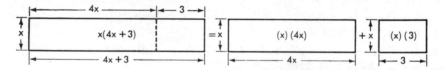

Since the area of the largest rectangle is equal to the sum of the areas of the two smaller rectangles, we see that $x(4x + 3) = (x)(4x) + (x)(3) = 4x^2 + 3x$.

To find the product $5(3x + 2y)$, we apply the distributive property of multiplication: $5(3x + 2y) = 5(3x) + 5(2y) = 15x + 10y$.

The multiplication may also be arranged vertically as shown at the right.

$$\begin{array}{r} 3x + 2y \\ 5 \\ \hline 15x + 10y \end{array}$$

Procedure. To multiply a polynomial by a monomial, use the distributive property: multiply each term of the polynomial by the monomial and add the resulting products.

MODEL PROBLEMS

In 1–3, multiply:

1. $8(3x - 2y + 4z) = 24x - 16y + 32z$

2. $-5x(x^2 - 2x + 4) = -5x^3 + 10x^2 - 20x$

3. $-3a^2b^2(4ab^2 - 3b^2) = -12a^3b^4 + 9a^2b^4$

Exercises

In 1–41, multiply:

1. $3(6c + 3d)$ **2.** $-5(4m - 6n)$ **3.** $-2(8a + 6b)$

4. $10(2x - \frac{1}{5}y)$ **5.** $18(2a - \frac{1}{6}b)$ **6.** $12(\frac{2}{3}m - 4n)$

7. $-8(4r - \frac{1}{4}s)$ **8.** $-27(\frac{2}{9}x - y)$ **9.** $-16(\frac{3}{4}c - \frac{5}{8}d)$

10. $4x(5x + 6)$ **11.** $8c(2c - 5)$ **12.** $5d(d^2 - 3d)$

13. $-5c^2(15c - 4c^2)$ **14.** $mn(m + n)$ **15.** $-ab(a - b)$

16. $3ab(5a^2 - 7b^2)$ **17.** $-8xy(-4xy^2 + 2x^2y)$

18. $-5c^3d^2(9cd^2 - 4c^3d)$ **19.** $-r^3s^3(6r^4s - 3s^4)$

20. $10m^4n(-5n^3 + 3m^2)$ **21.** $-a^4(10b^2 - a)$

22. $10d(2a - 3c + 4b)$ **23.** $-8(2x^2 - 3x - 5)$

24. $3d(d^2 - 2d + 8)$ **25.** $3t(1 - 2t + 3t^2)$

26. $-5s(2s^2 - 6s + 7)$ **27.** $-9e(4 - 2e - 6e^2)$

28. $3xy(x^2 + xy + y^2)$ **29.** $-6ab(2a^2 - 3ab + 5b^2)$

30. $5r^2s^2(-2r^2 + 3rs - 4s^2)$ **31.** $-15xyz(3xz - 5xy - yz)$

32. $16(\frac{1}{2}y^2 - \frac{3}{4}y + \frac{5}{8})$ **33.** $-24(\frac{1}{2}t^2 - \frac{3}{4}t + \frac{2}{3})$

34. $\frac{1}{2}(4x^2 - 6x + 14)$ **35.** $\frac{3}{4}(12 - 8x + 4x^2)$

36. $x^2 - 5x + 4$
$\underline{3x}$

37. $2y^2 - 5y - 3$
$\underline{-2y}$

38. $r^2 - rs + s^2$
$\underline{4r}$

39. $y^2 - 3yz + z^2$
$\underline{3yz}$

40. $2c^2 - 3c - 5$
$\underline{-3c^2}$

41. $5 - 6ab - 3b^2$
$\underline{-4ab}$

In 42–47, use grouping symbols to write an algebraic expression which represents the answer. Then simplify the expression.

42. Express the area of a rectangle whose length is $3x + 4y$ and whose width is $5z$.

43. Express the area of a rectangle whose length is $\frac{2}{3}r$ and whose width is $9r - 6s$.

44. A car travels $2x + 5$ miles per hour. Express the distance it travels in:
    a. 4 hours   *b.* 8 hours   *c.* 20 hours   *d. h* hours   *e. x* hours

45. A hat costs $2x - 1$ dollars. Express the cost of:
    a. 2 hats   *b.* 10 hats   *c. h* hats   *d. x* hats

46. A building is $5h + 3$ yards high. Express its height in feet.

47. A boy is y years old now. His father is 5 times as old as the boy will be 3 years from now. Express the father's present age.

48. If the length of one side of an equilateral triangle is represented by $5x - 4y$, represent the perimeter of the triangle.

49. If the length of one side of a square is represented by $3a + 4b$, represent the perimeter of the square.

4. Using Multiplication To Simplify Algebraic Expressions Containing Symbols of Grouping

To simplify the expression $3x + 7(2x + 3)$, we use the distributive property and then collect like terms. Thus:

$$3x + 7(2x + 3) = 3x + 7(2x) + 7(3) = 3x + 14x + 21 = 17x + 21$$

By using addition, we can simplify the expression $5 + (2x - 3)$ as shown at the right.

Since the multiplication property of 1 states that $1 \cdot x = x$ and $1 \cdot (2x - 3) = 2x - 3$, we can also simplify $5 + (2x - 3)$ using multiplication:

$$\begin{array}{r} 5 \\ 2x - 3 \\ \hline 2x + 2 \end{array}$$

$$5 + (2x - 3) = 5 + 1 \cdot (2x - 3) = 5 + 2x - 3 = 2x + 2$$

Likewise, we can simplify $5y - (2 - 7y)$ using multiplication:

$$5y - (2 - 7y) = 5y - 1 \cdot (2 - 7y) = 5y - 2 + 7y = 12y - 2$$

～～～～～ MODEL PROBLEMS ～～～～～

In 1–3, simplify the expression by using the distributive property of multiplication and collecting like terms.

1. $3(x + 5) - 10$ **2.** $2c + (7c - 4)$ **3.** $-2(3 - 2x) - (6 - 5x)$

Solution   *Solution*   *Solution*

$3(x + 5) - 10$ $2c + (7c - 4)$ $-2(3 - 2x) - (6 - 5x)$
$= 3x + 15 - 10$ $= 2c + 1(7c - 4)$ $= -2(3 - 2x) - 1 \cdot (6 - 5x)$
$= 3x + 5$ *Ans.* $= 2c + 7c - 4$ $= -6 + 4x - 6 + 5x$
                $= 9c - 4$ *Ans.* $= 9x - 12$ *Ans.*

4. Simplify: $6x - [+3x - 2(x - 5)]$

Solution: $6x - [+3x - 2(x - 5)] = 6x - [+3x - 2x + 10]$
$$= 6x - 1[3x - 2x + 10]$$
$$= 6x - 3x + 2x - 10$$
$$= 5x - 10 \quad Ans.$$

Exercises

In 1–30, simplify the expression.

1. $5(d + 3) - 10$
2. $3(2 - 3c) + 5c$
3. $7 + 2(7x - 5)$
4. $-2(x - 1) + 6$
5. $-4(3 - 6a) - 7a$
6. $5 - 4(3e - 5)$
7. $8 + (4e - 2)$
8. $a + (b - a)$
9. $(6b + 4) - 2b$
10. $9 - (5t + 6)$
11. $4 - (2 - 8s)$
12. $-(6x - 7) + 14$
13. $5x(2x - 3) + 9x$
14. $12y - 3y(2y - 4)$
15. $7x + 3(2x - 1) - 8$
16. $7c - 4d - 2(4c - 3d)$
17. $3a - 2a(5a - a) + a^2$
18. $(a + 3b) - (a - 3b)$
19. $4(2x + 5) - 3(2 - 7x)$
20. $r(s - t) - s(r - t)$
21. $5x(2 - 3x) - x(3x - 1)$
22. $y(y + 4) - y(y - 3) - 9y$
23. $7x(x + 3y) - 4y(-4x - y)$
24. $-2c(c + 2d) + 4d(2c - 3d)$
25. $ab(7a - 3c) - bc(2a - b)$
26. $mn(4m^2 - 2n^2) - 2mn(2m^2 - n^2)$
27. $7[5x + 2(x - 3) + 4]$
28. $-4[8y - 7 - 3(2y - 1)]$
29. $4x[2x^2 - 2x(x + 3) - 5]$
30. $x^2z - x[xy - x(y - z)]$

31. A carpenter has a piece of lumber which is $x + 2$ yards in length and another piece which is $2x - 1$ feet in length. Represent in simplest form the total number of inches of lumber that he has.

32. A girl has $3x - 4$ nickels and $2x + 2$ dimes. Represent in simplest form the total number of cents she has.

33. A man spent his vacation by staying at home for 10 days and traveling for $2x - 1$ weeks. Represent in simplest form the number of days he had as his vacation.

5. Multiplying a Polynomial by a Polynomial

To find the product $a(x + 3)$, we learned to use the distributive property of multiplication: $a(x + 3) = a(x) + a(3)$. Now let us find the product of two polynomials: $(x + 4)(x + 3)$.

Since $a(x + 3)$ $=$ $a(x)$ $+$ $a(3)$, if we replace a by $x + 4$, then

$$(x + 4)(x + 3) = (x + 4)(x) + (x + 4)(3) \qquad \text{Distributive property.}$$
$$= x^2 + 4x + 3x + 12 \qquad \text{Distributive property.}$$
$$= x^2 + 7x + 12 \qquad \text{Combining like terms.}$$

This result can also be illustrated geometrically.

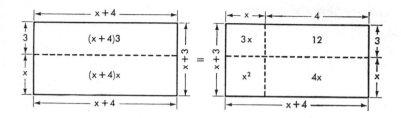

From the figures, we see that:

$$(x + 4)(x + 3)$$
$$= (x + 4)(x) + (x + 4)(3)$$
$$= x^2 + 4x + 3x + 12$$
$$= x^2 + 7x + 12$$

In general, for all numbers a, b, c, and d, $(a + b)(c + d) = (a + b)c + (a + b)d$, or

$$(a + b)(c + d) = ac + bc + ad + bd$$

Notice that each term of the first polynomial is multiplied by each term of the second.

At the right, we see a convenient vertical arrangement of the previous multiplication, similar to the arrangement used in arithmetic multiplication. Multiply from left to right.

$$
\begin{array}{r}
x + 4 \\
x + 3 \\
\hline
\end{array}
$$

$(x + 4)x \longrightarrow x^2 + 4x$
$(x + 4)3 \longrightarrow \quad\quad + 3x + 12$
Add like terms: $x^2 + 7x + 12$

Procedure. To multiply a polynomial by a polynomial, first arrange the multiplicand and multiplier according to descending or ascending powers of a common variable. Then use the distributive property: multiply each term of the multiplicand by each term of the multiplier. Finally, combine like terms.

Multiplication can be checked by interchanging the multiplicand and the multiplier and multiplying again. The product should remain the same. Multiplication can also be checked by substituting any convenient value (not 0 or 1) for each variable. The value of the multiplicand times the value of the multiplier should equal the value of the product.

~~~~~~~~~~~~~ **MODEL PROBLEMS** ~~~~~~~~~~~~~

1. Multiply and check: $(3x - 4)(4x + 5)$

Solution: *Check:*

$$\begin{array}{ll} 3x \; - \; 4 & \text{multiplicand} \\ 4x \; + \; 5 & \text{multiplier} \end{array}$$

$$\begin{array}{ll} \overline{12x^2 \, - \, 16x} & \text{partial product} \\ \quad + \, 15x \, - \, 20 & \text{partial product} \\ \overline{12x^2 \, - \quad x \, - \, 20} & \text{product} \end{array}$$

$$\begin{array}{l} 4x \; + \; 5 \\ 3x \; - \; 4 \\ \hline 12x^2 \, + \, 15x \\ \quad - \, 16x \, - \, 20 \\ \hline 12x^2 \, - \quad x \, - \, 20 \end{array}$$

Answer: $12x^2 - x - 20$

2. Multiply and check: $(x^2 + 3xy + 9y^2)(x - 3y)$

Solution: *Check:*

Let $x = 5, y = 2$

$$\begin{array}{l} x^2 + 3xy \, + 9y^2 \longrightarrow \quad 25 + 30 + 36 = \quad 91 \\ x \; - \, 3y \quad\quad\quad\longrightarrow \quad\quad\quad\quad 5 - 6 = - \, 1 \\ \hline x^3 + 3x^2y + 9xy^2 \\ \quad - \, 3x^2y - 9xy^2 - 27y^3 \quad\quad\quad\quad\quad\quad = -91 \quad \text{product} \\ \hline x^3 + 0 \quad\; + 0 \quad\; - \, 27y^3 \quad \text{product} \longrightarrow \quad 125 - 216 = -91 \end{array}$$

Answer: $x^3 - 27y^3$

Exercises

In 1–66, multiply:

1. $(a + 2)(a + 3)$ **2.** $(c + 6)(c + 1)$ **3.** $(x - 5)(x - 3)$

4. $(d - 6)(d - 5)$ **5.** $(c + 8)(c - 6)$ **6.** $(d + 9)(d - 3)$

7. $(x - 7)(x + 2)$ **8.** $(y - 4)(y + 12)$ **9.** $(m + 3)(m - 7)$

10. $(z - 5)(z + 8)$ **11.** $(s + 9)(s + 5)$ **12.** $(f + 10)(f - 8)$

13. $(t + 15)(t - 6)$ **14.** $(b - 8)(b - 10)$ **15.** $(w - 13)(w + 7)$

16. $(6 + y)(5 + y)$ **17.** $(8 - e)(6 - e)$ **18.** $(12 - r)(6 + r)$

19. $(x + 5)(x - 5)$ **20.** $(y + 7)(y - 7)$ **21.** $(a + 9)(a - 9)$

22. $(2x + 1)(x - 6)$ **23.** $(2y - 3)(y + 2)$ **24.** $(c - 5)(2c - 4)$

25. $(2a + 9)(3a + 1)$ **26.** $(3x - 4)(4x + 3)$ **27.** $(5y - 2)(3y - 1)$

28. $(2x + 3)(2x - 3)$ **29.** $(5z - 1)(5z + 1)$ **30.** $(3d + 8)(3d - 8)$

31. $(x + y)(x + y)$ **32.** $(a - b)(a - b)$ **33.** $(a + b)(a - b)$

34. $(a + 2b)(a + 3b)$ **35.** $(2c - d)(3c + d)$ **36.** $(x - 4y)(x + 4y)$

37. $(2z + 5w)(3z - 4w)$

38. $(5y + 12x)(7x - 2y)$

39. $(9x - 5y)(2x + 3y)$

40. $(5k + 2m)(3r + 4s)$

41. $(3x + 4y)(3x - 4y)$

42. $(6a - 5b)(6a + 5b)$

43. $(r^2 + 5)(r^2 - 2)$

44. $(s^2 - 2)(s^2 - 4)$

45. $(x^2 - y^2)(x^2 + y^2)$

46. $(r^3 - s^3)(r^3 + s^3)$

47. $(x^2 + 3x + 5)(x + 2)$

48. $(y^2 - 2y + 6)(y - 2)$

49. $(2c^2 - 3c - 1)(2c + 1)$

50. $(3 - 2d - d^2)(5 - 2d)$

51. $(c^2 - 2c + 4)(c + 2)$

52. $(d^2 - 3d + 9)(d + 3)$

53. $(2x^2 - 3x + 1)(3x - 2)$

54. $(3y^2 - 9y + 4)(4y + 5)$

55. $(3x^2 - 4xy + y^2)(4x + 3y)$

56. $(4a^2 - 3ab - 2b^2)(2a - 5b)$.

57. $(x^3 - 3x^2 + 2x - 4)(3x - 1)$

58. $(2x + 1)(3x - 4)(x + 3)$

59. $(x^2 - 4x + 1)(x^2 + 5x - 2)$

60. $(x + 4)(x + 4)(x + 4)$

61. $(a + 5)^3$

62. $(x - y)^3$

63. $(5 + x^2 - 2x)(2x - 3)$

64. $(5x - 4 + 2x^2)(3 + 4x)$

65. $(2xy + x^2 + y^2)(x + y)$

66. $(3b^2 - 2c^2 - bc)(3b - 2c)$

In 67–74, simplify the expression.

67. $(x + 7)(x - 2) - x^2$

68. $2(3x + 1)(2x - 3) + 14x$

69. $8x^2 - (4x + 3)(2x - 1)$

70. $(x + 4)(x + 3) - (x - 2)(x - 5)$

71. $(3y + 5)(2y - 3) - (y + 7)(5y - 1)$

72. $(y + 4)^2 - (y - 3)^2$

73. $(x + y)^2 + x(x + 3y)$

74. $r(r - 2s) - (r - s)$

In 75–79, use symbols of grouping to write an algebraic expression which represents the answer. Then simplify the expression.

75. The length of a rectangle is $2x - 5$ and its width is $x + 7$. Express the area of the rectangle.

76. The dimensions of a rectangle are represented by $11x - 8$ and $3x + 5$. Represent the area of the rectangle.

77. The dimensions of a rectangle are represented by $7c - 8d$ and $3c + 5d$. Represent the area of the rectangle.

78. The price of a coat is represented by $(2x + 5)$ dollars. Represent the amount a man paid for $(3x - 1)$ of these coats.

79. A plane travels at a rate represented by $(x + 100)$ miles per hour. Represent the distance it can travel in $(2x + 3)$ hours.

6. Dividing a Polynomial by a Monomial

Since division is the inverse operation of multiplication, if $(x + y)2 = 2x + 2y$, then $\dfrac{2x + 2y}{2} = x + y$.

We can obtain the same result by using the multiplicative inverse and the distributive property:

$$\frac{2x + 2y}{2} = \tfrac{1}{2}(2x + 2y) = \tfrac{1}{2}(2x) + \tfrac{1}{2}(2y) = x + y$$

Observe that the quotient $x + y$ can be obtained by dividing each term of $2x + 2y$ by 2. Thus, $\dfrac{2x + 2y}{2} = \dfrac{2x}{2} + \dfrac{2y}{2} = x + y$.

In general, for all numbers a, x, and y $(a \neq 0)$:

$$\frac{ax + ay}{a} = \frac{ax}{a} + \frac{ay}{a} = x + y$$

Usually, the middle step $\dfrac{ax}{a} + \dfrac{ay}{a}$ is done mentally.

Procedure. To divide a polynomial by a monomial, divide each term of the polynomial by the monomial.

~~~~~~~~~~~ **MODEL PROBLEMS** ~~~~~~~~~~~

In 1 and 2, divide:

1. $(8a^5 - 6a^4) \div 2a^2 = 4a^3 - 3a^2$

2. $\dfrac{24x^3y^4 - 18x^2y^2 - 6xy}{-6xy} = -4x^2y^3 + 3xy + 1$

Exercises

In 1–33, divide:

1. $(10x + 20y) \div 5$

2. $(18r - 27s) \div 9$

3. $(14x + 7) \div 7$

4. $(cm + cn) \div c$

5. $(xr - yr) \div r$

6. $(tr - r) \div r$

7. $\dfrac{12a - 6b}{-2}$

8. $\dfrac{8c^2 - 12d^2}{-4}$

9. $\dfrac{15x^2 - 5}{-5}$

10. $\dfrac{m^2 + 8m}{m}$

11. $\dfrac{p + prt}{p}$

12. $\dfrac{2e^2 - 5e}{e}$

13. $\dfrac{y^2 - 5y}{-y}$

14. $\dfrac{18d^3 + 12d^2}{6d}$

15. $\dfrac{-20x^2 + 15x}{-5x}$

16. $\dfrac{18r^5 + 12r^3}{6r^2}$

17. $\dfrac{16t^5 - 8t^4}{4t^2}$

18. $\dfrac{-40x^6 + 16x^4}{8x^4}$

19. $\dfrac{9y^9 - 6y^6}{-3y^3}$

20. $\dfrac{-15x^6 + 10x^4}{-5x^2}$

21. $\dfrac{8a^3 - 4a^2}{-4a^2}$

22. $\dfrac{3ab^2 - 4a^2b}{ab}$

23. $\dfrac{4c^2d - 12cd^2}{4cd}$

24. $\dfrac{2\pi r^2 + 2\pi rh}{2\pi r}$

25. $\dfrac{-6a^2b - 12ab^2}{-2ab}$

26. $\dfrac{-10a^3b^2 - 5a^2b^3}{-5a^2b^2}$

27. $\dfrac{36a^4b^2 - 18a^2b^2}{-18a^2b^2}$

28. $\dfrac{-5y^5 + 15y - 25}{-5}$

29. $\dfrac{-2a^2 - 3a + 1}{-1}$

30. $\dfrac{1.6a^6x^2 - .8a^5y^2 + 1.2a^4z^2}{.4a^2}$

31. $\dfrac{2.4y^5 + 1.2y^4 - .6y^3}{-.6y^3}$

32. $\dfrac{15r^4s^4 + 20r^3s^3 - 5r^2s^2}{-5r^2s^2}$

33. $\dfrac{x^3y^3 - x^2y^2 + xy}{xy}$

34. Represent in simplest form the number of weeks in $14x + 7$ days.

35. If $px + py$ represents the cost of p suits, represent in simplest form the cost of 1 suit.

36. The area of a rectangle is $75r^2 + 15r$. Represent in simplest form its width if its length is:

    a. 5   *b.* 3   *c.* r *d.* $15r$

37. If $60x^2 + 20x$ represents the distance traveled by a man, represent in simplest form the number of miles per hour he travels if the number of hours he travels is:

    a. 5   *b.* 20   *c.* x *d.* $10x$ *e.* $20x$

7. Dividing a Polynomial by a Polynomial

To divide one polynomial by another, we use a procedure similar to the one used when dividing one arithmetic number by another. When we divide 736 by 32, we discover through repeated subtractions how many times 32 is contained in 736. Likewise, when we divide $x^2 + 6x + 8$ by $x + 2$, we discover through repeated subtractions how many times $x + 2$ is contained in $x^2 + 6x + 8$.

See how dividing $x^2 + 6x + 8$ by $x + 2$ follows the same pattern as dividing 736 by 32:

How To Proceed	*Solution 1*	*Solution 2*

1. Write the usual division form.

$$32\overline{)736} \qquad x + 2\overline{)x^2 + 6x + 8}$$

2. Divide the left number of the dividend by the left number of the divisor to obtain the first number of the quotient.

$$\begin{array}{r} 2 \\ 32\overline{)736} \end{array} \qquad \begin{array}{r} x \\ x + 2\overline{)x^2 + 6x + 8} \end{array}$$

3. Multiply the whole divisor by the first number of the quotient.

$$\begin{array}{r} 2 \\ 32\overline{)736} \\ 64 \end{array} \qquad \begin{array}{r} x \\ x + 2\overline{)x^2 + 6x + 8} \\ x^2 + 2x \end{array}$$

4. Subtract this product from the dividend and bring down the next number of the dividend to obtain the new dividend.

$$\begin{array}{r} 2 \\ 32\overline{)736} \\ 64 \\ \hline 96 \end{array} \qquad \begin{array}{r} x \\ x + 2\overline{)x^2 + 6x + 8} \\ x^2 + 2x \\ \hline 4x + 8 \end{array}$$

5. Divide the left number of the new dividend by the left number of the divisor to obtain the next number of the quotient.

$$\begin{array}{r} 23 \\ 32\overline{)736} \\ 64 \\ \hline 96 \end{array} \qquad \begin{array}{r} x + 4 \\ x + 2\overline{)x^2 + 6x + 8} \\ x^2 + 2x \\ \hline 4x + 8 \end{array}$$

6. Repeat steps 3 and 4, multiplying the whole divisor by the second number of the quotient. Subtract the result from the new dividend. The last remainder is 0.

$$\begin{array}{r} 23 \\ 32\overline{)736} \\ 64 \\ \hline 96 \\ 96 \\ \hline \end{array} \qquad \begin{array}{r} x + 4 \\ x + 2\overline{)x^2 + 6x + 8} \\ x^2 + 2x \\ \hline 4x + 8 \\ 4x + 8 \\ \hline \end{array}$$

Ans. 23   *Ans.* $x + 4$

[*Note:* When the dividend is not exactly divisible by the divisor, the last remainder will not be zero.]

To check the division, test the relationship quotient $\times$ divisor $+$ remainder $=$ dividend as shown at the right.

23	$x + 4$
32	$x + 2$
46	$x^2 + 4x$
69	$\quad\quad + 2x + 8$
736	$x^2 + 6x + 8$

ARRANGING TERMS IN DIVISION

Division becomes more convenient if the terms of both the divisor and the dividend are arranged in descending or ascending powers of one variable.

For example, if $3x - 1 + x^3 - 3x^2$ is to be divided by $x - 1$, write:

$$x - 1 \overline{)x^3 - 3x^2 + 3x - 1}$$

MISSING POWERS IN DIVISION

If $x^3 + 8$ is to be divided by $x + 2$, note that the terms containing x^2 and x are missing in the dividend. In order to arrange the terms of the dividend in descending powers of x, we use a zero as the coefficient of each missing term in the dividend when we set down our division form. We write:

$$x + 2 \overline{)x^3 + 0x^2 + 0x + 8}$$

CHECKING DIVISION

Division may be checked by using the relationship:

$$\text{quotient} \times \text{divisor} + \text{remainder} = \text{dividend}$$

Division can also be checked by substituting any convenient value (not 0 or 1) for each variable. Do not use values which make the value of the divisor zero. When the dividend, divisor, quotient, and remainder are evaluated, their values must satisfy the following relationship:

$$\text{quotient} \times \text{divisor} + \text{remainder} = \text{dividend}$$

Procedure. To divide a polynomial by a polynomial:

1. **Arrange the terms of both divisor and dividend according to descending or ascending powers of one variable.**
2. **Divide the first term of the dividend by the first term of the divisor to obtain the first term of the quotient.**
3. **Multiply the whole divisor by the first term of the quotient.**
4. **Subtract this product from the dividend to obtain the new dividend.**
5. **Repeat steps 2 to 4 until the remainder is 0 or until the degree of the remainder is less than the degree of the divisor.**
6. **If the remainder is not 0, write the division as:**

$$\frac{\text{dividend}}{\text{divisor}} = \text{quotient} + \frac{\text{remainder}}{\text{divisor}}$$

MODEL PROBLEMS

1. Divide $5s + 6s^2 - 15$ by $2s + 3$. Check.

Solution:

Arrange terms of dividend in descending powers of s.

$$
\begin{array}{r}
3s - 2 \\
2s + 3\overline{)6s^2 + 5s - 15} \\
\underline{6s^2 + 9s} \\
-4s - 15 \\
\underline{-4s - 6} \\
-9
\end{array}
$$

Check:

$$
\begin{array}{ll}
2s + 3 & \text{divisor} \\
3s - 2 & \text{quotient} \\
\hline
6s^2 + 9s & \\
 -4s - 6 & \\
\hline
6s^2 + 5s - 6 & \\
 -9 & \text{remainder} \\
\hline
6s^2 + 5s - 15 & \text{dividend}
\end{array}
$$

Answer: $3s - 2 + \dfrac{-9}{2s + 3}$

2. Divide $3x^3 - 5y^3 + 18xy^2 - 14x^2y$ by $3x - 5y$.

Solution:

Arrange terms in descending powers of x.

$$
\begin{array}{r}
x^2 - 3xy + y^2 \\
3x - 5y\overline{)3x^3 - 14x^2y + 18xy^2 - 5y^3} \\
\underline{3x^3 - 5x^2y} \\
-9x^2y + 18xy^2 \\
\underline{-9x^2y + 15xy^2} \\
3xy^2 - 5y^3 \\
\underline{3xy^2 - 5y^3}
\end{array}
$$

Answer: $x^2 - 3xy + y^2$

3. Divide $x^3 + 8$ by $x + 2$.

Solution:

Use zeros as the coefficients of the missing terms.

$$
\begin{array}{r}
x^2 - 2x + 4 \\
x + 2\overline{)x^3 + 0x^2 + 0x + 8} \\
\underline{x^3 + 2x^2} \\
-2x^2 + 0x \\
\underline{-2x^2 - 4x} \\
4x + 8 \\
\underline{4x + 8}
\end{array}
$$

Answer: $x^2 - 2x + 4$

Exercises

In 1–34, divide and check.

1. $b^2 + 5b + 6$ by $b + 3$
2. $c^2 - 8c + 7$ by $c - 1$
3. $r^2 + 2r - 15$ by $r + 5$
4. $t^2 - 7t - 60$ by $t - 12$
5. $x^2 - 15x - 54$ by $x + 3$
6. $y^2 + 22y + 85$ by $y + 17$
7. $66 + 17x + x^2$ by $6 + x$
8. $30 - t - t^2$ by $5 - t$
9. $3t^2 - 8t + 4$ by $3t - 2$
10. $21a^2 - 10a + 1$ by $3a - 1$
11. $15x^2 - 19x - 56$ by $5x + 7$
12. $16y^2 - 46y + 15$ by $8y - 3$
13. $2x^2 - xy - 6y^2$ by $x - 2y$
14. $21x^2 - 72xy - 165y^2$ by $3x - 15y$
15. $45x^2 + 69xy - 10y^2$ by $3x + 5y$
16. $40x^2 + 11xy - 63y^2$ by $8x - 9y$
17. $56x^2 - 15 - 11x$ by $7x + 3$
18. $15 + 4a^2 - 16a$ by $2a - 3$
19. $a^2 - 8b^2 + 7ab$ by $a + 8b$
20. $cd + c^2 - 30d^2$ by $c - 5d$
21. $15ab + 9b^2 + 6a^2$ by $2a + 3b$
22. $5cd - 3d^2 + 2c^2$ by $2c - d$
23. $x^2 - 64$ by $x - 8$
24. $y^2 - 100$ by $y + 10$
25. $4m^2 - 49n^2$ by $2m + 7n$
26. $64a^2 - 81b^2$ by $8a - 9b$
27. $x^3 - 8x^2 + 17x - 10$ by $x - 5$
28. $6y^3 + y^2 - 28y - 30$ by $2y - 5$
29. $6b^3 - 8b^2 - 17b - 6$ by $3b + 2$
30. $2c^3 - 4c - c^2 + 3$ by $2c + 3$
31. $6y^3 + 11y^2 - 1$ by $3y + 1$
32. $d^3 - 64$ by $d - 4$
33. $8x^3 + 27$ by $2x + 3$
34. $a^3 - 8b^3$ by $a - 2b$

In 35–48, find the quotient and the remainder. Check the answer.

35. $(x^2 - 9x + 7) \div (x - 2)$
36. $(4x^2 + 6x + 9) \div (2x - 5)$
37. $(3x^2 + 9x - 4) \div (3x + 3)$
38. $(12x^2 - 9 + 24x) \div (6x - 3)$
39. $(c^3 - 8c^2 - 6c + 9) \div (c - 2)$
40. $(3c^3 + 14c^2 + 4c - 4) \div (c + 4)$
41. $(2 - 8a + 2a^3 - 5a^2) \div (2a + 3)$
42. $(6y^3 - 10 + 11y^2) \div (3y + 1)$
43. $(10x^2 - 3xy + 9y^2) \div (2x + y)$
44. $(6a^2 + 5ab - 4b^2) \div (3a - 2b)$
45. $(a^2 - 28b^2 + 3ab) \div (a - 6b)$
46. $(10x^2 - 5y^2 + 38xy) \div (2x + 8y)$
47. $(x^2 + 25) \div (x + 5)$
48. $(x^3 - 27) \div (x + 3)$

In 49–54, divide and check.

49. $\dfrac{x^3 + 2x^2 - 2x - 12}{x^2 + 4x + 6}$

50. $\dfrac{6r^3 - 30r + 14r^2 + 12}{2r^2 + 6r - 6}$

51. $\dfrac{2x^3 - x^2 - 4x + 3}{x^2 + 1 - 2x}$

52. $\dfrac{y^4 - 6y^2 + 8}{y^2 - 4}$

53. $\dfrac{4a^4 - 4a^2b^2 - 15b^4}{2a^2 + 3b^2}$

54. $\dfrac{4x^4 + 1}{2x^2 + 2x + 1}$

55. One factor of $x^2 - 8x - 9$ is $x + 1$. Find the other factor.
56. One factor of $3y^2 + 8y + 4$ is $3y + 2$. Find the other factor.
57. Is $x - 2$ a factor of $x^3 - 2x^2 + 4x - 6$? Why?

CHAPTER IX

FIRST-DEGREE EQUATIONS AND INEQUALITIES IN ONE VARIABLE

1. Using the Additive Inverse in Solving Equations

When we were dealing with the set of numbers of arithmetic, we used the addition property of equality to solve the first-degree equation $x - 4 = 7$ and the subtraction property to solve $x + 5 = 9$.

$$x - 4 = 7 \qquad\qquad x + 5 = 9$$
$$x - 4 + 4 = 7 + 4 \qquad x + 5 - 5 = 9 - 5$$
$$x = 11 \qquad\qquad x = 4$$

The addition and subtraction properties of equalities also hold true in the set of signed numbers. When the same signed number is added to both members of an equation or subtracted from both members of an equation, the equality is retained. However, with our knowledge of signed numbers, we can solve equations such as $x - 4 = 7$ and $x + 5 = 9$ using only the addition property of equality.

Remember that the sum of a number and its additive inverse (opposite) is 0; that is, $n + (-n) = 0$. The following model problems illustrate how the additive inverse is used in solving equations:

~~~~~~~~~~~~~~~~ *MODEL PROBLEMS* ~~~~~~~~~~~~~~~~

1. Solve and check: $x - 4 = 7$

How To Proceed	*Solution*	*Check*
To transform $x - 4$ to x, add $+4$, the additive inverse (opposite) of -4, to both members of the equation.	$x - 4 = 7$ $x - 4 + (+4) = 7 + (+4)$ $x + 0 = 11$ $x = 11$	$x - 4 = 7$ $11 - 4 \stackrel{?}{=} 7$ $7 = 7$ (true)

Answer: $x = 11$, or solution set is $\{11\}$.

2. Solve and check: $x + 5 = 3$

How To Proceed	*Solution*	*Check*
To eliminate $+5$, add its additive inverse (opposite) -5 to both members of the equation.	$x + 5 = 3$ $x + 5 + (-5) = 3 + (-5)$ $x + 0 = -2$ $x = -2$	$x + 5 = 3$ $(-2) + 5 \overset{?}{=} 3$ $3 = 3$ (true)

Answer: $x = -2$, or solution set is $\{-2\}$.

Exercises

In 1–20, solve for the variable and check.

1. $x - 5 = 13$ **2.** $y + 8 = 12$ **3.** $17 = t - 9$ **4.** $36 = c + 20$
5. $x + 6 = 4$ **6.** $x - 5 = -9$ **7.** $n + 7 = 4$ **8.** $3 = y + 12$
9. $5 + r = -9$ **10.** $-5 = -7 + c$ **11.** $-4 = d - 8$ **12.** $s + 12 = 8$
13. $x + .9 = .5$ **14.** $w - 1.6 = .3$ **15.** $.6 + y = .2$ **16.** $-.3 = s + .7$
17. $n + 3\frac{1}{2} = 2$ **18.** $x - 2\frac{1}{3} = -5$ **19.** $-\frac{1}{2} = n - 1\frac{3}{4}$ **20.** $3\frac{1}{4} = y + 6\frac{1}{2}$

In 21–26, determine the element(s) of the set if $x \in \{\text{signed numbers}\}$.

21. $\{x \mid x - 8 = 12\}$ **22.** $\{x \mid x + 3 = 10\}$ **23.** $\{x \mid x - 3 = -6\}$
24. $\{x \mid x + 7 = 2\}$ **25.** $\{x \mid 9 = x + 15\}$ **26.** $\{x \mid 10 = x + 10\}$

2. Using the Multiplicative Inverse in Solving Equations

The multiplication and division properties of equality hold true in the set of signed numbers as well as in the set of numbers of arithmetic. When both members of an equation are multiplied or divided by the same signed number (not zero), the equality is retained. However, with our knowledge of signed numbers, we can solve equations such as $5x = -20$ and $\dfrac{x}{3} = -2$ using only the multiplication property of equality.

Remember that the product of a number and its multiplicative inverse (reciprocal) is 1; that is, $(n)\left(\dfrac{1}{n}\right) = 1$. The following model problems illustrate how the multiplicative inverse is used in solving equations:

MODEL PROBLEMS

1. Solve and check: $5x = -20$

How To Proceed	*Solution*	*Check*
To transform $5x$ to x, multiply both members of the equation by $\frac{1}{5}$, the multiplicative inverse (reciprocal) of the coefficient 5.	$5x = -20$ $\frac{1}{5}(5x) = \frac{1}{5}(-20)$ $1 \cdot x = -4$ $x = -4$	$5x = -20$ $5(-4) \overset{?}{=} -20$ $-20 = -20$ (true)

Answer: $x = -4$, or solution set is $\{-4\}$.

2. Solve and check: $-\frac{2}{3}y = 18$

How To Proceed	*Solution*	*Check*
To transform $-\frac{2}{3}y$ to y, multiply both members of the equation by $-\frac{3}{2}$, the multiplicative inverse (reciprocal) of the coefficient $-\frac{2}{3}$.	$-\frac{2}{3}y = 18$ $(-\frac{3}{2})(-\frac{2}{3}y) = (-\frac{3}{2})(18)$ $1 \cdot y = -27$ $y = -27$	$-\frac{2}{3}y = 18$ $(-\frac{2}{3})(-27) \overset{?}{=} 18$ $18 = 18$ (true)

Answer: $y = -27$, or solution set is $\{-27\}$.

3. Solve and check: $\dfrac{x}{3} = -2$

How To Proceed	*Solution*	*Check*
In order to transform $\dfrac{x}{3}$, or $\frac{1}{3}x$, to x, multiply both members of the equation by 3, the multiplicative inverse (reciprocal) of $\frac{1}{3}$.	$\dfrac{x}{3} = -2$ $3\left(\dfrac{x}{3}\right) = 3(-2)$ $1 \cdot x = -6$ $x = -6$	$\dfrac{x}{3} = -2$ $\dfrac{-6}{3} \overset{?}{=} -2$ $-2 = -2$ (true)

Answer: $x = -6$, or solution set is $\{-6\}$.

Exercises

In 1–30, find the solution set of the sentence and check.

1. $3m = 15$ **2.** $9t = 36$ **3.** $15x = -45$ **4.** $23z = -46$

5. $-77 = 11k$ **6.** $4x = 9$ **7.** $-5 = 2y$ **8.** $9a = -6$

9. $-13a = 65$ **10.** $-8k = 8.8$ **11.** $-5m = -35$ **12.** $2x = -\frac{1}{9}$

13. $-x = 18$ **14.** $\frac{1}{4}y = 2$ **15.** $\frac{1}{3}z = 6$ **16.** $\frac{1}{2}c = -8$

17. $-20 = \frac{2}{5}d$ **18.** $\frac{5}{8}x = -10$ **19.** $12 = -\frac{2}{3}x$ **20.** $-\frac{3}{4}x = 36$

21. $\frac{1}{3}x = -1.8$ **22.** $\frac{3}{5}y = \frac{6}{8}$ **23.** $\dfrac{12}{9} = \dfrac{-4}{3}c$ **24.** $-\frac{3}{2}x = 1\frac{1}{2}$

25. $\dfrac{-25}{9} = 8\frac{1}{3}t$ **26.** $\dfrac{x}{2} = 12$ **27.** $\dfrac{y}{3} = -15$ **28.** $\dfrac{m}{-4} = -2\frac{1}{2}$

29. $\dfrac{c}{9} = -\dfrac{2}{3}$ **30.** $\dfrac{2x}{3} = \dfrac{4}{9}$

In 31–35, determine the elements of the set if $x \in$ {signed numbers}.

31. $\{x \mid 4x = 28\}$ **32.** $\{x \mid -3x = 15\}$ **33.** $\{x \mid \frac{1}{5}x = 25\}$

34. $\left\{x \mid \dfrac{x}{5} = -20\right\}$ **35.** $\{x \mid -\frac{4}{5}x = 40\}$

3. Using Both the Additive and Multiplicative Inverses in Solving Equations

When the solution of an equation requires the use of both the additive and the multiplicative inverses, either inverse may be used first. However, the solution is usually easier when the additive inverse is used first.

~~~~~~~~~~~ **MODEL PROBLEMS** ~~~~~~~~~~~

1. Solve and check: $2x + 3x + 4 = -6$

How To Proceed	*Solution*
1. Write the equation.	$2x + 3x + 4 = -6$
2. Combine like terms.	$5x + 4 = -6$
3. Add -4, the additive inverse of $+4$.	$5x + 4 + (-4) = -6 + (-4)$
	$5x = -10$
4. Multiply by $\frac{1}{5}$, the multiplicative inverse of 5.	$\frac{1}{5}(5x) = \frac{1}{5}(-10)$
	$x = -2$

Check

$$2x + 3x + 4 = -6$$
$$2(-2) + 3(-2) + 4 \overset{?}{=} -6$$
$$(-4) + (-6) + 4 \overset{?}{=} -6$$
$$-6 = -6 \quad \text{(true)}$$

Answer: $x = -2$, or solution set is $\{-2\}$.

[*Note:* In step 3, if we had subtracted 4 from both members of the equation, we would have obtained the same result, $5x = -10$. Also, in step 4, if we had divided both members of the equation by 5, we would have obtained the same result, $x = -2$.]

2. Solve and check: $\frac{3}{4}x - 4 = 17$

How To Proceed	*Solution*	*Check*
1. Write the equation.	$\frac{3}{4}x - 4 = 17$	$\frac{3}{4}x - 4 = 17$
2. Add $+4$, the additive inverse of -4.	$\frac{3}{4}x - 4 + (+4) = 17 + (+4)$	$\frac{3}{4}(28) - 4 \overset{?}{=} 17$
	$\frac{3}{4}x = 21$	$21 - 4 \overset{?}{=} 17$
3. Multiply by $\frac{4}{3}$, the multiplicative inverse of $\frac{3}{4}$.	$\frac{4}{3}(\frac{3}{4}x) = \frac{4}{3}(21)$	$17 = 17$
	$x = 28$	(true)

Answer: $x = 28$, or solution set is $\{28\}$.

Exercises

In 1–30, solve the equation and check.

1. $3x + 4 = 16$
2. $5x - 9 = 16$
3. $35 = 21y - 7$
4. $2c + 1 = -31$
5. $5t - 2 = -32$
6. $2y + 18 = 8$
7. $2x + 9 = 37$
8. $5x + 15 = 0$
9. $4x + 2 = -34$
10. $-42 = 5x + 28$
11. $-5x + 9 = 14$
12. $-34 = 2 - 6t$
13. $13 = 8x - 7$
14. $4y + 8 = 2$
15. $-32 = 24y - 20$
16. $\frac{1}{2}z + 6 = 15$
17. $9 = \frac{1}{3}c + 11$
18. $\frac{1}{5}y - 3 = -4$
19. $\frac{2}{3}m + 7 = 29$
20. $\frac{3}{4}a + 14 = 8$
21. $\frac{2}{5}r - 9 = -19$
22. $\frac{3}{2}x - 14 = 16$
23. $\frac{9}{5}c + 32 = -4$
24. $-25 = \frac{7}{3}r - 11$
25. $-5.4 = 2.6 + 2x$
26. $1\frac{1}{4} - 4x = 17\frac{1}{4}$
27. $9x - 5x + 9 = 1$
28. $5x + 2x - 17 = 53$
29. $2y - 8y + 29 = 5$
30. $8x - 21 - 5x = -15$

In 31–36, determine the element(s) of the set if $x \in \{$signed numbers$\}$.

31. $\{x \mid 2x + 3 = 11\}$
32. $\{x \mid 5x + 30 = 10\}$
33. $\{x \mid 15 = 6x - 15\}$
34. $\{x \mid \frac{2}{3}x - 12 = 60\}$
35. $\{x \mid -19 = \frac{2}{3}x + 17\}$
36. $\{x \mid 5x - 9x + 5 = -11\}$

4. Solving Equations Which Have the Variable in Both Members

A variable represents a number; as we know, any number may be added to or subtracted from both members of an equation without changing the solution set. Therefore, the same variable (or the same multiple of the same variable) may be added to or subtracted from both members of an equation without changing the solution set.

To solve $8x = 30 + 5x$, we first eliminate $5x$ from the right member of the equation by either of the following two methods:

Method 1	Method 2
Subtract $5x$ from both members of the equation, S_{5x}.	Add $-5x$, the additive inverse of $+5x$, to both members of the equation, A_{-5x}.
$8x = 30 + 5x$	$8x = 30 + 5x$
$8x - 5x = 30 + 5x - 5x$	$8x + (-5x) = 30 + 5x + (-5x)$
$3x = 30$	$3x = 30$
$x = 10$	$x = 10$

Answer: $x = 10$, or solution set is $\{10\}$. The check is left to the student.

Procedure. To solve an equation which has the variable in both members, transform it into an equivalent equation in which the variable appears only in one member. Then solve this equation.

~~~~~~~ MODEL PROBLEMS ~~~~~~~

1. Solve and check: $7x = 63 - 2x$

How To Proceed	*Solution*	*Check*
1. Write the equation.	$7x = 63 - 2x$	$7x = 63 - 2x$
		$7(7) \overset{?}{=} 63 - 2(7)$
2. A_{+2x}	$7x + (+2x) = 63 - 2x + (+2x)$	$49 \overset{?}{=} 63 - 14$
3. Collect like terms.	$9x = 63$	$49 = 49$ (true)
4. D_9 or $M_{\frac{1}{9}}$	$x = 7$	

Answer: $x = 7$, or solution set is $\{7\}$.

2. Solve and check: $5t - 12 = 8t + 24$

How To Proceed	*Solution*
1. Write the equation.	$5t - 12 = 8t + 24$
2. A_{+12}	$5t - 12 + (+12) = 8t + 24 + (+12)$
3. Collect like terms.	$5t = 8t + 36$
4. S_{8t} or A_{-8t}	$5t + (-8t) = 8t + 36 + (-8t)$
5. Collect like terms.	$-3t = 36$
6. D_{-3} or $M_{-\frac{1}{3}}$	$t = -12$

Answer: $t = -12$, or solution set is $\{-12\}$. The check is left to the student.

3. If five times a number is decreased by 13, the result is equal to twice the number increased by 11. Find the number.

Solution:

$$\text{Let } x = \text{the number.}$$
$$\text{Then } 5x - 13 = \text{five times the number decreased by 13.}$$
$$\text{And } 2x + 11 = \text{twice the number increased by 11.}$$

		Check
$5x - 13 = 2x + 11$		
$5x - 2x - 13 = 2x - 2x + 11$	S_{2x} or A_{-2x}	Show that 8 satisfies the
$3x - 13 = 11$		original question:
$3x - 13 + 13 = 11 + 13$	A_{13}	$5 \times 8 - 13 = 27$
$3x = 24$		$2 \times 8 + 11 = 27$
$x = 8$	D_3 or $M_{\frac{1}{3}}$	

Answer: The number is 8.

~~~~~~

Exercises

In 1–67, solve the equation and check.

1. $7x = 10 + 2x$	**2.** $9x = 44 - 2x$	**3.** $12y = 3y + 27$
4. $8c = 6 - c$	**5.** $6x = 2x + 20$	**6.** $5c = 28 + c$
7. $9x = 3x - 54$	**8.** $y = 4y + 30$	**9.** $2d = 36 + 5d$
10. $6\frac{1}{2}c = 7 - \frac{1}{2}c$	**11.** $2\frac{1}{4}y = 1\frac{1}{4}y - 8$	**12.** $.8m = .2m + 24$
13. $8y = 90 - 2y$	**14.** $4a - 55 = 9a$	**15.** $7m + 36 = 11m$
16. $4 - 2y = 6y$	**17.** $3 - y = 8y$	**18.** $2.3x + 36 = .3x$
19. $2\frac{3}{4}x + 24 = 3x$	**20.** $12 - 1\frac{1}{2}x = 2\frac{1}{2}x$	**21.** $81 - \frac{3}{4}x = 1\frac{1}{2}x$
22. $5a - 40 = 3a$	**23.** $5c = 2c - 81$	**24.** $x = 9x - 72$
25. $y = 9y - 56$	**26.** $.5m - 30 = 1.1m$	**27.** $4\frac{1}{4}c = 9\frac{3}{4}c + 44$

28. $7r + 10 = 3r + 50$ **29.** $8t + 17 = 5t + 35$

30. $4y + 20 = 5y + 9$ **31.** $8s + 56 = 14s + 26$

32. $37 + x = 5x + 9$ **33.** $6b + 11 = 2b + 47$

34. $7x + 8 = 6x + 1$ **35.** $x + 4 = 9x + 4$

36. $9x - 3 = 2x + 46$ **37.** $y + 30 = 12y - 14$

38. $6x - 7 = 4x + 3$ **39.** $2z + 1 = 10z - 1$

40. $c + 20 = 55 - 4c$ **41.** $9a - 23 = 5a - 11$

42. $2d + 36 = -3d - 54$ **43.** $-4d - 37 = 7d + 18$

44. $7y - 5 = 9y + 29$ **45.** $2m - 1 = 6m + 1$

46. $5c - 8 = 2c + 7$ **47.** $2 + 7y = 11 - 2y$

48. $4x - 3 = 47 - x$ **49.** $5c - 13 = 43 - 2c$

50. $3b - 8 = 14 - 8b$ **51.** $\frac{2}{3}t - 11 = 64 - 4\frac{1}{3}t$

52. $11y - 8 = 22 - y$ **53.** $10x - 21 = 2x - 5$

54. $18 - 4n = 6 - 16n$ **55.** $-2y - 39 = 5y - 18$

56. $7x - 4 = 5x - x + 35$ **57.** $10 - x - 3x = 7x - 23$

58. $8a - 15 - 6a = 85 - 3a$ **59.** $5d + 9 - 4d = 51 - 5d$

60. $5x - 2x + 13 = x + 1$ **61.** $8c + 1 = 7c - 14 - 2c$

62. $9c - 2c + 8 = 4c + 38$ **63.** $12x - 5 = 8x - x + 50$

64. $6d - 12 - d = 9d + 53 + d$ **65.** $8x - 4 + 7 = 6x + x + 9$

66. $3m - 5m - 12 = 7m - 88 - 5$ **67.** $5 - 3z - 18 = z - 1 + 8z$

68. Eight times a number equals 35 more than the number. Find the number.

69. Six times a number equals 3 times the number, increased by 24. Find the number.

70. Twice a number is equal to 35 more than 7 times the number. Find the number.

71. If a number is multiplied by 7, the result is the same as when 25 is added to twice the number. Find the number.

72. If 3 times a number is increased by 10, the result is equal to 8 times the number. Find the number.

73. If twice a number is subtracted from 132, the result equals four times the number. Find the number.

74. If 3 is added to 5 times a number, the result is the same as when 15 is added to twice the number. Find the number.

75. If 6 times a number is increased by 9, the result is the same as the number increased by 34. Find the number.

76. If 4 times a number is decreased by 9, the result is the same as when 3 times the number is decreased by 1. Find the number.

77. If 4 times a number is increased by 10, the result is the same as when 9 times the number is diminished by 50.

78. If 3 times a number is increased by 5, the result is the same as when 77 is decreased by 9 times the number. Find the number.

79. If six times a number is increased by 3, the result is equal to 9 times the number increased by 27. Find the number.

80. Seven times a number exceeds 150 by the same amount that 3 times the number exceeds 250. Find the number.
81. The excess of 50 over twice a number is equal to the excess of 6 times the number over 6. Find the number.

5. Solving Equations Containing Parentheses

Procedure. To solve an equation containing parentheses, transform it into an equation which does not contain parentheses. Do this by performing the indicated operation on the numbers and variables contained within the parentheses. Then solve the transformed equation.

~~~~~~~~~~~~ *MODEL PROBLEMS* ~~~~~~~~~~~~

1. Solve and check: $8x + (2x - 3) = 2$

        [*Note:* $8x + (2x - 3)$ means add $8x$ and $(2x - 3)$.]

How To Proceed	*Solution*
1. Write the equation.	$8x + (2x - 3) = 2$
2. Perform the addition.	$8x + 2x - 3 = 2$
3. Collect like terms.	$10x - 3 = 2$
4. A_{+3}	$10x - 3 + (+3) = 2 + (+3)$
5. Collect like terms.	$10x = 5$
6. D_{10} or $M_{\frac{1}{10}}$	$x = \frac{1}{2}$

Check

$$8x + (2x - 3) = 2$$
$$8 \times \tfrac{1}{2} + (2 \times \tfrac{1}{2} - 3) \overset{?}{=} 2$$
$$8 \times \tfrac{1}{2} + (1 - 3) \overset{?}{=} 2$$
$$4 + (-2) \overset{?}{=} 2$$
$$2 = 2 \quad \text{(true)}$$

Answer: $x = \frac{1}{2}$, or solution set is $\{\frac{1}{2}\}$.

2. Solve and check: $9t - (2t - 4) = 25$

[*Note:* $9t - (2t - 4)$ means from $9t$ subtract $(2t - 4)$.]

How To Proceed	*Solution*	*Check*
1. Write the equation.	$9t - (2t - 4) = 25$	$9t - (2t - 4) = 25$
		$9 \cdot 3 - (2 \cdot 3 - 4) \overset{?}{=} 25$
2. To subtract $(2t - 4)$, add its opposite $(-2t + 4)$.	$9t + (-2t + 4) = 25$	$9 \cdot 3 - (6 - 4) \overset{?}{=} 25$
	$9t - 2t + 4 = 25$	$27 - (2) \overset{?}{=} 25$
		$25 = 25$
3. Collect like terms.	$7t + 4 = 25$	(true)
4. S_4 or A_{-4}	$7t + 4 + (-4) = 25 + (-4)$	
5. Collect like terms.	$7t = 21$	
6. D_7 or $M_{\frac{1}{7}}$	$t = 3$	

Answer: $t = 3$, or solution set is $\{3\}$.

3. Solve and check: $5(3y - 2) = 5$

[*Note:* Since $5(3y - 2)$ means that 5 and $(3y - 2)$ are to be multiplied, we will use the distributive property of multiplication.]

How To Proceed	*Solution*	*Check*
1. Write the equation.	$5(3y - 2) = 5$	$5(3y - 2) = 5$
		$5(3 \cdot 1 - 2) \overset{?}{=} 5$
2. Use the distributive property.	$15y - 10 = 5$	$5(3 - 2) \overset{?}{=} 5$
		$5(1) \overset{?}{=} 5$
3. A_{+10}	$15y - 10 + (+10) = 5 + (+10)$	$5 = 5$
4. Collect like terms.	$15y = 15$	(true)
5. D_{15} or $M_{\frac{1}{15}}$	$y = 1$	

Answer: $y = 1$, or solution set is $\{1\}$.

4. Solve and check: $15x - 3(x + 6) = 6$

> [*Note:* Since $3(x + 6)$ means that 3 and $(x + 6)$ are to be multiplied, we will use the distributive property of multiplication.]

How To Proceed	*Solution*
1. Write the equation.	$15x - 3(x + 6) = 6$
2. Use the distributive property.	$15x - 3x - 18 = 6$
3. Collect like terms.	$12x - 18 = 6$
4. A_{+18}	$12x - 18 + (+18) = 6 + (+18)$
5. Collect like terms.	$12x = 24$
6. D_{12} or $M_{\frac{1}{12}}$	$x = 2$

Check

$$15x - 3(x + 6) = 6$$
$$15(2) - 3(2 + 6) \stackrel{?}{=} 6$$
$$15(2) - 3(8) \stackrel{?}{=} 6$$
$$30 - 24 \stackrel{?}{=} 6$$
$$6 = 6 \quad \text{(true)}$$

Answer: $x = 2$, or solution set is $\{2\}$.

Exercises

In 1–51, solve and check the equation.

1. $x + (x - 6) = 20$

2. $x - (12 - x) = 38$

3. $5y + (2y - 7) = 63$

4. $10y - (5y + 8) = 42$

5. $(15x + 7) - 12 = 4$

6. $(14 - 3c) + 7c = 94$

7. $x + (4x + 32) = 12$

8. $7x - (4x - 39) = 0$

9. $5(x + 2) = 20$

10. $3(y - 9) = 30$

11. $7(a + 3) = 28$

12. $4(b - 6) = 44$

13. $8(2c - 1) = 56$

14. $5(6y - 2) = 50$

15. $2(10 - 3d) = 80$

16. $6(3c - 1) = -42$

17. $7(x + 2) = 5(x + 4)$

18. $3(a - 5) = 2(2a + 1)$

19. $3(2b + 1) - 7 = 50$

20. $5(3c - 2) + 8 = 43$

21. $4(y - 3) + 3y = 16$

22. $6(2s + 3) - 2s = 28$

23. $8y - (6y - 3) = 9$

24. $7r - (6r - 5) = 7$

25. $8y - (5y + 2) = 16$

26. $8w - (3w + 6) = 19$

27. $41 + (3x + 4) = 8x$

28. $11x = 40 + (7x + 4)$

29. $10z - (3z - 11) = 17$

30. $3z = 18 + (5z - 10)$

31. $15a - 2(a + 6) = 14$

32. $8b - 4(b - 2) = 24$

33. $5m - 2(m - 5) = 17$

34. $8t = 23 + 3(2t - 5)$

35. $9 + 2(5v + 3) = 13v$

36. $15c - 4(3c + 2) = 13$

37. $28r - 6(3r - 5) = 40$

38. $22s - 3(5s + 4) = 16$

39. $3a + (2a - 5) = 13 - 2(a + 2)$

40. $2(t - 3) - 17 = 13 - 3(t + 2)$

41. $2(b + 1) - 3b = 3(3 + 2b)$

42. $4(2r + 1) - 3(2r - 5) = 29$

43. $2 - 7(d - 1) = 3(d - 2) - 5(d + 3)$

44. $4(y - 3) - 6(y + 1) = 4(3y + 4) - 2(8 + 6y)$

45. $6(2x + 1) - 3(4x - 3) - (6x + 10) = -(4x - 3) + 3$

46. $(x + 4)(x + 1) = x^2 + 59$

47. $x(x + 1) = (x - 6)(x + 4)$

48. $(y + 3)(y + 2) = y(y + 7)$

49. $(y - 5)(y - 1) - y^2 = -13$

50. $(a + 5)(a - 2) = (a + 1)^2$

51. $(4 - r)(6 + r) = 40 - (r^2 - 4r - 18)$

In 52–54, determine the element(s) of the set if $x \in$ {signed numbers}.

52. $\{x \mid 5x - (3x + 2) = 18\}$

53. $\{x \mid 5 + 3(x - 1) = 37\}$

54. $\{x \mid 6x - 4(2x - 6) = 10\}$

55. The larger of two numbers is 5 more than the smaller. The smaller number plus twice the larger equals 100. Find the numbers.

56. One number is 2 smaller than another. If 4 times the larger is subtracted from 5 times the smaller, the result is 10. Find the numbers.

57. A coat costs $15 more than a dress. Two coats and 4 dresses cost $150. Find the cost of each.

58. Sam is 4 years older than Catherine. If 4 times Catherine's age is subtracted from 5 times Sam's age, the difference is 32 years. Find the age of each.

59. Mr. Powers travels 12 miles less each day in going to and from his job than Mr. Clay does. The difference between the distance Mr. Clay travels in 6 days and the distance that Mr. Powers travels in 5 days is 96 miles. How far does each one travel each day?

6. Solving Equations Involving Absolute Values

Since $|{+}8| = 8$ and $|{-}8| = 8$, both $+8$ and -8 can replace x in the equation $|x| = 8$ and make the resulting sentence true. Therefore, $x = +8$ and $x = -8$ are solutions of $|x| = 8$, and the solution set is $\{+8, -8\}$.

If we apply the definition of absolute value, the two equations $x = 8$ and $x = -8$ together are equivalent to the equation $|x| = 8$.

Procedure. To solve an equation involving the absolute value symbol, first write two equations that do not contain the absolute value symbol and which together are equivalent to the given equation. Then solve the resulting equations.

~~~~~~~~~~ **MODEL PROBLEMS** ~~~~~~~~~~

1. Solve and check: $|5x| = 20$

> [*Note:* $5x = 20$ and $5x = -20$ together are equivalent to $|5x| = 20$.]

Solution

$5x = 20$

$x = 4$ D_5 or $M_{\frac{1}{5}}$

Check

For $x = 4$: $|5x| = 20$

$|5(4)| \overset{?}{=} 20$

$|20| = 20$ (true)

Solution

$5x = -20$

$x = -4$ D_5 or $M_{\frac{1}{5}}$

Check

For $x = -4$: $|5x| = 20$

$|5(-4)| \overset{?}{=} 20$

$|-20| = 20$ (true)

Answer: $x = 4$ and $x = -4$, or solution set is $\{4, -4\}$.

2. Solve and check: $4|x| = 24$

Solution

$4|x| = 24$

$\frac{1}{4} \cdot 4|x| = \frac{1}{4} \cdot 24$ $M_{\frac{1}{4}}$

$|x| = 6$

$x = 6$ and $x = -6$

Check

For $x = 6$: $4|x| = 24$

$4|6| \overset{?}{=} 24$

$4 \cdot 6 \overset{?}{=} 24$

$24 = 24$

(true)

Check

For $x = -6$: $4|x| = 24$

$4|-6| \overset{?}{=} 24$

$4 \cdot 6 \overset{?}{=} 24$

$24 = 24$

(true)

Answer: $x = 6$ and $x = -6$, or solution set is $\{6, -6\}$.

3. Solve and check: $|2x - 3| = 13$

[*Note:* $2x - 3 = 13$ and $2x - 3 = -13$ together are equivalent to $|2x - 3| = 13$.]

Solution	*Check*
$2x - 3 = 13$	For $x = 8$: $|2x - 3| = 13$
$2x - 3 + (+3) = 13 + (+3)$	$|2(8) - 3| \overset{?}{=} 13$
$2x = 16$	$|16 - 3| \overset{?}{=} 13$
$x = 8$	$13 = 13$ (true)

Solution	*Check*
$2x - 3 = -13$	For $x = -5$: $|2x - 3| = 13$
$2x - 3 + (+3) = -13 + (+3)$	$|2(-5) - 3| \overset{?}{=} 13$
$2x = -10$	$|-10 - 3| \overset{?}{=} 13$
$x = -5$	$13 = 13$ (true)

Answer: $x = 8$ and $x = -5$, or solution set is $\{8, -5\}$.

4. Solve and check: $\left|\dfrac{4x + 8}{3}\right| = 12$

[*Note:* $\dfrac{4x + 8}{3} = 12$ and $\dfrac{4x + 8}{3} = -12$ together are equivalent to $\left|\dfrac{4x + 8}{3}\right| = 12$.]

Solution	*Check*
$\dfrac{4x + 8}{3} = 12$	For $x = 7$: $\left|\dfrac{4x + 8}{3}\right| = 12$
$3\left(\dfrac{4x + 8}{3}\right) = 3(12)$	$\left|\dfrac{4(7) + 8}{3}\right| \overset{?}{=} 12$
$4x + 8 = 36$	$\left|\dfrac{28 + 8}{3}\right| \overset{?}{=} 12$
$4x + 8 + (-8) = 36 + (-8)$	$\left|\dfrac{36}{3}\right| \overset{?}{=} 12$
$4x = 28$	
$x = 7$	$|12| = 12$ (true)

Solution   *Check*

$$\frac{4x+8}{3} = -12 \qquad\qquad \text{For } x = -11: \left|\frac{4x+8}{3}\right| = 12$$

$$3\left(\frac{4x+8}{3}\right) = 3(-12) \qquad\qquad \left|\frac{4(-11)+8}{3}\right| \overset{?}{=} 12$$

$$4x + 8 = -36 \qquad\qquad \left|\frac{-44+8}{3}\right| \overset{?}{=} 12$$

$$4x + 8 + (-8) = -36 + (-8)$$

$$4x = -44 \qquad\qquad \left|\frac{-36}{3}\right| \overset{?}{=} 12$$

$$x = -11 \qquad\qquad |-12| = 12 \quad \text{(true)}$$

Answer: $x = 7$ and $x = -11$, or solution set is $\{7, -11\}$.

Exercises

In 1–8, write two equations that do not contain the absolute value symbol and which together are equivalent to the given equation.

1. $|y| = 7$ **2.** $|3x| = 15$ **3.** $|t + 6| = 8$ **4.** $|m - 4| = 7$

5. $|3c + 8| = 29$ **6.** $|6 - 2x| = 2$ **7.** $\left|\frac{2c}{3}\right| = 6$ **8.** $\left|\frac{5c + 1}{4}\right| = 9$

In 9–28, find the solution set of the equation.

9. $|x| = 14$ **10.** $|c| = 10$ **11.** $|3r| = 36$ **12.** $2|m| = 32$

13. $|x + 8| = 17$ **14.** $|r - 6| = 5$ **15.** $2|y + 1| = 8$ **16.** $4|4 - y| = 16$

17. $|2x + 1| = 13$ **18.** $|7 + 5y| = 32$ **19.** $|4c - 1| = 35$

20. $2|2t - 1| = 9$ **21.** $\left|\frac{x}{2}\right| = 10$ **22.** $4\left|\frac{y}{5}\right| = 20$

23. $\frac{1}{2}\left|\frac{t}{3}\right| = 8$ **24.** $-\left|\frac{2x}{3}\right| = -6$ **25.** $\left|\frac{2x + 3}{3}\right| = 3$

26. $\left|\frac{5m - 1}{6}\right| = 4$ **27.** $\left|\frac{2(x + 3)}{9}\right| = 2$ **28.** $\left|\frac{3(3x - 5)}{2}\right| = 15$

7. Solving Equations Containing More Than One Variable

An equation may contain more than one variable. Examples of such equations are $ax = b$, $x + c = d$, and $y - r = z$.

To solve such an equation for one of its variables means to express this particular variable in terms of the other variables. In order to plan the steps in the solution, it may be helpful to compare the equation with a similar equation which contains only the variable being solved for. For example, in solving $bx - c = d$ for x, compare it with $2x - 5 = 19$. The same operations are used in solving both equations.

━━━━━━━━━ **MODEL PROBLEMS** ━━━━━━━━━

1. Solve for x: $ax = b$

Solution

Compare with $2x = 7$.

$$2x = 7 \qquad ax = b$$

$$\frac{2x}{2} = 7 \quad \text{D}_2 \text{ or } \text{M}_{\frac{1}{2}} \qquad \frac{ax}{a} = \frac{b}{a} \quad \text{D}_a \text{ or } \text{M}_{\frac{1}{a}}$$

$$x = \frac{7}{2} \quad Ans. \qquad x = \frac{b}{a} \quad Ans.$$

Check

$$ax = b$$

$$a\left(\frac{b}{a}\right) \overset{?}{=} b$$

$$b = b \quad \text{(true)}$$

2. Solve for x: $x + a = b$

Solution

Compare with $x + 5 = 9$.

$$x + a = b$$

$$x + a + (-a) = b + (-a) \quad \text{S}_a \text{ or } \text{A}_{-a}$$

$$x = b - a \qquad Ans.$$

Check

$$x + a = b$$

$$b - a + a \overset{?}{=} b$$

$$b = b \quad \text{(true)}$$

3. Solve for x: $2ax = 10a^2 - 3ax$

How To Proceed

1. Write the equation.
2. A_{+3ax}
3. Collect like terms.

4. $\text{D}_{5a} \text{ or } \text{M}_{\frac{1}{5a}}$

5. Simplify.

Solution

Compare with $2x = 10 - 3x$.

$$2ax = 10a^2 - 3ax$$

$$2ax + (+3ax) = 10a^2 - 3ax + (+3ax)$$

$$5ax = 10a^2$$

$$\frac{5ax}{5a} = \frac{10a^2}{5a}$$

$$x = 2a \quad Ans.$$

Check

$$2ax = 10a^2 - 3ax$$
$$2a(2a) \stackrel{?}{=} 10a^2 - 3a(2a)$$
$$4a^2 \stackrel{?}{=} 10a^2 - 6a^2$$
$$4a^2 = 4a^2 \quad \text{(true)}$$

~~~~~~

Exercises

In 1–28, solve for x or y and check.

1. $5x = b$	**2.** $sx = 8$	**3.** $ry = s$
4. $3y = t$	**5.** $cy = 5$	**6.** $hy = m$
7. $x + 5 = r$	**8.** $x + a = 7$	**9.** $y + c = d$
10. $4 + x = k$	**11.** $d + y = 9$	**12.** $3x - q = p$
13. $x - 2 = r$	**14.** $y - a = 7$	**15.** $x - c = d$
16. $4x - 5c = 3c$	**17.** $bx = 9b^2$	**18.** $cx + c^2 = 5c^2 - 3cx$
19. $bx - 5 = c$	**20.** $a = by + 6$	**21.** $ry + s = t$
22. $abx - d = 5d$	**23.** $rsx - rs^2 = 0$	**24.** $m^2x - 3m^2 = 12m^2$

25. $9x - 24a = 6a + 4x$ **26.** $5y + 2b = y + 6b$

27. $8ax - 7a^2 = 19a^2 - 5ax$ **28.** $5by - 3b^2 = 2by + 6b^2$

8. Properties of Inequalities

THE ORDER PROPERTY OF NUMBER

If two signed numbers x and y are graphed on a number line, only one of the following situations can happen:

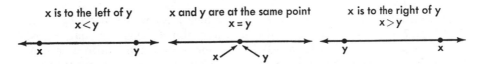

These graphs illustrate the **order property of number:**

If x and y are two signed numbers, then one and only one of the following sentences is true:

$$x < y \qquad\qquad x = y \qquad\qquad x > y$$

THE TRANSITIVE PROPERTY OF INEQUALITIES

From the graph at the right, we see that if x lies to the left of y, or $x < y$, and if y lies to the left of z, or $y < z$, then x lies to the left of z, or $x < z$. Likewise, if z lies to the right of y, or $z > y$, and if y lies to the right of x, or $y > x$, then z lies to the right of x, or $z > x$.

This graph illustrates the *transitive property of inequalities:*

If x, y, and z are signed numbers, then:

$$\text{if } x < y \text{ and } y < z, \text{ then } x < z$$
$$\text{if } z > y \text{ and } y > x, \text{ then } z > x$$

THE ADDITION PROPERTY OF INEQUALITIES

If 3 is added to both members of $9 > 2$, which is a true sentence, then $9 + (3) > 2 + (3)$, or $12 > 5$, is also a true sentence. Observe that $2 < 9$ is a true sentence and that $2 + (-3) < 9 + (-3)$, or $-1 < 6$, is also a true sentence.

These examples illustrate the *addition property of inequalities:*

If x, y, and z are signed numbers, then:

$$\text{if } x > y, \text{ then } x + z > y + z$$
$$\text{if } x < y, \text{ then } x + z < y + z$$

Since subtracting a signed number from both members of an inequality means adding its opposite to both members of the inequality, we can say:

When the same number is added to or subtracted from both members of an inequality, the order of the inequality remains unchanged.

THE MULTIPLICATION PROPERTY OF INEQUALITIES

If we multiply both members of $5 > 3$, which is a true sentence, by 7, then $7 \times 5 > 7 \times 3$, or $35 > 21$, is also a true sentence. Observe that $-2 < 4$ is a true sentence and that $5(-2) < 5(4)$, or $-10 < 20$, is also a true sentence. Notice that when both members of an equality were multiplied by the same positive number, the order of the inequality remained unchanged.

Now if we multiply both members of $5 > 3$ by -7, then $(-7)(5) > (-7)(3)$, or $-35 > -21$, is a false sentence. However, if we reverse the order in the resulting inequality $-35 > -21$, changing $>$ to $<$, we will have $-35 < -21$, a true sentence. Likewise, $-2 < 4$ is a true sentence, but $(-5)(-2) < (-5)(4)$, or $10 < -20$, is a false sentence. However, if we reverse the order in the resulting inequality $10 < -20$ and write $10 > -20$, we have a true sentence.

These examples illustrate the **multiplication property of inequalities:**

If x, y, and z are signed numbers, then:

        if $x > y$, then $xz > yz$ when z is positive $(z > 0)$

        if $x < y$, then $xz < yz$ when z is positive $(z > 0)$

        if $x > y$, then $xz < yz$ when z is negative $(z < 0)$

        if $x < y$, then $xz > yz$ when z is negative $(z < 0)$

Since dividing both members of an inequality by a non-zero signed number means to multiply by the reciprocal of the number, we can say:

When both members of an inequality are multiplied or divided by a positive number, the order of the inequality remains unchanged; when both members are multiplied or divided by a negative number, the order of the inequality is reversed.

Exercises

In 1–25, replace the question mark with the symbol $>$ or the symbol $<$ so that the resulting sentence will be true. All variables in exercises 9–25 are non-zero signed numbers.

1. Since $8 > 2$, $8 + 1 \ ? \ 2 + 1$.
2. Since $-6 < 2$, $-6 + (-4) \ ? \ 2 + (-4)$.
3. Since $9 > 5$, $9 - 2 \ ? \ 5 - 2$.
4. Since $-2 > -8$, $-2 - (4) \ ? \ -8 - (4)$.
5. Since $7 > 3$, $5(7) \ ? \ 5(3)$.
6. Since $-4 < 1$, $(-2)(-4) \ ? \ (-2)(1)$.
7. Since $-8 < 4$, $(-8) \div (4) \ ? \ (4) \div (4)$.
8. Since $9 > 6$, $(9) \div (-3) \ ? \ (6) \div (-3)$.
9. If $5 > x$, then $5 + 7 \ ? \ x + 7$.
10. If $y < 6$, then $y - 2 \ ? \ 6 - 2$.
11. If $20 > r$, then $4(20) \ ? \ 4(r)$.
12. If $t < 64$, then $t \div 8 \ ? \ 64 \div 8$.
13. If $x > 8$, then $-2x \ ? \ (-2)(8)$.

14. If $y < 8$, then $y \div (-4)$? $8 \div (-4)$.

15. If $x + 2 > 7$, then $x + 2 + (-2)$? $7 + (-2)$ and x ? 5.

16. If $y - 3 < 12$, then $y - 3 + 3$? $12 + 3$, or y ? 15.

17. If $x + 5 < 14$, then $x + 5 - 5$? $14 - 5$, or x ? 9.

18. If $2x > 8$, then $\dfrac{2x}{2}$? $\dfrac{8}{2}$, or x ? 4.

19. If $\frac{1}{3}y < 4$, then $3 \times \frac{1}{3}y$? 3×4, or y ? 12.

20. If $-3x < 36$, then $\dfrac{-3x}{-3}$? $\dfrac{36}{-3}$, or x ? $- 12$.

21. If $-2x > 6$, then $(-\frac{1}{2})(-2x)$? $(-\frac{1}{2})(6)$, or x ? -3.

22. If $x < 5$ and $5 < y$, then x ? y.

23. If $m > -7$ and $-7 > a$, then m ? a.

24. If $x < 10$ and $z > 10$, then x ? z.

25. If $a > b$ and $c < b$, then a ? c.

9. Finding the Solution Sets of Inequalities Containing One Variable

Let us find the solution set of the inequality $2x > 8$, when x is a member of the set of signed numbers. To do this, we must find the set of all numbers each of which can replace x in the sentence $2x > 8$ and result in a true sentence.

$$2x > 8$$

If $x = 1$, then $2(1) > 8$, or $2 > 8$, is a false sentence.

If $x = 2\frac{1}{2}$, then $2(2\frac{1}{2}) > 8$, or $5 > 8$, is a false sentence.

If $x = 3\frac{3}{4}$, then $2(3\frac{3}{4}) > 8$, or $7\frac{1}{2} > 8$, is a false sentence.

If $x = 4$, then $2(4) > 8$, or $8 > 8$, is a false sentence.

If $x = 4.1$, then $2(4.1) > 8$, or $8.2 > 8$, is a *true* sentence.

If $x = 5$, then $2(5) > 8$, or $10 > 8$, is a *true* sentence.

Notice that if x is replaced by any number greater than 4, the resulting sentence is true. Therefore, the solution set of $2x > 8$ is the set of all signed numbers greater than 4, written {all signed numbers greater than 4}. The solution set can also be described by the symbol $\{x \mid x > 4\}$ which is read "the set of all x such that x is greater than 4."

Observe that every member of the solution set of $x > 4$ is also a member of the solution set of $2x > 8$. Therefore, we call $2x > 8$ and $x > 4$ *equivalent inequalities.*

The inequality $2x > 8$ is called a **conditional inequality** because it is true for at least one but not all the elements of the replacement set (which was the set of signed numbers). Other examples of conditional inequalities are $x + 5 > 7$ and $2x - 1 < 9$.

If $x \in$ {signed numbers}, the inequality $x + 5 > x$ is true for every element of the replacement set. Such an inequality is called an **absolute inequality,** or an **unconditional inequality.** Other examples of absolute inequalities are $2x + 9 > 2x$ and $x - 7 < x$.

To find the solution set of an inequality, we will solve the inequality using methods similar to those used in solving an equation. We will use the properties of inequalities to transform the given inequality into a simpler equivalent inequality whose solution set is evident. Study the following model problems to learn how this is done.

-------------------- **MODEL PROBLEMS** --------------------

In 1–6, the domain of the variable is the set of signed numbers.

1. Find and graph the solution set of the inequality $x - 4 > 1$.

How To Proceed	*Solution*
1. Write the inequality.	$x - 4 > 1$
2. Add 4 to both members, and use the addition property of inequalities.	$x - 4 + 4 > 1 + 4$ $x > 5$

Answer: The solution set is {all signed numbers greater than 5}, or $\{x \mid x > 5\}$.

The graph of the solution set is shown below. Note that 5 is not included in the graph.

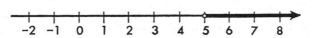

2. Find and graph the solution set of the inequality $x + 1 \leq 4$. (Remember that $x + 1 \leq 4$ means $x + 1 < 4$ or $x + 1 = 4$.)

How To Proceed	*Solution*	*Check*
1. Write the inequality.	$x + 1 \leq 4$	If $x = 3$, then $x + 1 = 4$.
2. Subtract 1 from both members, and use the subtraction property of inequalities.	$x + 1 - 1 \leq 4 - 1$ $x \leq 3$	If $x < 3$, then $x + 1 < 4$.

Answer: The solution set is {all signed numbers less than or equal to 3}, or $\{x \mid x \leq 3\}$.

[*Note:* This problem can also be solved by adding -1, which is the opposite, or additive inverse, of $+1$, to both members of the inequality.]

The graph of the solution set is shown at the right. Note that 3 is included in the graph.

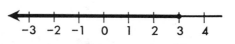

3. Find and graph the solution set of the inequality $\frac{1}{4}y \geq 1$.

How To Proceed	*Solution*
1. Write the inequality.	$\frac{1}{4}y \geq 1$
2. Multiply both members by 4, the reciprocal of $\frac{1}{4}$. Use the inequality property of multiplying by a positive number.	$4 \cdot \frac{1}{4}y \geq 4 \cdot 1$ $y \geq 4$ The check is left to the student.

Answer: The solution set is {all signed numbers greater than or equal to 4}, or $\{y \mid y \geq 4\}$.

[*Note:* This problem can also be solved by dividing both members of the inequality by $\frac{1}{4}$.]

The graph of the solution set is shown at the right. Note that 4 is included in the graph.

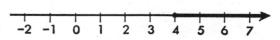

4. Find and graph the solution set of the inequality $-5z < 10$.

How To Proceed	*Solution*
1. Write the inequality.	$-5z < 10$
2. Divide both members by -5. Use the inequality property of division by a negative number. Remember to reverse the order of the inequality.	$\dfrac{-5z}{-5} < \dfrac{10}{-5}$ $z > -2$ The check is left to the student.

Answer: The solution set is {all signed numbers greater than -2}, or $\{z \mid z > -2\}$.

[*Note:* This problem can also be solved by multiplying both members of the inequality by $-\frac{1}{5}$, which is the reciprocal, or multiplicative inverse, of -5.]

The graph of the solution set is shown at the right. Note that -2 is not included in the graph.

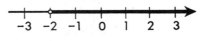

5. Find and graph the solution set of the inequality $5x + 4 \le 11 - 2x$.

How To Proceed	*Solution*
1. Write the inequality.	$5x + 4 \le 11 - 2x$
2. Add $2x$ to each member, and use the addition property of inequalities.	$5x + 4 + 2x \le 11 - 2x + 2x$ $7x + 4 \le 11$
3. Subtract 4 from both members, and use the subtraction property of inequalities.	$7x + 4 - 4 \le 11 - 4$ $7x \le 7$
4. Divide both members by 7, and use the property of dividing by a positive number.	$\dfrac{7x}{7} \le \dfrac{7}{7}$ $x \le 1$

The check is left to the student.

Answer: The solution set is {all signed numbers less than or equal to 1}, or $\{x \mid x \le 1\}$.

The graph of the solution set is shown at the right. Note that 1 is included in the graph.

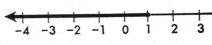

6. Find and graph the solution set of the inequality $2(2x - 8) - 8x \leq 0$.

How To Proceed	*Solution*
1. Write the inequality.	$2(2x - 8) - 8x \leq 0$
2. Use the distributive property.	$4x - 16 - 8x \leq 0$
3. Collect like terms.	$-4x - 16 \leq 0$
4. Add 16 to both members, and use the addition property of inequalities.	$-4x - 16 + 16 \leq 0 + 16$
	$-4x \leq 16$
5. Divide both members by -4, and use the property of division by a negative number.	$\dfrac{-4x}{-4} \geq \dfrac{16}{-4}$
	$x \geq -4$

The check is left to the student.

Answer: The solution set is {all signed numbers greater than or equal to -4}, or $\{x \mid x \geq -4\}$.

The graph of the solution set is shown at the right. Note that -4 is included in the graph.

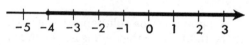

-5 -4 -3 -2 -1   0   1   2   3

Exercises

In 1–66, find and graph the solution set of the inequality. Use the set of signed numbers as the domain of the variable.

1. $x - 2 > 4$ **2.** $y - 5 > 7$ **3.** $z - 6 < 4$

4. $y - \frac{1}{2} > 2$ **5.** $x - 1.5 < 3.5$ **6.** $5\frac{3}{4} > w - 1\frac{1}{4}$

7. $x + 3 > 6$ **8.** $x + 5 > 12$ **9.** $19 < y + 17$

10. $d + \frac{1}{4} > 3$ **11.** $m + .1 < 2.1$ **12.** $-3\frac{1}{2} > c + \frac{1}{2}$

13. $y - 4 \geq 4$ **14.** $y + 3 \leq 8$ **15.** $25 \leq d + 22$

16. $3t > 6$ **17.** $4s > -8$ **18.** $2x \leq 12$

19. $15 \leq 3y$ **20.** $-24 > 6r$ **21.** $-10 \leq 4h$

22. $-3x > 21$ **23.** $-6y < 24$ **24.** $27 > -9y$

25. $-10x > -20$ **26.** $-12x \geq 30$ **27.** $12 \leq -1.2r$

28. $\frac{1}{3}x > 2$ **29.** $\frac{1}{2}y < -3$ **30.** $-\frac{2}{3}z \geq 6$

31. $\dfrac{x}{2} > 1$ **32.** $\dfrac{y}{3} \leq -1$ **33.** $\dfrac{1}{2} \leq \dfrac{z}{4}$

34. $1.5x > 6$ **35.** $-.4y \leq 4$ **36.** $-10 \geq 2.5z$

37. $2x - 1 > 5$ **38.** $4c - 3 > 17$ **39.** $3y - 6 \geq 12$

40. $5x - 1 > -31$ **41.** $2x - 3 < 12$ **42.** $-5 \leq 3y - 2$

43. $3x + 4 > 10$ **44.** $2y + 7 < 17$ **45.** $5y + 3 \geq 13$

46. $6c + 1 > -11$ **47.** $4d + 3 \leq 17$ **48.** $8h + 5 \geq -23$

49. $5x + 3x - 4 > 4$ **50.** $8y - 3y + 1 \leq 29$ **51.** $6x + 2 - 8x < 14$

52. $3x + 1 > 2x + 7$ **53.** $7y - 4 < 6 + 2y$ **54.** $4 - 3x \geq 16 + x$

55. $2x - 1 > 4 - \frac{1}{2}x$ **56.** $2c + 5 \geq 14 + 2\frac{1}{3}c$ **57.** $\frac{x}{3} - 1 \leq \frac{x}{2} + 3$

58. $4(x - 1) > 16$ **59.** $8x < 5(2x + 4)$ **60.** $12\left(\frac{1}{4} + \frac{x}{3}\right) > 15$

61. $8m - 2(2m + 3) \geq 0$ **62.** $12r - (8r - 20) > 12$

63. $3y - 6 \leq 3(7 + 2y)$ **64.** $5x \leq 10 + 2(3x - 4)$

65. $-3(4x - 8) > 2(3 + 2x)$ **66.** $4 - 5(y - 2) \leq -2(-9 + 2y)$

In 67–72, state whether the inequality is a conditional inequality or an absolute inequality. Use the set of signed numbers as the domain of the variable.

67. $x + 8 > x$ **68.** $x + 8 > 8$

69. $5x - 4 < 21$ **70.** $7x + x + 10 > 8x$

71. $2x + 3x < 4x + 1$ **72.** $6x + 3x - 1 < 8x + x$

73. Six times a number is less than 72. What numbers satisfy this condition?

74. A number increased by 10 is greater than 50. What numbers satisfy this condition?

75. A number decreased by 15 is less than 35. What numbers satisfy this condition?

76. Twice a number, increased by 6, is less than 48. What numbers satisfy this condition?

77. Five times a number, decreased by 24, is greater than 3 times the number. What numbers satisfy this condition?

CHAPTER X

SOLVING PROBLEMS BY USING FIRST-DEGREE OPEN SENTENCES IN ONE VARIABLE

We have already learned and practiced the procedure for solving verbal problems (see pages 88 and 89). In this chapter, we will deal with many different kinds of word problems. We will find it challenging to translate the verbal relationships into algebraic equations; then we will test our knowledge of algebra in solving these equations.

1. Number Problems

PREPARING TO SOLVE NUMBER PROBLEMS

Exercises

In exercises 1–10, represent in terms of x:
1. twice the number represented by x increased by 8
2. three times the number represented by x decreased by 12
3. 12 decreased by three times the number represented by x
4. four times the number which is 3 more than x
5. five times the number which is 3 less than $2x$
6. three times the number which exceeds x by 5
7. twice the number which exceeds $3x$ by 4
8. twice the sum of the number represented by x and 5
9. ten times the number obtained when twice x is decreased by 10
10. six times the number which is 4 less than one-third of x

11. If the smaller of two numbers is represented by x, represent the larger when their sum is:
    a. 10   *b.* 25   *c.* 36   *d.* 50   *e.* 100   *f.* 3000
12. If the sum of two numbers is represented by S, and the smaller number is represented by x, represent the larger in terms of S and x.
13. If the larger of two numbers is represented by l, represent the smaller when their sum is:
    a. 5   *b.* 12   *c.* 20   *d.* 40   *e.* 75   *f.* 1000
14. If the sum of two numbers is represented by S, and the larger number is represented by l, represent the smaller in terms of S and l.

SOLVING NUMBER PROBLEMS

~~~~~~~~~~~~~~~~ *MODEL PROBLEMS* ~~~~~~~~~~~~~~~~

1. The larger of two numbers is twice the smaller. If the larger is decreased by 10, the result is 5 more than the smaller. Find the numbers.

How To Proceed	*Solution*
1. Represent the smaller number by a variable and all the other described numbers in terms of the same variable.	Let $x =$ the smaller number. Then $2x =$ the larger number. Then $2x - 10 =$ the larger decreased by 10. Then $x + 5 = 5$ more than the smaller.
2. Write an open sentence which symbolizes the relationships stated in the problem.	$2x - 10 = x + 5$
3. Solve the open sentence.	$2x - 10 + 10 = x + 5 + 10$ $2x = x + 15$ $2x + (-x) = x + 15 + (-x)$ $x = 15$ $2x = 30$
4. Check the answers in the original problem.	The larger decreased by $10 = 30 - 10 = 20$. 5 more than the smaller $= 15 + 5 = 20$. The results are the same, 20.

Answer: The smaller number is 15; the larger number is 30.

2. Separate 38 into two parts such that 3 times the smaller is 16 less than twice the larger.

Solution:

$$\text{Let } s = \text{the smaller number.}$$
$$\text{Then } 38 - s = \text{the larger number.}$$
$$\text{Then } 3s = 3 \text{ times the smaller number.}$$
$$\text{Then } 2(38 - s) - 16 = 16 \text{ less than twice the larger number.}$$

$$3s = 2(38 - s) - 16$$
$$3s = 76 - 2s - 16$$
$$3s = 60 - 2s$$
$$3s + 2s = 60 - 2s + 2s$$
$$5s = 60$$
$$s = 12$$
$$38 - s = 26$$

Check: 3 times the smaller = $3(12) = 36$. 16 less than twice the larger = $2(26) - 16 = 36$. The results are the same, 36.

Answer: The smaller number is 12; the larger number is 26.

3. The larger of two numbers is 4 times the smaller. If the larger number exceeds the smaller number by 15, find the number.

> [*Note:* "The larger number exceeds the smaller by 15" has the following meanings. Use any one of them.
> 1. The larger equals 15 more than the smaller, written $4s = s + 15$.
> 2. The larger decreased by 15 equals the smaller, written $4s - 15 = s$.
> 3. The larger decreased by the smaller equals 15, written $4s - s = 15$.]

Solution:

Let s = the smaller number.
Then $4s$ = the larger number.

$$4s = s + 15$$
$$4s + (-s) = s + 15 + (-s)$$
$$3s = 15$$
$$s = 5$$
$$4s = 20$$

Check: The larger number, 20, is 4 times the smaller number, 5. The larger number, 20, exceeds the smaller number, 5, by 15.

Answer: The larger number is 20; the smaller number is 5.

Exercises

1. If 6 times a number is decreased by 6, the result is the same as when 3 times the number is increased by 12. Find the number.
2. If 5 times a number is increased by 50, the result is the same as when 200 is decreased by the number. Find the number.
3. If 10 times a certain number is increased by 4, the result is 12 more than 9 times the number. Find the number.
4. If 50 is decreased by 4 times a certain number, the result is 15 more than the number. Find the number.
5. If 3 times a number is increased by 22, the result is 14 less than 7 times the number. Find the number.
6. One number is twice another number. If the larger is diminished by 10, the result is 2 more than the smaller. Find the numbers.
7. The larger of two numbers is 20 more than the smaller. Four times the larger is 70 more than 5 times the smaller. Find the numbers.
8. If 14 is added to a certain number and the sum is multiplied by 2, the result is equal to 8 times the number decreased by 14. Find the number.
9. The larger of two numbers is 5 less than twice the smaller. If their sum is 70, find the numbers.
10. The difference between two numbers is 24. Find the numbers if their sum is 88.
11. Separate 160 into two parts such that the larger will be 3 times the smaller.
12. Separate 144 into two parts such that one part will be 12 less than twice the other.
13. Separate 45 into two parts such that 5 times the smaller is 6 less than twice the larger.
14. Separate 65 into two parts such that 3 times the larger will be 6 more than 6 times the smaller.
15. The larger of two numbers is 1 less than 3 times the smaller. If 3 times the larger is 5 more than 8 times the smaller, find the numbers.
16. The larger of two numbers is 1 more than 3 times the smaller. The difference between 8 times the smaller and 2 times the larger is 10. Find the numbers.
17. The larger of two numbers is 8 times the smaller. If the larger number exceeds the smaller by 56, find the numbers.
18. The smaller of two numbers is 12 less than the larger. Four times the larger exceeds 3 times the smaller by 90. Find the numbers.
19. The larger of two numbers is 1 more than twice the smaller. Three times the larger exceeds 5 times the smaller by 10. Find the numbers.
20. Separate 150 into two parts such that 4 times the larger exceeds 5 times the smaller by 60.

21. If 3 times a number is increased by 9, the result will be 6 times the excess of the number over 2. Find the number.

22. Find a number which exceeds 10 by as much as twice the number exceeds 38.

23. Find a number which is as much larger than 35 as 2 times the number is smaller than 190.

24. The second of three numbers is 2 more than the first. The third number is twice the first. The sum of the first and third exceeds the second by 2. Find the three numbers.

25. The second of three numbers is 1 less than the first. The third number is 5 less than twice the second. If the third number exceeds the first number by 12, find the three numbers.

2. Consecutive Integer Problems

PREPARING TO SOLVE CONSECUTIVE INTEGER PROBLEMS

As we know, an integer is any whole number, positive or negative, or zero. Examples of integers are 5, -3, and 0.

An *even integer* is an integer which is twice some integer. For example, 6 and -10 are even integers.

An *odd integer* is an integer which is not an even integer. For example, 7 and -5 are odd integers.

Consecutive integers are integers which follow one another in order. To obtain a set of consecutive integers, we start with any integer and count by ones. Each number in the set is 1 more than the previous number in the set. Each of the following is a set of consecutive integers:

$$\{5, 6, 7, 8\}$$
$$\{-5, -4, -3, -2\}$$
$$\{x, x + 1, x + 2, x + 3\} \qquad x \in \{\text{integers}\}$$

Consecutive even integers are even integers which follow one another in order. To obtain a set of consecutive even integers, we can start with any even integer and count by twos. Each number in the set is 2 more than the previous number in the set. Each of the following is a set of consecutive even integers:

$$\{2, 4, 6, 8\}$$
$$\{-12, -10, -8, -6\}$$
$$\{x, x + 2, x + 4, x + 6\} \qquad x \in \{\text{even integers}\}$$

Consecutive odd integers are odd integers which follow one another in order. To obtain a set of consecutive odd integers, we start with any odd integer and count by twos. Each number in the set is 2 more than the previous number in the set. Each of the following is a set of consecutive odd integers:

$$\{3,\ 5,\ 7,\ 9\}$$
$$\{-5,\ -3,\ -1,\ 1\}$$
$$\{x,\ x+2,\ x+4,\ x+6\} \qquad x \in \{\text{odd integers}\}$$

--- **KEEP IN MIND** ---

1. Consecutive integers differ by 1.
2. Consecutive even integers and also consecutive odd integers differ by 2.

Exercises

1. Write 4 consecutive integers beginning with each of the following integers (y is an integer):

    a. 15   *b.* 31   *c.* -10 *d.* -2 *e.* y *f.* $2y+1$ *g.* $3y-2$

2. Write 4 consecutive even integers beginning with each of the following integers (y is an even integer):

    a. 8   *b.* 26   *c.* -20 *d.* -4 *e.* y *f.* $2y$ *g.* $2y-6$

3. Write 4 consecutive odd integers beginning with each of the following integers (y is an odd integer):

    a. 9   *b.* 35   *c.* -15 *d.* -3 *e.* y *f.* $2y+1$ *g.* $2y-1$

4. If $2x-3$ is an odd integer, write the following two even integers.

5. If $2x+6$ is an even integer, write the following two odd integers.

In 6–12, give a replacement set each of whose elements can replace x and make the resulting sentence true.

6. $x+1$ represents an even integer.

7. $x+1$ represents an odd integer.

8. $2x$ represents an even integer.

9. x and $x+2$ represent two consecutive even integers.

10. x and $x+2$ represent two consecutive odd integers.

11. $2x$ and $2x+2$ represent two consecutive even integers.

12. $2x-1$ and $2x+1$ represent two consecutive odd integers.

In 13–15, answer (a) odd or (b) even so that the resulting sentence is true.

13. The sum of an even number of consecutive odd integers is an _____ integer.

14. The sum of an odd number of consecutive odd integers is an _____ integer.

15. The sum of any number of consecutive even integers is an _____ integer.

SOLVING CONSECUTIVE INTEGER PROBLEMS

~~~~~~~~~~~~~~~~ *MODEL PROBLEMS* ~~~~~~~~~~~~~~~~

1. Find two consecutive integers whose sum is 95.

   Solution:

   > Let n = the first integer.
   > Then $n + 1$ = the second integer.
   > Then $2n + 1$ = the sum of the two integers.

   The sum of the two integers is 95.

   $$2n + 1 = 95$$
   $$2n + 1 - 1 = 95 - 1$$
   $$2n = 94$$
   $$n = 47, \; n + 1 = 48$$

   Check: The sum of the consecutive integers, 47 and 48, is 95.

   Answer: 47 and 48

2. Find 3 consecutive even integers such that 4 times the first decreased by the second is 12 more than twice the third.

   Solution:

   > Let n = the first even integer.
   > Then $n + 2$ = the second even integer.
   > Then $n + 4$ = the third even integer.

   4 times the first decreased by the second is 12 more than twice the third.

   $$4n - (n + 2) = 2(n + 4) + 12$$
   $$4n - n - 2 = 2n + 8 + 12$$
   $$3n - 2 = 2n + 20$$
   $$3n - 2 + 2 = 2n + 20 + 2$$
   $$3n = 2n + 22$$
   $$3n + (-2n) = 2n + 22 + (-2n)$$
   $$n = 22$$
   $$n + 2 = 24, \; n + 4 = 26$$

   Check: Show that 22, 24, and 26 satisfy the conditions in the given problem.

   Answer: 22, 24, 26

~~~~~~

Exercises

1. Find two consecutive integers whose sum is:
   a. 61   *b.* 35   *c.* 91   *d.* 125   *e.* −17   *f.* −81
2. Find three consecutive integers whose sum is:
   a. 18   *b.* 48   *c.* 99   *d.* 303   *e.* −12   *f.* −57
3. Find four consecutive integers whose sum is 234.
4. Find two consecutive even integers whose sum is:
   a. 22   *b.* 38   *c.* 146   *d.* 206   *e.* −10   *f.* −34
5. Find three consecutive even integers whose sum is:
   a. 12   *b.* 48   *c.* 156   *d.* 258   *e.* −18   *f.* −60
6. Find four consecutive even integers whose sum is 60.
7. Find two consecutive odd integers whose sum is:
   a. 12   *b.* 20   *c.* 112   *d.* 224   *e.* −16   *f.* −32
8. Find three consecutive odd integers whose sum is:
   a. 33   *b.* 45   *c.* 159   *d.* 615   *e.* −27   *f.* −105
9. Find four consecutive odd integers whose sum is 112.
10. Find three consecutive integers such that the sum of the first and the third is 40.
11. Find four consecutive integers such that the sum of the second and fourth is 132.
12. Find three consecutive integers such that twice the smallest is 12 more than the largest.
13. Find three consecutive integers such that the sum of the first two integers is 24 more than the third integer.
14. Find three consecutive odd integers such that the sum of the first and second is 27 less than 3 times the third.
15. Find three consecutive even integers such that the sum of the smallest and twice the second is 20 more than the third.
16. Find two consecutive integers such that 4 times the larger exceeds 3 times the smaller by 23.
17. Find four consecutive odd integers such that the sum of the first three exceeds the fourth by 18.
18. Find three consecutive even integers such that twice the sum of the second and third exceeds 3 times the first by 34.
19. Find three consecutive integers such that the first increased by twice the second exceeds the third by 24.
20. Find three consecutive integers such that the sum of the second and third exceeds $\frac{1}{2}$ of the first by 33.
21. Is it possible to find 3 consecutive even integers whose sum is 40?
22. Is it possible to find 3 consecutive odd integers whose sum is 59?
23. How many sets of 3 consecutive integers are there in which the sum of the 3 integers does not equal three times the middle integer?

3. Motion Problems

PREPARING TO SOLVE MOTION PROBLEMS

If a car traveled at the rate of 30 miles per hour, in 2 hours it traveled 2(30), or 60 miles. In this case, the three quantities that are related are:

1. the *distance* traveled, 60 miles
2. the rate of speed, or *rate,* 30 miles per hour (mph)
3. the *time* traveled, 2 hours

The relation involving the distance, D, the rate, R, and the time, T, may be expressed in the following ways:

$$D = RT \qquad T = \frac{D}{R} \qquad R = \frac{D}{T}$$

In our work, *rate* will represent either of the following:

1. The *uniform rate of speed*, which represents a rate of speed which remains constant (does not change) throughout a trip. Thus, if a car is traveling at a uniform rate of 30 miles per hour on a 2-hour trip, the car is constantly traveling 30 miles per hour during the entire trip.
2. The *average rate of speed*, which represents the total distance traveled divided by the total time traveled. Thus, a car which traveled 120 miles in 3 hours was traveling at an average rate of 120 ÷ 3, or 40 miles per hour.

When any two of the three quantities, rate, time, and distance, have been represented, the third can be represented in terms of those two by using one of the three formulas previously stated. For example:

The distance traveled in 5 hours at an average rate of 40 mph equals 5(40) = 200 miles.   ($D = RT$)

The distance traveled in 7 hours at an average rate of $(x + 10)$ mph equals $7(x + 10)$ miles.   ($D = RT$)

The time required to travel 150 miles at an average rate of 30 mph is $\frac{150}{30} = 5$ hours. $\left(T = \frac{D}{R}\right)$

The time required to travel 200 miles at an average rate of $(x + 20)$ mph is $\frac{200}{x + 20}$ hours. $\left(T = \frac{D}{R}\right)$

The average rate of speed at which one travels when 60 miles are covered in 2 hours is $\dfrac{60}{2} = 30$ mph. $\left(R = \dfrac{D}{T} \right)$

The average rate of speed at which one travels when 100 miles are covered in x hours is $\dfrac{100}{x}$ mph. $\left(R = \dfrac{D}{T} \right)$

---KEEP IN MIND---

$$D = RT \qquad\qquad T = \frac{D}{R} \qquad\qquad R = \frac{D}{T}$$

Exercises

1. If a car is traveling 40 mph, represent how far it will go in:
   a. 5 hr.   b. 3 hr. 30 min.   c. x hr.   d. $(2x + 1)$ hr.   e. $(10 - x)$ hr.

2. A train traveled 300 miles. Represent how long the trip took if the train was traveling at a rate of:
   a. 50 mph   b. 70 mph   c. x mph   d. $(x + 10)$ mph   e. $(x - 5)$ mph

3. A plane flew 2400 miles. Represent how fast it was flying if it flew for:
   a. 4 hr.   b. 6 hr. 40 min.   c. x hr.   d. $(x + 40)$ hr.   e. $(x - 50)$ hr.

4. Find the average rate for the entire trip if a car travels:
   a. 1 hour at 40 mph and 1 hour at 50 mph
   b. 1 hour at 30 mph, 1 hour at 40 mph, and 1 hour at 50 mph
   c. 1 hour at 30 mph and 2 hours at 36 mph
   d. 2 hours at 40 mph and 3 hours at 50 mph

5. Two cars started from the same point and traveled for x hours in opposite directions at rates of 30 mph and 40 mph.
   a. Represent in terms of x the distance traveled by the slow car.
   b. Represent in terms of x the distance traveled by the fast car.
   c. Represent how far apart the two cars were at the end of x hours.
   d. Write an open sentence which would indicate that the two cars were 140 miles apart at the end of x hours.

6. Jack and Harry started on bicycles at the same time from two different places on a straight road and traveled toward each other. Jack traveled 8 mph and Harry traveled 10 mph. They met in x hours.

    a. Represent in terms of x the distance Jack traveled.

    b. Represent in terms of x the distance Harry traveled.

    c. Represent in terms of x the total distance they traveled.

    d. Write an open sentence which would indicate that Jack and Harry were originally 27 miles apart.

7. Mr. Sands left his home by car, traveling on a certain road at the rate of 40 mph. One hour later, his son Barry left home and started after him on the same road, traveling at the rate of 50 mph. Barry overtook his father in x hours.

    a. Represent in terms of x the number of hours Mr. Sands traveled.

    b. Represent in terms of x the distance Mr. Sands traveled.

    c. Represent in terms of x the distance Barry traveled.

    d. Write an open sentence which represents the relationship between the distances traveled by Mr. Sands and Barry.

8. Saul left his home and walked a distance of x miles at the rate of 3 mph. He then retraced his steps, walking home at the rate of 2 mph.

    a. Represent in terms of x the time Saul spent walking out.

    b. Represent in terms of x the time Saul spent walking back.

    c. Represent in terms of x the total time Saul spent on the trip.

    d. Write an open sentence which would indicate that the total time Saul spent on the trip was 4 hours.

9. Represent the missing quantities in the following table:

	Rate	Time	Distance
a.	40	x	?
b.	40	?	x
c.	?	2	x

	Rate	Time	Distance
d.	50	$x + 2$	?
e.	?	$x + 1$	150
f.	$x + 10$	?	200

SOLVING MOTION PROBLEMS

In solving motion problems, it is helpful to draw a diagram. The facts in the problem may be organized by using verbal sentences or by using a table.

～～～～～～～ *MODEL PROBLEMS* ～～～～～～～

1. Two cars start from the same point at the same time and travel in opposite directions. The slow car travels at 28 mph, and the fast car travels at 35 mph. In how many hours will the cars be 252 miles apart?

Solution: Since both cars start at the same time, they will travel the same number of hours.

Let h = the number of hours traveled by each car.

Then $28h$ = the distance traveled by the slow car.

And $35h$ = the distance traveled by the fast car.

The total distance traveled is 252 miles.

$$28h + 35h = 252$$
$$63h = 252$$
$$h = 4$$

Check

$$28(4) = 112$$
$$35(4) = \underline{140}$$
$$\text{Total} = 252$$

Answer: 4 hours

The following tabular arrangement may also be used:

Let h = the number of hours traveled by each car.

First fill in the rate and time for each car. Then represent the distance for each car.

	(mph) Rate	(hr.) Time	(mi.) Distance
Slow car	28	h	$28h$
Fast car	35	h	$35h$

The total distance traveled is 252 miles.

$$28h + 35h = 252$$

Complete the solution as before.

2. A passenger train and a freight train start at the same time from stations which are 405 miles apart and travel toward each other. The rate of the passenger train is twice the rate of the freight train. In 3 hours, the trains pass each other. Find the rate of each train.

Solution:

Let r = the rate of the freight train.

Then $2r$ = the rate of the passenger train.

And $3r$ = the distance traveled by the freight train.

And $3(2r)$ = the distance traveled by the passenger train.

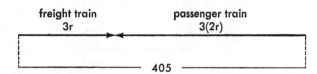

The total distance traveled was 405 miles.

$$3r + 3(2r) = 405$$
$$3r + 6r = 405$$
$$9r = 405$$
$$r = 45$$
$$2r = 90$$

Check

$$3(45) = 135$$
$$3(90) = \underline{270}$$
$$\text{Total} = 405$$

Answer: The rate of the freight train was 45 mph. The rate of the passenger train was 90 mph.

The following table may also be used:

Let r = the rate of the freight train.

Then $2r$ = the rate of the fast train.

First fill in the time and rate for each train. Then represent the distance for each train.

	(mph) Rate	(hr.) Time	(mi.) Distance
Freight train	r	3	$3r$
Passenger train	$2r$	3	$3(2r)$

The total distance traveled was 405 miles.

$$3r + 3(2r) = 405$$

Complete the solution as before.

3. Two trains started at the same time from stations which were 360 miles apart and traveled toward each other. The rate of the fast train exceeded the rate of the slow train by 10 mph. At the end of 2 hours, the trains were still 120 miles apart. Find the rate of each train.

Solution:

Let r = the rate of the slow train.
Then $r + 10$ = the rate of the fast train.

First fill in the time and rate for each train. Then represent the distance for each train.

	(mph) Rate	(hr.) Time	(mi.) Distance
Slow train	r	2	$2r$
Fast train	$r + 10$	2	$2(r + 10)$

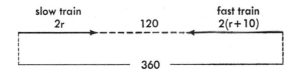

The total distance between the stations was 360 miles.

$$2r + 120 + 2(r + 10) = 360$$
$$2r + 120 + 2r + 20 = 360$$
$$4r + 140 = 360$$
$$4r + 140 - 140 = 360 - 140$$
$$4r = 220$$
$$r = 55$$
$$r + 10 = 65$$

Check

$$2(55) = 110$$
$$2(65) = \underline{130}$$
$$\text{Total} = 240$$
$$360 - 240 = 120$$

Answer: The rate of the slow train was 55 mph. The rate of the fast train was 65 mph.

4. Martin left his home by car, traveling on a certain road at the rate of 30 mph. Two hours later, his brother William left the home and started after him on the same road, traveling at the rate of 45 mph. In how many hours did William overtake Martin?

Solution: Since Martin started 2 hours earlier than William, he traveled 2 hours longer than William.

Let h = the number of hours William traveled.
Then $h + 2$ = the number of hours Martin traveled.

First fill in the rate and time for each boy. Then represent the distance for each boy.

	(mph) Rate	(hr.) Time	(mi.) Distance
Martin	30	$h + 2$	$30(h + 2)$
William	45	h	$45h$

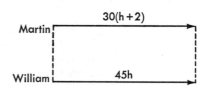

The distance traveled by William is the same as the distance traveled by Martin.

$$45h = 30(h + 2)$$
$$45h = 30h + 60$$
$$45h + (-30h) = 30h + 60 + (-30h)$$
$$15h = 60$$
$$h = 4$$

Check

$4 + 2 = 6$
$6(30) = 180$
$4(45) = 180$

Both boys travel the same distance.

Answer: William overtook Martin in 4 hours.

5. How far can a man drive out into the country at the average rate of 40 mph and return over the same road at the average rate of 30 mph if he travels a total of 7 hours?

Solution: *Method* 1

Let h = the number of hours he spent driving out.

Then $7 - h$ = the number of hours he spent driving back.

First fill in the rate and time for each trip. Then represent the distance for each trip.

	(mph) Rate	(hr.) Time	(mi.) Distance
Trip out	40	h	$40h$
Trip back	30	$7 - h$	$30(7 - h)$

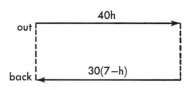

The distance out is the same as the distance back.

$$40h = 30(7 - h)$$
$$40h = 210 - 30h$$
$$40h + 30h = 210 - 30h + 30h$$
$$70h = 210$$
$$h = 3$$
$$40h = 120$$

Check

$7 - 3 = 4$

$3(40) = 120$

$4(30) = 120$

The distances are the same.

Answer: He can travel 120 miles out into the country.

Method 2

Since he drives out to a certain point and returns over the same road to his starting point, the distance traveled going out is the same as the distance traveled coming back.

Let d = the number of miles he can travel out into the country.

First fill in the rate and distance for each trip. Then represent the time for each trip.

	(mph) Rate	(hr.) Time	(mi.) Distance
Trip out	40	$\dfrac{d}{40}$	d
Trip back	30	$\dfrac{d}{30}$	d

Total time spent in traveling is 7 hours.

$$\frac{d}{40} + \frac{d}{30} = 7$$

$$120\left(\frac{d}{40} + \frac{d}{30}\right) = 120(7)$$

$$120\left(\frac{d}{40}\right) + 120\left(\frac{d}{30}\right) = 120(7)$$

$$3d + 4d = 840$$

$$7d = 840$$

$$d = 120$$

Check

$$\frac{120}{40} = 3$$

$$\frac{120}{30} = 4$$

$$3 + 4 = 7$$

Answer: He can travel 120 miles out into the country.

Exercises

1. A destroyer traveling 40 mph and a battleship traveling 30 mph left the same naval base at the same time and sailed in opposite directions. In how many hours were the ships 350 miles apart?
2. Two trains started at the same time from the same station and traveled in opposite directions. One traveled at the rate of 50 mph and the other at the rate of 60 mph. In how many hours were they 660 miles apart?
3. Two planes departed from an airport at the same time. One flew east at the rate of 180 mph; the other flew west at the rate of 330 mph. In how many hours were they 1530 miles apart?
4. At 8 A.M. two automobiles started from the same place. One traveled north at the rate of 35 mph, and the other traveled south at the rate of 40 mph. At what time were the automobiles 300 miles apart?
5. At 7 A.M. two freight trains started from the same station. One traveled east at the rate of 42 mph, and the other traveled west at the rate of 48 mph. At what time were the trains 390 miles apart?
6. One plane departed from New York, and at the same time another plane departed from Mexico City. They flew toward each other at rates of 650 mph and 550 mph. If New York and Mexico City are 3000 miles apart, in how many hours did the planes pass each other?
7. Two trains are at stations which are 800 miles apart. If they start traveling toward each other at the same time, one averaging 67 mph and the other averaging 53 mph, in how many hours will they pass each other?
8. Two trains are 515 miles apart. At 10 A.M. they start traveling toward each other at average rates of 48 and 55 mph. At what time will they pass each other?

9. Albany and New York are 150 miles apart. One car left Albany for New York, averaging 40 mph. At the same time, another car left New York for Albany, averaging 35 mph. How far from Albany did the cars pass each other?

10. Saratoga and New York are 180 miles apart. A truck traveled from New York toward Saratoga at the rate of 44 mph. Another truck traveled from Saratoga toward New York at the rate of 36 mph. How many miles did each travel before they met?

11. Two planes started at the same time from the same airport and flew in opposite directions. One flew 60 miles per hour faster than the other. In 5 hours, they were 2800 miles apart. Find the rate of each plane.

12. Two trains started from the same station at the same time and traveled in opposite directions. After traveling 10 hours, they were 850 miles apart. The rate of the fast train exceeded the rate of the slow train by 5 mph. Find the rate of each train.

13. Two trains started from the same place at the same time and traveled in opposite directions at rates which differed by 20 mph. In 5 hours, they were 500 miles apart. Find the rate of each train.

14. Two planes left at the same time from two airports which are 4500 miles apart and flew toward each other. In 5 hours, they passed each other. The rate of the fast plane was twice the rate of the slow plane. Find the rate of each plane.

15. Two cars started from the same place at the same time and traveled in opposite directions. At the end of 6 hours, they were 420 miles apart. If the average rate of the slow car exceeded $\frac{1}{2}$ of the average rate of the fast car by 13 mph, find the rate of each car.

16. At 7:00 A.M. two cars started from the same place, one traveling east and the other traveling west. At 10:30 A.M. they were 287 miles apart. If the rate of the fast car exceeded the rate of the slow car by 6 mph, find the rate of each car.

17. A salesman made a trip of 375 miles by bus and train. He traveled 3 hours by bus and 4 hours by train. If the train averaged 15 mph more than the bus, find the rate of each.

18. An airplane made a flight of 1600 miles in 5 hours. During the first 3 hours of the trip it had good weather. It then ran into bad weather, which decreased its rate by 75 mph for the rest of the flight. Find the rate on each part of the flight.

19. An autoist made a trip of 275 miles in 8 hours. Before noon he averaged 40 mph, and after noon he averaged 25 mph. At what time did he begin his trip and when did he end it?

20. Two planes started at the same time from two airports which are 1550 miles apart and flew toward each other. One plane flew 330 mph, and the other flew 370 mph. In how many hours were the planes still 150 miles apart?

21. At 3 P.M. two ships started sailing toward each other from ports which were 265 miles apart at average rates of 18 and 23 mph. At what time were the ships still 60 miles apart?

22. A destroyer traveling 40 mph and a battleship traveling 30 mph leave the same base at the same time and sail in the same direction. In how many hours will they be 70 miles apart?

23. At 9:00 A.M. two cars started from the same town and traveled north on the same road. One car averaged 36 mph, and the other car averaged 31 mph. In how many hours were the cars 30 miles apart?

24. At 6:00 A.M. two planes started from the same airport and flew west. One plane averaged 260 mph, and the other plane averaged 300 mph. At what time were the planes 140 miles apart?

25. A ship left a port and sailed east at the rate of 20 mph. One hour later, a second ship left the same port at the rate of 25 mph, also traveling east. In how many hours did the second ship overtake the first ship?

26. Susan left her home at 7 A.M., driving her car at the rate of 30 mph. At 9 A.M. her sister Marion drove after her along the same highway, traveling at the rate of 45 mph. In how many hours did Marion pass Susan?

27. A plane left LaGuardia Airport at 3 P.M., flying west at the rate of 200 mph. At 3:30 P.M. another plane left the same airport, flying west at the rate of 250 mph. At what time did the second plane overtake the first plane?

28. Mr. Stone started from home on a trip, planning to average 30 mph. How fast must his son Carl plan to travel in order to overtake him in 3 hours if Carl started 30 minutes after his father?

29. A cargo plane left an airport at noon and flew toward New York at the average rate of 300 mph. At 2 P.M. a jet plane left the same airport for New York and flew the same route as the cargo plane at the average rate of 500 mph. How many miles did the jet plane fly before it overtook the cargo plane?

30. Mr. Fields spent 6 hours on a trip out into the country and back. He walked out at the rate of 4 mph and walked back at the rate of 2 mph. How far out into the country did he go?

31. Ronald rode away from home in a car at the rate of 32 mph. He walked back at the rate of 4 mph. The round trip required $2\frac{1}{4}$ hours. How far did Ronald ride?

32. A round trip in a helicopter lasted 4 hours and 30 minutes. If the helicopter flew away from the airport at 100 mph and returned at the rate of 50 mph, what was its greatest distance from the airport?

33. A flyer on reconnaissance duty spent 5 hours on a mission. He flew out from his base with the wind at the rate of 360 mph and returned to his base over the same route, flying against the wind at the rate of 240 mph. How many miles did he fly out before he turned back?

34. A pilot plans to make a flight lasting 2 hours and 30 minutes. How far can he fly from his base at the rate of 300 mph and return over the same route at the rate of 200 mph?

35. Mr. West drove his car from his home to Chicago at the rate of 40 mph and returned at the rate of 45 mph. If his time going exceeded his time returning by 30 minutes, find his time going and his time returning.

4. Coin Problems

PREPARING TO SOLVE COIN PROBLEMS

In solving problems which deal with coins of different denominations—for example, nickels, dimes, and quarters—it is often helpful to represent the values of the coins in the same unit of money. In the following examples, the unit of money is cents:

The value of 3 nickels in cents is $3(5)$, or 15 cents.

The value of d dimes in cents is $d(10)$, or $10d$ cents.

The value of q quarters in cents is $q(25)$, or $25q$ cents.

```
┌──────────── KEEP IN MIND ────────────┐
│  Number of coins × Value of each = Total value of the │
│                    coin in cents       coins in cents │
└───────────────────────────────────────┘
```

Exercises

1. Represent the value of each of the following number of nickels in cents:
    a. 6   *b.* 10   *c.* x *d.* $3x$ *e.* $x + 3$ *f.* $2x - 1$

2. Represent the value of each of the following number of dimes in cents:
    a. 3   *b.* 8   *c.* y *d.* $2y$ *e.* $y + 2$ *f.* $3x - 2$

3. Represent the value of each of the following number of quarters in cents:
    a. 6   *b.* 13   *c.* q *d.* $5q$ *e.* $q + 5$ *f.* $2q - 3$

4. Represent the value of each of the following number of dollars in cents:
    a. 4   *b.* 15   *c.* D *d.* $4D$ *e.* $D + 4$ *f.* $3D - 4$

5. Represent the value of each of the following in cents:
    a. \$4.00   *b.* \$13.00   *c.* \$5.50   *d.* \$8.75   *e.* \$19.25   *f.* \$7.28

6. Represent the value of each of the following in cents:
   a. 8 pennies and 6 nickels　　　　b. 8 nickels and 7 dimes
   c. 13 nickels and 7 quarters　　　d. 3 dollars and 5 half-dollars
   e. x pennies and $2x$ nickels　　　f. n nickels and $(2n - 1)$ dimes
   g. q quarters and $(n + 5)$ dimes　h. x dollars and $(3x - 2)$ dimes
   i. x nickels and $(15 - x)$ dimes　j. y dimes and $(20 - y)$ quarters
7. Represent the value of each of the following in cents:
   a. x pennies, $3x$ dimes, and $(x + 3)$ quarters
   b. y nickels, $(2y + 1)$ quarters, and $(2y - 3)$ dollars

SOLVING COIN PROBLEMS

When solving coin problems, the facts in the problem may be organized by using verbal sentences or by using a table.

~~~~~~~~~~~~~~~ *MODEL PROBLEMS* ~~~~~~~~~~~~~~~

1. In a boy's bank, there is a collection of nickels, dimes, and quarters which amounts to $3.20. There are 3 times as many quarters as nickels, and 5 more dimes than nickels. How many coins of each kind are there?

Solution:

$$\text{Let } n = \text{the number of nickels.}$$
$$\text{Then } 3n = \text{the number of quarters.}$$
$$\text{And } n + 5 = \text{the number of dimes.}$$
$$\text{Then } 5n = \text{the value of nickels in cents.}$$
$$\text{And } 25(3n) = \text{the value of the quarters in cents.}$$
$$\text{And } 10(n + 5) = \text{the value of the dimes in cents.}$$

The total value of all the coins is 320 cents.

$$5n + 25(3n) + 10(n + 5) = 320$$
$$5n + 75n + 10n + 50 = 320$$
$$90n + 50 = 320$$
$$90n + 50 + (-50) = 320 + (-50)$$
$$90n = 270$$
$$n = 3$$
$$3n = 9$$
$$n + 5 = 8$$

Check

9 is 3 times 3
8 is 5 more than 3

Value of 3 nickels	= $ .15
Value of 9 quarters	= 2.25
Value of 8 dimes	= .80
Total value	= $3.20

Answer: There are 3 nickels, 9 quarters, and 8 dimes.

The following tabular arrangement may also be used. Let n = the number of nickels.

Kind of coin	Number of coins	Value of each coin in cents	Total value in cents
Nickel	n	5	$5n$
Quarter	$3n$	25	$25(3n)$
Dime	$n + 5$	10	$10(n + 5)$

The total value of all the coins is 320 cents.

$$5n + 25(3n) + 10(n + 5) = 320$$

Complete the solution as before.

2. A purse contains \$1.35 in nickels and dimes. In all there are 15 coins. How many coins of each kind are there?

Solution:

Let d = the number of dimes.

Then $15 - d$ = the number of nickels.

Kind of coin	Number of coins	Value of each coin in cents	Total value in cents
Dime	d	10	$10d$
Nickel	$15 - d$	5	$5(15 - d)$

The total value of all the coins is 135 cents.

$$10d + 5(15 - d) = 135$$
$$10d + 75 - 5d = 135$$
$$5d + 75 = 135$$
$$5d + 75 + (-75) = 135 + (-75)$$
$$5d = 60$$
$$d = 12$$
$$15 - d = 3$$

Check

$12 + 3 = 15$

Value of 12 dimes = \$1.20
Value of 3 nickels =   .15
Total value   = \$1.35

Answer: There are 12 dimes and 3 nickels.

Exercises

1. Bill has 4 times as many quarters as dimes. In all he has $2.20. How many coins of each type does he have?
2. May has 3 times as many dimes as nickels. In all she has $1.40. How many coins of each type does she have?
3. Paul has twice as many dimes as pennies and 3 times as many nickels as pennies. In all he has $1.80. How many coins of each type does he have?
4. Sally has three times as many dimes as nickels and twice as many quarters as dimes. In all she has $5.55. How many coins of each type does she have?
5. Sam has $2.05 in quarters and dimes. He has 4 more quarters than dimes. Find the number he has of each coin.
6. Helen has $1.35 in her bank in nickels and dimes. There are 9 more nickels than dimes. Find the number she has of each kind.
7. Bess has $2.80 in quarters and dimes. The number of dimes is 7 less than the number of quarters. Find the number she has of each kind.
8. Roger has $2.30 in dimes and nickels. The number of dimes exceeds the number of nickels by 5. Find the number he has of each kind.
9. Marie has $5.05 in quarters and dimes. The number of quarters exceeds twice the number of dimes by 1. Find the number she has of each kind.
10. Mr. Boyce deposited $170 in his bank. The number of $5 bills was 3 times the number of $10 bills, and the number of $1 bills was 30 more than the number of $5 bills. How many bills of each type did he deposit?
11. Harriet deposited $4.50 in nickels, quarters, and dimes in her savings account. The number of dimes exceeded the number of nickels by 5, and the number of quarters was 16 less than the number of nickels. Find the number of each kind of coin she deposited.
12. Mildred bought 2-cent stamps, 4-cent stamps, and 5-cent stamps for $4.35. The number of 2-cent stamps exceeded the number of 5-cent stamps by 50. The number of 4-cent stamps was 10 less than twice the number of 5-cent stamps. How many of each kind did she buy?
13. A class contributed $3.50 in nickels and dimes to the Red Cross. In all there were 45 coins. How many were there of each kind?
14. A purse containing $3.20 in quarters and dimes has, in all, 20 coins. Find the number of each kind of coin.
15. A purse contains $4.70 in nickels and quarters. There are 30 coins in all. How many of each kind are there?
16. James bought 80 postage stamps for which he paid $3.50. Some were 3-cent stamps and some were 5-cent stamps. How many of each kind did he buy?
17. A postal clerk sold 75 stamps for $4.80. Some were 5-cent and some were 8-cent stamps. How many of each kind did he sell?

18. Mr. Perkins cashed a $185 check in his bank. He received $1 bills, $5 bills, and $10 bills. In this order, the numbers of the three types of bills he received were three consecutive integers. How many bills of each type did he receive?

19. Saul paid a bill of $4.60 with nickels, dimes, and quarters. The number of nickels was 3 less than the number of dimes. The number of dimes was 5 more than the number of quarters. How many coins of each type did he use?

20. Roger has $3.10 consisting of quarters, dimes, and nickels. He has twice as many quarters as dimes and 3 more dimes than nickels. Find the number of each kind of coin.

21. In Paul's bank, there is $2.60 in pennies, nickels, and dimes. In all there are 45 coins. If there are twice as many nickels as pennies, find how many of each kind there are.

22. Selma paid a bill of $2.70 with quarters, dimes, and pennies. She had 5 less quarters than dimes and 4 less quarters than pennies. How many coins of each kind did she use to pay the bill?

23. Sue counted her money and found that her 25 coins which were nickels, dimes, and quarters were worth $3.20. The number of dimes exceeded the number of nickels by 4. How many coins of each kind did she have?

24. Is it possible to have $4.50 in dimes and quarters and have twice as many quarters as dimes?

25. Is it possible to spend $3.00 for 100 stamps consisting of 2-cent stamps and 5-cent stamps?

5. Per Cent and Percentage Problems

You have learned that **per cent** means *per hundred* or *hundredths*. For example, 13% is $\frac{13}{100}$ or .13. Likewise, 6% is $\frac{6}{100}$ or .06; 100% is $\frac{100}{100}$ or 1; 150% = $\frac{150}{100}$ or 1.50.

Problems dealing with interest, discounts, commissions, and taxes frequently involve per cents. For example, to find the amount of tax when $60 is taxed at a rate of 5%, we multiply $60 by 5%, .05 × 60, and get $3 as the result. In this case, the three quantities related are:

1. the sum of money being taxed, the **base,** which is $60
2. the rate of tax, the **rate,** which is 5% or .05
3. the amount of tax, the **percentage,** which is $3

The relation involving base, b, rate, r, and percentage, p, may be expressed as follows:

$$p = rb$$

~~~~~~~~~~~~~~~~ **MODEL PROBLEMS** ~~~~~~~~~~~~~~~~

1. If 25% of a number is 80, find the number.

Solution:

<table>
<tr><td align="center"><em>Method 1</em></td><td align="center"><em>Method 2</em></td></tr>
</table>

Let $n =$ the number.   Let $n =$ the number.

$\quad p = rb \qquad [p = 80,$ $\qquad p = rb \qquad [p = 80,$

$\qquad\qquad\qquad r = 25\% = .25]$ $\qquad\qquad\qquad r = 25\% = \frac{25}{100} = \frac{1}{4}]$

$\quad 80 = .25n$ $\qquad 80 = \frac{1}{4}n$

$\quad \dfrac{80}{.25} = \dfrac{.25n}{.25} \quad \text{D}_{.25}$ $\qquad 4(80) = 4(\frac{1}{4}n) \quad \text{M}_4$

$\quad 320 = n$ $\qquad 320 = n$

Check: 25% of 320 is 80.

Answer: The number is 320.

2. Of the 560 seniors in Village High School, 476 attended the senior prom. What per cent of the senior class attended the prom?

Solution:

Let $\dfrac{x}{100} =$ the per cent of the senior class that attended the dance.

<table>
<tr><td align="center"><em>Method 1</em></td><td align="center"><em>Method 2</em></td></tr>
</table>

$\quad p = br \quad [p = 476, b = 560]$ $\qquad p = br \quad [p = 476, b = 560]$

$\quad 476 = 560\left(\dfrac{x}{100}\right)$ $\qquad 476 = 560\left(\dfrac{x}{100}\right)$

$\quad 47600 = 560x \quad \text{M}_{100}$ $\qquad 476 = \dfrac{560}{100}x$

$\quad \dfrac{47600}{560} = \dfrac{560x}{560} \quad \text{D}_{560}$ $\qquad \dfrac{100}{560}(476) = \dfrac{100}{560}\left(\dfrac{560}{100}x\right) \quad \text{M}_{\frac{100}{560}}$

$\qquad 85 = x$ $\qquad\qquad 85 = x$

$\qquad \dfrac{x}{100} = \dfrac{85}{100} = 85\%$ $\qquad\qquad \dfrac{x}{100} = \dfrac{85}{100} = 85\%$

Check: 85% of 560 is 476.

Answer: 85% of the seniors attended.

3. A dealer sold a radio for $39.20, which was 40% above its cost to him. Find the cost of the radio to the dealer.

Solution:

Method 1

Let x = the cost of the radio to the dealer.

Since the dealer sold the radio 40% above its cost to him, he sold it for 100% + 40%, or 140% of the original cost.

$$p = br \qquad [p = \$39.20, \; r = 140\% = 1.40]$$
$$39.20 = 1.40x$$

$$\frac{39.20}{1.40} = \frac{1.40x}{1.40} \qquad D_{1.40}$$
$$28 = x$$

Check: 40% of $28 is $11.20. $28 + $11.20 = $39.20

Answer: The dealer paid $28 for the radio.

Method 2

Let x = the cost of the radio to the dealer.
$.40x$ = the amount of the dealer's markup.

Cost of the radio plus the markup equals the selling price.

$$x + .40x = 39.20$$
$$1.40x = 39.20$$

$$\frac{1.40x}{1.40} = \frac{39.20}{1.40} \qquad D_{1.40}$$
$$x = 28$$

Answer: The dealer paid $28 for the radio.

Exercises

In 1–15, use the formula $p = br$ to find the indicated percentage.

1. 2% of 36	2. 6% of 150	3. 15% of 48
4. 29% of 92	5. 60% of 56	6. 100% of 7.5
7. 2.5% of 400	8. $1\frac{1}{4}$% of 144	9. $4\frac{1}{2}$% of 200
10. $12\frac{1}{2}$% of 128	11. $33\frac{1}{3}$% of 72	12. $\frac{1}{4}$% of 2400
13. 150% of 18	14. 105% of 50	15. $166\frac{2}{3}$% of 99

In 16–25, use the formula $p = br$ to find the number.

16. 20 is 10% of what number?   **17.** 64 is 80% of what number?

18. 75% of what number is 3.6?   **19.** 6% of what number is 10.8?

20. 72 is 100% of what number?   **21.** 125% of what number is 45?

22. $37\frac{1}{2}$% of what number is 60?   **23.** $66\frac{2}{3}$% of what number is 54?

24. 3% of what number is 1.86?   **25.** $1\frac{1}{2}$% of what number is 240?

In 26–35, use the formula $p = br$ to find the rate.

26. 6 is what per cent of 12?   **27.** 9 is what per cent of 30?

28. What % of 10 is 6?   **29.** What % of 35 is 28?

30. 5 is what % of 15?   **31.** What % of 80 is 30?

32. 22 is what % of 22?   **33.** 18 is what % of 12?

34. 2 is what per cent of 400?   **35.** 3 is what % of 3000?

36. There were 120 planes on an airfield. If 75% of the planes took off for a flight, how many planes took off?

37. The price of a new car is $3450. Mr. Klein made a down payment of 15% of the price of the car when he bought it. How much was his down payment?

38. How much salt is in 30 ounces of a solution of salt and water which is 10% salt?

39. How much silver is in 75 pounds of an alloy which is 8% silver?

40. In a factory, 54,650 parts were made. When these were tested, 4% were found to be defective. How many parts were good?

41. A baseball team won 8 games, which was 50% of the total number of games it played. How many games did the team play?

42. In a school, there are 60 pupils who participate in a certain activity. If this is 12% of the student body, how many students are there in the school?

43. Helen bought a coat at a "20% off" sale and saved $12. What was the marked price of the coat?

44. A businessman is required to collect a 5% sales tax. One day he collected $281 in taxes. Find the total amount of sales he made that day.

45. A merchant sold a television set for $150, which was 25% above its cost to him. Find the cost of the television set to the dealer.

46. Mr. Tayler took a 2% discount on a bill. He paid the balance with a check for $76.44. What was the original amount of the bill?

47. After the price of a pound of meat was increased 10%, the new price was 99 cents. What was the price of a pound of meat before the increase?

48. It is estimated that in ten years the population of Keysport will increase 75% and will then be 2800. Find the present population of Keysport.

49. After Mr. Sims lost 15% of his investment, he had $2550 left. How much did he invest originally?

50. Bill had $300 on deposit in the bank. He then deposited $15 in the bank. This represented what per cent of the amount he had on deposit in the bank?

51. Mr. Todd bought a suit for $90 and paid $4.50 as a sales tax. What per cent is the tax?

52. When a salesman sold a vacuum cleaner for $110, he received a commission of $8.80. What was the rate of commission?

53. A man bought a car for $2400. At the end of a year, the value of the car had decreased $480. By what per cent had the car decreased in value?

54. Mr. Brown's salary increased from $75 per week to $90 per week. Find the per cent of increase in his salary.

55. During a sale, the price of a dress was decreased from $48 to $32. What was the per cent of the decrease in price?

6. Mixture Problems

PREPARING TO SOLVE MIXTURE PROBLEMS

Many problems deal with the mixing of ingredients which have different costs. In solving these problems, it is helpful to express the total value of each ingredient in the same unit of money, such as cents. For example:

The value of 3 pounds of coffee worth 75 cents per pound is 3(75), or 225 cents.

The value of x pounds of candy worth 40 cents per pound is $x(40)$, or $40x$ cents.

The value of $(20 - x)$ pounds of nuts worth $1.25 per pound is $(20 - x)125$ or $125(20 - x)$ cents.

```
┌──────────── KEEP IN MIND ────────────┐
│                                        │
│  Number of units  ×  Price per unit  =  Total value of │
│  of the same kind                       all of the units │
│                                        │
└────────────────────────────────────────┘
```

Exercises

1. A certain kind of candy is worth 65 cents a pound. Represent the total value of:

a. 2 lb.	*b.* 10 lb.	*c.* x lb.
d. $2x$ lb.	*e.* $(x + 5)$ lb.	*f.* $(20 - x)$ lb.

2. A certain kind of nut is worth 90 cents a pound. Represent the total value of:

a. 5 lb.	*b.* 12 lb.	*c.* x lb.
d. $3x$ lb.	*e.* $(x + 2)$ lb.	*f.* $(30 - x)$ lb.

3. Represent the total value of each of the following mixtures in cents:
- *a.* 10 lb. of candy worth 45 cents a pound and 30 lb. of candy worth 75 cents a pound.
- *b.* x lb. of 65-cent coffee and $(x + 5)$ lb. of 85-cent coffee.
- *c.* x gallons of 40-cent oil and $(50 - x)$ gallons of 65-cent oil.
- *d.* 80 lb. of nuts worth $1.50 per pound and x lb. of nuts worth $.95 per pound.

SOLVING MIXTURE PROBLEMS

---------------------- **MODEL PROBLEMS** ----------------------

1. A dealer wishes to mix coffee worth 65 cents per pound with coffee worth 90 cents per pound in order to produce 40 pounds of coffee which can be sold at 75 cents per pound. How many pounds of each type should he use?

Solution:

Let n = the number of lb. of the 90-cent coffee.
Then $40 - n$ = the number of lb. of the 65-cent coffee.
$90n$ = the value of the 90-cent coffee in cents.
$65(40 - n)$ = the value of the 65-cent coffee in cents.
$75(40)$ = the value of the mixture in cents.

The total value of the 90-cent coffee and the 65-cent coffee equals the value of the mixture.

$90n + 65(40 - n) = 75(40)$
$90n + 2600 - 65n = 3000$
$25n + 2600 = 3000$
$25n + 2600 - 2600 = 3000 - 2600$
$25n = 400$
$n = 16$
$40 - n = 24$

Check

$24 + 16 = 40$
Value of 24 lb. at 65¢ per lb. = $15.60
Value of 16 lb. at 90¢ per lb. = $\underline{14.40}$
Total value = $30.00
Value of 40 lb. at 75¢ per lb. = $30.00

Answer: 16 lb. of the 90-cent coffee; 24 lb. of the 65-cent coffee

The following tabular arrangement may also be used:
Let n = the number of pounds of the 90-cent coffee.
Then $40 - n$ = the number of pounds of the 65-cent coffee.

Kind of coffee	Number of pounds	Price per pound in cents	Total value in cents
90-cent	n	90	$90n$
65-cent	$40 - n$	65	$65(40 - n)$
Mixture	40	75	$75(40)$

The total value of the 90-cent coffee and the 65-cent coffee equals the value of the mixture.

$$90n + 65(40 - n) = 75(40)$$

Complete the solution as before.

2. How many pounds of candy worth 70 cents per pound must be mixed with 30 pounds of candy worth 90 cents per pound to produce a mixture which can be sold for 85 cents per pound?

Solution:

Let $n =$ the required number of pounds of the 70-cent candy.

Kind of candy	Number of pounds	Price per pound in cents	Total value in cents
70-cent	n	70	$70n$
90-cent	30	90	$90(30)$
Mixture	$n + 30$	85	$85(n + 30)$

The total value of the 70-cent candy and the 90-cent candy equals the value of the mixture.

$$70n + 90(30) = 85(n + 30)$$
$$70n + 2700 = 85n + 2550$$
$$70n + 2700 + (-70n) = 85n + 2550 + (-70n)$$
$$2700 = 15n + 2550$$
$$2700 + (-2550) = 15n + 2550 + (-2550)$$
$$150 = 15n$$
$$10 = n$$

Check: Value of 10 lb. at 70¢ per lb. = $ 7.00
        Value of 30 lb. at 90¢ per lb. = 27.00
        Total value   = $34.00
        Value of 40 lb. at 85¢ per lb. = $34.00

Answer: 10 pounds of the 70-cent candy are required.

~~~~~~

Exercises

1. A grocer mixed nuts worth 80 cents per pound with nuts worth 50 cents per pound. How many pounds of each did he use to make a mixture of 30 pounds to sell at 75 cents per pound?

2. How many gallons of gasoline worth 21 cents per gallon and how many gallons of gasoline worth 26 cents per gallon must be mixed to produce 500 gallons worth 24 cents per gallon?

3. If almonds sell at $1.20 per pound and walnuts sell for $.75 per pound, how many pounds of each must be used to make 45 pounds of a mixture to sell at $1.00 per pound?

4. How many pounds of 60-cent coffee and 87-cent coffee must a dealer mix to produce 90 pounds of coffee to sell for 69 cents per pound?

5. A seedman has seeds worth $.70 per pound and seeds worth $.90 per pound. How many pounds of each must he use to make 300 pounds worth $.75 per pound?

6. A dealer has some hard candy worth 45 cents per pound and some worth 70 cents per pound. He wishes to make a mixture of 120 pounds that will be worth 55 cents per pound. How many pounds of each kind should he use?

7. A dealer wishes to produce 300 gallons of oil worth 40 cents a quart by mixing oil worth 36 cents a quart with oil worth 52 cents a quart. How many quarts of each kind of oil should he use?

8. A dealer has tea worth $1.20 a pound and tea worth $1.90 a pound. How many pounds of each kind must he use to make 70 pounds that can be sold for $1.50 per pound?

9. A baker has cookies worth $.95 per pound and cookies worth $1.70 per pound. How many pounds of each kind must he use to produce a 45-pound mixture to sell for $1.25 per pound?

10. A candy dealer sells 5-cent chocolate bars and 10-cent chocolate bars. One day he sold 130 chocolate bars for which he received $9. How many bars of each kind did he sell?

11. A florist sold roses at $3.50 per dozen and carnations at $2.50 per dozen. In all he sold 14 dozen, and his total receipts were $43. How many dozen of each kind of flower did he sell?

12. At a high school baseball game, G.O. members paid 35 cents each and non-members paid 50 cents each. There were 20 more G.O. members at the game than non-members. If the total receipts were $75, how many tickets of each kind were sold?

13. One evening 478 tickets were sold at the local movie. The charges for admission were $.85 for adults and $.50 for children. The total receipts for the performance were $375.50. How many adults and how many children attended?

14. Is it possible for 150 people to pay $150 to attend a performance if adults pay $1.25 and children pay $.60 for admission?

15. How many pounds of 65-cent coffee must be mixed with 10 pounds of 90-cent coffee to make a mixture worth 70 cents a pound?

16. How many pounds of nuts worth 70 cents per pound must be mixed with 12 pounds of nuts worth 50 cents per pound to produce a mixture which can be sold for 65 cents per pound?

17. How many pounds of tea worth $1.80 a pound must be mixed with 15 pounds of tea worth $1.10 a pound to produce a mixture worth $1.50 a pound?

18. How many pounds of seed worth 60 cents per pound must be mixed with 300 pounds of seed worth 35 cents per pound to produce a mixture worth 50 cents per pound?

7. Per Cent Mixture Problems

PREPARING TO SOLVE PER CENT MIXTURE PROBLEMS

The per cent mixture problem is a type of mixture problem that involves per cents. For example:

The amount of pure salt in 25 oz. of a 20% solution of salt and water is $.20(25)$, or 5 oz.

The amount of butterfat in x lb. of milk testing 4% butterfat is $.04(x)$, or $.04x$ lb.

The amount of pure acid in $(100 - x)$ oz. of a 25% solution of acid in water is $.25(100 - x)$ oz.

```
┌─────────────────── KEEP IN MIND ───────────────────┐
│                                                     │
│     The number of units of a solution (mixture) which│
│   contains a given pure substance × the part of the solu-│
│   tion (mixture) which is that pure substance = the │
│   amount of that pure substance in the solution (mixture).│
│                                                     │
└─────────────────────────────────────────────────────┘
```

Exercises

1. A solution is 40% pure acid. Represent the number of pounds of pure acid in this solution if it weighs:

   a. 100 lb.   b. 60 lb.   c. 12 lb.   d. x lb.   e. $(x - 2)$ lb.

2. Represent the total amount of pure acid in a solution if the solution contains x ounces of acid which is 50% pure acid and $(20 - x)$ ounces of acid which is 30% pure acid.

3. A solution which is 20% pure iodine weighs 60 ounces.

   a. Represent the number of ounces of pure iodine in the solution.
   b. If x ounces of pure iodine are added to this solution, represent (1) the amount of pure iodine in the resulting solution and (2) the number of ounces in the resulting solution.

4. A solution of salt and water contains 25% pure salt. The solution weighs 120 ounces.

   a. Represent the number of ounces of pure salt in the solution.
   b. If x ounces of water are evaporated from the solution, represent the number of ounces in the resulting solution.
   c. If the resulting solution is 30% pure salt, represent in terms of x the number of ounces of salt in the resulting solution.

SOLVING PER CENT MIXTURE PROBLEMS

~~~~~~~~~~~~~~~~~~~~ MODEL PROBLEM ~~~~~~~~~~~~~~~~~~~~

How much pure acid must be added to 15 ounces of an acid solution which is 40% acid in order to produce a solution which is 50% acid?

Solution:

The number of ounces of pure acid in the given mixture is .40(15) = 6.
        Let n = the number of ounces of pure acid to be added.
Then $6 + n$ = the number of ounces of pure acid in the new mixture.
Also $15 + n$ = the total contents of the new mixture.

The number of ounces of pure acid in the new mixture
is 50% of the total contents of the new mixture.

$$6 + n = .50(15 + n)$$
$$6 + n = 7.50 + .50n$$
$$600 + 100n = 750 + 50n \qquad M_{100}$$
$$600 + 100n + (-50n) = 750 + 50n + (-50n)$$
$$600 + 50n = 750 \qquad\qquad Check$$
$$600 + 50n + (-600) = 750 + (-600) \qquad 40\% \text{ of } 15 = .40(15) = 6$$
$$50n = 150 \qquad\qquad 6 + 3 = 9$$
$$n = 3 \qquad\qquad 50\% \text{ of } (15 + 3) = .50(18) = 9$$

Answer: 3 ounces of pure acid must be added.

The following tabular arrangement may also be used:

Let $n =$ the number of ounces of pure acid to be added.

Kind of solution	Number of ounces	Part pure acid	Number of ounces of pure acid
Original solution	15	.40	6
Pure acid to be added	n	1.00	n
New mixture	$15 + n$	.50	$.50(15 + n)$

The total amount of pure acid in the original solution and in the pure
acid added is equal to the amount of pure acid in the new mixture.

$$6 + n = .50(15 + n)$$

Complete the solution as before.

Exercises

1. A chemist has one solution which is 30% pure acid and another solution which is 60% pure acid. How many pounds of each solution must be used to produce 60 pounds of a solution which is 50% pure acid?
2. A farmer has some cream which is 24% butterfat and some cream which is 18% butterfat. How many quarts of each must he use to produce 90 quarts of cream which is 22% butterfat?

3. A chemist has a solution which is 40% pure acid and another solution which is 15% pure acid. How many ounces of each solution should he use to make 40 ounces of a solution which is 25% pure acid?

4. How many pounds of a solution which is 75% pure acid must be mixed with 16 pounds of a solution which is 30% pure acid to produce a solution which is 55% pure acid?

5. How much pure acid must be added to 25 ounces of a solution of acid and water which is 20% pure acid in order to make a solution which is 50% pure acid?

6. How much salt must be added to 80 pounds of a 5% salt solution to make a 24% salt solution?

7. A chemist has 40 ounces of a solution of iodine and alcohol which is 15% iodine. How much pure iodine must he add to make a solution which is 20% iodine?

8. A solution of 70 pounds of acid contains 6 pounds of pure acid. How many pounds of pure acid must be added to make a solution which is 20% pure acid?

9. A solution of iodine and alcohol contains 3 ounces of iodine and 21 ounces of alcohol. How much pure iodine must be added to produce a solution which is 25% iodine?

10. A solution of alcohol and water which is 20% alcohol weighs 60 pounds. How much water must be added to make a solution which is 5% alcohol?

11. In a tank there are 100 pounds of a solution of acid and water which is 20% acid. How much water must be evaporated to produce a solution which is 50% acid?

12. A solution contains 8 pounds of acid and 32 pounds of water. How many pounds of water must be evaporated to produce a solution which will be 40% acid?

13. How much water must be added to 30 pounds of a solution of salt in water which contains 20% salt so that the resulting solution will be 15% salt?

8. Investment Problems

PREPARING TO SOLVE INVESTMENT PROBLEMS

Mr. Samuels invested $500 at 4%. His annual income was 4% of $500, which equals .04($500), or $20. In finding the annual income, we make use of the *annual interest formula* $i = pr$. In this formula, p represents the *principal*, or amount invested, $500; r represents the *annual rate of interest*, 4%; and i represents the *annual income*, $20.

┌──────────────── **KEEP IN MIND** ────────────────┐
│   │
│   Principal in $\times$ Annual rate = Annual income │
│   dollars   of income   in dollars │
│   │
└───┘

Exercises

1. Represent the annual income when the annual rate is 5% and the amount invested is:

   a. $600   *b.* $2500   *c.* $$x$ *d.* $$3x$ *e.* $$(x + 500)$ *f.* $$(5000 - x)$

2. Represent the annual income when the annual rate is $4\frac{1}{2}\%$ and the principal invested is:

   a. $800   *b.* $3000   *c.* $$x$ *d.* $$8x$ *e.* $$(2x + 400)$ *f.* $$(4000 - x)$

3. Represent the total annual income in each of the following:

   a. $4000 invested at 5% and $6500 invested at 4%
   b. $3500 invested at $3\frac{1}{2}\%$ and $4200 invested at $4\frac{1}{2}\%$
   c. $8000 invested at 6% and $$x$ invested at 8%
   d. $$x$ invested at 5% and $$4x$ invested at 6%
   e. $$x$ invested at 6% and $$(x + 2000)$ invested at 7%
   f. $$x$ invested at 4% and $$(8000 - x)$ invested at 10%

4. Mr. Walker invested $$x$ at 4%. He also invested $500 more than this sum at 6%.

   a. Represent the amount he invested at 6%.
   b. Represent the annual income from the 4% investment.
   c. Represent the annual income from the 6% investment.
   d. Represent the total annual income from both investments.
   e. Write an open sentence which would indicate that Mr. Walker's total annual income was $130.

5. Mr. Collins invested a portion of $9000 at 5% and the remainder at 10%. Let x represent the amount he invested at 5%.

   a. Represent the amount he invested at 10%.
   b. Represent the annual income from the 5% investment.
   c. Represent the annual income from the 10% investment.
   d. Write an open sentence which would indicate that the annual incomes from both investments are the same.

SOLVING INVESTMENT PROBLEMS

~~~~~~~~~~~~~~~~~ *MODEL PROBLEMS* ~~~~~~~~~~~~~

1. Mr. Parsons invested a sum of money at 6% and a second sum, $500 more than the first, at 4%. The total annual income was $50. How much did he invest at each rate?

Solution:

Let p = the number of dollars invested at 6%.
Then $p + 500$ = the number of dollars invested at 4%.
$.06p$ = the annual income from the 6% investment.
$.04(p + 500)$ = the annual income from the 4% investment.

The total annual income was $50.

$.06p + .04(p + 500) = 50$
$.06p + .04p + 20 = 50$
$.10p + 20 = 50$ *Check*
$.10p + 20 - 20 = 50 - 20$ $300 + $500 = $800
$.10p = 30$ $.06($300) = $18.00
$p = 300$ $.04($800) = $32.00
$p + 500 = 800$ Total   = $50.00

Answer: $300 was invested at 6%; $800 was invested at 4%.

The following tabular arrangement may also be used:
Let p = the number of dollars invested at 6%.
Then $p + 500$ = the number of dollars invested at 4%.

Investment	Principal in dollars	Annual rate of income	Annual income in dollars
6% investment	p	.06	$.06p$
4% investment	$p + 500$	.04	$.04(p + 500)$

The total annual income was $50.

$.06p + .04(p + 500) = 50$

Complete the solution as before.

2. Mr. Simpson invested $2000, part at 5% and the remainder at 3%. The total annual interest he received was $88. How much did he invest at each rate?

Solution:

$$\text{Let } p = \text{ the number of dollars invested at } 5\%.$$
$$\text{Then } 2000 - p = \text{ the number of dollars invested at } 3\%.$$
$$.05p = \text{ the annual income from the } 5\% \text{ investment.}$$
$$.03(2000 - p) = \text{ the annual income from the } 3\% \text{ investment.}$$

The total annual income was $88.

$$.05p + .03(2000 - p) = 88$$
$$.05p + 60 - .03p = 88$$
$$.02p + 60 = 88$$
$$.02p + 60 - 60 = 88 - 60$$
$$.02p = 28$$
$$p = 1400$$
$$2000 - p = 600$$

Check

$1400 + 600 = 2000$
$.05(1400) = 70.00$
$.03(600)\ \ = \underline{18.00}$
Total $= 88.00$

Answer: $1400 was invested at 5%; $600 was invested at 3%.

The following tabular arrangement may also be used:

$$\text{Let } p = \text{ the number of dollars invested at } 5\%.$$
$$\text{Then } 2000 - p = \text{ the number of dollars invested at } 3\%.$$

Investment	Principal in dollars	Annual rate of income	Annual income in dollars
5% investment	p	.05	$.05p$
3% investment	$2000 - p$	.03	$.03(2000 - p)$

The total annual income was $88.

$$.05p + .03(2000 - p) = 88$$

Complete the solution as before.

3. Mr. Harvey invested a part of $1000 at 4% and the remainder at 6%. The annual income from the 4% investment exceeded the annual income from the 6% investment by $30. Find the amount he invested at each rate.

Solution:

Let p = the amount invested at 4%.
Then $1000 - p$ = the amount invested at 6%.

Investment	Principal in dollars	Annual rate of income	Annual income in dollars
4% investment	p	.04	$.04p$
6% investment	$1000 - p$	.06	$.06(1000 - p)$

The annual income from the 4% investment exceeded the annual income from the 6% investment by $30.

$.04p = .06(1000 - p) + 30$
$.04p = 60 - .06p + 30$
$.04p = 90 - .06p$
$.04p + .06p = 90 - .06p + .06p$
$.10p = 90$
$p = 900$
$1000 - p = 100$

Check

$900 + 100 = 1000$
$.04(900) = 36$
$.06(100) = 6$
$36 exceeds $6 by $30.

Answer: $900 was invested at 4%; $100 was invested at 6%.

Exercises

1. Mr. Sawyer invested a sum of money at 4%. He invested twice as much at 5%. The total annual income from these investments was $210. Find the amount he invested at each rate.
2. Mr. Traynor invested a sum of money at 4%. He invested a second sum, $250 more than the first sum, at 6%. If his total annual income was $90, how much did he invest at each rate?
3. Mr. Wayne invested a sum of money at 3%. He invested a second sum, $150 less than the first sum, at 6%. The total annual income was $54. Find the amount invested at each rate.

4. Mr. Jones invested a sum of money in 6% bonds. He invested $400 more than this sum in 4% bonds. If his total annual income was $116, how much did he invest in each kind of bond?

5. Mr. Fox invested a sum of money at 6%. He invested a second sum, $2000 less than this sum, at 5%. He invested a third sum, which was $3000 less than the first sum, at 3%. His total annual income was $370. Find the amount he invested at each rate.

6. Mr. Ryan invested a sum of money at 6%. He invested a second sum, which exceeded twice the first sum by $1000, at 10%. His total annual income was $620. Find the amount he invested at each rate.

7. Mr. Hart made two investments, one at $4\frac{1}{2}\%$ and the other at 3%. The amount invested at 3% exceeded the amount invested at $4\frac{1}{2}\%$ by $300. If his total annual income was $84, find the amount invested at each rate.

8. Mrs. Johnson invested $4000, part at 5% and the remainder at 3%. The total annual income from both investments was $152. Find the amount invested at each rate.

9. Mr. Joyce invested $25,000, part at 4% and the remainder at 7%. The total income he received at the end of the year was $1,450. How much did he invest at each rate?

10. A sum of $3500 is invested in two parts. One part brings a return of 5% and the other a return of 8%. The total annual return is $250. Find the amount invested at each rate.

11. Mr. Carlson has invested $7,500 in two parts, one part at 6% and the other at 10%. Find the amount invested at each rate if the total yearly income is $590.

12. Mr. Sims has invested $8000. Part of his money is invested in bonds which yield 4% and the remainder is invested in bonds which yield 5%. His total annual income from these bonds is $380. Find the amount he has invested in each kind of bond.

13. Mr. Daniels had a sum of money to invest. He invested $\frac{1}{2}$ of the sum at 5%, $\frac{1}{3}$ of the sum at 6%, and the remainder at 3%. His total annual income was $300. What was the total sum that Mr. Daniels invested?

14. Mr. Thorpe inherited a sum of money. He invested $\frac{2}{5}$ of this sum at 4%, $\frac{1}{3}$ at 5%, and the rest at 3%. If the annual income from these investments was $610, find the amount of money he inherited.

15. Mr. Mack invested a sum of money at 6%. He invested $200 more than this sum at 4%. If the annual incomes from both investments were the same, find the amount invested at each rate.

16. Mr. West invested $7200, part at 4% and the remainder at 5%. If the annual incomes from both investments were equal, find the amount invested at each rate.

17. Mr. Doyle invested $7500 in two business enterprises. In one enterprise he made a 5% profit; in the other he had a 2% loss. His net profit for the year was $130. Find the amount invested at each rate.

18. Mr. Lamb has invested $18,000 in two parts. One part is invested at 8% and the other at 10%. The annual income from the 10% investment is $360 more than the annual income from the 8% investment. Find the amount invested at each rate.

19. The sum of $4000 is invested, part at 4% and the rest at 6%. The annual income from the 6% investment is $10 less than the annual income from the 4% investment. Find the amount invested at each rate.

20. Mr. Simpson invested $6,000, part at 4% and the rest at 3%. Each year the income from the 4% investment exceeded the income from the 3% investment by $2. Find the amount invested at each rate.

21. Mr. Jewel bought two bonds for $15,000. One bond pays 6% interest and the other pays 8% interest. The annual interest from the 8% bond exceeds the annual interest from the 6% bond by $500. Find the cost of each bond.

22. Mr. Crawford has invested $6,000 at 3%. How much additional money must he invest at 8% so that his total annual income will be 4% of his total investment?

23. Mr. Walker has $2000 invested at 7% and $5000 invested at 4%. How much additional money must he invest at 6% to make his total annual income 5% of his total investment?

24. Mr. Ryan invested $5000 at 6%. How much additional money must he invest at $3\frac{1}{2}$% to make his total annual income $4\frac{1}{2}$% of his total investment?

9. Age Problems

PREPARING TO SOLVE AGE PROBLEMS

If Ken is 20 years old now, 5 years ago Ken was $20 - 5$, or 15 years old; 5 years from now Ken will be $20 + 5$, or 25 years old.

KEEP IN MIND

1. To represent a past age, subtract from the present age.
2. To represent a future age, add to the present age.

Exercises

1. Thomas is x years old now. Represent his age 10 years from now.
2. Marion is y years old now. Represent her age 8 years ago.
3. Terry is $2x$ years old now. Represent her age 2 years hence.
4. Marilyn is $5y$ years old now. Represent her age 4 years ago.
5. Sue is $(2x - 3)$ years old now. Represent her age 8 years from now.
6. Robert is $(30 - x)$ years old now. Represent his age 7 years ago.
7. A man is x years old now. Represent his age y years from now.
8. A woman is x years old now. Represent her age y years ago.
9. Six years ago, Paul's age was $2x$. Represent his age 3 years from now.
10. Two years from now, Martin's age will be $3x + 5$. Represent his age 4 years ago.
11. Ted is now 7 years younger than his brother, whose age is $5x + 1$. Represent Ted's age 3 years from now.
12. Gloria is three times as old as Marie, whose age is x.

   a. Represent each girl's age 6 years from now.
   b. Represent each girl's age 3 years ago.

SOLVING AGE PROBLEMS

~~~~~~~~~~~~~ *MODEL PROBLEMS* ~~~~~~~~~~~~~

1. Bill is 3 times as old as Peter. Six years from now, Bill will be twice as old as Peter will be then. Find the present age of both Bill and Peter.

Solution:

$$\text{Let } x = \text{Peter's present age.}$$
$$\text{Then } 3x = \text{Bill's present age.}$$
$$\text{Then } x + 6 = \text{Peter's age 6 years from now.}$$
$$\text{Then } 3x + 6 = \text{Bill's age 6 years from now.}$$

Six years from now, Bill will be twice as old as Peter will be then.

$3x + 6 = 2(x + 6)$	
$3x + 6 = 2x + 12$	
$3x + 6 + (-6) = 2x + 12 + (-6)$	*Check*
$3x = 2x + 6$	$18 = 3(6)$
$3x + (-2x) = 2x + 6 + (-2x)$	$6 + 6 = 12$
$x = 6$	$18 + 6 = 24$
$3x = 18$	$24 = 2(12)$

Answer: Peter's age is 6 years. Bill's age is 18 years.

The following tabular arrangement may also be used:

Let x = Peter's present age.
Then $3x$ = Bill's present age.

Person	Present age in years	Future age, 6 years from now
Peter	x	$x + 6$
Bill	$3x$	$3x + 6$

Six years from now, Bill will be twice as old as Peter will be then.

$$3x + 6 = 2(x + 6)$$

Complete the solution as before.

2. Helen is now 20 years old and Arlene is 10 years old. How many years ago was Helen three times as old as Arlene was then?

Solution:

Let x = the required number of years ago.
Then $20 - x$ = Helen's age x years ago.
And $10 - x$ = Arlene's age x years ago.

Helen was three times as old as Arlene was then.

$$20 - x = 3(10 - x)$$
$$20 - x = 30 - 3x$$
$$20 - x + (+3x) = 30 - 3x + (+3x)$$
$$20 + 2x = 30$$
$$20 + 2x + (-20) = 30 + (-20)$$
$$2x = 10$$
$$x = 5$$

Check

$20 - 5 = 15$
$10 - 5 = 5$
$15 = 3(5)$

Answer: 5 years ago

The following tabular arrangement may also be used:

Let x = the required number of years ago.

Person	Present age in years	Past age, x years ago
Helen	20	$20 - x$
Arlene	10	$10 - x$

Helen was three times as old as Arlene was then.

$$20 - x = 3(10 - x)$$

Complete the solution as before.

~~~~~~

Exercises

1. John is now 4 times as old as his brother Sam. In 4 years, John will be twice as old as Sam will be then. Find their present ages.
2. A man is now 6 times as old as his son. In 6 years, the father will be 3 times as old as the son will be then. Find their present ages.
3. James is now 3 times as old as Arthur. In 10 years, James will be twice as old as Arthur will be then. Find their present ages.
4. Marie is one-ninth as old as her mother. In 3 years, she will be one-fifth as old as her mother will be then. Find their present ages.
5. A father is now 24 years older than his son. In 8 years, the father will be twice as old as his son will be then. Find their present ages.
6. Mr. Wilson is 15 years older than Mr. Connors. Five years from now, Mr. Wilson will be $1\frac{1}{2}$ times as old as Mr. Connors will be then. How old is each man now?
7. Marion is twice as old as Judy. Three years ago, Marion was three times as old as Judy was then. Find the age of each girl now.
8. A father is 3 times as old as his son. Fifteen years ago, the father was 9 times as old as his son was then. Find their present ages.
9. Selma is now 3 times as old as Joyce. Four years ago, Selma was 4 times as old as Joyce was then. Find their present ages.
10. Robert is one-half as old as his father. Twelve years ago, Robert was one-third as old as his father was then. Find their present ages.
11. Phil is 24 years older than Stanley. Four years ago, he was 7 times as old as Stanley was then. Find their present ages.

12. Mrs. Barry is 20 years older than Mrs. Cook. Sixteen years ago, Mrs. Barry was 3 times as old as Mrs. Cook was then. Find their present ages.

13. Josephine is 22 years old and Ruth is 10 years old. In how many years will Josephine be twice as old as Ruth will be then?

14. A man is 40 years old and his son is 8 years old. In how many years will the man be 3 times as old as his son will be then?

15. Gene is 23 years old and Stanley is 15 years old. How many years ago was Gene 3 times as old as Stanley was then?

16. Mr. Atkins is 33 years old and Mr. Speyer is 27 years old. How many years ago was Mr. Atkins $1\frac{1}{2}$ times as old as Mr. Speyer was then?

17. The sum of a man's age and his daughter's age is 50 years. Eight years from now, the man will be twice as old as his daughter will be then. Find the present age of each.

18. Mrs. Sanford is three times as old as Mrs. Fox. Eight years from now, Mrs. Sanford's age will exceed twice Mrs. Fox's age at that time by 14 years. Find the present age of each.

19. Hal is 10 years older than Gerald. In 6 years, Hal will be $1\frac{1}{2}$ times as old as Gerald will be then. Find their present ages.

20. Mrs. Watson was 25 years old when her daughter Rose was born. Now Mrs. Watson's age exceeds 4 times Rose's age by 10 years. Find their ages now.

21. The sum of Wilbur's age and Fred's age is 20 years. Wilbur's age 1 year from now will be 9 times Fred's age 1 year ago. Find the present age of each.

22. The sum of Carl's age and Ellen's age is 40 years. Carl's age 10 years from now will be 1 less than 4 times Ellen's age 6 years ago. Find their present ages.

23. Mark is 10 years younger than Larry. Larry's age 8 years from now will exceed twice Mark's age 3 years ago by 4 years. How old is each now?

10. Perimeter Problems

PREPARING TO SOLVE PERIMETER PROBLEMS

--- KEEP IN MIND ---

The perimeter of a geometric plane figure is the sum of the lengths of all of its sides.

Exercises

1. Represent the perimeter of each of the following figures:

(a)　　　　　　　(b)　　　　　　　(c)　　　　　　　(d)

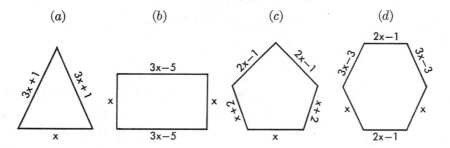

2. Represent the length and perimeter of a rectangle whose width is represented by x and whose length:

a. is twice its width
b. is 4 more than its width
c. is 5 less than twice its width
d. is 3 more than twice its width
e. is 4 times its width diminished by 1
f. exceeds three times its width by 6

SOLVING PERIMETER PROBLEMS

In solving problems dealing with the perimeters of geometric plane figures, it is helpful to draw the figures.

~~~~~~~~~~~~~~ **MODEL PROBLEM** ~~~~~~~~~~~~~~

The perimeter of a rectangle is 40 feet. The length is 2 more than 5 times the width. Find the dimensions of the rectangle.

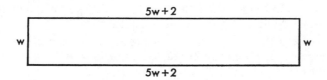

Solution:

Let w = the width of the rectangle.
Then $5w + 2$ = the length of the rectangle.

The sum of all the sides is 40.

$$w + 5w + 2 + w + 5w + 2 = 40$$
$$12w + 4 = 40$$
$$12w + 4 - 4 = 40 - 4$$
$$12w = 36$$
$$w = 3$$
$$5w + 2 = 17$$

Check

$$3 + 17 + 3 + 17 = 40$$
$$17 \overset{?}{=} 5(3) + 2$$
$$17 = 17 \qquad \text{(true)}$$

Answer: The width is 3 feet; the length is 17 feet.

Exercises

1. If the perimeter of an equilateral triangle is 24 inches, find a side of the triangle.

2. Each of the equal sides of an isosceles triangle is 4 times the third side. The perimeter of the triangle is 144 inches. Find the sides of the triangle.

3. The second side of a triangle is 3 times the first side. The third side of the triangle is $2\frac{1}{2}$ times the first side. If the perimeter of the triangle is 65 feet, find the length of each side.

4. The length of a rectangle is 3 times its width. The perimeter of the rectangle is 72 feet. Find the dimensions of the rectangle.

5. The length of a rectangle is 4 times its width. The perimeter of the rectangle is 150 feet. Find the dimensions of the rectangle.

6. The length of a rectangle is $2\frac{1}{2}$ times its width. The perimeter of the rectangle is 84 inches. Find the dimensions of the rectangle.

7. The length of a rectangle is 25% more than its width. The perimeter is 72 inches. Find the length and the width.

8. The length of a rectangle is 7 times its width. The perimeter of the rectangle is 40 feet. Find the dimensions of the rectangle.

9. The second side of a triangle is 8 inches less than the first side. The third side is 14 inches more than the first side. The perimeter of the triangle is 63 inches. Find each side of the triangle.

10. The lengths of the sides of a triangle are represented by three consecutive even integers. If the perimeter of the triangle is 96 feet, find the lengths of its sides.

11. The perimeter of a triangle is 40 inches. The second side exceeds twice the first side by 1 inch, and the third side is 2 inches less than the second side. Find the length of each side of the triangle.

12. Each of the equal sides of an isosceles triangle exceeds 3 times the base by 2 inches. If the perimeter is 60 inches, find the length of each side of the triangle.

13. The base of an isosceles triangle exceeds each of the equal sides by 3 feet. If the perimeter is 27 feet, find each side of the triangle.

14. The length of a rectangle is 5 inches more than its width. The perimeter is 66 inches. Find the dimensions of the rectangle.

15. The length of a rectangle exceeds its width by 8 inches. The perimeter is 80 inches. Find the length and the width of the rectangle.

16. The length of a rectangle exceeds the width by 5 inches. The perimeter of the rectangle is 168 inches. Find the dimensions of the rectangle.

17. The width of a rectangle is 3 inches less than its length. The perimeter is 130 inches. Find the length and the width of the rectangle.

18. The perimeter of a rectangular parking lot is 146 rods. Find its dimensions if the length is 7 rods less than 4 times the width.

19. The perimeter of a rectangular skating rink is 530 feet. If the length is 5 feet more than 3 times the width, what are the dimensions?

20. The perimeter of a rectangular garden is 110 feet. Find its dimensions if the length is 5 feet less than twice the width.

21. The perimeter of a rectangular tennis court is 228 feet. If the length of the court exceeds twice its width by 6 feet, find its dimensions.

22. The length of a rectangle is represented by $5x - 7$ and the width by $3x + 2$. Find its dimensions if the perimeter is 70 inches.

23. The length of a rectangle is twice the width. If the length is increased by 4 inches and the width is diminished by 1 inch, a new rectangle is formed whose perimeter is 198 inches. Find the dimensions of the original rectangle.

24. The length of a rectangle exceeds 3 times its width by 1 inch. If the length of the rectangle is diminished by 3 inches and the width is doubled, a new rectangle is formed whose perimeter is 46 inches. Find the dimensions of the original rectangle.

25. If one side of a square is increased by 4 inches and an adjacent side is multiplied by 4, the perimeter of the resulting rectangle is 3 times the perimeter of the square. Find a side of the original square.

26. The length of a rectangle exceeds its width by 4 feet. If the width is doubled and the length is diminished by 2 feet, a new rectangle is formed whose perimeter is 8 feet more than the perimeter of the original rectangle. Find the dimensions of the original rectangle.

27. Each side of a hexagon (a polygon which has 6 sides) is 4 inches less than a side of a square. The perimeter of the hexagon is equal to the perimeter of the square. Find a side of the hexagon and a side of the square.

28. One side of an equilateral triangle exceeds one side of a square by 8 inches. The perimeter of the equilateral triangle exceeds the perimeter of the square by 20 inches. Find the length of one side of the square and one side of the triangle.

11. Area Problems

PREPARING TO SOLVE AREA PROBLEMS

KEEP IN MIND

Area of a rectangle = Length $\times$ Width

Exercises

1. Represent the area of a rectangle whose length and width are represented by:

a. $l = 7, w = x$ b. $l = 5, w = x + 2$ c. $l = 10, w = 2x - 3$

d. $l = x, w = x - 1$ e. $l = x + 5, w = x$ f. $l = x + 3, w = x + 2$

2. The length of a rectangle is 10 more than its width, x. Represent the area of the rectangle.

3. The width of a rectangle is 8 less than twice its length, x. Represent the area of the rectangle.

4. The length of a rectangle exceeds 3 times its width, x, by 2. Represent the area of the rectangle.

5. The length of a rectangle is 2 inches more than the width, x. If the length of the rectangle is increased by 6 inches and the width is decreased by 3 inches, a new rectangle is formed.

a. Represent the dimensions of the original rectangle.

b. Represent the dimensions of the new rectangle.

c. Represent the area of the original rectangle.

d. Represent the area of the new rectangle.

e. Write an open sentence that would indicate that the area of the new and original rectangles are equal.

f. Write an open sentence that would indicate that the area of the new rectangle is 6 sq. in. more than the area of the original rectangle.

SOLVING AREA PROBLEMS

In solving problems dealing with areas of geometric figures, it is helpful to draw the figures.

~~~~~~~~~~~~~~~~~ **MODEL PROBLEM** ~~~~~~~~~~~~~~~~~

The length of a rectangle exceeds its width by 7 inches. If the length of the rectangle is decreased by 2 inches and the width is increased by 3 inches, a new rectangle is formed whose area is 20 square inches more than the area of the original rectangle. Find the dimensions of the original rectangle.

Solution: Let w = the width of the original rectangle.

Then $w + 7$ = the length of the original rectangle.

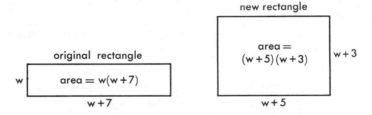

Figure	Length in inches	Width in inches	Area in square inches
Original rectangle	$w + 7$	w	$w(w + 7)$
New rectangle	$w + 5$	$w + 3$	$(w + 5)(w + 3)$

The area of the new rectangle is 20 sq. in. more
than the area of the old rectangle.

$$(w + 5)(w + 3) = w(w + 7) + 20$$
$$w^2 + 8w + 15 = w^2 + 7w + 20$$
$$w^2 + 8w + 15 + (-w^2) + (-7w) = w^2 + 7w + 20 + (-w^2) + (-7w)$$
$$w + 15 = 20$$
$$w + 15 + (-15) = 20 + (-15)$$
$$w = 5$$
$$w + 7 = 12$$

Check: In the old rectangle, $l = 12$, $w = 5$, and the area $= 12(5) = 60$.
In the new rectangle, $l = 10$, $w = 8$, and the area $= 10(8) = 80$.
80 is 20 more than 60.

Answer: The length of the rectangle is 12 inches; the width is 5 inches.

Exercises

1. The length of a rectangle is 8 inches more than its width. If the length is increased by 4 inches and the width is decreased by 1 inch, the area is unchanged. Find the dimensions of the rectangle.

2. The length of a rectangle exceeds 3 times the width by 1 foot. If the length is decreased by 5 feet and the width is increased by 2 feet, the area is unchanged. Find the dimensions of the rectangle.

3. If one side of a square is increased by 3 inches and the adjacent side is decreased by 2 inches, a rectangle is formed whose area is equal to the area of the square. Find a side of the square.

4. Each side of a square is increased by 3 feet. The area of the new square which is formed is 39 square feet more than the area of the original square. Find a side of the original square.

5. If one side of a square is increased by 3 inches and the adjacent side is decreased by 4 inches, a rectangle is formed whose area is 19 square inches less than the area of the square. Find a side of the original square.

6. The length of a rectangular garden exceeds its width by 8 feet. If each side of the garden is increased by 2 feet, the area of the garden will be increased by 60 square feet. Find the dimensions of the original garden.

7. The length of a rectangle is 2 inches less than its width. If the length is increased by 4 inches and the width is decreased by 2 inches, the area is increased by 8 square inches. Find the measurements of the rectangle.

8. The area of a square exceeds the area of a rectangle by 3 square inches. The width of the rectangle is 3 inches shorter and the length of the rectangle 4 inches longer than the side of the square. Find the side of the square.

9. The length of a rectangle is 3 inches more than the width. The side of a square is equal to the length of the rectangle. The area of the square exceeds the area of the rectangle by 24 square inches. Find the dimensions of the rectangle.

10. The length of a rectangle exceeds twice its width by 2 inches. If the length is increased by 5 inches and the width is decreased by 1 inch, a new rectangle is formed whose area exceeds the area of the original rectangle by 20 square inches. Find the dimensions of the original rectangle.

12. Lever Problems

A *lever* is a bar which can rotate about a fixed point called the *fulcrum.* A seesaw is an example of a lever.

Let a weight w_1 be placed on one arm of the lever at a distance d_1 from the fulcrum; let a weight w_2 be placed on the other arm of the lever at a distance d_2 from the fulcrum. In physics, it is shown that when a lever is in balance, the following relationship, called the *law of the lever,* is true:

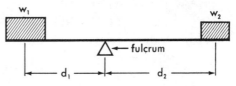

$$w_1 \times d_1 = w_2 \times d_2$$

~~~~~~~~~~ MODEL PROBLEMS ~~~~~~~~~~

1. Sid, who weighs 60 pounds, sits 3 feet from the fulcrum of a seesaw. Marion just balances him when she is sitting 4 feet from the fulcrum. Find Marion's weight.

Solution:

Let x = Marion's weight.

$w_1 \times d_1 = w_2 \times d_2$ [the law of the lever]

$w_1 = 60$, $d_1 = 3$, $w_2 = x$, $d_2 = 4$

$w_1 \times d_1 = w_2 \times d_2$

$\quad (60)(3) = (x)(4)$

$\qquad 180 = 4x$

$\qquad\ \ 45 = x$

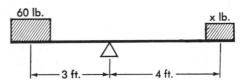

Check: Does $60 \times 3 = 45 \times 4$?
            Yes.

Answer: Marion weighs 45 pounds.

2. A plank 14 feet long is to be used as a seesaw by Harry and Ted. Harry weighs 120 pounds and Ted weighs 90 pounds. If the boys are to balance each other, how far from the fulcrum must each sit?

Solution:

Let x = Harry's distance from the fulcrum.
Then $14 - x$ = Ted's distance from the fulcrum.
$$w_1 \times d_1 = w_2 \times d_2 \qquad \text{[the law of the lever]}$$
$$w_1 = 120, \ d_1 = x, \ w_2 = 90, \ d_2 = 14 - x$$
$$w_1 \times d_1 = w_2 \times d_2$$

$$120x = 90(14 - x)$$
$$120x = 1260 - 90x$$
$$120x + 90x = 1260 \qquad A_{90x}$$
$$210x = 1260$$
$$x = 6$$
$$14 - x = 8$$

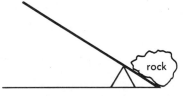

Check: Does $120 \times 6 = 90 \times 8$? Yes.

Answer: Harry sits 6 ft. from the fulcrum; Ted sits 8 ft. from the fulcrum.

Exercises

1. Sue, who weighs 80 pounds, sits 6 feet from the fulcrum of a seesaw and balances Lillian, who is sitting 8 feet from the fulcrum. Find Lillian's weight.

2. Robert weighs 180 lb.; Gene weighs 120 lb. How far from the fulcrum must Robert sit to balance Gene, who is sitting 6 feet from the fulcrum?

3. The figure shows how a crowbar 8 ft. long is used to lift a rock which weighs 450 lb. The fulcrum is placed 2 ft. from the rock. What weight must be applied at the upper end of the crowbar to lift the rock?

4. Marvin can exert a force of 180 lb. How heavy a rock can he lift if he uses a crowbar which is 5 ft. long and places the fulcrum so that it is 6 in. from the rock?

5. Martha and Ann use a plank 10 ft. long as a seesaw. Ann weighs 40 lb. and Martha weighs 60 lb. If the girls are to balance each other, how far from the fulcrum must each sit?

6. Fred, who weighs 100 lb., and Jack, who weighs 140 lb., use a 12-ft. plank as a seesaw. Where should the fulcrum be placed if the boys are to balance each other?

7. Bill wished to carry two bundles, one weighing 60 lb. and the other weighing 40 lb. He put one of them at each end of a bar 5 ft. long and placed the bar on his shoulder. If he balanced the weights, where did he place the fulcrum (his shoulder)?

8. Ronald, who can exert a force of 200 lb., wishes to raise an object which weighs 600 lb. using a 6-ft. bar and a block as a fulcrum. Where should he place the fulcrum?

13. Miscellaneous Problems

In solving the problems in this group, use the procedure described on page 88.

~~~~~~~~~~~~~~ *MODEL PROBLEM* ~~~~~~~~~~~~~~

Mr. Podell left an estate of \$90,000 to his wife, son, and daughter. The wife received \$10,000 less than 6 times the son's share. The daughter received \$20,000 more than the son's share. How much did each receive?

How To Proceed	*Solution*
1. Represent one unknown number by a variable and all the other described numbers in terms of the same variable.	Let x = the son's share. Then $6x - 10,000$ = the wife's share. Then $x + 20,000$ = the daughter's share. *The total of all three shares is \$90,000.*
2. Write an open sentence which symbolizes the relationships stated in the problem.	$x + 6x - 10,000 + x + 20,000 = 90,000$
3. Solve the open sentence.	$8x + 10,000 = 90,000$ $8x = 80,000$ $x = 10,000$ $6x - 10,000 = 50,000$ $x + 20,000 = 30,000$

4. Check the answers in the original problem.

Son received $10,000
Wife received
  6($10,000) − $10,000 .... $50,000
Daughter received
  $10,000 + $20,000 .... $30,000
Total estate $90,000

Answer: The son received $10,000; the daughter received $30,000; the wife received $50,000.

~~~~~~

Exercises

1. On Wednesday, Harry picked 3 times as many quarts of berries as on Tuesday. On Thursday, he picked 5 times as many quarts as on Wednesday. In all he picked 152 quarts. Find the number he picked each day.

2. In an algebra class of 36 pupils, there are 8 more girls than boys. How many boys and how many girls are in the class?

3. Bill has 5 times as many marbles as Fred. Tim has 3 fewer than 4 times as many marbles as Fred. In all they have 167 marbles. How many has each?

4. Four sections of a city salvaged 214 tons of tin cans. Section B collected three times as many as section A; section C collected 2 tons less than five times as many as section A; and section D collected 7 tons more than twice as many as section A. Find the number of tons collected in each section.

5. John gathered 3 times as many pounds of milkweed pods as James. Tom gathered 5 pounds more than James. In all they gathered 15 pounds. Find the number of pounds gathered by each.

6. John, James, and George sold tickets for the school baseball game. John sold 6 times as many as James. George sold 6 more than James. In all they sold 54 tickets. How many did each boy sell?

7. Mr. James and Mr. Frank bought the same number of E-bonds over a period of years. Mr. James still has all the bonds he bought. Mr. Frank has kept two-thirds of the number of bonds he bought. Together they now have 75 bonds. How many bonds did each man purchase?

8. Fred saved two-thirds as much money as John. John saved 5 times as much as Mary. Together they saved $14. How much did each save?

9. Buffalo contributed 6 more tons of clothing to a drive than did Troy. Endicott contributed half as much as Troy. In all they contributed 71 tons. How many tons were contributed by each?

10. The distance between two villages, L and M, is 8 miles less than the distance from M to the third village, S. One-half the distance between M and S is 6 miles less than the distance between L and M. Find the number of miles from L to M.

11. Mrs. Jones bought 36 yards of material that she used to make curtains. She used three-fourths as much in the dining room as in the living room and one-half as much in the kitchen as in the living room. How many yards did she use in each room?

12. Mr. Dwyer bought a house which he improved. The cost of the house and the cost of the improvements amounted to $23,100. The house cost $600 more than 6 times the cost of the interior improvements. The exterior improvements cost half as much as the interior improvements. Find the cost of the house, the interior improvements, and the exterior improvements.

13. Sam has twice as many marbles as Bill. If Bill wins 12 marbles from Sam, both boys will have the same number of marbles. How many marbles did each boy have originally?

14. In basketball, a foul basket counts 1 point and a field basket counts 2 points. A team scored 39 points in a game, making 6 more field baskets than foul baskets. How many baskets of each kind did they make?

15. In a schoolroom, there are two kinds of seats, single and double. There are three times as many single seats as double seats. The room can seat 70 pupils. How many seats of each kind are there?

16. The cost of 3 pens and 3 books is $6. If the cost of a pen exceeds the cost of a book by $1, find the cost of each.

17. At a sale, the price of a fur coat was reduced 20%. Mrs. Pearson bought the coat for $360. What was the original price of the coat?

18. Mr. Slater, a jeweler, bought a ring for $150. For how much must he sell it in order that his margin will be 40% of the selling price?

19. A dealer bought a coat for $37.50. For how much must he sell it in order that the margin should be 25% of the selling price?

20. Mr. Calvin sold a lot for $2400. If his profit was 50% of the cost of the lot, find the cost of the lot. (Assume there were no expenses other than the cost of the lot.)

14. Solving Verbal Problems by Using Inequalities

———————— MODEL PROBLEMS ————————

1. Sam is 5 years older than Tom. The sum of their ages is less than 33 years. Find each boy's age.

Solution:

Let x = Tom's age.
Then $x + 5$ = Sam's age.

The sum of the two ages is less than 33 years.

$$x + x + 5 < 33$$
$$2x + 5 < 33$$
$$2x < 28$$
$$x < 14$$
$$x + 5 < 19$$

Answer: Tom is less than 14 years old. Sam is less than 19 years old and is also 5 years older than Tom. (The check is left to the student.)

2. In a school, the number of girls is 50 more than twice the number of boys. If the school has at most 650 pupils, find the greatest possible number of boys and the greatest possible number of girls in the school.

Solution: If the school has at most 650 pupils, then the sum of the number of boys and the number of girls is either 650 or less than 650.

Let x = the number of boys.
Then $2x + 50$ = the number of girls.

The number of boys plus the number of girls is 650 or less than 650.

$$x + 2x + 50 \leq 650$$
$$3x + 50 \leq 650$$
$$3x \leq 600$$
$$x \leq 200 \quad \text{(There are at most 200 boys.)}$$
$$2x + 50 \leq 450 \quad \text{(There are at most 450 girls.)}$$

Answer: There are at most 200 boys and at most 450 girls in the school. (The check is left to the student.)

3. In a child's bank, there are twice as many nickels as quarters. If the value of all the coins is at least $7.00, find the smallest possible number of coins in the bank.

Solution: If the value of all the coins is at least $7.00, then the value of the nickels plus the value of the quarters is either 700 cents or more than 700 cents.

Let x = the number of quarters.

Then $2x$ = the number of nickels.

Then $25x$ = the value of the quarters in cents.

Then $10x$ = the value of the nickels in cents.

The value of the nickels plus the value of the quarters is 700 cents or more than 700 cents.

$$10x + 25x \geq 700$$
$$35x \geq 700$$
$$x \geq 20 \quad \text{(There are at least 20 quarters.)}$$
$$2x \geq 40 \quad \text{(There are at least 40 nickels.)}$$

Answer: There are at least 60 coins in the bank. (The check is left to the student.)

Exercises

1. Carol weighs 3 times as much as Sue. The sum of their weights is less than 100 lb. Find the weight of each girl.
2. Henry's age is 10 years less than 4 times Paul's age. If the sum of their ages is greater than 25 years, find the age of each boy.
3. 6 more than 2 times a certain number is less than the number increased by 20. Find the numbers that satisfy this condition.
4. If 19 more than a number is divided by 4, the result is greater than the original number decreased by 2. Find the numbers that satisfy this condition.
5. Mr. Burke had a sum of money in a bank. After he deposited an additional sum of $100, he had at least $550 in the bank. How much money did Mr. Burke have in the bank originally?
6. A club agreed to buy at least 250 tickets for a theatre party. If it agreed to buy 80 less orchestra tickets than balcony tickets, what was the least number of balcony tickets it could buy?
7. Mrs. Scott decided that she would spend no more than $120 to buy a coat and a dress. If the price of the coat was $20 more than 3 times the price of the dress, find the highest possible price of the dress.

8. The number of nickels in a boy's bank is 1 less than twice the number of dimes. If the total value of the coins in the bank is at least $4.35, find the smallest possible number of coins in the bank.

9. Bill received grades of 87, 92, 88, and 86 on four mathematics tests. Find the least grade that he must receive on a fifth test in order for him to have an average of at least 90 on the five tests.

10. The length of a rectangle is 10 in. less than 3 times its width. If the perimeter of the rectangle is at most 180 in., find the maximum length of the rectangle.

11. The cashier in a movie box office sold 200 more adult admission tickets at $2.00 each than children's admission tickets at $.75 each. What is the minimum number of each type of ticket that the cashier had to sell for the total receipts to be at least $620?

12. Mr. Drake wishes to save at least $1500 in 12 months. If he saved $300 during the first 4 months, what is the minimum average amount that he must save in each of the remaining 8 months?

13. Mr. Blake is 20 years younger than Mr. Sawyer, and Mr. Reid is one-third as old as Mr. Sawyer. The sum of Mr. Blake's age and Mr. Sawyer's age is at least 70 years more than Mr. Reid's age. Find Mr. Sawyer's minimum age.

14. Two consecutive even integers are such that their sum is more than 98 decreased by twice the larger. Find the smallest possible values for the integers.

15. Three consecutive integers are such that the sum of the two smaller integers is less than 32 decreased by half of the largest integer. Find the largest possible values for the integers.

CHAPTER XI

SPECIAL PRODUCTS AND FACTORING

1. Understanding the Meaning of Factoring

When two integers are multiplied, the result is called their **product.** The integers being multiplied are called the *factors* of the product. Since $3 \times 5 = 15$, then 3 and 5 are factors of the product 15. Since $3 \times 5 = 15$, then $15 \div 3 = 5$ and $15 \div 5 = 3$.

This illustrates that over the set of integers:
1. A factor of an integer is an exact divisor of the integer. In general, if an integer f is a factor of an integer n, then $n \div f$ represents an integer.
2. When the product of two integers is divided by one of its factors, the quotient is the other factor.

Factoring a number is the process of finding those numbers whose product is the given number. When we factor an integer, we will deal with integral factors only.

If an integer greater than 1 has no factors other than itself and 1, it is called a **prime number.** For example, the members of the set $\{2, 3, 5, 7, 11, 13, 17, \ldots\}$ are prime numbers.

Every integer can be expressed as the product of prime factors. Although the factors may be written in any order, there is one and only one combination of factors whose product is a

$$\boxed{\begin{aligned} 21 &= 3 \times 7 \\ 20 &= 2 \cdot 2 \cdot 5 \text{ or } 2^2 \cdot 5 \end{aligned}}$$

given integer. Study the examples at the right. Note that a prime factor may appear in the product more than once.

$$\boxed{\begin{aligned} 180 &= 2 \cdot 90 \\ 180 &= 2 \cdot 2 \cdot 45 \\ 180 &= 2 \cdot 2 \cdot 3 \cdot 15 \\ 180 &= 2 \cdot 2 \cdot 3 \cdot 3 \cdot 5 \text{ or} \\ 180 &= 2^2 \cdot 3^2 \cdot 5 \end{aligned}}$$

To express an integer, for example 180, as a product of primes, we test in order the primes 2, 3, 5, etc. until all factors are prime numbers. The smallest prime factor of 180 is 2. Then $180 \div 2 = 90$. Therefore, $180 = 2 \cdot 90$. The smallest prime factor of 90 is 2. Then $90 \div 2 = 45$. Therefore, $180 = 2 \cdot 2 \cdot 45$. The smallest prime factor of 45 is 3. Then $45 \div 3 = 15$. Therefore, $180 = 2 \cdot 2 \cdot 3 \cdot 15$. The smallest prime factor of 15 is 3. Then $15 \div 3 = 5$. Therefore, $180 = 2 \cdot 2 \cdot 3 \cdot 3 \cdot 5$ or $180 = 2^2 \cdot 3^2 \cdot 5$.

Expressing each of two integers as the product of prime factors makes it possible to discover the greatest integer which is a factor of both of them. We call this factor their **greatest common factor.**

Let us find the greatest common factor of 180 and 54.

$$180 = 2 \cdot 2 \cdot 3 \cdot 3 \cdot 5 \text{ or } 2^2 \cdot 3^2 \cdot 5 \qquad 54 = 2 \cdot 3 \cdot 3 \cdot 3 \text{ or } 2 \cdot 3^3$$

We see that the greatest number of times that 2 appears as a factor in both 180 and 54 is once; the greatest number of times that 3 appears as a factor in 180 and 54 is twice. Therefore, the greatest common factor of 180 and 54 is $2 \cdot 3 \cdot 3$, or $2 \cdot 3^2$, or 18.

To find the greatest common factor of two monomials, we find the greatest common factor of their numerical coefficients; then we find the greatest degree of each variable that is a factor of both monomials. For example, since $24a^3b^2 = 2 \cdot 2 \cdot 2 \cdot 3 \cdot a \cdot a \cdot a \cdot b \cdot b$ and $18a^2b = 2 \cdot 3 \cdot 3 \cdot a \cdot a \cdot b$, we see that $2 \cdot 3 \cdot a \cdot a \cdot b$, or $6a^2b$, is the greatest common factor of $24a^3b^2$ and $18a^2b$.

When we factor a monomial whose coefficients are integers, we will deal only with integral factors, that is, integers or monomials whose coefficients are integers.

~~~~~~~~~ MODEL PROBLEMS ~~~~~~~~~

1. Express 700 as a product of prime factors.

Solution:

$$700 = 2 \cdot 350$$
$$700 = 2 \cdot 2 \cdot 175$$
$$700 = 2 \cdot 2 \cdot 5 \cdot 35$$
$$700 = 2 \cdot 2 \cdot 5 \cdot 5 \cdot 7 \text{ or } 2^2 \cdot 5^2 \cdot 7 \quad Ans.$$

2. Find the greatest common factor of the monomials $60r^2s^4$ and $36rs^2t$.

Solution:

$60r^2s^4 = 2 \cdot 2 \cdot 3 \cdot 5 \cdot r \cdot r \cdot s \cdot s \cdot s \cdot s \text{ or } 2^2 \cdot 3 \cdot 5 \cdot r^2 \cdot s^4$

$36rs^2t = 2 \cdot 2 \cdot 3 \cdot 3 \cdot r \cdot s \cdot s \cdot t \text{ or } 2^2 \cdot 3^2 \cdot r \cdot s^2 \cdot t$

The greatest common factor is $2 \cdot 2 \cdot 3 \cdot r \cdot s \cdot s$ or $2^2 \cdot 3 \cdot r \cdot s^2$ or $12rs^2$. *Ans.*

Exercises

In 1–4, write all the prime numbers between the given numbers.

1. 1 and 10   **2.** 10 and 20   **3.** 20 and 30   **4.** 30 and 40

In 5–19, express the integer as a product of prime numbers.

5. 35   **6.** 9   **7.** 18   **8.** 108   **9.** 144

10. 250   **11.** 77   **12.** 128   **13.** 182   **14.** 400

15. 202   **16.** 222   **17.** 129   **18.** 590   **19.** 316

In 20–25, write all the positive integral factors of the number.

20. 26   **21.** 50   **22.** 36   **23.** 88   **24.** 100   **25.** 242

26. The product of two integers is 144. Find the second factor if the first factor is:

   a. 2   *b.* 8   *c.* 18   *d.* 36   *e.* 48

27. The product of two monomials is $36x^3y^4$. Find the second factor if the first factor is:

   a. $3x^2y^3$ *b.* $6x^3y^2$ *c.* $12xy^2$ *d.* $-9x^3y$ *e.* $18x^3y^2$

In 28–35, find the greatest common factor of the pair of integers.

28. 10; 15   **29.** 12; 28   **30.** 14; 35   **31.** 18; 24

32. 75; 50   **33.** 72; 108   **34.** 144; 200   **35.** 96; 156

In 36–44, find the greatest common factor of the pair of monomials.

36. $4x; 4y$ **37.** $6; 12a$ **38.** $4r; 6r^2$

39. $8xy; 6xz$ **40.** $10x^2; 15xy^2$ **41.** $7c^3d^3; -14c^2d$

42. $36xy^2z; -27xy^2z^2$ **43.** $50m^3n^2; 75m^3n$ **44.** $24ab^2c^3; 18ac^2$

2. Factoring Polynomials Whose Terms Have a Common Monomial Factor

Factoring a polynomial means expressing it as the indicated product of other polynomials.

Since the distributive property states that $2(x + y) = 2x + 2y$, we know that $2x + 2y = 2(x + y)$. Thus, we have used the distributive property to factor the polynomial $2x + 2y$. Notice that the monomial 2 is a factor of each term of the polynomial $2x + 2y$. Therefore, 2 is called a *common monomial factor* of the polynomial $2x + 2y$.

When we factor a polynomial, we look first for the **greatest common monomial factor**. For example, to factor $4rs + 8st$, we should observe that $4s$ is the greatest common monomial factor of the polynomial. When we divide $4rs + 8st$ by $4s$, we obtain the quotient $r + 2t$, which is the other factor.

Therefore, $4rs + 8st = 4s(r + 2t)$.

Procedure. To factor a polynomial whose terms have a common monomial factor:

1. **Find the greatest monomial that is a factor of each term of the polynomial.**
2. **Divide the polynomial by the monomial factor. The quotient is the other factor.**
3. **Express the polynomial as the indicated product of the two factors.**

MODEL PROBLEMS

1. Write in factored form: $5x - 5y$

   Solution:

   1. 5 is the greatest common factor of $5x$ and $5y$.
   2. To find the other factor, divide $5x - 5y$ by 5.
      $(5x - 5y) \div 5 = x - y$
   3. $5x - 5y = 5(x - y)$ *Ans.*

2. Write in factored form: $\frac{1}{2}na + \frac{1}{2}nl$

   Solution:

   1. $\frac{1}{2}n$ is the greatest common factor of $\frac{1}{2}na$ and $\frac{1}{2}nl$.
   2. To find the other factor, divide $\frac{1}{2}na + \frac{1}{2}nl$ by $\frac{1}{2}n$.
      $(\frac{1}{2}na + \frac{1}{2}nl) \div \frac{1}{2}n = a + l$
   3. $\frac{1}{2}na + \frac{1}{2}nl = \frac{1}{2}n(a + l)$ *Ans.*

3. Write in factored form: $6c^3d - 12c^2d^2 + 3cd$

   Solution:

   1. $3cd$ is the greatest common factor of $6c^3d$, $12c^2d^2$, and $3cd$.
   2. To find the other factor, divide $6c^3d - 12c^2d^2 + 3cd$ by $3cd$.
      $(6c^3d - 12c^2d^2 + 3cd) \div 3cd = 2c^2 - 4cd + 1$
   3. $6c^3d - 12c^2d^2 + 3cd = 3cd(2c^2 - 4cd + 1)$ *Ans.*

4. Use factoring to evaluate $87 \times 64 + 87 \times 36$.

   Solution: $87 \times 64 + 87 \times 36 = 87(64 + 36) = 87(100) = 8700$ *Ans.*

Exercises

In 1–57, write the expression in factored form.

1. $2a + 2b$ **2.** $5c + 5d$ **3.** $8m + 8n$

4. $3x - 3y$ **5.** $7l - 7n$ **6.** $6R - 6r$

7. $bx + by$ **8.** $sr - st$ **9.** $xc - xd$

10. $4x + 8y$ **11.** $3m - 6n$ **12.** $12t - 6r$

13. $15c - 10d$ **14.** $12x - 18y$ **15.** $18c - 27d$

16. $8x + 16$ **17.** $6x - 18$ **18.** $8x - 12$

19. $7y - 7$ **20.** $8 - 4y$ **21.** $6 - 18c$

22. $y^2 - 3y$ **23.** $2x^2 + 5x$ **24.** $3x^2 - 6x$

25. $32x + x^2$ **26.** $rs^2 - 2r$ **27.** $ax - 5ab$

28. $3y^4 + 3y^2$ **29.** $10x - 15x^3$ **30.** $2x - 4x^3$

31. $p + prt$ **32.** $s - sr$ **33.** $\frac{1}{2}hb + \frac{1}{2}hc$

34. $\pi r^2 + \pi R^2$ **35.** $\pi r^2 + \pi rl$ **36.** $\pi r^2 + 2\pi rh$

37. $4x^2 + 4y^2$ **38.** $3a^2 - 9$ **39.** $5x^2 + 5$

40. $3ab^2 - 6a^2b$ **41.** $10xy - 15x^2y^2$ **42.** $21r^3s^2 - 14r^2s$

43. $2x^2 + 8x + 4$ **44.** $3x^2 - 6x - 30$ **45.** $ay - 4aw - 12a$

46. $c^3 - c^2 + 2c$ **47.** $\frac{1}{4}ma + \frac{1}{4}mb + \frac{1}{4}mc$ **48.** $9ab^2 - 6ab - 3a$

49. $15x^3y^3z^3 - 5xyz$ **50.** $8a^4b^2c^3 + 12a^2b^2c^2$ **51.** $28m^4n^3 - 70m^2n^4$

52. $a(x + y) + b(x + y)$ **53.** $c(m - n) + d(m - n)$

54. $r(y + z) - s(y + z)$ **55.** $mx + my + nx + ny$

56. $av - aw + bv - bw$ **57.** $tc + sc - td - sd$

In 58–63, use factoring to simplify the computation involved in evaluating the number expression.

58. $35 \times 49 + 35 \times 51$ **59.** $85 \times 19 + 15 \times 19$

60. $63 \times 87 - 63 \times 77$ **61.** $\frac{1}{2} \times 153 + \frac{1}{2} \times 47$

62. $\frac{22}{7} \times 1600 - \frac{22}{7} \times 900$ **63.** $\frac{1}{2} \times 7 \times 6.3 + \frac{1}{2} \times 7 \times 1.7$

3. Squaring a Monomial

To square a monomial means to use that monomial as a factor two times. For example:

$$(3x)^2 = (3x)(3x) = (3)(3)(x)(x) = (3)^2(x)^2 \text{ or } 9x^2$$

$$(5y^2)^2 = (5y^2)(5y^2) = (5)(5)(y^2)(y^2) = (5)^2(y^2)^2 \text{ or } 25y^4$$

$$(-6b^4)^2 = (-6b^4)(-6b^4) = (-6)(-6)(b^4)(b^4) = (-6)^2(b^4)^2 \text{ or } 36b^8$$

$$(4c^2d^3)^2 = (4c^2d^3)(4c^2d^3) = (4)(4)(c^2)(c^2)(d^3)(d^3) = (4)^2(c^2)^2(d^3)^2 \text{ or } 16c^4d^6$$

Notice that when a product which has several factors is squared, the operation of squaring is distributed over each factor of the product.

In general, when a and b are signed numbers and m and n are positive integers:

$$(a^m b^n)^2 = a^{2m} b^{2n}$$

Observe that in the case we are discussing, when a monomial is a square, its numerical coefficient is a square and the exponent of each variable is an even number. This is the case with each of the previous results: $9x^2$, $25y^4$, $36b^8$, $16c^4 d^6$, $a^{2m} b^{2n}$.

━━━━━━━━━ **MODEL PROBLEMS** ━━━━━━━━━

In each of the following, square the monomial mentally.

1. $(3a^3)^2 = 9a^6$ **2.** $(\frac{2}{5}ab)^2 = \frac{4}{25}a^2 b^2$ **3.** $(-7xy^2)^2 = 49x^2 y^4$

━━━━━━━━━━━━━━━━━━━━━━━━━━━━━━━━━━

Exercises

In 1–28, square the monomial mentally.

1. $(a^2)^2$ **2.** $(b^3)^2$ **3.** $(c^4)^2$ **4.** $(-d^5)^2$

5. $(rs)^2$ **6.** $(m^2 n^2)^2$ **7.** $(cd^2)^2$ **8.** $(-x^3 y^2)^2$

9. $(2b)^2$ **10.** $(3x^2)^2$ **11.** $(-4m^3)^2$ **12.** $(-5y^4)^2$

13. $(9ab)^2$ **14.** $(10x^2 y^2)^2$ **15.** $(-12cd^3)^2$ **16.** $(-15r^2 s^4)^2$

17. $(\frac{3}{4}a)^2$ **18.** $(\frac{5}{7}xy)^2$ **19.** $(-\frac{7}{8}a^2 b^2)^2$ **20.** $(-\frac{9}{10}rs^2)^2$

21. $\left(\dfrac{x}{6}\right)^2$ **22.** $\left(\dfrac{5c}{3}\right)^2$ **23.** $\left(-\dfrac{7m}{8}\right)^2$ **24.** $\left(-\dfrac{4x^2}{5}\right)^2$

25. $(.8x)^2$ **26.** $(.5y^2)^2$ **27.** $(.1xy)^2$ **28.** $(-.6a^2 b)^2$

29. Represent the area of a square whose side is represented by:
     a. $4x$ *b.* $10y$ *c.* $\frac{2}{3}x$ *d.* $1.5x$

30. From a square piece of paper each of whose sides is represented by $10x$ is cut a square each of whose sides is represented by $9x$. Represent the area which is left.

4. Multiplying the Sum and Difference of Two Numbers

Let us multiply the sum of two numbers by the difference of the same two numbers. Study each of the following examples to see why the product contains two terms, not three:

$$
\begin{array}{lll}
a + 4 & a + b & 3x^2 + 5y \\
\underline{a - 4} & \underline{a - b} & \underline{3x^2 - 5y} \\
a^2 + 4a & a^2 + ab & 9x^4 + 15x^2y \\
\underline{ - 4a - 16} & \underline{ - ab - b^2} & \underline{ - 15x^2y - 25y^2} \\
a^2 - 16 & a^2 - b^2 & 9x^4 - 25y^2
\end{array}
$$

These examples illustrate the following procedure, which will enable us to find the products mentally:

Procedure. To multiply the sum of two numbers by the difference of the same two numbers, square the first number and from this result subtract the square of the second number.

KEEP IN MIND

$$(a + b)(a - b) = a^2 - b^2$$

MODEL PROBLEMS

1. Find the product mentally: $(y + 7)(y - 7)$

    Solution: $(y + 7)(y - 7) = (y)^2 - (7)^2 = y^2 - 49$

2. Find the product mentally: $(3a + 4b)(3a - 4b)$

    Solution: $(3a + 4b)(3a - 4b) = (3a)^2 - (4b)^2 = 9a^2 - 16b^2$

3. Find the product mentally: $(x^3 - 5y^2)(x^3 + 5y^2)$

    Solution: $(x^3 - 5y^2)(x^3 + 5y^2) = (x^3)^2 - (5y^2)^2 = x^6 - 25y^4$

4. In the expression 33×27, first express the factors as the sum and difference of the same two numbers. Then multiply mentally.

Solution: $33 \times 27 = (30 + 3)(30 - 3) = (30)^2 - (3)^2 = 900 - 9 = 891$

Exercises

In 1–28, find the product mentally.

1. $(x + 8)(x - 8)$ **2.** $(y + 10)(y - 10)$

3. $(m - 4)(m + 4)$ **4.** $(n - 9)(n + 9)$

5. $(10 + a)(10 - a)$ **6.** $(12 - b)(12 + b)$

7. $(c + d)(c - d)$ **8.** $(r - s)(r + s)$

9. $(3x + 1)(3x - 1)$ **10.** $(5c + 4)(5c - 4)$

11. $(11z - 7)(11z + 7)$ **12.** $(20x - 9)(20x + 9)$

13. $(8x + 3y)(8x - 3y)$ **14.** $(5r - 7s)(5r + 7s)$

15. $(x^2 + 8)(x^2 - 8)$ **16.** $(3 - 5y^2)(3 + 5y^2)$

17. $(a + \frac{1}{2})(a - \frac{1}{2})$ **18.** $(\frac{3}{4}c - d)(\frac{3}{4}c + d)$

19. $(r + .5)(r - .5)$ **20.** $(.3 + m)(.3 - m)$

21. $(ab + 8)(ab - 8)$ **22.** $(10 - cd)(10 + cd)$

23. $(r^3 - 2s^4)(r^3 + 2s^4)$ **24.** $(5c^2d^3 + 7e^5)(5c^2d^3 - 7e^5)$

25. $(a + 5)(a - 5)(a^2 + 25)$ **26.** $(x - 3)(x + 3)(x^2 + 9)$

27. $(a + b)(a - b)(a^2 + b^2)$ **28.** $(m^2 + n^2)(m^2 - n^2)(m^4 + n^4)$

In 29–36, first express the factors as the sum and difference of the same two numbers, then multiply mentally.

29. 22×18 **30.** 39×41 **31.** 53×47 **32.** 66×74

33. 38×42 **34.** 55×65 **35.** 88×92 **36.** 94×106

5. Factoring the Difference of Two Squares

An expression of the form $a^2 - b^2$ is called a **difference of two squares.** Factoring an expression which is the difference of two squares is the reverse of multiplying the sum of two numbers by the difference of the same two numbers. Since the product of $a + b$ and $a - b$ is $a^2 - b^2$, the factors of $a^2 - b^2$ are $a + b$ and $a - b$. Therefore:

$$a^2 - b^2 = (a + b)(a - b)$$

Remember that for a monomial to be a square (the case we have discussed), its numerical coefficient must be a square and the exponent of each of its variables must be an even number.

Procedure. To factor a binomial which is a difference of two squares, express each of its terms as the square of a monomial; then apply the rule $a^2 - b^2 = (a + b)(a - b)$.

~~~~~~~~~~~~ **MODEL PROBLEMS** ~~~~~~~~~~~~

Factor: **1.** $r^2 - 9$ **2.** $25x^2 - \frac{1}{49}y^2$ **3.** $.04 - c^6d^4$

Solution:

1. $r^2 - 9 = (r)^2 - (3)^2 = (r + 3)(r - 3)$ *Ans.*

2. $25x^2 - \frac{1}{49}y^2 = (5x)^2 - (\frac{1}{7}y)^2 = (5x + \frac{1}{7}y)(5x - \frac{1}{7}y)$ *Ans.*

3. $.04 - c^6d^4 = (.2)^2 - (c^3d^2)^2 = (.2 + c^3d^2)(.2 - c^3d^2)$ *Ans.*

~~~~~~

Exercises

In 1–9: If possible, express the binomial as the difference of the squares of monomials; if not possible, tell why.

1. $y^2 - 64$ **2.** $4r^2 - b^2$ **3.** $r^2 + s^2$
4. $t^2 - 7$ **5.** $9n^2 - 16m^2$ **6.** $c^2 - .09d^2$
7. $p^2 - \frac{9}{25}q^2$ **8.** $16a^4 - 25b^6$ **9.** $-9 + m^2$

In 10–48, factor the binomial.

10. $a^2 - 4$ **11.** $b^2 - 25$ **12.** $c^2 - 100$
13. $r^2 - 16$ **14.** $s^2 - 49$ **15.** $t^2 - 81$
16. $9 - x^2$ **17.** $144 - c^2$ **18.** $121 - m^2$
19. $16a^2 - b^2$ **20.** $25m^2 - n^2$ **21.** $d^2 - 4c^2$
22. $r^4 - 9$ **23.** $x^4 - 64$ **24.** $25 - s^4$
25. $100x^2 - 81y^2$ **26.** $64e^2 - 9f^2$ **27.** $r^2s^2 - 144$
28. $w^2 - \frac{1}{64}$ **29.** $s^2 - \frac{1}{100}$ **30.** $\frac{1}{81} - t^2$

31. $49x^2 - \frac{1}{9}$ **32.** $\dfrac{4}{25} - \dfrac{49d^2}{81}$ **33.** $\dfrac{1}{9}r^2 - \dfrac{64s^2}{121}$

34. $x^2 - .64$ **35.** $y^2 - 1.44$ **36.** $.04 - 49r^2$

37. $.16m^2 - 9$ **38.** $81n^2 - .01$ **39.** $.81x^2 - y^2$

40. $64a^2b^2 - c^2d^2$ **41.** $25r^2s^2 - 9t^2u^2$ **42.** $81m^2n^2 - 49x^2y^2$

43. $49m^4 - 64n^4$ **44.** $25x^6 - 121y^{10}$ **45.** $x^4y^8 - 144a^6b^{10}$

46. $(a + b)^2 - c^2$ **47.** $(x - y)^2 - 4$ **48.** $25 - (m + n)^2$

6. Finding the Product of Two Binomials

Let us learn how to find mentally the product of two binomials of the form $ax + b$ and $cx + d$.

Study carefully the multiplication example at the right, which makes use of the distributive property. Note:

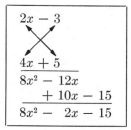

1. $8x^2$, the first term in the product, is equal to the product of $2x$ and $4x$, the first terms in the binomials.

2. -15, the last term in the product, is equal to the product of -3 and $+5$, the last terms in the binomials.

3. $-2x$, the middle term, is obtained by multiplying the first term of each binomial by the second term of the other and adding these products: $(-12x) + (+10x) = -2x$.

If we arrange the two multipliers horizontally, we can find the middle term by adding the product of the two inner terms of the binomials and the product of the two outer terms of the binomials.

$$-12x$$
$$(2x - 3)(4x + 5) \qquad \text{Think: } (-12x) + (+10x) = -2x$$
$$+10x$$

Procedure. To find the product of two binomials of the form $ax + b$ and $cx + d$:

1. **Multiply the first terms of the binomials.**
2. **Multiply the first term of each binomial by the last term of the other binomial and add these products.**
3. **Multiply the last terms of the binomials.**
4. **Add the results obtained in steps 1, 2, and 3.**

~~~~~ *MODEL PROBLEMS* ~~~~~

1. Multiply: $(x - 5)(x - 7)$

Solution: *Think:*

$$\overbrace{(x - 5)(x - 7)}^{-5x}_{-7x}$$

1. $(x)(x) = x^2$
2. $(-5x) + (-7x) = -12x$
3. $(-5)(-7) = +35$

Write: $(x - 5)(x - 7) = x^2 - 12x + 35$ *Ans.*

2. Multiply: $(3y - 8)(4y + 3)$

Solution: *Think:*

$$\overbrace{(3y - 8)(4y + 3)}^{-32y}_{+9y}$$

1. $(3y)(4y) = 12y^2$
2. $(-32y) + (+9y) = -23y$
3. $(-8)(+3) = -24$

Write: $(3y - 8)(4y + 3) = 12y^2 - 23y - 24$ *Ans.*

3. Multiply: $(5x + 2y)(5x + 2y)$

Solution: *Think:*

$$\overbrace{(5x + 2y)(5x + 2y)}^{+10xy}_{+10xy}$$

1. $(5x)(5x) = 25x^2$
2. $(+10xy) + (+10xy) = +20xy$
3. $(+2y)(+2y) = +4y^2$

Write: $(5x + 2y)(5x + 2y) = 25x^2 + 20xy + 4y^2$ *Ans.*

Exercises

In 1–36, multiply mentally.

1. $(x + 5)(x + 3)$ **2.** $(y + 9)(y + 2)$
3. $(6 + d)(3 + d)$ **4.** $(1 + m)(9 + m)$
5. $(y + 8)(y + 8)$ **6.** $(7 + r)(7 + r)$
7. $(x - 10)(x - 5)$ **8.** $(y - 1)(y - 9)$

9. $(8 - c)(3 - c)$ **10.** $(12 - d)(9 - d)$

11. $(z - 4)(z - 4)$ **12.** $(1 - t)(1 - t)$

13. $(x + 7)(x - 2)$ **14.** $(y + 11)(y - 4)$

15. $(m - 15)(m + 2)$ **16.** $(n - 20)(n + 3)$

17. $(5 - t)(9 + t)$ **18.** $(6 - s)(3 + s)$

19. $(3x + 2)(x + 5)$ **20.** $(2y + 1)(y + 6)$

21. $(c - 5)(3c - 3)$ **22.** $(x - 6)(2x - 1)$

23. $(m - 6)(3m + 2)$ **24.** $(-7m + 5)(m - 4)$

25. $(7x + 3)(2x - 1)$ **26.** $(2y + 3)(3y + 2)$

27. $(5z - 3)(2z - 5)$ **28.** $(3t^2 - 2)(4t^2 + 7)$

29. $(2x + 3)(2x + 3)$ **30.** $(-5y - 4)(-5y - 4)$

31. $(3x + y)(4x + 2y)$ **32.** $(2t - 3r)(5t - r)$

33. $(2c + 3d)(5c - 2d)$ **34.** $(4a - 3b)(3a + b)$

35. $(5a + 7b)(5a + 7b)$ **36.** $(-3r - 4s)(-3r - 4s)$

37. Represent the area of a rectangle whose length and width are represented by:

     a. $(x + 5)$ and $(x + 4)$ *b.* $(2x + 3)$ and $(x - 1)$

38. Represent the area of a square whose side is represented by:

     a. $(x + 6)$ *b.* $(x - 2)$ *c.* $(2x + 1)$ *d.* $(3x - 2)$

7. Factoring Trinomials of the Form $ax^2 + bx + c$

We have learned that $(x + 3)(x + 5) = x^2 + 8x + 15$. Therefore, the factors of $x^2 + 8x + 15$ are $(x + 3)$ and $(x + 5)$. Factoring a trinomial of the form $ax^2 + bx + c$ is the reverse of multiplying binomials of the form $(dx + e)$ and $(fx + g)$. When we factor a trinomial of this form, we list the possible pairs of factors and test them out one by one until we find the correct result.

Procedure. To factor a trinomial of the form $ax^2 + bx + c$, we must find two binomials which have the following characteristics:

1. **The product of the first terms of both binomials must be equal to the first term in the trinomial (ax^2).**
2. **The product of the last terms of both binomials must be equal to the last term of the trinomial (c).**
3. **When the first term of each binomial is multiplied by the second term of the other and the sum of these products is found, this result must be equal to the middle term of the trinomial (bx).**

~~~~~~~~~~~~~~~ **MODEL PROBLEMS** ~~~~~~~~~~~~~~~

1. Factor: $x^2 + 7x + 10$

   Solution:

   1. The product of the first terms of the binomials must be x^2. Therefore, each first term must be x. We write:
   $$x^2 + 7x + 10 = (x\quad)(x\quad)$$
   2. Since the product of the last terms of the binomials must be $+10$, these last terms must be either both positive or both negative. Since the middle term of the given trinomial, $+7x$, is positive, the last terms of the binomials must both be positive. The pairs of positive integers whose product is $+10$ are $(+10)$ and $(+1)$, $(+5)$ and $(+2)$.
   3. The possible factors are $(x + 10)(x + 1)$, $(x + 5)(x + 2)$.
   4. Test each pair of factors.

   $(x + 10)(x + 1)$ is not correct because the middle term, $(+10x) + (+1x)$, is $+11x$, not $+7x$.

   $$\overset{+10x}{\overbrace{(x + 10)(x + 1)}}$$
   $$\underset{+1x}{}$$

   $(x + 5)(x + 2)$ is correct because the middle term, $(+5x) + (+2x)$, is $+7x$.

   $$\overset{+5x}{\overbrace{(x + 5)(x + 2)}}$$
   $$\underset{+2x}{}$$

   5. $x^2 + 7x + 10 = (x + 5)(x + 2)$ *Ans.*

2. Factor: $y^2 - 8y + 12$

   Solution:

   1. The product of the first terms of the binomials must be y^2. Therefore, each first term must be y. We write:
   $$y^2 - 8y + 12 = (y\quad)(y\quad)$$
   2. Since the product of the last terms of the binomials must be $+12$, these last terms must be either both positive or both negative. Since the middle term of the given trinomial, $-8y$, is negative, the last terms of the binomials must both be negative. The pairs of negative integers whose product is $+12$ are (-1) and (-12), (-6) and (-2), (-4) and (-3).
   3. The possible factors are: $(y - 1)(y - 12)$, $(y - 6)(y - 2)$, and $(y - 4)(y - 3)$.
   4. When we find the middle term in each of the trinomial products, we find that only $(y - 6)(y - 2)$ yields a middle term of $-8y$.
   5. $y^2 - 8y + 12 = (y - 6)(y - 2)$ *Ans.*

3. Factor: $c^2 + 5c - 6$

Solution:

1. The product of the first terms of the binomials must be c^2. Therefore, each first term must be c. We write:
$$c^2 + 5c - 6 = (c \quad)(c \quad)$$

2. Since the product of the last terms of the binomials must be -6, one of these last terms must be positive, the other negative. The pairs of integers whose product is -6 are $(+1)$ and (-6), (-1) and $(+6)$, $(+3)$ and (-2), (-3) and $(+2)$.

3. The possible factors are: $(c + 1)(c - 6)$, $(c - 1)(c + 6)$, $(c + 3)(c - 2)$, and $(c - 3)(c + 2)$.

4. When we find the middle term of each of the trinomial products, we find that only $(c - 1)(c + 6)$ yields a middle term of $+5c$.

5. $c^2 + 5c - 6 = (c - 1)(c + 6)$ *Ans.*

4. Factor: $2x^2 - 7x - 15$

Solution:

1. Since the product of the first terms of the binomials must be $2x^2$, one of these terms must be $2x$, the other x. We write:
$$2x^2 - 7x - 15 = (2x \quad)(x \quad)$$

2. Since the product of the last terms of the binomials must be -15, one of these last terms must be positive, the other negative. The pairs of integers whose product is -15 are $(+1)$ and (-15), (-1) and $(+15)$, $(+3)$ and (-5), (-3) and $(+5)$.

3. The possible pairs of factors are:

$(2x + 1)(x - 15)$	$(2x - 1)(x + 15)$
$(2x + 15)(x - 1)$	$(2x - 15)(x + 1)$
$(2x + 3)(x - 5)$	$(2x - 3)(x + 5)$
$(2x + 5)(x - 3)$	$(2x - 5)(x + 3)$

4. When we find the middle term of each of the trinomial products, we find that only $(2x + 3)(x - 5)$ yields a middle term of $-7x$.

5. $2x^2 - 7x - 15 = (2x + 3)(x - 5)$ *Ans.*

┌───┐
── *KEEP IN MIND* ──

In factoring a trinomial of the form $ax^2 + bx + c$, when a is a positive integer $(a > 0)$:
1. If the last term, the constant c, is positive, the last terms of the binomial factors must be either both positive or both negative.
2. If the last term, the constant c, is negative, one of the last terms in the binomial factors must be positive, the other negative.

└───┘

Exercises

In 1–90, factor:

1. $a^2 + 3a + 2$
2. $b^2 + 4b + 3$
3. $c^2 + 6c + 5$
4. $x^2 + 8x + 7$
5. $y^2 + 10y + 9$
6. $r^2 + 12r + 11$
7. $m^2 + 5m + 4$
8. $t^2 + 7t + 10$
9. $x^2 + 9x + 18$
10. $x^2 + 12x + 27$
11. $c^2 + 8c + 15$
12. $y^2 + 12y + 35$
13. $x^2 + 11x + 24$
14. $y^2 + 15y + 36$
15. $z^2 + 13z + 40$
16. $a^2 + 11a + 18$
17. $b^2 + 13b + 30$
18. $16 + 17c + c^2$
19. $x^2 + 2x + 1$
20. $y^2 + 8y + 16$
21. $z^2 + 10z + 25$
22. $a^2 - 8a + 7$
23. $x^2 - 12x + 11$
24. $a^2 - 6a + 5$
25. $x^2 - 5x + 6$
26. $x^2 - 9x + 14$
27. $x^2 - 11x + 10$
28. $y^2 - 6y + 8$
29. $z^2 - 10z + 21$
30. $r^2 - 11r + 18$
31. $a^2 - 9a + 8$
32. $x^2 - 12x + 35$
33. $15 - 8y + y^2$
34. $x^2 - 10x + 24$
35. $y^2 - 13y + 36$
36. $c^2 - 14c + 40$
37. $t^2 - 18t + 72$
38. $r^2 - 16r + 60$
39. $x^2 - 16x + 48$
40. $x^2 - 14x + 49$
41. $y^2 - 16y + 64$
42. $z^2 - 20z + 100$
43. $x^2 - x - 2$
44. $x^2 - 3x - 4$
45. $x^2 - 6x - 7$
46. $y^2 + 4y - 5$
47. $y^2 + 8y - 9$
48. $z^2 - 12z - 13$
49. $a^2 - 3a - 10$
50. $b^2 - 2b - 8$
51. $c^2 - 2c - 15$
52. $c^2 + 2c - 35$
53. $r^2 + 4r - 21$
54. $t^2 + t - 6$
55. $x^2 - 7x - 18$
56. $y^2 - 5y - 24$
57. $z^2 + 9z - 36$
58. $m^2 - 6m - 27$
59. $x^2 + 3x - 40$
60. $x^2 - 13x - 48$
61. $x^2 - 6x - 72$
62. $x^2 + 11x - 60$
63. $x^2 - 2x - 80$
64. $2x^2 + 5x + 2$
65. $3x^2 + 10x + 3$
66. $2x^2 + 11x + 5$
67. $2x^2 + 7x + 6$
68. $2x^2 + 11x + 12$
69. $3x^2 + 10x + 8$

70. $2y^2 - 3y + 1$ **71.** $3y^2 - 8y + 4$ **72.** $14 - 13y + 3y^2$
73. $2x^2 + x - 3$ **74.** $3x^2 - 5x - 2$ **75.** $3x^2 + 2x - 5$
76. $2x^2 + x - 6$ **77.** $5x^2 - 3x - 8$ **78.** $3x^2 - 5x - 12$
79. $4x^2 - 12x + 5$ **80.** $6x^2 + 5x - 6$ **81.** $6x^2 + 5x - 4$
82. $10a^2 - 9a + 2$ **83.** $10x^2 + 49x - 5$ **84.** $18y^2 - 23y - 6$
85. $x^2 + 3xy + 2y^2$ **86.** $c^2 + 4cd - 5d^2$ **87.** $r^2 - 3rs - 10s^2$
88. $3a^2 - 7ab + 2b^2$ **89.** $5m^2 + 3mn - 2n^2$ **90.** $4x^2 - 5xy - 6y^2$

8. Factoring Completely

The polynomials $x^2 + 4$ and $x^2 + x + 1$ cannot be factored over the set of polynomials with integral coefficients. We say that these polynomials are *prime over this set of polynomials.*

To factor a polynomial completely means to find the *prime factors* of the polynomial. Therefore, whenever we factor a polynomial, we will continue the process of factoring until all factors other than monomial factors are prime factors.

Procedure. To factor a polynomial completely, use the following steps:
1. **Look for the greatest common factor. If there is one, factor the given polynomial. Then examine each factor.**
2. **If one of these factors is a binomial, see if it is a difference of two squares. If it is, factor it as such.**
3. **If one of these factors is a trinomial, see if it can be factored. If it can, find its binomial factors.**
4. **Write the answer as the product of all the factors. Make certain that in the answer all factors other than monomial factors are prime factors.**

~~~~~~~ MODEL PROBLEMS ~~~~~~~

1. Factor: $5x^2 - 45$

How To Proceed	*Solution*
1. Find the greatest common factor.	$5x^2 - 45 = 5(x^2 - 9)$
2. Factor the difference of 2 squares.	$5x^2 - 45 = 5(x + 3)(x - 3)$ *Ans.*

2. Factor: $3x^2 - 6x - 24$

How To Proceed	*Solution*
1. Find the greatest common factor.	$3x^2 - 6x - 24 = 3(x^2 - 2x - 8)$
2. Factor the trinomial.	$3x^2 - 6x - 24 = 3(x - 4)(x + 2)$ *Ans.*

3. Factor: $x^4 - 16$

How To Proceed	*Solution*
1. Factor the difference of 2 squares.	$x^4 - 16 = (x^2 + 4)(x^2 - 4)$
2. Factor the difference of 2 squares.	$x^4 - 16 = (x^2 + 4)(x + 2)(x - 2)$ *Ans.*

Exercises

In 1–36, factor completely.

1. $2a^2 - 2b^2$

2. $6x^2 - 6y^2$

3. $4x^2 - 4$

4. $ax^2 - ay^2$

5. $cm^2 - cn^2$

6. $st^2 - s$

7. $2x^2 - 18$

8. $2x^2 - 32$

9. $3x^2 - 27y^2$

10. $18m^2 - 8$

11. $12a^2 - 27b^2$

12. $63c^2 - 7$

13. $x^3 - 4x$

14. $y^3 - 25y$

15. $z^3 - z$

16. $4a^3 - ab^2$

17. $4c^3 - 49c$

18. $9db^2 - d$

19. $4a^2 - 36$

20. $u^4 - 1$

21. $y^4 - 81$

22. $\pi R^2 - \pi r^2$

23. $\pi c^2 - \pi d^2$

24. $100x^2 - 36y^2$

25. $ax^2 + 3ax + 2a$

26. $3x^2 + 6x + 3$

27. $4r^2 - 4r - 48$

28. $x^3 + 7x^2 + 10x$

29. $4x^2 - 6x - 4$

30. $2ax^2 - 2ax - 12a$

31. $abx^2 - ab$

32. $z^6 - z^2$

33. $16x^2 - x^2y^4$

34. $x^4 + x^2 - 2$

35. $a^4 - 10a^2 + 9$

36. $y^4 - 13y^2 + 36$

CHAPTER XII

OPERATIONS WITH FRACTIONS

1. The Meaning of an Algebraic Fraction

A fraction is a symbol which indicates the quotient of any two numbers (remember that division by zero is not possible). For example, the arithmetic fraction $\frac{3}{4}$ indicates the quotient of 3 and 4. Keep in mind that the symbol $\frac{3}{4}$ is a numeral representing an arithmetic number. In our work, the word *fraction* will be used to mean either the numeral or the number. The context will determine which meaning is intended.

An **algebraic fraction** is a quotient which involves algebraic expressions. Examples of algebraic fractions are: $\frac{2}{5}, \frac{x}{2}, \frac{2}{x}, \frac{a}{b}, \frac{4c}{3d}, \frac{x+5}{x-2}, \frac{x^2+4x+3}{x+1}$.

The fraction $\frac{a}{b}$ means that the number represented by a, the numerator, is to be divided by the number represented by b, the denominator. Since division by zero is not possible, the value of the denominator, b, may not be zero. In all our work with fractions, we will assume that the denominator is not zero.

~~~~~~~~~~~ **MODEL PROBLEM** ~~~~~~~~~~~

Find the value of x for which $\dfrac{12}{x-9}$ has no meaning.

Solution: $\dfrac{12}{x-9}$ is not defined when the denominator $x-9$ is equal to 0.

Let $x - 9 = 0$. Then $x = 9$.   *Ans.* 9

Exercises

In 1–9, represent the symbol as a fraction and give the value of the variable, if any, for which the fraction has no meaning.

1. $x \div 7$
2. $9 \div x$
3. $(-8) \div 3x$
4. $(x+6) \div x^2$
5. $15 \div (y-3)$
6. $(-7b) \div (b+8)$
7. $(x+4) \div (2x-6)$
8. $(5y+3) \div (3y+1)$
9. $(x-5) \div (x^2-25)$

In 10–17, find the value of the variable for which the fraction is not defined.

10. $\dfrac{2}{x}$ **11.** $\dfrac{-5}{6x}$ **12.** $\dfrac{12}{y^2}$ **13.** $\dfrac{x}{x-8}$

14. $\dfrac{y+5}{y+2}$ **15.** $\dfrac{x^2-9}{2x-1}$ **16.** $\dfrac{2y+3}{4y+2}$ **17.** $\dfrac{4x-5}{x^2-9}$

In 18–28, represent the answer to the problem as a fraction.

18. Represent the cost of 1 piece of candy if 5 pieces cost c cents.

19. Represent the cost of one pear if p pears cost 60 cents.

20. If string beans cost 19 cents a pound, represent the number of pounds that can be bought for y cents.

21. If x pencils cost y cents, represent the cost of one pencil.

22. If $(x + 1)$ dresses cost $(4x + 9)$ dollars, represent the cost of one dress.

23. If a car travels m miles in 4 hours, represent the number of miles it travels in 1 hour.

24. If a man walks at the rate of r miles per hour, represent the number of hours that he will require to travel d miles.

25. What fractional part of an hour is m minutes?

26. In a school there are b boys and g girls. What fractional part of the pupils is girls?

27. Sam can mow a lawn in 90 minutes. What part of the lawn can he mow in x minutes?

28. Harold can paint a fence in h hours. Represent the part of the fence that he can paint in 4 hours.

2. Reducing Fractions to Lowest Terms

A fraction is said to be ***reduced to lowest terms*** when its numerator and denominator have no common factor other than 1.

The fractions $\dfrac{5}{10}$ and $\dfrac{1a}{2a}$ each become the fraction $\dfrac{1}{2}$ when reduced to lowest terms. Let us use the multiplication property of 1 to show that $\dfrac{5}{10}$ names the same number as $\dfrac{1}{2}$ and that $\dfrac{1a}{2a}$ also names the same number as $\dfrac{1}{2}.$ Remember that any non-zero number divided by itself equals 1.

$$\frac{5}{10} = \frac{1 \cdot 5}{2 \cdot 5} = \frac{1}{2} \cdot \frac{5}{5} = \frac{1}{2} \cdot 1 = \frac{1}{2} \quad \text{AND} \quad \frac{1a}{2a} = \frac{1 \cdot a}{2 \cdot a} = \frac{1}{2} \cdot \frac{a}{a} = \frac{1}{2} \cdot 1 = \frac{1}{2}$$

These examples illustrate the ***division property of a fraction:*** If the numerator and denominator of a fraction are divided by the same non-zero number, the resulting fraction is equal to the original fraction.

In general, for any numbers x, y, and a, where $y \neq 0$ and $a \neq 0$:

$$\frac{x}{y} = \frac{x \div a}{y \div a}$$

Note the following examples of the division property of fractions:

$$\frac{15}{20} = \frac{15 \div 5}{20 \div 5} = \frac{3}{4}$$

$$\frac{4x}{5x} = \frac{4x \div x}{5x \div x} = \frac{4}{5}$$

$$\frac{cy}{dy} = \frac{cy \div y}{dy \div y} = \frac{c}{d}$$

$$\frac{2(x+5)}{3(x+5)} = \frac{2(x+5) \div (x+5)}{3(x+5) \div (x+5)} = \frac{2}{3}$$

When reducing a fraction, the division of the numerator and the denominator by a common factor may be indicated by a **cancellation**. For example, we may write:

$$\frac{2(x+5)}{3(x+5)} = \frac{2\overset{1}{\cancel{(x+5)}}}{3\underset{1}{\cancel{(x+5)}}} = \frac{2}{3}$$

Procedure: To reduce a fraction to its lowest terms:

Method 1

1. **Factor both its numerator and its denominator.**
2. **Examine the factors and determine the greatest common factor of the numerator and the denominator.**
3. **Express the given fraction as the product of two fractions, one of which has as its numerator and its denominator the greatest common factor determined in step 2.**
4. **Use the multiplication property of 1.**

Method 2

1. **Factor both its numerator and its denominator.**
2. **Divide both the numerator and the denominator by their greatest common factor.**

MODEL PROBLEMS

1. Reduce $\dfrac{27}{45}$ to lowest terms.

Solution:

Method 1

$$\frac{27}{45} = \frac{3}{5} \cdot \frac{9}{9} = \frac{3}{5} \cdot 1 = \frac{3}{5} \quad Ans.$$

Method 2

$$\frac{27}{45} = \frac{9(3)}{9(5)} = \frac{9(3) \div 9}{9(5) \div 9} = \frac{3}{5} \quad Ans.$$

2. Reduce $\dfrac{8x^3y^2}{12x^2y^4}$ to lowest terms.

Solution:

Method 1

$$\frac{8x^3y^2}{12x^2y^4} = \frac{2x}{3y^2} \cdot \frac{4x^2y^2}{4x^2y^2}$$

$$= \frac{2x}{3y^2} \cdot 1$$

$$= \frac{2x}{3y^2} \quad Ans.$$

Method 2

$$\frac{8x^3y^2}{12x^2y^4} = \frac{4x^2y^2 \cdot 2x}{4x^2y^2 \cdot 3y^2}$$

$$= \frac{4x^2y^2 \cdot 2x \div 4x^2y^2}{4x^2y^2 \cdot 3y^2 \div 4x^2y^2}$$

$$= \frac{2x}{3y^2} \quad Ans.$$

3. Reduce $\dfrac{4x - 4y}{x^2 - y^2}$ to lowest terms.

Solution:

Method 1

$$\frac{4x - 4y}{x^2 - y^2} = \frac{4(x - y)}{(x + y)(x - y)}$$

$$= \frac{4}{(x + y)} \cdot \frac{(x - y)}{(x - y)}$$

$$= \frac{4}{(x + y)} \cdot 1$$

$$= \frac{4}{x + y} \quad Ans.$$

Method 2

$$\frac{4x - 4y}{x^2 - y^2} = \frac{4(x - y)}{(x + y)(x - y)}$$

$$= \frac{4\overset{1}{\cancel{(x - y)}}}{(x + y)\underset{1}{\cancel{(x - y)}}}$$

$$= \frac{4}{x + y} \quad Ans.$$

4. Reduce $\dfrac{(x-4)^2}{x^2-5x+4}$ to lowest terms.

Solution:

Method 1

$$\frac{(x-4)^2}{x^2-5x+4} = \frac{(x-4)(x-4)}{(x-1)(x-4)}$$

$$= \frac{(x-4)}{(x-1)} \cdot 1$$

$$= \frac{x-4}{x-1} \quad Ans.$$

Method 2

$$\frac{(x-4)^2}{x^2-5x+4} = \frac{(x-4)(x-4)}{(x-1)(x-4)}$$

$$= \frac{(x-4)\overset{1}{(\cancel{x-4})}}{(x-1)\underset{1}{(\cancel{x-4})}}$$

$$= \frac{x-4}{x-1} \quad Ans.$$

5. Reduce $\dfrac{2-x}{4x-8}$ to lowest terms.

Solution:

$$\frac{2-x}{4x-8} = \frac{-x+2}{4x-8} = \frac{-1(x-2)}{4(x-2)} = \frac{-1}{4} \cdot \frac{(x-2)}{(x-2)} = -\frac{1}{4} \cdot 1 = -\frac{1}{4} \quad Ans.$$

WRONG METHODS OF REDUCING FRACTIONS

Students sometimes make mistakes when reducing fractions because they carelessly "cross off" or "cancel" the same quantity in some part of the numerator and in some part of the denominator. Remember that a fraction may be reduced by *dividing* the numerator and the denominator by a common factor. Thus, $\dfrac{\cancel{3}x}{\cancel{3}+y} = \dfrac{x}{y}$ is wrong, because 3 is not a factor of the denominator, $3+y$.

When the same number is subtracted from both terms of a fraction, the resulting fraction is not always equivalent to the original fraction. For example, $\dfrac{4}{5}$ does not equal $\dfrac{4-2}{5-2}$, or $\dfrac{2}{3}$. Also, $\dfrac{x+\cancel{2}}{y+\cancel{2}} = \dfrac{x}{y}$ is wrong, because the numerator and the denominator were not *divided* by a factor 2; since 2 was *subtracted* from the numerator and from the denominator, the result is not always an equivalent fraction.

Similarly, when the same number is added to both terms of a fraction, the resulting fraction is not always equivalent to the original fraction. For example, $\frac{5}{6}$ does not equal $\frac{5+4}{6+4}$, or $\frac{9}{10}$. Also, $\frac{x-\not{4}}{y-\not{4}} = \frac{x}{y}$ is wrong, because the numerator and the denominator were not *divided* by a factor 4; since 4 was *added* to the numerator and to the denominator, the result is not always an equivalent fraction.

KEEP IN MIND

The word *cancellation* may be used in reducing fractions provided that it means dividing both the numerator and the denominator of a fraction by the same factor.

Exercises

In 1–76, reduce the fraction to lowest terms.

1. $\dfrac{4}{12}$ **2.** $\dfrac{6}{8}$ **3.** $\dfrac{27}{36}$ **4.** $\dfrac{24}{32}$

5. $\dfrac{6x}{6y}$ **6.** $\dfrac{24c}{36d}$ **7.** $\dfrac{9r}{10r}$ **8.** $\dfrac{3m^2}{5m^2}$

9. $\dfrac{ab}{cb}$ **10.** $\dfrac{rs^2}{ts^2}$ **11.** $\dfrac{x^2y}{x^2z}$ **12.** $\dfrac{3ay^2}{6by^2}$

13. $\dfrac{5xy}{9xy}$ **14.** $\dfrac{4xyz}{7xyz}$ **15.** $\dfrac{2abc}{4abc}$ **16.** $\dfrac{6cde}{12cde}$

17. $\dfrac{15x^3}{5x}$ **18.** $\dfrac{18y^4}{6y^2}$ **19.** $\dfrac{5x^2}{25x^3}$ **20.** $\dfrac{27a}{36a^2}$

21. $\dfrac{8xy^2}{24x^2y}$ **22.** $\dfrac{36a^4y^2}{48ay^3}$ **23.** $\dfrac{18rs^3}{45r^2s}$ **24.** $\dfrac{64a^2b^2c^2}{24ab^2c^2}$

25. $\dfrac{+12a^2b}{-8ac}$ **26.** $\dfrac{-20x^2y^2}{-90xy^2}$ **27.** $\dfrac{-32a^3b^3}{+48a^3b^3}$ **28.** $\dfrac{+5xy}{+45x^2y^2}$

29. $\dfrac{5(x+2)}{7(x+2)}$ **30.** $\dfrac{4(m+1)}{8(m+1)}$ **31.** $\dfrac{15(y-3)}{20(y-3)}$ **32.** $\dfrac{18(5-x)}{27(5-x)}$

33. $\dfrac{m(a+b)}{n(a+b)}$ **34.** $\dfrac{x(r-s)}{x(r-s)}$ **35.** $\dfrac{m^2(x+y)}{m(x+y)}$ **36.** $\dfrac{6x^2(r-2s)}{3x(r-2s)}$

37. $\dfrac{5(x-7)}{5x}$ **38.** $\dfrac{8m}{8(m+5)}$ **39.** $\dfrac{2x(a+b)}{8x^2}$ **40.** $\dfrac{9x(x+2)}{9x}$

41. $\dfrac{5x+5y}{7x+7y}$ **42.** $\dfrac{9a-18}{4a-8}$ **43.** $\dfrac{6(x+2y)}{9x+18y}$ **44.** $\dfrac{(x+4)^2}{x+4}$

45. $\dfrac{ab+ac}{db+dc}$ **46.** $\dfrac{rx-ry}{sx-sy}$ **47.** $\dfrac{3x-3}{x^2-1}$ **48.** $\dfrac{y^2-25}{5y+25}$

49. $\dfrac{3m-9}{m^2-9}$ **50.** $\dfrac{64-r^2}{16+2r}$ **51.** $\dfrac{(x+y)^2}{x^2-y^2}$ **52.** $\dfrac{x^2-4}{(x-2)^2}$

53. $\dfrac{9y-18}{3y^2-12}$ **54.** $\dfrac{6y^2-6}{27y+27}$ **55.** $\dfrac{75-12x^2}{15-6x}$ **56.** $\dfrac{5a^2-20}{(a-2)^2}$

57. $\dfrac{1-x}{x-1}$ **58.** $\dfrac{3-b}{b^2-9}$ **59.** $\dfrac{2s-2r}{s^2-r^2}$ **60.** $\dfrac{x^2-y^2}{3y-3x}$

61. $\dfrac{x^2-3x}{2x}$ **62.** $\dfrac{6y-12y^2}{9y}$ **63.** $\dfrac{x}{x^2+\cdot x}$ **64.** $\dfrac{3m}{6m-9m^2}$

65. $\dfrac{3y-3}{y^2-2y+1}$ **66.** $\dfrac{x^2-3x}{x^2-4x+3}$ **67.** $\dfrac{x^2-25}{x^2-2x-15}$

68. $\dfrac{a^2-a-6}{a^2-9}$ **69.** $\dfrac{a^2-6a}{a^2-7a+6}$ **70.** $\dfrac{2x^2-50}{x^2+8x+15}$

71. $\dfrac{r^2-4r-5}{r^2-2r-15}$ **72.** $\dfrac{48+8x-x^2}{x^2+x-12}$ **73.** $\dfrac{2x^2-7x+3}{(x-3)^2}$

74. $\dfrac{3x^2-15x+18}{x^2-x-6}$ **75.** $\dfrac{x^2-7xy+12y^2}{x^2+xy-20y^2}$ **76.** $\dfrac{18c^2-32d^2}{6c^2-cd-12d^2}$

In 77–82, tell whether the solution is correct. State the reason for your answer.

77. $\dfrac{a+\cancel{7}}{b+\cancel{7}}=\dfrac{a}{b}$ **78.** $\dfrac{c-\cancel{d}}{d-\cancel{d}}=\dfrac{c}{d}$ **79.** $\dfrac{\overset{1}{\cancel{y}}(\overset{1}{\cancel{x+2}})}{2\cancel{y}(\underset{1}{\cancel{x+2}})}=\dfrac{1}{2}$

80. $\dfrac{\overset{1}{\cancel{d}}}{3\underset{1}{\cancel{d}}+e}=\dfrac{1}{3+e}$ **81.** $\dfrac{3\overset{1}{\cancel{x+y}}}{\underset{1}{\cancel{x+y}}}=3$ **82.** $\dfrac{\overset{x}{\cancel{x^2}}+\overset{y}{\cancel{y^2}}}{\underset{1}{\cancel{x}}+\underset{1}{\cancel{y}}}=\dfrac{x+y}{2}$

3. Multiplying Fractions

The product of two fractions is a fraction with the following characteristics:

1. The product's numerator is the product of the numerators of the given fractions.
2. The product's denominator is the product of the denominators of the given fractions.

In general, for any numbers a, b, x, and y, when $b \neq 0$ and $y \neq 0$:

$$\frac{a}{b} \cdot \frac{x}{y} = \frac{ax}{by}$$

We can find the product of $\frac{7}{27}$ and $\frac{9}{4}$ in lowest terms by using either one of the following two methods:

Method 1   *Method 2*

$$\frac{7}{27} \cdot \frac{9}{4} = \frac{7 \cdot 9}{27 \cdot 4} = \frac{63}{108} = \frac{7 \cdot \overset{1}{\cancel{9}}}{12 \cdot \underset{1}{\cancel{9}}} = \frac{7}{12} \qquad\qquad \frac{7}{27} \cdot \frac{9}{4} = \frac{7 \cdot \overset{1}{\cancel{9}}}{\underset{3}{\cancel{27}} \cdot 4} = \frac{7}{12}$$

Notice that method 2 requires less computation than method 1 since the reduced form of the product was obtained by dividing the numerator and the denominator by a common factor *before* the product was found. This method may be called the **cancellation method.**

When we multiply algebraic fractions, the product has the same characteristics as when we multiply arithmetic fractions.

Thus, to multiply $\dfrac{5x^2}{7y}$ by $\dfrac{14y^2}{15x^3}$, we may use either one of the following two methods:

Method 1

$$\frac{5x^2}{7y} \cdot \frac{14y^2}{15x^3} = \frac{5x^2 \cdot 14y^2}{7y \cdot 15x^3} = \frac{70x^2y^2}{105x^3y} = \frac{2y}{3x} \cdot \frac{35x^2y}{35x^2y} = \frac{2y}{3x} \cdot 1 = \frac{2y}{3x}$$

Method 2 (the cancellation method)

$$\frac{5x^2}{7y} \cdot \frac{14y^2}{15x^3} = \frac{\overset{1}{\cancel{5x^2}}}{\underset{1}{\cancel{7y}}} \cdot \frac{\overset{2y}{\cancel{14y^2}}}{\underset{3x}{\cancel{15x^3}}} = \frac{2y}{3x}$$

Procedure. To find the product of two fractions:
1. **Factor, when possible, the numerators and denominators of the fractions.**
2. **Divide both the numerator and the denominator by common factors.**
3. **Multiply the remaining factors of the numerators to find the numerator of the product.**
4. **Multiply the remaining factors of the denominators to find the denominator of the product.**

～～～～～～～～ MODEL PROBLEM ～～～～～～～～

Multiply and express the product in reduced form: $\dfrac{a^2 - b^2}{10x^3} \cdot \dfrac{5x^2}{2a + 2b}$

How To Proceed | *Solution*

1. Factor the numerators and the denominators.

$$\frac{a^2 - b^2}{10x^3} \cdot \frac{5x^2}{2a + 2b} = \frac{(a + b)(a - b)}{10x^3} \cdot \frac{5x^2}{2(a + b)}$$

2. Divide the numerators and the denominators by the common factors, $5x^2$ and $(a + b)$.

$$= \frac{\overset{1}{\cancel{(a + b)}}(a - b)}{\underset{2x}{\cancel{10x^3}}} \cdot \frac{\overset{1}{\cancel{5x^2}}}{\underset{1}{2\cancel{(a + b)}}}$$

3. Multiply the remaining numerators and then multiply the remaining denominators.

$$= \frac{a - b}{4x} \quad Ans.$$

～～～～～～～～～～～～～～～～～～～～～～～～～～～～～～～

── KEEP IN MIND ──

Any integer or polynomial may be expressed as a fraction whose denominator is 1. For example:

$$5 = \frac{5}{1} \qquad 3x^2 = \frac{3x^2}{1} \qquad 5y - 6 = \frac{5y - 6}{1}$$

Exercises

In 1–48, find the product in lowest terms.

1. $\dfrac{3}{5} \times \dfrac{7}{8}$

2. $\dfrac{8}{12} \times \dfrac{30}{36}$

3. $\dfrac{3}{8} \times 32$

4. $36 \times \dfrac{5}{9}$

5. $\dfrac{1}{2} \times 20x$

6. $40 \times \dfrac{b}{8}$

7. $\dfrac{5}{d} \times d^2$

8. $cd \times \dfrac{5}{c}$

9. $\dfrac{x^2}{36} \times 20$

10. $\dfrac{18}{a^2} \times 3a$

11. $6y^2 \times \dfrac{4}{3y}$

12. $mn \times \dfrac{8}{m^2 n^2}$

13. $\dfrac{3c}{4d} \cdot \dfrac{5r}{3s}$

14. $\dfrac{24x}{35y} \cdot \dfrac{14y}{8x}$

15. $\dfrac{ab}{c} \cdot \dfrac{c}{a}$

16. $\dfrac{12x}{5y} \cdot \dfrac{15y^2}{36x^2}$

17. $\dfrac{m^2}{8} \cdot \dfrac{32}{3m}$

18. $\dfrac{6r^2}{5s^2} \cdot \dfrac{10rs}{6r^3}$

19. $\dfrac{30m^2}{18n} \cdot \dfrac{6n}{5m}$

20. $\dfrac{24a^3b^2}{7c^3} \cdot \dfrac{21c^2}{12ab}$

21. $\dfrac{7}{x^2 - 4} \cdot \dfrac{2x + 4}{21}$

22. $\dfrac{3a + 9}{15a} \cdot \dfrac{a^2}{a^2 - 9}$

23. $\dfrac{5x - 5y}{x^2 y} \cdot \dfrac{xy^2}{x^2 - y^2}$

24. $\dfrac{x^2 - 1}{14} \cdot \dfrac{2}{x + 1}$

25. $\dfrac{x^2 - 9}{5c^5} \cdot \dfrac{10c^4}{x - 3}$

26. $\dfrac{a}{x^2 - 4} \cdot (2x + 4)$

27. $\dfrac{(a + 3)^2}{x^2} \cdot \dfrac{4x^2}{4a + 12}$

28. $\dfrac{6k^5}{(x - y)^2} \cdot \dfrac{x^2 - y^2}{9k}$

29. $\dfrac{a(a - b)^2}{4b} \cdot \dfrac{4b}{a(a^2 - b^2)}$

30. $\dfrac{(a - 2)^2}{4b} \cdot \dfrac{16b^3}{4 - a^2}$

31. $\dfrac{a^2 - 7a - 8}{2a + 2} \cdot \dfrac{5}{a - 8}$

32. $\dfrac{x^2 + 6x + 5}{9y^2} \cdot \dfrac{3y}{x + 1}$

33. $\dfrac{y^2 - 2y - 3}{2c^3} \cdot \dfrac{4c^2}{2y + 2}$

34. $\dfrac{4a - 6}{4a + 8} \cdot \dfrac{6a + 12}{5a - 15}$

35. $\dfrac{x^2 - 25}{4x^2 - 9} \cdot \dfrac{2x + 3}{x - 5}$

36. $\dfrac{4x + 8}{6x + 18} \cdot \dfrac{5x + 15}{x^2 - 4}$

37. $\dfrac{y^2 - 81}{(y + 9)^2} \cdot \dfrac{10y + 90}{5y - 45}$

38. $\dfrac{8x}{2x^2 - 8} \cdot \dfrac{8x + 16}{32x^2}$

39. $\dfrac{x + 2d}{5x^2 - 20d^2} \cdot \dfrac{25x - 50d}{25x}$

40. $\dfrac{(x - 4)^2}{2x^2 - 32} \cdot \dfrac{4x + 16}{20x}$

41. $\dfrac{x^2 - 7x + 12}{x^2 - 4} \cdot \dfrac{2x + 4}{x + 3}$

42. $\dfrac{x^2 - 3x - 18}{x - 6} \cdot \dfrac{6 - 2x}{x^2 - 9}$

43. $\dfrac{(x - 3)^2}{x^2 - x - 6} \cdot \dfrac{x + 2}{x - 3}$

44. $\dfrac{a - b}{a + b} \cdot \dfrac{a^2 - b^2}{a^2 - 2ab + b^2}$

45. $\dfrac{y^2 - 3y - 10}{y^2 + 3y + 2} \cdot \dfrac{y^2 + 8y + 7}{y^2 - 6y + 5}$

46. $\dfrac{a^2 + 8a + 12}{a^2 - 8a + 16} \cdot \dfrac{20 - a - a^2}{a^2 + 11a + 30}$

47. $\dfrac{2x - 2}{30x^2} \cdot \dfrac{9x^2 + 27x}{x^2 - 9} \cdot \dfrac{x^2 + 2x - 15}{x^2 + 4x - 5}$

48. $\dfrac{c^2 + 6cd + 9d^2}{c^2 - 4d^2} \cdot \dfrac{15c + 30d}{3c^2 + 9cd} \cdot \dfrac{c^2 - cd - 2d^2}{c^2 + 2cd - 3d^2}$

4. Dividing Fractions

We know that the operation of division may be defined by means of the multiplicative inverse, the reciprocal. A quotient can be expressed as the product of the dividend and the reciprocal of the divisor. Thus, $8 \div 5 = 8 \cdot \frac{1}{5} = \frac{8}{5}$ and $\frac{8}{7} \div \frac{5}{3} = \frac{8}{7} \cdot \frac{3}{5} = \frac{24}{35}$.

In general, for any numbers a, b, c, and d, when $b \neq 0$, $c \neq 0$, and $d \neq 0$:

$$\frac{a}{b} \div \frac{c}{d} = \frac{a}{b} \cdot \frac{d}{c} = \frac{ad}{bc}$$

Procedure. To divide by an algebraic fraction, multiply the dividend by the reciprocal of the divisor.

KEEP IN MIND

The reciprocal of $\dfrac{1}{n}$ is n, of $\dfrac{a}{b}$ is $\dfrac{b}{a}$, and of $\dfrac{a + b}{c + d}$ is $\dfrac{c + d}{a + b}$. In each example, the product of the two expressions is 1.

~~~~~~~~~~~ **MODEL PROBLEMS** ~~~~~~~~~~~

1. Divide: $\dfrac{16c^3}{21d^2} \div \dfrac{24c^4}{14d^3}$

How To Proceed	*Solution*
Multiply the dividend by the reciprocal of the divisor.	$\dfrac{16c^3}{21d^2} \div \dfrac{24c^4}{14d^3} = \dfrac{\overset{2}{\cancel{16c^3}}}{\underset{3}{\cancel{21d^2}}} \cdot \dfrac{\overset{2d}{\cancel{14d^3}}}{\underset{3c}{\cancel{24c^4}}} = \dfrac{4d}{9c}$ *Ans.*

2. Divide: $\dfrac{8x^2}{x^2 - 25} \div \dfrac{4x}{3x + 15}$

How To Proceed	*Solution*
1. Multiply the dividend by the reciprocal of the divisor.	$\dfrac{8x^2}{x^2 - 25} \div \dfrac{4x}{3x + 15}$ $= \dfrac{8x^2}{x^2 - 25} \cdot \dfrac{3x + 15}{4x}$
2. Factor the numerators and denominators. Divide by the common factors.	$= \dfrac{\overset{2x}{\cancel{8x^2}}}{\underset{1}{(x + 5)}(x - 5)} \cdot \dfrac{\overset{1}{3\cancel{(x + 5)}}}{\underset{1}{\cancel{4x}}}$
3. Multiply the remaining numerators and then the remaining denominators.	$= \dfrac{6x}{x - 5}$ *Ans.*

~~~~~~

Exercises

In 1–32, divide and express the quotient in lowest terms.

1. $\frac{7}{10} \div \frac{21}{5}$ **2.** $\frac{12}{35} \div \frac{4}{7}$ **3.** $8 \div \frac{1}{2}$ **4.** $\frac{3}{4} \div 6$

5. $\dfrac{x}{9} \div \dfrac{x}{3}$ **6.** $\dfrac{2}{b^2} \div \dfrac{2}{b}$ **7.** $\dfrac{3x}{5y} \div \dfrac{21x}{20y}$ **8.** $\dfrac{7ab^2}{10cd} \div \dfrac{14b^3}{5c^2d^3}$

9. $\dfrac{xy^2}{x^2y} \div \dfrac{x}{y^3}$ **10.** $\dfrac{8x^2}{3y^2} \div \dfrac{4x}{6y^3}$ **11.** $8rs \div \dfrac{24r}{s}$ **12.** $\dfrac{6a^2b^2}{8c} \div 3ab$

13. $\dfrac{9}{x^2 - 1} \div \dfrac{3}{x + 1}$

14. $\dfrac{y^2 - 25}{18} \div \dfrac{y - 5}{27}$

15. $\dfrac{3x - 3y}{xy^2} \div \dfrac{x^2 - y^2}{x^2 y}$

16. $\dfrac{3a + 12}{18} \div \dfrac{a - 2}{2}$

17. $\dfrac{x^2 - 36}{7y^3} \div \dfrac{x - 6}{14y^4}$

18. $\dfrac{b}{a^2 - 49} \div \dfrac{4b^3}{2a + 14}$

19. $\dfrac{(m + 1)^2}{n^2} \div \dfrac{6m + 6}{9n^2}$

20. $\dfrac{8r^4}{(s - 7)^2} \div \dfrac{20r}{s^2 - 49}$

21. $\dfrac{y^2 - 3y - 10}{8y^2} \div \dfrac{2y - 10}{16y^2}$

22. $\dfrac{a^2 - 1}{2a + 2} \div \dfrac{1 - a}{3}$

23. $\dfrac{y^2 - 16}{9y^2 - 25} \div \dfrac{y - 4}{3y + 5}$

24. $\dfrac{6x + 12}{2x + 6} \div \dfrac{x^2 - 4}{7x + 21}$

25. $\dfrac{y^2 - 49}{(y + 7)^2} \div \dfrac{3y - 21}{2y + 14}$

26. $\dfrac{2x^2 - 2y^2}{10x} \div \dfrac{6y - 6x}{15x^2}$

27. $\dfrac{(x - 2)^2}{4x^2 - 16} \div \dfrac{21x}{3x + 6}$

28. $\dfrac{x^2 - 2xy - 8y^2}{x^2 - 16y^2} \div \dfrac{5x + 10y}{3x + 12y}$

29. $(y^2 - 9) \div \dfrac{y^2 + 8y + 15}{2y + 10}$

30. $\dfrac{x^2 - 4x + 4}{3x - 6} \div (x - 2)$

31. $\dfrac{x - 1}{x + 1} \cdot \dfrac{2x + 2}{x + 2} \div \dfrac{4x - 4}{x + 2}$

32. $\dfrac{x + y}{x^2 + y^2} \cdot \dfrac{x}{x - y} \div \dfrac{(x + y)^2}{x^4 - y^4}$

5. Adding or Subtracting Fractions Which Have the Same Denominator

We know that the sum of two arithmetic fractions which have the same denominator is a fraction whose numerator is the sum of the numerators and whose denominator is the common denominator of the given fractions. We use the same rule to add algebraic fractions which have the same non-zero denominator. Thus:

Arithmetic fractions   *Algebraic fractions*

$$\frac{5}{7} + \frac{1}{7} = \frac{5 + 1}{7} = \frac{6}{7} \qquad \frac{a}{x} + \frac{b}{x} = \frac{a + b}{x} \qquad \frac{a}{x - y} + \frac{b}{x - y} = \frac{a + b}{x - y}$$

$$\frac{5}{7} - \frac{1}{7} = \frac{5 - 1}{7} = \frac{4}{7} \qquad \frac{a}{x} - \frac{b}{x} = \frac{a - b}{x} \qquad \frac{a}{x - y} - \frac{b}{x - y} = \frac{a - b}{x - y}$$

Procedure. To add (or subtract) fractions which have the same denominator:
1. **Write a fraction whose numerator is the sum (or difference) of the numerators and whose denominator is the common denominator of the given fractions.**
2. **Reduce the resulting fraction to lowest terms.**

MODEL PROBLEMS

Add or subtract as indicated. Reduce answers to lowest terms.

1. $\dfrac{5}{4x} + \dfrac{9}{4x} - \dfrac{8}{4x}$

2. $\dfrac{4x + 7}{x - 3} - \dfrac{2x - 5}{x - 3}$

Solution

$$\dfrac{5}{4x} + \dfrac{9}{4x} - \dfrac{8}{4x}$$

$$= \dfrac{5 + 9 - 8}{4x}$$

$$= \dfrac{6}{4x}$$

$$= \dfrac{3}{2x} \quad Ans.$$

Solution

$$\dfrac{4x + 7}{x - 3} - \dfrac{2x - 5}{x - 3}$$

$$= \dfrac{(4x + 7) - (2x - 5)}{x - 3}$$

$$= \dfrac{4x + 7 - 2x + 5}{x - 3}$$

$$= \dfrac{2x + 12}{x - 3} \quad Ans.$$

[*Note:* In model problem 2, since the fraction bar is a symbol of grouping, we place numerators which have more than one term in parentheses.]

KEEP IN MIND

When we add or subtract fractions, we are combining the fractions.

Exercises

In 1–54, add or subtract (combine) the fractions as indicated. Reduce answers to lowest terms.

1. $\dfrac{1}{8} + \dfrac{4}{8}$ **2.** $\dfrac{6}{12} - \dfrac{1}{12}$ **3.** $\dfrac{9}{15} - \dfrac{6}{15}$ **4.** $\dfrac{9}{16} - \dfrac{6}{16} + \dfrac{5}{16}$

5. $\dfrac{2}{x} + \dfrac{3}{x}$ **6.** $\dfrac{9}{y} - \dfrac{3}{y}$ **7.** $\dfrac{7}{3b} - \dfrac{2}{3b}$ **8.** $\dfrac{11}{4c} + \dfrac{5}{4c} - \dfrac{6}{4c}$

9. $\dfrac{3x}{4} + \dfrac{2x}{4}$ **10.** $\dfrac{12y}{5} - \dfrac{4y}{5}$ **11.** $\dfrac{11a}{9} - \dfrac{5a}{9}$ **12.** $\dfrac{7b}{8} + \dfrac{5b}{8} - \dfrac{6b}{8}$

13. $\dfrac{x}{3} + \dfrac{y}{3}$ **14.** $\dfrac{a}{10} - \dfrac{b}{10}$ **15.** $\dfrac{2c}{5} - \dfrac{3d}{5}$ **16.** $\dfrac{x}{2} - \dfrac{y}{2} + \dfrac{z}{2}$

17. $\dfrac{x}{a} + \dfrac{y}{a}$ **18.** $\dfrac{c}{b} - \dfrac{d}{b}$ **19.** $\dfrac{5r}{t} - \dfrac{2s}{t}$ **20.** $\dfrac{a}{n} + \dfrac{b}{n} - \dfrac{2c}{n}$

21. $\dfrac{9}{8x} + \dfrac{6}{8x}$ **22.** $\dfrac{8}{3z} - \dfrac{7}{3z}$ **23.** $\dfrac{6}{12x} - \dfrac{2}{12x}$ **24.** $\dfrac{8}{9y} + \dfrac{4}{9y} - \dfrac{3}{9y}$

25. $\dfrac{6a}{4x} + \dfrac{5a}{4x}$ **26.** $\dfrac{11b}{3y} - \dfrac{4b}{3y}$ **27.** $\dfrac{19c}{12d} + \dfrac{9c}{12d}$ **28.** $\dfrac{6}{10c} + \dfrac{9}{10c} - \dfrac{3}{10c}$

29. $\dfrac{5}{x+2} + \dfrac{3}{x+2}$ **30.** $\dfrac{2}{a-b} - \dfrac{1}{a-b}$ **31.** $\dfrac{r}{y-2} + \dfrac{x}{y-2}$

32. $\dfrac{x}{x+1} + \dfrac{1}{x+1}$ **33.** $\dfrac{2x}{x+3} + \dfrac{6}{x+3}$ **34.** $\dfrac{y}{y^2-4} - \dfrac{2}{y^2-4}$

35. $\dfrac{2x+1}{2} + \dfrac{3x+6}{2}$ **36.** $\dfrac{9x-3}{6} + \dfrac{5x+5}{6}$ **37.** $\dfrac{4x+12}{16x} + \dfrac{8x+4}{16x}$

38. $\dfrac{5x-4}{3} - \dfrac{2x+1}{3}$ **39.** $\dfrac{6x-9}{6} - \dfrac{4x-8}{6}$ **40.** $\dfrac{12a-15}{12a} - \dfrac{9a-6}{12a}$

41. $\dfrac{4x+1}{3x+2} + \dfrac{6x-3}{3x+2}$ **42.** $\dfrac{3c-7}{2c-3} + \dfrac{c+9}{2c-3}$ **43.** $\dfrac{6y-4}{4y+3} + \dfrac{7-2y}{4y+3}$

44. $\dfrac{9d+6}{2d+1} - \dfrac{7d+5}{2d+1}$ **45.** $\dfrac{8x-4}{2x+6} - \dfrac{4x-6}{2x+6}$ **46.** $\dfrac{6x-5}{x^2-1} - \dfrac{5x-6}{x^2-1}$

47. $\dfrac{a^2+3ab}{a+b} + \dfrac{b^2-ab}{a+b}$ **48.** $\dfrac{x^2-2xy}{x-2y} - \dfrac{xy-2y^2}{x-2y}$

49. $\dfrac{8x-8}{6x-5} - \dfrac{2x-7}{6x-5} + \dfrac{6x-9}{6x-5}$ **50.** $\dfrac{a+4b}{a^2-b^2} + \dfrac{4a-7b}{a^2-b^2} - \dfrac{3a-b}{a^2-b^2}$

51. $\dfrac{x}{(x+y)(x-y)} - \dfrac{y}{(x+y)(x-y)}$

52. $\dfrac{5a+b}{(2a+3b)(a-b)} - \dfrac{a-5b}{(2a+3b)(a-b)}$

53. $\dfrac{r^2+4r}{r^2-r-6} + \dfrac{8-r^2}{r^2-r-6}$

54. $\dfrac{4m^2+7m}{2m^2+5m+2} - \dfrac{1+7m}{2m^2+5m+2}$

6. Adding or Subtracting Fractions Which Have Different Denominators

Each of the fractions $\dfrac{2}{8}, \dfrac{3}{12}$, and $\dfrac{1a}{4a}$ is equal to the fraction $\dfrac{1}{4}$ since each one names the fraction $\frac{1}{4}$. Let us use the multiplication property of 1 to show that this statement is true $\left(\text{remember that } \dfrac{a}{a} = 1 \text{ when } a \neq 0\right)$:

$$\frac{1}{4} = \frac{1}{4} \cdot 1 = \frac{1}{4} \cdot \frac{2}{2} = \frac{2}{8} \qquad \frac{1}{4} = \frac{1}{4} \cdot 1 = \frac{1}{4} \cdot \frac{3}{3} = \frac{3}{12} \qquad \frac{1}{4} = \frac{1}{4} \cdot 1 = \frac{1}{4} \cdot \frac{a}{a} = \frac{1a}{4a}$$

These examples illustrate the **multiplication property of a fraction:** If the numerator and the denominator of a fraction are multiplied by the same non-zero number, the resulting fraction is equivalent to the original fraction.

To add $\frac{11}{24}$ and $\frac{7}{36}$, we first transform them to equivalent fractions which have a common denominator. Any integer which has both 24 and 36 as factors could become a common denominator. To simplify our work, we will use the **lowest common denominator** (L.C.D.), which can be found in the following manner:

1. Express each denominator as a product of prime factors.

   $24 = 2 \cdot 2 \cdot 2 \cdot 3 = 2^3 \cdot 3$ \qquad\qquad $36 = 2 \cdot 2 \cdot 3 \cdot 3 = 2^2 \cdot 3^2$

2. Write the product of the highest power of each of the different prime factors of the denominators.

   $\text{L.C.D.} = 2^3 \cdot 3^2 = 8 \cdot 9 = 72$

To find the integer by which to multiply the numerator and the denominator of $\frac{11}{24}$ to transform it into an equivalent fraction whose denominator is the L.C.D., 72, we divide 72 by the denominator 24. The result is 3. Then,
$$\frac{11}{24} = \frac{11 \cdot 3}{24 \cdot 3} = \frac{33}{72}.$$

To find the integer by which to multiply the numerator and the denominator of $\frac{7}{36}$ to transform it into an equivalent fraction whose denominator is the L.C.D., 72, we divide 72 by 36. The result is 2. Then, $\frac{7}{36} = \frac{7 \cdot 2}{36 \cdot 2} = \frac{14}{72}.$

Now we add $\frac{33}{72}$ and $\frac{14}{72}$ and obtain $\frac{47}{72}$ as the result.

The entire solution may be written as follows:

$$\frac{11}{24} + \frac{7}{36} = \frac{11 \cdot 3}{24 \cdot 3} + \frac{7 \cdot 2}{36 \cdot 2} = \frac{33}{72} + \frac{14}{72} = \frac{33 + 14}{72} = \frac{47}{72} \quad Ans.$$

Algebraic fractions are added in the same manner as arithmetic fractions.

Procedure. To add (or subtract) fractions which have different denominators:

1. **Factor each denominator in order to find the lowest common denominator, L.C.D.**
2. **Transform each fraction to an equivalent fraction by multiplying its numerator and denominator by the quotient that is obtained when the L.C.D. is divided by the denominator of the fraction.**
3. **Write a fraction whose numerator is the sum (or difference) of the numerators of the new fractions and whose denominator is the L.C.D.**
4. **Reduce the resulting fraction to lowest terms.**

~~~~~~~ MODEL PROBLEMS ~~~~~~~

1. Combine: $\dfrac{3x}{2} + \dfrac{7x}{4} - \dfrac{x}{6}$

2. Subtract: $\dfrac{5}{a^2b} - \dfrac{2}{ab^2}$

Solution

$2 = 2 \cdot 1; 4 = 2 \cdot 2 = 2^2;$
$\quad 6 = 2 \cdot 3$
L.C.D. $= 2^2 \cdot 3 = 12$
$12 \div 2 = 6; 12 \div 4 = 3;$
$\quad 12 \div 6 = 2$

Solution

$a^2b = a^2 \cdot b; ab^2 = a \cdot b^2$
L.C.D. $= a^2 \cdot b^2 = a^2b^2$
$a^2b^2 \div a^2b = b;$
$\quad a^2b^2 \div ab^2 = a$

$$\frac{3x}{2} + \frac{7x}{4} - \frac{x}{6}$$

$$= \frac{3x(6)}{2(6)} + \frac{7x(3)}{4(3)} - \frac{x(2)}{6(2)}$$

$$= \frac{18x}{12} + \frac{21x}{12} - \frac{2x}{12}$$

$$= \frac{18x + 21x - 2x}{12}$$

$$= \frac{37x}{12} \quad Ans.$$

$$\frac{5}{a^2b} - \frac{2}{ab^2}$$

$$= \frac{5(b)}{a^2b(b)} - \frac{2(a)}{ab^2(a)}$$

$$= \frac{5b}{a^2b^2} - \frac{2a}{a^2b^2}$$

$$= \frac{5b - 2a}{a^2b^2} \quad Ans.$$

3. Subtract: $\dfrac{2x + 5}{3} - \dfrac{x - 2}{4}$

Solution

$3 = 3 \cdot 1; 4 = 2 \cdot 2 = 2^2$

L.C.D. $= 3 \cdot 2^2 = 12$

$12 \div 3 = 4; 12 \div 4 = 3$

$$\frac{2x + 5}{3} - \frac{x - 2}{4}$$

$$= \frac{4(2x + 5)}{4(3)} - \frac{3(x - 2)}{3(4)}$$

$$= \frac{8x + 20}{12} - \frac{3x - 6}{12}$$

$$= \frac{(8x + 20) - (3x - 6)}{12}$$

$$= \frac{8x + 20 - 3x + 6}{12}$$

$$= \frac{5x + 26}{12} \quad Ans.$$

4. Add: $\dfrac{2a - 5}{18a} + \dfrac{3a + 2}{15a}$

Solution

$18a = 2 \cdot 3^2 \cdot a; 15a = 3 \cdot 5 \cdot a$

L.C.D. $= 2 \cdot 3^2 \cdot 5 \cdot a = 90a$

$90a \div 18a = 5; 90a \div 15a = 6$

$$\frac{2a - 5}{18a} + \frac{3a + 2}{15a}$$

$$= \frac{5(2a - 5)}{5(18a)} + \frac{6(3a + 2)}{6(15a)}$$

$$= \frac{10a - 25}{90a} + \frac{18a + 12}{90a}$$

$$= \frac{(10a - 25) + (18a + 12)}{90a}$$

$$= \frac{10a - 25 + 18a + 12}{90a}$$

$$= \frac{28a - 13}{90a} \quad Ans.$$

5. Add: $\dfrac{5}{3x - 15} + \dfrac{2}{5x - 25}$

Solution

$3x - 15 = 3(x - 5)$

$5x - 25 = 5(x - 5)$

L.C.D. $= 15(x - 5)$

6. Subtract: $\dfrac{5x}{x^2 - 4} - \dfrac{3}{x - 2}$

Solution

$x^2 - 4 = (x - 2)(x + 2)$

$x - 2 = 1 \cdot (x - 2)$

L.C.D. $= (x - 2)(x + 2)$

$$\frac{5}{3x - 15} + \frac{2}{5x - 25}$$

$$= \frac{5}{3(x - 5)} + \frac{2}{5(x - 5)}$$

$$[15(x - 5) \div 3(x - 5) = 5;$$
$$15(x - 5) \div 5(x - 5) = 3]$$

$$= \frac{5 \cdot 5}{5 \cdot 3(x - 5)} + \frac{3 \cdot 2}{3 \cdot 5(x - 5)}$$

$$= \frac{25}{15(x - 5)} + \frac{6}{15(x - 5)}$$

$$= \frac{25 + 6}{15(x - 5)}$$

$$= \frac{31}{15(x - 5)} \text{ or}$$

$$\frac{31}{15x - 75} \quad Ans.$$

$$\frac{5x}{x^2 - 4} - \frac{3}{x - 2}$$

$$= \frac{5x}{(x - 2)(x + 2)} - \frac{3}{(x - 2)}$$

$$[(x - 2)(x + 2) \div (x - 2) = (x + 2)]$$

$$= \frac{5x}{(x - 2)(x + 2)} - \frac{3(x + 2)}{(x - 2)(x + 2)}$$

$$= \frac{5x - (3x + 6)}{(x - 2)(x + 2)}$$

$$= \frac{5x - 3x - 6}{(x - 2)(x + 2)}$$

$$= \frac{2x - 6}{(x - 2)(x + 2)} \text{ or}$$

$$\frac{2x - 6}{x^2 - 4} \quad Ans.$$

Exercises

In 1–16, find the lowest common denominator for two fractions whose denominators are:

1. $10; 5$ **2.** $8; 12$ **3.** $6a; 2a$ **4.** $3; x$ **5.** $r; s$

6. $15a; 6b$ **7.** $xy; yz$ **8.** $m^2n; mn^2$ **9.** $12x^2; 18y^2$ **10.** $6c^2d^2; 10cd$

11. $x + 3; x - 3$ **12.** $4(c + 1); 6(c + 1)$ **13.** $3c + 9; 4c + 12$

14. $x; x + 5$ **15.** $x^2 - 1; 3x + 3$ **16.** $3x - 4; 4 - 3x$

In 17–33, transform the given fractions into equivalent fractions that have the L.C.D. as their denominators.

17. $\dfrac{3}{5}; \dfrac{4}{3}$ **18.** $\dfrac{5}{8}; \dfrac{9}{20}$ **19.** $\dfrac{5y}{3}; \dfrac{7y}{6}$ **20.** $\dfrac{3x}{12}; \dfrac{7x}{90}$

21. $\dfrac{5y}{3c}; \dfrac{7y}{6c}$ **22.** $\dfrac{8}{x^2}; \dfrac{2}{x}$ **23.** $\dfrac{a}{cd}; \dfrac{m}{bc}$ **24.** $\dfrac{7}{4c^2}; \dfrac{5}{18d^2}$

25. $\dfrac{a - 6}{2}; \dfrac{2a + 5}{4}$ **26.** $\dfrac{3c + 1}{18d}; \dfrac{5c - 3}{24d}$ **27.** $\dfrac{5x - 4}{20y}; \dfrac{3x + 7}{72y}$

28. $\dfrac{1}{x + 2}; \dfrac{3}{x - 2}$ **29.** $\dfrac{5m - 1}{3(m - 2)}; \dfrac{8}{2(m - 2)}$ **30.** $\dfrac{2t - 1}{8t - 8}; \dfrac{4t + 1}{6t - 6}$

31. $\dfrac{4}{y}; \dfrac{y - 1}{y + 2}$ **32.** $\dfrac{6x + 1}{x^2 - 9}; \dfrac{-3}{x - 3}$ **33.** $\dfrac{7}{1 - 3a}; \dfrac{2}{3a - 1}$

In 34–126, add or subtract (combine) the fractions as indicated. Reduce answers to lowest terms.

34. $\dfrac{5}{6} + \dfrac{1}{12}$

35. $\dfrac{7}{8} - \dfrac{1}{4}$

36. $\dfrac{2}{3} - \dfrac{1}{6}$

37. $\dfrac{5}{4} + \dfrac{3}{2} - \dfrac{1}{3}$

38. $\dfrac{3x}{10} + \dfrac{7x}{5}$

39. $\dfrac{10y}{7} - \dfrac{3y}{4}$

40. $\dfrac{ab}{5} + \dfrac{ab}{4}$

41. $\dfrac{8x}{5} - \dfrac{3x}{4} + \dfrac{7x}{10}$

42. $\dfrac{5a}{6} - \dfrac{3a}{4}$

43. $\dfrac{3m}{10} - \dfrac{m}{4}$

44. $\dfrac{5x}{6} - \dfrac{3x}{8}$

45. $\dfrac{7y}{8} + \dfrac{3y}{10} - \dfrac{y}{5}$

46. $\dfrac{a}{7} + \dfrac{b}{14}$

47. $\dfrac{c}{5} - \dfrac{2d}{3}$

48. $\dfrac{x}{18} - \dfrac{y}{4}$

49. $\dfrac{a}{3} + \dfrac{b}{4} - \dfrac{c}{5}$

50. $\dfrac{9}{4x} + \dfrac{3}{2x}$

51. $\dfrac{7}{8y} - \dfrac{3}{4y}$

52. $\dfrac{8}{5c} - \dfrac{1}{4c}$

53. $\dfrac{1}{2x} - \dfrac{1}{x} + \dfrac{3}{8x}$

54. $\dfrac{5x}{2d} + \dfrac{4x}{3d}$

55. $\dfrac{9a}{8b} - \dfrac{3a}{4b}$

56. $\dfrac{7x}{4y} - \dfrac{3x}{5y}$

57. $\dfrac{3r}{2s} - \dfrac{5r}{4s} - \dfrac{2r}{3s}$

58. $\dfrac{7}{x} - \dfrac{3}{y}$

59. $\dfrac{1}{a} + \dfrac{1}{b}$

60. $\dfrac{c}{a} - \dfrac{a}{b}$

61. $\dfrac{1}{x} + \dfrac{1}{y} + \dfrac{1}{z}$

62. $\dfrac{5}{y^2} - \dfrac{2}{y}$

63. $\dfrac{1}{r^2} - \dfrac{3}{r}$

64. $\dfrac{2}{a^2} - \dfrac{5}{b}$

65. $\dfrac{x}{a^2 b} + \dfrac{y}{ab^2}$

66. $\dfrac{1}{xy} + \dfrac{1}{yz}$

67. $\dfrac{2}{ab} - \dfrac{3}{bc}$

68. $\dfrac{5}{rs} + \dfrac{9}{st}$

69. $\dfrac{x}{3ab} - \dfrac{y}{2bc}$

70. $\dfrac{9}{ab} + \dfrac{2}{bc} - \dfrac{3}{ac}$

71. $\dfrac{2}{y^3} - \dfrac{3}{y^2} + \dfrac{7}{y}$

72. $\dfrac{1}{x^2} + \dfrac{3}{xy} - \dfrac{5}{y^2}$

73. $\dfrac{a-3}{3} + \dfrac{a+1}{6}$

74. $\dfrac{y-1}{2} - \dfrac{y-5}{8}$

75. $\dfrac{m+9}{2} + \dfrac{m-3}{3}$

76. $\dfrac{x+7}{3} - \dfrac{2x-3}{5}$

77. $\dfrac{3x-5}{4} + \dfrac{2x+3}{6}$

78. $\dfrac{3x-2}{7} + \dfrac{x+1}{14}$

79. $\dfrac{3y-4}{5} - \dfrac{y-2}{4}$

80. $\dfrac{3a-2}{5} - \dfrac{2a+3}{15}$

81. $\dfrac{x+y}{2} - \dfrac{2x-y}{6}$

82. $\dfrac{6a+b}{30} - \dfrac{2a-b}{10}$

83. $\dfrac{x+y}{8} - \dfrac{x+y}{10}$

84. $\dfrac{a-b}{4} - \dfrac{a+b}{6}$

85. $\dfrac{x+5}{2x} + \dfrac{2x-1}{4x}$

86. $\dfrac{9y-2}{12y} - \dfrac{4y+1}{6y}$

87. $\dfrac{3x-4}{5x} - \dfrac{2x-3}{20x} + \dfrac{5x}{2}$

88. $\dfrac{3b+1}{5b} - \dfrac{4b-3}{4b}$

89. $\dfrac{y-4}{4y^2} + \dfrac{3y-5}{3y}$

90. $\dfrac{2x+3}{12x} - \dfrac{3x-6}{8x} - \dfrac{5}{x}$

91. $5 + \dfrac{8a-6}{4}$

92. $\dfrac{3c-7}{4} - 2c$

93. $6x - \dfrac{4x-9}{5}$

94. $\dfrac{3x+5}{3} + \dfrac{2-5x}{4} - \dfrac{x-8}{5}$

95. $\dfrac{2x+3y}{6x} - \dfrac{4x-5y}{4x} - x$

96. $\dfrac{x+y}{x} - \dfrac{y-z}{y} - \dfrac{z-x}{z}$

97. $\dfrac{6}{ab} + \dfrac{a-3}{a^2} - \dfrac{7+b}{b^2}$

98. $\dfrac{2}{3y} - \dfrac{4y-7}{6y^2} + \dfrac{3y-2y^2}{4y^3}$

99. $\dfrac{4a+1}{6a^2b} - \dfrac{3b-5}{4ab^2} - \dfrac{2b+1}{9ab}$

100. $\dfrac{5}{x-3} + \dfrac{7}{2x-6}$

101. $\dfrac{9}{y+1} - \dfrac{3}{4y+4}$

102. $\dfrac{2}{3a-1} + \dfrac{7}{15a-5}$

103. $\dfrac{10}{3x-6} + \dfrac{3}{2x-4}$

104. $\dfrac{11x}{8x-8} - \dfrac{3x}{4x-4}$

105. $\dfrac{3}{2x-3y} + \dfrac{5}{3y-2x}$

106. $\dfrac{2a}{4a-8b} + \dfrac{3b}{3a-6b}$

107. $\dfrac{3x-2}{2x+2} + \dfrac{4x-1}{3x+3}$

108. $\dfrac{5x+2}{6x-3} - \dfrac{3x-5}{8x-4}$

109. $\dfrac{1}{x-5} + \dfrac{1}{x+5}$

110. $\dfrac{9}{y+4} - \dfrac{6}{y-4}$

111. $\dfrac{7}{a+3} + \dfrac{4}{2-a}$

112. $\dfrac{7}{x-2} + \dfrac{3}{x}$

113. $\dfrac{9}{c+8} - \dfrac{2}{c}$

114. $\dfrac{2a+b}{a-b} + \dfrac{a}{b}$

115. $\dfrac{5}{y^2-9} + \dfrac{3}{y-3}$

116. $\dfrac{6}{y^2-16} - \dfrac{5}{y+4}$

117. $\dfrac{9}{a^2-b^2} + \dfrac{3}{b-a}$

118. $\dfrac{3y}{y^2-4} - \dfrac{4}{2y-4}$

119. $\dfrac{x}{x^2-36} - \dfrac{4}{3x+18}$

120. $\dfrac{9}{a^2-ab} + \dfrac{3}{ab-b^2}$

121. $\dfrac{1}{y-3} + \dfrac{2}{y+4} + \dfrac{2}{3}$

122. $\dfrac{1}{(x+2)^3} - \dfrac{1}{(x+2)^2} + \dfrac{1}{x+2}$

123. $\dfrac{7a}{(a-1)(a+3)} + \dfrac{2a-5}{(a+3)(a+2)}$

124. $\dfrac{5}{r^2-4} - \dfrac{3}{r^2+3r-10}$

125. $\dfrac{x+2y}{3x+12y} - \dfrac{6x-y}{x^2+3xy-4y^2}$

126. $\dfrac{2a+7}{a^2-2a-15} - \dfrac{3a-4}{a^2-7a+10}$

7. Mixed Expressions

The mixed number $3\frac{1}{2}$, which means the sum of the integer 3 and the fraction $\frac{1}{2}$, can be expressed as a fraction. To do this, we express the integer 3 as the fraction $\frac{3}{1}$ and then add $\frac{3}{1}$ and $\frac{1}{2}$.

$$3\tfrac{1}{2} = \frac{3}{1} + \frac{1}{2} = \frac{3\cdot 2}{1\cdot 2} + \frac{1}{2} = \frac{6}{2} + \frac{1}{2} = \frac{6+1}{2} = \frac{7}{2}$$

The indicated sum or difference of a polynomial and a fraction is called a **mixed expression.** For example, $y + \dfrac{5}{y}$ is a mixed expression. A mixed expression can be changed to a fraction.

Procedure. To express a mixed expression as a fraction, write the polynomial of the expression as a fraction whose denominator is 1. Then add the two fractions.

MODEL PROBLEMS

In 1 and 2, express the mixed expression as a fraction.

1. $y + \dfrac{5}{y}$

Solution

$$y + \frac{5}{y} = \frac{y}{1} + \frac{5}{y}$$

$$= \frac{y \cdot y}{1 \cdot y} + \frac{5}{y}$$

$$= \frac{y^2}{y} + \frac{5}{y}$$

$$= \frac{y^2 + 5}{y} \quad Ans.$$

2. $y + 1 - \dfrac{1}{y-1}$

Solution

$$y + 1 - \frac{1}{y-1} = \frac{y+1}{1} - \frac{1}{y-1}$$

$$= \frac{(y+1)(y-1)}{1(y-1)} - \frac{1}{y-1}$$

$$= \frac{y^2 - 1}{y-1} - \frac{1}{y-1}$$

$$= \frac{y^2 - 1 - 1}{y-1}$$

$$= \frac{y^2 - 2}{y-1} \quad Ans.$$

Exercises

In 1–19, express the mixed expression as a fraction in its lowest terms.

1. $5\frac{2}{3}$

2. $9\frac{3}{4}$

3. $5 + \dfrac{1}{x}$

4. $9 - \dfrac{7}{s}$

5. $m + \dfrac{1}{m}$

6. $d - \dfrac{7}{5d}$

7. $\dfrac{a}{b} + c$

8. $3 + \dfrac{5}{x+1}$

9. $6 - \dfrac{4}{x-y}$

10. $7 + \dfrac{2a}{b+c}$

11. $t + \dfrac{1}{t+1}$

12. $s - \dfrac{1}{s-1}$

13. $5 - \dfrac{2x}{x+y}$

14. $\dfrac{4}{y-2} + 4$

15. $8 + \dfrac{c+2}{c-3}$

16. $7 - \dfrac{x+y}{x-y}$

17. $a + 1 + \dfrac{1}{a+1}$

18. $x - 5 - \dfrac{x}{x+3}$

19. $\dfrac{2x-1}{x+2} + 2x - 3$

8. Studying the Changes in the Value of a Fraction

If a variable appears in a fraction, the value of the fraction may change as the variable is replaced by different numbers.

The set of numbers $\frac{5}{10}$, $\frac{5}{9}$, $\frac{5}{8}$, $\frac{5}{7}$, etc. illustrates:

Principle 1. If the numerator of a fraction has a fixed positive value and the denominator is positive and decreases, then the value of the fraction increases.

Thus, the value of $\dfrac{5}{x}$ increases as x decreases from 10 to 1.

The set of numbers $\frac{4}{3}$, $\frac{4}{4}$, $\frac{4}{5}$, $\frac{4}{6}$, etc. illustrates:

Principle 2. If the numerator of a fraction has a fixed positive value and the denominator is positive and increases, then the value of the fraction decreases.

Thus, the value of $\dfrac{4}{x}$ decreases as x increases from 1 to 10.

The set of numbers $\frac{10}{3}$, $\frac{9}{3}$, $\frac{8}{3}$, $\frac{7}{3}$, etc. illustrates:

Principle 3. If the denominator of a fraction has a fixed positive value and the numerator is positive and decreases, then the value of the fraction decreases.

Thus, the value of $\dfrac{x}{3}$ decreases as x decreases from 10 to 1.

The set of numbers $\frac{3}{9}$, $\frac{4}{9}$, $\frac{5}{9}$, $\frac{6}{9}$, etc. illustrates:

Principle 4. If the denominator of a fraction has a fixed positive value and the numerator is positive and increases, then the value of the fraction increases.

Thus, the value of $\dfrac{x}{9}$ increases as x increases from 1 to 10.

~~~~~~~~~~ **MODEL PROBLEM** ~~~~~~~~~~

If $y = \dfrac{5}{x+2}$, does y increase or decrease as x decreases from 5 to 3?

Solution: In the equation $y = \dfrac{5}{x+2}$, replace x by the values 5, 4, and 3.

If $x = 5$, $y = \dfrac{5}{5+2} = \dfrac{5}{7}$.

If $x = 4$, $y = \dfrac{5}{4+2} = \dfrac{5}{6}$.

If $x = 3$, $y = \dfrac{5}{3+2} = \dfrac{5}{5} = 1$.

We see by principle 1 that y increases.

Answer: y increases.

~~~~~~~~~~~~~~~~~~~~~~~~~~~~~~~~~~~

Exercises

1. If x is positive and $y = \dfrac{1}{x}$, does y increase or decrease as x increases?

2. If x is positive and $y = \dfrac{12}{x}$, does y increase or decrease as x decreases?

3. If $y = \dfrac{5}{2x}$ and x is positive, does y increase or decrease as x increases?

4. If $y = \dfrac{3x}{2}$ and x is positive, does y increase or decrease as x increases?

5. If $y = \dfrac{5x}{3}$ and x is positive, does y increase or decrease as x decreases?

6. If x is positive, does the value of the fraction $\dfrac{12}{x+3}$ increase or decrease as x increases?

7. If x is positive and $y = \dfrac{2}{3x+1}$, does y increase or decrease as x decreases?

8. If $y = \dfrac{4x + 3}{5}$ and x is positive, does y increase or decrease as x increases?

9. If $y = \dfrac{5x - 1}{2}$ and x is positive, does y increase or decrease as x decreases?

10. If $y = \dfrac{x^2 - 5}{10}$ and x is positive and increases, does y increase or decrease as x increases?

11. Tell whether the value of the fraction $\dfrac{x}{y}$ increases or decreases when:

   a. x is positive and increasing, and y is positive and decreasing
   b. x is positive and decreasing, and y is positive and increasing

12. $\dfrac{y}{z}$ and $\dfrac{z}{y}$ are fractions in which y and z are positive integers and y is less than z $(y < z)$. Select the fraction which has the larger value.

13. Select the fraction which will have the least value if any pair of positive integers are substituted for x and y.

   a. $\dfrac{x}{y}$ b. $\dfrac{x + 2}{y}$ c. $\dfrac{x}{y - 2}$ d. $\dfrac{x + 2}{y - 2}$

14. Select the fraction which will have the greatest value if x and y are replaced by any pair of positive integers.

   a. $\dfrac{2x}{3y}$ b. $\dfrac{2x}{3y - 1}$ c. $\dfrac{2x + 1}{3y - 1}$ d. $\dfrac{2x + 1}{3y}$

In 15–17, select the choice which correctly completes the statement.

15. If positive integers are substituted for x and y in the fractions $\dfrac{x}{y}$ and $\dfrac{x + 5}{y + 5}$, then the second fraction as compared with the first will be (a) always equal (b) always greater (c) always less (d) sometimes greater and sometimes less.

16. If positive integers are substituted for r and s in the fractions $\dfrac{r}{s}$ and $\dfrac{r + 2}{s + 2}$, then the first fraction as compared to the second will be (a) always equal (b) sometimes equal (c) always greater (e) always less.

17. If positive integers are substituted for a, b, and c in the fractions $\dfrac{a}{b}$ and $\dfrac{a + c}{b + c}$, then the first fraction as compared to the second will be (a) always less (b) sometimes less and sometimes greater (c) always greater (d) always equal.

CHAPTER XIII

FIRST-DEGREE EQUATIONS AND INEQUALITIES INVOLVING FRACTIONS

1. Solving Equations Containing Fractional Coefficients

Examples of equations which contain fractional coefficients are:

$$\frac{1}{2}x = 10 \text{ or } \frac{x}{2} = 10 \qquad\qquad \frac{1}{3}x + 60 = \frac{5}{6}x \text{ or } \frac{x}{3} + 60 = \frac{5x}{6}$$

In solving such equations, we make use of the previously learned methods of solving equations.

Procedure. To solve an equation which contains fractional coefficients: First transform it into a simpler equation which does not contain fractions (clear the equation of fractions). Do this by multiplying both of its members by the lowest common denominator, L.C.D. Then solve the resulting equation by the usual methods.

> [*Note:* In solving an equation or an inequality involving fractions, the lowest common denominator (L.C.D.) that is used as a multiplier is sometimes called the lowest common multiple (L.C.M.) of the denominators in the equation or inequality.]

~~~~~~~~~~~~~~~ *MODEL PROBLEMS* ~~~~~~~~~~~~~~~

1. Solve and check: $\dfrac{3x}{4} = 20 + \dfrac{x}{4}$

How To Proceed	*Solution*
1. Write the equation.	$\dfrac{3x}{4} = 20 + \dfrac{x}{4}$
2. Multiply by the L.C.D., 4.	$4\left(\dfrac{3x}{4}\right) = 4\left(20 + \dfrac{x}{4}\right)$
3. Use the distributive property.	$4\left(\dfrac{3x}{4}\right) = 4(20) + 4\left(\dfrac{x}{4}\right)$
4. Multiply.	$3x = 80 + x$
5. S_x or A_{-x}.	$3x + (-x) = 80 + x + (-x)$
6. Collect like terms.	$2x = 80$
7. D_2 or $M_{\frac{1}{2}}$.	$x = 40$

301

Check

$$\frac{3x}{4} = 20 + \frac{x}{4}$$

$$\frac{3(40)}{4} \stackrel{?}{=} 20 + \frac{40}{4}$$

$$\frac{120}{4} \stackrel{?}{=} 20 + 10$$

$$30 \stackrel{?}{=} 20 + 10$$

$$30 = 30 \quad \text{(true)}$$

Answer: $x = 40$, or solution set is $\{40\}$.

2. Solve: $\dfrac{2x + 7}{6} - \dfrac{2x - 9}{10} = 3$

How To Proceed	*Solution*
1. Write the equation.	$\dfrac{2x + 7}{6} - \dfrac{2x - 9}{10} = 3$
2. Multiply by the L.C.D., 30.	$30\left(\dfrac{2x + 7}{6} - \dfrac{2x - 9}{10}\right) = 30(3)$
3. Use the distributive property.	$30\left(\dfrac{2x + 7}{6}\right) - 30\left(\dfrac{2x - 9}{10}\right) = 30(3)$
4. Multiply.	$5(2x + 7) - 3(2x - 9) = 90$
5. Use the distributive property.	$10x + 35 - 6x + 27 = 90$
6. Collect like terms.	$4x + 62 = 90$
7. S$_{62}$ or A$_{-62}$.	$4x + 62 + (-62) = 90 + (-62)$
8. Collect like terms.	$4x = 28$
9. D$_4$ or M$_{\frac{1}{4}}$.	$x = 7$

Check by substituting 7 for x in the given equation.

Answer: $x = 7$, or solution set is $\{7\}$.

Exercises

In 1–50, solve and check.

1. $\dfrac{x}{7} = 3$

2. $\dfrac{y}{4} = 16$

3. $\dfrac{t}{6} = 18$

4. $\dfrac{3x}{5} = 15$

5. $\dfrac{2m}{3} = 24$

6. $\dfrac{5n}{7} = 35$

7. $\dfrac{x + 8}{4} = 6$

8. $\dfrac{m - 2}{9} = 3$

9. $\dfrac{3x - 1}{5} = 7$

10. $\dfrac{2r + 6}{5} = -4$

11. $\dfrac{5y - 30}{7} = 0$

12. $\dfrac{7 - 2x}{5} = -1$

13. $\dfrac{x}{5} = \dfrac{8}{10}$

14. $\dfrac{y}{21} = \dfrac{3}{7}$

15. $\dfrac{5x}{2} = \dfrac{15}{4}$

16. $\dfrac{y + 2}{4} = \dfrac{5}{2}$

17. $\dfrac{m - 5}{35} = \dfrac{5}{7}$

18. $\dfrac{2c + 8}{28} = \dfrac{12}{7}$

19. $\dfrac{2x + 1}{3} = \dfrac{6x - 9}{5}$

20. $\dfrac{3y + 1}{4} = \dfrac{44 - y}{5}$

21. $\dfrac{2m}{3} = \dfrac{3m + 9}{4}$

22. $\dfrac{x}{5} + \dfrac{x}{3} = \dfrac{8}{15}$

23. $\dfrac{y}{3} + \dfrac{y}{2} = 40$

24. $10 = \dfrac{x}{3} + \dfrac{x}{7}$

25. $\dfrac{r}{3} - \dfrac{r}{6} = 2$

26. $\dfrac{2t}{5} - \dfrac{t}{4} = 3$

27. $1 = \dfrac{3r}{4} - \dfrac{2r}{3}$

28. $\dfrac{3t}{4} - 6 = \dfrac{t}{12}$

29. $\dfrac{2s}{3} = \dfrac{s}{4} + 10$

30. $\dfrac{y}{4} = \dfrac{3y}{5} - 2\dfrac{1}{10}$

31. $\dfrac{a}{2} + \dfrac{a}{3} + \dfrac{a}{4} = 26$

32. $\dfrac{5c}{8} - \dfrac{c}{3} = \dfrac{5c}{6} - 13$

33. $\dfrac{s}{3} + 7 = \dfrac{s}{5} - 3$

34. $\dfrac{3y}{2} - \dfrac{17}{3} = \dfrac{2y}{3} - \dfrac{3}{2}$

35. $\dfrac{7y}{12} - \dfrac{1}{4} = 2y - \dfrac{5}{3}$

36. $\dfrac{5c}{4} - \dfrac{1}{2} = \dfrac{2c}{3} + 6\dfrac{1}{2}$

37. $\dfrac{x}{3} - 2 = \dfrac{3x - 30}{6}$

38. $\dfrac{2y}{3} - \dfrac{7 - y}{4} = 1$

39. $\dfrac{y + 4}{4} + \dfrac{y - 2}{2} = 3$

40. $\dfrac{t + 1}{2} + \dfrac{2t - 3}{3} = 10$

41. $\dfrac{y + 2}{4} - \dfrac{y - 3}{3} = \dfrac{1}{2}$

42. $\dfrac{7s + 5}{8} - \dfrac{3s + 15}{10} = 2$

43. $\dfrac{6v - 3}{2} - \dfrac{v + 2}{5} = \dfrac{37}{10}$

44. $\dfrac{t - 3}{6} - \dfrac{t - 25}{5} = 4$

45. $\dfrac{2a - 3}{5} - \dfrac{a - 3}{3} = 2$

46. $\dfrac{5s - 3}{4} - \dfrac{3s + 5}{8} = 3$

47. $6 + \dfrac{x - 2}{4} = \dfrac{x + 3}{3}$

48. $\dfrac{3m + 1}{4} = 2 - \dfrac{3 - 2m}{6}$

49. $\dfrac{5x - 1}{9} + \dfrac{2x + 4}{6} = \dfrac{3x - 4}{3}$

50. $\dfrac{3c - 4}{3} - \dfrac{2c + 4}{6} = \dfrac{5c - 1}{9}$

51. If one-half of a number is increased by 20, the result is 35. Find the number.

52. If two-thirds of a number is decreased by 30, the result is 10. Find the number.

53. If 5 is added to one-half of a number, the result is the same as when three-fifths of the number is decreased by 3. Find the number.

54. If 3 times a number is decreased by 9, the result is $1\frac{1}{2}$. Find the number.

55. If 3 more than 3 times a number is divided by 15, the result is the same as when 18 less than twice the number is divided by 6. Find the number.

2. Solving Equations Containing Decimals

Decimals (decimal fractions) are fractions whose denominators are 10, 100, 1000, etc. For example:

$$.7 = \tfrac{7}{10} \qquad\qquad .21 = \tfrac{21}{100} \qquad\qquad .125 = \tfrac{125}{1000}$$

Procedure. To solve an equation containing decimals:

Method 1

Follow the same procedure that is used in solving equations which contain whole numbers.

Method 2

In order to clear the equation of decimals, multiply both members of the equation by the largest denominator among the decimal fractions in the equation. Then solve the resulting equation.

~~~~~~~~~~~~~~~~~ **MODEL PROBLEMS** ~~~~~~~~~~~~~~~

1. Solve and check: $1.5x = 54 + .6x$

Solution:

Method 1	*Method 2*

$$1.5x = 54 + .6x$$
$$1.5x + (-.6x) = 54 + .6x + (-.6x)$$
$$.9x = 54$$
$$x = 60 \quad \text{D}_{.9}$$

$$1.5x = 54 + .6x$$
$$10(1.5x) = 10(54 + .6x) \quad \text{M}_{10}$$
$$15x = 540 + 6x$$
$$15x + (-6x) = 540 + 6x + (-6x)$$
$$9x = 540$$
$$x = 60$$

Check by substituting 60 for x in the given equation.

Answer: $x = 60$, or solution set is $\{60\}$.

2. Solve and check: $.05x + .04(500 - x) = 22$

Solution:

Method 1

$$.05x + .04(500 - x) = 22$$
$$.05x + 20 - .04x = 22$$
$$.01x + 20 = 22$$
$$.01x + 20 + (-20) = 22 + (-20)$$
$$.01x = 2$$
$$x = 200 \quad \text{D}_{.01}$$

Method 2

$$.05x + .04(500 - x) = 22$$
$$100[.05x + .04(500 - x)] = 100(22)$$
$$5x + 4(500 - x) = 2200$$
$$5x + 2000 - 4x = 2200$$
$$x + 2000 = 2200$$
$$x + 2000 + (-2000) = 2200 + (-2000)$$
$$x = 200$$

Check by substituting 200 for x in the given equation.

Answer: $x = 200$, or solution set is $\{200\}$.

Exercises

In 1–39, solve and check.

1. $3x = .9$	**2.** $.8 = 8y$	**3.** $2z = .08$	**4.** $6t = 18.6$
5. $.3m = 2.4$	**6.** $.4r = 16$	**7.** $1.3t = .39$	**8.** $.25a = 6$
9. $.04z = 6$	**10.** $.45c = 9$	**11.** $.5x = 1.5$	**12.** $8.7 = 3w$
13. $.06a = 1.2$	**14.** $1.68 = .08b$	**15.** $.4t = .012$	**16.** $.09d = .018$

17. $.7x - .4 = 1$ **18.** $.03y - 1.2 = 8.7$ **19.** $.4x + .08 = 4.24$

20. $.5x - .3x = 8$ **21.** $2c + .5c = 50$ **22.** $.08y - .9 = .02y$

23. $1.7x = 30 + .2x$ **24.** $1.5y - 1.69 = .2y$ **25.** $.08c = 1.5 + .07c$

26. $.8m + 2.6 = .2m + 9.8$ **27.** $.05x - .25 = .02x + .44$

28. $.13x - 1.4 = .08x + 7.6$ **29.** $.06y + 40 - .03y = 70$

30. $.02(x + 5) = 8$ **31.** $.05(x - 8) = .07x$

32. $.4(x - 9) = .3(x + 4)$ **33.** $.06(x - 5) = .04(x + 8)$

34. $.04x + .03(2000 - x) = 75$ **35.** $.02x + .04(1500 - x) = 48$

36. $.05x + 10 = .06(x + 50)$ **37.** $.08x = .03(x + 200) - 4$

38. $.07x + .04(9000 - x) = 450$ **39.** $.06x - .04(3500 - x) = 160$

40. Three times a number equals 14.4. Find the number.

41. Nine-tenths of a number is .45. Find the number.

42. Seven-hundredths of a number increased by 2.5 equals eight-hundredths of the number. Find the number.

43. If seventeen-hundredths of a number is decreased by 1.4, the result is the same as when twelve-hundredths of the number is increased by 7.6. Find the number.

44. 25% of a number equals 32. Find the number.

45. 15% of a number decreased by 40 is equal to 7% of the number. Find the number.

3. Solving Inequalities Containing Fractional Coefficients

Procedure. To solve an inequality which contains fractional coefficients: First transform it into a simpler inequality which does not contain fractions (clear the inequality of fractions). Do this by multiplying both of its members by the lowest common denominator, L.C.D. (a positive number). Then solve the resulting inequality by the usual methods.

~~~~~~~~~~~~~ *MODEL PROBLEMS* ~~~~~~~~~~~~~

1. Solve: $\dfrac{x}{3} - \dfrac{x}{6} > 12$

              Solution

$$\frac{x}{3} - \frac{x}{6} > 12$$

$$6\left(\frac{x}{3} - \frac{x}{6}\right) > 6(12)$$

$$6\left(\frac{x}{3}\right) - 6\left(\frac{x}{6}\right) > 72$$

$$2x - x > 72$$

$$x > 72$$

Answer: $x > 72$

2. Solve: $\dfrac{3y}{2} + \dfrac{8 - 4y}{7} \le 3$

              Solution

$$\frac{3y}{2} + \frac{8 - 4y}{7} \le 3$$

$$14\left(\frac{3y}{2} + \frac{8 - 4y}{7}\right) \le 14(3)$$

$$14\left(\frac{3y}{2}\right) + 14\left(\frac{8 - 4y}{7}\right) \le 42$$

$$21y + 16 - 8y \le 42$$

$$13y \le 26$$

$$y \le 2$$

Answer: $y \le 2$

Exercises

In 1–20, solve the inequality.

1. $\frac{1}{4}x - \frac{1}{5}x > \frac{9}{20}$

2. $y - \frac{2}{3}y < 5$

3. $\frac{5}{6}c > \frac{1}{3}c + 3$

4. $\dfrac{x}{4} - \dfrac{x}{8} \le \dfrac{5}{8}$

5. $\dfrac{y}{6} \ge \dfrac{y}{12} + 1$

6. $\dfrac{y}{9} - \dfrac{y}{4} > \dfrac{5}{36}$

7. $\dfrac{t}{10} \le 4 + \dfrac{t}{5}$

8. $1 + \dfrac{2x}{3} \ge \dfrac{x}{2}$

9. $2.5x - 1.6x > 4$

10. $2y + 3 \ge .2y$

11. $\dfrac{3x - 1}{7} > 5$

12. $\dfrac{5y - 30}{7} \le 0$

13. $2d + \dfrac{1}{4} < \dfrac{7d}{12} + \dfrac{5}{3}$

14. $\dfrac{4c}{3} - \dfrac{7}{9} \geq \dfrac{c}{2} + \dfrac{7}{6}$

15. $\dfrac{2m}{3} \geq \dfrac{7 - m}{4} + 1$

16. $\dfrac{3x - 30}{6} < \dfrac{x}{3} - 2$

17. $\dfrac{6x - 3}{2} > \dfrac{37}{10} + \dfrac{x + 2}{5}$

18. $\dfrac{2y - 3}{3} + \dfrac{y + 1}{2} < 10$

19. $\dfrac{2r - 3}{5} - \dfrac{r - 3}{3} \leq 2$

20. $\dfrac{3t - 4}{3} \geq \dfrac{2t + 4}{6} + \dfrac{5t - 1}{9}$

4. Solving Fractional Equations

An equation is called a ***fractional equation*** when a variable appears in the denominator of one, or more than one, of its terms. For example, $\dfrac{1}{3} + \dfrac{1}{x} = \dfrac{1}{2}$ and $\dfrac{6}{x} = \dfrac{7}{x + 2}$ are called fractional equations. To solve such equations, we use the same methods as those used in solving equations containing fractional coefficients.

~~~~~~~~~~ MODEL PROBLEMS ~~~~~~~~~~

1. Solve and check: $\dfrac{1}{3} + \dfrac{1}{x} = \dfrac{1}{2}$

Solution: Multiply both members of the equation by the L.C.D., $6x$.

$$\frac{1}{3} + \frac{1}{x} = \frac{1}{2}$$

$$6x\left(\frac{1}{3} + \frac{1}{x}\right) = 6x\left(\frac{1}{2}\right) \quad \text{M}_{6x}$$

$$6x\left(\frac{1}{3}\right) + 6x\left(\frac{1}{x}\right) = 6x\left(\frac{1}{2}\right)$$

$$2x + 6 = 3x$$

$$6 = x$$

Check

$$\frac{1}{3} + \frac{1}{x} = \frac{1}{2}$$

$$\frac{1}{3} + \frac{1}{6} \overset{?}{=} \frac{1}{2}$$

$$\frac{3}{6} \overset{?}{=} \frac{1}{2}$$

$$\frac{1}{2} = \frac{1}{2} \quad \text{(true)}$$

Answer: $x = 6$, or solution set is $\{6\}$.

2. Solve and check: $\dfrac{2}{3d} + \dfrac{1}{3} = \dfrac{11}{6d} - \dfrac{1}{4}$

Solution: Multiply both members of the equation by the L.C.D., $12d$.

$$\frac{2}{3d} + \frac{1}{3} = \frac{11}{6d} - \frac{1}{4}$$

Check

$$12d\left(\frac{2}{3d} + \frac{1}{3}\right) = 12d\left(\frac{11}{6d} - \frac{1}{4}\right) \quad \mathrm{M}_{12d}$$

$$12d\left(\frac{2}{3d}\right) + 12d\left(\frac{1}{3}\right) = 12d\left(\frac{11}{6d}\right) - 12d\left(\frac{1}{4}\right)$$

$$8 + 4d = 22 - 3d$$
$$8 + 4d + (-8) = 22 - 3d + (-8)$$
$$4d = 14 - 3d$$
$$4d + (3d) = 14 - 3d + (3d)$$
$$7d = 14$$
$$d = 2$$

$$\frac{2}{3d} + \frac{1}{3} = \frac{11}{6d} - \frac{1}{4}$$
$$\frac{2}{3(2)} + \frac{1}{3} \overset{?}{=} \frac{11}{6(2)} - \frac{1}{4}$$
$$\frac{2}{6} + \frac{1}{3} \overset{?}{=} \frac{11}{12} - \frac{1}{4}$$
$$\frac{4}{12} + \frac{4}{12} \overset{?}{=} \frac{11}{12} - \frac{3}{12}$$
$$\frac{8}{12} = \frac{8}{12} \quad \text{(true)}$$

Answer: $d = 2$, or solution set is $\{2\}$.

3. Solve and check: $\dfrac{3x - 5}{3x + 5} = \dfrac{1}{2}$

Solution: Multiply both members of the equation by the L.C.D., $2(3x + 5)$.

$$\frac{3x - 5}{3x + 5} = \frac{1}{2}$$

Check

$$2(3x + 5)\left(\frac{3x - 5}{3x + 5}\right) = 2(3x + 5)\left(\frac{1}{2}\right) \quad \mathrm{M}_{2(3x+5)}$$

$$2(3x - 5) = 1(3x + 5)$$
$$6x - 10 = 3x + 5$$
$$6x - 3x = 5 + 10$$
$$3x = 15$$
$$x = 5$$

$$\frac{3x - 5}{3x + 5} = \frac{1}{2}$$
$$\frac{3(5) - 5}{3(5) + 5} \overset{?}{=} \frac{1}{2}$$
$$\frac{10}{20} \overset{?}{=} \frac{1}{2}$$
$$\frac{1}{2} = \frac{1}{2} \quad \text{(true)}$$

Answer: $x = 5$, or solution set is $\{5\}$.

┌───┐
│ ──────────── **KEEP IN MIND** ──────────── │
│   │
│   When both members of an equation are multiplied by │
│ a variable expression which may represent zero, the re- │
│ sulting equation may not be equivalent to the given │
│ equation. Each solution, therefore, must be checked in │
│ the given equation. │
└───┘

Exercises

In 1–40, solve and check.

1. $\dfrac{10}{x} = 5$ **2.** $\dfrac{15}{y} = 3$ **3.** $\dfrac{6}{x} = 12$ **4.** $\dfrac{8}{b} = -2$

5. $\dfrac{3}{2x} = \dfrac{1}{2}$ **6.** $\dfrac{15}{4x} = \dfrac{1}{8}$ **7.** $\dfrac{7}{3y} = -\dfrac{1}{3}$ **8.** $\dfrac{4}{5y} = -\dfrac{1}{10}$

9. $\dfrac{10}{x} + \dfrac{8}{x} = 9$ **10.** $\dfrac{15}{y} - \dfrac{3}{y} = 4$ **11.** $\dfrac{7}{c} + \dfrac{1}{c} = 16$ **12.** $\dfrac{9}{2x} = \dfrac{7}{2x} + 2$

13. $\dfrac{30}{x} = 7 + \dfrac{18}{2x}$ **14.** $\dfrac{3}{a} = \dfrac{19}{3a} - \dfrac{5}{3}$ **15.** $\dfrac{4}{c} - \dfrac{1}{2} = \dfrac{5}{12} - \dfrac{3}{2c}$

16. $\dfrac{y+9}{2y} + 3 = \dfrac{15}{y}$ **17.** $\dfrac{3}{2x} - 1 = \dfrac{x+1}{x}$ **18.** $\dfrac{2+x}{6x} = \dfrac{3}{5x} + \dfrac{1}{30}$

19. $\dfrac{15}{a+1} = 3$ **20.** $\dfrac{12}{x-2} = 4$ **21.** $\dfrac{10}{x+2} = 2$

22. $\dfrac{9}{2x+1} = 3$ **23.** $\dfrac{10}{2t-1} = 2$ **24.** $\dfrac{16}{1-3t} = 4$

25. $\dfrac{6}{3x-1} = \dfrac{3}{4}$ **26.** $\dfrac{2}{3x-4} = \dfrac{1}{4}$ **27.** $\dfrac{5x}{x+1} = 4$

28. $\dfrac{3}{5-3a} = \dfrac{1}{2}$ **29.** $\dfrac{4z}{7+5z} = \dfrac{1}{3}$ **30.** $\dfrac{1-r}{1+r} = \dfrac{2}{3}$

31. $\dfrac{3}{y} = \dfrac{2}{5-y}$ **32.** $\dfrac{5}{a} = \dfrac{7}{a-4}$ **33.** $\dfrac{2}{m} = \dfrac{5}{3m-1}$

34. $\dfrac{b+1}{b-3} = \dfrac{b-3}{b+1}$ **35.** $\dfrac{y-2}{y+4} = \dfrac{y-3}{y+1}$ **36.** $\dfrac{x-2}{x+1} = \dfrac{x+1}{x-2}$

37. $\dfrac{1}{d-1} = \dfrac{4}{d^2-1} - \dfrac{1}{d+1}$

38. $\dfrac{5}{x^2-4} - \dfrac{x+12}{x+2} + \dfrac{x-1}{x-2} = 0$

39. $\dfrac{y}{y+1} - \dfrac{1}{y} = 1$

40. $\dfrac{x-3}{x-1} - \dfrac{x-1}{x} = \dfrac{5}{x^2-x}$

5. Solving More Difficult Equations Involving Several Variables

When we solve an equation involving several variables for one of those variables, we express this variable in terms of the other variables.

Procedure. To solve an equation which involves several variables for one of those variables:

1. **If the equation contains fractions, clear the fractions by multiplying both members of the equation by the L.C.D. of the denominators.**
2. **If the equation contains parentheses, use the distributive property to remove them.**
3. **Collect on one side of the equation all terms involving the variable for which we are solving. Collect all other terms on the other side.**
4. **Find the coefficient of this variable. If necessary, use the distributive property or factoring.**
5. **Divide both members of the equation by the coefficient found in step 4.**
6. **Simplify the answer if necessary.**

~~~~~~~~~~ **MODEL PROBLEMS** ~~~~~~~~~~

1. Solve for y and check: $\dfrac{y}{r} = s$ $\left(\text{Compare with } \dfrac{y}{9} = 7.\right)$

How To Proceed	Solution	Check
1. Write the equation.	$\dfrac{y}{r} = s$	$\dfrac{y}{r} = s$
2. Multiply by the L.C.D., r.	$r\left(\dfrac{y}{r}\right) = r(s)$	$\dfrac{rs}{r} \overset{?}{=} s$
3. Simplify.	$y = rs$ *Ans.*	$s = s$ (true)

2. Solve for x and check: $cx + d^2 = c^2 + dx$

Solution

$$cx + d^2 = c^2 + dx$$
$$cx + d^2 - dx = c^2 + dx - dx$$
$$cx + d^2 - dx = c^2$$
$$cx + d^2 - dx - d^2 = c^2 - d^2$$
$$cx - dx = c^2 - d^2$$
$$x(c - d) = c^2 - d^2$$

$$\frac{\overset{1}{x\cancel{(c-d)}}}{\cancel{(c-d)}} = \frac{\overset{1}{\cancel{(c-d)}(c+d)}}{\cancel{(c-d)}}$$
$$_1_1$$

$$x = c + d \quad Ans.$$

Check

$$cx + d^2 = c^2 + dx$$
$$c(c + d) + d^2 \overset{?}{=} c^2 + d(c + d)$$
$$c^2 + cd + d^2 = c^2 + cd + d^2 \quad \text{(true)}$$

3. Solve for y and check: $\dfrac{y}{b} + \dfrac{y}{a} = a + b$

Solution

$$\frac{y}{b} + \frac{y}{a} = a + b$$

$$ab\left(\frac{y}{b} + \frac{y}{a}\right) = ab(a + b) \quad \text{M}_{ab} \ \ \text{(ab is the L.C.D.)}$$

$$ab\left(\frac{y}{b}\right) + ab\left(\frac{y}{a}\right) = ab(a) + ab(b)$$

$$ay + by = a^2b + ab^2$$

$$y(a + b) = ab(a + b)$$

$$\frac{\overset{1}{y\cancel{(a+b)}}}{\cancel{(a+b)}} = \frac{\overset{1}{ab\cancel{(a+b)}}}{\cancel{(a+b)}}$$
$$_1_1$$

$$y = ab \quad Ans.$$

Check

$$\frac{y}{a} + \frac{y}{b} = a + b$$

$$\frac{ab}{a} + \frac{ab}{b} \overset{?}{=} a + b$$

$$b + a \overset{?}{=} a + b$$

$$a + b = a + b \quad \text{(true)}$$

Exercises

In 1–51, solve for x or y and check.

1. $\dfrac{x}{5} = t$

2. $\dfrac{x}{c} = 8$

3. $\dfrac{y}{r} = s$

4. $\dfrac{x}{3a} = b$

5. $s = \dfrac{y}{5t}$

6. $\dfrac{x}{ab} = c$

7. $\dfrac{x}{2} - c = d$

8. $2m = \dfrac{y}{5} + n$

9. $\dfrac{x}{3} + b = 4b$

10. $\dfrac{x}{3} = \dfrac{b}{4}$

11. $\dfrac{y}{2} - \dfrac{b}{3} = 0$

12. $\dfrac{x}{6} + \dfrac{c}{4} = 0$

13. $\dfrac{x}{a} = \dfrac{b}{c}$

14. $\dfrac{x}{n} = \dfrac{s}{n^2}$

15. $\dfrac{y}{t^2} - \dfrac{h}{t} = 0$

16. $\dfrac{mx}{r} + c = d$

17. $a = \dfrac{by}{c} - d$

18. $t = s - \dfrac{nx}{d}$

19. $\dfrac{5}{x} = a$

20. $\dfrac{r}{x} = t$

21. $\dfrac{t}{y} - r = 0$

22. $\dfrac{x - 4b}{5} = 8b$

23. $\dfrac{2x + c}{3} = 9c$

24. $\dfrac{3y - 2a}{4} - 7a = 0$

25. $\dfrac{a + b}{x} = c$

26. $\dfrac{m + n}{y} - a = 0$

27. $\dfrac{a}{b} = \dfrac{c + d}{x}$

28. $\dfrac{y}{4} + \dfrac{y}{6} = 5b$

29. $\dfrac{x}{3a} + \dfrac{x}{5a} = 8$

30. $\dfrac{y}{2a} - \dfrac{y}{3a} = 3a^2$

31. $\dfrac{8}{x} - \dfrac{7}{x} = e$

32. $\dfrac{r}{y} + s = \dfrac{t}{y}$

33. $\dfrac{c}{y} = \dfrac{d}{y} + h$

34. $ax + bx = 4a + 4b$

35. $cy + dy = r$

36. $3x - a = 3 - ax$

37. $ax - b = bx$

38. $ax + b^2 = a^2 - bx$

39. $cx - c^2 = dx - d^2$

40. $a(x + b) = 6ax - 9ab$

41. $8x = 2x - 4(x - 5c)$

42. $(x - a)(x - b) = x^2$

43. $c(c - y) = d(d + y)$

44. $\dfrac{x}{a} + \dfrac{x}{b} = 1$

45. $\dfrac{1}{x} = \dfrac{1}{c} + \dfrac{1}{d}$

46. $\dfrac{x}{d} - \dfrac{x}{c} = c - d$

47. $\dfrac{1}{a} + \dfrac{1}{x} = \dfrac{1}{b} - \dfrac{1}{x}$

48. $x = \dfrac{a - x}{b}$

49. $\dfrac{x + s}{r} = \dfrac{r - x}{s}$

50. $\dfrac{y - 1}{y - 3} = a$

51. $\dfrac{y + m}{y + n} = \dfrac{y + n}{y + m}$

6. Solving Verbal Problems Involving Fractions

NUMBER PROBLEMS

~~~~~~~~~~~~~~~~ *MODEL PROBLEMS* ~~~~~~~~~~~~~~~~

1. The larger of two numbers is 5 more than four times the smaller. If the smaller number is equal to one-fifth of the larger number, find the numbers.

   Solution:

   > Let x = the smaller number.
   >
   > Then $4x + 5$ = the larger number.

   > *The smaller number is equal to one-fifth of the larger number.*

$$x = \tfrac{1}{5}(4x + 5)$$
$$5 \cdot x = 5 \cdot \tfrac{1}{5}(4x + 5) \qquad \text{M}_5$$
$$5x = 4x + 5$$
$$x = 5$$
$$4x + 5 = 25$$

   Check: The larger number, 25, is 5 more than 4 times the smaller number, 5. The smaller number, 5, is equal to $\frac{1}{5}$ of 25, the larger number.

   Answer: The smaller number is 5; the larger number is 25.

2. The denominator of a fraction exceeds the numerator by 7. If 3 is subtracted from the numerator of the fraction and the denominator is unchanged, the value of the resulting fraction becomes $\frac{1}{3}$. Find the original fraction.

   Solution:

   > Let x = the numerator of the original fraction.
   >
   > Then $x + 7$ = the denominator of the original fraction.

   And $\dfrac{x}{x + 7}$ = the original fraction.

   And $\dfrac{x - 3}{x + 7}$ = the new fraction.

The value of the new fraction is $\frac{1}{3}$.

$$\frac{x-3}{x+7} = \frac{1}{3}$$

$$3(x+7)\left(\frac{x-3}{x+7}\right) = 3(x+7)\left(\frac{1}{3}\right) \qquad \mathrm{M}_{3(x+7)}$$

$$3(x-3) = 1(x+7)$$

$$3x - 9 = x + 7$$

$$3x - x = 7 + 9$$

$$2x = 16$$

$$x = 8,\ x + 7 = 15$$

Check: The original fraction was $\frac{8}{15}$. The new fraction is $\frac{8-3}{15} = \frac{5}{15} = \frac{1}{3}$.

Answer: The original fraction was $\frac{8}{15}$.

3. The larger of two numbers is 2 less than 4 times the smaller. When the larger number is divided by the smaller number, the quotient is 3 and the remainder is 5. Find the numbers.

Solution:

[*Note:* When 17 is divided by 3, the quotient is 5 and the remainder is 2. This may be written as follows: $\frac{17}{3} = 5 + \frac{2}{3}$. Similarly, "when D is divided by d, the quotient is Q and the remainder is R" may be written as: $\dfrac{D}{d} = Q + \dfrac{R}{d}$.]

Let $x =$ the smaller number. Then $4x - 2 =$ the larger number.

When the larger number is divided by the smaller,
the quotient is 3 and the remainder is 5.

$$\frac{4x-2}{x} = 3 + \frac{5}{x}$$

$$x\left(\frac{4x-2}{x}\right) = x\left(3 + \frac{5}{x}\right) \qquad \mathrm{M}_x$$

$$4x - 2 = 3x + 5$$

$$4x - 3x = 5 + 2,\ x = 7,\ 4x - 2 = 26$$

Check: The larger number, 26, is 2 less than 4 times the smaller number, 7. When 26 is divided by 7, the quotient is 3 and the remainder is 5.

Answer: The larger number is 26; the smaller number is 7.

Exercises

1. If 3 times a number is increased by one-third of itself, the result is 280. Find the number.

2. If one-half of a number is 8 more than one-third of the number, find the number.

3. The larger of two numbers is 12 less than 5 times the smaller. If the smaller number is equal to $\frac{1}{3}$ of the larger number, find the numbers.

4. The larger of two numbers exceeds the smaller by 14. If the smaller number is equal to $\frac{3}{5}$ of the larger number, find the numbers.

5. Separate 90 into two parts such that one part is $\frac{1}{2}$ of the other part.

6. Separate 150 into two parts such that one part is two-thirds of the other part.

7. One-third of the result obtained by adding 5 to a certain number is equal to one-half of the result obtained when 5 is subtracted from the number. Find the number.

8. The numerator of a fraction is 8 less than the denominator of the fraction. The value of the fraction is $\frac{3}{5}$. Find the fraction.

9. The denominator of a fraction exceeds twice the numerator of the fraction by 10. The value of the fraction is $\frac{5}{12}$. Find the fraction.

10. The denominator of a fraction is 30 more than the numerator of the fraction. If 10 is added to the numerator of the fraction and the denominator is unchanged, the value of the resulting fraction becomes $\frac{3}{5}$. Find the original fraction.

11. The numerator of a certain fraction is three times the denominator. If the numerator is decreased by 1 and the denominator is increased by 2, the value of the resulting fraction is $\frac{5}{2}$. Find the original fraction.

12. What number must be added to both the numerator and denominator of the fraction $\frac{7}{19}$ to make the value of the resulting fraction $\frac{3}{4}$?

13. The numerator of a fraction exceeds the denominator by 3. If 3 is added to the numerator and 3 is subtracted from the denominator, the resulting fraction is equal to $\frac{5}{2}$. Find the original fraction.

14. The numerator of a fraction is 7 less than the denominator. If 3 is added to the numerator and 9 is subtracted from the denominator, the resulting fraction is equal to $\frac{3}{2}$. Find the original fraction.

15. If 1 less than 4 times a certain number is divided by 9, the quotient is 3. Find the number.

16. One number is 8 more than another. When the larger is divided by the smaller, the quotient is $\frac{7}{5}$. Find the numbers.

17. Separate 96 into two parts such that when the larger part is divided by the smaller part, the quotient is 7.

18. The larger of two numbers is 25 more than the smaller. If the larger is divided by the smaller, the quotient is 5 and the remainder is 1. Find the numbers.

19. The larger of two numbers is 2 less than 7 times the smaller. If the larger is divided by the smaller, the quotient is 6 and the remainder is 5. Find the numbers.

20. The larger of two numbers exceeds twice the smaller by 9. The larger divided by the smaller gives a quotient of 3 and a remainder of 4. Find the numbers.

21. When the reciprocal of a number is decreased by 2, the result is 5. Find the number.

22. When the reciprocal of a number is increased by $\frac{1}{4}$, the result is 3. Find the number.

23. One-half of the reciprocal of a number exceeds one-third of the reciprocal of the number by 2. Find the number.

7. Average Problems

PREPARING TO SOLVE AVERAGE PROBLEMS

Bill received marks of 80, 90, 70, and 80 on his four algebra tests. To find his average for these four tests, he added the four marks and divided by 4, giving $\frac{80 + 90 + 70 + 80}{4} = \frac{320}{4} = 80$. To find the average of several marks, we find the sum of all the marks and divide the sum by the number of marks.

Exercises

1. Sid received marks of 75, 85, and 89 on three tests. Find his average.

2. Harold received marks of 90, 70, 75, and x on four tests. Represent his average in terms of x.

3. Carl received marks of x, y, and z on the three tests which he took. Represent his average in terms of x, y, and z.

4. Sarah received the mark x on each of two tests and the mark y on each of three tests. Represent her average for all the tests in terms of x and y.

5. Paul has an average of 75 for the 6 tests that he has taken. What is the sum of all his marks?

6. Richard has an average of $x + y$ for the five tests that he has taken. Represent in terms of x and y the sum of all his marks.

SOLVING AVERAGE PROBLEMS

—————————————— **MODEL PROBLEM** ——————————————

A boy has marks of 75 in English, 82 in Latin, and 90 in algebra. What mark must he obtain in social studies to have an average of 85 for all four subjects?

Solution: Let x = the boy's mark in social studies.

The sum of the four marks divided by 4 is 85.

$$\frac{75 + 82 + 90 + x}{4} = 85$$

Check

$$\frac{247 + x}{4} = 85 \qquad\qquad \frac{75 + 82 + 90 + 93}{4} \stackrel{?}{=} 85$$

$$247 + x = 340 \quad \text{M}_4 \qquad\qquad \frac{340}{4} \stackrel{?}{=} 85$$

$$x = 93 \quad \text{S}_{247} \qquad\qquad 85 = 85 \quad \text{(true)}$$

Answer: He must obtain a mark of 93 in social studies.

———————————————————————————————————

Exercises

1. A boy received marks of 85%, 95%, and 80% in his first three spelling tests. How much must he receive on his next test to obtain an average of 90% for all four tests?

2. Richard has marks of 73 in English, 80 in French, and 89 in geometry. What mark must he obtain in history to have an average of 85 for these four tests?

3. A boy received the following marks in algebra: 72, 90, 70, 80. What must be his fifth mark if his average for the five tests is to be 80%?

4. William has received 85 in each of three tests and 95 in a fourth test in geometry. What mark must he receive in a fifth test in order to have an average of 90% for all five tests?

5. The total of all the marks that Harry has received in his three tests in English is 215. What must Harry receive in his fourth test in order that his average for the four tests should be 75?

6. Sam, William, and Bob together weigh 340 pounds. How much does Ray weigh if the average of the weights of all four boys is 120 pounds?

7. The average of the weights of Sue, Mary, and Betty is 110 pounds. How much does Agnes weigh if the average of the weights of the four girls is 120 pounds?

8. The average of the heights of three boys is 5 feet 4 inches. What is the height of a fourth boy if the average of the heights of the four boys is $5\frac{1}{2}$ feet?

9. Robert drove 280 miles on the first day of a trip and 320 miles on the second day of the trip. How many miles must he drive on the third day so that he will average 325 per day for the entire trip?

10. The average of three consecutive even numbers is 20. Find the numbers.

11. The average of three numbers is 31. The second is 1 more than twice the first. The third is 4 less than three times the first. Find the numbers.

12. Laura has marks of 95, 70, 85 in her history tests. On how many successive tests must she receive 100 in order to have an average of 90 for all her history tests?

13. Sue has taken 20 subjects in high school and has an average of 80. This term she is taking 5 subjects. What must her average for these 5 subjects be in order to raise her average for all of her high school work to 82?

8. Motion Problems

~~~~~~~~~~~~~~~~ **MODEL PROBLEMS** ~~~~~~~~~~~~~~~~

1. On a trip, a motorist traveled 50 miles before lunch and 150 miles after lunch. His average rate after lunch was twice his average rate before lunch. He spent 5 hours on the entire trip, not counting the time spent in eating lunch. Find his average rate on each part of the trip.

Solution:

Let r = the average rate before lunch in miles per hour.
Then $2r$ = the average rate after lunch in miles per hour.

	(mi.) Distance	(mph) Rate	(hr.) Time
Before lunch	50	r	$\dfrac{50}{r}$
After lunch	150	$2r$	$\dfrac{150}{2r}$

$$\text{Time} = \frac{\text{Distance}}{\text{Rate}}$$

The total time spent in traveling was 5 hours.

$$\frac{50}{r} + \frac{150}{2r} = 5$$

$$2r\left(\frac{50}{r} + \frac{150}{2r}\right) = 2r(5) \qquad \text{M}_{2r}$$

$$100 + 150 = 10r$$

$$250 = 10r$$

$$25 = r$$

$$50 = 2r$$

Check: Time spent in traveling before lunch was $\frac{50}{25}$ = 2 hours. Time spent in traveling after lunch was $\frac{150}{50}$ = 3 hours. Total time was 3 + 2, or 5 hours.

Answer: The average rate before lunch was 25 mph. The average rate after lunch was 50 mph.

2. A man traveled 120 miles at a certain average rate. By increasing his average rate by 10 mph, he traveled 160 miles in the same time that he spent on the 120-mile trip. Find his average rate on the first trip.

Solution:

Let r = the average rate on the first trip in miles per hour.

Then $r + 10$ = the average rate on the second trip in miles per hour.

	(mi.) Distance	(mph) Rate	(hr.) Time
First trip	120	r	$\dfrac{120}{r}$
Second trip	160	$r + 10$	$\dfrac{160}{r + 10}$

$$\text{Time} = \frac{\text{Distance}}{\text{Rate}}$$

The time for the first trip was the same as the time for the second trip.

$$\frac{120}{r} = \frac{160}{r + 10}$$

$$r(r + 10)\left(\frac{120}{r}\right) = r(r + 10)\left(\frac{160}{r + 10}\right) \qquad \text{M}_{r(r+10)}$$

$$120(r + 10) = 160r$$

$$120r + 1200 = 160r \qquad \text{S}_{120r} \text{ or } \text{A}_{-120r}$$

$$1200 = 40r$$

$$30 = r$$

$$40 = r + 10$$

Check: Time for first trip is $\frac{120}{30}$, or 4 hours. Time for second trip is $\frac{160}{40}$, or 4 hours also.

Answer: Average rate on the first trip was 30 mph.

3. A boat can travel 20 mph in still water. It can travel 75 miles downstream in the same time that it requires to travel 45 miles upstream. Find the rate of the stream.

Solution:

Let c = the rate of the stream in miles per hour.
Then $20 + c$ = the rate of the boat downstream in miles per hour.
And $20 - c$ = the rate of the boat upstream in miles per hour.

	(mi.) Distance	(mph) Rate	(hr.) Time
Downstream	75	$20 + c$	$\dfrac{75}{20 + c}$
Upstream	45	$20 - c$	$\dfrac{45}{20 - c}$

$$\text{Time} = \frac{\text{Distance}}{\text{Rate}}$$

*The time spent traveling upstream is the same
as the time spent traveling downstream.*

$$\frac{45}{20 - c} = \frac{75}{20 + c}$$

Multiply by the L.C.D., $(20 - c)(20 + c)$.

$$(20 - c)(20 + c)\left(\frac{45}{20 - c}\right) = (20 - c)(20 + c)\left(\frac{75}{20 + c}\right)$$
$$45(20 + c) = 75(20 - c)$$
$$900 + 45c = 1500 - 75c$$
$$45c + 75c = 1500 - 900$$
$$120c = 600, \ c = 5$$

Check: Time spent traveling downstream is $\dfrac{75}{20 + 5} = \dfrac{75}{25}$, or 3 hours.

Time spent traveling upstream is $\dfrac{45}{20 - 5} = \dfrac{45}{15}$, or 3 hours also.

Answer: Rate of the stream is 5 mph.

Exercises

1. Mr. Stewart rode a distance of 12 miles out into the country on a bicycle and returned on foot. His rate on the bicycle was 4 times his rate on foot. He spent 5 hours on the entire trip. Find his rate of walking.

2. Mr. Carlson drove a distance of 1000 miles to another city. He returned by plane. The rate of the plane was 10 times the rate at which he drove. He spent 22 hours on the trip. Find the rate at which he drove and the rate of the plane.

3. A man traveled a distance of 640 miles by ship to an island. He returned by plane. The rate of the plane was 20 times the rate of the ship. He spent 42 hours on the trip. Find the rate of the ship and the rate of the plane.

4. A man made a 70-mile trip at a certain average rate. By increasing his average rate by 5 miles per hour, he traveled 80 miles in the same time that he spent on the 70-mile trip. Find his average rate on each trip.

5. Mr. James is traveling 15 miles per hour slower than Mr. Kenton. Mr. James can travel 150 miles in the same time that Mr. Kenton can travel 225 miles. Find the rate at which each man is traveling.

6. One automobile party averages 8 mph less than another. It travels 160 miles in the same time that the other travels 200 miles. Find their rates.

7. The rate at which a jet plane is traveling exceeds twice the rate at which a cargo plane is traveling by 100 miles per hour. The jet plane can fly 1800 miles in the same time that the cargo plane requires to fly 750 miles. Find the rate of each plane.

8. The rate of a passenger train is 20 mph more than the rate of a freight train. It takes the passenger train $\frac{1}{2}$ as much time to travel 160 miles as it does the freight train. Find the rate of each train.

9. A boat can travel 8 mph in still water. If it can travel 15 miles downstream in the same time that it can travel 9 miles up the stream, what is the rate of the stream?

10. A plane can fly 320 miles per hour in still air. Flying with the wind, the plane can fly 1400 miles in the same time that it requires to fly 1160 miles against the wind. Find the rate of the wind.

11. A light private plane can fly 120 miles per hour in still air. Flying with the wind, it can fly 640 miles in a certain time. Flying against the wind, it can fly only half of this distance in the same time. Find the rate of the wind.

9. Work Problems

PREPARING TO SOLVE WORK PROBLEMS

If Harry can paint a wall in 40 minutes, then in 1 minute he will complete $\frac{1}{40}$ of the job. The part of a job that can be completed in 1 unit of time is called the **rate of work**. Thus, $\frac{1}{40}$ is Harry's rate of work. In 2 minutes Harry will complete $2(\frac{1}{40})$ or $\frac{2}{40}$ of the job; in x minutes he will complete $x\left(\dfrac{1}{40}\right)$ or $\dfrac{x}{40}$ of the job. Therefore, we see that:

$$\textit{Rate of work} \times \textit{Time of work} = \textit{Part of the work done}$$

If Sam can paint the same wall in 60 minutes, then in 1 minute he will complete $\frac{1}{60}$ of the job; in two minutes he will complete $2(\frac{1}{60})$ or $\frac{2}{60}$ of the job; in x minutes he will complete $x\left(\dfrac{1}{60}\right)$ or $\dfrac{x}{60}$ of the job.

If Harry and Sam both start painting the wall at the same time, at the end of 1 minute, working together, they will finish $\frac{1}{40} + \frac{1}{60}$ or $\frac{5}{120}$ of the job. At the end of two minutes, they will finish $\frac{2}{40} + \frac{2}{60}$ or $\frac{10}{120}$ of the job. At the end of x minutes, they will finish $\dfrac{x}{40} + \dfrac{x}{60}$ or $\dfrac{5x}{120}$ of the job.

After Harry and Sam have worked for 24 minutes, Harry has finished $\frac{24}{40}$ or $\frac{72}{120}$ of the job and Sam has finished $\frac{24}{60}$ or $\frac{48}{120}$ of the job. Together they finished $\frac{72}{120} + \frac{48}{120}$ or $\frac{120}{120}$ of the job, or the whole job. Notice that in order for Harry and Sam to complete the whole job, the sum of the fractional part of the job that Harry finished and the fractional part of the job that Sam finished must be a fraction whose value is 1.

Exercises

1. *a.* If Sid can mow a lawn in 80 minutes, what part of the lawn can he mow in   (1) 1 minute?   (2) x minutes?
   b. If Gene can mow the same lawn in 120 minutes, what part of the lawn can he mow in   (1) 1 minute?   (2) x minutes?
   c. Represent the part of the job that Sid and Gene, working together, completed in x minutes.
   d. If Sid and Gene mowed the entire lawn in x minutes, what must be the value of the answer given in part *c*?
   e. Write an equation whose solution would reveal the number of minutes that Sid and Gene, working together, would require to mow the entire lawn.

2. *a.* A large pipe can fill a tank in 2 hours. What part of the tank can the pipe fill in   (1) 1 hour?   (2) x hours?
   b. If a smaller pipe can fill the same tank in 3 hours, what part of the tank can this pipe fill in   (1) 1 hour?   (2) x hours?
   c. Represent the part of the tank that is filled in x minutes when both pipes are being used.
   d. Write an equation whose solution would reveal the number of hours that both pipes, being used together, would require to fill the entire tank.
3. A tank can be filled in 4 hours by one pipe and emptied by another pipe in 6 hours. The tank is empty and the faucets of both pipes are opened.
   a. Represent the part of the tank that is filled in 1 hour.
   b. Represent the part of the tank that is filled in x hours.
   c. Write an equation whose solution would reveal the number of hours that would be required to fill the tank.

SOLVING WORK PROBLEMS

------------------- **MODEL PROBLEMS** -------------------

1. Sam can mow a lawn in 20 minutes. Bob can mow the same lawn in 30 minutes. If they work together, how long will it take them to complete the job?

   Solution:

   Let x = number of minutes required to complete the job when both boys work together.

   20 = number of minutes Sam needs to do the job alone.

   30 = number of minutes Bob needs to do the job alone.

   Then $\dfrac{1}{20}$ = part of the job finished by Sam in 1 minute (Sam's rate of work).

   And $\dfrac{1}{30}$ = part of the job finished by Bob in 1 minute (Bob's rate of work).

   Then $x\left(\dfrac{1}{20}\right)$ or $\dfrac{x}{20}$ = part of the job finished by Sam in x minutes.

   And $x\left(\dfrac{1}{30}\right)$ or $\dfrac{x}{30}$ = part of the job finished by Bob in x minutes.

If the job is finished, the sum of the fractional part of the job finished by Sam and the fractional part finished by Bob must equal 1.

$$\frac{x}{20} + \frac{x}{30} = 1$$

$$60\left(\frac{x}{20} + \frac{x}{30}\right) = 60(1)$$

$$3x + 2x = 60$$

$$5x = 60$$

$$x = 12$$

Check: In 12 minutes, Sam will mow $\frac{12}{20}$ or $\frac{36}{60}$ of the lawn.

In 12 minutes, Bob will mow $\frac{12}{30}$ or $\frac{24}{60}$ of the lawn.

In 12 minutes, together, they will mow $\frac{36}{60} + \frac{24}{60} = \frac{60}{60}$, or the whole lawn.

Answer: 12 minutes

Alternate Solution: Let x = number of minutes required to complete the job when both boys work together.

Worker	(part of job per min.) Rate of work	(min.) Time of work	(part of job) Work done
Sam	$\dfrac{1}{20}$	x	$\dfrac{x}{20}$
Bob	$\dfrac{1}{30}$	x	$\dfrac{x}{30}$

Rate of work $\times$ Time of work = Work done

If the job is finished, the sum of the fractional parts done by each must be 1.

$$\frac{x}{20} + \frac{x}{30} = 1$$

The remaining steps are the same as in the previous solution.

2. Mr. Cooper can paint a fence in 2 hours. His son Bill can paint the fence in 6 hours. Mr. Cooper painted alone for 1 hour and stopped working. How many hours would Bill require to finish the job?

Solution:

Let x = number of hours required by Bill to finish the job.

  2 = number of hours required by Mr. Cooper to do the job alone.

  6 = number of hours required by Bill to do the job alone.

Then $\dfrac{1}{2}$ = part of job finished by Mr. Cooper in 1 hour.

And $\dfrac{1}{6}$ = part of job finished by Bill in 1 hour.

And $\dfrac{x}{6}$ = part of job finished by Bill in x hours.

If the job is finished, the sum of the fractional part of the job finished by Mr. Cooper and the fractional part finished by Bill must equal 1.

$$\frac{1}{2} + \frac{x}{6} = 1$$

$$6\left(\frac{1}{2} + \frac{x}{6}\right) = 6(1)$$

$$3 + x = 6$$

$$x = 3$$

Check: In 1 hour, Mr. Cooper finished $\frac{1}{2}$ of the job.

In 3 hours, the son finished $\frac{3}{6}$ or $\frac{1}{2}$ of the job.

Therefore, Mr. Cooper and his son finished $\frac{1}{2} + \frac{1}{2}$, or the whole job.

Answer: 3 hours

Alternate Solution: Let x = number of hours required by Bill to finish the job.

Worker	(part of job per hr.) Rate of work	(hr.) Time of work	(part of job) Work done
Mr. Cooper	$\dfrac{1}{2}$	1	$\dfrac{1}{2}$
Bill	$\dfrac{1}{6}$	x	$\dfrac{x}{6}$

Rate of work $\times$ Time of work = Work done

If the job is finished, the sum of the
fractional parts done by each must be 1.

$$\frac{1}{2} + \frac{x}{6} = 1$$

The remaining steps are the same as in the previous solution.

3. The larger of two pipes can fill a tank twice as fast as the smaller. Together the two pipes require 20 minutes to fill the tank. Find the number of minutes required for the larger pipe, operating alone, to fill the tank.

Solution:

Let x = number of minutes required for the larger pipe, operating alone, to fill the tank.

Then $2x$ = number of minutes required for the smaller pipe, operating alone, to fill the tank.

Then $\dfrac{1}{x}$ = part of the tank filled by the larger pipe in 1 minute.

And $\dfrac{1}{2x}$ = part of the tank filled by the smaller pipe in 1 minute.

Then $\dfrac{20}{x}$ = part of the tank filled by the larger pipe in 20 minutes.

And $\dfrac{20}{2x}$ = part of the tank filled by the smaller pipe in 20 minutes.

If the tank is filled, the sum of the fractional part of
the tank filled by the larger pipe and the fractional part
filled by the smaller pipe must equal 1.

$$\frac{20}{x} + \frac{20}{2x} = 1$$

$$2x\left(\frac{20}{x} + \frac{20}{2x}\right) = 2x(1)$$

$$40 + 20 = 2x$$
$$60 = 2x$$
$$30 = x$$

Answer: 30 minutes (The check is left to the student.)

Alternate Solution:

Let x = number of minutes required for the larger pipe, operating alone, to fill the tank.

Then $2x$ = number of minutes required for the smaller pipe, operating alone, to fill the tank.

Size of pipe	(part of job per min.) Rate of work	(min.) Time of work	(part of job) Work done
Larger pipe	$\dfrac{1}{x}$	20	$\dfrac{20}{x}$
Smaller pipe	$\dfrac{1}{2x}$	20	$\dfrac{20}{2x}$

Rate of work $\times$ Time of work = Work done

If the tank is filled, the sum of the fractional parts filled by each pipe must be 1.

$$\frac{20}{x} + \frac{20}{2x} = 1$$

The remaining steps are the same as in the previous solution.

Exercises

1. Mrs. Saunders can clean the windows of her house in 3 hours. Her daughter can clean the windows in 6 hours. How long will it take them to clean the windows if they work together?
2. Mr. Ford can paint the fence around his house in 6 hours. His son needs 12 hours to do the job. How many hours would it take them to do the job if they worked together?
3. One printing press can print the weekly edition of the local newspaper in 12 hours. Another press can do the job in 18 hours. How long would it take both presses, working together, to do the job?
4. A newsboy can deliver his papers in 80 minutes. His friend can take care of the same route in 2 hours. How long would it take them to do the job together?

5. A mason can make a concrete walk in 6 hours. His helper requires 9 hours to do the same job. In how many hours can they make the walk if they work together?

6. One pipe can fill a tank in 8 minutes, a second can fill it in 12 minutes, and a third can fill it in 24 minutes. If the tank is empty, how long will it take the three pipes, operating together, to fill it?

7. A farmer, working together with his son, needs 3 hours to plow a field. Working alone, the farmer can plow the field in 4 hours. How long would it take the son, working alone, to plow the field?

8. Two printing presses, working together, can complete a job in 2 hours. If one press requires 6 hours to do the job alone, how many hours would the second press need to complete the job alone?

9. Mr. Downey can build a brick wall in 9 hours. His son Carl can build the same wall in 18 hours. Mr. Downey started to build the wall, worked for 3 hours, and then stopped working. How many hours would Carl require to complete the wall?

10. A farmer can plow a field with a tractor in 4 hours. He requires 12 hours to plow the same field with a team of horses. After working for 2 hours, the tractor broke down. How long will it take him to complete the job with the team of horses?

11. An old machine requires three times as many hours to complete a job as a new machine. When both machines work together, they require 9 hours to complete a job. How many hours would it take the new machine to finish the job operating alone?

12. Mr. Curie shovels snow twice as fast as Mrs. Curie. They require 16 minutes to clear the walk around their house when they work together. How long would it take Mrs. Curie to clear the walk working alone?

13. A large pipe can fill a tank 4 times as rapidly as a small pipe. When both pipes are operating, they require 4 hours to fill the tank. How many hours would the small pipe require to fill the tank operating alone?

14. An inlet pipe can fill a tank in 3 hours. An outlet pipe can empty the tank in 6 hours. If the tank is empty and both pipes are opened, how many hours will it take to fill the tank?

15. A bathtub can be filled by the hot water pipe in 20 minutes, and it can be filled by the cold water pipe in 10 minutes. It can be drained in 12 minutes. If the tank is empty and the pipes and drain are opened, in how many hours will the bathtub be filled?

16. A printing press can print an edition of a newspaper in 4 hours. After the press has been at work for 1 hour, another press also starts to print the edition and together both presses require 1 more hour to finish the job. How long would it take the second press to print the edition alone?

17. Miss Allison is asked to do a job that she can complete in 8 hours. After she has been working for 2 hours, Miss Rogers, who is able to do this job alone in 10 hours, is asked to help Miss Allison. In how many hours will both girls, working together, finish the job?

18. Howard and Edward, working together, can complete a job in 12 hours. Edward requires 18 hours to do this job alone. Howard and Edward start the job. After they worked for 4 hours, Howard left the job. How many hours will Edward require to finish the job working alone?

19. A new printing machine can do a job in 6 hours. An old machine can complete the same job in 16 hours. If 3 new machines and 4 old machines are used to do the job, how many hours will be required to finish it?

10. Miscellaneous Problems

Exercises

1. What number added to 8% of itself is 64.8?
2. One part of 480 is $\frac{1}{3}$ of the other. Find the smaller part.
3. Find a number such that $\frac{1}{4}$ of the number is 50 less than $\frac{2}{3}$ of the number.
4. The denominator of a fraction exceeds the numerator of the fraction by 25. The value of the fraction is $\frac{3}{8}$. Find the fraction.
5. What number must be subtracted from both the numerator and the denominator of $\frac{17}{25}$ so that the value of the resulting fraction will become $\frac{3}{7}$?
6. The denominator of a fraction is 3 times the numerator. If 8 is added to the numerator and 6 is subtracted from the denominator, the value of the resulting fraction is $\frac{8}{9}$. Find the original fraction.
7. In a cash register there are nickels, dimes, and quarters. One-half of the coins are nickels, one-fifth of the coins are dimes, and the rest are quarters. The total value of the coins is $6.00. Find the total number of coins in the cash register.
8. Mr. Ray invested $\frac{1}{3}$ of a sum of money at 6%, $\frac{1}{2}$ of the sum of money at 5%, and the remainder at 3%. His total annual income was $600. Find the sum he invested.
9. Mr. Ives invested $\frac{2}{5}$ of a sum of money at 4%, $\frac{1}{3}$ of the sum at 5%, and the remainder at 3%. If his annual income was $1,220, find the amount he invested.
10. Mr. Brink is 24 years older than his son, Stanley. Four years from now, Stanley will be $\frac{2}{5}$ of his father's age at that time. Find Mr. Brink's present age.

11. The width of a rectangle is $\frac{3}{5}$ of its length. If the perimeter of the rectangle is 192 feet, find its length and its width.

12. Find Alice's present age if $\frac{1}{6}$ of her present age is $\frac{1}{4}$ of her age 6 years ago.

13. The sum of two numbers is 44. If $\frac{1}{4}$ of the larger is subtracted from $\frac{1}{2}$ of the smaller, the result is 4. Find the numbers.

14. A farmer wishes to produce 100 lb. of milk which will test 3.2% butterfat by mixing milk testing 3.8% butterfat with milk testing 2.8% butterfat. How many pounds of each type of milk should he use?

15. A pharmacist has 20 ounces of a 30% Argyrol solution. How many ounces of a 40% Argyrol solution should he add to produce a 32% Argyrol solution?

16. How much water must be added to 40 ounces of a 5% solution of salt in water so that the resulting solution will be 3% salt?

17. Mr. Reynolds drove a distance of 240 miles at a certain rate of speed. He covered the first 150 miles in 2 hours more time than was required for the rest of the trip. Find the rate of speed at which he was traveling.

18. Sue is 11 years older than Rose. One-half of Sue's age exceeds one-third of Rose's age by 7 years. Find Sue's age and Rose's age.

19. A certain fraction is equivalent to $\frac{2}{5}$. If the numerator of this fraction is decreased by 4 and its denominator is increased by 14, the resulting fraction is equivalent to $\frac{1}{4}$. Find the numerator and denominator of the original fraction.

20. Mr. Blackstone drove from his city home to his country home, stopping for lunch on the way. Before lunch, he traveled 80 miles farther than he did after lunch. Before lunch, he averaged 40 mph; after lunch, he averaged 50 mph. His traveling time, not including the time spent for lunch, was $6\frac{1}{2}$ hours. Find the number of miles he drove before lunch and also after lunch.

21. In a purse which contains only nickels and dimes, the number of nickels is 2 less than twice the number of dimes. If there had been one-half as many dimes and one-third as many nickels, the total value of the coins would have been $.80. How many coins of each type are there in the purse?

CHAPTER XIV

THE FORMULA

1. Translating Verbal Sentences Into Formulas

A formula uses mathematical language to express the relationship between two or more variables. Let us learn how to translate verbal sentences into formulas.

~~~~~~~~~~~~~~~~ *MODEL PROBLEMS* ~~~~~~~~~~~~~~~~

1. Write a formula for each of the following relationships:

a. The perimeter, P, of a square is equal to 4 times the length of each side, s.

Answer: $P = 4s$

b. The cost, C, of a number of articles is the product of the number of articles, n, and the price, p, of each article.

Answer: $C = np$

c. The area, A, of a circle is equal to π times the square of the radius, r.

Answer: $A = \pi r^2$

2. Write a formula which expresses the number of months, m, that there are in y years, in terms of y.

Solution: First discover the rule which states the relation between the variables m and y. Then write this rule as a formula.

Since there are 12 months in a year, the number of months, m, that there are in y years is equal to 12 times the number of years, y.

Answer: $m = 12y$

Exercises

In 1–25, write a formula which expresses the relationship.

1. The total length, l, of 10 pieces of lumber, each f feet in length, is 10 times the length of each piece of lumber.
2. The total cost, C, of 8 hats, each of which costs d dollars, equals 8 times the cost of each hat.
3. The total weight, w, of n cars, each weighing p pounds, is n times the weight of each car.
4. The selling price of an article, s, equals its cost, c, plus the margin, m.
5. The selling price of an article, s, equals its cost, c, minus the loss, l.
6. The perimeter, p, of a rectangle is equal to the sum of twice its length, l, and twice its width, w.
7. The number of diagonals, d, that can be drawn from one vertex of a polygon to all the other vertices, is two less than the number of sides of the polygon, n.
8. The average, M, of three numbers, a, b, c, is their sum divided by 3.
9. The area, A, of a triangle is equal to one-half the base, b, multiplied by the altitude, h.
10. The area, A, of a square is equal to the square of a side, s.
11. The volume, V, of a cube is equal to the cube of an edge, e.
12. The surface, S, of a cube is equal to 6 times the square of an edge, e.
13. The surface, S, of a sphere is equal to the product of 4π and the square of the radius, r.
14. The average weight, w, of 11 men of a football team is the total of all their weights, T, divided by 11.
15. The average rate of speed, R, is equal to the distance that is traveled, D, divided by the time spent on the trip, T.
16. The Fahrenheit temperature, F, is 32° more than nine-fifths of the centigrade temperature, C.
17. The average weight, w, of 2 boys is equal to one-half the sum of their weights, a and b.
18. The number of cents change, C, to be received from a one-dollar bill is equal to 100 decreased by the price of the article purchased, p, when p is less than \$1.00.
19. The distance, d, which a body will fall from rest is one-half the product of the gravitational constant, g, and the square of the time, t.
20. The centigrade temperature, C, is equal to five-ninths of the difference between the Fahrenheit temperature, F, and 32.
21. To find the approximate number of bushels, n, in a bin, multiply the length, l, by the width, w, by the height, h, each expressed in feet, and divide this product by 1.25.

22. The dividend, D, equals the product of the divisor, d, and the quotient, Q, plus the remainder, R.

23. A worker's earnings during a week, E, is equal to his weekly salary, S, increased by $1\frac{1}{2}$ times his hourly rate of pay, P, times the number of hours he works overtime, H.

24. A sales tax, T, that must be paid when an article is purchased is equal to 4% of the value of the article, V.

25. A salesman's weekly earnings, E, is equal to his weekly salary, S, increased by 2% of his total volume of sales, V.

In 26–38, each required formula will express one of the variables in terms of the others.

26. Write a formula for finding the number of trees, n, in an orchard containing r rows of t trees each.

27. Write the formula for the total number of seats, n, in the school auditorium, if it has two sections, each with r rows having s seats in each row.

28. Write a formula for the number of students, n, that may be seated in a room in which there are S single seats and T double seats.

29. Write a formula for the number of inches, i, in y yards.

30. Write a formula for the number of feet, f, in i inches.

31. Write a formula for the number of ounces, o, in p pounds.

32. Write a formula for the number of days, n, in w weeks and 5 days.

33. Write a formula for the surface area, A, of the four side walls of a room whose length is L, width W, and height H.

34. A group of n persons in an automobile crosses the Hudson River on a ferry. Write a formula for the total ferry charge, c, in cents, if the charge is 50 cents for the car and driver and t cents for each additional person.

35. Write a formula for the cost in cents, c, of a telephone conversation lasting 9 minutes if the charge for the first 3 minutes is x cents and the cost for each additional minute is y cents.

36. Write a formula for the cost in cents, c, of sending a telegram of 18 words if the cost of sending the first 10 words is a cents and each additional word costs b cents.

37. Write a formula for the cost in cents, c, of a telephone conversation which lasts m minutes, m being greater than 3, if the charge for the first 3 minutes is x cents and the cost for each additional minute is y cents.

38. A gasoline dealer is allowed a profit of 2 cents a gallon for each gallon he sells. If he sells more than 25,000 gallons in a year, he is given an additional profit of 1 cent for every gallon over that number. Assuming that he always sells more than 25,000 gallons a year, express as a formula the number of dollars, D, in his yearly income in terms of the number, N, of gallons sold.

2. Evaluating the Subject of a Formula

The variable for which a formula is solved is called the **subject of the formula**. For example, P is the subject of $P = 4s$, the formula for the perimeter, P, of a square each of whose sides has a length represented by s.

$P = 4s$ is an open sentence because there are pairs of numbers which, when they replace s and P, result in a true sentence; and there are pairs of numbers which, when they replace s and P, result in a false sentence. For example, when $s = 3$ and $P = 12$, the resulting sentence $12 = 4 \times 3$ is true; when $s = 5$ and $P = 30$, the resulting sentence $30 = 4 \times 5$ is false.

The solution set of the open sentence $P = 4s$ has a limitless number of elements. Each element is a pair of numbers in which the second number, the value of P, is always 4 times the first number, the value of s. For example, the pairs of numbers $(1, 4)$, $(2, 8)$, and $(3, 12)$ are elements of the solution set of the formula $P = 4s$.

Since the side of a square and the perimeter of a square cannot be negative numbers or 0, the largest possible replacement set for s and also for P is {all positive numbers}. The domains of the variables in any formula are determined by the nature of the quantities which they represent.

If the values of all the variables of a formula except the subject are known, we can compute its value; that is, we can evaluate the subject of the formula.

Procedure. To evaluate the subject of a formula, replace the other variables in the formula by their values. Then perform the indicated operations.

EVALUATING PERIMETER FORMULAS

~~~~~~~~~~~~~~~ **MODEL PROBLEMS** ~~~~~~~~~~~~~~~

1. If $P = 3s$, find P when $s = 5$.

Solution

$P = 3s$
$P = 3(5)$ $[s = 5]$
$P = 15$ *Ans.*

2. If $P = 2b + 2h$, find P when $b = 3$ and $h = 7$.

Solution

$P = 2b + 2h$
$P = 2(3) + 2(7)$ $[b = 3, h = 7]$
$P = 6 + 14$
$P = 20$ *Ans.*

Exercises

1. The formula for the perimeter of a triangle is $P = a + b + c$. Find P when:

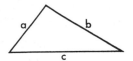

a. $a = 12$ ft., $b = 8$ ft., $c = 6$ ft.
b. $a = 15$ in., $b = 10$ in., $c = 7$ in.
c. $a = 4.5$ ft., $b = 1.7$ ft., $c = 3.8$ ft.
d. $a = 7\frac{1}{2}$ ft., $b = 5\frac{3}{4}$ ft., $c = 6\frac{1}{2}$ ft.
e. $a = 9$ ft., $b = 8$ ft., $c = 18$ in.
f. $a = 36$ in., $b = 5$ ft., $c = 4$ ft.

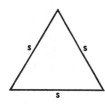

2. The formula for the perimeter of an equilateral triangle is $P = 3s$. Find P when s equals:

a. 6 ft.   b. 12 in.   c. 4.8 in.   d. $9\frac{1}{3}$ ft.   e. $8\frac{1}{2}$ in.

3. The formula for the perimeter of an isosceles triangle is $P = 2a + b$. Find P when:

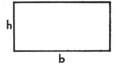

a. $a = 6'$, $b = 4'$
b. $a = 8''$, $b = 7''$
c. $a = 3\frac{1}{2}''$, $b = 5''$
d. $a = 7.5'$, $b = 5.4'$
e. $a = 12.6''$, $b = 7.3''$
f. $a = 21.9'$, $b = 35.2'$

4. The formula for the perimeter of a square is $P = 4s$. Find P when s equals:

a. 7 in.   b. 4 ft.   c. 3.5 ft.   d. $8\frac{3}{4}$ in.   e. $5\frac{1}{8}$ in.

5. The formula for the perimeter of a rectangle is $P = 2b + 2h$. Find P when:

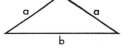

a. $b = 20''$, $h = 9''$
b. $b = 38'$, $h = 25'$
c. $b = 8.2''$, $h = 9.3''$
d. $b = 7.3'$, $h = 6.9'$
e. $b = 5\frac{1}{2}''$, $h = 5\frac{1}{4}''$
f. $b = 5\frac{1}{3}'$, $h = 6\frac{1}{2}''$

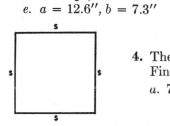

6. The formula for the circumference of a circle is $C = \pi d$. Find C when $\pi = \frac{22}{7}$ and d equals:

a. 14 ft.   b. 7 yd.   c. 21 in.   d. 3 ft.   e. 10 in.

7. The formula for the circumference of a circle is $C = 2\pi r$. Find C when $\pi = 3.14$ and r equals:

a. 10 ft.   b. 5 yd.   c. 40 in.   d. 13 ft.   e. 5.6 in.

EVALUATING AREA FORMULAS

--------------------------------- **MODEL PROBLEMS** ---------------------------------

1. If $A = s^2$, find A when $s = 7$.

Solution

$A = s^2$

$A = (7)^2 \quad [s = 7]$

$A = (7)(7)$

$A = 49 \quad Ans.$

2. If $A = \frac{1}{2}h(b + c)$, find A when $h = 3$, $b = 4$, and $c = 5$.

Solution

$A = \frac{1}{2}h(b + c)$

$A = \frac{1}{2}(3)(4 + 5) \quad [h = 3, b = 4, c = 5]$

$A = \frac{1}{2}(3)(9)$

$A = \frac{1}{2}(27) = 13.5 \quad Ans.$

Exercises (continued)

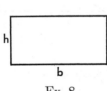

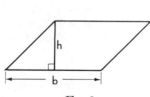

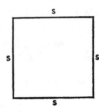

Ex. 8   Ex. 9   Ex. 10

8. The formula for the area of a rectangle is $A = bh$. Find A when:
   a. $b = 10$ in., $h = 8$ in.   b. $b = 15$ ft., $h = 13$ ft.
   c. $b = 7.5$ yd., $h = 3.4$ yd.   d. $b = 8\frac{1}{2}$ ft., $h = 6$ ft.
   e. $b = 4$ ft., $h = 10$ in.   f. $b = 4\frac{1}{3}$ yd., $h = 8$ ft.
   g. $b = 4\frac{1}{2}$ in., $h = 5\frac{1}{2}$ in.   h. $b = 12\frac{1}{2}$ in., $h = 7\frac{1}{4}$ in.

9. The formula for the area of a parallelogram is $A = bh$. Find A when:
   a. $b = 8$ ft., $h = 12$ ft.   b. $b = 11$ yd., $h = 9$ yd.
   c. $b = 3.5$ ft., $h = 6.4$ ft.   d. $b = 7\frac{1}{2}$ in., $h = 8$ in.
   e. $b = 3$ ft., $h = 10$ in.   f. $b = 2\frac{1}{3}$ yd., $h = 6$ ft.
   g. $b = 7\frac{1}{2}$ in., $h = 4\frac{1}{2}$ in.   h. $b = 5\frac{1}{2}$ in., $h = 8\frac{1}{4}$ in.

10. The formula for the area of a square is $A = s^2$. Find A when s equals:
   a. 25 in.   b. 32 ft.   c. 9 yd.   d. $2\frac{1}{2}$ ft.   e. 6.1 in.

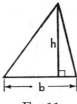

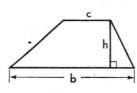

Ex. 11   Ex. 12   Ex. 13

11. The formula for the area of a triangle is $A = \frac{1}{2}bh$. Find A when:

a. $b = 10'$, $h = 6'$ b. $b = 7''$, $h = 14''$
c. $b = 3$ yd., $h = 5$ yd.   d. $b = 8.2''$, $h = 14''$
e. $b = 10.5$ yd., $h = 7.6$ yd.   f. $b = 9.3''$, $h = 5.5''$
g. $b = 3\frac{1}{2}'$, $h = 8'$ h. $b = 4\frac{1}{2}''$, $h = 7\frac{3}{4}''$
i. $b = 3\frac{1}{2}'$, $h = 19''$ j. $b = 1'$, $h = 5\frac{1}{2}''$

12. The formula for the area of a trapezoid is $A = \frac{1}{2}h(b + c)$. Find A when:

a. $h = 10''$, $b = 8''$, $c = 6''$ b. $h = 8''$, $b = 12''$, $c = 5''$
c. $h = 9''$, $b = 14''$, $c = 8''$ d. $h = 7''$, $b = 9''$, $c = 4''$
e. $h = 5''$, $b = 3\frac{1}{4}''$, $c = \frac{3}{4}''$ f. $h = 9''$, $b = 7.6''$, $c = 4.4''$

13. The formula for the area of a circle is $A = \pi r^2$. Find A when $\pi = \frac{22}{7}$ and r equals:

a. 7 ft.   b. 14 in.   c. 5.6 ft.   d. $3\frac{1}{2}$ yd.   e. 10 in.

EVALUATING FORMULAS FOR SURFACES OF SOLIDS

14. The formula for the surface area of a rectangular solid is $S = 2LW + 2HL + 2HW$. Find S when:

a. $L = 6'$, $W = 5'$, $H = 3'$
b. $L = 7''$, $W = 6''$, $H = 9''$
c. $L = 4.5'$, $W = 1.4'$, $H = 2.6'$
d. $L = 3\frac{1}{2}''$, $W = 4''$, $H = 4\frac{1}{4}''$

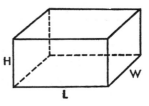

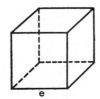

15. The formula for the surface area of a cube is $S = 6e^2$. Find S when e equals:

a. 6 in.   b. 5 yd.   c. 9 in.
d. $\frac{1}{4}$ ft.   e. 4.5 in.

16. The formula for the surface area of a sphere is
$S = 4\pi r^2$. Find S when:

   a. $\pi = \frac{22}{7}$, $r = 14$ in.
   b. $\pi = \frac{22}{7}$, $r = 3\frac{1}{2}$ ft.
   c. $\pi = 3.14$, $r = 10$ in.
   d. $\pi = 3.14$, $r = 20$ in.

17. The formula for the surface area of a cylinder
is $S = 2\pi r(r + h)$. Find S when:

   a. $\pi = \frac{22}{7}$, $r = 4''$, $h = 3''$
   b. $\pi = \frac{22}{7}$, $r = 2'$, $h = 1\frac{1}{2}'$
   c. $\pi = 3.14$, $r = 5''$, $h = 5''$
   d. $\pi = 3.14$, $r = 2.5''$, $h = 7.5''$

EVALUATING FORMULAS FOR VOLUMES OF SOLIDS

18. The formula for the volume of a rectangular
solid is $V = LWH$. Find V when:

   a. $L = 5'$, $W = 4'$, $H = 7'$
   b. $L = 8''$, $W = 7''$, $H = 5''$
   c. $L = 8.5''$, $W = 4.2''$, $H = 6.0''$
   d. $L = 2\frac{1}{2}''$, $W = 8''$, $H = 5\frac{1}{4}''$

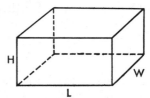

19. The formula for the volume of a cube is $V = e^3$.
Find V when e equals:

   a. 2 in.   *b.* 3 yd.   *c.* 8 in.
   d. $\frac{1}{3}$ ft.   *e.* 1.5 in.

20. The formula for the volume of a sphere is
$V = \frac{4}{3}\pi r^3$. Find V when:

   a. $\pi = \frac{22}{7}$, $r = 7$ ft.
   b. $\pi = \frac{22}{7}$, $r = 2\frac{1}{3}$ ft.
   c. $\pi = 3.14$, $r = 10$ in.
   d. $\pi = 3.14$, $r = 30$ in.

21. The formula for the volume of a cylinder is
$V = \pi r^2 h$. Find V when $\pi = \frac{22}{7}$ and:

   a. $r = 21''$, $h = 10''$ *b.* $r = 35''$, $h = 12''$
   c. $r = 28''$, $h = \frac{3}{4}''$ *d.* $r = 1.4'$, $h = 8'$
   e. $r = 10''$, $h = 2.1''$ *f.* $r = 9''$, $h = 5.6''$

EVALUATING MISCELLANEOUS FORMULAS

~~~~~~~~~~~ *MODEL PROBLEMS* ~~~~~~~~~~~

1. If $F = \frac{9}{5}C + 32$, find F
when $C = 40°$.

Solution

$F = \frac{9}{5}C + 32$
$F = \frac{9}{5}(40) + 32$ $[C = 40]$
$F = 9(8) + 32$
$F = 72 + 32$
$F = 104°$ *Ans.*

2. If $C = \frac{5}{9}(F - 32)$, find C
when $F = -13°$.

Solution

$C = \frac{5}{9}(F - 32)$
$C = \frac{5}{9}(-13 - 32)$ $[F = -13]$
$C = \frac{5}{9}(-45)$
$C = 5(-5)$
$C = -25°$ *Ans.*

~~~~~~~~~~~~~~~~~~~~~~~~~~~~~~~~~~~~~~~

Exercises (continued)

22. If $E = \dfrac{360}{n}$, find E when:

   a. n $= 4$ *b. n* $= 6$ *c. n* $= 8$ *d. n* $= 10$ *e. n* $= 12$

23. If $I = prt$, find I when:
   a. $p = \$200$, $r = 4\%$, $t = 4$ yr.   *b.* $p = \$800$, $r = 3\%$, $t = 5$ yr.
   c. $p = \$640$, $r = 6\%$, $t = 2\frac{3}{4}$ yr.   *d.* $p = \$1200$, $r = 5\%$, $t = 3.5$ yr.

24. If $A = p + prt$, find A when:
   a. $p = \$600$, $r = 3\%$, $t = 2$ yr.   *b.* $p = \$4000$, $r = 5\%$, $t = 8$ yr.
   c. $p = \$1250$, $r = 4\%$, $t = 2\frac{1}{4}$ yr.   *d.* $p = \$3500$, $r = 2\%$, $t = 4.5$ yr.

25. If $S = \frac{1}{2}gt^2$, find S when $g = 32$ and t equals:
   a. 2   *b.* 3   *c.* 4   *d.* 6   *e.* 10   *f.* 1.5   *g.* $3\frac{1}{2}$ *h.* $1\frac{3}{4}$

26. If F represents a Fahrenheit temperature and C represents the equivalent centigrade temperature, $F = \frac{9}{5}C + 32$. Find F when:
   a. $C = 20°$ *b.* $C = 35°$ *c.* $C = 0°$ *d.* $C = 22°$ *e.* $C = 41°$
   f. $C = -5°$ *g.* $C = -15°$ *h.* $C = -20°$ *i.* $C = -9°$ *j.* $C = -27°$

27. If C represents a centigrade temperature and F represents the equivalent Fahrenheit temperature, $C = \frac{5}{9}(F - 32)$. Find C when:
   a. $F = 50°$ *b.* $F = 86°$ *c.* $F = 32°$ *d.* $F = 56°$ *e.* $F = 40°$
   f. $F = -4°$ *g.* $F = -22°$ *h.* $F = -40°$ *i.* $F = -7°$ *j.* $F = -19°$

28. If $S = \dfrac{n}{2}(a + l)$, find S when:

a. $n = 20$, $a = 2$, $l = 40$ b. $n = 11$, $a = 4$, $l = 44$
c. $n = 15$, $a = 10$, $l = 80$ d. $n = 8$, $a = 5$, $l = 33$
e. $n = 12$, $a = 4.5$, $l = 20.5$ f. $n = 7$, $a = 1.3$, $l = 1.9$
g. $n = 10$, $a = 18$, $l = -8$ h. $n = 9$, $a = -17$, $l = 1$

29. The lifting force on an airfoil is given by the formula $L = KAV^2$. Find L when:

a. $K = .0025$, $A = 350$, $V = 100$ b. $K = .0027$, $A = 200$, $V = 150$

30. The horsepower required for flight is given by the formula $H = \dfrac{DV}{375}$.
Find H when:

a. $D = 187.5$ lb., $V = 200$ mph   b. $D = 160$ lb., $V = 240$ mph

31. In the formula $L = a + (n - 1)d$, find the value of L when $a = 7$, $n = 13$, and $d = 3$.

32. In the formula $K = 2a - 5(n - 1)$, find the value of K when $a = 8$ and $n = 3$.

33. If $S = \dfrac{a}{1 - r}$, find S when $a = 8$ and $r = .5$.

34. If $S = \dfrac{rl - a}{r - 1}$, find S when $r = 3$, $l = 15$, and $a = 5$.

In 35–39: From the given domains, choose a replacement for each variable which will make the formula a true statement.

35. $C = 5n$ C: $\{3, 7, 15, 22\}$ n: $\{1, 2, 3, 4\}$
36. $P = 3s$ P: $\{2, 4, 6, 8\}$ s: $\{1, 2, 3, 4\}$
37. $A = e^2$ A: $\{10, 15, 20, 25\}$ e: $\{4, 5, 6, 7\}$
38. $A = bh$ A: $\{11, 13, 15, 17\}$ b: $\{3, 4, 5, 6\}$ h: $\{1, 2, 3, 4\}$
39. $C = \frac{5}{9}(F - 32)$ C: $\{5, 10, 15, 20\}$ F: $\{40, 50, 60, 70\}$

3. Evaluating a Formula by Solving an Equation

If the value of the subject of a formula and all its other variables but one are known, the value of the remaining variable can be computed.

Procedure. To find the value of a variable in a formula when the values of the other variables including the subject of the formula are given, substitute the given values in the formula. Then solve the resulting equation.

~~~~~~~~~~~~~~~~ **MODEL PROBLEMS** ~~~~~~~~~~~~~~~~

1. If $A = \frac{1}{2}bh$, find h when $A = 60$ and $b = 10$.

Solution	*Check*
$A = \frac{1}{2}bh$	$A = \frac{1}{2}bh$
$60 = \frac{1}{2}(10)h \quad [A = 60, b = 10]$	$60 \overset{?}{=} \frac{1}{2}(10)(12)$
$60 = 5h$	$60 = 60 \quad \text{(true)}$
$12 = h \quad Ans.$	

2. If $S = \dfrac{n}{2}(a + l)$, find a when $S = 40$, $n = 8$, and $l = 6$.

Solution	*Check*
$S = \dfrac{n}{2}(a + l)$	$S = \dfrac{n}{2}(a + l)$
$40 = \dfrac{8}{2}(a + 6) \quad [S = 40, n = 8, l = 6]$	$40 \overset{?}{=} \dfrac{8}{2}(4 + 6)$
$40 = 4(a + 6)$	$40 \overset{?}{=} 4(10)$
$40 = 4a + 24$	$40 = 40 \quad \text{(true)}$
$40 - 24 = 4a + 24 - 24$	
$16 = 4a$	
$4 = a \quad Ans.$	

~~~~~~

Exercises

1. If $p = a + b + c$, find c when $p = 80$, $a = 20$, and $b = 25$.

2. If $p = a + b + c$; find b when $p = 9.7$, $a = 3.1$, and $c = 2.4$.

3. If $p = 4s$, find s when (a) $p = 20$ (b) $p = 32$ (c) $p = 6.4$.

4. If $nE = 360$, find n when (a) $E = 90$ (b) $E = 45$ (c) $E = 12$.

5. If $A = lw$, find w when (a) $A = 80$, $l = 10$ (b) $A = 100$, $l = 5$ (c) $A = 3.6$, $l = .9$.

6. If $D = RT$, find R when (a) $D = 120$, $T = 3$ (b) $D = 40$, $T = \frac{1}{2}$.

7. If $C = \pi D$, find D when $C = 44$ and $\pi = \frac{22}{7}$.

8. If $C = 2\pi R$, find R when $C = 628$ and $\pi = 3.14$.

9. If $A = \frac{1}{2}bh$, find h when (a) $A = 24$, $b = 8$ (b) $A = 36$, $b = 18$ (c) $A = 12$, $b = 3$.

10. If $S = 2\pi rh$, find h when $S = 440$, $\pi = \frac{22}{7}$, $r = 5$.

11. If $V = lwh$, find h when $V = 200$, $l = 10$, and $w = 4$.
12. If $V = lwh$, find w when $V = 72$, $l = \frac{3}{4}$, $h = 12$.
13. If $I = prt$, find t when $I = \$12$, $r = 2\%$, and $p = \$300$.
14. If $I = prt$, find p when $I = \$45$, $r = 3\%$, and $t = 3$ yr.
15. If $I = prt$, find r when $I = \$80$, $p = \$1000$, $t = 2$ yr.
16. If $p = 2a + b$, find b when $p = 80$ and $a = 30$.
17. If $p = 2a + b$, find b when $p = 12.4$ and $a = 4.3$.
18. If $p = 2a + b$, find a when $p = 32$ and $b = 14$.
19. If $p = 2a + b$, find a when $p = 18.6$ and $b = 5.8$.
20. If $F = \frac{9}{5}C + 32$, find C when   (a) $F = 95°$ (b) $F = 68°$ (c) $F = 59°$.
21. If $A = p + prt$, find t when $A = \$600$, $p = \$500$, $r = 4\%$.

22. If $S = \dfrac{n}{2}(a + l)$, find n when $S = 30$, $a = 4$, $l = 6$.

23. If $S = \dfrac{n}{2}(a + l)$, find n when $S = 100$, $a = 20$, $l = 30$.

24. If $S = \dfrac{n}{2}(a + l)$, find l when $S = 36$, $n = 4$, $a = 5$.

25. If $S = \dfrac{n}{2}(a + l)$, find a when $S = 42$, $n = 14$, $l = 2$.

26. If $C = \frac{5}{9}(F - 32)$, find F when   (a) $C = 5°$ (b) $C = 10°$ (c) $C = 77°$.
27. If $A = \frac{1}{2}h(b + c)$, find h when $A = 24$, $b = 9$, $c = 3$.
28. If $A = \frac{1}{2}h(b + c)$, find h when $A = 35$, $b = 6$, $c = 4$.
29. If $A = \frac{1}{2}h(b + c)$, find b when $A = 50$, $h = 4$, $c = 11$.
30. If $A = \frac{1}{2}h(b + c)$, find c when $A = 54$, $h = 12$, $b = 5.5$.

4. Transforming Simple Formulas

A formula may be expressed in more than one form. Sometimes it is desirable to solve a formula for a variable different from the one for which it is solved. This is called **transforming** the formula, or **changing the subject** of the formula. For example, the formula $D = 40t$ can be transformed into the equivalent formula $\dfrac{D}{40} = t$. In the formula $D = 40t$, D is expressed in terms of t; in the formula $t = \dfrac{D}{40}$, t is expressed in terms of D. If we know the value of D and wish to find the value of t, the computation is more convenient when we use the formula $t = \dfrac{D}{40}$. (See the first model problem following the Procedure on the next page.)

Procedure. To transform a formula so that it is solved for a particular variable, consider the formula as an equation with several variables and solve it for the indicated variable in terms of the others.

~~~~~~~~~~~~~~~~~ **MODEL PROBLEMS** ~~~~~~~~~~~~~~~~~

1. *a.* Solve the formula $D = 40t$ for t.
   b. Use the answer found in *a* to find the value of t when $D = 200$.

Solution:

a. $D = 40t$

$$\frac{D}{40} = \frac{40t}{40} \quad \mathrm{D}_{40}$$

$$\frac{D}{40} = t$$

$$t = \frac{D}{40} \quad Ans.$$

b. $t = \dfrac{D}{40}$

$$t = \frac{200}{40} \quad [D = 200]$$

$$t = 5 \quad Ans.$$

2. Solve the formula
   $V = \frac{1}{3}Bh$ for B.

   Solution

   $V = \frac{1}{3}Bh$

   $3V = 3 \cdot \frac{1}{3}Bh \quad \mathrm{M}_3$

   $3V = Bh$

   $\dfrac{3V}{h} = \dfrac{Bh}{h} \quad \mathrm{D}_h$

   $\dfrac{3V}{h} = B \quad Ans.$

3. Solve the formula $P = 2(L + W)$ for W.

   Solution

   $P = 2(L + W)$

   $P = 2L + 2W \quad$ [distributive property]

   $P + (-2L) = 2L + 2W + (-2L) \quad \mathrm{A}_{-2L}$

   $P - 2L = 2W$

   $\dfrac{P - 2L}{2} = \dfrac{2W}{2} \quad \mathrm{D}_2$

   $\dfrac{P - 2L}{2} = W \quad Ans.$

~~~~~~

Exercises

In 1–37, transform the given formula by solving for the indicated letter.
1. $A = 6h$ for h
2. $36 = bh$ for h
3. $P = 4s$ for s
4. $P = ns$ for s
5. $D = 60t$ for t
6. $D = rt$ for t
7. $A = bh$ for h
8. $D = RT$ for R
9. $C = \pi D$ for π

10. $A = BH$ for B

11. $p = br$ for b

12. $D = dq$ for q

13. $E = ir$ for i

14. $V = nc$ for c

15. $A = lw$ for l

16. $V = lwh$ for h

17. $C = 2\pi r$ for r

18. $i = prt$ for p

19. $V = lwh$ for w

20. $CN = 360$ for N

21. $400 = BH$ for B

22. $A = \frac{1}{2}bh$ for h

23. $A = \frac{1}{3}BH$ for H

24. $K = \dfrac{AP}{2}$ for A

25. $S = \frac{1}{2}gt^2$ for g

26. $E = \frac{1}{2}mv^2$ for m

27. $S = \pi \dfrac{R^2 A}{90}$ for A

28. $S = c + g$ for g

29. $l = c - s$ for c

30. $P = 2l + 2w$ for l

31. $F = \frac{9}{5}C + 32$ for C

32. $2S = n(a + l)$ for a

33. $2S = n(a + l)$ for l

34. $A = \dfrac{h}{2}(b + c)$ for b

35. $A = \dfrac{h}{2}(b + c)$ for c

36. $T = m(g - b)$ for g

37. $E = I(R + r)$ for R

38. If $A = BH$, express H in terms of A and B. (Solve for H.)

39. If $P = nS$, express n in terms of P and S. (Solve for n.)

40. If $P = 2a + b$, express b in terms of P and a.

41. If $A = \frac{1}{2}rp$, express r in terms of A and p.

42. If $P = 2a + b + c$, express a in terms of the other variables.

In 43–49:   (a) Transform the given formula by solving for the variable to be evaluated.   (b) Substitute the given values (in the result obtained in part a) to find the value of this variable.

43. If $nE = 360$, find E when $n = 20$.

44. If $LWH = 144$, find W when $L = 3$ and $H = 6$.

45. If $A = \frac{1}{2}bh$, find h when $A = 15$ and $b = 5$.

46. If $F = \frac{9}{5}C + 32$, find C when $F = 95$.

47. If $P = 2L + 2W$, find L when $P = 64$ and $W = 13$.

48. If $S = \dfrac{n}{2}(a + l)$, find l when $S = 36$, $n = 4$, and $a = 5$.

49. If $A = P(1 + rt)$, find r when $A = 200$, $P = 100$, and $t = 10$.

50. The formula for finding the area of a rectangle is $A = bh$. Rewrite this formula if $b = 4h$.

51. The formula for the area of a triangle is $A = \frac{1}{2}bh$. Rewrite this formula if $h = 4b$.

52. The formula for the area of a trapezoid is $A = \dfrac{h}{2}(b + c)$. If $h = 3b$ and $c = 5b$, express A in terms of b.

5. Transforming More Difficult Formulas

~~~~~~~~~~~~~~~~~~ MODEL PROBLEMS ~~~~~~~~~~~~~~~~~~

1. *a.* Solve the formula $\dfrac{D}{R} = T$ for R in terms of D and T.

    b. Find R when $D = 200$ and $T = 5$.

Solution:

  a. $\dfrac{D}{R} = T$ *b.* $R = \dfrac{D}{T}$ $[D = 200, T = 5]$

    $R \cdot \dfrac{D}{R} = R \cdot T$ M_R $R = \dfrac{200}{5}$

        $D = RT$ $R = 40$ *Ans.*

        $\dfrac{D}{T} = \dfrac{RT}{T}$ D_T

        $\dfrac{D}{T} = R$ *Ans.*

2. *a.* Solve the formula $C = \frac{5}{9}(F - 32)$ for F in terms of C.

    b. Find F when $C = 10$.

Solution:

  a. $C = \dfrac{5}{9}(F - 32)$ *b.* $F = \dfrac{9C + 160}{5}$ $[C = 10]$

    $9 \times C = 9 \times \dfrac{5}{9}(F - 32)$ M_9 $F = \dfrac{9(10) + 160}{5}$

        $9C = 5(F - 32)$ $F = \dfrac{90 + 160}{5}$

        $9C = 5F - 160$

    $9C + 160 = 5F$ A_{160} $F = \dfrac{250}{5}$

    $\dfrac{9C + 160}{5} = F$ D_5 $F = 50$ *Ans.*

      $F = \dfrac{9C + 160}{5}$ *Ans.*

3. Solve the formula $R = \dfrac{gs}{g+s}$ for s.

Solution:

$$R = \frac{gs}{g+s} \, .$$

$$R(g+s) = \frac{gs}{\cancel{(g+s)}}_{1} \cdot \overset{1}{\cancel{(g+s)}} \quad \text{M}_{(g+s)}$$

$$Rg + Rs = gs \qquad\qquad \text{[distributive property]}$$

$$Rg = gs - Rs \quad \text{S}_{Rs} \text{ or } \text{A}_{-Rs}$$

$$Rg = s(g - R) \quad \text{[factoring]}$$

$$\frac{Rg}{(g-R)} = \frac{s\cancel{(g-R)}}{\cancel{(g-R)}}_{1} \quad \text{D}_{(g-R)}$$

$$\frac{Rg}{(g-R)} = s$$

Answer: $s = \dfrac{Rg}{g-R}$

Exercises

In 1–27, solve the formula for the indicated variable.

1. $C = \dfrac{360}{n}$ for n **2.** $R = \dfrac{E}{I}$ for I **3.** $B = \dfrac{P}{R}$ for R

4. $v = \dfrac{s}{t}$ for t **5.** $F = \dfrac{mv^2}{gr}$ for m **6.** $V^2 = \dfrac{L}{KA}$ for A

7. $H = \dfrac{3V}{\pi R^2}$ for V **8.** $\dfrac{P}{N} = \dfrac{p}{n}$ for N **9.** $t = \dfrac{V - K}{g}$ for g

10. $\dfrac{E}{R+r} = I$ for r **11.** $F = 32 + \tfrac{9}{5}C$ for C **12.** $\dfrac{D}{d} = q + \dfrac{r}{d}$ for d

13. $S = \dfrac{n}{2}(a + l)$ for a **14.** $S = \dfrac{n}{2}(a + l)$ for l **15.** $A = \frac{1}{2}h(b + c)$ for b

16. $A = P(1 + rt)$ for P **17.** $S = \dfrac{n}{2}(a + l)$ for n **18.** $A = p + prt$ for p

19. $n = \dfrac{a - W}{6W}$ for W **20.** $\dfrac{1}{f} = \dfrac{1}{p} + \dfrac{1}{q}$ for p **21.** $I = \dfrac{E}{R + r}$ for r

22. $I = \dfrac{E}{R + r}$ for R **23.** $R = \dfrac{gs}{g + s}$ for g **24.** $C = \dfrac{nE}{R + nr}$ for n

25. $\dfrac{1}{f} - \dfrac{1}{q} = \dfrac{1}{p}$ for q **26.** $S = \dfrac{rl - a}{r - l}$ for r **27.** $I = \dfrac{E}{r_1 + r_2}$ for r_2

28. If $S = \frac{1}{2}at^2$, express a in terms of S and t.

29. If $A = p + prt$, express t in terms of A, r, and p.

30. If $V = \dfrac{h}{6}(B + B' + 4m)$, express h in terms of V, B, B', and m.

In 31–40: (a) Transform the given formula into a formula which is solved for the variable to be evaluated. (b) Substitute the given values (in the result obtained in part a) to find the value of this variable.

31. If $\dfrac{D}{T} = R$, find T when $D = 120$ and $R = 30$.

32. If $\dfrac{P}{B} = r$, find B when $P = 80$ and $r = .04$.

33. If $A = p(1 + rt)$, find p when $A = 230$, $r = .05$, and $t = 3$.

34. If $S = \dfrac{n}{2}(a + l)$, find n when $S = 150$, $a = 25$, and $l = 75$.

35. If $A = \frac{1}{2}h(b + c)$, find h when $A = 48$, $b = 12$, and $c = 4$.

36. If $A = \dfrac{h}{2}(b + c)$, find c when $A = 36$, $h = 12$, and $b = 2$.

37. If $n = \dfrac{a - K}{5K}$, find K when $a = 33$ and $n = 2$.

38. If $\dfrac{1}{F} = \dfrac{1}{g} + \dfrac{1}{h}$, find F when $g = \frac{1}{2}$ and $h = \frac{2}{5}$.

39. If $S = \dfrac{n}{2}(a + l)$, express S in terms of a when $n = 3a$ and $l = 5a$.

40. If $A = \frac{1}{2}h(b + c)$, express A in terms of c when $h = 5c$ and $b = 9c$.

6. Writing Formulas for Tables of Values of Related Variables

In the table at the right are summarized the lengths of the sides, s, of different squares and the perimeters, P, of these squares. If we notice that every value of P in this table is 4 times the corresponding value of s, we see that $P = 4s$ is a formula which expresses the relation between P and s.

s	1	2	3	4	10
P	4	8	12	16	40

Procedure. To write a formula for a table of values of related variables:

1. **Study the table carefully to discover the relationship between the corresponding values of the two variables in the table.**
2. **Express the relationship as a rule.**
3. **Test the rule for all sets of values in the table.**
4. **Translate the rule into a formula.**

～～～～～～ MODEL PROBLEMS ～～～～～～

Write a formula which expresses the relationship between the numbers in each of the following tables. Then find the missing number.

1.

Number of hours traveled, h	1	2	3	4	5
Distance traveled in miles, d	30	60	90	120	?

Solution: Notice that the distance, d, is always 30 times the number of hours, h.

$$30 \times 1 = 30, \quad 30 \times 2 = 60, \quad 30 \times 3 = 90, \quad 30 \times 4 = 120$$

Therefore, the formula is: $d = 30h$.   *Ans.*

If $h = 5$, $d = 30 \times 5 = 150$.   *Ans.*

2.

Harry's age, H, in years	7	8	9	10	11
Tom's age, T, in years	15	16	17	18	?

Solution: Notice that Tom's age, T, is always 8 years more than Harry's age, H.

$$15 = 7 + 8, \qquad 16 = 8 + 8, \qquad 17 = 9 + 8, \qquad 18 = 10 + 8$$

Therefore, the formula is: $T = H + 8$.   *Ans.*
If $H = 11$, $T = 11 + 8 = 19$.   *Ans.*

Exercises

Study each of the following tables and write a formula to represent the relationship between the numbers in each of the tables. Find the missing number.

1.

n	3	4	5	6	7
c	9	12	15	18	?

2.

r	6	7	10	15	20
d	12	14	20	30	?

3.

h	3	5	8	10	25
d	45	75	120	150	?

4.

w	1	2	3	4	7
d	7	14	21	28	?

5.

y	1	2	4	8	15
f	3	6	12	24	?

6.

h	2	4	6	8	12
s	3	6	9	12	?

7.

s	3	5	7	10	20
p	12	20	28	40	?

8.

i	12	24	36	48	96
f	1	2	3	4	?

9.

s	3	4	5	6	7
t	1	2	3	4	?

10.

d	3	4	5	6	7
m	25	26	27	28	?

11.

b	8	10	12	15	20
s	5	7	9	12	?

12.

s	3	5	8	12	20
d	1	3	6	10	?

13.

S	1	2	3	4	5
A	1	4	9	16	?

14.

e	1	2	3	4	5
v	1	8	27	64	?

15.

x	3	4	5	6	8
y	7	9	11	13	?

16.

s	1	2	3	5	8
r	2	5	8	14	?

17.

m	1	2	3	5	7
n	4	7	10	16	?

18.

c	1	2	4	7	15
d	1	3	7	13	?

19.

x	1	2	3	4	5
y	2	8	18	32	?

20.

h	2	3	4	5	6
d	5	10	17	26	?

7. Using Formulas To Study Related Changes

The formula $P = 4s$ states the relationship between the side of a square, s, and its perimeter, P. A change in the value of the variable s will bring about a change in the value of the variable P. A table of values prepared from the formula can help us study the effect that a change in one variable has upon the other variable.

~~~~~~~~~~~~~~~~ MODEL PROBLEMS ~~~~~~~~~~~~~~~~

1. The formula for the perimeter of a square is $P = 4s$. If s increases, what change takes place in P?

   Solution: Assume a set of increasing values for s; for example, 3, 4, and 5. Use the formula to find the corresponding values for P. The table shows that the values for P increase.

   Answer: If s increases, then P increases.

s	P
3	12
4	16
5	20

2. The formula for the perimeter of a square is $P = 4s$. If s is doubled, what change takes place in P?

Solution: Assume a set of values for s in which each number after the first is double the previous one; for example, 4, 8, 16. Find the corresponding values for P. The table shows that each value for P is double the previous value.

s	P
4	16
8	32
16	64

Answer: If s is doubled, then P is doubled.

It is also possible to use algebraic representation to study the effect that a change in one variable in a formula has upon the other variable.

MODEL PROBLEMS

1. If the side of a square is doubled, what change takes place in its perimeter?

Solution: The formula for the perimeter of a square is $P = 4s$. Since the side of the square, s, is to be doubled, the side of the new square can be represented by $2s$. The perimeter of the new square, P', can be found by substituting $2s$ for s in the formula $P = 4s$.

$$P' = 4(2s)$$
$$P' = 8s$$

Since $8s$ is twice $4s$, then P' is twice P.

Answer: The perimeter is doubled.

2. If the side of a square is multiplied by 2, what change takes place in its area?

Solution: The formula for the area of a square is $A = s^2$. Represent the side of the new square by $2s$. Find the area of the new square, A', by substituting $2s$ for s in the formula $A = s^2$.

$$A' = (2s)^2$$
$$A' = (2s)(2s)$$
$$A' = 4s^2$$

Since $4s^2$ is 4 times s^2, then A' is 4 times A.

Answer: The area is multiplied by 4.

Exercises

In 1–16, prepare a table of values to help you complete each statement correctly. In the formula:

1. $p = 3s$, if s is positive and increases, then p _____.
2. $C = 5n$, if n is positive and decreases, then C _____.
3. $D = 50t$, if t is positive and is doubled, then D is _____.
4. $A = 6b$, if b is positive and multiplied by 3, then A is _____.
5. $A = 8h$, if h is positive and is halved, then A is _____.
6. $I = .06p$, if p is positive and divided by 3, then I is _____.
7. $A = s^2$, if s is positive and increases, then A _____.
8. $S = 6e^2$, if e is positive and decreases, then S _____.
9. $V = e^3$, if e is positive and is doubled, then V is _____.

10. $a = \dfrac{360}{n}$, if n is positive and increases, then a _____.

11. $R = \dfrac{60}{I}$, if I is positive and decreases, then R _____.

12. $T = \dfrac{60}{R}$, if R is positive and is doubled, then T is _____.

13. $C = \dfrac{40}{n}$, if n is positive and is halved, then C is _____.

14. $A = 12 - 2b$, if b is positive and increases, then A _____.
15. $A = BH$, if B is positive and remains unchanged and H is positive and increases, then A _____.
16. $D = RT$, if T is positive and remains unchanged and R is positive and decreases, then D _____.

In 17–26, use algebraic representation to discover how to complete the statement correctly. In the formula:

17. $P = 6s$, if s is multiplied by 4, then P is _____.
18. $E = 60R$, if R is divided by 2, then E is _____.
19. $A = 20h$, if h is tripled, then A is _____.
20. $A = s^2$, if s is multiplied by 5, then A is _____.
21. $P = ns$, if n remains unchanged and s is multiplied by 6, then P is _____.
22. $A = lw$, if l remains unchanged and w is halved, then A is _____.
23. $A = \frac{1}{2}bh$, if h remains unchanged and b is doubled, then A is _____.
24. $I = prt$, if p and r are unchanged and t is multiplied by 3, then I is _____.
25. $D = RT$, if R is doubled and T is tripled, then D is multiplied by _____.
26. $p = br$, if b is doubled and r is halved, then p is _____.

27. The formula for the perimeter of a square is $P = 4s$. If the side of the square, s, is multiplied by 10, what change takes place in the perimeter, P?

28. The formula for the area of a square is $A = s^2$. If the side of the square, s, is multiplied by 10, what change takes place in the area, A?

29. The formula for the volume of a cube is $V = e^3$. If the edge of the cube, e, is multiplied by 10, what change takes place in the volume, V?

30. The formula for the area of a rectangle is $A = lw$. Find the change that takes place in the area, A, when:

  a. the length, l, is multiplied by 4 and the width, w, is multiplied by 3.
  b. the length, l, remains unchanged and the width, w, is multiplied by 4.
  c. the length, l, is multiplied by 3 and the width, w, is divided by 3.

8. More Algebraic Representation

If you have difficulty working with the variables in the following questions, it may be helpful to solve similar questions involving arithmetic numbers.

～～～～～～ MODEL PROBLEM ～～～～～～

If 5 pears cost c cents, represent the cost of n pears.

Solution: The cost of 5 pears is c cents. The cost of 1 pear is $\frac{1}{5}$ of c cents, or $\frac{c}{5}$ cents. The cost of n pears is n times the cost of 1 pear, or $n\left(\frac{c}{5}\right)$ cents.

Answer: $n\left(\frac{c}{5}\right)$ cents, or $\frac{nc}{5}$ cents

Exercises

1. If one book costs d dollars, what is the cost of n of these books?

2. A carton contains r cans of sardines. Represent the number of cans in t cartons.

3. Sally's allowance each week is m cents. Represent her allowance for b weeks.

4. A pound of apples costs 17 cents and a pound of peaches costs 29 cents. Represent the cost of r pounds of apples and w pounds of peaches.

5. Represent the cost of k pounds of butter at f cents per pound and t pounds of cheese at m cents per pound.

6. A dealer bought e dozen eggs at r cents per dozen and c pounds of coffee at s cents per pound. Represent the cost of the merchandise.

7. A man bought d dozen apples at c cents an apple and had 15 cents left. Represent the number of cents he had before making the purchase.

8. A man earns d dollars a month and spends s dollars a month. Represent the number of dollars he will save in 3 years.

9. If 8 books cost m dollars, represent the cost of a book.

10. If t toys cost q dollars, represent the cost of one toy.

11. If 3 pens cost n dollars, represent the cost of 5 pens.

12. If 6 boxes of candy cost r dollars, represent the cost of z boxes of this candy.

13. If t pounds of sugar cost 90 cents, represent the cost of 1 pound of sugar.

14. If m chairs weigh 360 pounds, represent the weight of p of these chairs.

15. If n shirts cost c dollars, represent the cost of d shirts.

16. If g gallons of gasoline cost q dollars, represent the cost of s gallons of this gasoline.

17. If t tons of coal cost S dollars, represent the cost of g tons.

18. Two numbers are represented by x and y. Represent the average of the two numbers.

19. A basketball player in 3 games scored P, S, and T points. Represent his average score for the three games.

20. If four boys weigh w, x, y, and z pounds respectively, represent the average of their weights.

21. A ship sailed r miles the first day, s miles the second day, and t miles the third day. Represent the average number of miles it sailed in a day.

22. Represent the width of a rectangle whose area is K and whose length is L.

23. An automobile travels at the average rate of m miles per hour. Represent the distance it travels in h hours.

24. If a plane flies m miles in h hours, represent the average number of miles it flies in 1 hour.

25. Express the number of miles per hour a boat travels if it covers 150 miles in y hours.

26. Represent the number of hours it will take a train to travel 240 miles if it travels at the average rate of h miles per hour.

27. If a car travels b miles in c hours, represent the number of hours required to travel d miles at the same rate of speed.

28. A team won A games and lost B games. What fractional part of all the games played did the team win?

29. In a class, there are b boys and g girls. Represent the fractional part of the class which is girls.

30. In a school, there are x boys, y girls, and z teachers. Represent the number of pupils in every teacher's class if all classes have the same number of pupils.

9. Writing Formulas for Areas

Irregularly shaped geometric plane figures may be formed by combining polygons, circles, and parts of polygons and circles.

To find the area of an irregularly shaped figure, find the areas of the polygons and circles which compose it. Then add or subtract the results as the shape of the irregular figure requires.

~~~~~~~~~~~~~~~~~ **MODEL PROBLEM** ~~~~~~~~~~~~~~~

Write the formula for the area, A, of the shaded figure.

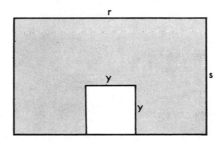

Solution:

Shaded area = area of rectangle — area of square.
Area of rectangle = base × altitude = rs.
Area of square = side × side = $y × y = y^2$.

Answer: $A = rs - y^2$

~~~~~~

Exercises

In 1–18, write the formula for the area, A, of the following shaded figures:

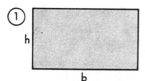

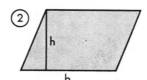

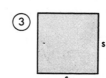

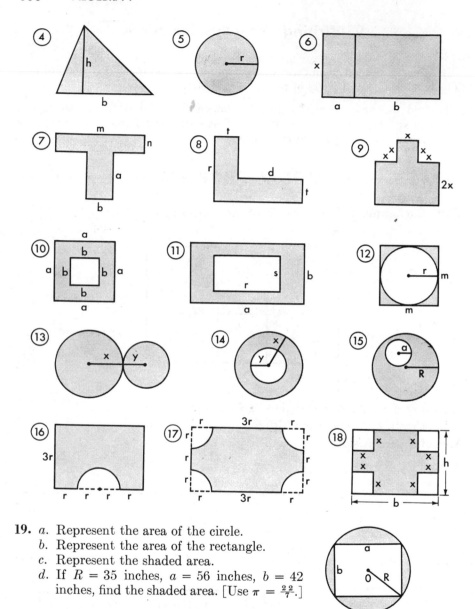

19. a. Represent the area of the circle.
    b. Represent the area of the rectangle.
    c. Represent the shaded area.
    d. If $R = 35$ inches, $a = 56$ inches, $b = 42$
    inches, find the shaded area. [Use $\pi = \frac{22}{7}$.]

20. The dimensions of a rectangle are p and $2q$. From it a circle of radius q and a square of side s are cut.

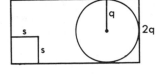

a. Represent the area of the rectangle.
b. Represent the area of the square.
c. Represent the area of the circle.
d. Represent the waste.
e. If $p = 28$ in., $q = 7$ in., $s = 6$ in., and $\pi = \frac{22}{7}$, find the area of the waste.

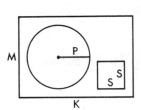

21. Using the diagram at the left:

a. Represent the area of the rectangle.
b. Represent the area of the circle.
c. Represent the area of the square.
d. If the circle and the square are cut from the rectangle, what represents the waste?
e. If $K = 24$ in., $M = 18$ in., $P = 7$ in., $S = 6$ in., and $\pi = \frac{22}{7}$, find the area of the waste.

CHAPTER XV

GRAPHS OF LINEAR OPEN SENTENCES IN TWO VARIABLES

1. Using Ordered Number Pairs To Describe Points on a Map

The figure shows a small part of a map of Watertown. The tourist information center is located at O, the intersection of Main Street and Broadway. From O, a tourist can be directed to any one of four points of interest—A, B, C, or D—by a pair of instructions. For example, to direct a tourist to point A, the instructions might be, "travel east 1 block and then north 3 blocks." These instructions may be written (east 1, north 3).

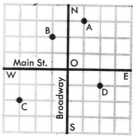

If signed numbers are used to show the direction of travel, distances east of Broadway can be indicated by positive numbers, distances west of Broadway by negative numbers. Also, distances north of Main Street can be indicated by positive numbers, distances south of Main Street by negative numbers. Therefore, the instructions (east 1, north 3) may be represented by the number pair $(+1, +3)$, or simply $(1, 3)$.

It is understood in all such number pairs that the first number always represents a distance east or west of Broadway; the second always represents a distance north or south of Main Street. For this reason $(1, 3)$ is called an **ordered number pair.** We must be careful not to interchange the numbers 1 and 3 in the ordered number pair $(1, 3)$ because the resulting ordered number pair $(3, 1)$ would represent a different point in Watertown. It would represent a point 3 blocks east of Broadway and 1 block north of Main Street.

The instructions to go from O to B can be represented by the ordered number pair $(-1, 2)$, from O to C by $(-3, -2)$, and from O to D by $(2, -1)$.

Exercises

In 1–8, refer to the map of Watertown on page 360. Write an ordered number pair to describe each of the sets of directions which locates a point in Watertown. Always start from the information center, O.

1. Go 2 blocks east, then 1 block north.
2. Go 4 blocks east, then 3 blocks south.
3. Go 3 blocks west, then 2 blocks north.
4. Go 5 blocks west, then 4 blocks south.
5. Stay on Broadway and go 5 blocks north.
6. Stay on Broadway and go 1 block south.
7. Stay on Main Street and go 6 blocks east.
8. Stay on Main Street and go 3 blocks west.

In 9–16, each number pair represents a point in Watertown. Give a set of verbal instructions that would direct a tourist from the information center to the point.

9. $(3, 5)$ 10. $(2, -3)$ 11. $(-6, 4)$ 12. $(-6, -2)$
13. $(0, 4)$ 14. $(5, 0)$ 15. $(-1, 0)$ 16. $(-3, 0)$

17. If you were at the information center and followed the directions represented by the ordered number pair $(0, 0)$, where would you be?

2. Ordered Number Pairs and Points in a Plane

The method used to describe points on a map will now be extended to describe points in a plane. We start with two signed number lines, called **coordinate axes,** drawn at right angles to each other. The horizontal line is called the x-axis. The vertical line is called the y-axis. In a **coordinate plane,** or **Cartesian plane,** the point O at which the two axes intersect is called the **origin.**

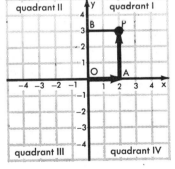

The x-axis and the y-axis divide the plane into 4 regions called **quadrants.** These quadrants are numbered I, II, III, and IV in a counterclockwise order as shown in the drawing.

Point P in the plane can be located by starting at the origin, moving 2 units to the right along the x-axis, then moving 3 units upward in a direction parallel to the y-axis.

Distances measured to the *right* of the y-axis, along the x-axis or along a line parallel to the x-axis, are considered to be *positive;* distances measured to the *left* of the y-axis are considered to be *negative.* Distances measured *upward* from the x-axis, along the y-axis or along a line parallel to the y-axis, are considered to be *positive;* distances measured *downward* from the x-axis are considered to be *negative.*

The distance of a point from the y-axis, measured either along the x-axis or along a line parallel to it, is called the **x-coordinate,** or **abscissa.** The distance of a point from the x-axis, measured either along the y-axis or along a line parallel to it, is called the **y-coordinate,** or **ordinate.** For example, consider point P previously discussed (page 361). The abscissa, BP, which can be read along the x-axis as OA, is $+2$, or 2; the ordinate, AP, which can be read along the y-axis as OB, is $+3$, or 3.

The two numbers which are associated with any particular point, the abscissa and ordinate of the point, are called the **coordinates** of the point. The coordinates of a point may be written as an ordered number pair in which the first number is always the abscissa and the second number is always the ordinate. Thus, the coordinates of point P in the graph at the right may be written (2, 3). The point P is called the **graph** of the ordered number pair (2, 3).

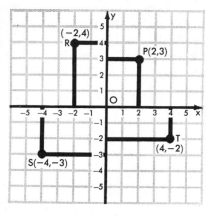

We must be careful not to interchange the numbers 2 and 3 in the number pair (2, 3) because the resulting number pair (3, 2) would be associated with a different point. Each ordered number pair corresponds to only one point in the plane. Also, each point in the plane corresponds to only one ordered number pair. In general, the coordinates of a point may be represented as (x, y).

In the preceding graph, point R in quadrant II is 2 units to the left of the y-axis; thus, the abscissa of point R is -2. Since point R is 4 units above the x-axis, its ordinate is 4. The coordinates of point R may be written $(-2, 4)$. Point R is the graph of the number pair $(-2, 4)$.

Similarly, the point described by $(-4, -3)$ is point S in quadrant III, and the point described by $(4, -2)$ is point T in quadrant IV. When we graph the point described by an ordered number pair, we are **plotting the point.**

Exercises

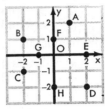

1. Write as ordered number pairs the coordinates of points A, B, C, D, E, F, G, H, and O in the graph.

In 2–26, draw a pair of coordinate axes on a sheet of graph paper and graph the point associated with the ordered number pair.

2. $(5, 4)$	**3.** $(-3, 2)$	**4.** $(2, -6)$	**5.** $(-4, -5)$
6. $(2\frac{1}{4}, -3\frac{3}{4})$	**7.** $(1, 6)$	**8.** $(-8, 5)$	**9.** $(4, -4)$
10. $(-2, -7)$	**11.** $(-1.5, -2.5)$	**12.** $(5, 0)$	**13.** $(-3, 0)$
14. $(8, 0)$	**15.** $(-10, 0)$	**16.** $(3\frac{1}{3}, 0)$	**17.** $(0, 4)$
18. $(0, -6)$	**19.** $(0, 1)$	**20.** $(0, -4)$	**21.** $(0, 0)$
22. $(|2|, |4|)$	**23.** $(|-5|, |3|)$	**24.** $(|1|, |-2|)$	
25. $(|-3|, |-11|)$	**26.** $(-5, |-2|)$		

In 27–31, name the quadrant in which the graph of the point described appears.

27. $(5, 7)$ **28.** $(-3, -2)$ **29.** $(-7, 4)$ **30.** $(1, -3)$ **31.** $(|-2|, |-3|)$

32. Graph the following points: $A(5, 3)$, $B(-5, 3)$, $C(-5, -3)$, $D(5, -3)$. Connect these points with straight lines in the order given. What kind of quadrilateral is $ABCD$?

33. Locate the points described by $(2, -3)$ and $(-3, 2)$. Join them with a straight line. At what point does the line cut the y-axis?

34. Plot the points described by $x = 12$, $y = 5$; and $x = 4$, $y = -3$. What is the value of x where the line joining these two points crosses the x-axis?

35. Plot the points described by $(-1, 2)$ and $(3, -2)$. Join them with a straight line. Where does this line cut the x-axis?

36. Plot the points described by $x = 4$, $y = 2$; and $x = -5$, $y = 5$. Draw the line joining these points. What is the y-value of the point on this line for which the x-value is 1?

37. Graph several points on the x-axis. What is the value of the ordinate for every point in the set of points on the x-axis?

38. Graph several points on the y-axis. What is the value of the abscissa for every point in the set of points on the y-axis?

39. What are the coordinates of the origin on the coordinate axes?

40. The coordinates of point P are (x, y). Name the set of numbers of which the abscissa must be a member, and the set of which the ordinate must be a member if the graph of P is not on the coordinate axes and is in:

   $a.$ quadrant I $b.$ quadrant II $c.$ quadrant III $d.$ quadrant IV

41. Name the quadrant in which the graph of point $P(x, y)$ lies when:

    a. $x > 0$ and $y > 0$ *b.* $x > 0$ and $y < 0$

    c. $x < 0$ and $y > 0$ *d.* $x < 0$ and $y < 0$

42. Name the quadrant in which the graph of the point $P(|x|, |y|)$ lies when:

    a. $x > 0$ and $y > 0$ *b.* $x > 0$ and $y < 0$

    c. $x < 0$ and $y > 0$ *d.* $x < 0$ and $y < 0$

3. Finding Solution Sets of Open Sentences in Two Variables

There are some replacements for x and y that cause $y = 3x$ to become a true sentence. For example, if x is replaced by 1 and y by 3, the resulting sentence $3 = 3 \times 1$ is a true sentence. Therefore, the pair of numbers $x = 1$, $y = 3$ is said to **satisfy** the open sentence in two variables $y = 3x$. Such a pair of numbers is called a **root,** or **solution,** of $y = 3x$. We can write the solution $x = 1$, $y = 3$ as an ordered pair $(1, 3)$ if we agree that the first value in the pair always represents a value of the variable x and the second value always represents a value of the variable y.

On the other hand, there are some replacements for x and y that cause $y = 3x$ to become a false sentence. For example, when x is replaced by 3 and y is replaced by 1, $y = 3x$ becomes $1 = 3 \times 3$, which is a false sentence. Therefore, the pair of numbers $x = 3$, $y = 1$, which may be written as the ordered pair $(3, 1)$, is not a solution of the sentence $y = 3x$.

Since the ordered pair of numbers $(1, 3)$ is a solution of $y = 3x$, while the ordered pair $(3, 1)$ is not, we see that $(1, 3) \neq (3, 1)$. We must be careful not to interchange numbers when dealing with ordered pairs of numbers.

Two ordered pairs of numbers are equal when their first members are equal and when their second members are equal. For example, $(1, 3) = (\frac{5}{5}, \frac{9}{3})$ because $1 = \frac{5}{5}$ and $3 = \frac{9}{3}$.

In general, for all real numbers a, b, c, and d:

$$(a, b) = (c, d) \text{ when } a = c \text{ and } b = d$$

The solutions of $y = 3x$, when the replacement set for x and for y is $\{1, 2, 3, 4, 5, 6, 7, 8, 9\}$, are the ordered pairs $(1, 3)$, $(2, 6)$, and $(3, 9)$. We call this set of ordered pairs $\{(1, 3), (2, 6), (3, 9)\}$ the **solution set** of the sentence $y = 3x$. The solution set of a sentence involving two variables is the set whose members are all the ordered pairs that are solutions of the sentence. If there are no ordered pairs which are solutions of the sentence, we say the solution set is the empty set, $\varnothing$.

If the replacement set is the set of positive numbers, negative numbers, and zero, there are many more members in the solution set of $y = 3x$ than when the replacement set was $\{1, 2, 3, \ldots, 9\}$. Some members of this new solution set are $(-2, -6)$, $(-1, -3)$, $(\frac{1}{3}, 1)$, $(\frac{2}{3}, 2)$, $(10, 30)$. It is impossible to list all the members of the solution set because there are an infinite number of them. In such a case, we can describe the solution set as $\{(x, y) \mid y = 3x\}$, which is read "the set of all ordered pairs (x, y) such that $y = 3x$."

The solution set of $y > 3x$, when the replacement set for x and for y is $\{1, 2, 3, 4, 5, 6, 7, 8, 9\}$, is the set of ordered pairs $\{(1, 4), (1, 5), (1, 6), (1, 7), (1, 8), (1, 9), (2, 7), (2, 8), (2, 9)\}$.

To verify that $(1, 9)$ is a solution of $y > 3x$, we replace x by 1 and y by 9. We obtain $9 > 3 \times 1$, which is a true sentence. All the other ordered pairs of the solution set can be verified in the same way.

If the replacement set is the set of positive numbers, negative numbers, and zero, there are many more members in the solution set of $y > 3x$ than when the replacement set was $\{1, 2, 3, \ldots, 9\}$. Some members of this new solution set are $(-2, -4)$, $(-1, -2)$, $(-1, 2)$, $(-\frac{1}{3}, 1)$, $(\frac{2}{3}, 3)$, $(5, 16)$. It is impossible to list all the members of the solution set because there are an infinite number of them. In such a case, we can describe the solution set as $\{(x, y) \mid y > 3x\}$, which is read "the set of all ordered pairs (x, y) such that $y > 3x$."

~~~~~~~~~~ MODEL PROBLEMS ~~~~~~~~~~

1. Find the value of x and the value of y for which $(2x, 3y) = (10, 2y + 1)$.

   Solution: The ordered pairs $(2x, 3y)$ and $(10, 2y + 1)$ are equal when their first members, $2x$ and 10, are equal. Also, their second members, $3y$ and $2y + 1$, must be equal. Therefore, we solve the equations $2x = 10$ and $3y = 2y + 1$ as follows:

$2x = 10$	$3y = 2y + 1$	*Check*
$x = 5$	$3y - 2y = 2y + 1 - 2y$	$(2x, 3y) = (10, 2y + 1)$
	$y = 1$	$(2 \times 5, 3 \times 1) \stackrel{?}{=} (10, 2 \times 1 + 1)$
		$(10, 3) = (10, 3)$ (true)

   Answer: $x = 5$, $y = 1$

2. Find the solution set of $y - 2x = 4$ when the replacement set for x is $R = \{1, 2, 3, 4, 5\}$ and the replacement set for y is $S = \{6, 7, 8, 9, 10\}$.

How To Proceed	*Solution*
1. Transform the sentence into an equivalent sentence which has y alone as one member.	$y - 2x = 4$ $y - 2x + 2x = 4 + 2x$ $y = 2x + 4$

2. Replace x by each member of R, the replacement set for x. Then compute each of the corresponding y-values.

3. Determine whether or not each y-value computed in step 2 is a member of S, the replacement set for y. If the y-value belongs to S, then the ordered pair of the corresponding x- and y-values is a solution of the sentence.

Answer: Solution set is
$\{(1, 6), (2, 8), (3, 10)\}$.

x	$2x + 4$	y
1	$2 \times 1 + 4$	6 is a member of S
2	$2 \times 2 + 4$	8 is a member of S
3	$2 \times 3 + 4$	10 is a member of S
4	$2 \times 4 + 4$	12 is not a member of S
5	$2 \times 5 + 4$	14 is not a member of S

3. Find the solution set of $y - 2x > 4$ when the replacement set for x is $R = \{1, 2, 3, 4, 5\}$ and the replacement set for y is $S = \{6, 7, 8, 9, 10\}$.

How To Proceed

1. Transform the sentence into an equivalent sentence which has y alone as one member.

2. Replace x by each member of R, the replacement set for x. Then compute the corresponding y-values.

3. If any y-values computed in step 2 are members of S (S is the replacement set for y), then each ordered pair of the corresponding x- and y-values is a solution of the sentence.

Solution

$$y - 2x > 4$$
$$y - 2x + 2x > 4 + 2x$$
$$y > 2x + 4$$

x	$2x + 4$	$y > 2x + 4$	y
1	$2 \times 1 + 4$	$y > 6$	7, 8, 9, 10
2	$2 \times 2 + 4$	$y > 8$	9, 10
3	$2 \times 3 + 4$	$y > 10$	no values in S
4	$2 \times 4 + 4$	$y > 12$	no values in S
5	$2 \times 5 + 4$	$y > 14$	no values in S

Answer: Solution set is $\{(1, 7), (1, 8), (1, 9), (1, 10), (2, 9), (2, 10)\}$.

Exercises

In 1–10, find the missing member in each ordered pair if the second member of the pair is twice the first member.

1. $(3, ?)$ **2.** $(\frac{1}{2}, ?)$ **3.** $(0, ?)$ **4.** $(-2, ?)$ **5.** $(a, ?)$
6. $(?, 10)$ **7.** $(?, 11)$ **8.** $(?, 0)$ **9.** $(?, -8)$ **10.** $(?, a)$

In 11–20, find the missing member in each ordered pair if the first member of the pair is 4 more than the second member.

11. $(?, 5)$ **12.** $(?, \frac{1}{2})$ **13.** $(?, 0)$ **14.** $(?, -6)$ **15.** $(?, a)$
16. $(12, ?)$ **17.** $(9\frac{1}{4}, ?)$ **18.** $(0, ?)$ **19.** $(-8, ?)$ **20.** $(a, ?)$

In 21–26, find the value for x and the value for y for which the ordered pairs of numbers are equal.

21. $(x, 15)$ and $(10, y)$
22. $(2x, 21)$ and $(20, 7y)$
23. $(5x, 4y)$ and $(2x + 12, 3y + 6)$
24. $(3x - 1, y - 3)$ and $(x + 7, 4y + 12)$
25. $(\frac{1}{2}x, 6)$ and $(4, \frac{2}{3}y)$
26. $(\frac{1}{3}x, y + 20)$ and $(x - 12, \frac{1}{5}y - 5)$

27. State the relationship that must exist between x and y in order that $(x, y) = (y, x)$.

In 28–41, state whether the given ordered pair of numbers is a solution of the sentence. The replacement set for x and for y is the set of whole numbers.

28. $y = 5x$; $(3, 15)$ **29.** $y = 4x$; $(16, 4)$
30. $y = 3x + 1$; $(7, 22)$ **31.** $y = x - 3$; $(4, 7)$
32. $2x + 3y = 13$; $(5, 1)$ **33.** $4x - 5y = 18$; $(7, 2)$
34. $3x - 2y = 0$; $(3, 2)$ **35.** $6y = 5x + 5$; $(2, 1)$
36. $y > 4x$; $(2, 10)$ **37.** $y < 2x + 3$; $(0, 2)$
38. $3y > 2x + 1$; $(4, 3)$ **39.** $x + 3y < 10$; $(2, 3)$
40. $2x + 3y \leq 9$; $(0, 3)$ **41.** $5x - 4y \geq 23$; $(4, 3)$

In 42–49, state whether the given ordered pair of numbers is a solution of the sentence. The replacement set for x and for y is the set of positive numbers, negative numbers, and zero.

42. $x + y = 8$; $(4, 5)$ **43.** $4x + 3y = 2$; $(\frac{1}{4}, \frac{1}{3})$
44. $3x = y + 4$; $(-7, -1)$ **45.** $x - 2y = 15$; $(1, -7)$
46. $y > 6x$; $(-1, -2)$ **47.** $3x < 4y$; $(5, 2)$
48. $y \geq 3 - 2x$; $(-1, 6)$ **49.** $5x - 2y \leq 19$; $(3, -2)$

In 50–57, find the solution set of the sentence.

50. $y = 2x$ when the replacement set for x is $\{1, 2\}$ and the replacement set for y is $\{1, 2, 3, 4, 5\}$.
51. $x + y = 4$ when the replacement set for x is $\{5, 7\}$ and the replacement set for y is {natural numbers}.

52. $y = 3x - 1$ when the replacement set for x is $\{-3, -1, 2\}$ and the replacement set for y is $\{$positive numbers, negative numbers, zero$\}$.

53. $4x + y = 2$ when the replacement set for x is $\{5, 6, 7\}$ and the replacement set for y is $\{$positive numbers$\}$.

54. $y > x + 2$ when the replacement set for x is $\{2, 3, 4\}$ and the replacement set for y is $\{5, 6\}$.

55. $y < 2x - 1$ when the replacement set for x is $\{5, 6\}$ and the replacement set for y is $\{8, 9, 10, 11\}$.

56. $x + y \geq 12$ when the replacement set for x is $\{-7, 10, 12\}$ and the replacement set for y is $\{-2, 2, 6, 10\}$.

57. $y - 3 \leq 2x$ when the replacement set for x is $\{-1, 0, 1, 2\}$ and the replacement set for y is $\{-1, 0, 1, 2\}$.

In 58–63, use set notation to describe the solution set when the replacement set for x and for y is the set of positive numbers, negative numbers, and zero.

58. $y = 6x$ **59.** $y = x + 9$ **60.** $3x + y = 11$

61. $y > 10x$ **62.** $y < 3x - 1$ **63.** $y - x \geq 4$

4. Graphing a Linear Equation in Two Variables by Means of Its Solutions

If we wish to find number pairs which satisfy the equation $x + y = 6$, we can replace one variable, for example x, by a convenient value. Then we can solve the resulting equation for the value of the other variable, y. If we let $x = 1$, then $1 + y = 6$ and $y = 5$. Thus, the ordered pair $(1, 5)$ is a solution of $x + y = 6$.

We can also transform the equation $x + y = 6$ into an equivalent equation in which y stands alone on one side of the equation. Then we can assign a value to x and find the corresponding value of y. For example:

$$x + y = 6$$
$$y = 6 - x$$
$$\text{Let } x = 1: \quad y = 6 - 1$$
$$y = 5$$

Thus, a solution of $x + y = 6$ is $(1, 5)$, the same result as before.

If the replacement set for both x and y is $\{$signed numbers$\}$, we can find an infinite number of ordered pairs that are solutions of $x + y = 6$. Some of these solutions are shown in the table on the following page.

x	7	6	5	4	3	$2\frac{1}{2}$	2	1	$\frac{1}{2}$	0	-1
y	-1	0	1	2	3	$3\frac{1}{2}$	4	5	$5\frac{1}{2}$	6	7

Let us plot the points associated with the ordered number pairs that are shown in the table. Notice that these points seem to lie on a straight line. In fact, if {signed numbers} is the replacement set for both x and y, then the following is true:

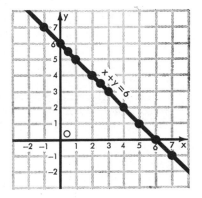

The graphs of all ordered pairs (x, y) which are solutions of $x + y = 6$ lie on this same line; the graphs of all ordered pairs which are not solutions of $x + y = 6$ do not lie on this line.

This line, which is the set of all those points and only those points whose coordinates satisfy the equation $x + y = 6$, is called the **graph** of $x + y = 6$.

A first-degree equation in two variables, such as $x + y = 6$, may be written in the form $Ax + By + C = 0$, where A, B, and C are signed numbers, with A and B not both zero. It can be proved that the graph of such an equation is a straight line. We therefore call such an equation a **linear equation.**

When we graph a linear equation, we may determine the straight line by plotting two points whose coordinates satisfy that equation. However, we always plot a third point as a check on the first two. If the third point lies on the line determined by the first two points, we have probably made no error.

[*Note:* When we graph a linear equation, the replacement set of the variables is {signed numbers} unless otherwise indicated.]

KEEP IN MIND

1. Every ordered pair of numbers which satisfies an equation represents the coordinates of a point on the graph of the equation.
2. Every point on the graph of an equation has as its coordinates an ordered pair of numbers which satisfies the equation.

MODEL PROBLEM

a. Write the following verbal sentence as an equation: "The sum of twice the abscissa of a point and the ordinate of that point is 4."

b. Graph the equation written in part *a.*

a. Solution: Let x = the abscissa of the point.

Let y = the ordinate of the point.

Then $2x + y = 4$ *Ans.*

b.   *How To Proceed*   *Solution*

1. Transform the equation into an equivalent equation which has y alone as one member.

$$2x + y = 4$$
$$y = -2x + 4$$

x	$-2x + 4$	y
0	$-2(0) + 4$	4
1	$-2(1) + 4$	2
2	$-2(2) + 4$	0

2. Determine 3 solutions of the equation by assuming values for x and computing the corresponding values for y.

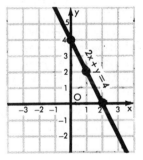

3. Plot the points which are associated with the 3 solutions found previously.

4. Draw a straight line through the points which were plotted.

Exercises

1. In each part, state whether the pair of values for x and y satisfies the equation $2x - y = 6$.

   a. $x = 0, y = 6$ *b.* $x = 2, y = 2$

   c. $x = 4, y = 2$ *d.* $x = 4, y = -2$

In 2–4, plot the points that are associated with the ordered number pairs in the table and draw the line on which they seem to lie.

2.
x	0	1	2
y	0	4	8

3.
x	-1	0	1
y	-1	1	3

4.
x	-1	4	2
y	-6	9	3

In 5–13, solve the equation for y in terms of x.

5. $y - x = 5$ **6.** $3x + y = -1$ **7.** $4x - y = 6$
8. $2y = 6x$ **9.** $6x + 3y = 0$ **10.** $12x = \frac{3}{2}y$
11. $4x + 2y = 8$ **12.** $6x - 3y = 5$ **13.** $3x + 2y + 8 = 0$

In 14–16, find the missing values of the variable needed to complete the table. Plot the points described by the pairs of values in the completed table; then draw the line on which they seem to lie.

14. $y = 4x$

x	y
0	?
1	?
2	?

15. $y = 3x + 1$

x	y
-1	?
0	?
1	?

16. $x + 2y = 3$

x	y
-1	?
2	?
5	?

In 17–40, graph the equation.

17. $y = 2x$ **18.** $y = 5x$ **19.** $y = -3x$
20. $y = -x$ **21.** $x = 2y$ **22.** $x = 3y$
23. $x = -y$ **24.** $x = \frac{1}{2}y$ **25.** $y = x + 3$
26. $y = 2x - 1$ **27.** $y = 3x + 1$ **28.** $y = -2x + 4$
29. $x + y = 8$ **30.** $y + x = 4$ **31.** $x - y = 5$
32. $y - x = 0$ **33.** $2x + y = 10$ **34.** $x + 3y = 12$
35. $x - 2y = 0$ **36.** $y - 3x = -5$ **37.** $2x + 3y = 6$
38. $3x + 4y = 12$ **39.** $3x - 2y = -6$ **40.** $4x + 3y = -12$

In 41–46, state whether the point whose coordinates are given is on the graph of the given equation.

41. $x + y = 7$; $(4, 3)$ **42.** $x - y = 5$; $(9, 4)$
43. $2y + x = 7$; $(1, 3)$ **44.** $3x - 2y = 8$; $(2, 1)$
45. $4x + y = 10$; $(2, -2)$ **46.** $2y = 3x - 5$; $(-1, -4)$

In 47–49, a point is to lie on the graph of each equation. Find its abscissa (x-value) if its ordinate (y-value) is the number indicated in the parentheses.

47. $x + y = 12$; (5) **48.** $2x - y = 8$; (-2) **49.** $3x + 2y = 24$; (3)

In 50–55: *a.* Write the verbal sentence as an equation.

           b. Graph the equation.

50. The ordinate of a point is equal to the abscissa.

51. The ordinate of a point is twice the abscissa.

52. The ordinate of a point is 2 more than the abscissa.

53. The ordinate of a point is 4 less than 3 times the abscissa.

54. The sum of the ordinate and abscissa of a point is 6.

55. Twice the ordinate of a point decreased by 3 times the abscissa is 6.

In 56–58, a point is to lie on the graph of each equation. Find its ordinate if its abscissa is the number indicated in the parentheses.

56. $x + 2y = 9$; (3)   **57.** $4x - y = 7$; (-1)   **58.** $2x + 3y = 5$; (-2)

In 59–61, find a value which can replace k so that the graph of the resulting equation will pass through the point whose coordinates are given.

59. $x + y = k$; (2, 5)   **60.** $x - y = k$; (5, -3)   **61.** $5y - 2x = k$; (-2, -1)

5. Graphing a Linear Equation in Two Variables by the Intercepts Method

The ***x-intercept*** of a line is the x-coordinate of the point at which the line intersects the x-axis. The graph of the equation $y = \frac{2}{3}x + 2$, shown in the figure, intersects the x-axis at $A(-3, 0)$. Therefore, the x-intercept of the graph of $y = \frac{2}{3}x + 2$ is -3. Notice that the value of y at point A must be zero since A is on the x-axis.

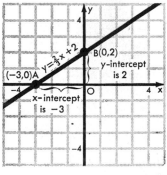

The ***y-intercept*** of a line is the y-coordinate of the point at which the line intersects the y-axis. The graph of $y = \frac{2}{3}x + 2$ intersects the y-axis at $B(0, 2)$. Therefore, the y-intercept of the graph of $y = \frac{2}{3}x + 2$ is 2. Notice that the value of x at point B must be 0 since B is on the y-axis.

FINDING THE INTERCEPTS OF A LINE

Procedure. To find the *x*-intercept of a line, substitute 0 for *y* in the equation of the line. Then solve the resulting equation for *x*.

To find the *y*-intercept of a line, substitute 0 for *x* in the equation of the line. Then solve the resulting equation for *y*.

Study the model problem on the following page to learn how to graph a linear equation by the intercepts method.

～～～～～～～～～ MODEL PROBLEM ～～～～～～～～～

Find the x- and y-intercepts of the line $2x - y = 4$. Then use these intercepts to graph the equation.

How To Proceed   *Solution*

1. Find the x-intercept by substituting 0 for y; find the y-intercept by substituting 0 for x.

<table>
<tr><td>*x-intercept*</td><td>*y-intercept*</td></tr>
<tr><td>$2x - y = 4$</td><td>$2x - y = 4$</td></tr>
<tr><td>$2x - 0 = 4$</td><td>$2(0) - y = 4$</td></tr>
<tr><td>$2x = 4$</td><td>$-y = 4$</td></tr>
<tr><td>$x = 2$</td><td>$y = -4$</td></tr>
</table>

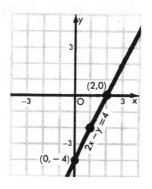

2. On the x-axis, graph a point whose abscissa is the x-intercept. Since $x = 2$ when $y = 0$, the point is $(2, 0)$. On the y-axis, graph a point whose ordinate is the y-intercept. Since $y = -4$ when $x = 0$, the point is $(0, -4)$.

3. Draw a line through these points.

4. To check, find a third pair of values that satisfies the equation. The graph of this pair of values must be on the line.

Check

$$2x - y = 4$$
$$\text{Let } x = 1: 2(1) - y = 4$$
$$-y = 2$$
$$y = -2$$

The point $(1, -2)$ is on the graph of the line.

～～～～～～～～～～～～～～～～～～～～～～～～～～～～～～

Exercises

In 1–6, find the x-intercept and y-intercept of the line which is the graph of the equation.

1. $x + y = 8$ 2. $x - 5y = 10$ 3. $y = 4x + 12$
4. $y = 6x$ 5. $4x - 3y = -12$ 6. $5x + 3y = 8$

In 7–15, draw the graph of the equation by the intercepts method.

7. $x + y = 3$ **8.** $2x + y = 8$ **9.** $3x - y = 12$

10. $y = 2x + 8$ **11.** $y = -3x + 6$ **12.** $x = 4y - 12$

13. $2x + 3y = 6$ **14.** $5x - 4y = 20$ **15.** $3x - 6y = 9$

16. *a.* Find the x-intercept and y-intercept for the graph of the equation $y = 3x$.

    b. Can you graph the equation $y = 3x$ by the intercepts method?

    c. Draw the graph of $y = 3x$ using another method.

6. Graphing Lines Parallel to the X-Axis or Y-Axis

LINES PARALLEL TO THE X-AXIS

Study the graph. Line AB, whose y-intercept is 2, is parallel to the x-axis. Notice that the y-value of each ordered pair that is associated with a point on line AB equals 2. This is true no matter what the value of x is. Therefore, an equation of line AB is written simply $y = 2$. Similarly, $y = -2$ represents an equation of a line (CD) whose graph is parallel to the x-axis and whose y-intercept is -2.

An equation for a line parallel to the x-axis, when its y-intercept is a, is $y = a$.

LINES PARALLEL TO THE Y-AXIS

Study the graph. Line EF, whose x-intercept is 2, is parallel to the y-axis. Notice that the x-value of each ordered pair that is associated with a point of line EF equals 2. This is true no matter what the value of y is. Therefore, an equation of line EF is written simply $x = 2$. Similarly, $x = -2$ represents an equation of a line (GH) whose graph is parallel to the y-axis and whose x-intercept is -2.

An equation for a line parallel to the y-axis, when its x-intercept is b, is $x = b$.

Exercises

In 1–10, draw the graph of the equation.

1. $x = 6$ **2.** $x = \frac{2}{3}$ **3.** $x = 0$ **4.** $x = -3$ **5.** $x = -5$

6. $y = 4$ **7.** $y = 2\frac{1}{4}$ **8.** $y = 0$ **9.** $y = -4$ **10.** $y = -7$

11. Write an equation of a line that is parallel to the x-axis and whose y-intercept is:

    a. 1   *b.* 5   *c.* -4 *d.* -8 *e.* -2.5

12. Write an equation of a line that is parallel to the y-axis and whose x-intercept is:

    a. 3   *b.* 10   *c.* $4\frac{1}{2}$ *d.* -6 *e.* -10

7. The Slope of a Line

MEANING OF THE SLOPE OF A LINE

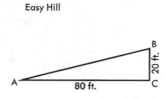
Easy Hill

Tough Hill

It is more difficult to hike up Tough Hill than it is to hike up Easy Hill. Tough Hill rises 40 ft. vertically over a horizontal distance of 80 ft., whereas Easy Hill rises only 20 ft. vertically over the same horizontal distance of 80 ft. Therefore, Tough Hill is steeper than Easy Hill. To compare the steepness of roads AB and DE, roads which lead up the two hills, we compare their **slopes.**

The slope of road AB is the ratio of the change in vertical distance, CB, to the change in horizontal distance, AC:

$$\text{slope of road } AB = \frac{\text{change in vertical distance, } CB}{\text{change in horizontal distance, } AC} = \frac{20 \text{ ft.}}{80 \text{ ft.}} = \frac{1}{4}$$

Also:

$$\text{slope of road } DE = \frac{\text{change in vertical distance, } FE}{\text{change in horizontal distance, } DF} = \frac{40 \text{ ft.}}{80 \text{ ft.}} = \frac{1}{2}$$

Since road DE rises $\frac{1}{2}$ ft. vertically for each 1 ft. of horizontal distance, whereas road AB rises only $\frac{1}{4}$ ft. vertically for each 1 ft. of horizontal distance, road DE is steeper than road AB.

FINDING THE SLOPE OF A LINE

Procedure. To find the slope of a line:
1. **Select any two points on the line.**
2. **Find the horizontal change, the change in *x*-values, in going from the point on the left to the point on the right.**
3. **Find the vertical change, the change in *y*-values, in going from the point on the left to the point on the right.**
4. **Divide the vertical change by the horizontal change.**

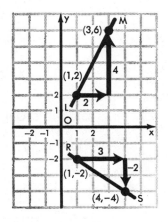

For example, in the figure:

$$\text{slope of } LM = \frac{\text{vertical change}}{\text{horizontal change}} = \frac{4}{2} = 2$$

$$\text{slope of } RS = \frac{\text{vertical change}}{\text{horizontal change}} = \frac{-2}{3} = -\frac{2}{3}$$

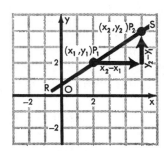

In general, the slope, m, of a line RS which passes through two points $P_1(x_1, y_1)$ and $P_2(x_2, y_2)$ is the ratio of the difference of the y-values of these points to the difference of the corresponding x-values. Thus:

$$\textbf{slope of line} = \frac{\textbf{difference in } y\textbf{-values}}{\textbf{difference in } x\textbf{-values}}$$

$$m = \frac{y_2 - y_1}{x_2 - x_1}$$

The expression "difference in x-values," $x_2 - x_1$, is usually represented by Δx, read "delta x." Similarly, the "difference in y-values," $y_2 - y_1$, is usually represented by Δy, read "delta y." Therefore, we write:

$$\textbf{slope of line} = \textbf{\textit{m}} = \frac{\Delta y}{\Delta x}$$

POSITIVE SLOPES

As a point moves along line AB from left to right, for example, from C to D, the line is rising. As the x-values increase, the y-values also increase. Between point C and point D, the change in y (Δy) is 1; the change in x (Δx) is 2. Since both Δy and Δx are positive, the slope of line AB must be positive.

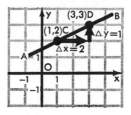

$$\text{slope} = m = \frac{\Delta y}{\Delta x} = \frac{1}{2}$$

This example illustrates:

Principle 1. As a point moves from left to right along a line that is rising, y increases as x increases and the slope of the line is positive.

NEGATIVE SLOPES

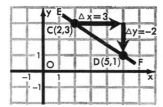

As a point moves along line EF from left to right, for example, from C to D, the line is falling. As the x-values increase, the y-values decrease. Between point C and point D, the change in y (Δy) is -2; the change in x (Δx) is 3. Since Δy is negative and Δx is positive, the slope of line EF must be negative.

$$\text{slope} = m = \frac{\Delta y}{\Delta x} = \frac{-2}{3} = -\frac{2}{3}$$

This example illustrates:

Principle 2. As a point moves from left to right along a line that is falling, y decreases as x increases and the slope of the line is negative.

ZERO SLOPE

Line GH is parallel to the x-axis. Consider a point moving along GH from left to right, for example, from C to D: As the x-values increase, the y-values are unchanged. Between point C and point D, the change in y (Δy) is 0, and the change in x (Δx) is 3. Since Δy is 0 and Δx is 3, the slope of line GH must be 0.

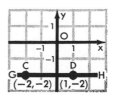

$$\text{slope} = m = \frac{\Delta y}{\Delta x} = \frac{0}{3} = 0$$

The preceding example illustrates:

Principle 3. If a line is parallel to the x-axis, its slope is 0.

[*Note:* The slope of the x-axis itself is also 0.]

NO SLOPE

Line LM is parallel to the y-axis. Consider a point moving upward along LM, for example, from C to D: The x-values are unchanged, but the y-values increase. Between point C and point D, the change in y (Δy) is 3 and the change in x (Δx) is 0. Since the slope of line $LM = \dfrac{\Delta y}{\Delta x} = \dfrac{3}{0}$, and a non-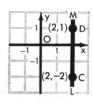
zero number cannot be divided by 0, line LM has no defined slope.

. This example illustrates:

Principle 4. If a line is parallel to the y-axis, it has no defined slope.

[*Note:* The y-axis itself has no defined slope.]

~~~~~~~~~~~~~~~ **MODEL PROBLEMS** ~~~~~~~~~~~~~~~

1. Find the slope of the straight line which passes through the points $(-2, 4)$ and $(4, 2)$.

   Solution: Plot the points $(-2, 4)$ and $(4, 2)$. Let the point $(-2, 4)$ be $P_1(x_1, y_1)$, and let the point $(4, 2)$ be $P_2(x_2, y_2)$. Then $x_1 = -2$, $y_1 = 4$; $x_2 = 4$, $y_2 = 2$.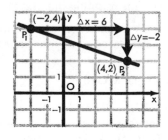

   $$\text{slope of line } P_1P_2 = \frac{\Delta y}{\Delta x} = \frac{y_2 - y_1}{x_2 - x_1}$$

   $$= \frac{(2) - (4)}{(4) - (-2)}$$

   $$= \frac{2 - 4}{4 + 2}$$

   $$= \frac{-2}{6} = -\frac{1}{3}$$

   Answer: $-\frac{1}{3}$

2. Through the point $(2, -1)$, draw a line whose slope is $\frac{3}{2}$.

How To Proceed Solution

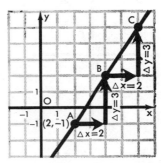

1. Graph the point $A(2, -1)$.

2. Since slope $= \dfrac{\Delta y}{\Delta x} = \dfrac{\to 3}{\to 2}$, when x changes 2, then y changes 3.

3. Start at point $A(2, -1)$ and move 2 units to the right and 3 units upward to locate point B. Start at B and repeat these movements to locate point C.

4. Draw a straight line which passes through points A, B, and C.

KEEP IN MIND

A fundamental property of a straight line is that its slope is constant. Therefore, any two points on a line may be used to compute the slope of the line.

Exercises

1. In a–f, tell whether the line has a positive slope, a negative slope, a slope of zero, or no slope.

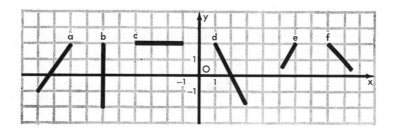

2. In a–f, find the slope of the line; if the line has no slope, indicate that fact.

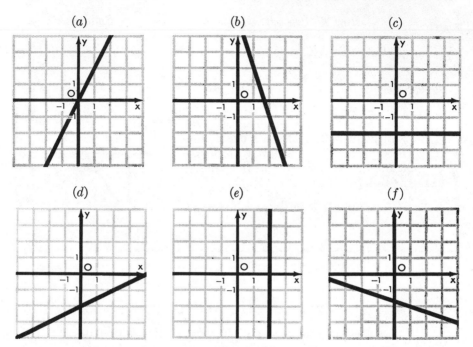

(a)　　　　　　　(b)　　　　　　　(c)

(d)　　　　　　　(e)　　　　　　　(f)

In 3–14, plot both points, draw the straight line which joins them, and find the slope of this line.

3. $(0, 0)$ and $(4, 4)$　　　**4.** $(0, 0)$ and $(4, 8)$　　　**5.** $(0, 0)$ and $(9, 3)$

6. $(0, 0)$ and $(3, -6)$　　**7.** $(1, 5)$ and $(3, 9)$　　　**8.** $(5, 8)$ and $(4, 3)$

9. $(7, 3)$ and $(1, -1)$　　**10.** $(-2, 4)$ and $(0, 2)$　　**11.** $(5, -2)$ and $(7, -8)$

12. $(4, 2)$ and $(8, 2)$　　　**13.** $(-1, 3)$ and $(2, 3)$　　**14.** $(6, -1)$ and $(-2, -1)$

15. Find the value of y so that the slope of the line passing through the points $(2, y)$ and $(6, 10)$ will be:

　　$a.$ 1　　　$b.$ 2　　　$c.$ $\frac{1}{2}$　　　$d.$ 0

In 16–19, use the definition of the slope of a line to determine whether the points lie on the same line (are *collinear*).

16. $(1, 3)$; $(2, 5)$; $(3, 7)$　　　　　**17.** $(-1, 5)$; $(0, 2)$; $(1, -1)$

18. $(2, 5)$; $(4, 9)$; $(6, 15)$　　　　　**19.** $(-4, -1)$; $(0, 3)$; $(2, 5)$

In 20–28, draw a line with the given slope, m, through the given point.

20. $(0, 0)$; $m = 2$ **21.** $(1, 3)$; $m = 3$ **22.** $(2, -5)$; $m = 4$

23. $(4, 6)$; $m = \frac{2}{3}$ **24.** $(-4, 5)$; $m = \frac{1}{2}$ **25.** $(-3, -4)$; $m = -2$

26. $(1, -5)$; $m = -1$ **27.** $(2, 4)$; $m = -\frac{3}{2}$ **28.** $(-2, 3)$; $m = -\frac{1}{3}$

8. The Slope and Y-Intercept of a Line

Figure 1

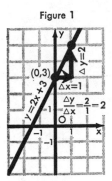

Figure 2

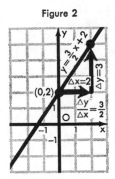

Figure 3

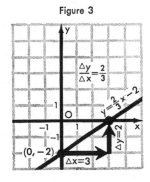

Each of the preceding figures shows the line which is the graph of the indicated equation. We can see that the slope of each line is the coefficient of the x-term in the equation and that the y-intercept of each line is the *constant* which follows the x-term in the equation.

	Equation	Slope $\left(\dfrac{\Delta y}{\Delta x}\right)$	y-intercept
In Fig. 1:	$y = 2x + 3$	2	3
In Fig. 2:	$y = \frac{3}{2}x + 2$	$\frac{3}{2}$	2
In Fig. 3:	$y = \frac{2}{3}x - 2$	$\frac{2}{3}$	-2

These examples illustrate the following general principle:

If a linear equation is expressed in the form $y = mx + b$, then the slope of the line is m, the coefficient of x; the y-intercept is b, the constant term.

~~~~~~~~~~ **MODEL PROBLEM** ~~~~~~~~~~

Find the slope and y-intercept of the line which is the graph of $4x + 2y = 10$.

How To Proceed	*Solution*
1. Transform the equation into an equivalent equation of the form $y = mx + b$ by solving for y in terms of x.	$4x + 2y = 10$ $2y = -4x + 10$ $y = -2x + 5$
2. The coefficient of x is the slope.	slope $= -2$
3. The constant term is the y-intercept.	y-intercept $= 5$

Answer: slope $= -2$, y-intercept $= 5$

~~~~~~

Exercises

In 1–21, find the slope and y-intercept of the line which is the graph of the equation.

1. $y = 3x + 1$ **2.** $y = x - 3$ **3.** $y = 2x$

4. $y = x$ **5.** $y = \frac{1}{2}x + 5$ **6.** $y = \frac{3}{4}x - \frac{1}{2}$

7. $y = -2x + 3$ **8.** $y = -x - 4$ **9.** $y = -3x$

10. $y = -2$ **11.** $y = -\frac{2}{3}x + 4$ **12.** $y = -\frac{1}{2}x - 2$

13. $y - 3x = 7$ **14.** $2x + y = 5$ **15.** $3x - y = 4$

16. $3y = 6x + 9$ **17.** $2y = 5x - 4$ **18.** $2x + 3y = 6$

19. $\frac{1}{2}x + \frac{3}{4} = \frac{1}{3}y$ **20.** $4x - 3y = 0$ **21.** $2y = 5(x + 1)$

In 22–33, write an equation of the line whose slope and y-intercept are respectively:

22. 2 and 7   **23.** 3 and -5 **24.** -4 and 2

25. -1 and -3 **26.** -2 and 4   **27.** -3 and 0

28. $\frac{2}{3}$ and 1   **29.** $\frac{3}{5}$ and -2 **30.** $\frac{1}{2}$ and 0

31. $-\frac{1}{3}$ and 2   **32.** $-\frac{4}{3}$ and $-\frac{1}{3}$ **33.** $-\frac{3}{2}$ and 0

34. Write equations for three lines so that the slope of each line is 2.

35. Write equations for three lines so that the y-intercept of each line is -4.

36. What do the graphs of the lines described by the equations $y = 4x$, $y = 4x + 2$, and $y = 4x - 2$ all have in common?

37. How are the graphs of $y = mx + b$ affected when m is always replaced by the same number and b is replaced by different numbers?

38. What do the lines which are the graphs of the equations $y = 2x + 1$, $y = 3x + 1$, and $y = -4x + 1$ all have in common?

39. How are the graphs of $y = mx + b$ affected when b is always replaced by the same number and m is replaced by different numbers?

40. If two lines are parallel, what is the relation of their slopes?
41. What will be true of two lines whose slopes are equal?

In 42–45, state whether the sets of lines are parallel.
42. $y = 3x + 2$, $y = 3x - 5$ **43.** $y = -2x - 6$, $y = 2x + 6$
44. $y = 4x - 8$, $y - 4x = 3$ **45.** $y = 2x$, $2y - 4x = 9$

9. Graphing a Linear Equation in Two Variables by the Slope-Intercept Method

The slope and y-intercept of a line can be used to draw the graph of a linear equation.

~~~~~~~~~~~~~ MODEL PROBLEM ~~~~~~~~~~~~

Draw the graph of $2x + 3y = 9$ using the slope-intercept method.

How To Proceed	Solution

1. Transform the equation to the form $y = mx + b$.

$$2x + 3y = 9$$
$$3y = -2x + 9$$
$$y = \frac{-2}{3}x + 3$$

2. Find the slope of the line.

$$\text{slope} = \frac{-2}{3}$$

3. Find the y-intercept of the line.

$$y\text{-intercept} = 3$$

4. Graph a point A on the y-axis whose ordinate is the y-intercept.
5. Use the slope to find two more points on the line. Since slope $= \dfrac{\Delta y}{\Delta x} \to \dfrac{-2}{3}$, when x changes 3, y changes -2. Start at point A and move 3 units to the right and 2 units down to locate point B. Start at point B and repeat this procedure to locate point C.
6. Draw the line which passes through the three points.

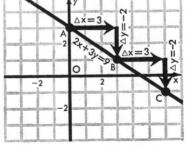

~~~~~~

Exercises

In 1–24, graph the equation using the slope and the y-intercept of each line (the slope-intercept method).

1. $y = 2x + 3$
2. $y = 2x - 5$
3. $y = 2x$
4. $y = x - 2$
5. $y = 2x - 2$
6. $y = 3x - 2$
7. $y = 3x$
8. $y = 5x$
9. $y = -2x$
10. $y = \frac{2}{3}x + 2$
11. $y = \frac{1}{2}x - 1$
12. $y = \frac{3}{2}x$
13. $y = \frac{1}{3}x$
14. $y = -\frac{4}{3}x + 5$
15. $y = -\frac{3}{4}x$
16. $y - 2x = 8$
17. $3x + y = 4$
18. $2y = 4x + 6$
19. $3y = 4x + 9$
20. $4x - y = 3$
21. $3x + 4y = 12$
22. $2x = 3y + 6$
23. $4x + 3y = 0$
24. $2x - 3y - 6 = 0$

10. Writing an Equation for a Line

Procedure. To write an equation for a line, determine its slope and y-intercept. Then use the slope-intercept formula $y = mx + b$.

～～～～～～～ MODEL PROBLEMS ～～～～～～～

1. Write an equation of a line whose slope is 4 and which passes through the point (3, 5).

How To Proceed	*Solution*
1. In the equation of a line $y = mx + b$, replace m by the given slope, 4.	$y = mx + b$ $y = 4x + b$
2. Since the given point (3, 5) is on the line, its coordinates satisfy the equation $y = 4x + b$. Replace x by 3 and y by 5.	$5 = 4(3) + b$ $5 = 12 + b$ $-7 = b$
3. In $y = 4x + b$, replace b by -7.	$y = 4x - 7$

Answer: $y = 4x - 7$

2. Write an equation of a line which passes through the points (2, 5) and (4, 11).

How To Proceed	*Solution*
1. Find the slope of the line which passes through the two given points, (2, 5) and (4, 11).	Let P_1 be (2, 5). Let P_2 be (4, 11). $m = \dfrac{y_2 - y_1}{x_2 - x_1}$ $m = \dfrac{11 - 5}{4 - 2} = \dfrac{6}{2} = 3$

2. In $y = mx + b$, replace m by the slope, 3. $\qquad$ $y = mx + b$
$$y = 3x + b$$

3. Select one point which is on the line, for example $(2, 5)$. Its coordinates must satisfy the equation $y = 3x + b$. Replace x by 2 and y by 5.

$$5 = 3(2) + b$$
$$5 = 6 + b$$
$$-1 = b$$

4. In $y = 3x + b$, replace b by -1. $\qquad$ $y = 3x - 1$

5. Check whether the coordinates of the second point $(4, 11)$ satisfy the equation $y = 3x - 1$.

$$11 \overset{?}{=} 3(4) - 1$$
$$11 = 11 \quad \text{(true)}$$

Answer: $y = 3x - 1$

Exercises

In 1–9, write an equation of the line which has the given slope, m, and which passes through the given point.

1. $m = 2;\ (1, 4)$ $\qquad$ **2.** $m = 2;\ (-3, 4)$ $\qquad$ **3.** $m = -1;\ (0, -2)$

4. $m = -3;\ (-2, -1)$ $\quad$ **5.** $m = \frac{1}{2};\ (4, 2)$ $\qquad$ **6.** $m = \frac{2}{3};\ (-6, 4)$

7. $m = \dfrac{-3}{4};\ (0, 0)$ $\qquad$ **8.** $m = \dfrac{-5}{3};\ (-3, 0)$ $\qquad$ **9.** $m = 0;\ (3, -6)$

In 10–18, write an equation of the line which passes through the given points.

10. $(1, 4);\ (3, 8)$ $\qquad$ **11.** $(1, 0);\ (3, 6)$ $\qquad$ **12.** $(3, 1);\ (9, 7)$

13. $(1, 2);\ (10, 14)$ $\qquad$ **14.** $(0, -1);\ (6, 8)$ $\qquad$ **15.** $(3, 6);\ (6, 0)$

16. $(-3, 11);\ (6, 5)$ $\qquad$ **17.** $(-2, -5);\ (-1, -2)$ $\quad$ **18.** $(0, 0);\ (-3, 5)$

19. Write an equation of the line which is:

a. parallel to the line $y = 2x - 4$ and whose y-intercept is 7

b. parallel to the line $y - 3x = 6$ and whose y-intercept is -2

c. parallel to the line $2x + 3y = 12$ and which passes through the origin

20. Write an equation of the line which is:

a. parallel to the line $y = 4x + 1$ and which passes through the point $(2, 3)$

b. parallel to the line $y - 3x = 5$ and which passes through the point $(-1, 6)$

c. parallel to the line $2y - 6x = 9$ and which passes through the point $(-2, 1)$

d. parallel to the line $y = 4x + 3$ and which has the same y-intercept as the line $y = 5x - 3$

11. Graphing Open Sentences Involving Absolute Values

~~~~~~~~~~~~~~ *MODEL PROBLEMS* ~~~~~~~~~~~~~~

1. Graph the equation $|x| = 3$.

Solution:

1. The sentence $|x| = 3$ is equivalent to "$x = 3$ or $x = -3$."
2. The graph of each of the equations $x = 3$ and $x = -3$ is a line parallel to the y-axis.
3. The graph of $|x| = 3$ consists of two lines as shown in the figure.

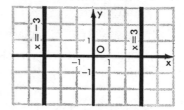

2. Graph the equation $|y - 1| = 2$.

Solution:

1. The sentence $|y - 1| = 2$ is equivalent to:

$$y - 1 = 2 \qquad \text{OR} \qquad y - 1 = -2$$
$$y = 3 \qquad\qquad\qquad y = -1$$

2. The graph of each of the equations $y = 3$ and $y = -1$ is a line parallel to the x-axis.
3. The graph of $|y - 1| = 2$ consists of two lines as shown in the figure.

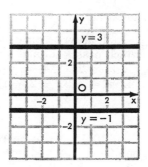

3. Graph the equation $y = |x|$.

Solution:

1. Find several solutions of $y = |x|$ by replacing x with signed numbers and finding the corresponding values of y. Notice that y must be a non-negative number.
2. List these solutions as shown in the table.

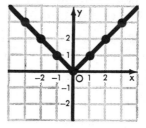

x	-3	-2	-1	0	1	2	3
y	3	2	1	0	1	2	3

3. Plot the ordered pairs in the table as shown in the figure.

~~~~~~

Exercises

In 1–8, graph the equation.

1. $|x| = 1$ 2. $|x| = 4$ 3. $|y| = 2$ 4. $|y| = 0$
5. $|x - 1| = 4$ 6. $|x + 3| = 6$ 7. $|y - 3| = 5$ 8. $|y + 2| = 3$

In 9–28, graph the open sentence.

9. $y = 3|x|$ 10. $y = \frac{1}{2}|x|$ 11. $y = -|x|$ 12. $y = -3|x|$
13. $x = |y|$ 14. $x = 2|y|$ 15. $x = |-y|$ 16. $x = -2|y|$
17. $y = |x| + 2$ 18. $y = |x| - 3$ 19. $y = 2|x| + 1$ 20. $x = -|y| + 2$
21. $y = |x - 4|$ 22. $y = |x + 1|$ 23. $y = 2|x + 4|$ 24. $x = |y + 2| - 3$
25. $|x| = |y|$ 26. $|x| + |y| = 4$ 27. $|x| + |y| = 6$ 28. $|x| - |y| = 6$

12. Graphing an Inequality in Two Variables

Figure 1

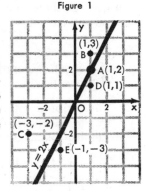

The line which is the graph of the equation $y = 2x$ (figure 1) is the set of all points each of whose ordinate is equal to twice its abscissa. For example, at point $A(1, 2)$, the ordinate (2) is equal to twice the abscissa (1), $2 = 2 \times 1$. This line divides the plane into two regions called *half-planes*.

Figure 2

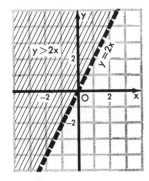

The half-plane above the line $y = 2x$ (figure 1) is the set of all points each of whose ordinate y is greater than twice its abscissa x. For example, at point $B(1, 3)$, the ordinate (3) is greater than twice the abscissa (1), $3 > 2 \times 1$, or $y > 2x$. The coordinates of point $C(-3, -2)$ also satisfy $y > 2x$ because $-2 > 2 \times (-3)$ is a true sentence. The graph of $y > 2x$ is the shaded half-plane above the line $y = 2x$ (figure 2). Notice that the line is dashed to indicate that the line is not part of the graph. To graph $y \geq 2x$, we draw a solid line to indicate that the line $y = 2x$ is part of the graph.

The half-plane below the line $y = 2x$ (figure 1) is the set of all points each of whose ordinate y is less than twice its abscissa x. For example, at point $D(1, 1)$, the ordinate (1) is less than twice the abscissa (1), $1 < 2 \times 1$, or $y < 2x$. The coordinates of point $E(-1, -3)$ also satisfy $y < 2x$ because $-3 < 2 \times (-1)$ is a true sentence. The graph of $y < 2x$ is the shaded half-plane below the line $y = 2x$ (figure 3). Notice that the line is dashed to indicate that the line is not part of the graph. To graph $y \leq 2x$, we draw a solid line to indicate that the line $y = 2x$ is part of the graph.

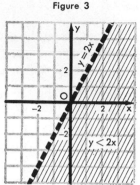

Figure 3

From the study of the graphs of $y = 2x$, $y > 2x$, and $y < 2x$, we see that the line which is the graph of $y = 2x$ acts as a **plane divider.** It divides the plane into two regions. The region above the line is the graph of $y > 2x$; the region below it is the graph of $y < 2x$.

In general, the graph of $y = mx + b$ is a line which divides the coordinate plane into three sets of points:

1. The set of points on the line. Each ordered pair which describes a member of this set of points is a solution of $y = mx + b$. The line is the graph of the equation $y = mx + b$.

2. The set of points in the half-plane above the line. Each ordered pair which describes a member of this set of points is a solution of $y > mx + b$. The half-plane is the graph of the inequality $y > mx + b$.

3. The set of points in the half-plane below the line. Each ordered pair which describes a member of this set of points is a solution of $y < mx + b$. The half-plane is the graph of the inequality $y < mx + b$.

KEEP IN MIND

To graph $Ax + By + C > 0$ or $Ax + By + C < 0$, transform the inequality so that the left member is y alone: $y > rx + s$ or $y < rx + s$. This enables us first to graph the plane divider $y = rx + s$.

~~~~~~~~~~~~~~~ **MODEL PROBLEMS** ~~~~~~~~~~~~~~~

1. Graph the inequality $y - 2x \geq 2$.

How To Proceed	*Solution*

1. Transform the sentence into one having y as the left member.

$$y - 2x \geq 2$$
$$y \geq 2x + 2$$

2. Graph the resulting inequality by first graphing the plane divider, $y = 2x + 2$.

$$y = 2x + 2$$

x	-1	0	1
y	0	2	4

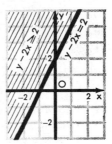

3. Shade the half-plane above the line. This region and the line are the required graph; the half-plane is the graph of $y - 2x > 2$, and the line is the graph of $y - 2x = 2$. Note that the line is drawn solid to show that it is part of the graph.

2. Graph each of the following sentences in the coordinate plane:

    a. $x > 1$ *b.* $x \leq 1$ *c.* $y \geq 1$ *d.* $y < 1$

Solution

     (a)   (b)   (c)   (d)

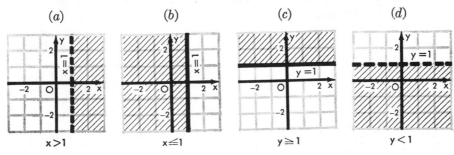

Exercises

In 1–9, transform the sentence into one whose left member is y.

1. $y - 2x > 0$ **2.** $y + 3x \leq 0$ **3.** $5x > 2y$
4. $y - x \geq 3$ **5.** $2x + y \leq 0$ **6.** $3x - y \geq 4$
7. $4y - 3x \leq 12$ **8.** $3x + 2y > 6$ **9.** $10 \geq 2x + 5y$

In 10–33, graph the sentence in the coordinate plane.

10. $x > 4$ **11.** $x \leq -2$ **12.** $y > 5$
13. $y \leq -3$ **14.** $x \geq 6$ **15.** $y \leq 0$
16. $y > 4x$ **17.** $y \leq 3x$ **18.** $y < x - 2$
19. $y \geq \frac{1}{2}x + 3$ **20.** $x + y < 4$ **21.** $x + y \geq 4$
22. $x + y \leq -3$ **23.** $y - x \geq 5$ **24.** $x - y > 6$
25. $x - y \leq -1$ **26.** $y - 3x > 3$ **27.** $x - 2y \leq 4$
28. $2x + y - 4 \leq 0$ **29.** $y - x + 6 > 0$ **30.** $2y - 6x > 0$
31. $3x + 4y \leq 0$ **32.** $2x - 3y \geq 6$ **33.** $10 \leq 5x - 2y$

In 34–39: a. Write the verbal sentence as an open sentence.
            b. Graph the open sentence in the coordinate plane.

34. The ordinate of a point is greater than the abscissa.
35. The ordinate of a point is less than four times the abscissa.
36. The ordinate of a point is equal to or greater than 3 more than the abscissa.
37. The sum of the abscissa and ordinate of a point is less than or equal to 5.
38. The ordinate of a point decreased by three times the abscissa is greater than or equal to 2.
39. The sum of three times the abscissa of a point and twice the ordinate is less than or equal to 12.

CHAPTER XVI

SYSTEMS OF LINEAR OPEN SENTENCES IN TWO VARIABLES

1. Graphic Solution of a System of Linear Equations in Two Variables

CONSISTENT EQUATIONS

We have learned that there are an infinite number of ordered pairs of numbers (x, y) which are solutions of the equation $x + y = 4$. Among the many ordered pairs that satisfy this equation is (3, 1). We know that all the elements of the solution set of the equation $x + y = 4$ describe the points on the line which is the graph of $x + y = 4$.

Similarly, there are an infinite number of solutions of the equation $x - y = 2$, among them being the ordered number pair (3, 1). All the ordered number pairs (x, y) which are solutions of $x - y = 2$ will describe the points on the line which is the graph of $x - y = 2$.

Since the ordered pair (3, 1) satisfies both equations $x + y = 4$ and $x - y = 2$, it is called a ***common solution*** of this pair of linear equations. The figure shows the graphs of the equations $x + y = 4$ and $x - y = 2$ when they are both drawn in a co-ordinate plane using the same set of axes. Notice that S, the point of intersection of the lines, is the one point common to both graphs. The coordinates of the point of intersection (3, 1) represent the one common solution that satisfies both equations. The solution set of this pair of equations is $\{(3, 1)\}$.

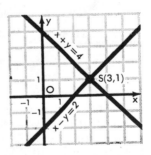

The two linear equations $x + y = 4$ and $x - y = 2$ impose on the variables x and y two conditions which must both hold at the same time. Therefore, these equations are called a ***system of simultaneous linear equations,*** or a ***system of linear equations.***

391

If a system of linear equations such as $x + y = 4$ and $x - y = 2$ has one common solution, it is called a **system of consistent equations.** These equations are also called **independent equations** because their solution sets are not identical. The graphs of two consistent linear equations are straight lines which have unequal slopes and which intersect in one point.

INCONSISTENT EQUATIONS

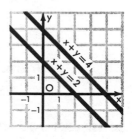

Sometimes, when two linear equations are graphed in a coordinate plane using the same set of axes, the lines are parallel and fail to intersect. This happens in the case of $x + y = 2$ and $x + y = 4$. There is no common solution for the system of equations $x + y = 2$ and $x + y = 4$. It is obvious that there can be no ordered number pair (x, y) such that the sum of those numbers, $x + y$, is both 2 and 4. Since the solution set of the system has no members, it is the empty set $\varnothing$.

If a system of linear equations such as $x + y = 2$ and $x + y = 4$ has no common solution, it is called a **system of inconsistent equations.** The graphs of two inconsistent linear equations are straight lines which have equal slopes and which are parallel.

DEPENDENT EQUATIONS

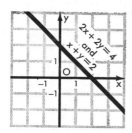

Sometimes, when two linear equations are graphed in a coordinate plane using the same set of axes, they turn out to be the same line; that is, they coincide. This happens in the case of $x + y = 2$ and $2x + 2y = 4$. Every one of the infinite number of solutions of $x + y = 2$ is also a solution of $2x + 2y = 4$. We see that $2x + 2y = 4$ and $x + y = 2$ are equivalent equations with identical solutions. Note that when both members of the equation $2x + 2y = 4$ are divided by 2, the result is $x + y = 2$.

If a system of two linear equations, for example $x + y = 2$ and $2x + 2y = 4$, is such that every solution of either one of the equations is also a solution of the other, it is called a **system of dependent equations.**

Procedure. To solve a pair of linear equations graphically:

1. **Graph one equation in a coordinate plane.**
2. **Graph the second equation in a coordinate plane using the same set of coordinate axes.**

3. **Read the ordered number pair associated with the point of intersection of the two graphs to determine the common solution.**
4. **Check the apparent solution by verifying that the ordered pair satisfies both equations.**

```
┌──────────────── KEEP IN MIND ────────────────┐
│                                               │
│    The solution set of a system of two linear equations │
│  is the intersection of the solution sets of the individual │
│  equations.                                   │
│                                               │
└───────────────────────────────────────────────┘
```

MODEL PROBLEM

Solve graphically and check: $2x + y = 8$
$$y - x = 2$$

Solution:

1. Graph $2x + y = 8$, or $y = -2x + 8$.

x	1	3	4
y	6	2	0

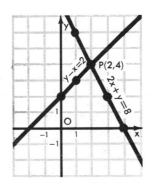

2. Graph $y - x = 2$, or $y = x + 2$.

x	0	1	2
y	2	3	4

3. Read the coordinates of the point of intersection P (2, 4).

4. *Check:* $(x = 2, y = 4)$

$$2x + y = 8 \qquad\qquad\qquad y - x = 2$$
$$2(2) + 4 \stackrel{?}{=} 8 \qquad\qquad 4 - 2 \stackrel{?}{=} 2$$
$$8 = 8 \quad \text{(true)} \qquad\qquad 2 = 2 \quad \text{(true)}$$

Answer: The common solution is (2, 4). The solution set is $\{(2, 4)\}$.

Exercises

In 1–27, solve the systems of equations graphically. Check.

1. $y = 2x$
   $y = 3x - 3$

2. $y = x + 4$
   $y = 2x + 5$

3. $y = -2x + 3$
   $y = \frac{1}{2}x + 3$

4. $x + y = 7$
   $x - y = 1$

5. $x + y = 4$
   $x - y = 0$

6. $x + y = -4$
   $x - y = 6$

7. $x + 2y = 7$
   $y = 2x + 1$

8. $y = 3x$
   $2x + y = 10$

9. $x + 3y = 9$
   $x = 3$

10. $y - x = -2$
    $x - 2y = 4$

11. $3x + y = 6$
    $y = 3$

12. $4x - y = 9$
    $2x + y = 12$

13. $y = 2x + 4$
    $x = y - 5$

14. $x + y = 3$
    $2x - y = -9$

15. $y - 3x = 12$
    $y = -3$

16. $2x - y = -1$
    $x = y + 1$

17. $3x + y = -9$
    $x + 3y = -11$

18. $x = 3$
    $y = 4$

19. $y = \frac{1}{3}x - 3$
    $2x - y = 8$

20. $3x + y = 13$
    $x + 6y = -7$

21. $x = 0$
    $y = -5$

22. $2x = y + 9$
    $6x + 3y = 15$

23. $5x - 3y = 9$
    $5y = 13 - x$

24. $x = 0$
    $y = 0$

25. $x + y + 2 = 0$
    $x = y - 8$

26. $y + 2x + 6 = 0$
    $y = 2x$

27. $7x - 4y + 7 = 0$
    $3x - 5y + 3 = 0$

In 28–33, graph both equations. Determine whether the system is consistent, inconsistent, or dependent.

28. $x + y = 1$
    $x + y = 3$

29. $x + y = 5$
    $2x + 2y = 10$

30. $y = 2x + 1$
    $y = 3x + 3$

31. $2x - y = 1$
    $2y = 4x - 2$

32. $y - 3x = 2$
    $y = 3x - 2$

33. $x + 4y = 6$
    $x = 2$

34. Are there any ordered number pairs which satisfy both equations $2x + y = 7$ and $2x = 5 - y$?

35. Are there any ordered number pairs which satisfy the equation $y - x = 4$ but which do not satisfy the equation $2y = 8 + 2x$?

2. Algebraic Solution of a System of Simultaneous Linear Equations by Using Addition or Subtraction

We will now learn algebraic methods for solving a system of linear equations in two variables. Solutions by these methods usually take less time and lead to more accurate results than the graphic method previously used.

~~~~~~~~~~~~~~~ **MODEL PROBLEMS** ~~~~~~~~~~~~~~~

1. Solve the system of equations and check: $x + 3y = 13$
$$x + y = 5$$

How To Proceed	*Solution*

1. The coefficients of the variable x are the same in both equations. Therefore, subtracting the members of equation B from the corresponding members of equation A will eliminate the variable x and will result in an equation which involves one variable, y.

$$\begin{array}{ll} x + 3y = 13 & (A) \\ \underline{x + y = 5} & (B) \\ 2y = 8 & \end{array}$$

2. Solve the resulting equation for the variable, y.

$$y = 4$$

3. Replace y by its value in any equation involving both variables.

$$\begin{array}{l} x + y = 5 \quad (B) \\ x + 4 = 5 \end{array}$$

4. Solve the resulting equation for the remaining variable, x.

$$x = 1$$

5. *Check:* Substitute 1 for x and 4 for y in each of the given equations to verify that the resulting sentences are true.

$$\begin{array}{ll} x + 3y = 13 & x + y = 5 \\ 1 + 3(4) \overset{?}{=} 13 & 1 + 4 \overset{?}{=} 5 \\ 13 = 13 \quad \text{(true)} & 5 = 5 \quad \text{(true)} \end{array}$$

Answer: Since $x = 1$ and $y = 4$, the solution is $(1, 4)$, or solution set is $\{(1, 4)\}$.

2. Solve the system of equations and check: $5a + b = 13$
$$4a - 3b = 18$$

How To Proceed	*Solution*

1. Multiply both members of equation A by 3. This yields an equivalent equation C in which the coefficient of b has the same absolute value as the coefficient of b in equation B.

$$\begin{array}{ll} 5a + b = 13 & (A) \\ 4a - 3b = 18 & (B) \\ \underline{15a + 3b = 39} & (C) \end{array}$$

2. Add the corresponding members of equations B and C to eliminate the variable b.

$$19a = 57$$

3. Solve the resulting equation for the variable a.

$$a = 3$$

4. Replace a by its value in any equation involving both variables.

$$\begin{array}{l} 5a + b = 13 \quad (A) \\ 5(3) + b = 13 \end{array}$$

5. Solve the resulting equation for the remaining variable, b.

$$\begin{array}{l} 15 + b = 13 \\ b = -2 \end{array}$$

6. *Check:* Substitute 3 for a and -2 for b in each of the given equations to verify that the resulting sentences are true. This is left to the student.

Answer: Since $a = 3$ and $b = -2$, the solution is $(3, -2)$, or solution set is $\{(3, -2)\}$.

3. Solve the system of equations and check: $7x = 5 - 2y$
$$3y = 16 - 2x$$

How To Proceed	*Solution*

1. Transform each of the given equations (A and B) into equivalent equations (C and D) in which the terms containing the variables appear on one side and the constant appears on the other side.

$$7x = 5 - 2y \quad (A)$$
$$3y = 16 - 2x \quad (B)$$
$$7x + 2y = 5 \quad\;\; (C)$$
$$2x + 3y = 16 \quad\;\; (D)$$

2. To eliminate y, multiply both members of equation C by 3; multiply both members of equation D by 2. In the resulting equivalent equations (E and F), the absolute values of the coefficients of y are equal.

$$21x + 6y = 15 \quad (E)$$
$$\underline{4x + 6y = 32} \quad (F)$$

3. Subtract the members of equation F from the corresponding members of equation E to eliminate the variable y.

$$17x \qquad\quad = -17$$

4. Solve the resulting equation for the variable x.

$$x = -1$$

5. Replace x by its value in any equation containing both variables.

$$3y = 16 - 2x \quad (B)$$
$$3y = 16 - 2(-1)$$

6. Solve the resulting equation for the remaining variable, y.

$$3y = 16 + 2$$
$$3y = 18$$
$$y = 6$$

7. *Check:* Substitute -1 for x and 6 for y in each of the given equations to verify that the resulting sentences are true. This is left to the student.

Answer: Since $x = -1$ and $y = 6$, the solution is $(-1, 6)$, or solution set is $\{(-1, 6)\}$.

Procedure. To solve a system of simultaneous linear equations in two variables by the method of elimination using addition or subtraction:

1. Transform each equation into an equivalent equation in which the variables appear on one side and the constant appears on the other side.
2. If necessary, multiply both members of each of the resulting equations by such numbers as will make the coefficients of one of the variables the same in absolute value.
3. If one of these coefficients is positive and the other negative, add the corresponding members of the two resulting equations. If these coefficients are either both positive or both negative, subtract the corresponding members of the resulting equations. Thus, one of the variables is eliminated.
4. Solve the resulting equation which has one variable for the value of that variable.
5. Substitute the value of the variable obtained in step 4 in any equation containing both variables. Solve the resulting equation for the remaining variable.
6. Check the common solution by substituting the values of the variables in each of the given equations to verify that the resulting sentences are true.

Exercises

In 1–63, solve each system of equations by eliminating one of the variables using addition or subtraction. Check.

1. $x + y = 12$
   $x - y = 4$

2. $a + b = 13$
   $a - b = 5$

3. $r + s = -6$
   $r - s = -10$

4. $3x + y = 16$
   $2x + y = 11$

5. $m + 2n = 14$
   $3n + m = 18$

6. $c - 2d = 14$
   $c + 3d = 9$

7. $x + y = 10$
   $x - y = 0$

8. $s + r = 0$
   $r - s = 6$

9. $a - 4b = -8$
   $a - 2b = 0$

10. $x + 2y = 8$
    $x - 2y = 4$

11. $4r + 3s = 29$
    $2r - 3s = 1$

12. $8a + 5b = 9$
    $2a - 5b = -4$

13. $4x + 5y = 23$
    $4x - y = 5$

14. $2a + 3b = 2$
    $5a + 3b = 14$

15. $-2m + 4n = 13$
    $6m + 4n = 9$

16. $3a - b = 3$
    $a + 3b = 11$

17. $3r + s = 6$
    $r + 3s = 10$

18. $4x - y = 10$
    $2x + 3y = 12$

19. $5m + 3n = 14$
$2m + n = 6$

20. $5x + 4y = 27$
$x - 2y = 11$

21. $2c - d = -1$
$c + 3d = 17$

22. $2m + n = 12$
$m + 2n = 9$

23. $3a - b = 13$
$2a + 3b = 16$

24. $r - 3s = -11$
$3r + s = 17$

25. $a + 3b = 4$
$2a - b = 1$

26. $3x - y = 5$
$5x - 2y = 8$

27. $3x + 4y = 26$
$x - 3y = 0$

28. $5x + 8y = 1$
$3x + 4y = -1$

29. $x - y = -1$
$3x - 2y = 3$

30. $5a - 2b = 3$
$2a - b = 0$

31. $5x - 2y = 20$
$2x + 3y = 27$

32. $3x + 7y = 22$
$2x - 8y = 2$

33. $5a + 3b = 17$
$4a - 5b = 21$

34. $2x + 3y = 6$
$3x + 5y = 15$

35. $5r - 2s = 8$
$3r - 7s = -1$

36. $3x + 7y = -2$
$2x + 3y = -3$

37. $4x + 3y = -1$
$5x + 4y = 1$

38. $4a - 6b = 15$
$6a - 4b = 10$

39. $3x + 8y = 16$
$5x + 10y = 25$

40. $2x + y = 17$
$5x = 25 + y$

41. $5r + 3s = 30$
$2r = 12 - 3s$

42. $x - 2y = 8$
$2y = 3x - 16$

43. $3x + 4y = 16$
$4x = 2y + 14$

44. $6r = s$
$5r = 2s - 14$

45. $3a - 7 = 7b$
$4a = 3b + 22$

46. $3x - 4y = 2$
$x = 2(7 - y)$

47. $3(y - 6) = 2x$
$3x + 5y = 11$

48. $3x + 5(y + 2) = 1$
$8y = -3x$

49. $\frac{1}{3}x + \frac{1}{4}y = 10$
$\frac{1}{3}x - \frac{1}{2}y = 4$

50. $\frac{2}{3}x + \frac{3}{4}y = 2$
$\frac{1}{6}x + \frac{1}{2}y = -2$

51. $\frac{1}{2}a + \frac{1}{3}b = 8$
$\frac{3}{2}a - \frac{4}{3}b = -4$

52. $c - 2d = 1$
$\frac{2}{3}c + 5d = 26$

53. $a - \frac{2}{3}b = 4$
$\frac{3}{5}a + b = 15$

54. $2a = 3b$
$\frac{2}{3}a - \frac{1}{2}b = 2$

55. $.04x + .06y = 26$
$x + y = 500$

56. $.03x + .05y = 17$
$x + y = 400$

57. $.03x = .06y + 9$
$x + y = 600$

58. $x + 2y = 12$

$\dfrac{x}{y} = 1 + \dfrac{6}{y}$

59. $x - 8y = -2$

$\dfrac{3x}{2y} + 1 = \dfrac{10}{y}$

60. $2x + y = 23$

$\dfrac{x - 6}{3y} = \dfrac{1}{5}$

61. $3d = 13 - 2c$

$\dfrac{3c + d}{2} = 8$

62. $3x = 4y$

$\dfrac{3x + 8}{5} = \dfrac{3y - 1}{2}$

63. $\dfrac{a}{3} + \dfrac{a + b}{6} = 3$

$\dfrac{b}{3} - \dfrac{a - b}{2} = 6$

3. Algebraic Solution of a System of Simultaneous Linear Equations by Using Substitution

There is another algebraic method that can be used to eliminate one of the variables when solving a system of equations. It is the method of substitution.

━━━━━━━━━━ **MODEL PROBLEMS** ━━━━━━━━━━

1. Solve the system of equations and check: $4x + 3y = 27$
$$y = 2x - 1$$

How To Proceed	*Solution*
1. In equation B, both y and $2x - 1$ name the same number when the values of the common solution replace x and y. Therefore, eliminate y in equation A by replacing y by $2x - 1$.	$4x + 3y = 27 \qquad (A)$ $y = 2x - 1 \quad (B)$ $4x + 3(2x - 1) = 27$
2. Solve the resulting equation for x.	$4x + 6x - 3 = 27$ $10x = 30$ $x = 3$
3. Replace x by its value in any equation involving both variables.	$y = 2x - 1 \quad (B)$ $y = 2(3) - 1$
4. Solve the resulting equation for y.	$y = 6 - 1$ $y = 5$

5. *Check:* Substitute 3 for x and 5 for y in each of the given equations to verify that the resulting sentences are true.

$$4x + 3y = 27 \qquad\qquad y = 2x - 1$$
$$4(3) + 3(5) \overset{?}{=} 27 \qquad\qquad 5 \overset{?}{=} 2(3) - 1$$
$$12 + 15 \overset{?}{=} 27 \qquad\qquad 5 \overset{?}{=} 6 - 1$$
$$27 = 27 \quad \text{(true)} \qquad\qquad 5 = 5 \quad \text{(true)}$$

Answer: Since $x = 3$ and $y = 5$, the solution is $(3, 5)$, or solution set is $\{(3, 5)\}$.

2. Solve the system of equations and check: $3x - 4y = 26$
$$x + 2y = 2$$

How To Proceed	*Solution*
1. Transform one of the equations (B) into an equivalent equation (C) in which one of the variables is expressed in terms of the other. In equation B, solve for x in terms of y.	$3x - 4y = 26 \quad (A)$ $x + 2y = 2 \quad (B)$ $x = 2 - 2y \quad (C)$
2. Eliminate x in equation A by replacing it with $2 - 2y$, the expression for x in equation C.	$3(2 - 2y) - 4y = 26$
3. Solve the resulting equation for y.	$6 - 6y - 4y = 26$ $-10y = 20$ $y = -2$
4. Replace y by its value in any equation involving both variables.	$x = 2 - 2y \quad (C)$ $x = 2 - 2(-2)$
5. Solve the resulting equation for x.	$x = 2 + 4$ $x = 6$

6. *Check:* Substitute 6 for x and -2 for y in each of the given equations to verify that the resulting sentences are true. This is left to the student.

Answer: Since $x = 6$ and $y = -2$, the solution is $(6, -2)$, or solution set is $\{(6, -2)\}$.

Procedure. To solve a system of simultaneous linear equations in two variables by the method of elimination using substitution:
1. **Solve for one of the variables in terms of the other variable in one of the given equations.**
2. **Substitute this solution in the other equation; that is, replace the variable for which you solved with the expression to which it is equal. Thus, one of the variables is eliminated.**
3. **Solve the resulting equation, which has one variable, for the value of that variable.**
4. **Substitute the value of the variable obtained in step 3 in any equation containing both variables. Solve the resulting equation for the remaining variable.**
5. **Check the common solution by substituting the values of the variables in each of the given equations to verify that the resulting sentences are true.**

Exercises

In 1–39, solve each system of equations by eliminating one of the variables by the substitution method. Check.

1. $y = x$
   $x + y = 14$

2. $x = y$
   $2x + 3y = 15$

3. $x = y$
   $5x - 4y = -2$

4. $y = 2x$
   $x + y = 21$

5. $y = 3x$
   $y - x = 18$

6. $x = 4y$
   $2x + 3y = 22$

7. $a = -2b$
   $5a - 3b = 13$

8. $r = -3s$
   $3r + 4s = -10$

9. $-2c = d$
   $6c + 5d = -12$

10. $y = x + 1$
   $x + y = 9$

11. $x = y - 2$
   $x + y = 18$

12. $x = 5 - y$
   $x - y = 1$

13. $y = x + 3$
   $3x + 2y = 26$

14. $y = x - 2$
   $3x - y = 16$

15. $x = y + 4$
   $2x - 5y = 8$

16. $y = 2x + 1$
   $x + y = 7$

17. $y = 3x - 1$
   $7x + 2y = 37$

18. $a = 3b + 1$
   $5b - 2a = 1$

19. $a + b = 11$
   $3a - 2b = 8$

20. $r - s = 7$
   $3r - 2s = 18$

21. $x + y = 0$
   $3x + 2y = 5$

22. $3m - 2n = 11$
   $m + 2n = 9$

23. $3c - d = 1$
   $c + 2d = 12$

24. $a - 2b = -2$
   $2a - b = 5$

25. $7x - 3y = 23$
   $x + 2y = 13$

26. $3s - 2t = 4$
   $2s - t = 1$

27. $3x + 2y = 23$
   $x + 3y = 17$

28. $2x = 3y$
   $4x - 3y = 12$

29. $4y = -3x$
   $5x + 8y = 4$

30. $3a = 4b$
   $4a - 5b = 2$

31. $2x + 3y = 7$
   $4x - 5y = 25$

32. $7x + 3y = 3$
   $5x + 6y = 6$

33. $2a + 3b = 3$
   $3a + 4b = 3$

34. $y = 3x$
   $\frac{1}{3}x + \frac{1}{2}y = 11$

35. $t + u = 12$
   $t = \frac{1}{3}u$

36. $10t + u = 24$
   $t + u = \frac{1}{7}(10u + t)$

37. $x + y = 500$
   $y = 1.5x$

38. $x + y = 1000$
   $.06x = .04y$

39. $x + y = 300$
   $.25x + .75y = 195$

4. Solving Verbal Problems by Using Two Variables

Now we will learn how to solve verbal problems by using a system of two equations involving two variables. Frequently, a problem can be solved more easily by using two variables rather than one variable.

NUMBER PROBLEMS

~~~~~~~~~~~~~~~~~ *MODEL PROBLEM* ~~~~~~~~~~~~~~~~~

The sum of two numbers is 10. Three times the larger decreased by twice the smaller is 15. Find the numbers.

Solution:

Let x = larger number.

Let y = smaller number.

The sum of two numbers is 10.

$$x + y = 10 \ (A)$$

Three times the larger decreased by twice the smaller is 15.

$$3x - 2y = 15 \ (B)$$

Solve the system of equations: $x + y = 10 \ (A)$

Multiply both members of equation A by 2, and add the members of the resulting equation to the corresponding members of equation B.

$$3x - 2y = 15 \ (B)$$
$$2x + 2y = 20$$
$$\overline{5x = 35}$$
$$x = 7$$

$$x + y = 10 \ (A)$$
$$7 + y = 10$$

The check is left to the student.

$$y = 3$$

Answer: The larger number is 7; the smaller number is 3.

~~~~~~

Exercises

In 1–5, solve the problem by using two variables.

1. The sum of two numbers is 36. Their difference is 24. Find the numbers.
2. The sum of two numbers is 104. The larger number is 1 less than twice the smaller number. Find the numbers.
3. The difference between two numbers is 34. The larger exceeds 3 times the smaller by 4. Find the numbers.
4. The sum of two numbers is 50. If twice the larger is subtracted from 4 times the smaller, the result is 8. Find the numbers.
5. If 5 times the smaller of two numbers is subtracted from twice the larger, the result is 16. If the larger is increased by 3 times the smaller, the result is 63. Find the numbers.

COIN PROBLEMS

~~~~~~~~~~~~~~~~~~ *MODEL PROBLEM* ~~~~~~~~~~~~~~~

Marvin deposited $6.50, consisting of dimes and quarters, in a bank. The number of quarters was 10 less than twice the number of dimes. How many coins of each kind did he deposit?

Solution:

Let d = the number of dimes.

Let q = the number of quarters.

Kind of coin	Number of coins	Value of each coin in cents	Total value in cents
Dime	d	10	$10d$
Quarter	q	25	$25q$

The total value of the coins was 650 cents.

$$10d + 25q = 650$$

The number of quarters was 10 less than twice the number of dimes.

$$q = 2d - 10$$

$$
\begin{aligned}
10d + 25q &= 650 && (A) \\
q &= 2d - 10 && (B) \\
-2d + q &= -10 && (C)
\end{aligned}
$$

$$
\begin{aligned}
-10d + 5q &= -50 && [\text{In } C, \text{M}_5.] \\
10d + 25q &= 650 && (A) \\
\hline
30q &= 600 \\
q &= 20
\end{aligned}
$$

$$
\begin{aligned}
q &= 2d - 10 && (B) \\
20 &= 2d - 10 \\
30 &= 2d \\
15 &= d
\end{aligned}
$$

Check

Value of 15 dimes = $1.50
Value of 20 quarters = $5.00
Total value = $6.50

The number of quarters, 20, is 10 less than twice 15, the number of dimes.

Answer: He deposited 15 dimes and 20 quarters.

~~~~~~

Exercises

In 1–5, solve the problem by using two variables.

1. Irene has $4.50 in her coin bank in nickels and dimes. The number of dimes is twice the number of nickels. How many coins of each type does Irene have?
2. Rae has $5.70 in quarters and dimes. The number of quarters is 6 more than the number of dimes. How many coins of each kind does Rae have?
3. A purse contains $7.60 in quarters and dimes. In all, there are 40 coins. How many coins of each kind are there?
4. A class contributed $6.10 in nickels and dimes to a welfare fund. In all, there were 80 coins. How many coins of each kind were there?
5. Mr. Charles cashed a $135 check in his bank. He received $5 bills and $10 bills. The number of $5 bills exceeded twice the number of $10 bills by 3. How many bills of each type did Mr. Charles receive?

MIXTURE PROBLEMS

～～～～～～～～～ MODEL PROBLEM ～～～～～～～～～

A dealer wishes to obtain 50 pounds of mixed cookies to sell for $1.00 per pound. If he mixes cookies worth $1.20 per pound with cookies worth $.70 per pound, find the number of pounds of each kind he should use.

Solution:

Let x = the number of pounds of the $1.20 cookies to be used.
Let y = the number of pounds of the $.70 cookies to be used.

Kind of cookie	Number of pounds	Price per pound in cents	Total value in cents
$1.20 cookies	x	120	$120x$
$.70 cookies	y	70	$70y$
Mixture	50	100	100(50)

The total number of pounds of cookies is 50.

$$x + y = 50$$

The total value of the $1.20 cookies and $.70 cookies is 100(50) cents.

$$120x + 70y = 100(50)$$

$120x + 70y = 100(50)$ (A)
$x + y = 50$ (B)

$$\begin{array}{rl} 70x + 70y = & 3500 \quad [\text{In } B, \text{M}_{70}] \\ 120x + 70y = & 5000 \quad (A) \\ \hline -50x \quad\quad = & -1500 \\ x = & 30 \end{array}$$

$x + y = 50$ (B)
$30 + y = 50$
$y = 20$

Check

$30 + 20 = 50$
Value of 30 lb. at $1.20 per lb. = $36.00
Value of 20 lb. at $.70 per lb.   = $14.00
Value of 50 lb. at $1.00 per lb. = $50.00

Answer: He should use 30 lb. of the $1.20 cookies and 20 lb. of the $.70 cookies.

~~~~~~

Exercises

In 1–5, solve the problem by using two variables.

1. A grocer mixed nuts worth 85 cents per pound with nuts worth 55 cents per pound. How many pounds of each kind did he use to make a mixture of 60 pounds to sell at 75 cents per pound?

2. A dealer has some hard candy worth 50 cents per pound and some worth 75 cents per pound. He wishes to make a mixture of 80 pounds that he can sell for 55 cents per pound. How many pounds of each kind should he use?

3. A cake shop has cookies worth $.90 per pound and cookies worth $1.50 per pound. How many pounds of each kind should the manager of the shop use in order to have 120 pounds of cookies to sell at $1.25 per pound?

4. A dealer mixed some coffee worth 80 cents per pound with coffee worth 50 cents per pound to make a mixture to be sold for 70 cents per pound. If the number of pounds of 80-cent coffee was 10 more than the number of pounds of the 50-cent coffee, how many pounds of each kind did he use?

5. How many pounds of seed worth $1.05 per pound must be mixed with 30 pounds of seed worth $.90 per pound in order to produce a mixture to sell for $1.00 per pound?

INVESTMENT PROBLEMS

~~~~~~~~~~~~~~~~~~~~~ **MODEL PROBLEM** ~~~~~~~~~~~~~~~

Mr. Trask invested a sum of money in 4% bonds and twice as much in 6% bonds. His annual income from these bonds was $240. Find the amount he invested in each type of bond.

Solution:

Let x = the number of dollars invested in 4% bonds.
Let y = the number of dollars invested in 6% bonds.

Investment	Principal in dollars	Annual rate of income	Annual income in dollars
4% bond	x	.04	$.04x$
6% bond	y	.06	$.06y$

The amount invested at 6% is twice the amount invested at 4%.

$$y = 2x$$

The total annual income was $240.

$$.04x + .06y = 240$$

$y = 2x$ (A)	*Check*
$.04x + .06y = 240$ (B)	The amount invested in 6% bonds,
$4x + 6y = 24000$ [In B, M_{100}]	$3000, is twice $1500, the amount
$4x + 6(2x) = 24000$ $(y = 2x)$	invested in 4% bonds.
$4x + 12x = 24000$	4% of $1500 = .04($1500) = $ 60.00
$16x = 24000$	6% of $3000 = .06($3000) = $180.00
$x = 1500$	Total = $240.00
$y = 2x$ (A)	
$y = 2(1500)$	
$y = 3000$	

Answer: The amount invested in 4% bonds is $1500; the amount invested in 6% bonds is $3000.

~~~~~~

Exercises

In 1–5, solve the problem by using two variables.

1. Mr. Morton invested $1400, part at 5% and the rest at 8%. His total annual income from these investments was $100. Find the amount he invested at each rate.

2. Mr. Salz invested a sum of money in bonds yielding 4% a year and another sum in bonds yielding 6% a year. In all, he had $4000 invested. If his total annual income from the two investments was $188, how much is invested at each rate?

3. Mr. Decker invested a certain amount of money in bonds yielding 3% a year and twice as much in bonds yielding 5% a year. If his total annual income from the two investments was $208, how much did he invest in each type of bond?

4. Mr. May invested $20,000, part at 4% and the rest at 6%. If the annual incomes from both investments were equal, find the amount he invested at each rate.

5. Mr. Burnside invested $8000 at 7%. How much additional money must he invest at 4% in order that his total annual income may equal 5% of his entire investment?

BUSINESS PROBLEMS

~~~~~~~~~~~~~~~~ **MODEL PROBLEM** ~~~~~~~~~~~~~~~

The owner of a men's clothing store bought 6 shirts and 8 hats for $70. A week later, at the same prices, he bought 9 shirts and 6 hats for $66. Find the price of a shirt and the price of a hat.

Solution:

$$\text{Let } s = \text{the price of a shirt in dollars.}$$
$$\text{Let } h = \text{the price of a hat in dollars.}$$

6 shirts and 8 hats cost $70.

$$6s + 8h = 70 \quad (A)$$

9 shirts and 6 hats cost $66.

$$9s + 6h = 66 \quad (B)$$

1. In order to eliminate h, multiply both members of equation B by 4 and both members of equation A by 3.

$$36s + 24h = 264$$
$$18s + 24h = 210$$
$$\overline{18s \qquad = 54}$$
$$s = 3$$

2. In equation A, substitute 3 for s.

$$18 + 8h = 70$$
$$8h = 52$$
$$h = 6\tfrac{1}{2}$$

Check: 6 shirts and 8 hats cost $6(\$3) + 8(\$6.50) = \$18 + \$52 = \$70$.
9 shirts and 6 hats cost $9(\$3) + 6(\$6.50) = \$27 + \$39 = \$66$.

Answer: A shirt costs \$3; a hat costs \$6.50.

~~~~~~

Exercises

In 1–10, solve the problem by using two variables.

1. Six boxes of oranges and 5 boxes of grapefruits cost \$61. At the same time and place, 3 boxes of oranges and 2 boxes of grapefruits cost \$28. Find the cost of one box of each.
2. On one day, 4 plumbers and 5 helpers earned \$182. On another day, working the same number of hours and at the same rate of pay, 5 plumbers and 6 helpers earned \$224. How much does a plumber and how much does a helper earn each day?
3. A basketball manager bought 7 shirts and 4 pairs of shoes for \$81. Another manager, who paid the same prices, paid \$54 for 5 shirts and 2 pairs of shoes. Find the cost of a shirt and the cost of a pair of shoes.
4. A baseball manager bought 4 bats and 9 balls for \$33.75. On another day, he bought 3 bats and 1 dozen balls at the same prices and paid \$34.50. How much did he pay for each bat and each ball?
5. A customer bought 3 cans of corn and 5 cans of tomatoes for \$1.82. The next customer bought 2 cans of corn and 3 cans of tomatoes for \$1.11. Find the cost of one can of each.
6. Find the cost of one pound of butter and the cost of one pound of lard if 2 pounds of butter and 3 pounds of lard cost \$2.15, while 3 pounds of butter and 2 pounds of lard cost \$2.60.
7. Fifteen bars of soap and 4 cans of cleanser cost \$1.86. In the same store, at the same time, 8 bars of soap and 7 cans of cleanser cost \$1.43. What is the cost of one bar of soap and the cost of one can of cleanser?
8. Mrs. Jones paid \$5.45 for 4 pounds of walnuts and 3 pounds of pecans. At the same time, Mrs. Kay paid \$4.20 for 5 pounds of walnuts and one pound of pecans. Find the price per pound of each kind.
9. Five pounds of ham and 2 pounds of smoked tongue cost \$3.85. At the same time, 3 pounds of ham and 1 pound of smoked tongue cost \$2.22. Find the cost of 1 pound of ham and the cost of 1 pound of tongue.
10. Eight roses and 9 carnations cost \$3.35. At the same time and place, one dozen roses and 5 carnations cost \$3.75. Find the cost of a rose and the cost of a carnation.

DIGIT PROBLEMS

PREPARING TO SOLVE DIGIT PROBLEMS

In our decimal number system, every integer can be written by using only the symbols 0, 1, 2, 3, 4, 5, 6, 7, 8, 9. These ten number symbols are called **digits.**

When we write an integer, each place is given a value which is ten times the value of the place immediately at its right. For example, 734 means 7 hundreds plus 3 tens plus 4 ones. Therefore, $734 = 7(100) + 3(10) + 4(1)$. Similarly, 68 means 6 tens $+$ 8 ones, or $6(10) + 8(1)$. In the number 68, we call 6 the tens' digit and 8 the units' digit. The value of the tens' digit 6 is 60. The value of the units' digit 8 is 8.

If we wish to represent a two-digit number whose tens' digit is represented by t and whose units' digit is represented by u, we write $t(10) + u(1)$, or more simply $10t + u$. Notice that we may not represent the two-digit number by tu because tu means "t times u."

KEEP IN MIND

If t represents the tens' digit and u represents the units' digit of a two-digit number:

$10t + u$ represents the original number.

$10u + t$ represents the original number with its digits reversed.

$t + u$ represents the sum of the digits of the original number.

Exercises

In 1–5, give the value of each digit in each of the numbers.

1. 39   **2.** 625   **3.** 7803   **4.** 905   **5.** 25013

In 6–10, represent the number which is described.

6. The number whose tens' digit is 9 and whose units' digit is 1.
7. The number whose units' digit is 7 and whose tens' digit is 5.
8. The number obtained by reversing the digits of 38.
9. The number whose hundreds' digit is represented by h, whose tens' digit is represented by t, and whose units' digit is represented by u.
10. The number obtained by reversing the digits of the number described in exercise 9.

SOLVING DIGIT PROBLEMS

~~~~~~~~~~~~ **MODEL PROBLEM** ~~~~~~~~~~~~

In a two-digit number, the sum of the digits is 9. The number is 12 times the tens' digit. Find the number.

Solution:

Using One Variable	*Using Two Variables*

Using One Variable

Let x = the tens' digit.

Then $9 - x$ = the units' digit.

And $10x + (9 - x)$ = the number.

The number is 12 times the tens' digit.

$$10x + (9 - x) = 12x$$
$$10x + 9 - x = 12x$$
$$9 + 9x = 12x$$
$$9 = 3x \quad A_{-9x}$$
$$x = 3$$
$$9 - x = 6$$
$$10x + (9 - x) = 10(3) + 6 = 36$$

Using Two Variables

Let t = the tens' digit.

Let u = the units' digit.

$10t + u$ = the number.

The sum of the digits is 9.

$$t + u = 9 \quad (A)$$

The number is 12 times the tens' digits.

$$10t + u = 12t \quad (B)$$

$$\begin{array}{l} -2t + u = 0 \quad A_{-12t} \\ \underline{2t + 2u = 18} \quad [\text{In } A, \text{ M}_2.] \\ 3u = 18 \\ u = 6 \end{array}$$

In A, let $u = 6$.

$$t + 6 = 9$$
$$t = 3$$
$$10t + u = 10(3) + 6 = 36$$

Check: $3 + 6 = 9$ and $36 = 12(3)$

Answer: The number is 36.

~~~~~~

Exercises

1. In a two-digit number, the sum of the digits is 10 and the difference of the digits is 4. Find the number if the tens' digit is larger than the units' digit.
2. The tens' digit in a two-digit number is 2 more than twice the units' digit. The sum of the digits is 11. Find the number.

3. The units' digit in a two-digit number exceeds the tens' digit by 6. The sum of the digits is 10. Find the number.

4. The tens' digit of a two-digit number is 2 less than 4 times the units' digit. The difference between the tens' digit and the units' digit is 4. Find the number.

5. The units' digit of a two-digit number exceeds twice the tens' digit by 3. The sum of the digits is 6. Find the number.

6. The units' digit of a two-digit number is 4 more than the tens' digit. The number is 6 times the units' digit. Find the number.

7. The tens' digit of a two-digit number is 2 less than the units' digit. The number is 4 times the sum of the digits. Find the number.

8. The tens' digit of a two-digit number exceeds 3 times the units' digit by 1. The number is 8 times the sum of the digits. Find the number.

9. The tens' digit of a two-digit number exceeds the units' digit by 3. The number is 1 more than 8 times the sum of the digits. Find the number.

10. The units' digit of a two-digit number is 11 less than twice the tens' digit. The number is 6 less than 7 times the sum of the digits. Find the number.

11. The sum of the digits of a two-digit number is 11. If 45 is added to the number, the order of the digits is reversed. Find the number.

12. The tens' digit of a two-digit number is 1 more than 4 times the units' digit. If 63 is subtracted from the number, the order of the digits is reversed. Find the number.

MOTION PROBLEMS INVOLVING WATER CURRENTS AND AIR CURRENTS

PREPARING TO SOLVE MOTION PROBLEMS INVOLVING CURRENTS

Let us suppose that the motors of a boat supply enough power for the boat to travel at the rate of 20 mph in a body of still water, where there is no current. When the boat travels in a body of water where there is a current, the boat will move faster than 20 mph when it is traveling downstream with the current. It will move slower than 20 mph when it is traveling upstream against the current. For example, if the boat is traveling in a river which is flowing at the rate of 3 mph, the rate of the boat traveling downstream with the current will be 20 + 3, or 23 mph. Its rate traveling upstream against the current will be 20 − 3, or 17 mph.

The rate of speed of an airplane is similarly affected by an air current. Suppose the motors of a plane supply enough power for a plane to travel at the rate of 300 mph in still air, and there is a wind blowing at the rate of 20 mph. When flying with the wind, the plane will be traveling at the rate of 300 + 20, or 320 mph. When flying against the wind, the plane will be traveling at the rate of 300 − 20, or 280 mph.

KEEP IN MIND

If r = the rate in still water or in still air,
and c = the rate of the water current or air current,
then $r + c$ = the rate traveling with the current
and $r − c$ = the rate traveling against the current.

Exercises

1. A boy who can row 3 mph in still water is rowing in a stream which is flowing at the rate of 1 mph.
   a. Find his rate rowing downstream.
   b. Find his rate rowing upstream.
   c. How long would it take him to row 4 miles downstream?
   d. How long would it take him to return to his starting point rowing upstream?
   e. What is his total time going and returning?

2. A plane which can fly 250 mph in still air is flying at a time when the wind is blowing at the rate of 50 mph.
   a. Find the rate of the plane with the wind.
   b. Find the rate of the plane against the wind.
   c. How long would it take the plane to fly 600 miles with the wind?
   d. How long would it take the plane to return to its starting point flying against the wind?
   e. What is the total time going and returning?

3. A motorboat which can travel 35 mph in still water is traveling downstream at the rate of 38 mph. Find the rate of the stream.

4. A plane which was flying against a 35-mph wind traveled 318 miles in 1 hour. How far would the plane have traveled in 1 hour if there had been no wind?

5. If x represents the rate of a boat in still water and y represents the rate of the current of a river in which it is traveling, represent:
   a. the rate of the boat traveling downstream
   b. the rate of the boat traveling upstream
   c. the distance the boat would travel in 2 hours going downstream
   d. the distance the boat would travel in 3 hours going upstream

SOLVING MOTION PROBLEMS INVOLVING CURRENTS

—————————— *MODEL PROBLEM* ——————————

A motorboat can travel 60 miles downstream in 3 hours. It requires 5 hours
to make the return trip against the current. Find the rate of the boat
in still water and the rate of the current.

Solution:

Let r = the rate of the boat in still water.

Let c = the rate of the current.

	(mph) Rate	(hr.) Time	(mi.) Distance
Downstream	$r + c$	3	$3r + 3c$
Upstream	$r - c$	5	$5r - 5c$

The distance downstream is 60 miles.

$$3r + 3c = 60 \ (A)$$

The distance upstream is 60 miles.

$$5r - 5c = 60 \ (B)$$

1. In order to eliminate c in equation A, multiply both
   members by 5; in equation B, multiply both members by 3.

$$15r + 15c = 300$$
$$15r - 15c = 180$$
$$\overline{30r \qquad\quad = 480}$$
$$r = 16$$

2. In equation A, let $r = 16$.

$$3(16) + 3c = 60$$
$$48 + 3c = 60$$
$$3c = 12$$
$$c = 4$$

Check: Rate downstream = 16 + 4 or 20 mph.
Rate upstream = 16 − 4 or 12 mph.
Distance downstream = 3(20) = 60 miles.
Distance upstream = 5(12) = 60 miles.

Answer: The rate of the boat in still water is 16 mph; the rate of the current
is 4 mph.

Exercises

In 1–10, solve each problem by using two variables.

1. Mr. Turner has a motorboat that can travel 14 mph in still water. He wishes to take a trip on a river whose current flows at the rate of 2 mph. If he has 7 hours at his disposal, how many hours should he spend on the first part of his trip going downstream before returning upstream to his starting point?

2. A plane which can fly 275 mph in still air flies for 3 hours against a wind and for 2 hours with the same wind. The total distance it covers is 1300 miles. Find the rate of the wind.

3. A flyer on a reconnaissance flight has 4 hours for a round trip. His plane can fly 200 mph in still air. He flies out from his base against a 20-mph wind and immediately returns to his base, flying with the same wind. How many hours did he take for his flight out?

4. A plane flew for 4 hours against a 10-mph wind. It then flew for 3 hours with the same wind. In all, the plane flew 1390 miles. Find the rate of the plane in still air.

5. A boat is rowed downstream a distance of 16 miles in 2 hours. It is then rowed the same distance upstream in 8 hours. Find the rate of rowing in still water and the rate of the current.

6. A boat travels 18 miles downstream in 2 hours. It requires 6 hours to travel back to its starting point upstream. What is the rate of the boat in still water and what is the rate of the current?

7. A plane left an airport and flew with the wind for 4 hours, covering 2000 miles. It then returned over the same route to the airport against the same wind in 5 hours. Find the rate of the plane in still air and the speed of the wind.

8. Flying with a wind, a plane traveled 1080 miles in 6 hours. Flying against the same wind, the plane covered only $\frac{2}{3}$ of this distance in the same time. Find the speed of the plane in still air and the speed of the wind.

9. In 3 hours, a plane flew 720 miles with a wind. It then flew $\frac{4}{9}$ of this distance against the same wind in 2 hours. Find the speed of the plane in still air and the speed of the wind.

10. A plane flew a distance of 1555 miles in 5 hours. During the first 3 hours of the flight, it flew with a wind a distance of 975 miles. During the remainder of the flight, the plane flew against a wind whose average speed was 5 mph less than what it had been during the first part of the flight. Find the rate of the plane in still air and the original speed of the wind.

MISCELLANEOUS PROBLEMS

In 1–13, solve each problem by using two variables.

1. Tickets for a high school football game cost 50 cents each if purchased at the advanced sale before the day of the game. They cost 75 cents each if bought at the gate on the day of the game. For a particular game, 600 tickets were sold and the receipts were $350. How many tickets were sold at the gate for this game?

2. Mr. Vogel left $25,000 to be divided between his son and daughter. The son received $5000 less than the daughter. How much did each receive?

3. The perimeter of a rectangle is 78 inches. The length of the rectangle is twice its width. Find the dimensions of the rectangle.

4. The perimeter of a rectangle is 28 feet. Three times the length increased by 4 times the width is 48 feet. Find the dimensions of the rectangle.

5. Mr. Straton traveled for 7 hours and covered 260 miles on the trip. During the first part of the trip, he averaged 40 mph. During the second part, he averaged 30 mph. How many hours did he spend on each part of the trip?

6. Mr. Paley hiked from his summer cabin to town at the rate of 3 miles per hour. He came back in a car which averaged 36 miles per hour. If the total time he traveled was $3\frac{1}{4}$ hours, find the amount of time he spent on each part of the trip.

7. The sum of Godfrey's age and Marilyn's age is 60 years. Ten years ago, Godfrey was 3 times as old as Marilyn was then. How old is each now?

8. Four years ago, Mike was 5 times as old as Daniel was then. Eight years from now, Mike will be twice as old as Daniel will be then. Find the age of each now.

9. Henry bought 100 stamps for $8.00. Some were 5-cent stamps. The rest were 10-cent stamps. How many of each kind did he buy?

10. A dealer has a solution which is 60% pure acid and another solution which is 35% pure acid. How many ounces of each solution should he use to make 100 ounces of a solution which is 50% pure acid?

11. If 3 is subtracted from the numerator of a certain fraction, the value becomes $\frac{2}{3}$. If 10 is added to the denominator of the original fraction, the value becomes $\frac{1}{2}$. Find the original fraction.

12. If 3 is added to both numerator and denominator of a fraction, it becomes equal to $\frac{3}{4}$. When 5 is subtracted from both numerator and denominator of the original fraction, it becomes equal to $\frac{1}{4}$. Find the original fraction.

13. If the numerator of a fraction is decreased by 1 and the denominator is increased by 5, the value of the fraction becomes $\frac{1}{2}$. If the numerator of the original fraction is increased by 1 and the denominator of the original fraction is decreased by 6, the value of the resulting fraction becomes $\frac{4}{3}$. Find the original fraction.

5. Graphing Solution Sets of Systems of Inequalities

In order to find the solution set of a system of inequalities, we must find the ordered pairs that satisfy all the open sentences of the system. We do this by a graphic method that is similar to the method used in finding the solution set of a system of equations.

~~~~~~~~~ MODEL PROBLEMS ~~~~~~~~~

1. Graph the solution set of the system: $x > 2$
$$y < -2$$

Solution:

1. Graph $x > 2$ by first graphing the plane divider $x = 2$. (In the figure, see the dashed line labeled A.) The half-plane to the right of this line is the graph of the solution set of $x > 2$.

2. Using the same set of axes, graph $y < -2$ by first graphing the plane divider $y = -2$. (In the figure, see the dashed line labeled B.) The half-plane below this line is the graph of the solution set of $y < -2$.

3. The solution set of the system $x > 2$ and $y < -2$ consists of the intersection of the solution sets of $x > 2$ and $y < -2$. Therefore, the crosshatched region, which is the intersection of both graphs made in steps 1 and 2, is the graph of the solution set of the system $x > 2$ and $y < -2$. All points in this region, and no others, satisfy both sentences of the system. For example, the point $(4, -3)$, which lies in the region, satisfies both sentences of the system because its x-value $4 > 2$, and its y-value $-3 < -2$.

2. Graph the solution set of $3 < x < 5$.

Solution:

1. The sentence $3 < x < 5$ means $3 < x$
   and $x < 5$. This may be written $x > 3$
   and $x < 5$. Therefore, graph $x > 3$ by
   first graphing the plane divider $x = 3$.
   (In the figure, see the dashed line labeled A.) The half-plane to the right
   of the line $x = 3$ is the graph of the
   solution set of $x > 3$.

   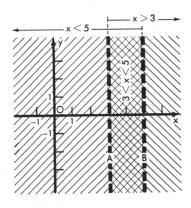

2. Using the same set of axes, graph $x < 5$
   by first graphing the plane divider
   $x = 5$. (In the figure, see the dashed
   line labeled B.) The half-plane to the
   left of the line $x = 5$ is the graph of the
   solution set of $x < 5$.

3. The crosshatched region, which is the intersection of the graphs made
   in steps 1 and 2, is the graph of the solution set of $x > 3$ and $x < 5$,
   or $3 < x < 5$.

3. Graph the solution set of the system: $x + y \geq 4$
$$y \leq 2x - 3$$

Solution:

1. Graph $x + y \geq 4$ by first graphing the
   plane divider $x + y = 4$. (In the figure, see
   the solid line labeled R.) The line $x + y = 4$
   and the half-plane above this line together
   form the graph of the solution set of
   $x + y \geq 4$.

   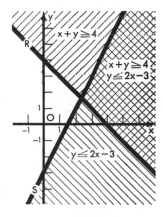

2. Using the same set of axes, graph $y \leq 2x - 3$
   by first graphing the plane divider $y =
   2x - 3$. (In the figure, see the solid line
   labeled S.) The line $y = 2x - 3$ and the
   half-plane below this line together form the
   graph of the solution set of $y \leq 2x - 3$.

3. The crosshatched region, which is the intersection of both graphs made in steps 1 and 2,
   is the graph of the solution set of the system $x + y \geq 4$ and $y \leq 2x - 3$.

4. Graph the solution set of the system: $3x + 5y \geq 15$
$$y \leq x + 2$$
$$x \leq 3$$

Solution:

1. Graph $3x + 5y \geq 15$ by first graphing the plane divider $3x + 5y = 15$. (See line R.) The line $3x + 5y = 15$ and the half-plane above this line together form the graph of the solution set of $3x + 5y \geq 15$.

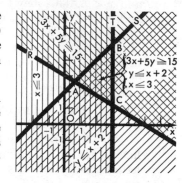

2. Using the same set of axes, graph $y \leq x + 2$ by first graphing the plane divider $y = x + 2$. (See line S.) The line $y = x + 2$ and the half-plane below this line together form the graph of the solution set of $y \leq x + 2$.

3. Using the same set of axes, graph $x \leq 3$ by first graphing the plane divider $x = 3$. (See line T.) The line $x = 3$ and the half-plane to the left of this line together form the graph of the solution set of $x \leq 3$.

4. The crosshatched region with all three types of hatching is the graph of the solution set of the system $3x + 5y \geq 15$, $y \leq x + 2$, $x \leq 3$. Notice that this region includes the interior of triangle ABC as well as all points on the lines AB, BC, and AC which form the sides of the triangle. Every point in this region is common to all three graphs made in steps 1, 2, and 3.

Exercises

In 1–21, graph the solution set of each system in a coordinate plane.

1. $x > 1$
$y > -2$

2. $x \leq 2$
$y \geq 3$

3. $x > 0$
$y < 0$

4. $x < 0$
$y > 0$

5. $y \geq x$
$x < 2$

6. $y \leq x$
$x \geq -1$

7. $y \geq 2x$
$y > x + 3$

8. $y \leq 2x + 3$
$y \geq -x$

9. $y - x \geq 5$
$y - 2x \leq 7$

10. $x + y > 3$
$x - y < 6$

11. $x - y \leq -2$
$x + y \geq 2$

12. $2x + y > -4$
$x - y \leq 1$

13. $2x + y \leq 6$
$\quad x + y - 2 > 0$

14. $2x + 3y \geq 6$
$\quad x + y - 4 \leq 0$

15. $5x - 3y - 2 \geq 0$
$\quad 4x + 2y + 2 < 0$

16. $y \geq x$
$\quad x = 0$

17. $x + y \leq 3$
$\quad y - 2x = 0$

18. $y - 2x - 2 > 0$
$\quad x + y - 2 = 0$

19. $x \leq 2$
$\quad y \leq 2$
$\quad x + y \geq 2$

20. $x + 3y \leq 6$
$\quad 2y \geq 2$
$\quad x \geq -2$

21. $y \geq x$
$\quad x + y - 3 \geq 0$
$\quad x - 4 \leq 0$

In 22–25, graph the solution set in a coordinate plane.

22. $1 < x < 4$

23. $-5 \leq x \leq -1$

24. $2 < y \leq 6$

25. $-2 \leq y \leq 3$

CHAPTER XVII

RATIO, PROPORTION, AND VARIATION

1. Ratio

The **ratio** of one number to another is the quotient of the first number divided by the second. For example, if Paul is 10 years old and Marion is 2 years old, the ratio of Paul's age to Marion's age is $10 \div 2$, or $\frac{10}{2}$. The quotient is equivalent to $\frac{5}{1}$, or 5. To compare Paul's age to Marion's age, we say the ratio of Paul's age to Marion's age is 5 to 1. We may also say Paul is 5 times as old as Marion.

Another way to express the ratio $\frac{10}{2}$ is to use the ratio symbol ":" and write "10:2."

In general, the ratio of a to b can be expressed as $\frac{a}{b}$, $a \div b$, or $a:b$. The numbers a and b are called the **terms** of the ratio.

A ratio is the quotient of two numbers in a definite order. The ratio of 5 to 1 is written $\frac{5}{1}$ or 5:1, whereas the ratio of 1 to 5 is written $\frac{1}{5}$ or 1:5. Therefore, a ratio may be considered as an ordered pair of numbers.

To find the ratio of two quantities, both quantities must be expressed in the same unit of measure before we find their quotient. For example, to compare a nickel with a penny, we first convert the nickel to 5 pennies and then find the ratio, which is $\frac{5}{1}$, or 5:1. Therefore, a nickel is worth 5 times as much as a penny.

Since the ratio $\frac{5}{1}$ is a fraction, we can use the multiplication property of 1 to find many equivalent ratios. For example:

$$\frac{5}{1} = \frac{5}{1} \cdot \frac{2}{2} = \frac{10}{2} \qquad \frac{5}{1} = \frac{5}{1} \cdot \frac{3}{3} = \frac{15}{3} \qquad \frac{5}{1} = \frac{5}{1} \cdot \frac{x}{x} = \frac{5x}{1x} \quad (x \neq 0)$$

From the last example, we see that $5x$ and $1x$ represent two numbers whose ratio is 5:1.

In general, if a, b, and x are numbers ($b \neq 0$, $x \neq 0$), ax and bx represent two numbers whose ratio is $a:b$ because:

$$\frac{a}{b} = \frac{a}{b} \cdot \frac{x}{x} = \frac{ax}{bx}$$

Also, since a ratio such as $\frac{24}{16}$ is a fraction, we can use the division property of a fraction to find equivalent ratios. For example:

$$\frac{24}{16} = \frac{24 \div 2}{16 \div 2} = \frac{12}{8} \qquad \frac{24}{16} = \frac{24 \div 4}{16 \div 4} = \frac{6}{4} \qquad \frac{24}{16} = \frac{24 \div 8}{16 \div 8} = \frac{3}{2}$$

A ratio is expressed in simplest form when both terms of the ratio are whole numbers and when there is no whole number other than 1 which is a common divisor of these terms. Thus, to express the ratio $\frac{24}{16}$ in simplest form, we divide both terms by their greatest common divisor, 8. We obtain the ratio $\frac{3}{2}$ (as shown in the last example).

If Ted weighs 50 lb., May weighs 40 lb., and Sue weighs 30 lb., the ratio of Ted's weight to May's weight is 50:40 and the ratio of May's weight to Sue's weight is 40:30. We can write these two ratios in an abbreviated form as the **continued ratio** 50:40:30. We say that the ratio of the weights of Ted, May, and Sue is 50:40:30.

In general, the ratio of the numbers a, b, and c $(b \neq 0,\ c \neq 0)$ is $a:b:c$.

~~~~~~~~ MODEL PROBLEMS ~~~~~~~~

1. Phil's forearm is $1\frac{1}{2}$ ft. long. In a photograph, his forearm is 1 in. long. What is the ratio of the actual length of Phil's forearm to the length of the forearm in the picture?

   Solution:

   $$\text{ratio} = \frac{\text{actual length of Phil's forearm}}{\text{length of forearm in picture}} = \frac{1\frac{1}{2}\text{ ft.}}{1\text{ in.}} = \frac{18\text{ in.}}{1\text{ in.}} = \frac{18}{1}$$

   Answer: 18:1

2. Express the ratio $1\frac{3}{4}$ to $1\frac{1}{2}$ in simplest form.

   Solution:

   Method 1

   $$\text{ratio} = 1\tfrac{3}{4} : 1\tfrac{1}{2} = \frac{1\frac{3}{4}}{1\frac{1}{2}} = \frac{\frac{7}{4}}{\frac{3}{2}} = \frac{\frac{7}{4}}{\frac{3}{2}} \cdot \frac{4}{4} = \frac{\frac{7}{4} \cdot \frac{4}{1}}{\frac{3}{2} \cdot \frac{4}{1}} = \frac{7}{6} \quad Ans.$$

   Method 2

   $$\text{ratio} = 1\tfrac{3}{4} : 1\tfrac{1}{2} = 1\tfrac{3}{4} \div 1\tfrac{1}{2} = \tfrac{7}{4} \div \tfrac{3}{2} = \tfrac{7}{4} \times \tfrac{2}{3} = \tfrac{14}{12} = \tfrac{7}{6} \quad Ans.$$

Exercises

1. Express each ratio as a fraction.
   a. 36 to 12   b. 48 to 24   c. 40 to 25   d. 2 to 3   e. 5 to 4

2. Write each ratio using a colon.
   a. 15 to 30   b. 90 to 45   c. 49 to 14   d. 5 to 3   e. 7 to 9

3. Express each ratio in simplest form.
   a. $\frac{8}{32}$ b. $\frac{40}{5}$ c. $\frac{12}{28}$ d. $\frac{36}{27}$ e. $\frac{36}{24}$
   f. 20:10   g. 15:45   h. 18:18   i. 48:20   j. 21:35
   k. $3x:2x$ l. $1y:4y$ m. $3c:5c$ n. $7x:7y$ o. $12s:4s^2$

4. The larger number is how many times the smaller number?
   a. 10, 5   b. 18, 6   c. 12, 8   d. 25, 10   e. 15, 25

5. If the ratio of two numbers is 4:1, how many times the smaller number is the larger number?

6. What fractional part of the larger number is the smaller number?
   a. 8, 24   b. 7, 14   c. 50, 10   d. 12, 18   e. 36, 27

7. If the ratio of two numbers is 8:1, the smaller number is what fractional part of the larger number?

8. In each part, tell whether the ratio is equal to $\frac{3}{2}$.
   a. $\frac{30}{20}$ b. $\frac{9}{4}$ c. $\frac{8}{12}$ d. 9:6   e. $\frac{45}{30}$ f. 18:6

9. In each part, name the ratios that are equal.
   a. $\frac{2}{3}, \frac{6}{9}, \frac{10}{30}, \frac{28}{36}, \frac{50}{75}$ b. 10:8, 20:16, 15:13, 4:5, 50:40

10. In each part, find the number which can replace the question mark and make the resulting statement true.
    a. $\dfrac{1}{2} = \dfrac{?}{24}$ b. $\dfrac{2}{3} = \dfrac{10}{?}$ c. $\dfrac{4}{5} = \dfrac{?}{100}$ d. $\dfrac{5}{8} = \dfrac{25}{?}$

11. Find four pairs of numbers, the ratio of each pair of numbers being:
    a. $\frac{1}{2}$ b. $\frac{1}{5}$ c. 3:1   d. 4:1   e. $\frac{3}{4}$ f. 2:3

12. Using a colon, express in simplest form the ratio of all pairs of   (a) equal numbers (not zero) and   (b) non-zero numbers whose difference is 0.

13. Express each ratio in simplest form.
    a. $\frac{3}{4}$ to $\frac{1}{4}$ b. $1\frac{1}{8}$ to $\frac{3}{8}$ c. $1\frac{1}{6}:2\frac{5}{6}$ d. $\frac{3}{4}$ to $\frac{5}{8}$ e. $1\frac{2}{3}:2\frac{1}{2}$
    f. 1.2 to 2.4   g. .75 to .25   h. 1.2:4   i. 6:.25   j. .05 to .01

14. Express each ratio in simplest form.

a. $1\frac{1}{2}$ hr. to $\frac{1}{2}$ hr.   b. $\frac{2}{3}$ yd. to $\frac{5}{8}$ yd.   c. 3 in. to $\frac{1}{2}$ in.

d. 1 ft. to 1 in.   e. 1 yd. to 1 ft.   f. $\frac{1}{3}$ yd. to 6 in.

g. 12 oz. to 3 lb.   h. 1 hr. to 15 min.   i. 12 hr. to 4 days

j. $6 to 50 cents   k. $\frac{2}{3}$ min. to 10 sec.   l. 2 mi. to 880 yd.

15. In a class, there are 20 boys and 10 girls.

a. What is the ratio of the number of boys to the number of girls?

b. For one girl in the class, how many boys are there?

c. What is the ratio of the number of girls to the number of boys?

d. What is the ratio of the number of boys to the total number of pupils in the class?

e. What is the ratio of the number of girls to the total number of pupils in the class?

16. A baseball team played 144 games and won 96.

a. What is the ratio of the number of games won to the number of games played?

b. For every 3 games played, how many games were won?

17. A student did 6 out of 10 problems correctly.

a. What is the ratio of the number right to the number wrong?

b. For every two answers that were wrong, how many answers were right?

18. A cake recipe calls for $1\frac{1}{2}$ cups of milk to $1\frac{3}{4}$ cups of flour. What is the ratio of the number of cups of milk to the number of cups of flour in this recipe?

19. The perimeter of a rectangle is 30 ft. and the width is 5 ft. Find the ratio of the length of the rectangle to its width.

20. In a freshman class, there are b boys and g girls. Express the ratio of the number of boys to the total number of pupils.

21. The length of a rectangle is represented by $3x$ and its width by $2x$. Find the ratio of the width of the rectangle to its perimeter.

22. Represent in terms of x two numbers whose ratio is:

a. 3 to 4   b. 4 to 7   c. 5 to 3   d. 3 to 1   e. 1 to 4

f. 1:2   g. 3:5   h. 2:3   i. 7:1   j. 9:5

23. Represent in terms of x three numbers which have the continued ratio:

a. 1 to 2 to 3   b. 3 to 4 to 5   c. 1 to 3 to 2   d. 7 to 3 to 1

e. 1:3:4   f. 2:3:5   g. 1:5:4   h. 9:5:2

2. Solving Verbal Problems Involving Ratios

~~~~~~~~~~~~~~~ **MODEL PROBLEMS** ~~~~~~~~~~~~~~~

1. Tom and his helper Bill agreed to do a job for $120. They also agreed to share this money in the ratio 3:1. How much money did each receive?

Solution:

Let $3x$ = the number of dollars Tom received.
Then $1x$ = the number of dollars Bill received.

The total of the two amounts is $120.

$$3x + 1x = 120$$
$$4x = 120$$
$$x = 30$$
$$3x = 90$$

Check

$$90 + 30 = 120$$
$$90:30 = 3:1$$

Answer: Tom received $90 and Bill received $30.

2. In a class, the ratio of the number of boys to the number of girls is $\frac{3}{2}$. If there are 14 girls in the class, how many boys are in the class?

Solution:

Let x = the number of boys.

Then $\dfrac{x}{14}$ = the ratio of the number of boys to the number of girls.

The ratio of the number of boys to the number of girls is $\frac{3}{2}$.

$$\frac{x}{14} = \frac{3}{2}$$

$$14\left(\frac{x}{14}\right) = 14\left(\frac{3}{2}\right) \quad \text{M}_{14}$$

$$x = 21$$

Check

$$\frac{21}{14} = \frac{3}{2}$$

Answer: 21 boys

3. Two numbers have the ratio 2:3. The larger is 30 more than $\frac{1}{2}$ of the smaller. Find the numbers.

Solution:

Let $2x$ = the smaller number.
Then $3x$ = the larger number.

The larger number is 30 more than $\frac{1}{2}$ of the smaller number.

$$3x = \tfrac{1}{2}(2x) + 30$$
$$3x = x + 30$$
$$3x - x = x + 30 - x$$
$$2x = 30$$
$$x = 15$$
$$2x = 30$$
$$3x = 45$$

Check

The ratio of 30 to 45 is 30:45 or 2:3. The larger number, 45, is 30 more than 15, which is $\frac{1}{2}$ of the smaller number.

Answer: The numbers are 30 and 45.

Exercises

1. Two numbers have the ratio 4:3. Their sum is 70. Find the numbers.
2. Find two numbers in the ratio 1:3 whose sum is 24.
3. Find two numbers whose sum is 160 and which have the ratio 5:3.
4. Two numbers have the ratio 7:5. Their difference is 12. Find the numbers.
5. Find two numbers whose ratio is 4:1 and whose difference is 36.
6. Mr. Gray and Mr. Charles are business partners. They agree to share the business profits in the ratio 4:3. One year the profits amounted to $35,000. How much money did each partner receive?
7. A line segment 32 inches in length is divided into two parts which are in the ratio 3:5. Find the length of each part.
8. An angle whose measure is 120° is divided into three parts in the ratio 2:3:7. Find the number of degrees in each part.
9. The ratio of the number of boys in a school to the number of girls is 11 to 10. If there are 525 pupils in the school, how many of them are boys?
10. The perimeter of a triangle is 48 in. The lengths of the sides are in the ratio 3:4:5. Find the length of each side.
11. The ratio of the number of pupils in the seventh grade of a school to the number of pupils in the eighth grade is $\frac{4}{5}$. If the number of pupils in the eighth grade is 125, find the number of pupils in the seventh grade.
12. The ratio of a father's age to his son's age is $\frac{7}{2}$. If the son's age is 10 years, how old is the father?

13. Mr. Corliss is following a budget in which the ratio of the amount paid for rent to the total monthly income is 1:4. If Mr. Corliss earns $400 a month, what is his monthly rent?

14. The weight of dried apples to the weight of the fresh apples from which they were dried is in the ratio of 2:5. How many pounds of fresh apples are needed to produce 98 pounds of dried apples?

15. The ratio of Carl's money to Donald's money is 7:3. If Carl gives Donald $20, the two then have equal amounts. Find the original amount that each one had.

16. Two numbers are in the ratio 3:7. The larger exceeds the smaller by 12. Find the numbers.

17. Two numbers are in the ratio 4:3. One-half of the larger exceeds one-third of the smaller by 5. Find the numbers.

18. Two numbers are in the ratio 4:15. If 25 is added to the smaller and the larger is diminished by 30, the resulting numbers are equal. Find the original numbers.

19. Two numbers are in the ratio 3:5. If 9 is added to their sum, the result is 41. Find the numbers.

20. John's age and Helen's age are in the ratio 3:5. Two years ago, Helen was twice as old as John was then. Find their present ages.

21. In a basketball foul shooting contest, the points made by Sam and Wilbur were in the ratio 7:9. Wilbur made 6 more points than Sam. Find the number of points made by each.

22. A chemist wishes to make $12\frac{1}{2}$ quarts of an acid solution by using water and acid in the ratio 3:2. How many quarts of each should he use?

23. The numerator and denominator of a fraction are in the ratio 3:5. If 2 is subtracted from the numerator and 6 is added to the denominator, the resulting fraction has the value $\frac{1}{3}$. Find the original fraction.

24. The numerator and the denominator of a fraction are in the ratio 3:7. If 2 is added to both the numerator and denominator, the ratio becomes 1:2. Find the original fraction.

25. Carl has $2.50 in his bank in nickels and dimes. The number of nickels and the number of dimes have the ratio 3:1. How many coins of each type does he have?

26. Two motorboats start at the same time from the same place and travel in opposite directions. The ratio of their rates of speed is 2:3. In 3 hours, they are 60 miles apart. Find the rate of each boat.

27. The ratio of Sue's age to Betty's age is 4:1. Twenty years from now, Sue will be twice as old as Betty will be then. Find their present ages.

28. The perimeter of a rectangle is 360 feet. If the ratio of its length to its width is 11:4, find the dimensions of the rectangle.

29. The ratio of a leg of an isosceles triangle to the base of the triangle is 4:3. If the perimeter of the triangle is 66, find the three sides of the triangle.

3. Proportion

Since the ratio $\frac{4}{20}$ is equal to the ratio $\frac{1}{5}$, we may write $\frac{4}{20} = \frac{1}{5}$. The equation $\frac{4}{20} = \frac{1}{5}$ is called a **proportion.** A proportion is an equation which states that two ratios are equal.

Another way of writing the proportion $\frac{4}{20} = \frac{1}{5}$ is 4:20 = 1:5. Both these equations are read "4 is to 20 as 1 is to 5."

The proportion $\frac{a}{b} = \frac{c}{d}$ ($b \neq 0$, $d \neq 0$), or $a:b = c:d$, is read "a is to b as c is to d." There are four terms in this proportion, namely, a, b, c, and d. The first and fourth terms, a and d, are called the **extremes** of the proportion. The second and third terms are called the **means.**

$$a : b = c : d$$

Observe that in the proportion 4:20 = 1:5 the product of the two means, 20 × 1, is equal to the product of the two extremes, 4 × 5, because each product is 20.

Likewise, in the proportion $\frac{5}{15} = \frac{10}{30}$ the product of the means, 15 × 10, is equal to the product of the extremes, 5 × 30, each product being 150.

In the proportion $\frac{a}{b} = \frac{c}{d}$ we can also show that the product of the means is equal to the product of the extremes, $ad = bc$.

Since $\frac{a}{b} = \frac{c}{d}$ is an equation, we can multiply both members by the L.C.D., bd, as follows:

$$\frac{a}{b} = \frac{c}{d}$$

$$bd\left(\frac{a}{b}\right) = bd\left(\frac{c}{d}\right)$$

$$ad = bc$$

Therefore, we have shown that the following statement is always true:

In a proportion, the product of the means is equal to the product of the extremes.

If a sentence states that two ratios are equal, and if the product of the first and fourth terms does not equal the product of the second and third terms, then the sentence is not a true proportion.

~~~~~~~~~~~~~~~~~~~ **MODEL PROBLEMS** ~~~~~~~~~~~~~~~~~~~

1. Tell whether $\frac{4}{16} = \frac{5}{20}$ is a true proportion.

Solution:

Method 1

$\frac{4}{16} = \frac{1}{4}$ and $\frac{5}{20} = \frac{1}{4}$

Therefore, $\frac{4}{16}$ and $\frac{5}{20}$ are equal ratios and $\frac{4}{16} = \frac{5}{20}$ is a true proportion.

Method 2

In the equation $\frac{4}{16} = \frac{5}{20}$, the product of the second and third terms is 16×5, or 80. The product of the first and fourth terms, 4×20, is also 80. Therefore, $\frac{4}{16} = \frac{5}{20}$ is a true proportion.

Answer: Yes

2. Solve for q in the proportion $25:q = 5:2$.

Solution

If $25:q = 5:2$ is a true proportion, then $5q = 25 \times 2$ (the product of the means is equal to the product of the extremes).

$$5q = 25 \times 2$$
$$5q = 50$$
$$q = 10$$

Answer: $q = 10$

Check

$25:q = 5:2$
$25:10 \overset{?}{=} 5:2$
$5:2 = 5:2$ (true)

3. Solve for x: $\dfrac{12}{x-2} = \dfrac{32}{x+8}$

Solution

$$\frac{12}{x-2} = \frac{32}{x+8}$$

In a proportion, the product of the means is equal to the product of the extremes.

$$32(x-2) = 12(x+8)$$
$$32x - 64 = 12x + 96$$
$$32x - 12x = 96 + 64$$
$$20x = 160$$
$$x = 8$$

Answer: $x = 8$

Check

$$\frac{12}{x-2} = \frac{32}{x+8}$$
$$\frac{12}{8-2} \overset{?}{=} \frac{32}{8+8}$$
$$\frac{12}{6} \overset{?}{=} \frac{32}{16}$$
$$2 = 2 \quad \text{(true)}$$

Exercises

In 1–15, state whether the given ratios may form a true proportion.

1. $\frac{2}{3}, \frac{10}{5}$ **2.** $\frac{3}{4}, \frac{30}{40}$ **3.** $\frac{4}{5}, \frac{16}{25}$ **4.** $\frac{2}{7}, \frac{16}{49}$ **5.** $\frac{3}{5}, \frac{9}{15}$

6. $\frac{10}{15}, \frac{12}{20}$ **7.** $\frac{2}{5}, \frac{5}{2}$ **8.** $\frac{20}{30}, \frac{4}{12}$ **9.** $\frac{14}{18}, \frac{28}{36}$ **10.** $\frac{12}{15}, \frac{36}{30}$

11. $\frac{5x}{9x}, \frac{10}{18}$ **12.** $\frac{y}{3y}, \frac{4}{16}$ **13.** $\frac{x}{2x}, \frac{10}{20}$ **14.** $\frac{3x}{y}, \frac{6x}{2y}$ **15.** $\frac{5a}{6b}, \frac{10b}{12a}$

In 16–23, use the given numbers to form a true proportion.

16. 1, 3, 30, 10   **17.** 2, 3, 18, 12   **18.** 4, 1, 3, 12   **19.** 12, 2, 1, 6

20. 15, 40, 8, 3   **21.** 28, 6, 24, 7   **22.** 5, 4, 8, 10   **23.** 24, 36, 9, 6

In 24–31, find the number which can replace the question mark and make the result a true proportion.

24. $\frac{1}{2} = \frac{?}{8}$ **25.** $\frac{3}{5} = \frac{18}{?}$ **26.** $1:4 = 6:?$ **27.** $4:6 = ?:42$

28. $\frac{4}{?} = \frac{12}{60}$ **29.** $\frac{?}{9} = \frac{35}{63}$ **30.** $?:60 = 6:10$ **31.** $16:? = 12:9$

In 32–51, solve the equation.

32. $\frac{x}{5} = \frac{3}{20}$ **33.** $\frac{5}{4} = \frac{x}{12}$ **34.** $\frac{90}{81} = \frac{10}{3x}$

35. $\frac{30}{4x} = \frac{10}{24}$ **36.** $\frac{5}{15} = \frac{x}{x+8}$ **37.** $\frac{x+10}{x} = \frac{18}{12}$

38. $\frac{x}{12-x} = \frac{10}{30}$ **39.** $\frac{16}{8} = \frac{21-x}{x}$ **40.** $5:x = 9:27$

41. $12:15 = x:45$ **42.** $18:15 = x:45$ **43.** $8:2x = 15:60$

44. $19:4 = x:8$ **45.** $19:x = 57:15$ **46.** $\frac{5}{x+2} = \frac{4}{x}$

47. $\frac{3x+3}{3} = \frac{7x-1}{5}$ **48.** $\frac{2x-1}{21} = \frac{3x-7}{15}$ **49.** $\frac{x}{x+4} = \frac{x+1}{x+6}$

50. $\frac{x+1}{x-2} = \frac{x+3}{x-1}$ **51.** $\frac{3x+1}{5x-7} = \frac{3x+6}{5x-3}$

In 52–54, solve for x in terms of the other variables.

52. $a:b = c:x$ **53.** $2r:s = x:t$ **54.** $2x:m = 4r:s$

4. Solving Verbal Problems by Using Proportions

~~~~~~~~~~~~~~~~ *MODEL PROBLEMS* ~~~~~~~~~~~~~~~~

1. A man received $20 for working 8 hours. How much would he receive for working 14 hours at the same rate of pay?

Solution: The ratio of the corresponding number of hours worked equals the ratio of the number of dollars earned.

$$\frac{\text{number of hours worked on 1st job}}{\text{number of hours worked on 2nd job}} = \frac{\text{number of dollars earned on 1st job}}{\text{number of dollars earned on 2nd job}}$$

Let $d =$ the number of dollars he would receive.

$$\frac{8}{14} = \frac{20}{d}$$

Check

In a proportion, the product of the means is equal to the product of the extremes.

$$\frac{8}{14} \overset{?}{=} \frac{20}{35}$$

$$8d = 14 \times 20$$
$$8d = 280, \; d = 35$$

$$\frac{4}{7} = \frac{4}{7} \quad \text{(true)}$$

Answer: $35

2. A board 12 feet long is cut into two pieces whose lengths are in the ratio $3:1$. Find the length of each piece.

Solution:

Let $x =$ the length of the longer piece.

Then $12 - x =$ the length of the shorter piece.

Then $\dfrac{x}{12 - x} =$ the ratio of the lengths of the two pieces.

The lengths of the two pieces are in the ratio 3:1.

$$\frac{x}{12 - x} = \frac{3}{1}$$

Check

In a proportion, the product of the means is equal to the product of the extremes.

$$9 + 3 = 12$$

$$1(x) = 3(12 - x)$$

$$9:3 \overset{?}{=} 3:1$$

$$x = 36 - 3x$$

$$3:1 = 3:1 \quad \text{(true)}$$

$$x + 3x = 36 - 3x + 3x$$
$$4x = 36, \; x = 9, \; 12 - x = 3$$

Answer: The lengths of the pieces are 9 ft. and 3 ft.

Note: Previously, we have learned the following solution for the second model problem:

Let $3x =$ the length of the longer piece.
Then $1x =$ the length of the shorter piece.

The sum of the lengths of the two pieces is 12 feet.

$$3x + 1x = 12$$
$$4x = 12$$
$$x = 3, 3x = 9$$

Exercises

Solve each of the following problems algebraically.

1. If 3 apples cost 17 cents, find the cost of 15 apples at the same rate.
2. If 3 tickets to a show cost $13.20, find the cost of 7 such tickets.
3. If beans are being sold at the rate of 3 cans for 55 cents, how many cans can be bought for $2.20?
4. How much would you pay for 5 apples at the rate of 96 cents a dozen?
5. Henry scores an average of 7 foul shots out of every 10 attempts. At the same rate, how many shots would he score in 200 attempts?
6. A 40-acre field yields 600 bushels of wheat. At the same rate, what will a 75-acre field yield?
7. A boy can travel 11 miles on his bicycle in 2 hours. At the same rate, how far can he travel in 5 hours?
8. A train traveled 90 miles in $1\frac{1}{2}$ hours. How many miles will the train go in 6 hours, traveling at the same rate?
9. A boy traveled 11 miles on his bicycle in 2 hours. At the same rate, how long will it take him to travel 44 miles?
10. The weight of 50 feet of copper wire is 2 pounds. Find the weight of 325 feet of the same wire.
11. A workman received $28 for working 20 hours. At the same rate of pay, how many hours must he work to earn $49?
12. A recipe calls for $1\frac{1}{2}$ cups of sugar for a 3-pound cake. How many cups of sugar should be used for a 5-pound cake?
13. A house which is assessed for $8000 pays $240 in taxes. What should be the tax on a house assessed at $10,500?
14. The scale on a map is 1 inch = 500 miles. If two cities are 875 miles apart, how far apart are they on this map?
15. The scale on a blueprint is 1 inch = 20 feet. If on the blueprint the length of a room is $1\frac{1}{4}$ inches, what is the actual length of the room?

16. A picture $3\frac{1}{4}$ inches long and $2\frac{1}{8}$ inches wide is to be enlarged so that its length will become $6\frac{1}{2}$ inches. What will be the width of the enlarged picture?

17. Two numbers are in the ratio 3:2. The smaller number is 36. Find the larger number.

18. In a certain concrete mixture, the ratio of cement to sand is 1:4. How many bags of cement would be used with 100 bags of sand?

19. In a school, the ratio of the number of boys to the number of girls is 5:4. If 560 girls attend the school, what is the number of boys attending the school?

20. The ratio of the length of a rectangle to its width is 10:7. If the width of the rectangle is 70 feet, find its length.

21. A team played 144 games. The ratio of the number of games won to the number of games lost was 3:1. Find the number of games the team won.

22. A board 12 feet long is to be cut into two pieces having the ratio 5:1. Find the length of each piece.

23. If a man can buy p pounds of candy for d dollars, represent the cost of n pounds of candy.

24. If a family consumes q quarts of milk in d days, represent the amount of milk consumed in h days.

5. Direct Variation

If the length of a side of a square, s, is 1 in., then the perimeter of the square, p, is 4 in. Also, if s is 2 in., p is 8 in.; if s is 3 in., p is 12 in. These pairs of values are shown in the table at the right.

s	1	2	3
p	4	8	12

In the table, observe that as s varies, p also varies.

Let us find the value of the ratio $\frac{p}{s}$ for each pair of values in the table. Let us represent the three values of s by s_1, s_2, and s_3; and the corresponding values of p by p_1, p_2, and p_3. Then:

$$\frac{p_1}{s_1} = \frac{4}{1} \qquad\qquad \frac{p_2}{s_2} = \frac{8}{2} = \frac{4}{1} \qquad\qquad \frac{p_3}{s_3} = \frac{12}{3} = \frac{4}{1}.$$

Observe that the ratio $\frac{p}{s}$ is always the same, $\frac{4}{1}$. We say that the ratio $\frac{p}{s}$ is a **constant**.

Thus, in each case, $\dfrac{p}{s} = 4$. This result may be written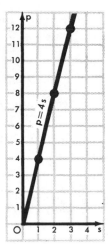
as $p = 4s$, which is the formula for the perimeter of a
square. Such a relation is called a *direct variation.* The
graph of $p = 4s$ is a straight line as is shown at the right.

When two variables are related so that the ratio of the
value of one variable to the corresponding value of the
other variable is constant, we say that one variable *varies
directly* as the other. We also say that one variable is
directly proportional to the other. The constant ratio is
called the *constant of variation.* In the preceding exam-

ple, the constant of variation is 4 $\left(\text{because } \dfrac{p}{s} = 4 \right)$.

In general, if y varies directly as x, the following ***principles of direct variation*** hold true:

Principle 1. The ratio $y : x$ is constant. $\dfrac{y}{x} = k$ or $y = kx$, where k $(k \neq 0)$ is
the constant of variation.

Principle 2. The ratio of y_1 and x_1, any pair of values for the variables,
is equal to the ratio of y_2 and x_2, any other pair of values for the variables.
Thus, $\dfrac{y_1}{x_1} = \dfrac{y_2}{x_2}$.

Principle 3. If x is *multiplied* by a number, y is *multiplied* by the same
number. Thus, if x is multiplied by 2 (doubled), then y is also multiplied by 2
(doubled).

Principle 4. If x is *divided* by a non-zero number, y is *divided* by the same
number. Thus, if x is divided by 2 (halved), y is also divided by 2 (halved).

Principle 5. The graph of $y = kx$ is a straight line whose slope is k and
which passes through the origin.

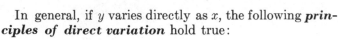

MODEL PROBLEMS

1. Express the following relation as a formula: The salary a man earns, S,
   varies directly as the number of hours, n, which he works.

   Solution: The ratio of S to n must be constant. Let $k = $ the constant.

   Answer: $\dfrac{S}{n} = k$, or $S = kn$

2. If d varies directly as t and if $d = 60$ when $t = 2$, find the value of d when $t = 7$.

Solution:

Method 1

Since d varies directly as t,
$$d = kt$$
If $d = 60$ when $t = 2$,
$$60 = 2k$$
$$30 = k$$
In $d = kt$, replace k by 30.
Hence, $d = 30t$.
If $t = 7$, then
$$d = 30(7)$$
$$d = 210$$

Answer: $d = 210$

Method 2

Let x = the unknown value of d.
Since d varies directly as t,

$$\frac{d_1}{t_1} = \frac{d_2}{t_2}$$

$$\frac{60}{2} = \frac{x}{7}$$

$$2x = 420$$
$$x = 210$$

d	60	x
t	2	7

Check

$$\frac{60}{2} \overset{?}{=} \frac{210}{7}$$

$$30 = 30 \quad \text{(true)}$$

Exercises

In 1–6, tell whether one variable varies directly as the other. If it does, express the relation between the variables by means of a formula.

1.

p	3	6	9
s	1	2	3

2.

n	3	4	5
c	6	8	10

3.

x	4	5	6
y	6	8	10

4.

t	1	2	3
d	20	40	60

5.

x	2	3	4
y	-6	-9	-12

6.

x	1	2	3
y	1	4	9

In 7–9, one variable varies directly as the other. Find the missing numbers and write the formula which relates the variables.

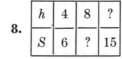

7.

h	1	2	?
A	5	?	25

8.

h	4	8	?
S	6	?	15

9.

L	2	8	?
W	1	?	7

In 10–12, write the relation as a formula using k as the constant of variation.
10. The perimeter, P, of an equilateral triangle varies directly as a side, s.
11. The circumference of a circle, C, varies directly as the radius, r.
12. The resistance, R, of a copper wire, varies directly as its length, l.

In 13–15, write the relation as a formula. Use k as the constant of variation and tell what each variable represents.
13. The length of the shadow of an object at a given time varies directly as the height of the object.
14. If a car travels at a constant rate of speed, the distance covered varies directly as the time that it travels.
15. The income of a man who works at a fixed hourly rate of pay is directly proportional to the number of hours that he works.

16. $C = 7N$ is a formula for the cost of any number of articles which sell for $7 each.
  a. How do C and N vary?
  b. How will the cost of 9 articles compare with the cost of 3 articles?
  c. If N is doubled, what change takes place in C?
17. $A = 12L$ is a formula for the area of any rectangle whose width is 12.
  a. Describe how A and L vary.
  b. How will the area of a rectangle whose length is 8 in. compare with the area of a rectangle whose length is 4 in.?
  c. If L is tripled, what change takes place in A?

In 18–21, state whether the relation between the variables is a direct variation. Give a reason for your answer.

18. $R + T = 80$ **19.** $15T = D$ **20.** $\dfrac{e}{i} = 20$ **21.** $bh = 36$

22. The weight, w, of a pipe varies directly as its length, l.
  a. Write a formula relating w and l.
  b. If $w = 6$ when $l = 8$, find w when $l = 20$.
  c. If $w = 5$ when $l = 10$, find l when $w = 12.5$.

23. The circumference, c, of a circle varies directly as the diameter, d.
    a. Write a formula relating c and d.
    b. If $c = 44$ when $d = 14$, find c when $d = 21$.
    c. If $c = 6.28$ when $d = 2$, find d when $c = 62.8$.

24. A salesman's commission, c, varies directly as his sales, s.
    a. Write a formula relating c and s.
    b. If $c = \$100$ when $s = \$1000$, find c when $s = \$1250$.
    c. If $c = \$240$ when $s = \$4000$, find s when $c = \$300$.

25. The cost of a railroad ticket, C, is directly proportional to the number of miles in the trip, n.
    a. Write a formula relating C and n.
    b. If $C = \$20.00$ when $n = 400$, find C when $n = 250$.
    c. If $C = \$6.00$ when $n = 150$, find n when $C = \$15.00$.

26. Y varies directly as x. If $Y = 35$ when $x = -5$, find Y when $x = -20$.

27. A varies directly as h. $A = 48$ when $h = 4$. Find h when $A = 36$.

28. N varies directly as d. $N = 10$ when $d = 8$. Find N when $d = 12$.

29. If 3 men earn \$210 in a week, what will 21 men working at the same rate of pay earn in a week?

30. x varies directly as $y + 1$. If $y = 3$ when $x = 2$, find y when $x = 6$.

31. $R + 2$ varies directly as $2S - 3$. If $S = 4$ when $R = 3$, find S when $R = 9$.

32. If 5 hats cost \$35, how much will 9 hats of the same kind cost?

33. If a train travels 240 miles in 4 hours, how far will it travel in 7 hours if it travels at the same rate of speed?

6. Inverse Variation

If the length of a rectangle, L, is 1 in. and its width, W, is 12 in., its area is 12 sq. in. If L is 2 in. and W is 6 in., the area is once again 12 sq. in. In the following table are listed pairs of numbers, each pair representing the length and width of a rectangle whose area is 12 sq. in.

L	1	2	3	4	6	12
W	12	6	4	3	2	1

In the table, observe that as L varies, W also varies. Remember that L and W represent the dimensions of a rectangle whose area is 12 sq. in. Therefore, for each pair of numbers in the table, the product LW is always the same, 12. That is, the product LW is a constant:

$$L_1W_1 = 1 \times 12 = 12 \quad L_2W_2 = 2 \times 6 = 12 \quad L_3W_3 = 3 \times 4 = 12$$
$$L_4W_4 = 4 \times 3 = 12 \quad L_5W_5 = 6 \times 2 = 12 \quad L_6W_6 = 12 \times 1 = 12$$

Thus, in each case $LW = 12$. Such a relation is called an **inverse variation**. The graph of $LW = 12$ is a curve, not a straight line, as shown on the right.

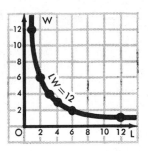

When two variables are related so that the product of the value of one variable and the corresponding value of the other variable is constant, we say that one variable **varies inversely** as the other. We also say that one variable is **inversely proportional** to the other. The constant product is called the **constant of variation**.

In the preceding table, which lists pairs of numbers that satisfy the equation $LW = 12$, notice that $\dfrac{L_1}{W_1}$ does not equal $\dfrac{L_2}{W_2}$. $\dfrac{L_1}{W_1}$ equals $\dfrac{1}{12}$, but $\dfrac{L_2}{W_2}$ equals $\dfrac{2}{6}$. However, notice that $\dfrac{L_1}{L_2}$, or $\dfrac{1}{2}$, does equal $\dfrac{W_2}{W_1}$, or $\dfrac{6}{12}$. That is, $\dfrac{L_1}{L_2} = \dfrac{W_2}{W_1}$.

In general, if y varies inversely as x, the following **principles of inverse variation** hold true:

Principle 1. The product of y and x is constant. $xy = k$ ($k \neq 0$), or $y = \dfrac{k}{x}$ ($x \neq 0$), where k is the constant of variation. We know that $y = \dfrac{k}{x}$ may be written $y = k\left(\dfrac{1}{x}\right)$. Therefore, when y varies inversely as x, we can also say that y varies directly as the reciprocal of x, or as the (multiplicative) inverse of x.

Principle 2. The product of x_1 and y_1, any pair of values for the variables, is equal to the product of x_2 and y_2, any other pair of values for the variables. Thus, $x_1 y_1 = x_2 y_2$. This relation may also be written as the proportion $\dfrac{x_1}{x_2} = \dfrac{y_2}{y_1}$.

Principle 3. If x is *multiplied* by a non-zero number, y is *divided* by the same number. Thus, if x is multiplied by 2, then y is divided by 2. (We can also say that y is multiplied by the reciprocal of 2, or $\frac{1}{2}$.)

Principle 4. If x is *divided* by a non-zero number, y is *multiplied* by the same number. Thus, if x is divided by 2, then y is multiplied by 2. (We can also say that y is divided by the reciprocal of 2, or $\frac{1}{2}$.)

Principle 5. The graph of $xy = k$ is a curve, not a straight line, since $xy = k$ is not a first-degree (linear) equation.

MODEL PROBLEMS

1. Express the following relation as a formula: The number of articles, n, that can be bought with a fixed sum of money varies inversely as the cost of each article, c.

   Solution: The product of n and c must be constant. Let $k =$ the constant.

   Answer: $nc = k$

2. If y varies inversely as x and if $y = 5$ when $x = 8$, find y when $x = 4$.

   Solution:

Method 1	*Method 2*

   Method 1

   Since y varies inversely as x,
   $$xy = k$$
   If $y = 5$ when $x = 8$,
   $$(8)(5) = k$$
   $$40 = k$$
   Hence, $xy = 40$.
   If $x = 4$, then
   $$4y = 40$$
   $$y = 10$$

   Method 2

   Let $y_2 =$ the unknown value of y.
   Since y varies inversely as x,

   $$\frac{x_1}{x_2} = \frac{y_2}{y_1}$$

x	8	4
y	5	y_2

   $$\frac{8}{4} = \frac{y_2}{5}$$
   $$4y_2 = 40$$
   $$y_2 = 10$$

   Check

   $$8 \times 5 \overset{?}{=} 4 \times 10$$
   $$40 = 40 \quad \text{(true)}$$

   Answer: $y = 10$

Exercises

In 1–6, tell whether one variable varies inversely as the other. If it does, express the relation between the variables by means of a formula.

1.

n	2	4	6
c	18	9	6

2.

R	10	20	40
T	4	2	1

3.

x	1	2	3
y	8	7	6

4.

l	2	4	8
w	$\frac{1}{2}$	$\frac{1}{4}$	$\frac{1}{8}$

5.

x	3	6	9
y	-12	-6	-4

6.

C	12	24	36
D	6	3	2

In 7–9, one variable varies inversely as the other. Find the missing numbers and write the formula which relates the variables.

7.

w	2	?	6
d	12	8	?

8.

R	2	6	?
T	72	?	12

9.

l	2	4	?
w	32	?	8

In 10–12, write the relation as a formula using k as the constant of variation.

10. If the area of a rectangle is constant, the altitude, h, varies inversely as the base, b.

11. The time, t, required to travel a fixed distance varies inversely as the rate of motion, r.

12. If a fixed sum of money is to be spent, the number of articles, N, that can be bought is inversely proportional to the cost, C, of an article.

In 13–15, write the relation as a formula. Use k as the constant of variation and tell what each variable represents.

13. When the temperature of a gas is constant, its volume varies inversely as the pressure.

14. The principal that must be invested to yield a fixed annual income varies inversely as the rate of interest.

15. The number of hours required to complete a certain job varies inversely as the number of persons doing the work if all persons work at the same rate.

16. $RT - 200$ is the formula showing the relation between rate and time in traveling a distance of 200 miles.

  a. How do T and R vary?

  b. How will the time required to travel 200 miles when the rate is 40 miles per hour compare with the time required when the rate is 20 miles per hour?

  c. If the rate is doubled, what change takes place in the time?

17. $LW = 144$ is the formula showing the relation between the length and width of a rectangle whose area is 144 square feet.

  a. Describe how L and W vary.

  b. How will the length of a rectangle whose width is 6 compare with the length of a rectangle whose width is 12?

  c. If L is trebled, what change takes place in W?

In 18–21, state whether the relation between the variables is an inverse variation. Give a reason for your answer.

18. $N - C = 40$ **19.** $NC = 40$ **20.** $t = \dfrac{60}{r}$ **21.** $h = 60b$

22. The number of days, d, necessary to finish a job varies inversely as the number of men working, n, if all men are working at the same rate.
   a. Write a formula relating d and n.
   b. If $d = 2$ when $n = 12$, find d when $n = 6$.
   c. If $d = 4$ when $n = 9$, find n when $d = 3$.

23. The number of times a wheel must turn, n, to cover a given distance varies inversely as the radius of the wheel, r.
   a. Write a formula relating n and r.
   b. If $n = 10$ when $r = 14$, find n when $r = 7$.
   c. If $n = 40$ when $r = 100$, find r when $n = 10$.

24. If x varies inversely as y and if $x = 8$ when $y = 9$, find x when $y = 18$.

25. If n varies inversely as c and if $n = 50$ when $c = 4$, find n when $c = 40$.

26. If R varies inversely as T and if $R = 80$ when $T = \frac{1}{4}$, find R when $T = 2$.

27. If y is inversely proportional to z and if $y = 6$ when $z = -4$, find y when $z = -3$.

28. If P varies inversely as r and if $P = 1000$ when $r = .06$, find r when $P = 3000$.

29. If x varies inversely as $y + 5$ and if $y = 1$ when $x = 2$, find y when $x = 1$.

30. If $M + 1$ varies inversely as $2N - 1$ and if $N = 13$ when $M = 3$, find N when $M = 24$.

31. A man invested \$10,000 at 6% per year. At what annual rate would he have to invest \$7500 to have the same annual income?

32. Ten printing presses, all alike, can do a job in 3 hours. How many hours would it take 6 of these printing presses to do the same job?

CHAPTER XVIII

THE REAL NUMBERS

1. The Set of Rational Numbers

The numbers with which you are familiar consist of positive and negative integers, fractions, and zero. Examples of these numbers are 5, -3, $\dfrac{7}{4}$, $\dfrac{-5}{4}$, and 0. Each of these numbers can be expressed in the form $y = \dfrac{a}{b}$ where a and b are integers and $b \neq 0$. $\Big($Remember that 5 may be expressed as $\dfrac{5}{1}$, -3 as $\dfrac{-3}{1}$, and 0 as $\dfrac{0}{1}\Big)$ Numbers which can be expressed in this form are called *rational numbers.*

PROPERTIES OF THE SET OF RATIONAL NUMBERS

The set of rational numbers has all the properties of the set of positive integers, zero, and negative integers. This set also has other properties:

Property 1. The set of rational numbers is closed under division as well as under addition, multiplication, and subtraction. When we divide one integer by another non-zero integer, we always get a unique rational number as the result. For example, -3 divided by 2 is $\dfrac{-3}{2}$; 5 divided by -4 is $\dfrac{5}{-4}$.

Property 2. For every non-zero rational number, there is a unique corresponding number such that the product of these numbers is 1, the identity element of multiplication. For example, for the given number $\frac{2}{3}$, there is the unique corresponding number $\frac{3}{2}$ such that $\frac{2}{3} \times \frac{3}{2} = 1$. The number $\frac{3}{2}$ is called the *reciprocal,* or *multiplicative inverse,* of $\frac{2}{3}$.

Property 3. The set of rational numbers can be associated with points on a number line.

Property 4. The set of rational numbers is an ordered set. Given any two unequal rational numbers, we can tell which is the greater of the numbers.

Study the following model problems to see how different methods may be used to order rational numbers:

~~~~~~~~~~~~~~~~~ **MODEL PROBLEMS** ~~~~~~~~~~~~~~~~~

1. Which is the greater of the numbers $\frac{1}{2}$ and -1?

   How To Proceed: Graph the numbers on a number line. Then determine which number is at the right. The number at the right is the greater number.

   Solution:

   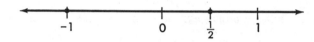

   We see that the number $\frac{1}{2}$ is to the right of the number -1.

   Answer: $\frac{1}{2} > -1$

2. In each part, determine which is the greater of the numbers:

   a. $\frac{5}{3}$ and $\frac{-5}{3}$ *b.* $\frac{1}{2}$ and $\frac{1}{3}$

   How To Proceed: Express the numbers as fractions which have the same positive denominator. Then compare the numerators of the resulting fractions.

   Solution:

   a. $\frac{5}{3} > \frac{-5}{3}$ because $5 > -5$. $\frac{5}{3} > \frac{-5}{3}$ *Ans.*

   b. $\frac{1}{2} = \frac{3}{6}$, and $\frac{1}{3} = \frac{2}{6}$. Since $\frac{3}{6} > \frac{2}{6}$, then $\frac{1}{2} > \frac{1}{3}$. $\frac{1}{2} > \frac{1}{3}$ *Ans.*

3. Which is the greater of the numbers $\frac{7}{9}$ and $\frac{8}{11}$?

   How To Proceed: Express the numbers as decimals and then compare the decimals. [See pages 443 and 444 for examples of expressing rational numbers as decimals.]

   Solution: By performing the indicated divisions:

   $\frac{7}{9} = .7777\ldots$ and $\frac{8}{11} = .7272\ldots$.
   Since $.7777\ldots > .7272\ldots$, then $\frac{7}{9} > \frac{8}{11}$. $\frac{7}{9} > \frac{8}{11}$ *Ans.*

Property 5. The set of rational numbers is everywhere dense. That is, given any two unequal rational numbers, it is always possible to find many rational numbers between them. The number midway between them is one such number.

ᨁᨁᨁᨁᨁᨁᨁᨁᨁ MODEL PROBLEM ᨁᨁᨁᨁᨁᨁᨁᨁᨁ

Find a rational number between $\frac{1}{4}$ and $\frac{3}{4}$.

How To Proceed	*Solution*
1. Find the difference between $\frac{3}{4}$ and $\frac{1}{4}$.	$\frac{3}{4} - \frac{1}{4} = \frac{2}{4}$
2. Find half of the difference.	$\frac{1}{2} \cdot \frac{2}{4} = \frac{1}{4}$
3. Add the result to the smaller number.	$\frac{1}{4} + \frac{1}{4} = \frac{2}{4} = \frac{1}{2}$

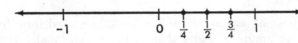

Answer: $\frac{1}{2}$ is a rational number between $\frac{1}{4}$ and $\frac{3}{4}$.

[*Note:* We can also find a number midway between $\frac{1}{4}$ and $\frac{3}{4}$ by finding their average: $(\frac{1}{4} + \frac{3}{4}) \div 2 = (1) \div 2 = \frac{1}{2}$.]

EXPRESSING A RATIONAL NUMBER AS A DECIMAL

To express a rational number as a decimal, we simply perform the indicated division.

ᨁᨁᨁᨁᨁᨁᨁᨁᨁ MODEL PROBLEM ᨁᨁᨁᨁᨁᨁᨁᨁᨁ

Express as a decimal: *a.* $\frac{1}{2}$ *b.* $\frac{3}{4}$ *c.* $\frac{1}{16}$

Solution:

$$a.\ \tfrac{1}{2} = 2\overline{)1.000000}\quad .500000$$

$$b.\ \tfrac{3}{4} = 4\overline{)3.000000}\quad .750000$$

$$c.\ \tfrac{1}{16} = 16\overline{)1.000000}\quad .062500$$

In each of the examples $\frac{1}{2}$, $\frac{3}{4}$, and $\frac{1}{16}$, when we perform the division, we reach a point after which we continually obtain only zeros in the quotient. Decimals which result from such divisions, for example, .5, .75, and .0625, are called **terminating decimals.**

Not all rational numbers can be expressed as terminating decimals.

~~~~~~~~~~~~~~~ **MODEL PROBLEM** ~~~~~~~~~~~~~~~

Express as a decimal: *a.* $\frac{1}{3}$ *b.* $\frac{2}{11}$ *c.* $\frac{1}{6}$

Solution:

$$a.\ \tfrac{1}{3} = 3)\overline{1.000000}^{\ .333333\ \ldots} \qquad b.\ \tfrac{2}{11} = 11)\overline{2.000000}^{\ .181818\ \ldots} \qquad c.\ \tfrac{1}{6} = 6)\overline{1.000000}^{\ .166666\ \ldots}$$

~~~~~~

In each of the examples, $\frac{1}{3}$, $\frac{2}{11}$, and $\frac{1}{6}$, when we perform the division, we find, in the quotient, that the same group of digits is continually repeated in the same order. Decimals which keep repeating endlessly, such as .333333 . . . , .181818 . . . , and .166666 . . . , are known as **repeating decimals,** or **periodic decimals.**

A repeating decimal may be written in an abbreviated form by placing a bar ($^{-}$) over the group of digits that is to be continually repeated. For example:

$$.333333 \ldots = .\overline{3} \qquad\qquad .181818 \ldots = .\overline{18} \qquad\qquad .166666 \ldots = .1\overline{6}$$

The six examples in the two preceding model problems illustrate the truth of the following statement:

Every rational number can be expressed as either a terminating decimal or a repeating decimal.

EXPRESSING A DECIMAL AS A RATIONAL NUMBER

In our study of arithmetic, we have learned how to express a terminating decimal as a rational number.

~~~~~~~~~~~~~~~ **MODEL PROBLEM** ~~~~~~~~~~~~~~~

Express as a rational number: *a.* .3   *b.* .37   *c.* .139   *d.* .0777

Solution:

$$a.\ .3 = \frac{3}{10} \qquad b.\ .37 = \frac{37}{100} \qquad c.\ .139 = \frac{139}{1000} \qquad d.\ .0777 = \frac{777}{10,000}$$

~~~~~~

Study the following model problem to learn how to express a repeating decimal as a rational number.

~~~~~~~~~~~~~~~~~~~ **MODEL PROBLEM** ~~~~~~~~~~~~~~~~~~~

Express as a rational number: *a.* .6666 . . .   *b.* .4141 . . .   *c.* .8333 . . .

Solution:

a. Let $N = .6666\ldots$ (A)

Multiply both members of (A) by 10.

Then $10N = 6.6666\ldots$ (B)

Subtract (A) from (B).

$$10N = 6.6666\ldots \quad (B)$$
$$\underline{N = .6666\ldots \quad (A)}$$
$$9N = 6$$
$$N = \tfrac{6}{9} = \tfrac{2}{3}$$

Answer (a): .6666 . . . $= \tfrac{2}{3}$

b. Let $N = .4141\ldots$ (A)

Multiply both members of (A) by 100.

Then $100N = 41.4141\ldots$ (B)

Subtract (A) from (B).

$$100N = 41.4141\ldots \quad (B)$$
$$\underline{N = .4141\ldots \quad (A)}$$
$$99N = 41$$
$$N = \tfrac{41}{99}$$

Answer (b): .4141 . . . $= \tfrac{41}{99}$

c. Let $N = .8333\ldots$ (A)

Multiply both members of (A) by 10.

Then $10N = 8.3333\ldots$ (B)

Subtract (A) from (B).

$$10N = 8.3333\ldots \quad (B)$$
$$\underline{N = .8333\ldots \quad (A)}$$
$$9N = 7.5$$
$$N = \frac{7.5}{9} = \frac{75}{90} = \frac{5}{6}$$

Answer (c): .8333 . . . $= \tfrac{5}{6}$

~~~~~~

The seven examples in the two preceding model problems illustrate the truth of the following statement:

Every terminating or repeating decimal represents a rational number.

Exercises

In 1–20, state which of the given numbers is the greater.

1. $\dfrac{5}{2}, \dfrac{7}{2}$ 2. $\dfrac{-9}{3}, \dfrac{-11}{3}$ 3. $\dfrac{5}{6}, -\dfrac{13}{6}$ 4. $2, \dfrac{5}{2}$

5. $-4, \dfrac{2}{3}$ 6. $-\dfrac{1}{5}, -5$ 7. $3, \dfrac{10}{3}$ 8. $\dfrac{5}{2}, \dfrac{7}{4}$

9. $\dfrac{-10}{3}, \dfrac{-13}{6}$ 10. $\dfrac{-8}{5}, \dfrac{1}{10}$ 11. $\dfrac{2}{3}, \dfrac{1}{4}$ 12. $\dfrac{5}{2}, \dfrac{-1}{7}$

13. $\dfrac{-4}{9}, \dfrac{-9}{4}$ 14. $\dfrac{13}{6}, \dfrac{15}{10}$ 15. $\dfrac{-5}{8}, \dfrac{-5}{12}$ 16. $1.4, 1\frac{3}{5}$

17. $-3.4, -3\frac{1}{3}$ 18. $-1\frac{1}{2}, 1.6$ 19. $.06, \dfrac{1}{6}$ 20. $\dfrac{-15}{11}, \dfrac{-11}{15}$

In 21–30, find a rational number midway between the given numbers.

21. $5, 6$ 22. $-4, -3$ 23. $-1, 0$ 24. $\frac{1}{4}, \frac{1}{2}$ 25. $\frac{1}{2}, \frac{7}{8}$

26. $\dfrac{-3}{4}, \dfrac{-2}{3}$ 27. $-2.1, -2.2$ 28. $2\frac{1}{2}, 2\frac{5}{8}$ 29. $-1\frac{1}{3}, -1\frac{1}{4}$ 30. $3.05, 3\frac{1}{10}$

In 31–40, write the rational number as a terminating decimal or as a repeating decimal.

31. $\frac{5}{8}$ 32. $\frac{9}{4}$ 33. $-5\frac{1}{2}$ 34. $\frac{13}{8}$ 35. $-\frac{7}{12}$

36. $\frac{5}{3}$ 37. $\frac{7}{9}$ 38. $\dfrac{-7}{6}$ 39. $\frac{35}{99}$ 40. $\frac{11}{6}$

In 41–50, express the decimal as a fraction.

41. $.5$ 42. $.555\ldots$ 43. $-.\overline{2}$ 44. $.125$ 45. $.2525\ldots$

46. $.\overline{07}$ 47. $3.666\ldots$ 48. $.\overline{579}$ 49. $1.5666\ldots$ 50. $-2.7\overline{23}$

2. The Set of Irrational Numbers

There are decimals which are non-terminating and non-repeating. An example of such a decimal is:

$$.03003000300003\ldots$$

Observe that, in this numeral, only the digits 0 and 3 appear. First we have a 3 preceded by one 0, then a 3 preceded by two 0's, then a 3 preceded by three 0's, and so on. At no time can we be certain that the decimal will repeat. Since this numeral does not represent a terminating or repeating decimal, it cannot represent a rational number.

A number represented by a non-terminating decimal which is also a non-repeating decimal is called an **irrational number**. An irrational number cannot be expressed in the form $\frac{a}{b}$ where a and b are integers.

Irrational numbers may be positive or negative. For example, .030030003 . . . represents a positive irrational number; −.030030003 . . . represents a negative irrational number.

Exercises

In 1–3, tell how the numeral is formed. Then write the next five digits.

1. .272272227 . . .   **2.** .656556555 . . .   **3.** .95969798 . . .

4. Write two numerals which represent irrational numbers.

In 5–12, tell whether the number is rational or irrational.

5. .36   **6.** .363636 . . .   **7.** .363363336 . . .   **8.** $-.\overline{945}$

9. $.8\overline{3}$ **10.** .989889888 . . .   **11.** .16171819 . . .   **12.** 5.08

In 13–16: (*a*) Find a rational number between the given numbers. (*b*) Find an irrational number between the two numbers.

13. .7777 . . . and .868686 . . .   **14.** .151551555 . . . and .161661666 . . .

15. 3.6464 . . . and $3.\overline{125}$ **16.** 2.343343334 . . . and 2.414114111 . . .

3. The Set of Real Numbers

The set of all rational numbers and all irrational numbers, taken together, is called the set of **real numbers**.

PROPERTIES OF REAL NUMBERS

The following properties are assumed for the set of real numbers under the operations of addition and multiplication. They are used in operations with real numbers.

In the eleven statements on the next page, a, b, and c represent any numbers which are members of the set of real numbers.

Property	*Symbolization*
1. Addition is closed.	1. $a + b = c$ (c is a unique number.)
2. Addition is commutative.	2. $a + b = b + a$
3. Addition is associative.	3. $(a + b) + c = a + (b + c)$
4. Zero is the additive identity.	4. $a + 0 = a$ and $0 + a = a$
5. Every number a has an additive inverse $-a$.	5. $a + (-a) = 0$
6. Multiplication is closed.	6. $ab = c$ (c is a unique number.)
7. Multiplication is commutative.	7. $ab = ba$
8. Multiplication is associative.	8. $(ab)c = a(bc)$
9. The number one is the multiplicative identity.	9. $a \times 1 = a$ and $1 \times a = a$
10. Every non-zero number a has a unique multiplicative inverse $\frac{1}{a}$.	10. $a \times \frac{1}{a} = 1$
11. Multiplication is distributive over addition.	11. $a(b + c) = ab + ac$

[*Note:* Subtraction can be performed by means of addition. We assume that $a - b = a + (-b)$. Division can be performed by means of multiplication. We assume that $a \div b = a \times \frac{1}{b}$ ($b \neq 0$).]

ORDERING REAL NUMBERS

When the set of real numbers is associated with the points on the number line, every real number, rational or irrational, corresponds to a unique point on the line; also, every point on the number line corresponds to a unique real number, rational or irrational.

Real numbers can be ordered by using a number line. The graph of the greater of two unequal real numbers is always at the right of the graph of the smaller number.

Given any two unequal real numbers, we can determine which is the larger by expressing each number as a decimal. Then we compare the resulting decimals.

~~~~~~~~~~~~~~~~~~~~ **MODEL PROBLEM** ~~~~~~~~~~~~~~~~~~~~

Which is the greater of the two numbers $\frac{13}{99}$ and .131331333 . . . ?

Solution:

$$\frac{13}{99} = .131313 \ldots \qquad\qquad \text{Compare:} \begin{array}{l} .131331333 \ldots \\ .131313131 \ldots \end{array}$$

The first four digits of the two decimals are the same. However, the fifth digit in .131331333 . . . is 3, whereas the fifth digit in .131313 . . . is 1. Therefore, .131331333 . . . > .131313 . . . , and .131331333 . . . > $\frac{13}{99}$.

Answer: .131331333 . . . > $\frac{13}{99}$

~~~~~~

Exercises

In 1–10, tell why the number is a real number.

1. 5   **2.** $-\frac{4}{3}$ **3.** $\frac{533}{629}$ **4.** .777 . . .   **5.** 2.137137 . . .

6. $-.\overline{67}$ **7.** 0   **8.** -3.72 **9.** .85353 . . .   **10.** .858558555 . . .

In 11–16, determine which is the greater number.

11. 2 and 2.25   **12.** -5.7 and -5.9 **13.** .5353 and .5353 . . .

14. .7 and .$\overline{7}$ **15.** $-.\overline{53}$ and $-.\overline{531}$ **16.** .2121 . . . and .212112111 . . .

In 17–20, arrange the set of real numbers in order from smallest to largest:

17. $\{.3, .31, .333 \ldots, .313113111 \ldots\}$ **18.** $\{.\overline{25}, .20, .\overline{2}, .202002000 \ldots\}$

19. $\{\frac{2}{7}, .27, .\overline{27}, .272272227 \ldots\}$ **20.** $\{-\frac{3}{5}, -.\overline{61}, -.\overline{6}, -.60616263 \ldots\}$

21. Consider the set of positive integers, the set of negative integers, the set of odd integers, the set of even integers, the set of rational numbers, and the set of real numbers. Which sets are closed under (*a*) addition (*b*) subtraction (*c*) multiplication (*d*) division?

22. Tell which of the following sets of numbers are dense:
     a. positive integers   *b.* negative integers   *c.* rational numbers
     d. irrational numbers   *e.* real numbers

23. Eleven properties of real numbers are listed on page 448. State which, if any, of these eleven properties do *not* hold for the set of integers $\{\ldots, -3, -2, -1, 0, 1, 2, 3, \ldots\}$.

24. The following chain of equations can be used to show that $x(yz) = (xz)y$ when x, y, and z are members of the set of real numbers. State the reason for each of the steps from a through c.

a. $x(yz) = x(zy)$

b. $x(zy) = (xz)y$

c. $x(yz) = (xz)y$

In 25–32, all variables represent members of the set of real numbers. Use the properties of real numbers to prove that the sentence is true. Justify each statement with a reason.

25. $(ab)c = a(cb)$

26. $(a + b) + c = c + (b + a)$

27. $a(b + c) = ab + ca$

28. $\dfrac{1}{n}(mn) = m \ \ (n \neq 0)$

29. $m + n + (-m) = n$

30. $\dfrac{1}{n}(m + n) = 1 + m \cdot \dfrac{1}{n}$

31. $-a + a(bc + 1) = cab$

32. $(a + b)(c + d) = ac + cb + bd + da$

In 33–36, all variables represent members of the set of real numbers.

33. If we assume that $\dfrac{1}{b} \cdot \dfrac{1}{d} = \dfrac{1}{bd}$, prove that $\dfrac{a}{b} \cdot \dfrac{c}{d} = \dfrac{ac}{bd}$ ($b \neq 0$, $d \neq 0$).

Justify each step with a reason. $\left[Hint: \dfrac{a}{b} = a \cdot \dfrac{1}{b} \right]$

34. Prove that $\dfrac{a}{b} + \dfrac{c}{b} = \dfrac{a + c}{b}$ ($b \neq 0$). Justify each step with a reason.

$\left[Hint: \dfrac{a}{b} = a \cdot \dfrac{1}{b} \right]$

35. Prove that if $a + x = b + x$, then $a = b$. Justify each step with a reason. [*Hint:* Add $(-x)$ to both members of the equation.]

36. Prove that $\dfrac{ax + ay}{a} = x + y$ ($a \neq 0$). $\left[Hint: \dfrac{r}{s} = r \cdot \dfrac{1}{s} \right]$

4. Finding a Root of a Number

To **square** a number is to use it as a factor twice. For example, the square of 5 is $5 \times 5 = 25$, or $5^2 = 25$.

To **cube** a number is to use it as a factor three times. For example, the cube of 2 is $2 \times 2 \times 2 = 8$, or $2^3 = 8$.

Finding a **square root** of a number is to find one of its two equal factors. For example, "a square root of 25," written $\sqrt{25}$, is 5 because $5 \times 5 = 25$, or $5^2 = 25$. Finding a square root of a number is the inverse operation of squaring.

Finding a **cube root** of a number is to find one of its three equal factors. For example, "a cube root of 8," written $\sqrt[3]{8}$, is 2 because $2 \times 2 \times 2 = 8$, or $2^3 = 8$. Finding a cube root is the inverse operation of cubing.

Similarly, for any positive integer n: if $x^n = a$, then x is an nth root of a, written $\sqrt[n]{a}$. Finding a root of a number, called **evolution,** is the inverse operation of raising a number to a power, called **involution.**

To indicate a root of a number, a **radical sign,** $\sqrt{}$, is used. The symbol $\sqrt{25}$ is called a **radical;** 25, the number under the radical sign, is called the **radicand.** The number which indicates the root to be taken is called the **index** of the radical. In $\sqrt[3]{8}$, the index is 3; in $\sqrt[4]{16}$, the index is 4. When no index appears, a square root is indicated. For example, $\sqrt{25}$ indicates a square root of 25.

Since a square root of 25 is a number whose square is 25, we can write $(\sqrt{25})^2 = 25$.

In general, for every real non-negative number n:

$$(\sqrt{n})^2 = n$$

Since $(+5)(+5) = 25$ and $(-5)(-5) = 25$, both $+5$ and -5 are square roots of 25. This example illustrates the truth of the following statement:

Every positive number has two square roots which have the same absolute value, one root being a positive number, the other root being a negative number.

The positive square root of a number is called the **principal square root.** To indicate that the principal square root of a number is to be found, a radical sign, $\sqrt{}$, is placed over the number. For example:

$$\sqrt{25} = 5 \qquad \sqrt{\tfrac{9}{16}} = \tfrac{3}{4} \qquad \sqrt{.49} = .7$$

To indicate that the negative square root of a number is to be found, we place a minus sign in front of the radical sign. For example:

$$-\sqrt{25} = -5 \qquad -\sqrt{\tfrac{9}{16}} = -\tfrac{3}{4} \qquad -\sqrt{.49} = -.7$$

To indicate that both square roots are to be found, we place a plus sign and a minus sign in front of the radical. For example:

$$\pm\sqrt{25} = \pm5 \qquad \pm\sqrt{\tfrac{9}{16}} = \pm\tfrac{3}{4} \qquad \pm\sqrt{.49} = \pm.7$$

Since the square of any real number is never negative, no negative number has a square root in the set of real numbers. For example, $\sqrt{-25}$ does not exist in the set of real numbers; there is no real number whose square is -25.

However, $\sqrt[3]{-8}$ does exist in the set of real numbers: Since $(-2)^3 = -8$, then $\sqrt[3]{-8} = -2$.

~~~~~~ MODEL PROBLEMS ~~~~~~

1. Find the principal square root of 64.

Solution: Since $8 \times 8 = 64$, then $\sqrt{64} = 8$.   8   *Ans.*

2. Find the value of $\sqrt[3]{27}$.

Solution: Since $3 \times 3 \times 3 = 27$, then $\sqrt[3]{27} = 3$.   3   *Ans.*

3. Find the value of $(\sqrt{13})^2$.

Solution: Since $(\sqrt{n})^2 = n$, then $(\sqrt{13})^2 = 13$.   13   *Ans.*

4. Solve for x: $x^2 = 36$

Solution: If $x^2 = a$, then $x = \pm\sqrt{a}$ when a is a positive number.

$x^2 = 36$	*Check:*	$x^2 = 36$		$x^2 = 36$	
$x = \pm\sqrt{36}$		$(+6)^2 \overset{?}{=} 36$		$(-6)^2 \overset{?}{=} 36$	
$x = \pm6$		$36 = 36$	(true)	$36 = 36$	(true)

Answer: $x = +6$ or $x = -6$; solution set is $\{+6, -6\}$.

Exercises

In 1–5, state the index and the radicand of the radical.

1. $\sqrt{36}$ **2.** $\sqrt[3]{125}$ **3.** $\sqrt[4]{81}$ **4.** $\sqrt[5]{32}$ **5.** $\sqrt[n]{1}$

In 6–15, find the principal square root of the number.

6. 81   **7.** 1   **8.** 121   **9.** 225   **10.** 900

11. $\frac{1}{9}$ **12.** $\frac{4}{25}$ **13.** .49 ·   **14.** 1.44   **15.** .04

In 16–40, express the radical as integer(s), fraction(s), or decimal(s).

16. $\sqrt{16}$ **17.** $\sqrt{81}$ **18.** $\sqrt{121}$ **19.** $-\sqrt{64}$ **20.** $-\sqrt{144}$

21. $\sqrt{0}$ **22.** $\pm\sqrt{100}$ **23.** $\pm\sqrt{169}$ **24.** $\sqrt{400}$ **25.** $-\sqrt{625}$

26. $\sqrt{\frac{1}{4}}$ **27.** $-\sqrt{\frac{9}{16}}$ **28.** $\pm\sqrt{\frac{25}{81}}$ **29.** $\sqrt{\frac{49}{100}}$ **30.** $\pm\sqrt{\frac{144}{169}}$

31. $\sqrt{.64}$ **32.** $-\sqrt{1.44}$ **33.** $\pm\sqrt{.09}$ **34.** $-\sqrt{.01}$ **35.** $\pm\sqrt{.0004}$

36. $\sqrt[3]{1}$ **37.** $\sqrt[4]{81}$ **38.** $\sqrt[5]{32}$ **39.** $\sqrt[3]{-8}$ **40.** $-\sqrt[3]{-125}$

In 41–54, find the value of the expression.

41. $\sqrt{(8)^2}$ **42.** $\sqrt{(\frac{1}{2})^2}$ **43.** $\sqrt{(.7)^2}$ **44.** $\sqrt{(-4)^2}$ **45.** $\sqrt{(-5)^2}$

46. $(\sqrt{4})^2$ **47.** $(\sqrt{36})^2$ **48.** $(\sqrt{11})^2$ **49.** $(\sqrt{39})^2$ **50.** $(\sqrt{97})(\sqrt{97})$

51. $\sqrt{36} + \sqrt{49}$ **52.** $\sqrt{100} - \sqrt{25}$

53. $(\sqrt{17})^2 + (\sqrt{7})(\sqrt{7})$ **54.** $\sqrt{(-9)^2} - (\sqrt{83})^2$

In 55–62, solve for the variable when the replacement set is the set of real numbers.

55. $x^2 = 4$ **56.** $y^2 = 100$ **57.** $z^2 = \frac{4}{81}$ **58.** $x^2 = .49$

59. $x^2 - 16 = 0$ **60.** $y^2 - 36 = 0$ **61.** $2x^2 = 50$ **62.** $3x^2 - 75 = 0$

In 63–66, find the length of each side of a square which has the given area.

63. 36 sq. ft.   **64.** 196 sq. ft.   **65.** 1600 sq. ft.   **66.** 441 sq. ft.

5. Square Roots Which Are Irrational Numbers

Positive rational numbers such as 9 and $\frac{4}{49}$ (also the number 0) are called **perfect squares** because they are squares of rational numbers. For example, $\sqrt{9} = 3$, and 3 is a rational number; $\sqrt{\frac{4}{49}} = \frac{2}{7}$, and $\frac{2}{7}$ is a rational number; $\sqrt{0} = 0$, and 0 is a rational number. Similarly, if any non-negative rational number n is a perfect square, then $\sqrt{n}$ is a rational number.

Suppose n is a non-negative rational number which is not a perfect square, for example, 2. What kind of number is $\sqrt{n}$? What is the value of $\sqrt{2}$?

Since $1 \times 1 = 1$ and $2 \times 2 = 4$, then $\sqrt{2}$ must be a number between 1 and 2: $1 < \sqrt{2} < 2$.

Since $1.4 \times 1.4 = 1.96$ and $1.5 \times 1.5 = 2.25$, then $\sqrt{2}$ must be a number between 1.4 and 1.5: $1.4 < \sqrt{2} < 1.5$.

Since $1.41 \times 1.41 = 1.9881$ and $1.42 \times 1.42 = 2.0164$, then $\sqrt{2}$ must be a number between 1.41 and 1.42: $1.41 < \sqrt{2} < 1.42$.

Regardless of how far we continue this work, we will never reach a point where the number $\sqrt{2}$ is expressed as a terminating or a repeating decimal. Therefore, we call $\sqrt{2}$ an **irrational number.** We have been finding only approximations of $\sqrt{2}$; the value of $\sqrt{2}$ cannot be expressed as a rational number.

If a number cannot be expressed in the form $\frac{a}{b}$, where a and b are integers, it is an irrational number.

It can be proved that if n is a non-negative number which is not a perfect square, then $\sqrt{n}$ is an irrational number. Examples of irrational numbers are $\sqrt{2}$, $\sqrt{3}$, $\sqrt{5}$, $\sqrt{7}$, and $\sqrt{8}$.

Even though the value of an irrational number can be only approximated, every square root which is an irrational number can be associated with a point on the real number line.

MODEL PROBLEMS

1. Between which consecutive integers is $\sqrt{42}$?

   Solution: Since $6 \times 6 = 36$ and $7 \times 7 = 49$, then $\sqrt{42}$ is between 6 and 7

   Answer: $\sqrt{42}$ is between 6 and 7, or $6 < \sqrt{42} < 7$.

2. State whether $\sqrt{56}$ is a rational or an irrational number.

   Solution: Since 56 is not a perfect square, $\sqrt{56}$ is an irrational number.

   Answer: $\sqrt{56}$ is an irrational number.

Exercises

In 1–15, between which consecutive integers is each given number?

1. $\sqrt{5}$ 2. $\sqrt{11}$ 3. $\sqrt{13}$ 4. $\sqrt{23}$ 5. $\sqrt{40}$

6. $-\sqrt{2}$ 7. $-\sqrt{14}$ 8. $-\sqrt{20}$ 9. $\sqrt{52}$ 10. $-\sqrt{60}$

11. $\sqrt{73}$ 12. $\sqrt{95}$ 13. $-\sqrt{125}$ 14. $\sqrt{143}$ 15. $-\sqrt{150}$

In 16–21, order the given numbers, starting with the smallest.

16. $2, \sqrt{3}, -1$ 17. $4, \sqrt{17}, 3$ 18. $-\sqrt{15}, -3, -4$

19. $0, \sqrt{7}, -\sqrt{7}$ 20. $5, \sqrt{21}, \sqrt{30}$ 21. $-\sqrt{11}, -\sqrt{23}, -\sqrt{19}$

In 22–36, state whether the number is rational or irrational.

22. $\sqrt{25}$ 23. $\sqrt{40}$ 24. $\sqrt{38}$ 25. $-\sqrt{36}$ 26. $-\sqrt{54}$

27. $\sqrt{100}$ 28. $-\sqrt{105}$ 29. $\sqrt{144}$ 30. $-\sqrt{150}$ 31. $\sqrt{400}$

32. $\sqrt{\frac{1}{2}}$ 33. $-\sqrt{\frac{4}{9}}$ 34. $\sqrt{\frac{1}{3}}$ 35. $\sqrt{.36}$ 36. $\sqrt{.1}$

6. Estimating Approximate Square Roots

To approximate the square root of a number which has only two or three digits, we can make an intelligent estimate and check by squaring the estimated value. This process can be continued until we have obtained the desired number of decimal places in our approximation.

~~~~~~~~~~~~~~~~ **MODEL PROBLEM** ~~~~~~~~~~~~~~~~

Approximate $\sqrt{38}$ to (a) the *nearest integer* and (b) the *nearest tenth*.

Solution:

a. $\sqrt{38}$ is not an integer because $6^2 = 36$ and $7^2 = 49$. Since 38 is between 36 and 49, $\sqrt{38}$ is between 6 and 7. Therefore, we test 6.5, the number midway between 6 and 7. Since $(6.5)^2 = 42.25$, and 38 is less than 42.25, then $\sqrt{38}$ is less than 6.5 and must be closer to 6 than to 7. Therefore, the value of $\sqrt{38}$, approximated to the nearest integer, is 6.

Answer: $\sqrt{38} \approx 6$

[*Note:* The symbol "$\approx$" means "is approximately equal to."]

b. Since we know from part *a* that $\sqrt{38}$ is a little greater than 6, we test 6.1. When we square 6.1, we get $(6.1)^2 = 37.21$, which is less than 38. We then test 6.2. When we square 6.2, we get $(6.2)^2 = 38.44$, which is greater than 38. Since $\sqrt{38}$ lies between 6.1 and 6.2, we test 6.15, the number midway between 6.1 and 6.2. Since $(6.15)^2 = 37.8225$, and 38 is greater than 37.8225, then $\sqrt{38}$ is greater than 6.15 and must be closer to 6.2 than to 6.1. Therefore, the value of $\sqrt{38}$, approximated to the nearest tenth, is 6.2.

Answer: $\sqrt{38} \approx 6.2$

Exercises

In 1–10, approximate the value of the expression to the *nearest integer*.

1. $\sqrt{5}$ **2.** $\sqrt{19}$ **3.** $\sqrt{22}$ **4.** $\sqrt{34}$ **5.** $-\sqrt{55}$

6. $\sqrt{93}$ **7.** $\sqrt{105}$ **8.** $-\sqrt{116}$ **9.** $\sqrt{157}$ **10.** $\sqrt{218}$

In 11–20, approximate the value of the expression to the *nearest tenth*.

11. $\sqrt{2}$ **12.** $\sqrt{12}$ **13.** $\sqrt{45}$ **14.** $-\sqrt{67}$ **15.** $-\sqrt{86}$

16. $\sqrt{106}$ **17.** $\sqrt{125}$ **18.** $-\sqrt{137}$ **19.** $\sqrt{152}$ **20.** $\sqrt{175}$

7. Using Division To Find Approximate Square Roots

Consider 144 and its square root, 12. $144 \div 12 = 12$ illustrates:

Principle 1. When a divisor of a number and the quotient are equal, the square root of the number is either the divisor or the quotient.

$144 \div 9 = 16$ and $144 \div 18 = 8$ illustrate:

Principle 2. When a divisor of a number and the quotient are unequal, the square root of the number lies between the divisor and the quotient.

The square root of a number may be approximated to any number of decimal places by applying the two preceding principles and using estimates, divisions, and averages.

~~~~~~~~~~~~~~~~~~~~ **MODEL PROBLEM** ~~~~~~~~~~~~~~~~~~~~

Approximate $\sqrt{14}$ to the nearest (a) integer   (b) tenth   (c) hundredth
(d) thousandth.

How To Proceed	*Solution*

1. Approximate the square root of the number 14 by estimation.

> Since $3^2 = 9$ and $4^2 = 16$, then $\sqrt{14}$ lies between 3 and 4, closer to 4. Estimate $\sqrt{14} \approx 3.8$.

2. Divide the number 14 by the estimate, 3.8, finding the quotient to one more decimal place than there is in the divisor.

$$
\begin{array}{r}
3.68 \\
3.8_\wedge\overline{)14.0_\wedge00} \\
11\ 4 \\
\hline
2\ 6\ 0 \\
2\ 2\ 8 \\
\hline
3\ 20 \\
3\ 04 \\
\hline
16
\end{array}
$$

[*Note:* The quotient is 3.68, not 3.8. This tells us that $\sqrt{14}$ is not 3.8, but lies between 3.68 and 3.8. Therefore, $3.68 < \sqrt{14} < 3.8$.]

3. Find the average of the divisor, 3.8, and the quotient, 3.68 (found in step 2).

$$\frac{3.8 + 3.68}{2} = \frac{7.48}{2} = 3.74$$

4. Divide the number 14 by the average, 3.74 (see step 3), finding the quotient to one more decimal place than there is in the divisor. Since $14 \div 3.74 \approx 3.743$, then $3.74 < \sqrt{14} < 3.743$.

$3.74\overline{)14.} \approx 3.743$
(The division is left to the student.)

5. Find the average of the divisor, 3.74, and the quotient, 3.743 (found in step 4).

$$\frac{3.74 + 3.743}{2} = \frac{7.483}{2} = 3.7415$$

[*Note:* This process may be continued to obtain as close an approximation as is desired.]

Since $\sqrt{14} \approx 3.7415$, we obtain the following approximations when we round off:

Answer: a. $\sqrt{14} \approx 4$ (nearest integer)
   b. $\sqrt{14} \approx 3.7$ (nearest tenth)
   c. $\sqrt{14} \approx 3.74$ (nearest hundredth)
   d. $\sqrt{14} \approx 3.742$ (nearest thousandth)

Exercises

In 1–10, approximate each expression to the *nearest integer*.

1. $\sqrt{39}$ 2. $\sqrt{80}$ 3. $\sqrt{155}$ 4. $-\sqrt{273}$ 5. $\sqrt{2348}$

6. $\sqrt{4389}$ 7. $\sqrt{1455}$ 8. $-\sqrt{6258}$ 9. $\sqrt{67.24}$ 10. $\sqrt{134.56}$

In 11–20, approximate each expression to the *nearest tenth*.

11. $\sqrt{6}$ 12. $\sqrt{11}$ 13. $\sqrt{18}$ 14. $\sqrt{21}$ 15. $-\sqrt{34}$

16. $\sqrt{53}$ 17. $\sqrt{90}$ 18. $-\sqrt{108}$ 19. $\sqrt{19.5}$ 20. $\sqrt{41.7}$

In 21–30, approximate each expression to the *nearest hundredth*.

21. $\sqrt{7}$ 22. $\sqrt{19}$ 23. $\sqrt{28}$ 24. $-\sqrt{61}$ 25. $\sqrt{74}$

26. $\sqrt{106}$ 27. $\sqrt{111}$ 28. $-\sqrt{127}$ 29. $\sqrt{23.5}$ 30. $\sqrt{88.2}$

In 31–35, approximate each expression to the *nearest thousandth*.

31. $\sqrt{3}$ 32. $\sqrt{15}$ 33. $\sqrt{89}$ 34. $-\sqrt{133}$ 35. $\sqrt{29.2}$

36. How many digits are there in the integral part of the square root of every positive integer less than 100?

37. What is the smallest positive integer whose square root is (*a*) a two-digit integer?   (*b*) a three-digit integer?

In 38–47, tell whether the number has a square root which is less than 10, greater than 10 but less than 100, or greater than 100 but less than 1000.

38. 49   39. 121   40. 8100   41. 14,400   42. 225,000
43. 87   44. 271   45. 4723   46. 18,625   47. 910,500

8. Using Another Method for Computing the Square Root of a Number

We will now illustrate still another method that can be used to compute the square root of a number to as many places as may be desired. The difficult reasoning which justifies the method will not be given here.

COMPUTING THE SQUARE ROOT OF A PERFECT SQUARE

~~~~~~~~~~~~~~~ *MODEL PROBLEMS* ~~~~~~~~~~~~~~~

1. Compute the positive square root of 1764.

How To Proceed	*Solution*
1. Starting at the decimal point and moving to the left, group the digits of the number in pairs of two digits. Place a decimal point directly above the decimal point in the number.	$\sqrt{\overline{17}\ \overline{64}.}$
2. Below the first group at the left, write the largest perfect square which is not more than that group. Write the square root of the perfect square above the first group.	$\begin{array}{r} 4 \\ \sqrt{\overline{17}\ \overline{64}.} \\ \underline{16} \end{array}$
3. Subtract the perfect square from the first group and bring down and annex the next group to the remainder.	$\begin{array}{r} 4 \\ \sqrt{\overline{17}\ \overline{64}.} \\ \underline{16} \\ 1\ 64 \end{array}$
4. Form a trial divisor by doubling (multiplying by 2) the part of the root already found in step 3 and annexing a 0.	$4 \times 2 = 8$ Trial divisor is 80. $\begin{array}{r} 4 \\ \sqrt{\overline{17}\ \overline{64}.} \\ \underline{16} \\ 80\ \overline{\left|\ 1\ 64\right.} \end{array}$
5. Divide the remainder found in step 3 by the trial divisor found in step 4. Annex the quotient to the part of the root already found; also, add it to the trial divisor to form the complete divisor.	$164 \div 80 = 2+$ Complete divisor is $80 + 2 = 82.$ $\begin{array}{r} 4\ 2. \\ \sqrt{\overline{17}\ \overline{64}.} \\ \underline{16} \\ 82\ \overline{\left|\ 1\ 64\right.} \end{array}$

6. Multiply the complete divisor by the last digit which was placed in the root, and subtract the product from the remainder found in step 3. The remainder is 0. The required root is 42.

$$2 \times 82 = 164$$

$$
\begin{array}{r}
4\ \ 2. \\
\sqrt{17\ \overparen{64}.} \\
16 \\
\end{array}
$$

$$
82\ \begin{array}{|l} 1\ 64 \\ \overline{1\ 64} \end{array}
$$

Check: Since $(42)^2 = 1764$, then $\sqrt{1764} = 42$.

Answer: $\sqrt{1764} = 42$

[*Note:* When necessary, the procedure given in steps 4, 5, 6 is repeated until the remainder is 0.]

2. Compute: $\sqrt{552.25}$

Solution:

1. Starting at the decimal point, moving first to the left and then to the right, group the digits in pairs. The first group on the left may have one digit. If the last digit on the right has one digit, annex a 0 to form a two-digit group.

2. The largest perfect square not more than 5 is 4. Write 4 below 5. $\sqrt{4} = 2$. Write 2 above 5.

$$
\begin{array}{r}
2\ \ 3.\ \ 5 \\
\sqrt{5\ \overparen{52}.\overparen{25}} \\
4 \\
\end{array}
$$

$$
43\ \begin{array}{|l} 1\ 52 \\ \overline{1\ 29} \end{array}
$$

$$
465\ \begin{array}{|l} 23\ 25 \\ \overline{23\ 25} \end{array}
$$

3. Subtract 4 from 5, obtaining 1. Bring down the next group, 52, and annex it to 1, forming 152.

4. Find the first trial divisor by doubling 2 and annexing a 0: $2 \times 2 = 4$; the trial divisor is 40.

5. Divide the remainder, 152, by the trial divisor, 40. The quotient is 3. Therefore, the complete first divisor is $40 + 3$, or 43.

6. $3 \times 43 = 129$. Subtract: $152 - 129 = 23$. Bring down the next group, 25, and annex it to 23, forming 2325.

7. Find the second trial divisor by doubling 23 and annexing a 0: $2 \times 23 = 46$; the trial divisor is 460.

8. Divide the remainder, 2325, by the trial divisor, 460. The quotient is 5. Therefore, the complete divisor is $460 + 5$, or 465.

9. $5 \times 465 = 2325$. Subtract: $2325 - 2325 = 0$. The required root is 23.5.

Check: Since $(23.5)^2 = 552.25$, then $\sqrt{552.25} = 23.5$.

Answer: $\sqrt{552.25} = 23.5$

COMPUTING THE APPROXIMATE SQUARE ROOT OF A NUMBER

~~~~~~~~~~~~~~~~~ **MODEL PROBLEMS** ~~~~~~~~~~~~~~~~

1. Find $\sqrt{42}$ correct to the *nearest tenth*.

Solution:

1. In order to approximate $\sqrt{42}$ correct to the nearest tenth, we carry the work to two decimal places and then round off the result to the nearest tenth.

$$
\begin{array}{r}
6.\ \ 4\ \ \ 8 \\
\sqrt{42.\widehat{00}\ \widehat{00}} \\
36 \\
\end{array}
$$

2. Since we wish to carry the result to two decimal places, we annex to 42 (at the right of the decimal point) two groups, each containing two zeros. Since $42 = 42.0000$, then $\sqrt{42} = \sqrt{42.0000}$.

$$
\begin{array}{r|l}
124 & 6\ 00 \\
 & 4\ 96 \\
\hline
1288 & 1\ 04\ 00 \\
 & 1\ 03\ 04 \\
\hline
 & 96
\end{array}
$$

3. Perform the computation and round off the answer to the nearest tenth. Since $6.48 \approx 6.5$, the required root is 6.5.

Answer: $\sqrt{42} = 6.5$ to the nearest tenth

2. Find $\sqrt{65}$ correct to the *nearest hundredth*.

Solution:

1. In order to carry the work in the result to three decimal places, we annex three groups, each containing two zeros, at the right of 65.

$$
\begin{array}{r}
8.\ \ 0\ \ \ 6\ \ \ 2 \\
\sqrt{65.\widehat{00}\ \widehat{00}\ \widehat{00}} \\
64 \\
\end{array}
$$

2. The first trial divisor is 160. Since $100 \div 160$ is less than 1, we say the quotient is 0. Therefore, the complete first divisor is $160 + 0 = 160$.

$$
\begin{array}{r|l}
160 & 1\ 00 \\
 & 0\ 00 \\
\hline
1606 & 1\ 00\ 00 \\
 & 96\ 36 \\
\hline
16122 & 3\ 64\ 00 \\
 & 3\ 22\ 44 \\
\hline
 & 41\ 56
\end{array}
$$

3. Complete the computation and round off the answer to the nearest hundredth. Since $8.062 \approx 8.06$, the required root is 8.06.

Answer: $\sqrt{65} = 8.06$ to the nearest hundredth

Exercises

In 1–16, find the square root.

1. $\sqrt{289}$ **2.** $\sqrt{324}$ **3.** $\sqrt{784}$ **4.** $-\sqrt{1296}$

5. $\sqrt{4225}$ **6.** $\sqrt{9801}$ **7.** $\sqrt{11{,}025}$ **8.** $\sqrt{16{,}900}$

9. $\sqrt{9.61}$ **10.** $\sqrt{90.25}$ **11.** $-\sqrt{56.25}$ **12.** $\sqrt{161.29}$

13. $\sqrt{1.1025}$ **14.** $\sqrt{16.1604}$ **15.** $\sqrt{1.7689}$ **16.** $\sqrt{.667489}$

In 17–31, find the square root correct to the *nearest tenth*.

17. $\sqrt{12}$ **18.** $\sqrt{19}$ **19.** $\sqrt{37}$ **20.** $-\sqrt{58}$ **21.** $\sqrt{60}$

22. $\sqrt{79}$ **23.** $\sqrt{108}$ **24.** $\sqrt{150}$ **25.** $\sqrt{200}$ **26.** $-\sqrt{416}$

27. $\sqrt{18.25}$ **28.** $\sqrt{205.78}$ **29.** $-\sqrt{8.5}$ **30.** $\sqrt{61.7}$ **31.** $\sqrt{4.052}$

In 32–36, find the square root correct to the *nearest hundredth*.

32. $\sqrt{2}$ **33.** $\sqrt{54}$ **34.** $\sqrt{77}$ **35.** $\sqrt{8.25}$ **36.** $\sqrt{9.5}$

In 37–41, find the length of a side of a square whose area is the given measure. Round off your answers to the *nearest tenth of an inch*.

37. 8 sq. in.   **38.** 29 sq. in.   **39.** 96 sq. in.

40. 140 sq. in.   **41.** 200 sq. in.

9. Using a Table To Find Squares and Square Roots

When computing the square or the square root of a number, much time can be saved by using a table of squares and square roots such as the one that appears on page 581.

━━━━━━━ MODEL PROBLEMS ━━━━━━━

1. Find the square of 58.

> *Solution:* In the table on page 581, in the column headed "No.," we find 58. We look to the right of 58 in the column headed "Square" and find 3,364.

> *Answer:* $(58)^2 = 3{,}364$

2. Approximate $\sqrt{48}$ (*a*) to the *nearest tenth* and (*b*) to the *nearest hundredth*.

> *Solution:* In the table on page 581, in the column headed "No.," we find 48. We look to the right of 48 in the column headed "Square Root" and find 6.928. Then we round off the decimal.

> *Answer:* (*a*) $\sqrt{48} = 6.9$ to the nearest tenth
>
>   (*b*) $\sqrt{48} = 6.93$ to the nearest hundredth

3. Find $\sqrt{15,376}$.

Solution: Since 15,376 is greater than 150, it does not appear in the column headed "No." In the column headed "Square," find 15,376. To its left, in the column headed "No.," appears 124. Since $(124)^2 = 15,376$, then $\sqrt{15,376} = 124$.

Answer: $\sqrt{15,376} = 124$

4. Find $\sqrt{3,000}$ correct to the *nearest integer*.

Solution: Since 3,000 is greater than 150, we look for 3,000 in the column headed, "Square," but do not find it there. In that column, the number just smaller than 3,000 is 2,916, which is 54^2; and the number just larger than 3,000 is 3,025, which is 55^2. Since $(54.5)^2 = 2970.25$ and 3,000 is greater than 2970.25, then the square root of 3,000 is greater than 54.5, or $54.5 < \sqrt{3,000} < 55$. We see that $\sqrt{3,000}$ is closer to 55 than to 54. Therefore, the square root of 3,000, to the nearest integer, is 55.

No.	Square
55	3,025
?	3,000
54	2,916

Answer: $\sqrt{3,000} = 55$ to the nearest integer

Exercises

In 1–6, use the table on page 581 to find the square of the number.

1. 27   **2.** 68   **3.** 94   **4.** 119   **5.** 132   **6.** 147

In 7–21, use the table on page 581 to approximate the square root to the *nearest tenth*.

7. $\sqrt{13}$ **8.** $\sqrt{53}$ **9.** $-\sqrt{63}$ **10.** $\sqrt{135}$ **11.** $-\sqrt{87}$

12. $\sqrt{5}$ **13.** $\sqrt{91}$ **14.** $\sqrt{85}$ **15.** $-\sqrt{111}$ **16.** $\sqrt{141}$

17. $2 + \sqrt{3}$ **18.** $9 - \sqrt{17}$ **19.** $\sqrt{55} + 7$ **20.** $\sqrt{120} - 4$ **21.** $-2 - \sqrt{13}$

In 22–31, use the table on page 581 to approximate the square root to the *nearest hundredth*.

22. $\sqrt{8}$ **23.** $\sqrt{17}$ **24.** $\sqrt{29}$ **25.** $\sqrt{78}$ **26.** $-\sqrt{93}$

27. $-\sqrt{31}$ **28.** $\sqrt{103}$ **29.** $\sqrt{120}$ **30.** $\sqrt{138}$ **31.** $\sqrt{147}$

In 32–41, use the table on page 581 to express the square root as an integer.

32. $\sqrt{961}$ **33.** $\sqrt{1,156}$ **34.** $\sqrt{4,356}$ **35.** $\sqrt{7,921}$ **36.** $\sqrt{9,409}$

37. $\sqrt{12,996}$ **38.** $\sqrt{15,625}$ **39.** $\sqrt{18,769}$ **40.** $\sqrt{19,321}$ **41.** $\sqrt{15,625}$

In 42–46, use the table on page 581 to approximate the square root to the *nearest integer*.

42. $\sqrt{170}$ **43.** $\sqrt{1,865}$ **44.** $\sqrt{5,420}$ **45.** $-\sqrt{9,325}$ **46.** $\sqrt{13,524}$

In 47–50, find c if $c = \sqrt{a^2 + b^2}$ and a and b have the given values. Use the table on page 581.

47. $a = 6, b = 8$ **48.** $a = 5, b = 12$
49. $a = 15, b = 20$ **50.** $a = 15, b = 36$

In 51–54, find b if $b = \sqrt{c^2 - a^2}$ and a and c have the given values. Use the table on page 581.

51. $c = 10, a = 6$ **52.** $c = 26, a = 10$
53. $c = 17, a = 8$ **54.** $c = 50, a = 30$

In 55–58, use the table on page 581 to find the value of $\sqrt{b^2 - 4ac}$ when:

55. $a = 5, b = 6, c = 1$ **56.** $a = 2, b = 9, c = -5$
57. $a = 1, b = 2, c = -24$ **58.** $a = 5, b = 0, c = -20$

In 59–62, approximate a to the *nearest tenth* if $a = \sqrt{c^2 - b^2}$ and b and c have the given values. Use the table on page 581.

59. $b = 5, c = 7$ **60.** $b = 3, c = 6$
61. $b = 9, c = 13$ **62.** $b = 8, c = 14$

In 63–66, approximate $\sqrt{b^2 - 4ac}$ to the *nearest tenth* when a, b, and c have the given values. Use the table on page 581.

63. $a = 1, b = 7, c = 2$ **64.** $a = 3, b = -6, c = 1$
65. $a = 5, b = -9, c = 3$ **66.** $a = 3, b = -8, c = -1$

10. Finding the Principal Square Root of a Monomial

Since we know that the principal square root of 49 is the positive number 7, we may write $\sqrt{49} = 7$. However, we do not know whether the principal square root of x^2 is $+x$ or $-x$ until we know whether x is a positive or a negative number. For example:

$$\text{If } x = 5, \text{ then } \sqrt{x^2} = \sqrt{(5)^2} = \sqrt{25} = 5 = x.$$
$$\text{If } x = -5, \text{ then } \sqrt{x^2} = \sqrt{(-5)^2} = \sqrt{25} = 5 = -x.$$

Therefore:

$$\sqrt{x^2} = x \text{ if } x \text{ is a positive number or zero.}$$
$$\sqrt{x^2} = -x \text{ if } x \text{ is a negative number.}$$

We could use an absolute value symbol to show that $\sqrt{x^2}$ is a positive number. If we write $\sqrt{x^2} = |x|$, then the result will be a positive number, the principal square root. In our work, however, we will not use absolute value symbols. Rather, we will limit the domain of the variables which appear under the radical sign to non-negative numbers only. Therefore, we will write $\sqrt{x^2} = x$, and $\sqrt{64y^4} = 8y^2$.

Procedure. To find the square root of a monomial which has more than one factor, write the indicated product of the square roots of its factors.

KEEP IN MIND
We limit the domain of the variables which appear under a radical sign to non-negative numbers only.

MODEL PROBLEM

In each part, find the principal square root.

a. $\sqrt{25y^2}$ b. $\sqrt{16m^6}$ c. $\sqrt{\frac{4}{9}a^2b^4}$ d. $\sqrt{.81y^8}$

Solution:

a. Since $(5y)(5y) = 25y^2$, then $\sqrt{25y^2} = 5y$. $5y$ *Ans.*
b. Since $(4m^3)(4m^3) = 16m^6$, then $\sqrt{16m^6} = 4m^3$. $4m^3$ *Ans.*
c. Since $(\frac{2}{3}ab^2)(\frac{2}{3}ab^2) = \frac{4}{9}a^2b^4$, then $\sqrt{\frac{4}{9}a^2b^4} = \frac{2}{3}ab^2$. $\frac{2}{3}ab^2$ *Ans.*
d. Since $(.9y^4)(.9y^4) = .81y^8$, then $\sqrt{.81y^8} = .9y^4$. $.9y^4$ *Ans.*

Exercises

In 1–25, find the indicated root.

1. $\sqrt{9c^2}$ 2. $\sqrt{36y^4}$ 3. $\sqrt{64c^6}$ 4. $\sqrt{100x^{10}}$ 5. $\sqrt{81t^8}$

6. $\sqrt{c^2d^2}$ 7. $\sqrt{x^4y^2}$ 8. $\sqrt{r^8s^6}$ 9. $\sqrt{x^{16}y^4}$ 10. $\sqrt{x^6y^2z^4}$

11. $\sqrt{4x^2y^2}$ 12. $\sqrt{36a^6b^4}$ 13. $\sqrt{144a^4b^2}$ 14. $\sqrt{169x^4y^2}$

15. $\sqrt{25r^8s^{16}t^{12}}$ 16. $\sqrt{\frac{1}{4}y^2}$ 17. $\sqrt{\frac{25}{36}x^2y^2}$ 18. $\sqrt{\frac{49}{9}a^4b^2}$

19. $\sqrt{\frac{81}{121}a^6b^2}$ 20. $\sqrt{\frac{64}{169}x^8y^{10}z^{16}}$ 21. $\sqrt{.36m^2}$ 22. $\sqrt{.49a^2b^2}$

23. $\sqrt{.04x^2y^6}$ 24. $\sqrt{.01x^4y^2}$ 25. $\sqrt{1.21a^4b^{16}c^{36}}$

11. Simplifying a Radical Whose Radicand Has a Perfect Square Factor

Since $\sqrt{4 \cdot 9} = \sqrt{36} = 6$, and $\sqrt{4} \cdot \sqrt{9} = 2 \cdot 3 = 6$, then $\sqrt{4 \cdot 9} = \sqrt{4} \cdot \sqrt{9}$.

Since $\sqrt{16 \cdot 25} = \sqrt{400} = 20$, and $\sqrt{16} \cdot \sqrt{25} = 4 \cdot 5 = 20$, then $\sqrt{16 \cdot 25} = \sqrt{16} \cdot \sqrt{25}$.

These examples illustrate the following property of radicals:

The square root of a product of non-negative numbers is equal to the product of the square roots of the numbers.

In general, if a and b are non-negative numbers:

$$\sqrt{a \cdot b} = \sqrt{a} \cdot \sqrt{b} \quad \text{AND} \quad \sqrt{a} \cdot \sqrt{b} = \sqrt{a \cdot b}$$

To simplify a square-root radical whose radicand has a perfect square factor, we transform it and express it in terms of a radical whose radicand has no perfect square factor other than 1.

If we wish to find $\sqrt{200}$, correct to the nearest hundredth, by the use of the table on page 581, we can first simplify the radical as follows:

$$\sqrt{200} = \sqrt{100 \cdot 2} = \sqrt{100} \cdot \sqrt{2} = 10\sqrt{2} \approx 10(1.414) \approx 14.14$$

Note that 100 is the largest perfect square factor of 200.

Procedure. To simplify the square root of a product:
1. **Find two factors of the radicand, one of which is the largest perfect square factor of the radicand.**
2. **Express the square root of the product as the product of the square roots of the factors.**
3. **Find the square root of the factor which is a perfect square.**

~~~~~~~~~~ **MODEL PROBLEM** ~~~~~~~~~~

In each part, simplify the expression.

a. $\sqrt{18}$ b. $4\sqrt{50}$ c. $\frac{1}{2}\sqrt{48}$ d. $-\sqrt{4y^3}$ e. $\sqrt{75x^2y^3z^7}$

Solution:

a. $\sqrt{18} = \sqrt{9 \cdot 2} = \sqrt{9} \cdot \sqrt{2} = 3\sqrt{2}$ *Ans.*

b. $4\sqrt{50} = 4\sqrt{25 \cdot 2} = 4\sqrt{25} \cdot \sqrt{2} = 4 \cdot 5\sqrt{2} = 20\sqrt{2}$ *Ans.*

c. $\frac{1}{2}\sqrt{48} = \frac{1}{2}\sqrt{16 \cdot 3} = \frac{1}{2}\sqrt{16} \cdot \sqrt{3} = \frac{1}{2} \cdot 4\sqrt{3} = 2\sqrt{3}$ *Ans.*

d. $-\sqrt{4y^3} = -\sqrt{4y^2 \cdot y} = -\sqrt{4y^2} \cdot \sqrt{y} = -2y\sqrt{y}$ *Ans.*

e. $\sqrt{75x^2y^3z^7} = \sqrt{25x^2y^2z^6 \cdot 3yz} = \sqrt{25x^2y^2z^6} \cdot \sqrt{3yz} = 5xyz^3\sqrt{3yz}$ *Ans.*

Exercises

In 1–60, simplify the expression.

1. $\sqrt{8}$ 2. $\sqrt{12}$ 3. $\sqrt{20}$ 4. $-\sqrt{24}$

5. $\sqrt{28}$ 6. $\sqrt{40}$ 7. $\sqrt{27}$ 8. $-\sqrt{45}$

9. $\sqrt{54}$ 10. $\sqrt{63}$ 11. $\sqrt{90}$ 12. $-\sqrt{72}$

13. $\sqrt{98}$ 14. $\sqrt{99}$ 15. $\sqrt{108}$ 16. $-\sqrt{128}$

17. $\sqrt{162}$ 18. $\sqrt{175}$ 19. $\sqrt{300}$ 20. $-\sqrt{500}$

21. $3\sqrt{8}$ 22. $4\sqrt{12}$ 23. $2\sqrt{20}$ 24. $-5\sqrt{24}$

25. $4\sqrt{90}$ 26. $2\sqrt{45}$ 27. $3\sqrt{200}$ 28. $-6\sqrt{98}$

29. $\frac{1}{3}\sqrt{45}$ 30. $\frac{1}{2}\sqrt{72}$ 31. $\frac{1}{4}\sqrt{48}$ 32. $\frac{1}{2}\sqrt{18}$

33. $\frac{3}{4}\sqrt{96}$ 34. $\frac{2}{3}\sqrt{63}$ 35. $\frac{3}{8}\sqrt{80}$ 36. $-\frac{2}{5}\sqrt{125}$

37. $\sqrt{a^3}$ 38. $2\sqrt{b^5}$ 39. $\sqrt{r^2s}$ 40. $3\sqrt{mn^2}$

41. $\sqrt{x^2y^3}$ 42. $4\sqrt{x^3y^3}$ 43. $\sqrt{3x^3y}$ 44. $-4\sqrt{2a^2b^3}$

45. $\sqrt{49a}$ 46. $\sqrt{36r^2s}$ 47. $\sqrt{9x^2y^3}$ 48. $5\sqrt{4x^3y^3}$

49. $\sqrt{27m^2}$ 50. $6\sqrt{8r^3}$ 51. $\sqrt{20x^2y^3}$ 52. $-7\sqrt{24a^3b^3}$

53. $\sqrt{4x^2y^4z^3}$ 54. $\sqrt{9a^3b^3c^2}$ 55. $\sqrt{12r^4s^3t^6}$ 56. $5\sqrt{18y^3u^6z^8}$

57. $\frac{1}{2}\sqrt{16a^3b^2c^2}$ 58. $\frac{2}{3}\sqrt{72x^5y^4z^7}$ 59. $\frac{3}{5}\sqrt{50r^3s^3t^3}$ 60. $-\frac{4}{7}\sqrt{147x^2y^6z^{11}}$

In 61–72, use the table on page 581 to approximate the expression to the *nearest tenth.*

61. $\sqrt{300}$ 62. $\sqrt{180}$ 63. $\sqrt{640}$ 64. $\sqrt{405}$

65. $2\sqrt{288}$ 66. $\frac{1}{3}\sqrt{252}$ 67. $\frac{3}{4}\sqrt{176}$ 68. $-\frac{2}{5}\sqrt{175}$

69. $3 + \sqrt{8}$ 70. $7 - \sqrt{28}$ 71. $-4 + \sqrt{200}$ 72. $-5 - \sqrt{500}$

73. Use the properties of the set of real numbers to prove that $\sqrt{a \cdot b} = \sqrt{a} \cdot \sqrt{b}$ when a and b are non-negative. [*Hint:* Show $(\sqrt{a} \cdot \sqrt{b})^2 = ab$.]

12. Simplifying a Radical Whose Radicand Is a Fraction

Since $\sqrt{\dfrac{4}{9}} = \dfrac{2}{3}$ and $\dfrac{\sqrt{4}}{\sqrt{9}} = \dfrac{2}{3}$, then $\sqrt{\dfrac{4}{9}} = \dfrac{\sqrt{4}}{\sqrt{9}}$.

Since $\sqrt{\dfrac{16}{25}} = \dfrac{4}{5}$ and $\dfrac{\sqrt{16}}{\sqrt{25}} = \dfrac{4}{5}$, then $\sqrt{\dfrac{16}{25}} = \dfrac{\sqrt{16}}{\sqrt{25}}$.

These examples illustrate the following property of radicals:

The square root of a fraction is equal to the square root of its numerator divided by the square root of its denominator.

In general, if a is non-negative and b is positive:

$$\sqrt{\dfrac{a}{b}} = \dfrac{\sqrt{a}}{\sqrt{b}} \quad \text{AND} \quad \dfrac{\sqrt{a}}{\sqrt{b}} = \sqrt{\dfrac{a}{b}}$$

To simplify a square-root radical whose radicand is a fraction, we transform it and express it in terms of a radical whose radicand is not a fraction.

If we wish to find $\sqrt{\frac{1}{8}}$, correct to the nearest hundredth, by the use of the table on page 581, we first simplify the radical as follows:

$$\sqrt{\dfrac{1}{8}} = \sqrt{\dfrac{1}{8} \cdot \dfrac{2}{2}} = \sqrt{\dfrac{2}{16}} = \dfrac{\sqrt{2}}{\sqrt{16}} = \dfrac{\sqrt{2}}{4} \approx \dfrac{1.414}{4} \approx .353 \approx .35$$

Note that we multiply the radicand $\frac{1}{8}$ by $\frac{2}{2}$, which is another symbol for 1. We choose $\frac{2}{2}$ because it is the fraction whose numerator and denominator are the least number which makes the denominator of the product a perfect square.

Procedure. To simplify the square root of a fraction:
1. **If the denominator of the radicand is not a perfect square, multiply the radicand by 1 represented as a fraction whose numerator and denominator are the least number which makes the denominator of the product a perfect square.**
2. **Express the square root of the resulting fraction as the square root of its numerator divided by the square root of its denominator.**
3. **Find the square root of the denominator and if possible simplify the result.**

~~~~~~~~~~ MODEL PROBLEM ~~~~~~~~~~

In each part, simplify the expression.

a. $\sqrt{\frac{3}{4}}$ b. $6\sqrt{\frac{1}{3}}$ c. $\sqrt{\frac{9}{5}}$ d. $\sqrt{\frac{c}{d}}$

Solution:

a. $\sqrt{\frac{3}{4}} = \frac{\sqrt{3}}{\sqrt{4}} = \frac{\sqrt{3}}{2}$ or $\frac{1}{2}\sqrt{3}$ *Ans.*

b. $6\sqrt{\frac{1}{3}} = 6\sqrt{\frac{1}{3} \cdot \frac{3}{3}} = 6\sqrt{\frac{3}{9}} = \frac{6\sqrt{3}}{\sqrt{9}} = \frac{6\sqrt{3}}{3} = 2\sqrt{3}$ *Ans.*

c. $\sqrt{\frac{9}{5}} = \sqrt{\frac{9}{5} \cdot \frac{5}{5}} = \sqrt{\frac{45}{25}} = \frac{\sqrt{45}}{\sqrt{25}} = \frac{\sqrt{9} \cdot \sqrt{5}}{5} = \frac{3\sqrt{5}}{5}$ or $\frac{3}{5}\sqrt{5}$ *Ans.*

d. $\sqrt{\frac{c}{d}} = \sqrt{\frac{c}{d} \cdot \frac{d}{d}} = \sqrt{\frac{cd}{d^2}} = \frac{\sqrt{cd}}{\sqrt{d^2}} = \frac{\sqrt{cd}}{d}$ or $\frac{1}{d}\sqrt{cd}$ *Ans.*

~~~~~~~~~~~~~~~~~~~~~~~~~~~~~~~~~~~~~~~

Exercises

In 1–36, simplify the expression.

1. $\sqrt{\frac{5}{9}}$ 2. $4\sqrt{\frac{5}{16}}$ 3. $\sqrt{\frac{8}{49}}$ 4. $10\sqrt{\frac{24}{25}}$

5. $\sqrt{\frac{1}{2}}$ 6. $\sqrt{\frac{1}{5}}$ 7. $12\sqrt{\frac{1}{6}}$ 8. $21\sqrt{\frac{1}{7}}$

9. $\sqrt{\frac{3}{2}}$ 10. $\sqrt{\frac{7}{5}}$ 11. $10\sqrt{\frac{3}{5}}$ 12. $8\sqrt{\frac{7}{2}}$

13. $\sqrt{\frac{12}{5}}$ 14. $\sqrt{\frac{8}{7}}$ 15. $4\sqrt{\frac{25}{2}}$ 16. $15\sqrt{\frac{16}{3}}$

17. $\sqrt{\frac{7}{12}}$ 18. $\sqrt{\frac{5}{18}}$ 19. $\sqrt{\frac{3}{32}}$ 20. $10\sqrt{\frac{25}{20}}$

21. $\sqrt{\frac{a}{3}}$ 22. $6\sqrt{\frac{b}{2}}$ 23. $12\sqrt{\frac{c}{6}}$ 24. $8\sqrt{\frac{x^2}{2}}$

25. $\sqrt{\frac{c}{d^2}}$ 26. $\sqrt{\frac{1}{y}}$ 27. $\sqrt{\frac{1}{a}}$ 28. $\sqrt{\frac{a}{b}}$

29. $\sqrt{\frac{m}{n}}$ 30. $\sqrt{\frac{A}{\pi}}$ 31. $\sqrt{\frac{2s}{g}}$ 32. $\sqrt{\frac{x^2}{y}}$

33. $\sqrt{\frac{5a}{2b}}$ 34. $\sqrt{\frac{7x}{5y}}$ 35. $\sqrt{\frac{9m}{8n}}$ 36. $\sqrt{\frac{25r^2}{12s^3}}$

In 37–44, use the table on page 581 to approximate the expression to the *nearest tenth.*

37. $\sqrt{\frac{7}{9}}$ **38.** $\sqrt{\frac{17}{81}}$ **39.** $\sqrt{\frac{1}{2}}$ **40.** $15\sqrt{\frac{1}{3}}$

41. $8\sqrt{\frac{5}{8}}$ **42.** $6\sqrt{\frac{7}{12}}$ **43.** $\frac{5}{3}\sqrt{\frac{9}{50}}$ **44.** $\frac{2}{5}\sqrt{\frac{25}{24}}$

45. Use the properties of the set of real numbers to prove that $\sqrt{\dfrac{a}{b}} = \dfrac{\sqrt{a}}{\sqrt{b}}$ when a is non-negative and b is positive.

13. Adding and Subtracting Radicals

ADDING AND SUBTRACTING LIKE RADICALS

Like radicals are radicals which have the *same index* and the *same radicand.* For example, $3\sqrt{2}$ and $5\sqrt{2}$ are like radicals, as are $4\sqrt[3]{7}$ and $9\sqrt[3]{7}$. However, $3\sqrt{5}$ and $5\sqrt{2}$ are unlike radicals, as are $\sqrt[3]{2}$ and $\sqrt{2}$.

To add or subtract like radicals, we use the distributive property as follows:

$$7\sqrt{2} + 3\sqrt{2} = (7 + 3)\sqrt{2} = 10\sqrt{2}$$
$$5\sqrt{3} - \sqrt{3} = (5 - 1)\sqrt{3} = 4\sqrt{3}$$

Procedure. To add or subtract like radicals:
1. **Add or subtract the coefficients of the radicals.**
2. **Multiply the sum or difference obtained by the common radical.**

ADDING AND SUBTRACTING UNLIKE RADICALS

The sum of the unlike radicals $\sqrt{5}$ and $\sqrt{2}$ is indicated as $\sqrt{5} + \sqrt{2}$, which cannot be expressed as a single term. Similarly, the difference of $\sqrt{5}$ and $\sqrt{2}$ is indicated as $\sqrt{5} - \sqrt{2}$.

However, when it is possible to transform unlike radicals into equivalent radicals which are like radicals, the resulting like radicals can be added or subtracted. For example, it would appear that the sum of $2\sqrt{3}$ and $\sqrt{27}$ can be indicated only as $2\sqrt{3} + \sqrt{27}$ since $2\sqrt{3}$ and $\sqrt{27}$ are unlike radicals. However, since $\sqrt{27} = \sqrt{9 \cdot 3} = \sqrt{9} \cdot \sqrt{3} = 3\sqrt{3}$, we can express $2\sqrt{3} + \sqrt{27}$ as $2\sqrt{3} + 3\sqrt{3}$ and then add the like radicals:

$$2\sqrt{3} + \sqrt{27} = 2\sqrt{3} + 3\sqrt{3} = (2 + 3)\sqrt{3} = 5\sqrt{3}$$

Procedure. To combine unlike radicals:
1. **Simplify each radical.**
2. **Combine like radicals by using the distributive property.**
3. **Indicate the sum or difference of the unlike radicals.**

MODEL PROBLEMS

1. Combine: $8\sqrt{5} + 3\sqrt{5} - 2\sqrt{5}$

   Solution: $8\sqrt{5} + 3\sqrt{5} - 2\sqrt{5} = (8 + 3 - 2)\sqrt{5} = 9\sqrt{5}$ *Ans.*

2. Simplify: $8\sqrt{3} + 4\sqrt{2} - \sqrt{2} + \sqrt{3}$

   Solution: $8\sqrt{3} + 4\sqrt{2} - \sqrt{2} + \sqrt{3} = (8\sqrt{3} + \sqrt{3}) + (4\sqrt{2} - \sqrt{2})$
   $$= (8 + 1)\sqrt{3} + (4 - 1)\sqrt{2}$$
   $$= 9\sqrt{3} + 3\sqrt{2}\quad Ans.$$

3. Combine: $5\sqrt{3} + 4\sqrt{12} - 2\sqrt{75}$

   Solution: $5\sqrt{3} + 4\sqrt{12} - 2\sqrt{75} = 5\sqrt{3} + 4\sqrt{4 \cdot 3} - 2\sqrt{25 \cdot 3}$
   $$= 5\sqrt{3} + 4\sqrt{4} \cdot \sqrt{3} - 2\sqrt{25} \cdot \sqrt{3}$$
   $$= 5\sqrt{3} + 4 \cdot 2 \cdot \sqrt{3} - 2 \cdot 5 \cdot \sqrt{3}$$
   $$= 5\sqrt{3} + 8\sqrt{3} - 10\sqrt{3}$$
   $$= (5 + 8 - 10)\sqrt{3}$$
   $$= 3\sqrt{3}\quad Ans.$$

4. Combine: $6\sqrt{8} - 4\sqrt{\frac{1}{2}}$

   Solution: $6\sqrt{8} - 4\sqrt{\frac{1}{2}} = 6\sqrt{4 \cdot 2} - 4\sqrt{\frac{1}{2} \cdot \frac{2}{2}}$
   $$= 6\sqrt{4} \cdot \sqrt{2} - 4 \cdot \frac{\sqrt{2}}{\sqrt{4}}$$
   $$= 6 \cdot 2 \cdot \sqrt{2} - \frac{4\sqrt{2}}{2}$$
   $$= 12\sqrt{2} - 2\sqrt{2}$$
   $$= (12 - 2)\sqrt{2}$$
   $$= 10\sqrt{2}\quad Ans.$$

5. Combine: $2\sqrt{2x} + 7\sqrt{8x} - 4\sqrt{50x}$

$Solution:$ $2\sqrt{2x} + 7\sqrt{8x} - 4\sqrt{50x} = 2\sqrt{2x} + 7\sqrt{4 \cdot 2x} - 4\sqrt{25 \cdot 2x}$

$$= 2\sqrt{2x} + 7\sqrt{4} \cdot \sqrt{2x} - 4\sqrt{25} \cdot \sqrt{2x}$$

$$= 2\sqrt{2x} + 7 \cdot 2 \cdot \sqrt{2x} - 4 \cdot 5 \cdot \sqrt{2x}$$

$$= 2\sqrt{2x} + 14\sqrt{2x} - 20\sqrt{2x}$$

$$= (2 + 14 - 20)\sqrt{2x}$$

$$= -4\sqrt{2x} \quad Ans.$$

Exercises

In 1–51, combine the radicals.

1. $8\sqrt{2} + 7\sqrt{2}$

2. $8\sqrt{5} + \sqrt{5}$

3. $5\sqrt{3} + 2\sqrt{3} + 8\sqrt{3}$

4. $14\sqrt{6} - 2\sqrt{6}$

5. $7\sqrt{2} - \sqrt{2}$

6. $4\sqrt{3} + 2\sqrt{3} - 6\sqrt{3}$

7. $5\sqrt{3} + \sqrt{3} - 2\sqrt{3}$

8. $4\sqrt{7} - \sqrt{7} - 5\sqrt{7}$

9. $3\sqrt{5} + 6\sqrt{2} - 3\sqrt{2} + \sqrt{5}$

10. $9\sqrt{x} + 3\sqrt{x}$

11. $15\sqrt{y} - 7\sqrt{y}$

12. $7\sqrt{x} + 3\sqrt{y} - \sqrt{x} - 3\sqrt{y}$

13. $\sqrt{2} + \sqrt{50}$

14. $\sqrt{27} + \sqrt{75}$

15. $\sqrt{5} + \sqrt{45} + \sqrt{80}$

16. $\sqrt{80} - \sqrt{5}$

17. $\sqrt{72} - \sqrt{50}$

18. $\sqrt{12} - \sqrt{48} + \sqrt{3}$

19. $3\sqrt{2} + 2\sqrt{32}$

20. $3\sqrt{32} - 6\sqrt{8}$

21. $5\sqrt{27} - \sqrt{108} + 2\sqrt{75}$

22. $3\sqrt{40} - \sqrt{90}$

23. $3\sqrt{8} - \sqrt{2}$

24. $5\sqrt{8} - 3\sqrt{18} + \sqrt{3}$

25. $3\sqrt{50} - 5\sqrt{18}$

26. $3\sqrt{28} - 2\sqrt{63}$

27. $\sqrt{98} - 4\sqrt{8} + 3\sqrt{128}$

28. $\frac{1}{2}\sqrt{20} + \sqrt{45}$

29. $\frac{2}{3}\sqrt{18} - \sqrt{72}$

30. $4\sqrt{18} - \frac{3}{4}\sqrt{32} - \frac{1}{2}\sqrt{8}$

31. $4\sqrt{3} + 6\sqrt{\frac{1}{3}}$

32. $\sqrt{20} - 10\sqrt{\frac{1}{5}}$

33. $5\sqrt{\frac{3}{5}} + \sqrt{60} - \sqrt{15}$

34. $3\sqrt{12} + 6\sqrt{\frac{1}{3}}$

35. $4\sqrt{8} - \sqrt{\frac{1}{2}}$

36. $\frac{1}{2}\sqrt{20} - \sqrt{\frac{1}{5}} + \frac{1}{5}\sqrt{80}$

37. $\sqrt{7a} + \sqrt{28a}$

38. $\sqrt{81x} + \sqrt{25x}$

39. $\sqrt{100b} - \sqrt{64b} + \sqrt{9b}$

40. $3\sqrt{3x} - \sqrt{12x}$

41. $5\sqrt{8b} + 3\sqrt{32b}$

42. $5\sqrt{3y} - \sqrt{27x} + \sqrt{12y}$

43. $\sqrt{3a^2} + \sqrt{12a^2}$

44. $4\sqrt{5y^2} - \sqrt{20y^2}$

45. $4\sqrt{12r^2} + 2\sqrt{75r^2} - 3\sqrt{27r^2}$

46. $\sqrt{7x^3} + \sqrt{28x^3}$

47. $3\sqrt{2y^3} - \sqrt{8y^3}$

48. $5\sqrt{12a^3} - 2\sqrt{3a^3} + \sqrt{27a^3}$

49. $x\sqrt{8y} + 3\sqrt{2x^2y}$

50. $b\sqrt{27a} - 6\sqrt{3ab^2}$

51. $\sqrt{3x^3} + 3\sqrt{12x^3} - x\sqrt{75}$

14. Multiplying Radicals

MULTIPLYING MONOMIALS CONTAINING RADICALS

We have learned that $\sqrt{a} \cdot \sqrt{b} = \sqrt{ab}$ when a and b are non-negative numbers. For example, $\sqrt{3} \cdot \sqrt{7} = \sqrt{3 \cdot 7} = \sqrt{21}$.

To multiply $4\sqrt{2}$ by $5\sqrt{3}$, we use the commutative and associative laws of multiplication as follows:

$$(4\sqrt{2})(5\sqrt{3}) = (4)(5)(\sqrt{2})(\sqrt{3}) = (4 \cdot 5)(\sqrt{2 \cdot 3}) = 20\sqrt{6}$$

In general, if a and b are non-negative numbers:

$$x\sqrt{a} \cdot y\sqrt{b} = xy\sqrt{ab}$$

Procedure. To multiply two monomial square roots:
1. **Multiply the coefficients to find the coefficient of the product.**
2. **Multiply the radicands to find the radicand of the product.**
3. **If possible, simplify the result.**

————— *MODEL PROBLEMS* —————

1. Multiply: $3\sqrt{6} \cdot 5\sqrt{2}$

Solution: $3\sqrt{6} \cdot 5\sqrt{2} = 3 \cdot 5\sqrt{6 \cdot 2} = 15\sqrt{12}$
$= 15\sqrt{4} \cdot \sqrt{3} = 15 \cdot 2 \cdot \sqrt{3} = 30\sqrt{3}$ *Ans.*

2. Find the value of $(2\sqrt{3})^2$.

Solution: $(2\sqrt{3})^2 = 2\sqrt{3} \cdot 2\sqrt{3}$
$$= 2 \cdot 2\sqrt{3 \cdot 3} = 4\sqrt{9} = 4 \cdot 3 = 12 \quad Ans.$$

3. Find the indicated product: $\sqrt{3x} \cdot \sqrt{6x}$

Solution: $\sqrt{3x} \cdot \sqrt{6x} = \sqrt{3x \cdot 6x}$
$$= \sqrt{18x^2} = \sqrt{9x^2 \cdot 2} = \sqrt{9x^2} \cdot \sqrt{2} = 3x\sqrt{2} \quad Ans.$$

MULTIPLYING POLYNOMIALS CONTAINING RADICALS

To find the product $\sqrt{3}(\sqrt{2} + \sqrt{5})$, we use the distributive property of multiplication as follows:

$$\sqrt{3}(\sqrt{2} + \sqrt{5}) = (\sqrt{3})(\sqrt{2}) + (\sqrt{3})(\sqrt{5}) = \sqrt{6} + \sqrt{15}$$

To find the product $(5 + \sqrt{2})(7 - \sqrt{2})$, we use the distributive property of multiplication and arrange the solution in the same way that was previously used in finding the product of two binomials.

$$\begin{array}{r} 7 - \sqrt{2} \\ 5 + \sqrt{2} \\ \hline 35 - 5\sqrt{2} \\ + 7\sqrt{2} - \sqrt{4} \\ \hline 35 + 2\sqrt{2} - 2 = 33 + 2\sqrt{2} \end{array}$$

--- **MODEL PROBLEMS** ---

1. Find the product:
$$2\sqrt{2}(\sqrt{6} + 3\sqrt{24})$$

Solution:

$$\begin{array}{r} \sqrt{6} \ + 3\sqrt{24} \\ 2\sqrt{2} \\ \hline 2\sqrt{12} + 6\sqrt{48} \end{array}$$
$$= 2\sqrt{4} \cdot \sqrt{3} + 6\sqrt{16} \cdot \sqrt{3}$$
$$= 4\sqrt{3} + 24\sqrt{3}$$
$$= 28\sqrt{3} \quad Ans.$$

2. Perform the indicated operation: $(2\sqrt{3} + 7)^2$

Solution:

$$\begin{array}{r} 2\sqrt{3} + \ 7 \\ 2\sqrt{3} + \ 7 \\ \hline 4\sqrt{9} + 14\sqrt{3} \\ + 14\sqrt{3} + 49 \\ \hline 12 + 28\sqrt{3} + 49 \end{array}$$
$$= 61 + 28\sqrt{3} \quad Ans.$$

─────── *KEEP IN MIND* ───────

The product of the square roots of two non-negative numbers is equal to the square root of the products of the numbers.

Exercises

In 1–61: Multiply, or raise to the power, as indicated. Then simplify the result.

1. $\sqrt{5} \cdot \sqrt{5}$ 2. $\sqrt{71} \cdot \sqrt{71}$ 3. $\sqrt{113} \cdot \sqrt{113}$

4. $\sqrt{a} \cdot \sqrt{a}$ 5. $\sqrt{r} \cdot \sqrt{r}$ 6. $\sqrt{2x} \cdot \sqrt{2x}$

7. $\sqrt{12} \cdot \sqrt{3}$ 8. $\sqrt{32} \cdot \sqrt{2}$ 9. $2\sqrt{18} \cdot 3\sqrt{8}$

10. $\sqrt{14} \cdot \sqrt{2}$ 11. $\sqrt{21} \cdot \sqrt{3}$ 12. $\sqrt{60} \cdot \sqrt{5}$

13. $3\sqrt{6} \cdot \sqrt{3}$ 14. $5\sqrt{8} \cdot 7\sqrt{3}$ 15. $3\sqrt{3} \cdot \sqrt{18}$

16. $\frac{2}{3}\sqrt{24} \cdot 9\sqrt{3}$ 17. $5\sqrt{6} \cdot \frac{2}{3}\sqrt{15}$ 18. $\frac{1}{3}\sqrt{18} \cdot 12\sqrt{3}$

19. $6\sqrt{\frac{1}{3}} \cdot 4\sqrt{12}$ 20. $7\sqrt{56} \cdot 3\sqrt{\frac{1}{2}}$ 21. $8\sqrt{225} \cdot 3\sqrt{\frac{1}{3}}$

22. $(5\sqrt{x})(3\sqrt{x})$ 23. $(-4\sqrt{a})(3\sqrt{a})$ 24. $(-\frac{1}{2}\sqrt{y})(-6\sqrt{y})$

25. $(\sqrt{3})^2$ 26. $(\sqrt{5})^2$ 27. $(\sqrt{y})^2$

28. $(\sqrt{t})^2$ 29. $(3\sqrt{6})^2$ 30. $(\frac{1}{3}\sqrt{3})^2$

31. $\sqrt{25x} \cdot \sqrt{4x}$ 32. $\sqrt{27a} \cdot \sqrt{3a}$ 33. $\sqrt{15x} \cdot \sqrt{3x}$

34. $\sqrt{9a} \cdot \sqrt{ab}$ 35. $\sqrt{5x^2y} \cdot \sqrt{10y}$ 36. $\sqrt{3a^2} \cdot \sqrt{18b^2}$

37. $(\sqrt{3a})^2$ 38. $(\sqrt{5x})^2$ 39. $(\sqrt{6z})^2$

40. $(3\sqrt{r})^2$ 41. $(2\sqrt{t})^2$ 42. $(5\sqrt{3m})^2$

43. $(\sqrt{2x+1})^2$ 44. $(\sqrt{3x-2})^2$ 45. $(\sqrt{5x-3})^2$

46. $5(\sqrt{7} + \sqrt{3})$ 47. $6(2\sqrt{5} - 3\sqrt{2} + 6)$

48. $\sqrt{5}(\sqrt{5} + \sqrt{11})$ 49. $\sqrt{2}(\sqrt{8} - 2\sqrt{2} + 5)$

50. $\sqrt{2}(8\sqrt{2} + 2\sqrt{8} - 3\sqrt{32})$ 51. $2\sqrt{3}(3\sqrt{5} - 2\sqrt{20} - \sqrt{45})$

52. $(5 + \sqrt{2})(6 + \sqrt{2})$ 53. $(3 + \sqrt{5})(7 - \sqrt{5})$

54. $(5 + \sqrt{3})(5 - \sqrt{3})$ 55. $(\sqrt{7} - 4)(\sqrt{7} + 4)$

56. $(\sqrt{a} + \sqrt{b})(\sqrt{a} + \sqrt{b})$ 57. $(\sqrt{a} - \sqrt{b})(\sqrt{a} + \sqrt{b})$

58. $(\sqrt{3} - 2)^2$ 59. $(3 + \sqrt{7})^2$ 60. $(3\sqrt{2} + 5)^2$ 61. $(x - \sqrt{y})^2$

In 62–65, find the area of a square whose side is:

62. $\sqrt{2}$ **63.** $2\sqrt{3}$ **64.** $6\sqrt{2}$ **65.** $5\sqrt{3}$

66. Find, in simplest radical form, the value of the expression $x^2 - 3x + 2$ when x is equal to:

  a. $\sqrt{2}$ *b.* $\sqrt{3}$ *c.* $\sqrt{5}$ *d.* $3\sqrt{2}$ *e.* $2\sqrt{3}$ *f.* $3 + \sqrt{2}$ *g.* $5 - \sqrt{3}$

67. Show, by substitution, that if $y = 3\sqrt{2}$, the expression $y^2 - 3y - 6$ has the value $3(4 - 3\sqrt{2})$.

68. Show, by substitution, that if $x = 1 + \sqrt{3}$, the expression $x^2 - 2x - 2$ has the value 0.

15. Dividing Radicals

We have learned that $\dfrac{\sqrt{a}}{\sqrt{b}} = \sqrt{\dfrac{a}{b}}$ (when a is non-negative and b is positive).

For example, $\dfrac{\sqrt{72}}{\sqrt{8}} = \sqrt{\dfrac{72}{8}} = \sqrt{9} = 3$.

To divide $6\sqrt{10}$ by $3\sqrt{2}$, we use the property of fractions, $\dfrac{ac}{bd} = \dfrac{a}{b} \cdot \dfrac{c}{d}$. See how the division is performed:

$$\frac{6\sqrt{10}}{3\sqrt{2}} = \frac{6}{3} \cdot \frac{\sqrt{10}}{\sqrt{2}} = \frac{6}{3} \cdot \sqrt{\frac{10}{2}} = 2\sqrt{5}$$

In general, if a is non-negative, b is positive, and $y \neq 0$:

$$\frac{x\sqrt{a}}{y\sqrt{b}} = \frac{x}{y}\sqrt{\frac{a}{b}}$$

Procedure. To divide two monomial square roots:
1. Divide the coefficients to find the coefficient of the quotient.
2. Divide the radicands to find the radicand of the quotient.
3. If possible, simplify the result.

MODEL PROBLEMS

1. Divide: $8\sqrt{48} \div 4\sqrt{2}$

Solution: $8\sqrt{48} \div 4\sqrt{2} = \frac{8}{4}\sqrt{\frac{48}{2}} = 2\sqrt{24} = 2\sqrt{4 \cdot 6} = 2 \cdot \sqrt{4} \cdot \sqrt{6} =$
$2 \cdot 2 \cdot \sqrt{6} = 4\sqrt{6}$ *Ans.*

2. Divide: $\sqrt{6x^3} \div \sqrt{2x}$

Solution: $\sqrt{6x^3} \div \sqrt{2x} = \sqrt{\dfrac{6x^3}{2x}} = \sqrt{3x^2} = \sqrt{x^2 \cdot 3} =$

$\sqrt{x^2} \cdot \sqrt{3} = x\sqrt{3}$ *Ans.*

3. Divide: $\dfrac{\sqrt{21} + \sqrt{35}}{\sqrt{7}}$

Solution: $\dfrac{\sqrt{21} + \sqrt{35}}{\sqrt{7}} = \dfrac{\sqrt{21}}{\sqrt{7}} + \dfrac{\sqrt{35}}{\sqrt{7}} = \sqrt{\dfrac{21}{7}} + \sqrt{\dfrac{35}{7}} = \sqrt{3} + \sqrt{5}$ *Ans.*

KEEP IN MIND

The quotient of the square roots of two positive numbers is equal to the square root of the quotient of the numbers.

Exercises

In 1–27, divide. Then simplify the quotient.

1. $\sqrt{72} \div \sqrt{2}$ **2.** $\sqrt{75} \div \sqrt{3}$ **3.** $\sqrt{18} \div \sqrt{3}$ **4.** $\sqrt{70} \div \sqrt{10}$

5. $\sqrt{14} \div \sqrt{2}$ **6.** $8\sqrt{48} \div 2\sqrt{3}$ **7.** $\sqrt{24} \div \sqrt{2}$ **8.** $\sqrt{150} \div \sqrt{3}$

9. $21\sqrt{40} \div \sqrt{5}$ **10.** $9\sqrt{6} \div 3\sqrt{6}$ **11.** $7\sqrt{3} \div 3\sqrt{3}$ **12.** $2\sqrt{2} \div 8\sqrt{2}$

13. $\sqrt{9y} \div \sqrt{y}$ **14.** $8\sqrt{3a} \div 2\sqrt{a}$ **15.** $5\sqrt{24x} \div 10\sqrt{6x}$

16. $\dfrac{12\sqrt{20}}{3\sqrt{5}}$ **17.** $\dfrac{20\sqrt{50}}{4\sqrt{2}}$ **18.** $\dfrac{4\sqrt{48}}{8\sqrt{3}}$

19. $\dfrac{25\sqrt{24}}{5\sqrt{2}}$ **20.** $\dfrac{14\sqrt{150}}{7\sqrt{2}}$ **21.** $\dfrac{3\sqrt{54}}{6\sqrt{3}}$

22. $\dfrac{\sqrt{y^3}}{\sqrt{y}}$

23. $\dfrac{6\sqrt{27a^5}}{2\sqrt{3a^3}}$

24. $\dfrac{5\sqrt{48a^3b}}{10\sqrt{3ab}}$

25. $\dfrac{\sqrt{27} + \sqrt{75}}{\sqrt{3}}$

26. $\dfrac{\sqrt{24} - \sqrt{6}}{\sqrt{2}}$

27. $\dfrac{20\sqrt{15} + 15\sqrt{60}}{5\sqrt{3}}$

In 28–33, simplify the expression. Then approximate the result to the *nearest tenth.*

28. $\dfrac{\sqrt{8} + \sqrt{16}}{\sqrt{2}}$

29. $\dfrac{\sqrt{125} - \sqrt{10}}{\sqrt{5}}$

30. $\dfrac{6\sqrt{27} + 12\sqrt{15}}{3\sqrt{3}}$

31. $\dfrac{4 + \sqrt{8}}{2}$

32. $\dfrac{6 - \sqrt{27}}{3}$

33. $\dfrac{-5 - \sqrt{50}}{5}$

16. Rationalizing an Irrational Radical Denominator

To find the approximate value of $\dfrac{1}{\sqrt{3}}$, we can use 1.732 as the approximate value of $\sqrt{3}$, and then divide 1 by 1.732. The result is .577, but the four-digit divisor makes this an inconvenient computation. To simplify the computation, we multiply $\dfrac{1}{\sqrt{3}}$ by 1 in the form of $\dfrac{\sqrt{3}}{\sqrt{3}}$. We obtain:

$$\frac{1}{\sqrt{3}} = \frac{1}{\sqrt{3}} \cdot \frac{\sqrt{3}}{\sqrt{3}} = \frac{\sqrt{3}}{3} \approx \frac{1.732}{3} \approx .577$$

We transformed the fraction $\dfrac{1}{\sqrt{3}}$, which has an irrational denominator, $\sqrt{3}$, to an equivalent fraction, $\dfrac{\sqrt{3}}{3}$, which has a rational denominator, 3. This process is called ***rationalizing the denominator*** of the fraction.

When a fraction has a radical which represents an irrational number in the denominator, it is not in simplest form. To simplify such a fraction, we rationalize the denominator.

Procedure. To rationalize an irrational radical denominator of a fraction, multiply the fraction by 1 represented as a fraction whose numerator and denominator are the least radical that will make the denominator of the resulting fraction a rational number.

~~~~~~~~~~~~~~ **MODEL PROBLEM** ~~~~~~~~~~~~~~

Rationalize the denominator of (a) $\dfrac{12}{\sqrt{2}}$ and (b) $\dfrac{4}{\sqrt{12}}$.

Solution:

a. $\dfrac{12}{\sqrt{2}} = \dfrac{12}{\sqrt{2}} \cdot \dfrac{\sqrt{2}}{\sqrt{2}} = \dfrac{12\sqrt{2}}{\sqrt{4}} = \dfrac{12\sqrt{2}}{2} = 6\sqrt{2}$ *Ans.*

b. $\dfrac{4}{\sqrt{12}} = \dfrac{4}{\sqrt{12}} \cdot \dfrac{\sqrt{3}}{\sqrt{3}} = \dfrac{4\sqrt{3}}{\sqrt{36}} = \dfrac{4\sqrt{3}}{6} = \dfrac{2\sqrt{3}}{3}$ or $\frac{2}{3}\sqrt{3}$ *Ans.*

~~~~~~

Exercises

In 1–25, rationalize the denominator and simplify the resulting fraction.

1. $\dfrac{1}{\sqrt{2}}$ 2. $\dfrac{1}{\sqrt{5}}$ 3. $\dfrac{1}{\sqrt{7}}$ 4. $\dfrac{1}{\sqrt{x}}$ 5. $\dfrac{1}{\sqrt{a}}$

6. $\dfrac{3}{\sqrt{2}}$ 7. $\dfrac{5}{\sqrt{3}}$ 8. $\dfrac{7}{\sqrt{5}}$ 9. $\dfrac{9}{\sqrt{7}}$ 10. $\dfrac{8}{\sqrt{11}}$

11. $\dfrac{8}{\sqrt{2}}$ 12. $\dfrac{9}{\sqrt{3}}$ 13. $\dfrac{25}{\sqrt{5}}$ 14. $\dfrac{6}{\sqrt{6}}$ 15. $\dfrac{7}{\sqrt{7}}$

16. $\dfrac{12}{\sqrt{8}}$ 17. $\dfrac{6}{\sqrt{12}}$ 18. $\dfrac{36}{\sqrt{18}}$ 19. $\dfrac{25}{\sqrt{20}}$ 20. $\dfrac{30}{\sqrt{50}}$

21. $\dfrac{12}{2\sqrt{3}}$ 22. $\dfrac{18}{3\sqrt{2}}$ 23. $\dfrac{60}{3\sqrt{8}}$ 24. $\dfrac{\sqrt{6}}{\sqrt{5}}$ 25. $\dfrac{15\sqrt{3}}{\sqrt{5}}$

In 26–30, transform the fraction into an equal fraction which does not have a radical in the denominator.

26. $\dfrac{1}{\sqrt{y}}$ 27. $\dfrac{\sqrt{r}}{\sqrt{s}}$ 28. $\dfrac{ab}{\sqrt{b}}$ 29. $\dfrac{8}{\sqrt{2a}}$ 30. $\dfrac{\sqrt{2s}}{\sqrt{g}}$

In 31–34, rationalize the denominator and simplify the resulting fraction.

31. $\dfrac{\sqrt{8} + \sqrt{18}}{\sqrt{2}}$ 32. $\dfrac{\sqrt{7} - 1}{\sqrt{7}}$ 33. $\dfrac{4\sqrt{3} + 2}{\sqrt{3}}$ 34. $\dfrac{\sqrt{5} - \sqrt{7}}{\sqrt{5}}$

In 35–39, approximate the value of the fraction to the *nearest tenth.*

35. $\dfrac{12}{\sqrt{3}}$ 36. $\dfrac{4}{\sqrt{2}}$ 37. $\dfrac{8}{\sqrt{8}}$ 38. $\dfrac{5}{\sqrt{2}}$ 39. $\dfrac{\sqrt{2} - 1}{\sqrt{2}}$

17. Solving Radical Equations

A *radical equation* is an equation in which a variable appears under a radical. For example, $\sqrt{x} = 2$ is a radical equation.

The method used to solve a radical equation, in which the radical is by itself in one member, depends on the following principle:

If two numbers are equal, the squares of these numbers are equal.

For example, if $(4 + 3) = (6 + 1)$ because each numeral represents the number 7, then $(4 + 3)^2 = (6 + 1)^2$ because both numerals represent the same number, 7^2, or 49.

In general, if $a = b$, then $a^2 = b^2$.

Let us solve the radical equation $\sqrt{x} = 2$.

Solution	*Check*
$\sqrt{x} = 2$	$\sqrt{x} = 2$
$(\sqrt{x})^2 = (2)^2$	$\sqrt{4} \overset{?}{=} 2$
$x = 4$	$2 = 2$ (true)

Since 4 can replace x in the original equation, 4 is a root of $\sqrt{x} = 2$.

Let us now consider the radical equation $\sqrt{x} = -2$.

Solution	*Check*
$\sqrt{x} = -2$	$\sqrt{x} = -2$
$(\sqrt{x})^2 = (-2)^2$	$\sqrt{4} \overset{?}{=} -2$
$x = 4$	$2 = -2$ (false)

We see that 4 is not a root of $\sqrt{x} = -2$.

Let us see why this happened. If $a^2 = b^2$, it is not necessarily true that $a = b$. For example, $(-7)^2 = (+7)^2$, but $-7 \neq +7$. Therefore, when we square both members of an equation, the solution set of the "squared" equation may not be the same as the solution set of the original equation. That is, the "squared" equation and the original equation may not be equivalent equations.

Whenever we solve an equation by squaring both members, we must be very careful to check the roots of the "squared" equation in the given equation to see that these roots also satisfy the given equation.

Procedure. To solve a radical equation:
1. **Isolate the radical in one member of the equation.**
2. **If the radical is a square root, square both members of the equation.**
3. **Solve the "squared" equation.**
4. **Check the roots of the "squared" equation in the given equation.**

~~~~~~~~~~~~~~~~~ **MODEL PROBLEMS** ~~~~~~~~~~~~~~~~~

1. Solve and check: $\sqrt{3x} = 12$

How To Proceed	*Solution*	*Check*
Write the equation.	$\sqrt{3x} = 12$	$\sqrt{3x} = 12$
Square both members.	$(\sqrt{3x})^2 = (12)^2$	$\sqrt{3 \times 48} \overset{?}{=} 12$
Simplify.	$3x = 144$	$\sqrt{144} \overset{?}{=} 12$
D_3	$x = 48$	$12 = 12$ (true)

Answer: $x = 48$, or solution set is $\{48\}$.

2. Solve and check: $\sqrt{2x - 1} = 3$

How To Proceed	*Solution*	*Check*
Write the equation.	$\sqrt{2x - 1} = 3$	$\sqrt{2x - 1} = 3$
Square both members.	$(\sqrt{2x - 1})^2 = (3)^2$	$\sqrt{(2)(5) - 1} \overset{?}{=} 3$
Simplify.	$2x - 1 = 9$	$\sqrt{10 - 1} \overset{?}{=} 3$
A_1	$2x = 10$	$\sqrt{9} \overset{?}{=} 3$
D_2	$x = 5$	$3 = 3$ (true)

Answer: $x = 5$, or solution set is $\{5\}$.

3. Solve and check: $3\sqrt{x} + 1 = 3$

How To Proceed	*Solution*	*Check*
Write the equation.	$3\sqrt{x} + 1 = 3$	$3\sqrt{x} + 1 = 3$
S_1 to isolate the radical term.	$3\sqrt{x} = 2$	$3\sqrt{\frac{4}{9}} + 1 \overset{?}{=} 3$
Square both members.	$(3\sqrt{x})^2 = (2)^2$	$3(\frac{2}{3}) + 1 \overset{?}{=} 3$
Simplify.	$9x = 4$	$2 + 1 \overset{?}{=} 3$
D_9	$x = \frac{4}{9}$	$3 = 3$ (true)

Answer: $x = \frac{4}{9}$, or solution set is $\{\frac{4}{9}\}$.

4. Solve and check: $\sqrt{3x + 4} - 3 = -7$

How To Proceed	*Solution*	*Check*
Write equation.	$\sqrt{3x + 4} - 3 = -7$	$\sqrt{3x + 4} - 3 = -7$
A_3	$\sqrt{3x + 4} = -4$	$\sqrt{(3)(4) + 4} - 3 \overset{?}{=} -7$
Square.	$(\sqrt{3x + 4})^2 = (-4)^2$	$\sqrt{12 + 4} - 3 \overset{?}{=} -7$
Simplify.	$3x + 4 = 16$	$\sqrt{16} - 3 \overset{?}{=} -7$
S_4	$3x = 12$	$4 - 3 \overset{?}{=} -7$
D_3	$x = 4$	$1 = -7$ (false)

Since 4 does not satisfy the equation $\sqrt{3x + 4} - 3 = -7$, it is not a root of that equation. The given equation has no root.

Answer: No root, or solution set is the empty set, $\varnothing$.

Exercises

In 1–42, solve and check the equation. If there is no root, write "no root."

1. $\sqrt{x} = 5$
2. $\sqrt{y} = 8$
3. $\sqrt{z} = -4$

4. $\sqrt{a} = 1.2$
5. $\sqrt{b} = \frac{1}{4}$
6. $\sqrt{c} = \frac{2}{9}$

7. $\sqrt{5x} = 5$
8. $\sqrt{2x} = 8$
9. $\sqrt{3y} = 4$

10. $2\sqrt{x} = 6$
11. $5\sqrt{y} = 10$
12. $4\sqrt{a} = 36$

13. $2\sqrt{y} = 1$
14. $3\sqrt{m} = 4$
15. $5\sqrt{r} = -2$

16. $\sqrt{\dfrac{x}{4}} = 6$
17. $\sqrt{\dfrac{y}{3}} = 5$
18. $\sqrt{\dfrac{3z}{2}} = 6$

19. $3\sqrt{2x} = 12$
20. $2\sqrt{5x} = 20$
21. $4\sqrt{3x} = -9$

22. $\sqrt{x + 1} = 4$
23. $\sqrt{b - 1} = 8$
24. $\sqrt{r + 3} = 5$

25. $\sqrt{2x - 1} = 7$
26. $\sqrt{3a + 3} = 6$
27. $\sqrt{2b - 4} = 10$

28. $\sqrt{x + 3} = 8$
29. $\sqrt{m - 6} = 2$
30. $\sqrt{2r + 7} = 8$

31. $2\sqrt{x + 1} = 5$
32. $3\sqrt{x - 2} = 10$
33. $4\sqrt{y + 1} = 8$

34. $\sqrt{2x + 1} - 1 = 4$
35. $\sqrt{5y - 1} - 3 = 0$
36. $5 + \sqrt{2x - 4} = 1$

37. $\dfrac{10}{\sqrt{x}} = \sqrt{x}$
38. $\dfrac{3}{\sqrt{y - 5}} = \sqrt{y - 5}$
39. $\sqrt{2x + 1} = \dfrac{7}{\sqrt{2x + 1}}$

40. $\sqrt{3x - 8} = \sqrt{x}$
41. $\sqrt{5y} = \sqrt{2y + 6}$
42. $\sqrt{4z - 3} = \sqrt{3z + 4}$

In 43–45, solve the equation for the indicated variable.

43. $s = \sqrt{A}$ for A
44. $R = \sqrt{\dfrac{A}{\pi}}$ for A
45. $e = \sqrt{\dfrac{s}{6}}$ for s

CHAPTER XIX

QUADRATIC EQUATIONS

1. The Standard Form of a Quadratic Equation

A *polynomial equation* is an equation which involves polynomials. When all terms of a polynomial equation in one variable are collected in one member of the equation and the other member is 0, we say the polynomial equation is in *standard form*. For example, the equation $x^2 - 3x - 10 = 0$ is in standard form.

The *degree of a polynomial equation* in standard form is the degree of the polynomial. For example, $x^2 - 3x - 10 = 0$ is an equation of the second degree. An equation of the second degree, such as $x^2 - 3x - 10 = 0$, is called a *quadratic equation*.

In general, the standard form of a quadratic equation in one variable is:

$$ax^2 + bx + c = 0$$

where a, b, and c are real numbers and $a \neq 0$.

———————— MODEL PROBLEMS ————————

1. In each part, tell whether the equation is a quadratic equation.

   a. $3x^2 - 5x + 2 = 0$ *Ans.* Yes   b. $x^3 + 2x^2 - 9 = 0$ *Ans.* No
   c. $x^2 - 4 = 0$ *Ans.* Yes   d. $2x - 4 = 0$ *Ans.* No

2. Transform the equation $x(x - 4) = 5$ into an equivalent quadratic equation which is in the standard form $ax^2 + bx + c = 0$.

   Solution

   $$x(x - 4) = 5$$
   $$x^2 - 4x = 5$$
   $$x^2 - 4x - 5 = 0 \quad Ans.$$

Exercises

In 1–9, tell whether the equation is a quadratic equation.

1. $x^2 + 2x + 1 = 0$
2. $x^2 + 2x = 0$
3. $2x + 1 = 0$

4. $4 + x^2 = 7x$
5. $4x^3 + 7x^2 = 5$
6. $x^2 + 8 = x + x^2$

7. $\frac{1}{3}x^2 = \frac{1}{2}x$
8. $\frac{8}{x} = 5$
9. $x(x - 4) = 12$

In 10–18, transform the equation into an equivalent equation in the standard form $ax^2 + bx + c = 0$.

10. $x^2 + 9x = 10$
11. $2x^2 + 7x = 3x$
12. $x^2 = 3x - 8$

13. $4x + 3 = x^2$
14. $3x^2 = 27x$
15. $x(x - 3) = 10$

16. $x^2 = 5(x + 4)$
17. $\frac{x^2}{2} + 3 = \frac{x}{4}$
18. $x^2 = 6 - \frac{x}{2}$

2. Using Factoring To Solve a Quadratic Equation

Consider the following products:

$$5 \times 0 = 0 \qquad \tfrac{1}{2} \times 0 = 0 \qquad (-2) \times 0 = 0$$
$$0 \times 7 = 0 \qquad 0 \times \tfrac{1}{3} = 0 \qquad 0 \times (-3) = 0$$

These examples illustrate the following principle:

The product of 0 and any other real number is 0.

Consider the equation $ab = 0$: If $a = 5$, then $b = 0$; if $a = -4$, then $b = 0$; if $b = 3$, then $a = 0$; if $b = -\frac{1}{2}$, then $a = 0$.

These examples illustrate the following principle:

If the product of two real numbers is 0, then at least one of the numbers is 0.

In general, if a and b are real numbers, then:

$$ab = 0 \text{ if, and only if, } a = 0 \text{ or } b = 0$$

This principle will now be applied to solving quadratic equations.

Let us first solve the equation $(x - 2)(x - 1) = 0$. Since $(x - 2)(x - 1) = 0$, then either $x - 2$ must be 0 or $x - 1$ must be 0. If $x - 2 = 0$, then $x = 2$. If $x - 1 = 0$, then $x = 1$.

Check

$$(x - 2)(x - 1) = 0$$

If $x = 2$, $(2 - 2)(2 - 1) \overset{?}{=} 0$

$$(0)(1) \overset{?}{=} 0$$

$$0 = 0 \quad \text{(true)}$$

$$(x - 2)(x - 1) = 0$$

If $x = 1$, $(1 - 2)(1 - 1) \overset{?}{=} 0$

$$(-1)(0) \overset{?}{=} 0$$

$$0 = 0 \quad \text{(true)}$$

Since both 2 and 1 satisfy the equation $(x - 2)(x - 1) = 0$, the solution set of this equation is $\{2, 1\}$. We may also say that the roots of the equation are 2 or 1.

Let us now solve the equation $x^2 - 3x + 2 = 0$. If we factor the left member of the equation, we get an equivalent equation $(x - 2)(x - 1) = 0$. The solution set of this equation, as we just saw, is $\{2, 1\}$. Therefore, the solution set of the given equation $x^2 - 3x + 2 = 0$ is also $\{2, 1\}$. This quadratic equation, like all others, has two roots.

The two roots of a quadratic equation are not always different numbers, as in the preceding case. Sometimes the roots are the same number. Such a root is called a ***double root*** and is written only once in the solution set.

Procedure. To solve a quadratic equation by using factoring:
1. **If necessary, transform the equation into standard form. Do this by removing parentheses, clearing fractions and combining like terms in the left member, and making the right member zero.**
2. **Factor the left member of the equation.**
3. **Set each factor containing the variable equal to zero.**
4. **Solve each of the resulting equations.**
5. **Check by substituting each value of the variable in the original equation.**

～～～～～～～～～ **MODEL PROBLEMS** ～～～～～～～～～

1. Solve and check: $x^2 - 7x = -10$

How To Proceed

Solution

$$x^2 - 7x = -10$$

1. Transform into standard form.

$$x^2 - 7x + 10 = 0$$

2. Factor the left member.

$$(x - 2)(x - 5) = 0$$

3. Let each factor $= 0$.

$$x - 2 = 0 \mid x - 5 = 0$$

4. Solve each equation.

$$x = 2 \mid \quad x = 5$$

Check

$$x^2 - 7x = -10$$

If $x = 2$, $(2)^2 - 7(2) \overset{?}{=} -10$

$$4 - 14 \overset{?}{=} -10$$

$$-10 = -10 \quad \text{(true)}$$

$$x^2 - 7x = -10$$

If $x = 5$, $(5)^2 - 7(5) \overset{?}{=} -10$

$$25 - 35 \overset{?}{=} -10$$

$$-10 = -10 \quad \text{(true)}$$

Answer: $x = 2$ or $x = 5$; solution set is $\{2, 5\}$.

2. Solve and check: $x^2 = 9$

How To Proceed   *Solution*

$$x^2 = 9$$

1. Transform into standard form. $x^2 - 9 = 0$

2. Factor the left member. $(x - 3)(x + 3) = 0$

3. Let each factor $= 0$. $x - 3 = 0 \mid x + 3 = 0$

4. Solve each equation. $x = 3 \quad \mid \quad x = -3$

Check

$$x^2 = 9 \qquad\qquad\qquad x^2 = 9$$

If $x = 3$, $(3)^2 \overset{?}{=} 9$ If $x = -3$, $(-3)^2 \overset{?}{=} 9$

$$9 = 9 \quad \text{(true)} \qquad\qquad 9 = 9 \quad \text{(true)}$$

Answer: $x = 3$ or $x = -3$; solution set is $\{3, -3\}$.

3. Find the solution set of $2x^2 = 3x$.

How To Proceed   *Solution*

$$2x^2 = 3x$$

1. Transform into standard form. $2x^2 - 3x = 0$

2. Factor the left member. $x(2x - 3) = 0$

3. Let each factor $= 0$. $x = 0 \mid 2x - 3 = 0$

4. Solve each equation. $2x = 3$

                                                  $x = \frac{3}{2}$

Check

$$2x^2 = 3x$$

If $x = 0$, $2(0)^2 \stackrel{?}{=} 3(0)$

$$2(0) \stackrel{?}{=} 0$$

$$0 = 0 \quad \text{(true)}$$

$$2x^2 = 3x$$

If $x = \frac{3}{2}$, $2(\frac{3}{2})^2 \stackrel{?}{=} 3(\frac{3}{2})$

$$2(\frac{9}{4}) \stackrel{?}{=} \frac{9}{2}$$

$$\frac{9}{2} = \frac{9}{2} \quad \text{(true)}$$

Answer: Solution set is $\{0, \frac{3}{2}\}$.

4. Solve and check: $x(x - 6) = -9$

How To Proceed

1. Use the distributive property.
2. Transform into standard form.
3. Factor the left member.
4. Let each factor = 0.
5. Solve each equation.

Solution

$$x(x - 6) = -9$$

$$x^2 - 6x = -9$$

$$x^2 - 6x + 9 = 0$$

$$(x - 3)(x - 3) = 0$$

$$x - 3 = 0 \mid x - 3 = 0$$

$$x = 3 \mid \quad x = 3$$

Check

$$x(x - 6) = -9$$

If $x = 3$, $3(3 - 6) \stackrel{?}{=} -9$

$$3(-3) \stackrel{?}{=} -9$$

$$-9 = -9 \quad \text{(true)}$$

Answer: $x = 3$ or $x = 3$; solution set is $\{3\}$.

KEEP IN MIND

To solve a quadratic equation by using factoring, one member of the equation must be zero.

Exercises

In 1–72, solve and check the equation.

1. $x^2 - 3x + 2 = 0$ **2.** $y^2 - 7y + 6 = 0$ **3.** $z^2 - 5z + 4 = 0$

4. $x^2 - 8x + 16 = 0$ **5.** $p^2 - 8p + 12 = 0$ **6.** $r^2 - 12r + 35 = 0$

7. $c^2 + 6c + 5 = 0$ **8.** $m^2 + 8m + 7 = 0$ **9.** $m^2 + 10m + 9 = 0$

10. $x^2 + 2x + 1 = 0$ **11.** $x^2 + 8x + 15 = 0$ **12.** $y^2 + 11y + 24 = 0$

13. $x^2 - 4x - 5 = 0$ **14.** $x^2 - 5x - 6 = 0$ **15.** $x^2 - 2x - 35 = 0$

16. $x^2 + x - 6 = 0$ **17.** $q^2 + q - 72 = 0$ **18.** $x^2 + 2x - 15 = 0$

19. $r^2 - r - 72 = 0$ **20.** $x^2 - x - 12 = 0$ **21.** $y^2 - 3y - 10 = 0$

22. $x^2 - 49 = 0$ **23.** $y^2 - 81 = 0$ **24.** $z^2 - 4 = 0$

25. $m^2 - 64 = 0$ **26.** $2r^2 - 18 = 0$ **27.** $3x^2 - 12 = 0$

28. $d^2 - 2d = 0$ **29.** $m^2 - 5m = 0$ **30.** $s^2 - s = 0$

31. $x^2 + 3x = 0$ **32.** $y^2 + 7y = 0$ **33.** $z^2 + 8z = 0$

34. $2x^2 - 5x + 2 = 0$ **35.** $3x^2 - 10x + 3 = 0$ **36.** $2x^2 + x - 3 = 0$

37. $3x^2 - 8x + 4 = 0$ **38.** $2x^2 + x - 10 = 0$ **39.** $5x^2 + 11x + 2 = 0$

40. $x^2 - x = 6$ **41.** $y^2 - 4y = 12$ **42.** $y^2 - 3y = 28$

43. $c^2 - 8c = -15$ **44.** $d^2 + 5d = 14$ **45.** $2m^2 + 7m = -6$

46. $r^2 = 4$ **47.** $x^2 = 25$ **48.** $3x^2 = 12$

49. $y^2 = 6y$ **50.** $t^2 = 8t$ **51.** $s^2 = -4s$

52. $y^2 = 8y + 20$ **53.** $z^2 = 15 - 2z$ **54.** $2x^2 - x = 15$

55. $x^2 = 9x - 20$ **56.** $30 + x = x^2$ **57.** $2y^2 = 7y - 3$

58. $x^2 + 3x - 4 = 50$ **59.** $x^2 - 8x + 28 = 3x$ **60.** $2x^2 + 7 = 5 - 5x$

61. $\frac{1}{3}x^2 + \frac{4}{3}x + 1 = 0$ **62.** $\frac{1}{2}x^2 + \frac{9}{2}x + 4 = 0$ **63.** $\frac{1}{2}x^2 - \frac{7}{6}x = 1$

64. $x(x - 2) = 35$ **65.** $y(y - 3) = 4$ **66.** $x(x + 3) = 40$

67. $\frac{x}{2} + 1 - \frac{12}{x} = 0$ **68.** $\frac{y}{3} + 1 = \frac{6}{y}$ **69.** $\frac{m}{3} + \frac{9}{m} = 4$

70. $\frac{16}{y} = \frac{y}{4}$ **71.** $x = \frac{40}{x - 3}$ **72.** $\frac{x}{3} = \frac{8}{x + 2}$

In 73–81, solve for x in terms of the other variable(s).

73. $x^2 - b^2 = 0$ **74.** $4x^2 = c^2$ **75.** $x^2 + ax = 0$

76. $x^2 = cx$ **77.** $rx^2 = sx$ **78.** $x^2 - 5bx + 6b^2 = 0$

79. $x^2 + 4ax = 21a^2$ **80.** $\frac{a}{x} = \frac{x}{a}$ **81.** $x = \frac{bx}{x + 3b}$

3. Solving Incomplete Quadratic Equations

A quadratic equation in which the first-degree term is missing is called an *incomplete quadratic equation,* or a *pure quadratic equation.* For example, $x^2 - 36 = 0$ (in general, $ax^2 + c = 0$ when $a \neq 0$) is an incomplete quadratic equation.

One method of solving $x^2 - 36 = 0$ is to factor the left member. We obtain $(x + 6)(x - 6) = 0$, from which we find that the solution set is $\{-6, 6\}$.

Another method which we may use to solve $x^2 - 36 = 0$ makes use of the following principle:

Every positive real number has two real square roots, one of which is the opposite of the other.

Solution

$$x^2 - 36 = 0$$
$$x^2 = 36$$
$$x = \sqrt{36} \text{ or } x = -\sqrt{36}$$
$$x = 6 \text{ or } x = -6$$

Check

$x^2 - 36 = 0$	$x^2 - 36 = 0$
If $x = 6$, $(6)^2 - 36 \overset{?}{=} 0$	If $x = -6$, $(-6)^2 - 36 \overset{?}{=} 0$
$36 - 36 \overset{?}{=} 0$	$36 - 36 \overset{?}{=} 0$
$0 = 0$ (true)	$0 = 0$ (true)

Answer: $x = 6$ or $x = -6$, which may be written $x = \pm 6$; solution set is $\{6, -6\}$.

Procedure. To solve an incomplete quadratic equation:
1. **Transform the equation into the form $x^2 = n$, where n is a non-negative real number.**
2. **Let $x = \sqrt{n}$ and let $x = -\sqrt{n}$.**
3. **Check the resulting values for x in the original equation.**

~~~~~~~~~~~~~~ **MODEL PROBLEMS** ~~~~~~~~~~~~~~

1. Find the solution set of $7y^2 = 3y^2 + 36$.

Solution

$$7y^2 = 3y^2 + 36$$
$$7y^2 - 3y^2 = 36$$
$$4y^2 = 36$$
$$y^2 = 9$$
$$y = \sqrt{9} = 3 \text{ or}$$
$$y = -\sqrt{9} = -3$$

Answer: Solution set is $\{3, -3\}$.

Check

$$7y^2 = 3y^2 + 36$$
If $y = -3$, $7(-3)^2 \overset{?}{=} 3(-3)^2 + 36$
$$7(9) \overset{?}{=} 3(9) + 36$$
$$63 \overset{?}{=} 27 + 36$$
$$63 = 63 \quad \text{(true)}$$
Similarly, check $y = +3$.

2. Solve and check: $4x^2 - 14 = 2x^2$

<table>
<tr><td colspan="2" align="center">*Solution*</td><td align="center">*Check*</td></tr>
</table>

$$4x^2 - 14 = 2x^2$$
$$4x^2 - 2x^2 - 14 = 0$$
$$2x^2 - 14 = 0$$
$$2x^2 = 14$$
$$x^2 = 7$$
$$x = \sqrt{7} \text{ or}$$
$$x = -\sqrt{7}$$

$4x^2 - 14 = 2x^2$

If $x = -\sqrt{7}$, $4(-\sqrt{7})^2 - 14 \overset{?}{=} 2(-\sqrt{7})^2$
$$4(7) - 14 \overset{?}{=} 2(7)$$
$$28 - 14 \overset{?}{=} 14$$
$$14 = 14 \quad \text{(true)}$$

Similarly, check $x = \sqrt{7}$.

Answer: $x = \pm\sqrt{7}$, or solution set is $\{\sqrt{7}, -\sqrt{7}\}$.

Exercises

In 1–33, solve and check the equation.

1. $x^2 = 4$
2. $y^2 = 64$
3. $\frac{1}{2}z^2 = 8$
4. $a^2 - 1 = 0$
5. $a^2 - 25 = 0$
6. $b^2 - .49 = 0$
7. $\frac{1}{2}x^2 = 50$
8. $5y^2 = 45$
9. $3m^2 = 75$
10. $3k^2 = 147$
11. $5x^2 = 405$
12. $27r^2 = 243$
13. $2x^2 - 8 = 0$
14. $5y^2 - 5 = 0$
15. $3y^2 - 300 = 0$
16. $x^2 + 9 = 25$
17. $y^2 + 25 = 169$
18. $z^2 + .01 = .37$
19. $y^2 - 6 = 58$
20. $r^2 - 11 = 70$
21. $y^2 - 100 = 44$
22. $4x^2 + 5 = 21$
23. $2x^2 - 11 = 39$
24. $.05x^2 - 3 = 2$
25. $2x^2 + 3x^2 = 45$
26. $6x^2 - 4x^2 = 98$
27. $7x^2 = 4x^2 + .75$
28. $4y^2 - 13 = y^2 + 14$
29. $2y^2 - 5 = 15 - 3y^2$
30. $2z^2 + 7 = 10 - z^2$
31. $\dfrac{y^2}{3} = 12$
32. $\dfrac{x}{9} = \dfrac{4}{x}$
33. $\dfrac{4x}{25} = \dfrac{4}{x}$

In 34–63, solve for x in simplest radical form.

34. $x^2 = 3$
35. $x^2 = 10$
36. $x^2 = 35$
37. $x^2 = 12$
38. $x^2 = 20$
39. $x^2 = 27$

40. $3x^2 = 6$

41. $2x^2 = 100$

42. $\frac{1}{2}x^2 = 6$

43. $2x^2 - 16 = 0$

44. $3x^2 - 60 = 0$

45. $4x^2 - 48 = 0$

46. $x^2 + 4 = 16$

47. $x^2 + 25 = 100$

48. $x^2 + 49 = 196$

49. $x^2 - 4 = 4$

50. $x^2 - 25 = 25$

51. $\frac{1}{3}x^2 - 3 = 3$

52. $3x^2 + 5 = 29$

53. $2x^2 - 30 = 70$

54. $5x^2 - 40 = 100$

55. $3x^2 + 4x^2 = 35$

56. $8x^2 - 6x^2 = 54$

57. $9x^2 = 4x^2 + 100$

58. $3x^2 - 28 = 2x^2 + 33$

59. $3x^2 - 6 = 34 - 2x^2$

60. $x^2 - 4 = 80 - 2x^2$

61. $\dfrac{x}{3} = \dfrac{5}{x}$

62. $\dfrac{x}{8} = \dfrac{4}{x}$

63. $\dfrac{2x}{9} = \dfrac{6}{x}$

In 64–81, find the positive value of x correct to the *nearest tenth*.

64. $x^2 = 7$

65. $x^2 = 24$

66. $\frac{1}{3}x^2 = 31$

67. $3x^2 = 45$

68. $10x^2 = 264$

69. $4x^2 - 160 = 0$

70. $x^2 + 9 = 36$

71. $x^2 + 16 = 64$

72. $x^2 - 16 = 16$

73. $2x^2 + 7 = 67$

74. $3x^2 - 9 = 87$

75. $5x^2 + 3x^2 = 320$

76. $7x^2 = x^2 + 198$

77. $5x^2 - 29 = x^2 + 11$

78. $x^2 - 42 = 82 - 3x^2$

79. $\dfrac{x}{5} = \dfrac{11}{x}$

80. $\dfrac{x}{9} = \dfrac{6}{x}$

81. $\dfrac{2x}{43} = \dfrac{8}{x}$

In 82–90, solve for x, expressing irrational answers in radical form.

82. $(x - 1)^2 = 4$

83. $(x - 3)^2 = 49$

84. $(x + 2)^2 = 16$

85. $(x - 2)^2 = 3$

86. $(x - 4)^2 = 11$

87. $(x + 5)^2 = 23$

88. $\dfrac{4}{x - 1} = \dfrac{x - 1}{9}$

89. $\dfrac{x + 3}{2} = \dfrac{8}{x + 3}$

90. $\dfrac{x - 2}{3} = \dfrac{5}{x - 2}$

In 91–96, solve for x in terms of the other variable(s).

91. $x^2 = b^2$

92. $x^2 = 25a^2$

93. $9x^2 = r^2$

94. $4x^2 - a^2 = 0$

95. $x^2 + a^2 = c^2$

96. $x^2 + b^2 = c^2$

In 97–104, solve for the indicated variable in terms of the other variable(s).

97. Solve for S: $S^2 = A$

98. Solve for e: $S = 6e^2$

99. Solve for r: $A = \pi r^2$

100. Solve for r: $S = 4\pi r^2$

101. Solve for I: $W = I^2 R$

102. Solve for r: $V = \pi r^2 h$

103. Solve for t: $s = \frac{1}{2}gt^2$

104. Solve for v: $F = \dfrac{mv^2}{gr}$

4. Completing a Trinomial Square

At the right, we see that $(x + 3)^2 = x^2 + 6x + 9$. Since the expression $x^2 + 6x + 9$ represents $(x + 3)^2$, it is called a **trinomial square.**

$$
\begin{array}{r}
x + 3 \\
x + 3 \\
\hline
x^2 + 3x \\
+ 3x + 9 \\
\hline
x^2 + 6x + 9
\end{array}
$$

Study the trinomial $x^2 + 6x + 9$ and the binomial $x + 3$. Notice that the constant 9 in the trinomial is equal to the square of the 3 in the binomial. Also, notice that the coefficient of x, which is 6 in the trinomial, is twice the 3 in the binomial. We will now use these facts to solve a problem.

Find the number that must be added to $x^2 - 8x$ to make the resulting trinomial a perfect square. First we square $\frac{1}{2}$ of (-8), the coefficient of x. We see that $[\frac{1}{2}(-8)]^2 = (-4)^2 = 16$. Therefore, we must add 16 to $x^2 - 8x$ to obtain the trinomial square $x^2 - 8x + 16$, which represents $(x - 4)^2$. This process is called **completing a trinomial square.**

Procedure. To form a trinomial square starting with a binomial of the form $x^2 + px$: Add to the binomial the square of one-half of p, the coefficient of x.

~~~~~~~~~~~ **MODEL PROBLEMS** ~~~~~~~~~~~

1. Find the value of k which will make the trinomial $x^2 + 6x + k$ a perfect square.

   Solution: $k = [\frac{1}{2}(6)]^2 = (3)^2 = 9$

   Answer: $k = 9$

2. Add a number to $x^2 + 10x$ which will complete the square. Also, express the resulting trinomial as the square of a binomial.

   Solution: $[\frac{1}{2}(10)]^2 = (5)^2 = 25$. Add 25 to $x^2 + 10x$.

   Answer: $x^2 + 10x + 25 = (x + 5)^2$

3. Add a number to $x^2 - 3x$ which will complete the square. Also, express the resulting trinomial as the square of a binomial.

   Solution: $[\frac{1}{2}(-3)]^2 = (-\frac{3}{2})^2 = \frac{9}{4}$. Add $\frac{9}{4}$ to $x^2 - 3x$.

   Answer: $x^2 - 3x + \frac{9}{4} = (x - \frac{3}{2})^2$

Exercises

In 1–3, find the value of k which will make the trinomial a perfect square.

1. $x^2 + 4x + k$ **2.** $x^2 - 12x + k$ **3.** $x^2 + 3x + k$

In 4–15, replace the question mark with a number which will complete the square. Also, express the resulting trinomial as the square of a binomial.

4. $x^2 - 4x + ?$ **5.** $c^2 + 14c + ?$ **6.** $x^2 - 18x + ?$
7. $r^2 + 5r + ?$ **8.** $x^2 - 9x + ?$ **9.** $x^2 - x + ?$
10. $x^2 + \frac{1}{2}x + ?$ **11.** $y^2 - \frac{1}{3}y + ?$ **12.** $x^2 - \frac{4}{5}x + ?$
13. $x^2 + (?)x + 9$ **14.** $x^2 + (?)x + 25$ **15.** $x^2 - (?)x + 64$

In 16–21, determine whether the trinomial is a perfect square.

16. $x^2 + 4x + 4$ **17.** $x^2 - 14x + 49$ **18.** $x^2 - 6x + 6$
19. $x^2 - 10x - 25$ **20.** $x^2 - 3x + 2.25$ **21.** $x^2 - x + 1$

In 22–27, factor the trinomial and determine whether it is a perfect square.

22. $x^2 - 2x + 1$ **23.** $x^2 + 4x + 4$ **24.** $x^2 + 6x - 16$
25. $x^2 + 12x + 36$ **26.** $x^2 - 8x - 9$ **27.** $x^2 - 16x + 64$

5. Solving Quadratic Equations by Completing the Square

We have learned that to solve the equation $x^2 = 16$, we use the property of square roots: $x = \sqrt{16} = 4$, or $x = -\sqrt{16} = -4$.

Similarly, to solve $(x - 1)^2 = 16$, we also use the property of square roots:

$$x - 1 = \sqrt{16} \text{ OR } x - 1 = -\sqrt{16}$$
$$x - 1 = 4 \qquad\qquad x - 1 = -4$$
$$x = 5 \qquad\qquad x = -3$$

Since both $x = 5$ and $x = -3$ satisfy the equation $(x - 1)^2 = 16$, the solution set of this equation is $\{5, -3\}$.

To solve $x^2 - 2x + 1 = 16$, we first represent $x^2 - 2x + 1$ as $(x - 1)^2$. Then we solve the equivalent equation $(x - 1)^2 = 16$ as before.

To solve $x^2 - 2x = 15$, we add a number to both members of the equation so that the left member, $x^2 - 2x$, becomes a trinomial square. The number we add is the square of one-half of the coefficient of x: $[\frac{1}{2}(-2)]^2 = (-1)^2 = 1$

Thus, we have $x^2 - 2x + 1 = 15 + 1$, or $(x - 1)^2 = 16$. This equivalent equation is solved as before.

When we solve a quadratic equation by expressing its left members as a trinomial square, we are solving it by the method of **completing the square**.

Procedure. To solve a quadratic equation by completing the square:

1. Transform the equation to the form $x^2 + px = q$. Do this by collecting all terms containing the variable in the left member of the equation, the constant being in the right member. When the coefficient of x^2 is not 1, divide both members of the equation by that coefficient.

2. Complete the trinomial square by adding the square of one-half the coefficient of x to both members of the equation.

3. Express the resulting equation in the form $(x + d)^2 = n$. That is, write the square of a binomial equal to a positive number n.

4. Use the property of square roots to write the equations $x + d = \sqrt{n}$ and $x + d = -\sqrt{n}$. Solve these equations.

5. Check the resulting values for x in the given equation.

--------------- **MODEL PROBLEMS** ---------------

In 1–4, solve by completing the square. Give irrational answers in radical form.

1. $x^2 - 6x + 8 = 0$

  Solution:

$$x^2 - 6x + 8 = 0$$
$$x^2 - 6x = -8$$
$$[\tfrac{1}{2}(-6)]^2 = (-3)^2 = 9$$
$$x^2 - 6x + 9 = -8 + 9$$
$$(x - 3)^2 = 1$$

$$x - 3 = \sqrt{1} \mid x - 3 = -\sqrt{1}$$
$$x - 3 = 1 \quad \mid \quad x - 3 = -1$$
$$x = 4 \quad \mid \quad x = 2$$

The check is left to the student.

Answer: Solution set is $\{4, 2\}$.

2. $2x^2 + 3x - 2 = 0$

  Solution:

$$2x^2 + 3x - 2 = 0$$
$$2x^2 + 3x = 2$$
$$x^2 + \tfrac{3}{2}x = 1 \quad D_2$$
$$[\tfrac{1}{2}(\tfrac{3}{2})]^2 = (\tfrac{3}{4})^2 = \tfrac{9}{16}$$
$$x^2 + \tfrac{3}{2}x + \tfrac{9}{16} = 1 + \tfrac{9}{16}$$
$$(x + \tfrac{3}{4})^2 = \tfrac{25}{16}$$

$$x + \tfrac{3}{4} = \sqrt{\tfrac{25}{16}} \mid x + \tfrac{3}{4} = -\sqrt{\tfrac{25}{16}}$$
$$x + \tfrac{3}{4} = \tfrac{5}{4} \quad \mid \quad x + \tfrac{3}{4} = -\tfrac{5}{4}$$
$$x = \tfrac{5}{4} - \tfrac{3}{4} \quad \mid \quad x = -\tfrac{5}{4} - \tfrac{3}{4}$$
$$x = \tfrac{2}{4} = \tfrac{1}{2} \quad \mid \quad x = -\tfrac{8}{4} = -2$$

The check is left to the student.

Answer: Solution set is $\{\tfrac{1}{2}, -2\}$.

3. $x^2 + 4 = 6x$

Solution:

$$x^2 + 4 = 6x$$
$$x^2 - 6x + 4 = 0$$
$$x^2 - 6x = -4$$
$$[\tfrac{1}{2}(-6)]^2 = (-3)^2 = 9$$
$$x^2 - 6x + 9 = -4 + 9$$
$$(x - 3)^2 = 5$$

$$x - 3 = \sqrt{5} \qquad x - 3 = -\sqrt{5}$$
$$x = 3 + \sqrt{5} \qquad x = 3 - \sqrt{5}$$

The check is left to the student.

Answer: Solution set is
$$\{3 + \sqrt{5}, 3 - \sqrt{5}\}.$$

We may also say that the roots are
$x = 3 \pm \sqrt{5}.$

Note: If we wish to approximate the roots of this equation to the nearest tenth, we approximate $\sqrt{5}$ to two decimal places,
$$\sqrt{5} \approx 2.23.$$
Then:

$$3 + \sqrt{5} \approx 3 + 2.23 \approx 5.23 \approx 5.2$$
$$3 - \sqrt{5} \approx 3 - 2.23 \approx .77 \approx .8$$

4. $3x^2 - 2x - 2 = 0$

Solution:

$$3x^2 - 2x - 2 = 0$$
$$3x^2 - 2x = 2$$
$$x^2 - \tfrac{2}{3}x = \tfrac{2}{3} \quad D_3$$
$$[\tfrac{1}{2}(-\tfrac{2}{3})]^2 = (-\tfrac{1}{3})^2 = \tfrac{1}{9}$$
$$x^2 - \tfrac{2}{3}x + \tfrac{1}{9} = \tfrac{2}{3} + \tfrac{1}{9}$$
$$(x - \tfrac{1}{3})^2 = \tfrac{7}{9}$$

$$x - \frac{1}{3} = \sqrt{\frac{7}{9}} \qquad x - \frac{1}{3} = -\sqrt{\frac{7}{9}}$$

$$x = \frac{1}{3} + \frac{\sqrt{7}}{3} \qquad x = \frac{1}{3} - \frac{\sqrt{7}}{3}$$

$$x = \frac{1 + \sqrt{7}}{3} \qquad x = \frac{1 - \sqrt{7}}{3}$$

The check is left to the student.

Answer: Solution set is

$$\left\{ \frac{1 + \sqrt{7}}{3}, \frac{1 - \sqrt{7}}{3} \right\}.$$

We may also say that the roots are

$$x = \frac{1}{3} \pm \frac{\sqrt{7}}{3}, \text{ or } x = \frac{1 \pm \sqrt{7}}{3}.$$

Exercises

In 1–6, solve the equation by using the square root property.

1. $(x - 5)^2 = 7^2$ 2. $(z + 3)^2 = 25$ 3. $(b - 4)^2 = 100$
4. $(x - 2)^2 = (\frac{1}{2})^2$ 5. $(y + 1)^2 = \frac{4}{9}$ 6. $(x - 3)^2 = 6$

In 7–12, solve the equation by expressing the left member as the square of a binomial and then by using the square root property.

7. $x^2 - 2x + 1 = 4$ 8. $z^2 + 4z + 4 = 49$ 9. $y^2 - 10y + 25 = 50$
10. $x^2 - x + \frac{1}{4} = \frac{9}{4}$ 11. $x^2 + 3x + \frac{9}{4} = \frac{49}{4}$ 12. $x^2 + 5x + \frac{25}{4} = \frac{3}{4}$

In 13–33, solve the equation by completing the square. [Express irrational answers in simplest radical form.]

13. $x^2 + 2x = 8$ 14. $z^2 - 4z = 21$ 15. $x^2 - 4x + 3 = 0$
16. $x^2 = 6x + 40$ 17. $y^2 - 5y - 14 = 0$ 18. $z^2 = 6 - z$
19. $x^2 - 4x = -4$ 20. $y^2 - 9 = 6y$ 21. $2c^2 - 3c - 2 = 0$
22. $2x^2 + 7x + 3 = 0$ 23. $3r^2 = 5r + 2$ 24. $5y^2 + 9y - 2 = 0$
25. $x^2 + 2x = 1$ 26. $x^2 - 4x + 2 = 0$ 27. $x^2 + 3x - 5 = 0$
28. $m^2 - 1 = 4m$ 29. $a^2 = 6a + 19$ 30. $2x^2 - 4x = 1$
31. $3x^2 - 12x + 5 = 0$ 32. $3x^2 - 2 = 6x$ 33. $5x^2 = 3x + 1$

In 34–39, solve the equation by completing the square. [Approximate the answers correct to the *nearest tenth.*]

34. $x^2 - 6x + 9 = 7$ 35. $x^2 + 4x + 4 = 3$ 36. $x^2 - 2x = 4$
37. $x^2 = 8x + 2$ 38. $2x^2 - 20x = 5$ 39. $3x^2 - 4x - 2 = 0$

6. Solving Quadratic Equations by Formula

Since any quadratic equation can be solved by the method of completing the square, we can solve the general quadratic equation $ax^2 + bx + c = 0$ ($a \neq 0$) for x in terms of a, b, and c. Then the general roots may be used as formulas for finding the roots of any quadratic equation. Examine carefully the parallel solutions on the next page to see how the same method is used in solving a particular quadratic equation and the general quadratic equation.

$$3x^2 + 5x + 1 = 0$$
$$3x^2 + 5x = -1$$

$$x^2 + \frac{5}{3}x = -\frac{1}{3}$$

$$\left[\frac{1}{2}\left(\frac{5}{3}\right)\right]^2 = \left(\frac{5}{6}\right)^2 = \frac{25}{36}$$

$$x^2 + \frac{5}{3}x + \frac{25}{36} = \frac{25}{36} - \frac{1}{3}$$

$$\left(x + \frac{5}{6}\right)^2 = \frac{25}{36} - \frac{1}{3}$$

$$\left(x + \frac{5}{6}\right)^2 = \frac{13}{36}$$

$$x + \frac{5}{6} = \pm\sqrt{\frac{13}{36}}$$

$$x = -\frac{5}{6} \pm \frac{\sqrt{13}}{6}$$

$$x = \frac{-5 \pm \sqrt{13}}{6}$$

$$ax^2 + bx + c = 0 \quad (a \neq 0)$$
$$ax^2 + bx = -c$$

$$x^2 + \frac{b}{a}x = \frac{-c}{a}$$

$$\left[\frac{1}{2}\left(\frac{b}{a}\right)\right]^2 = \left(\frac{b}{2a}\right)^2 = \frac{b^2}{4a^2}$$

$$x^2 + \frac{b}{a}x + \frac{b^2}{4a^2} = \frac{b^2}{4a^2} - \frac{c}{a}$$

$$\left(x + \frac{b}{2a}\right)^2 = \frac{b^2}{4a^2} - \frac{c}{a}$$

$$\left(x + \frac{b}{2a}\right)^2 = \frac{b^2 - 4ac}{4a^2}$$

$$x + \frac{b}{2a} = \pm\sqrt{\frac{b^2 - 4ac}{4a^2}}$$

$$x = -\frac{b}{2a} \pm \frac{\sqrt{b^2 - 4ac}}{2a}$$

$$x = \frac{-b \pm \sqrt{b^2 - 4ac}}{2a}$$

The last step, $x = \dfrac{-b \pm \sqrt{b^2 - 4ac}}{2a}$, which is an abbreviated way of

writing $x = \dfrac{-b + \sqrt{b^2 - 4ac}}{2a}$ and $x = \dfrac{-b - \sqrt{b^2 - 4ac}}{2a}$, is called the

quadratic formula. This formula may be used in solving any quadratic equation.

Procedure. To solve a quadratic equation by the quadratic formula:

1. **Transform the given equation into an equivalent equation in the standard form $ax^2 + bx + c = 0$. Do this by collecting all terms in the left member; the right member is zero.**
2. **Compare the resulting equation with the standard equation $ax^2 + bx + c = 0$ to determine the values of a, b, and c.**
3. **Substitute the values of a, b, and c in the quadratic formula:**

$$x = \frac{-b \pm \sqrt{b^2 - 4ac}}{2a}$$

4. **Perform the necessary arithmetic to find the values of x.**

MODEL PROBLEMS

1. Solve by using the quadratic formula: $2x^2 = 5 - 9x$

   Solution:

   $$2x^2 = 5 - 9x$$

   Transform the equation to standard form: $2x^2 + 9x - 5 = 0$

   Compare with $ax^2 + bx + c = 0$: $a = 2$, $b = 9$, $c = -5$

   The quadratic formula is $x = \dfrac{-b \pm \sqrt{b^2 - 4ac}}{2a}$.

   Substituting: $x = \dfrac{-9 \pm \sqrt{(9)^2 - 4(2)(-5)}}{2(2)}$

   $$x = \frac{-9 \pm \sqrt{81 + 40}}{4}$$

   $$x = \frac{-9 \pm \sqrt{121}}{4}$$

   $$x = \frac{-9 \pm 11}{4}$$

$x = \dfrac{-9 + 11}{4}$	$x = \dfrac{-9 - 11}{4}$
$x = \dfrac{2}{4}$	$x = \dfrac{-20}{4}$
$x = \dfrac{1}{2}$	$x = -5$

   Check

   $$2x^2 = 5 - 9x \qquad\qquad 2x^2 = 5 - 9x$$

   If $x = \frac{1}{2}$, $2(\frac{1}{2})^2 \overset{?}{=} 5 - 9(\frac{1}{2})$ ⎪ If $x = -5$, $2(-5)^2 \overset{?}{=} 5 - 9(-5)$

   $$\tfrac{2}{4} \overset{?}{=} 5 - 4\tfrac{1}{2} \qquad\qquad 2(25) \overset{?}{=} 5 + 45$$

   $$\tfrac{1}{2} = \tfrac{1}{2} \quad \text{(true)} \qquad\qquad 50 = 50 \quad \text{(true)}$$

   Answer: $x = \frac{1}{2}$ or $x = -5$; solution set is $\{\frac{1}{2}, -5\}$.

2. Use the quadratic formula to approximate the roots of the equation $2x^2 - 3x = 4$ correct to the *nearest tenth.*

Solution:

$$2x^2 - 3x = 4$$

Transform the equation to standard form: $2x^2 - 3x - 4 = 0$

Compare with $ax^2 + bx + c = 0$: $a = 2, b = -3, c = -4$

The quadratic formula is

$$x = \frac{-b \pm \sqrt{b^2 - 4ac}}{2a}.$$

Substituting:

$$x = \frac{-(-3) \pm \sqrt{(-3)^2 - 4(2)(-4)}}{2(2)}$$

$$x = \frac{3 \pm \sqrt{9 + 32}}{4}$$

$$x = \frac{3 \pm \sqrt{41}}{4}$$

$$x \approx \frac{3 \pm 6.40}{4}$$

```
          6. 4  0
     √41.00 00
          36
 124 │ 5 00
     │ 4 96
1280 │    4 00
     └       0
            4 00
```

$$x \approx \frac{3 + 6.40}{4} \qquad x \approx \frac{3 - 6.40}{4}$$

$$x \approx \frac{9.40}{4} \approx 2.35 \qquad x \approx \frac{-3.40}{4} \approx -.85$$

$$x \approx 2.4 \qquad\qquad x \approx -.9$$

Answer: $x \approx 2.4$ or $x \approx -.9$

Exercises

In 1–27, solve the equation by using the quadratic formula. [Express irrational roots in simplest radical form.]

1. $x^2 + 2x - 24 = 0$ **2.** $x^2 - 9x + 20 = 0$ **3.** $x^2 - 6x + 9 = 0$

4. $x^2 + 12 = 7x$ **5.** $x^2 - 30 = x$ **6.** $x^2 = 5x + 14$

7. $2x^2 - 5x + 2 = 0$ **8.** $3x^2 - 10x + 3 = 0$ **9.** $5x^2 = 3x + 2$

10. $x^2 - 8x = 0$ **11.** $x^2 - 9 = 0$ **12.** $4x^2 = 25$

13. $x^2 + 2x - 1 = 0$ **14.** $y^2 - 2y - 2 = 0$ **15.** $z^2 + 3z = 5$

16. $x^2 - 4x + 1 = 0$ **17.** $x^2 + 5x = 2$ **18.** $y^2 = 5y + 2$

19. $2x^2 - 3x - 1 = 0$ **20.** $2x^2 + x - 4 = 0$ **21.** $3x^2 - 2y - 3 = 0$

22. $2y^2 + y = 5$ **23.** $5y^2 - 1 = 2y$ **24.** $2x^2 = 6x - 1$

25. $\frac{1}{4}x^2 - \frac{3}{2}x - 1 = 0$ **26.** $1 + \dfrac{7}{x} + \dfrac{2}{x^2} = 0$ **27.** $2x = 5 + \dfrac{4}{x}$

In 28–42, solve the equation by using the quadratic formula. [Approximate irrational roots correct to the *nearest tenth.*]

28. $x^2 + 3x - 3 = 0$ **29.** $y^2 - 4y + 2 = 0$ **30.** $2c^2 - 7c + 1 = 0$

31. $x^2 + 2x - 4 = 0$ **32.** $3x^2 - 2x - 6 = 0$ **33.** $2x^2 - 8x + 1 = 0$

34. $3x^2 + 5x - 1 = 0$ **35.** $2x^2 + 4x = 3$ **36.** $2x^2 - 10x = 9$

37. $2x^2 - 2x = 3$ **38.** $x^2 = 20x + 10$ **39.** $x^2 = 12 - 9x$

40. $x(x - 3) = -2$ **41.** $x(2x + 9) = 3$ **42.** $x = 4 + \dfrac{2}{x}$

7. Using the Theorem of Pythagoras

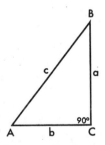

The figure represents a **right triangle.** Such a triangle contains one and only one right angle, an angle whose measure is 90°. In right triangle ABC, side AB, which is opposite the right angle, is called the **hypotenuse.** The hypotenuse is the longest side of the triangle. The other two sides of the triangle, AC and BC, form the right angle; they are called the **legs,** or **arms,** of the right triangle.

The following relation, known as the **theorem of Pythagoras,** is true for all right triangles:

In a right triangle, the square of the length of the hypotenuse is equal to the sum of the squares of the lengths of the other two sides.

In preceding right triangle ABC, if the length of the hypotenuse is represented by c and the lengths of the other two sides by a and b, then the theorem of Pythagoras can be represented by the following formula:

$$c^2 = a^2 + b^2$$

When the lengths of two sides of a right triangle are known, the theorem of Pythagoras can be used to find the length of the third side.

It is also true that:

If the square of the length of the largest side of a triangle is equal to the sum of the squares of the lengths of the other two sides, then the triangle is a right triangle.

When the lengths of the three sides of a triangle are known, this relation can be used to discover whether the triangle is a right triangle.

～～～～～～ MODEL PROBLEMS ～～～～～～

1. Find the hypotenuse of a right triangle in which the lengths of the other two sides are 5 inches and 12 inches.

   Solution: Let hypotenuse $= c$, side $a = 5$,
   side $b = 12$.

   $c^2 = a^2 + b^2$ [theorem of Pythagoras]

   $c^2 = 5^2 + 12^2$

   $c^2 = 25 + 144$

   $c^2 = 169$

   $c = \sqrt{169} = 13$ or

   $c = -\sqrt{169} = -13$ [Reject the negative value because the length of the hypotenuse cannot be a negative number.]

   Answer: 13 inches

2. The hypotenuse of a right triangle is 20 inches long and one leg is 16 inches long. Find the length of the other leg.

   Solution: Let the unknown leg $= a$, hypotenuse $c = 20$, side $b = 16$.

   $c^2 = a^2 + b^2$ [theorem of Pythagoras]

   $20^2 = a^2 + 16^2$

   $400 = a^2 + 256$

   $144 = a^2$

   $12 = a$ or

   $-12 = a$ [Reject.]

   Answer: 12 inches

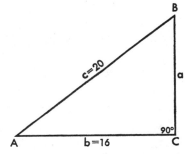

3. Approximate, correct to the *nearest inch*, the base of a rectangle whose altitude is 4 inches and whose diagonal is 10 inches.

Solution: Since *PQRS* is a rectangle, angle *PQR* is a right angle. Therefore, triangle *PQR* is a right triangle. Let $x =$ the length of base *PQ*.

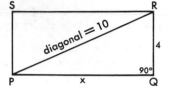

$$a^2 + b^2 = c^2 \qquad [a = 4,\ b = x,\ c = 10]$$
$$4^2 + x^2 = 10^2$$
$$16 + x^2 = 100$$
$$x^2 = 84$$
$$x = \pm\sqrt{84} \approx \pm 9.1 \quad \text{[Use the table on page 581 or compute. Re-}$$
$$x \approx 9 \qquad\qquad\qquad \text{ject the negative value.]}$$

Answer: The base is 9 inches.

4. Approximate, correct to the *nearest tenth of an inch*, the side of a square whose diagonal is 10 inches.

Solution: In square *QRST*, angle *QRS* is a right angle. Therefore, triangle *QRS* is a right triangle. Let $x =$ the length of each side of the square.

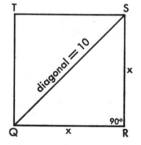

$$a^2 + b^2 = c^2 \qquad [a = x,\ b = x,\ c = 10]$$
$$x^2 + x^2 = 10^2$$
$$2x^2 = 100$$
$$x^2 = 50$$
$$x = \pm\sqrt{50} \approx \pm 7.07 \quad \text{[Use the table on}$$
$$x \approx 7.1 \qquad\qquad\qquad \text{page 581 or com-}$$
$$\text{pute. Reject the negative value.]}$$

Answer: The side of the square is 7.1 inches.

5. Is a triangle whose sides are 10 in., 7 in., and 4 in. a right triangle?

Solution: The square of 10, the longest side, $= 10^2 = 100$. The sum of the squares of the other two sides $= 7^2 + 4^2 = 49 + 16 = 65$.

Answer: Since 100 does not equal 65, the triangle is not a right triangle.

Exercises

In 1–9, find the third side of the right triangle whose hypotenuse is represented by c and whose other sides are represented by a and b.

1. $a = 3, b = 4$

2. $a = 8, b = 15$

3. $c = 10, a = 6$

4. $c = 13, a = 12$

5. $c = 17, b = 15$

6. $c = 25, b = 20$

7. $a = \sqrt{2}, b = \sqrt{2}$

8. $a = 4, b = 4\sqrt{3}$

9. $a = 5\sqrt{3}, c = 10$

In 10–15, express in simplest radical form the third side of the right triangle whose hypotenuse is represented by c and whose other sides are represented by a and b.

10. $a = 2, b = 3$

11. $a = 3, b = 3$

12. $a = 4, c = 8$

13. $a = 7, b = 1$

14. $b = \sqrt{3}, c = \sqrt{15}$

15. $a = 4\sqrt{2}, c = 8$

In 16–24, approximate, correct to the *nearest tenth*, the third side of the right triangle whose hypotenuse is represented by c and whose other sides are represented by a and b.

16. $a = 5, b = 7$

17. $a = 4, b = 9$

18. $c = 15, a = 5$

19. $c = 23, a = 9$

20. $c = 12, b = 3$

21. $c = 35, b = 25$

22. $a = 7, b = 7$

23. $a = 3, c = 6$

24. $a = 5\sqrt{2}, c = 10$

In 25–28, find x and express irrational results in simplest radical form.

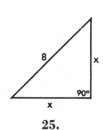

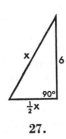

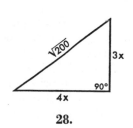

25.   **26.**   **27.**   **28.**

29. A ladder 39 feet long leans against a building and reaches the ledge of a window. If the foot of the ladder is 15 feet from the foot of the building, how high is the window ledge above the ground?

30. A wire stretches from the top of a pole 24 feet high to a stake in the ground which is 18 feet from the foot of the pole. Find the length of the wire.

31. A man traveled 24 miles north and then 10 miles east. How far was he from his starting point?

32. Tom and Henry started from the same place. Tom traveled west at the rate of 30 miles per hour and Henry traveled south at the rate of 40 miles per hour. How far apart were they at the end of one hour?

In 33–36, find the diagonal of a rectangle whose sides are the given measurements.

33. 8 in. and 15 in.   **34.** 15 in. and 20 in.
35. 10 ft. and 24 ft.   **36.** 9 yd. and 40 yd.

37. The diagonal of a rectangle is 13 in. One side is 12 in. Find the other side.

38. The diagonal of a rectangle is 34 in. One side is 16 in. Find the other side.

39. Approximate, to the *nearest foot*, the diameter of the largest round table which can be taken through a rectangular doorway whose base is 4 feet and whose height is 7 feet.

40. Approximate, to the *nearest inch*, the base of a rectangle whose diagonal is 25 inches and whose altitude is 18 inches.

In 41–45, approximate, to the *nearest tenth of an inch*, the diagonal of a square whose side is the given measurement.

41. 2 in.   **42.** 4 in.   **43.** 5 in.   **44.** 6 in.   **45.** 7 in.

In 46–50, approximate, to the *nearest tenth of an inch*, the side of a square whose diagonal is the given measurement.

46. 6 in.   **47.** 2 in.   **48.** 4 in.   **49.** 10 in.   **50.** 5 in.

In the figure, ABC is an equilateral triangle (it has 3 equal sides). CD, which is drawn so that angle CDB is a right angle, is called the altitude. When altitude CD is drawn, it divides AB into two equal parts, $AD = DB$. In 51–55, approximate, to the *nearest tenth of an inch*, the altitude of equilateral triangle ABC when each of its sides is the given measurement.

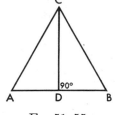

Ex. 51–55

51. 4 in.   **52.** 6 in.   **53.** 8 in.   **54.** 10 in.   **55.** 5 in.

56. In the figure, ABC is an isosceles triangle with $AC = CB$. CD, which is drawn so that angle CDB is a right angle, is called the altitude drawn to the base of the triangle. When altitude CD is drawn, it divides the base AB into two equal parts, $AD = DB$. Each of the two equal sides of isosceles triangle ABC is 26 in. and the base of the triangle is 20 in.

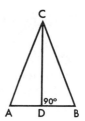

    a. Find the altitude drawn to the base.
    b. Find the area of triangle ABC.

57. In an isosceles triangle, the base is 12 in. and the altitude drawn to the base is 8 in. Find each of the equal sides of the triangle.

58. In an isosceles triangle, each of the equal sides is 17 in. and the altitude drawn to the base is 15 in.

    a. Find the base of the triangle.
    b. Find the area of the triangle.

59. A baseball diamond is a square 90 feet on each side. Approximate, to the *nearest tenth of a foot*, the distance from home plate to second base.

60. The hypotenuse of a right triangle is 25 in. One of the legs is 5 in. longer than the other. Find the length of each leg.

61. The ratio of two legs of a right triangle is $3:4$. Find each leg when the hypotenuse is:

    a. 10 in.   *b.* 20 in.   *c.* 25 in.   *d.* 100 in.

62. The ratio of the hypotenuse of a right triangle to one of its legs is $13:5$. If the other leg of the triangle is 24, find the hypotenuse of the triangle.

63. The perimeter of a right triangle is 30 inches. If the hypotenuse is 13 inches, find the length of each leg.

64. The side of a square is represented by s and the diagonal by d.

    a. Show that $d = s\sqrt{2}$.
    b. Show that $s = \tfrac{1}{2}d\sqrt{2}$.

In 65–68, tell whether the measurements can be the lengths of the sides of a right triangle.

65. 6 yd., 10 yd., 8 yd.   **66.** 7 ft., 4 ft., 5 ft.

67. 12 in., 16 in., 20 in.   **68.** 10 ft., 15 ft., 20 ft.

8. Locating Irrational Square Roots on a Number Line

Consider a right triangle in which each leg is 1. Using the theorem of Pythagoras, we discover that the hypotenuse of the right triangle is $\sqrt{2}$.

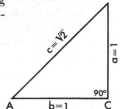

$$c^2 = (1)^2 + (1)^2$$
$$c^2 = 2$$
$$c = \sqrt{2}$$

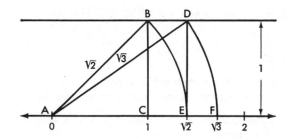

Let us associate the irrational number $\sqrt{2}$ with a point on a number line without using approximations. First we construct right triangle ACB using the length of the segment from 0 to 1 as legs AC and CB. Then with A as the center and a radius equal to AB (remember that the length of AB is $\sqrt{2}$), we construct an arc of a circle which intersects the number line at E. The coordinate of point E is $\sqrt{2}$.

To locate $\sqrt{3}$ on a number line, we first construct right triangle AED in which leg $AE = \sqrt{2}$ (which we constructed previously) and leg $ED = 1$. In this triangle, hypotenuse $AD = \sqrt{3}$:

$$(AD)^2 = (\sqrt{2})^2 + (1)^2, \ (AD)^2 = 3, \ AD = \sqrt{3}$$

On the number line, we can now locate point F, whose coordinate is $\sqrt{3}$.

In a similar manner, we can locate $\sqrt{5}$, $\sqrt{6}$, etc.

Exercises

In 1–10, without using approximations, locate on a number line the point associated with the given number.

1. $\sqrt{5}$ **2.** $\sqrt{8}$ **3.** $\sqrt{10}$ **4.** $\sqrt{13}$ **5.** $\sqrt{17}$
6. $\sqrt{18}$ **7.** $\sqrt{20}$ **8.** $\sqrt{32}$ **9.** $\sqrt{6}$ **10.** $\sqrt{7}$

9. Graphing a Quadratic Equation in Two Variables of the Form $y = ax^2 + bx + c$

We have learned that the graph of every first-degree equation in two variables is a straight line. For example, the graph $x + y = 6$ is a straight line.

Let us graph the quadratic equation $y = 2x^2$. We will use values for x from $x = -3$ to $x = 3$ inclusive, that is, $-3 \le x \le 3$.

Solution:

1. Develop the following table of values: $y = 2x^2$

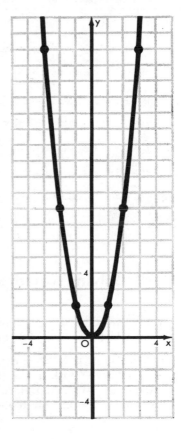

x	$2x^2$	$= y$
-3	$2(-3)^2$	18
-2	$2(-2)^2$	8
-1	$2(-1)^2$	2
0	$2(0)^2$	0
1	$2(1)^2$	2
2	$2(2)^2$	8
3	$2(3)^2$	18

2. Plot the point associated with each ordered number pair (x, y): $(-3, 18)$, $(-2, 8)$, $(-1, 2)$, etc.

3. Draw a smooth curve through the points. Notice that the graph of $y = 2x^2$ is a curve; it is not a straight line. This curve is called a **parabola.**

The graph of every quadratic equation of the form $y = ax^2 + bx + c$ (where a, b, and c are real numbers and $a \ne 0$) is a parabola.

Exercises

In 1–28, graph the quadratic equation. Use the integral values for x indicated in parentheses to prepare the necessary table of values.

1. $y = x^2$ $(-3 \leq x \leq 3)$ **2.** $y = 3x^2$ $(-2 \leq x \leq 2)$

3. $4x^2 = y$ $(-2 \leq x \leq 2)$ **4.** $5x^2 = y$ $(-2 \leq x \leq 2)$

5. $y = -x^2$ $(-3 \leq x \leq 3)$ **6.** $y = -2x^2$ $(-2 \leq x \leq 2)$

7. $-3x^2 = y$ $(-2 \leq x \leq 2)$ **8.** $-4x^2 = y$ $(-2 \leq x \leq 2)$

9. $y = \frac{1}{2}x^2$ $(-4 \leq x \leq 4)$ **10.** $-\frac{1}{2}x^2 = y$ $(-2 \leq x \leq 2)$

11. $y = x^2 + 1$ $(-3 \leq x \leq 3)$ **12.** $x^2 - 1 = y$ $(-3 \leq x \leq 3)$

13. $x^2 + 4 = y$ $(-3 \leq x \leq 3)$ **14.** $y = x^2 - 4$ $(-3 \leq x \leq 3)$

15. $-x^2 + 4 = y$ $(-3 \leq x \leq 3)$ **16.** $-x^2 - 4 = y$ $(-3 \leq x \leq 3)$

17. $y = x^2 - 2x$ $(-1 \leq x \leq 3)$ **18.** $x^2 + 2x = y$ $(-3 \leq x \leq 1)$

19. $y = -x^2 + 2x$ $(-1 \leq x \leq 3)$ **20.** $-x^2 - 2x = y$ $(-3 \leq x \leq 1)$

21. $y = x^2 - 6x + 8$ $(0 \leq x \leq 6)$ **22.** $y = x^2 - 4x + 3$ $(-1 \leq x \leq 5)$

23. $x^2 - 2x - 3 = y$ $(-2 \leq x \leq 4)$ **24.** $x^2 - 2x + 1 = y$ $(-2 \leq x \leq 4)$

25. $y = x^2 - 3x + 2$ $(-1 \leq x \leq 4)$ **26.** $x^2 + x - 6 = y$ $(-4 \leq x \leq 3)$

27. $y = -x^2 + 6x - 8$ $(0 \leq x \leq 6)$ **28.** $-x^2 + 4x - 3 = y$ $(-1 \leq x \leq 5)$

10. Solving Quadratic Equations by Using Graphs

When we solve the equation $x^2 - 2x - 8 = 0$, we are finding the values of x for which $x^2 - 2x - 8$ equals 0.

Let us graph $x^2 - 2x - 8 = y$. We will use values for x from $x = -3$ to $x = 5$ inclusive. Both in the table that we develop and on the graph which we draw, we will find the values of x for which $x^2 - 2x - 8$ equals zero. These values of x are the roots of the equation $x^2 - 2x - 8 = 0$.

Solve graphically $x^2 - 2x - 8 = 0$.

Solution:

1. Let $x^2 - 2x - 8 = y$.
2. Develop the following table of values:

$x^2 - 2x - 8 = y$

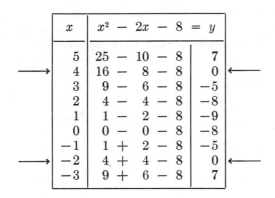

x	$x^2 - 2x - 8 = y$	
5	$25 - 10 - 8$	7
4	$16 - 8 - 8$	0
3	$9 - 6 - 8$	-5
2	$4 - 4 - 8$	-8
1	$1 - 2 - 8$	-9
0	$0 - 0 - 8$	-8
-1	$1 + 2 - 8$	-5
-2	$4 + 4 - 8$	0
-3	$9 + 6 - 8$	7

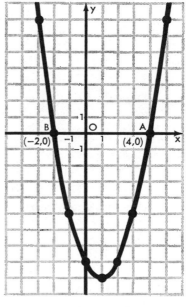

3. Plot the point associated with each ordered number pair (x, y): $(5, 7)$, $(4, 0)$, etc. Draw a smooth curve through the points.
4. We are looking for values of x for which $x^2 - 2x - 8 = 0$. In the table, we see that when $x = 4$, $y = 0$ (that is, when $x = 4$, $x^2 - 2x - 8 = 0$). Also, when $x = -2$, $y = 0$ (that is, when $x = -2$, $x^2 - 2x - 8 = 0$). Therefore, 4 and -2 are the roots of $x^2 - 2x - 8 = 0$.
5. As we know, every point on the graph $y = x^2 - 2x - 8$ has an x-coordinate and a y-coordinate (x, y). Inspection reveals that the y-coordinate has a value of 0 at $A(4, 0)$ and at $B(-2, 0)$. That is, y or $x^2 - 2x - 8$ is equal to 0 at A, where $x = 4$, and at B, where $x = -2$. Therefore, 4 and -2 are roots of $x^2 - 2x - 8 = 0$.
6. Also, notice that the roots of $x^2 - 2x - 8 = 0$ (4 and -2) are the x-values of the two points at which the graph of $x^2 - 2x - 8 = y$ intersects the x-axis $(y = 0)$.

Answer: $x = 4$ or $x = -2$; solution set is $\{4, -2\}$.

Procedure. To solve a quadratic equation by using a graph:
1. **Transform the equation into an equivalent equation in standard form: $ax^2 + bx + c = 0$. $(a \neq 0)$**
2. **Let $ax^2 + bx + c = y$.**
3. **Develop a table, choosing convenient values for x, and draw the graph of $ax^2 + bx + c = y$.**
4. **Read the x-values, or abscissas, of the points where the graph of $ax^2 + bx + c = y$ intersects the x-axis $(y = 0)$. These x-values are the roots of the quadratic equation that is being solved.**

Exercises

1. *a.* Draw the graph of $x^2 - 4 = y$ using integral values of x from $x = -3$ to $x = 3$ inclusive.

   b. Use the graph made in answer to part *a* to solve the equation $x^2 - 4 = 0$.

2. *a.* Draw the graph of $x^2 - 6x + 8 = y$ using integral values of x from $x = 0$ to $x = 6$ inclusive.

   b. Use the graph made in answer to part *a* to solve the equation $x^2 - 6x + 8 = 0$.

3. *a.* Draw the graph of $x^2 - 3x = y$ using integral values of x from $x = -1$ to $x = 4$ inclusive.

   b. Use the graph made in answer to part *a* to solve the equation $x^2 - 3x = 0$.

In 4–12, use a graph to solve the equation.

4. $x^2 - 4x + 3 = 0$ **5.** $x^2 + 2x - 8 = 0$ **6.** $x^2 - 16 = 0$

7. $x^2 - 25 = 0$ **8.** $x^2 - 2x = 0$ **9.** $x^2 + 3x = 0$

10. $x^2 - x - 6 = 0$ **11.** $x^2 - 2x = 8$ **12.** $x^2 - 3 = 2x$

11. Solving Verbal Problems by Using Quadratic Equations

The solutions of some verbal problems involve the solution of a quadratic equation. The most convenient method of solving the quadratic equation should be used.

NUMBER PROBLEMS

~~~~~~~~~~~~~~~~~ *MODEL PROBLEMS* ~~~~~~~~~~~~~~~

1. The square of a number decreased by 4 times the number equals 21. Find the number.

Solution: Let x = the number.

The square of the number decreased by 4 times the number equals 21.

$$x^2 - 4x = 21$$
$$x^2 - 4x - 21 = 0$$
$$(x - 7)(x + 3) = 0$$
$$x - 7 = 0 \quad | \quad x + 3 = 0$$
$$x = 7 \quad | \quad x = -3$$

Check for the number 7:

$(7)^2 - 4(7) \overset{?}{=} 21$

$49 - 28 \overset{?}{=} 21$

$21 = 21$ (true)

Check for the number -3:

$(-3)^2 - 4(-3) \overset{?}{=} 21$

$9 + 12 \overset{?}{=} 21$

$21 = 21$ (true)

Answer: The number is 7 or -3.

2. The product of two positive consecutive even numbers is 80. Find the numbers.

Solution:

Let x = the first positive even number.

Then $x + 2$ = the next consecutive positive even number.

The product of two positive consecutive even numbers is 80.

$$x(x + 2) = 80$$
$$x^2 + 2x = 80$$
$$x^2 + 2x - 80 = 0$$
$$(x - 8)(x + 10) = 0$$
$$x - 8 = 0 \quad | \quad x + 10 = 0$$
$$x = 8 \quad | \quad x = -10 \quad \text{[Reject because the number}$$
$$x + 2 = 10 \quad | \qquad\qquad \text{must be positive.]}$$

Check: The product of the two positive consecutive even numbers 8 and 10 is (8)(10), or 80.

Answer: The numbers are 8 and 10.

3. The sum of two numbers is 8. The sum of the squares of the numbers is 34. Find the numbers.

Solution:

Let x = the first number.
Then $8 - x$ = the second number.

The sum of the squares of the numbers is 34.

$$x^2 + (8 - x)^2 = 34$$

$x^2 + 64 - 16x + x^2 = 34$	Squaring $8 - x$
$2x^2 - 16x + 64 = 34$	Collecting like terms
$2x^2 - 16x + 30 = 0$	S_{34}
$x^2 - 8x + 15 = 0$	D_2
$(x - 5)(x - 3) = 0$	Factoring

$$x - 5 = 0 \quad | \quad x - 3 = 0$$
$$x = 5 \quad\quad | \quad\quad x = 3$$
$$8 - x = 3 \quad | \quad 8 - x = 5$$

Check: The sum of 5 and 3, $5 + 3 = 8$. The sum of $(5)^2$ and $(3)^2$, $25 + 9 = 34$.

Answer: The numbers are 5 and 3.

Exercises

1. The square of a number increased by 3 times the number is 28. Find the number.

2. When the square of a certain number is diminished by 9 times the number, the result is 36. Find the number.

3. A certain number added to its square is 30. Find the number.

4. The square of a number exceeds the number by 72. Find the number.

5. The square of a number exceeds 5 times the number by 24. Find the number.

6. The square of a number decreased by the number is 90. Find the number.

7. The square of a number decreased by 15 is equal to twice the number. Find the number.

8. The square of a number is equal to the sum of 21 and 4 times the number. Find the number.

9. Find two positive numbers whose ratio is 2:3 and whose product is 600.

10. The larger of two positive numbers is 5 more than the smaller. The product of the numbers is 36. Find the numbers.

11. In the balcony of a theatre, there are 240 seats. The number of seats in each row is 14 more than the number of rows. Find the number of rows.

12. The sum of two numbers is 9. Their product is 14. Find the numbers.

13. The product of two consecutive integers is 56. Find the integers.

14. The product of two consecutive odd integers is 99. Find the integers.

15. Find two consecutive even integers such that the square of the smaller is 10 more than the larger.

16. Twice the square of a certain number decreased by 6 times the number is 80. Find the number.

17. Nine times a certain number is 5 less than twice the square of the number. Find the number.

18. Four times the square of a certain positive number exceeds 8 times the number by 12. Find the number.

19. If 5 times the square of a certain number is decreased by twice the number, the result is 16. Find the number.

20. The sum of the squares of two positive consecutive integers is 41. Find the integers.

21. The sum of the squares of two positive consecutive even integers is 100. Find the integers.

22. Find three consecutive odd integers such that the square of the first increased by the product of the other two is 224.

23. The sum of two numbers is 10. The sum of their squares is 52. Find the numbers.

24. The sum of two numbers is 12. The sum of their squares is 104. Find the numbers.

25. The difference between two numbers is 3. The sum of the squares of the numbers is 89. Find the numbers.

26. The sum of a number and its reciprocal is $\frac{5}{2}$. Find the number.

27. The sum of a number and its reciprocal is $\frac{-10}{3}$. Find the number.

28. The sum of a number and its reciprocal is $2\frac{1}{6}$. Find the number.

GEOMETRIC PROBLEMS

~~~~~~~~~~~~~~~~~~~~~~ *MODEL PROBLEM* ~~~~~~~~~~~~~~~~~~~~~~

The base of a rectangle is 7 inches more than its height. If the area of the rectangle is 30 square inches, find its base and its height.

Solution:

Let x = the number of inches in the height of the rectangle.

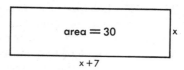

Then $x + 7$ = the number of inches in the base of the rectangle.

The area of the rectangle is 30.

$$x(x + 7) = 30 \qquad [\text{area} = \text{base} \times \text{height}]$$
$$x^2 + 7x = 30$$
$$x^2 + 7x - 30 = 0$$
$$(x - 3)(x + 10) = 0$$

$$
\begin{array}{c|c}
x - 3 = 0 & x + 10 = 0 \\
x = 3 & x = -10 \quad [\text{Reject because the height cannot} \\
x + 7 = 10 & \text{be a negative number.}]
\end{array}
$$

Check: When the base of a rectangle is 10 and its height is 3, the area is 10×3, or 30.

Answer: The height is 3 inches; the base is 10 inches.

~~~~~~

Exercises

1. The length of a rectangle is 2 times its width. The area of the rectangle is 72 square inches. Find the dimensions of the rectangle.
2. The length of a rectangle is 4 times its width. The area is 144 sq. in. Find the dimensions of the rectangle.
3. The width of a rectangle is $\frac{1}{3}$ of its length. The area of the rectangle is 75 sq. yd. Find the dimensions of the rectangle.
4. The ratio of the base and height of a rectangle is 3:4. The area of the rectangle is 1200 sq. ft. Find the dimensions of the rectangle.
5. The ratio of the length of a rectangle to its width is 5:2. If the area of the rectangle is 300 square feet, find its dimensions.
6. The length of a rectangular garden is 4 yards more than its width. The area of the garden is 60 square yards. Find the dimensions of the garden.

7. The width of a rectangle is 11 inches less than its length. Find the dimensions of the rectangle if its area is 80 square inches.

8. The length of a rectangle exceeds its width by 3 inches. If the area of the rectangle is 70 square inches, find its dimensions.

9. The perimeter of a rectangle is 20 inches and its area is 16 square inches. Find the dimensions of the rectangle.

10. Find the dimensions of a rectangle whose perimeter is 28 feet and whose area is 48 square feet.

11. If one side of a square is increased by 2 inches and an adjacent side is decreased by 2 inches, the area of the resulting rectangle is 32 square inches. Find one side of the square.

12. The length of a rectangle is three times its width. If the width is diminished by 1 inch and the length is increased by 3 inches, the area of the new rectangle is 72 square inches. Find the dimensions of the original rectangle.

13. A rectangle is 6 ft. long and 4 ft. wide. If each dimension is increased by the same number of feet, a new rectangle is formed whose area is 39 square feet more than the area of the original rectangle. By how many feet was each dimension increased?

14. A rectangle is 8 ft. long and 6 ft. wide. If each dimension is increased by the same number of feet, a new rectangle is formed whose area exceeds the area of the original rectangle by 72 sq. ft. Find the dimensions of the new rectangle.

15. Harry's garden is 6 yards long and 4 yards wide. He wishes to double the area of his garden by increasing its length and width by the same amount. Find the number of yards by which each dimension must be increased.

16. A picture 6 in. by 12 in. is surrounded by a frame of uniform width. If the area of the frame is twice the area of the picture, find the width of the frame.

17. The base of a parallelogram is twice its altitude. The area of the parallelogram is 50 square inches. Find its base and altitude. [Remember: Area of a parallelogram = base × altitude.]

18. The base of a parallelogram exceeds its altitude by 4 inches. The area of the parallelogram is 96 square inches. Find the base and altitude of the parallelogram.

19. The base of a triangle is 4 times its altitude. The area of the triangle is 72 sq. in. Find its base and altitude. [Remember: Area of a triangle = $\frac{1}{2}$ base × altitude.]

20. The altitude of a triangle is 5 inches less than its base. The area of the triangle is 42 sq. in. Find its base and altitude.

21. One leg of a right triangle is 1 inch longer than the other leg. The hypotenuse is 5 inches. Find each leg of the triangle.

22. One leg of a right triangle exceeds the other leg by 2 inches. The hypotenuse of the triangle is 10 inches. Find the legs of the triangle.

23. Find the legs of a right triangle if their difference is 7 and the hypotenuse of the triangle is 13.

24. The hypotenuse of a right triangle is 2 inches longer than one leg and 4 inches longer than the other leg. Find each side of the triangle.

MISCELLANEOUS PROBLEMS

25. The square of Clara's age 2 years from now is equal to 20 times her age 3 years ago. Find Clara's present age.

26. Harry and Saul start from the point of intersection of two straight roads which cross at right angles. Harry travels along one road at the rate of 5 mph and Saul travels along the other road at the rate of 12 miles per hour. In how many hours will they be 26 miles apart?

27. Arthur and Ben start from the same point and travel at the rates of 30 mph and 40 mph along straight roads that are at right angles to each other. In how many hours will they be 100 miles apart?

28. Perry and Stuart started from the same point at the same time. Perry traveled south and Stuart traveled west. Perry traveled 3 mph faster than Stuart. At the end of 2 hours, they were 30 miles apart. Find their rates.

29. Mr. Perkins drove from his home to Boston, 40 miles away, at a certain rate of speed. He then returned home from Boston, traveling over the same road at an average rate of speed which was 30 mph faster than his rate going to Boston. He spent 2 hours traveling. Find his rate of speed each way.

30. The rate of a motorboat in still water is 10 mph. The boat traveled 24 miles upstream and returned the same distance downstream. The round trip required 5 hours. Find the rate of the current.

31. Two cars made the same trip of 60 miles. One traveled 10 mph faster than the other and took 1 hour less time to make the trip. Find the rate of each car.

32. Two cities are 150 miles apart. The time required to travel from one city to the other by train is 2 hours less than the time required by bus. The average rate of the bus is 20 mph less than the average rate of the train. Find the rate of the train.

33. If Sid and Ted work together, they can paint a fence in 4 hours. If they work alone, Sid needs 6 hours more than Ted to paint the fence. How many hours would each boy working alone need to complete the job?

34. Tom requires 3 hours less than Bill to mow a certain lawn. If the two boys work together, they can mow the lawn in 2 hours. How many hours would each boy working alone need to mow the lawn?

CHAPTER XX

GEOMETRY

1. The Angle

A **point** may be pictured as a dot on a piece of paper. A point is usu-
ally named by a capital letter. For example, the point shown is called
"point P."

•P

A **line** is a set of points containing at least two points. A straight line may be named by naming two points on it. The figure shows "line AB." A line may also be named by placing a lower case (small)letter next to it. The figure also shows "line m." In each figure, the arrowheads show that the line extends indefinitely in both directions.

A **line segment,** or **segment,** is part of a line which con-
sists of two points on the line, called **endpoints,** and the
set of points on the line between the endpoints. The figure
shows line segment CD, which is part of line m and whose endpoints are
C and D. When there can be no confusion, a line segment may be referred
to simply as a **line.** To determine the length of a line segment, we determine
the number of units of measure it contains.

A **ray** is a part of a line consisting of one endpoint and the infinite set of
points that extends from the endpoint in only one direction.

The figure shows ray AB, whose endpoint is A and which
extends in only one direction through point B to the right.

An **angle** is a figure formed by two rays which have the same endpoint.

In the illustration, rays AB and AC, which
form an angle, are called the **sides** of the angle.
A, the endpoint of each ray, is called the **vertex**
of the angle. The symbol for angle is ∠ (plural,
∡).

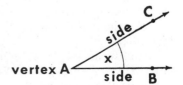

An angle, such as the one illustrated on the preceding page, may be named in any of the following ways:

1. By a capital letter which names its vertex. For example, $\angle A$.
2. By a lower case letter or by a number placed inside the angle. For example, $\angle x$.
3. By three capital letters, one naming the vertex of the angle and the others naming points on the two sides of the angle. The letter at the vertex of the angle is always the middle letter. For example, $\angle BAC$ or $\angle CAB$.

We can think of $\angle TOS$ as having been formed by revolving ray OT. If ray OT is revolved in a counterclockwise direction about vertex O, it will assume the position OS, thus forming $\angle TOS$. OT is called the *initial side* of $\angle TOS$; OS is called the *terminal side*.

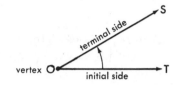

MEASURING ANGLES

To measure an angle means to determine the number of units of measure it contains. A common unit of measure of an angle is a degree, written as $1°$. A degree is $\frac{1}{360}$ of a complete revolution of a ray about a point. The *protractor* is an instrument used to measure angles. Study the model protractor.

The two scales on the protractor show divisions starting at $0°$ and going up to $180°$. One scale starts at $0°$ at the right and continues around to $180°$ at the left. The other scale starts at $0°$ at the left and continues around to $180°$ at the right. These two scales make it conven-ient to measure an angle easily, regard-less of its position.

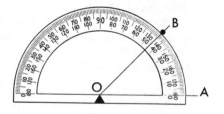

To measure an angle, place the center of the protractor on the vertex of the angle. Place the upper part of the base of the protractor on one side of the angle. This side of the angle cuts across $0°$ on one scale. Notice that the other side of the angle also cuts across that scale. At the point that the other side of the angle cuts across the scale, there is a reading that gives the measure of the angle. If the sides of the angle do not reach the scale, extend them until they do so.

In measuring angle AOB in the illustration, place the protractor so that side OA passes through the $0°$ reading on the inner scale. Side OB cuts across this scale at a point marked $45°$. Therefore, angle AOB contains $45°$.

Note that when the angle being measured is less than one-quarter of a complete revolution, the reading on the scale must be less than 90°. When the angle being measured is greater than one-quarter of a complete revolution and less than one-half of a complete revolution, the reading on the scale must be greater than 90° and less than 180°.

TYPES OF ANGLES

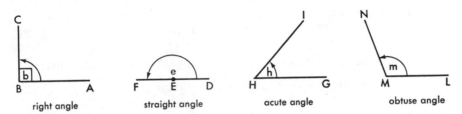

right angle   straight angle   acute angle   obtuse angle

A *right angle* is an angle that is formed by one-quarter of a complete revolution. $\angle ABC$ is a right angle. A right angle contains 90°; $\angle b = 90°$. It follows that:

All right angles are equal in measure.

Note that the symbol ⌐ at B is used to show that $\angle ABC$ is a right angle.

A *straight angle* is an angle that is formed by one-half of a complete revolution. $\angle DEF$ is a straight angle. A straight angle contains 180°; $\angle e = 180°$. It follows that:

All straight angles are equal in measure.

An *acute angle* is an angle that is greater than 0° and less than 90°. $\angle GHI$ is an acute angle; $0° < \angle h < 90°$.

An *obtuse angle* is an angle that is greater than a right angle and less than a straight angle. $\angle LMN$ is an obtuse angle; $90° < \angle m < 180°$.

Exercises

1. Use a protractor to measure each of the following angles:

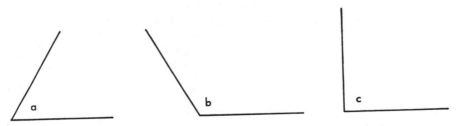

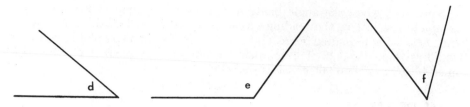

2. Use a protractor to draw an angle of:
   a. 30°   b. 80°   c. 90°   d. 65°   e. 48°   f. 24°
   g. 120°   h. 150°   i. 165°   j. 115°   k. 96°   l. 138°

3. What kind of angle is formed at each corner of a basketball court?

4. What kind of angle is each angle of a rectangle?

5. In triangle *ABC*, what kinds of angles do ∠*A*, ∠*B*, and ∠*C* appear to be?

6. In triangle *DEF*, what kinds of angles do ∠*D*, ∠*E*, and ∠*F* appear to be?

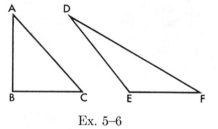

Ex. 5–6

7. Name the kind of angle that is formed between the hands of a clock when they show: (*a*) 3 o'clock   (*b*) 6 o'clock   (*c*) 1 o'clock   (*d*) 5 o'clock

8. Order the measures of the following types of angles, naming the smallest angle first: right angle, straight angle, obtuse angle, acute angle.

9. Draw an acute angle. Name it, using one capital letter.

10. Draw an obtuse angle. Name it, using one small letter.

11. Draw a right angle. Name it, using three capital letters.

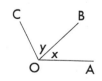

12. Using the figure shown:
    a. Name angle *x*, using three capital letters.
    b. Give the shorter name for angle *COB*.
    c. Name one acute angle.
    d. Name one obtuse angle.

13. Find the number of degrees there are in: (*a*) $\frac{1}{3}$ of a right angle   (*b*) $\frac{3}{5}$ of a right angle   (*c*) $\frac{3}{4}$ of a straight angle

14. Find the ratio of the number of degrees in the measure of a right angle to the number of degrees in the measure of a straight angle.

15. Find the number of degrees through which the earth rotates in:
    a. 24 hours   *b.* 12 hours   *c.* 1 hour   *d.* 4 minutes

16. Find the number of degrees formed by the hands of a clock at:
    a. 1 P.M.   *b.* 2 P.M.   *c.* 3 P.M.   *d.* 4 P.M.   *e.* 5 P.M.

    f. 6 P.M.   *g.* 12:30 P.M.   *h.* 5:30 P.M.   *i.* 2:20 P.M.   *j.* 4:15 P.M.

In 17–21, graph the open sentence on a number line and tell whether the graph is a point, a ray, a line, or a line segment.

17. $x \geq 3$ **18.** $x = 3$ **19.** $-3 \leq x \leq 3$ **20.** $|x| \geq 0$ **21.** $|x| \leq 3$

PAIRS OF ANGLES

If the sum of the measures of two angles is 90°, the angles are called **complementary angles.** Each angle is the **complement** of the other. If an angle contains 50°, its complement contains 90° − 50°, or 40°; if an angle contains $x°$, its complement contains $(90 − x)°$.

If the sum of the measures of two angles is 180°, the angles are called **supplementary angles.** Each angle is the **supplement** of the other. If an angle contains 70°, its supplement contains 180° − 70°, or 110°; if an angle contains $x°$, its supplement contains $(180 − x)°$.

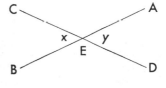

If two straight lines AB and CD intersect at E, $\angle x$ and $\angle y$ are opposite each other. They are called a pair of **vertical angles.** When we measure $\angle x$ and $\angle y$, we find that each angle is 50°. Therefore, $\angle x = \angle y$. Also, $\angle CEA$ and $\angle BED$ are a pair of vertical angles, each of which measures 130°. Therefore, $\angle CEA = \angle BED$. We can now understand the following property of vertical angles:

If two straight lines intersect, the vertical angles formed are equal.

~~~~~~~~~~~~~~~~~~~~~~ **MODEL PROBLEMS** ~~~~~~~~~~~~~~~~~~~~~~

1. Find the number of degrees in an angle which is four times as large as its complement.

Solution:

Let $x =$ the number of degrees in the complement of the angle.
Then $4x =$ the number of degrees in the angle.

The sum of the measures of the two complementary angles is 90°.

$$x + 4x = 90$$
$$5x = 90$$
$$x = 18$$
$$4x = 72$$

Check

$$72° = 4 \times 18°$$
$$72° + 18° = 90°$$

Answer: The angle contains 72°.

2. Find the number of degrees in an angle which exceeds its supplement by 42°.

Solution:

Let $x =$ the number of degrees in the supplement of the angle.
Then $x + 42 =$ the number of degrees in the angle.

The sum of the measures of the two supplementary angles is 180°.

$$x + x + 42 = 180$$
$$2x + 42 = 180$$
$$2x = 138$$
$$x = 69$$
$$x + 42 = 111$$

Check

111° exceeds 69° by 42°.
$$111° + 69° = 180°$$

Answer: The angle contains 111°.

~~~~~~

Exercises

COMPLEMENTARY ANGLES

In 1–4, tell whether the angles are complementary.

1. 10° and 80°   **2.** 55° and 45°   **3.** 37° and 53°
4. 18°22′ and 71°38′ [Remember that 1° = 60′.]

In 5–9, find the complement of the angle.

5. 40°   **6.** 25°   **7.** 72°   **8.** 31°30′   **9.** 69°17′

10. Represent the complement of an angle whose measure is represented by:
(a) $m°$ (b) $(90 - y)°$ (c) $(x + 10)°$

11. Two angles are complementary. One angle is twice as large as the other. Find the number of degrees in each angle.

12. The complement of an angle is 8 times as large as the angle. Find the number of degrees in the complement.

13. The complement of an angle is one-fifth of the angle. Find the number of degrees in the angle.

14. The complement of an angle is 20° more than the angle. Find the number of degrees in the angle.

15. Find the number of degrees in an angle which is 8° less than its complement.

16. Find the number of degrees in an angle which exceeds twice its complement by 36°.

17. Two complementary angles are in the ratio 7:2. Find the number of degrees in each angle.

18. The number of degrees in two complementary angles can be represented by two consecutive even numbers. Find the number of degrees in each angle.

19. Two angles are complementary. The larger exceeds three times the smaller by 10°. Find the number of degrees in each angle.

20. Find two complementary angles such that $\frac{2}{3}$ of the smaller is equal to $\frac{1}{2}$ of the result obtained when the larger is diminished by 20°.

SUPPLEMENTARY ANGLES

In 21–24, tell whether the angles are supplementary.

21. 20° and 160°   **22.** 150° and 40°   **23.** 124° and 56°   **24.** 81°30′ and 98°30′

In 25–30, find the supplement of the angle.

25. 40°   **26.** 80°   **27.** 90°   **28.** 110°   **29.** 55°30′   **30.** 148°25′

31. Represent the supplement of an angle whose measure is represented by:
(a) $m°$ (b) $(180 - y)°$ (c) $(x - 40)°$

32. Two angles are supplementary. One angle is twice as large as the other. Find the number of degrees in each angle.

33. The supplement of an angle is 5 times as large as the angle. Find the number of degrees in the angle.

34. The supplement of an angle is one-half of the angle. Find the number of degrees in the angle.

35. The supplement of an angle is 40° more than the angle. Find the number of degrees in the supplement.

36. Find the number of degrees in an angle which exceeds its supplement by 10°.

37. Find the number of degrees in an angle which is 20° less than 4 times its supplement.

38. Two supplementary angles are in the ratio 2:3. Find the number of degrees in each angle.

39. Find two supplementary angles such that $\frac{1}{4}$ of the smaller is equal to $\frac{1}{3}$ of the result obtained when the larger is diminished by 110°.

VERTICAL ANGLES

In 40–44, lines AB and CD intersect at E. Find the measure of angle BEC when angle AED measures:

40. 30°   **41.** 65°   **42.** 90°   **43.** 128°   **44.** 175°

In 45–48, lines MN and RS intersect at T.

45. If $\angle RTM = 5x°$ and $\angle NTS = (3x + 10)°$, find the number of degrees in $\angle RTM$.

46. If $\angle MTS = (4x - 60)°$ and $\angle NTR = 2x°$, find the number of degrees in $\angle MTS$.

47. If $\angle RTM = (7x + 16)°$ and $\angle NTS = (3x + 48)°$, find the number of degrees in $\angle NTS$.

48. If $\angle RTM = (\frac{3}{2}x + 10)°$ and $\angle STN = (x + 36)°$, find the number of degrees in $\angle STN$ and $\angle NTR$.

2. The Triangle

A **triangle** is a set of points, a figure, consisting of three points which do not lie on a straight line and the line segments determined by these points.

Consider triangle ABC ($\triangle ABC$). In triangle ABC, the points A, B, and C are the vertices of the triangle. Line segments AB, BC, and CA are the sides of the triangle. $\angle A$, $\angle B$, and $\angle C$ are the angles of the triangle.

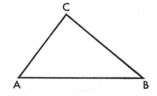

We say that side AB is included between $\angle A$ and $\angle B$, side BC is included between $\angle B$ and $\angle C$, and side CA is included between $\angle C$ and $\angle A$. We also say that $\angle A$ is included between sides AB and AC, $\angle B$ is included between sides BA and BC, and $\angle C$ is included between sides CB and CA.

KINDS OF TRIANGLES

isosceles triangle

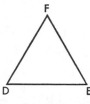

equilateral triangle

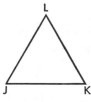

equiangular triangle

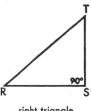

right triangle

An *isosceles triangle* is a triangle that has two equal sides.

An *equilateral triangle* is a triangle that has three equal sides.

An *equiangular triangle* is a triangle that has three equal angles.

A *right triangle* is a triangle that has one and only one right angle.

THE SUM OF THE MEASURES OF THE ANGLES OF A TRIANGLE

In each of the preceding triangles, when the three angles are measured and these measures are added, the sum is 180°. All triangles, regardless of their size or shape, have the following property:

The sum of the measures of the angles of a triangle is 180°.

[*Note:* If the sum of the measures of three angles is not 180°, these angles cannot be the angles of a triangle.]

——————— MODEL PROBLEMS ———————

1. Two angles of a triangle measure 35° and 75°. How many degrees does the third angle contain?

Solution: Let x = the number of degrees in the third angle.

The sum of the measures of the angles of a triangle is 180°.

$$x + 35 + 75 = 180$$
$$x + 110 = 180$$
$$x = 70$$

Check

$$35° + 75° + 70° = 180°$$

Answer: 70°

2. In triangle ABC, angle B is twice angle A, and angle C is three times angle A. Find the number of degrees in each angle of the triangle.

Solution:

Let x = the number of degrees in angle A.
Then $2x$ = the number of degrees in angle B.
Then $3x$ = the number of degrees in angle C.

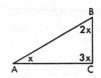

The sum of the measures of the angles of a triangle is 180°.

$$x + 2x + 3x = 180$$

	Check
$6x = 180$	$60° = 2 \times 30°$
$x = 30$	$90° = 3 \times 30°$
$2x = 60$	$30° + 60° + 90° = 180°$
$3x = 90$	

Answer: $\angle A = 30°$, $\angle B = 60°$, $\angle C = 90°$

Exercises

In 1–4, discover whether the set of angles can be the three angles of a triangle.

1. 30°, 70°, 80°

2. 70°, 80°, 90°

3. 30°, 110°, 40°

4. 20°, 100°, 70°

In 5–10, find the third angle of the triangle if the first two angles contain:

5. 60°, 40°

6. 100°, 20°

7. 55°, 85°

8. 24°, 82°

9. 81°, 92°

10. 59°, 28°

11. Find the number of degrees in each angle of an equiangular triangle.

12. Can a triangle have: (*a*) two right angles?   (*b*) two obtuse angles?
(*c*) one right and one obtuse angle? Why?

13. What is the sum of the two acute angles of a right triangle?

14. If two angles in one triangle contain the same number of degrees as two angles in another triangle, what must be true of the third pair of angles in the two triangles? Why?

15. In a triangle, the second angle is 3 times the first angle, and the third angle is 5 times the first angle. Find the number of degrees in each angle of the triangle.

16. In triangle RST, angle R is $\frac{1}{2}$ of angle S, and angle T is 3 times angle S. Find each angle of the triangle.

17. In triangle ABC, angle B is twice angle A, and angle C is three times angle B. Find each angle of the triangle.

18. In a triangle, the second angle is 4 times the first angle. The third angle is equal to the sum of the first two angles. Find the number of degrees in each angle of the triangle.

19. In triangle LMN, angle M is 6 times angle L. Angle N is equal to the difference between angle M and angle L. Find the number of degrees in each angle of the triangle.

20. In a triangle, the second angle is 30° more than the first angle, and the third angle is 45° more than the first angle. Find the number of degrees in each angle of the triangle.

21. In a triangle, the second angle is 24° less than the first angle, and the third angle is 36° less than the second angle. Find the three angles of the triangle.

22. In a triangle, the second angle exceeds twice the first angle by 5°. The third angle is 35° less than 3 times the first angle. Find the number of degrees in each angle of the triangle.

23. The two acute angles of a right triangle are in the ratio 8:1. Find the number of degrees in each acute angle.

In 24–27, find the number of degrees in each angle of a triangle if the measures of the three angles are in the ratio:

24. 2:3:4   **25.** 2:5:8   **26.** 2:2:5   **27.** 1:5:3

28. In a triangle, the ratio of two angles is 5:1. The third angle is equal to the difference between the other two. Find the number of degrees in each angle.

29. The second angle of a triangle is 20° less than the first angle. The third angle is one-half of the first angle. Find the three angles of the triangle.

30. The second angle of a triangle is one-third of the first angle, and the third angle is one-sixth of the first angle. Find the three angles of the triangle.

THE ISOSCELES TRIANGLE

In isosceles triangle RST, the two equal sides, TR and TS, are called **legs,** or **arms,** of the triangle. The remaining side, RS, is called the **base.**

The angle opposite the base of the triangle, which is the angle formed by the two equal sides, $\angle T$, is called the **vertex angle** of the isosceles triangle.

The angles opposite the equal sides of the triangle, which are the angles at the ends of the base of the triangle, $\angle R$ and $\angle S$, are called the **base angles** of the isosceles triangle.

In isosceles triangle RST, if we measure $\angle S$ and $\angle R$ (which are opposite the equal sides TR and TS), we find that each angle contains 65°. Therefore, $\angle S = \angle R$. All isosceles triangles, regardless of their size or shape, have the following property:

If two sides of a triangle are equal, the angles opposite these sides are equal.

Since $\angle S$ and $\angle R$ are the base angles of isosceles triangle RST, we may also state this property of isosceles triangles as follows:

The base angles of an isosceles triangle are equal.

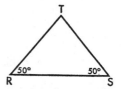

In triangle RST, $\angle R = 50°$ and $\angle S = 50°$. If we measure the sides opposite these equal angles, $\angle R$ and $\angle S$, we find that the measure (length) of TR equals the measure (length) of TS. This example illustrates the following property of triangles:

If two angles of a triangle are equal, the sides opposite those angles are equal. We may also say:

If two angles of a triangle are equal, the triangle is an isosceles triangle.

PROPERTIES OF TRIANGLES

1. The sum of the measures of the angles of a triangle is 180°.
2. The acute angles of a right triangle are complementary.
3. If two angles of one triangle are equal, respectively, to two angles of another triangle, then the remaining angles are equal.
4. If two sides of a triangle are equal, the angles opposite these sides are equal. (Base angles of an isosceles triangle are equal.)
5. If two angles of a triangle are equal, the sides opposite these angles are equal and the triangle is an isosceles triangle.

~~~ MODEL PROBLEMS ~~~

1. In isosceles triangle ABC, vertex angle B measures 70°. Find the number of degrees in each base angle.

Solution:

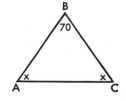

Let x = the number of degrees in base angle A.
Then x = the number of degrees in base angle C.

The sum of the measures of the angles of a triangle is 180°.

$$x + x + 70 = 180$$
$$2x + 70 = 180$$
$$2x = 110$$
$$x = 55$$

Check

$$55° + 55° + 70° = 180°$$

Answer: 55°

2. In isosceles triangle ABC, vertex angle C exceeds each base angle by 30°. Find the number of degrees in each angle of the triangle.

Solution:

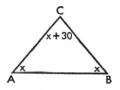

Let x = the number of degrees in one base angle, A.

Then x = the number of degrees in the other base angle, B.

Then $x + 30$ = the number of degrees in the vertex angle, C.

The sum of the measures of the angles of a triangle is 180°.

$$x + x + x + 30 = 180$$
$$3x + 30 = 180$$
$$3x = 150$$
$$x = 50$$
$$x + 30 = 80$$

Check

$$50° + 50° + 80° = 180°$$

Answer: $\angle A = 50°$, $\angle B = 50°$, $\angle C = 80°$

Exercises

1. Name the legs, base, vertex angle, and base angles in each of the following isosceles triangles:

(a) 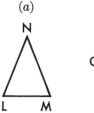   (b) 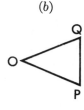   (c) 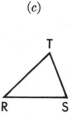   (d)

2. In $\triangle ABC$, $AC = 4$ in., $CB = 6$ in., and $AB = 6$ in.
   a. What type of triangle is $\triangle ABC$?
   b. Name two equal angles in $\triangle ABC$.
   c. Why are they equal?

3. In $\triangle RST$, $\angle R = 70°$ and $\angle T = 40°$.
   a. Find the measure of $\angle S$.
   b. Name two equal sides in $\triangle RST$.
   c. Why are they equal?
   d. What type of triangle is $\triangle RST$?

4. Draw a right triangle that is isosceles.

5. Two angles of a triangle are 50° and 80°.   (a) Find the third angle. (b) What kind of triangle is it?

6. Two angles of a triangle are 38° and 52°. What kind of triangle is it?

7. Find the vertex angle of an isosceles triangle if the measure of each base angle is:
   a. 80°   b. 55°   c. 42°   d. $22\frac{1}{2}°$ e. 51.5°

8. Find the measure of each base angle of an isosceles triangle if the vertex angle measures:
   a. 40°   b. 50°   c. 76°   d. 100°   e. 65°

9. What is the number of degrees in each angle of an equiangular triangle?

10. What is the number of degrees in each acute angle of an isosceles right triangle?

11. What is the number of degrees in each angle of an equilateral triangle?

12. Can a base angle of an isosceles triangle be a right angle? Why?

13. Can a base angle of an isosceles triangle be an obtuse angle? Why?

14. Each base angle of an isosceles triangle is seven times the vertex angle. Find each angle of the triangle.

15. Each of the equal angles of an isosceles triangle is 4 times the vertex angle. Find the angles of the triangle.

16. Each of the equal angles of an isosceles triangle is one-half of the vertex angle. Find the angles of the triangle.

17. The vertex angle of an isosceles triangle is 3 times as large as each base angle. Find the number of degrees in each angle of the triangle.

18. The vertex angle of an isosceles triangle is one-fourth of a base angle. Find the number of degrees in each angle of the triangle.

19. The vertex angle of an isosceles triangle is 15° more than each base angle. Find the number of degrees in each angle of the triangle.

20. Each of the equal angles of an isosceles triangle is 6° less than the vertex angle. Find the angles of the triangle.

21. Each of the equal angles of an isosceles triangle is 9° less than 4 times the vertex angle. Find the angles of the triangle.

22. The vertex angle of an isosceles triangle exceeds 3 times a base angle by 5°. Find the angles of the triangle.

23. Each of the equal angles of an isosceles triangle exceeds twice the vertex angle by 15°. Find the angles of the triangle.

3. Similar Triangles

Let us set up a correspondence between triangles ABC and DEF by pairing vertex A and vertex D, vertex B and vertex E, vertex C and vertex F. We call the angles whose vertices we have paired a pair of **corresponding angles.** For example, $\angle A$ and $\angle D$, $\angle B$ and $\angle E$, $\angle C$ and $\angle F$ are pairs of corresponding angles. Consider the sides which are opposite two vertices that were paired. We call these sides a pair of **corresponding sides.** For example, BC and EF, AC and DF, AB and DE are pairs of corresponding sides.

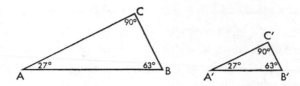

Two triangles may have the same shape although they do not have the same size. We call such triangles *similar triangles.* When all pairs of corresponding angles of two triangles are equal, the triangles have the same shape and are similar triangles. In the preceding figure, for example, examine triangle ABC and triangle $A'B'C'$. Note that $\angle A = \angle A'$ (each measures 27°), $\angle B = \angle B'$ (each measures 63°), and $\angle C = \angle C'$ (each measures 90°). Therefore, triangle ABC is similar to triangle $A'B'C'$, written $\triangle ABC \sim \triangle A'B'C'$. This example illustrates the following property of triangles:

Two triangles are similar if three pairs of corresponding angles are equal.

If we apply the property "the sum of the measures of the angles of a triangle is 180°," we can explain the following two properties of triangles:

Two triangles are similar if two pairs of corresponding angles are equal.

Two right triangles are similar if one pair of corresponding acute angles is equal.

In $\triangle ABC$ and $\triangle A'B'C'$ (see the preceding figure), if we measure AB and $A'B'$, BC and $B'C'$, AC and $A'C'$, we find that the ratio of the measures of each pair of corresponding sides is 2:1; that is, $\dfrac{AB}{A'B'} = \dfrac{2}{1}$, $\dfrac{BC}{B'C'} = \dfrac{2}{1}$, and $\dfrac{AC}{A'C'} = \dfrac{2}{1}$, or $\dfrac{AB}{A'B'} = \dfrac{BC}{B'C'} = \dfrac{AC}{A'C'}$. This example illustrates the following property of similar triangles:

If two triangles are similar, the ratio of any pair of corresponding sides is equal to the ratio of any other pair of corresponding sides.

Another way of expressing this property is:

The corresponding sides of similar triangles are in proportion.

A proportion involving two pairs of corresponding sides in two similar triangles may be written in more than one way. In the preceding figure, for example, the proportion $\dfrac{AB}{A'B'} = \dfrac{BC}{B'C'}$, which involves sides AB, $A'B'$, BC, and $B'C'$, may also be written $\dfrac{AB}{BC} = \dfrac{A'B'}{B'C'}$.

～～～～～～～ MODEL PROBLEM ～～～～～～～

In triangle ABC, $\angle A = 35°$, $\angle B = 90°$. In triangle DEF, $\angle F = 55°$, $\angle E = 90°$.

   a. Is triangle ABC similar to triangle DEF? Why?

   b. If $AB = 40$ ft., $BC = 28$ ft.,
and $DE = 60$ ft., find EF.

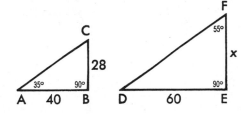

Solution:

   a. The triangles will be similar
if two angles in triangle ABC
are equal to two angles in triangle DEF.

     1. $\angle B = 90°$ and $\angle E = 90°$. Therefore, $\angle B = \angle E$.
     2. In $\triangle ABC$, $\angle A + \angle B = 35° + 90° = 125°$. $\angle C = 180° - 125° = 55°$.
     3. $\angle C = 55°$ and $\angle F = 55°$. Therefore, $\angle C = \angle F$.
     4. Therefore, $\triangle ABC$ is similar to $\triangle DEF$.   *Ans.*

   b. If triangles ABC and DEF are similar, their corresponding sides are
in proportion.

     1. $\dfrac{EF}{BC} = \dfrac{DE}{AB}$ $AB = 40$ ft., $BC = 28$ ft., $DE = 60$ ft.
                                 Let x = length of EF in ft.

     2. $\dfrac{x}{28} = \dfrac{60}{40}$

     3. $40x = (28)(60)$
     4. $40x = 1680$
     5. $x = 42$

Answer: Length of EF is 42 ft.

――――――――――――――――――――――

Exercises

1. In triangle ABC, angle $A = 40°$ and angle $B = 30°$.
In triangle DEF, angle $D = 30°$ and angle $E = 40°$.
Is triangle ABC similar to triangle DEF? Why?

2. In triangle RST, angle $R = 90°$ and angle $S = 40°$.
In triangle XYZ, angle $X = 40°$ and angle $Y = 50°$.
Is triangle RST similar to triangle XYZ? Why?

In 3–5, select the triangles that are similar and tell why they are similar.

3.

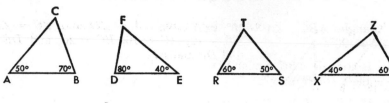

4.

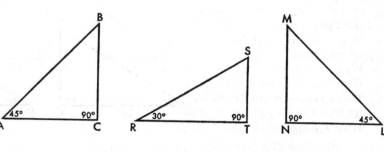

5.

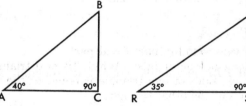

6. Are all equiangular triangles similar? Why?

7. In $\triangle ABC$ and $\triangle RST$, A corresponds to R, B to S, and C to T. If $\triangle ABC \sim \triangle RST$ and if $AB = 9$ in., $AC = 6$ in., and $RS = 3$ in., find RT.

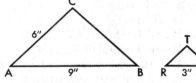

8. *a.* In the figure below, is triangle ABC similar to triangle DEF? Why?
b. Find the length of BC.

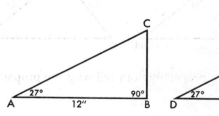

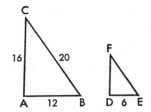

9. In the figure, $\angle A = \angle D$ and $\angle C = \angle F$. If $AB = 12$, $AC = 16$, $BC = 20$, and $DE = 6$, find DF and EF.

10. In the figure:

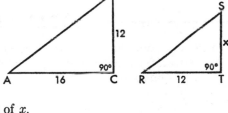

a. Why is triangle ABC similar to triangle $A'B'C'$?

b. Write the ratio of BC to $B'C'$.

c. Write the ratio of AC to $A'C'$.

d. Why are the ratios found in part a and part b equal?

e. Find the value of x.

f. Find the ratio of BC to AC.

g. Find the ratio of $B'C'$ to $A'C'$.

h. What is true of the ratios found in part f and part g?

i. Is the following statement true or false? Why? "If two triangles are similar, the ratio of two sides of one triangle is equal to the ratio of the corresponding sides of the other triangle."

11. In triangles ABC and RST, $\angle A = \angle R$.

a. Why is triangle ABC similar to triangle RST?

b. Write the ratio of BC to AC.

c. Write the ratio of ST to RT.

d. Use the answers found in part b and part c to write a proportion and find the value of x.

12. In triangles LMN and DEF, $\angle L = \angle D$.

a. Write the ratio of MN to ML.

b. Write the ratio of EF to ED.

c. Use the results found in part a and part b to write a proportion and tell why the proportion is true.

d. Find the value of x.

13. In triangles ABC and RST, $\angle A = \angle S$.

a. Why is triangle ABC similar to triangle RST?

b. Write a proportion involving x by setting the ratio of two sides in triangle ABC equal to the ratio of the two corresponding sides in triangle RST.

c. Find the value of x.

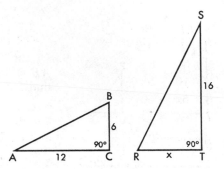

In 14–17, use the figure at the left.

14. If $BC = 3$ in., $AC = 4$ in., and $AC' = 8$ in., find $B'C'$.

15. If $AC = 5$ ft., $BC = 2$ ft., and $B'C' = 7$ ft., find AC'.

16. If $B'C' = 12$ in., $AC = 6$ in., $CC' = 3$ in., find BC.

17. If $BC = 10$ ft. and $AC = 8$ ft., find the ratio of $B'C'$ to AC'.

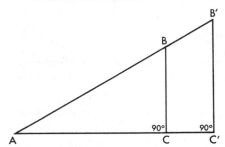

4. Using Similar Triangles in Indirect Measurement

Similar triangles may sometimes be used to discover by **indirect measurement** the measurements of line segments and angles which cannot be measured conveniently by direct measurement.

~~~~~~~~ **MODEL PROBLEM** ~~~~~~~~

At the same time that a vertical flagpole casts a shadow 10 ft. long, a nearby vertical pole that is 6 ft. high casts a shadow 5 ft. long. Find the height of the flagpole.

Solution:

1. Since the sun is at a very great distance from the earth, the sun's rays, AC and DF, are for all practical purposes parallel. Hence, $\angle A = \angle D$.

2. Since the poles are vertical, $\angle B$ and $\angle E$ are right angles. Hence, $\angle B = \angle E$.

3. Since two right triangles are similar if one pair of corresponding angles is equal, $\triangle DEF \sim \triangle ABC$.

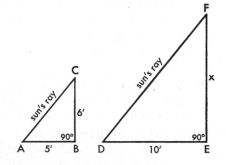

4. $\dfrac{EF}{DE} = \dfrac{BC}{AB}$ [Let x = the length of the flagpole.]

5. $\dfrac{x}{10} = \dfrac{6}{5}$

6. $5x = 60$

7. $x = 12$

Answer: The height of the flagpole is 12 ft.

~~~~~~

Exercises

1. A vertical flagpole casts a shadow 12 ft. long at the same time that a nearby vertical post 5 ft. high casts a shadow 3 ft. long. Find the height of the flagpole.

2. A vertical rod 8 ft. high casts a shadow 6 ft. long. At the same time, a nearby vertical tree casts a shadow 15 ft. long. Find the height of the tree.

3. A vertical yardstick casts a shadow $2\frac{1}{2}$ ft. long. At the same time, a nearby vertical pole casts a shadow 15 ft. long. Find the length of the pole.

4. A vertical tree casts a shadow 40 ft. long. At the same time, a nearby boy 5 ft. 6 in. tall casts a shadow 8 ft. long. Find the height of the tree.

5. In the figure, AB represents the width of a river. Angle B and angle D are right angles. AE and BD are line segments. $BC = 60'$, $CD = 30'$, and $DE = 15'$.

   a. Is triangle ABC similar to triangle CDE? Why?

   b. Find AB, the width of the river.

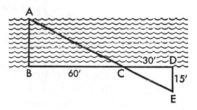

6. Using the figure in exercise 5, find AB, the width of the river, if $BC = 240'$, $CD = 80'$, and $DE = 25'$.

7. In the figure, AD and CB are line segments and $\angle ABE = \angle DCE$. Find AB, the distance across the pond, if:

   a. $CE = 40$ ft., $EB = 120$ ft., and $CD = 50$ ft.

   b. $AE = 75$ yd., $ED = 30$ yd., and $CD = 36$ yd.

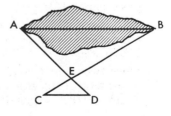

CHAPTER XXI

TRIGONOMETRY OF THE RIGHT TRIANGLE

In our study of trigonometry of the right triangle, we will develop new relations from the properties of similar triangles. These relations will provide additional methods for measuring segments and angles indirectly.

Let us review some of the facts we learned about the right triangle (pages 500 and 501).

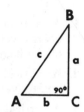

In the figure, triangle ABC is a right triangle in which angle C is the right angle. AB, the side opposite right angle C, is the hypotenuse of the right triangle; the length of AB is represented by c. The sides of the triangle which form the right angle, BC and AC, are called the *legs* of the triangle. We call BC the leg opposite angle A; the length of BC is represented by a. We call AC the leg opposite angle B; the length of AC is represented by b. We may also call AC the leg adjacent to (next to) angle A. We may also call BC the leg adjacent to (next to) angle B.

1. The Tangent Ratio

Each of the following triangles represents a right triangle in which there is a 31° angle. In each figure, the lengths of the leg opposite the 31° angle and the leg adjacent to the 31° angle are shown. In each triangle, let us find the ratio of the length of the leg opposite the 31° angle to the length of the leg adjacent to the 31° angle.

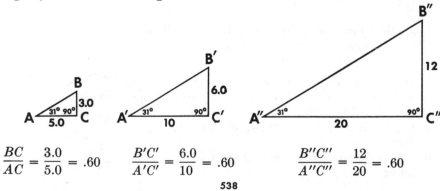

$$\frac{BC}{AC} = \frac{3.0}{5.0} = .60 \qquad \frac{B'C'}{A'C'} = \frac{6.0}{10} = .60 \qquad \frac{B''C''}{A''C''} = \frac{12}{20} = .60$$

Notice that in all three cases, the ratio is:

$$\frac{\text{length of the leg opposite the 31}^\circ \text{ angle}}{\text{length of the leg adjacent to the 31}^\circ \text{ angle}} = .60, \text{ a constant}$$

We might have expected that the three ratios $\frac{BC}{AC}, \frac{B'C'}{A'C'},$ and $\frac{B''C''}{A''C''}$ would be equal because the right triangles ABC, $A'B'C'$, and $A''B''C''$, each of which contains an angle of 31°, are similar, and the ratios of corresponding sides in these similar triangles must be equal.

In fact, in all right triangles which contain an angle of 31°, the value of the ratio $\frac{\text{length of the leg opposite the 31}^\circ \text{ angle}}{\text{length of the leg adjacent to the 31}^\circ \text{ angle}}$ is constant (approximately .60), no matter what the size of the triangle.

What we have shown to be true for a 31° angle would be true for any other acute angle in a right triangle. In general, in every right triangle having a particular acute angle, the ratio of the length of the leg opposite the acute angle to the length of the leg adjacent to the acute angle is constant. This is true because every right triangle containing a particular acute angle is similar to every other right triangle containing the same acute angle. For different acute angles, the ratio is a different constant.

In a right triangle, the ratio of the length of the leg opposite an acute angle to the length of the leg adjacent to the acute angle is called the **tangent of the angle.**

In right triangle ABC, with $\angle C = 90°$, the tangent of angle A, abbreviated "tan A," is:

$$\tan A = \frac{\text{length of leg opposite } \angle A}{\text{length of leg adjacent to } \angle A} = \frac{a}{b}$$

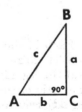

THE TABLE OF TANGENTS

As angle A changes, the tangent ratio for angle A also changes. The tangent ratio for angle A depends upon the size of angle A, not upon the size of the right triangle which contains angle A. Mathematicians have constructed a table which contains approximations of tangent ratios for all acute angles between 0° and 90°. This table, which is called a table of trigonometric functions, is found on page 582 in the fourth column.

To find tan 28° from this table, for example, first look in the column headed "Angle" for the angle 28°. Then, in the fourth column headed "Tan," on the same horizontal line as 28°, find the number .5317. Thus, tan 28° = .5317 to the *nearest ten-thousandth.*

[*Note:* Although .5317 is an approximation of tan 28°, we wrote tan 28° = .5317 rather than tan 28° ≈ .5317. In our trigonometry work, we will use "=" rather than "≈" in order to simplify the symbolism in the computations. We will keep in mind that the trigonometric ratios in the tables are approximations.]

The table may also be used to find an angle when its tangent ratio is known. Thus, if tan x = 1.5399, we see from the table that angle x must be 57°.

Sometimes the value of the tangent of an angle is not in the table. In such a case, we can approximate the value of the angle to the *nearest degree*. For example, suppose we wish to find angle x when tan x = .5000. This value is not in the table of tangent ratios. In the table, we find the number which is just larger than .5000 and the number which is just smaller than .5000, and we then discover to which of these two ratios .5000 is closer.

Angle	Tangent	Difference		
27°	.5095		.5095	.5000
		.0095	−.5000	−.4877
x	.5000		.0095	.0123
		.0123		
26°	.4877			

Since .0095 is less than .0123, then .5000 is closer to .5095 than it is to .4877.

Hence, angle x is closer to 27° than it is to 26°. We now know that angle x is 27° approximated to the *nearest degree*.

Exercises

In 1–4, name the hypotenuse, the leg opposite, and the leg adjacent to each acute angle of the right triangle.

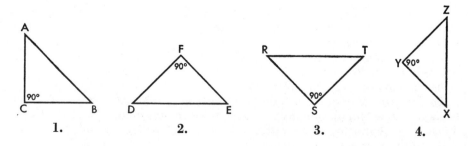

1.   2.   3.   4.

In 5–8, represent the tangent ratio for each acute angle.

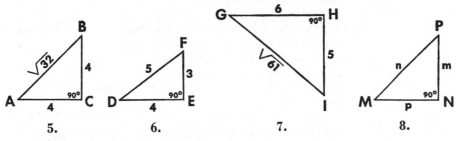

5.   **6.**   **7.**   **8.**

9. In triangle ABC, $\angle C = 90°$, $AC = 6$, and $AB = 10$. Find $\tan A$.
10. In triangle RST, $\angle T = 90°$, $RS = 13$, and $ST = 12$. Find $\tan S$.

In 11–15, use the table on page 582 to find:
11. $\tan 15°$ **12.** $\tan 32°$ **13.** $\tan 45°$ **14.** $\tan 74°$ **15.** $\tan 89°$

In 16–21, use the table on page 582 to find angle x if:
16. $\tan x = .1763$ **17.** $\tan x = .3443$ **18.** $\tan x = .8098$
19. $\tan x = 1.0000$ **20.** $\tan x = 2.3559$ **21.** $\tan x = 4.3315$

In 22–27, use the table on page 582 to find angle x to the *nearest degree* if:
22. $\tan x = .3285$ **23.** $\tan x = .7773$ **24.** $\tan x = 1.4000$
25. $\tan x = .2281$ **26.** $\tan x = 3.6231$ **27.** $\tan x = 2.3604$

28. *a.* Use the table on page 582 to discover whether $\tan 80°$ is twice $\tan 40°$.
   b. If an angle is doubled, is the tangent of the angle also doubled?
29. In triangle ABC, $\angle C = 90°$, $AC = 5$, and $BC = 5$.
   a. Find $\tan A$.   *b.* Find angle A.
30. In triangle RST, $\angle S = 90°$, $TS = 4$, and $RS = 3$.
   a. Find $\tan T$ to the *nearest ten-thousandth*.
   b. Find angle T to the *nearest degree*.

ANGLE OF ELEVATION AND ANGLE OF DEPRESSION

In the figure at the right, if a person using a telescope or some similar instrument wishes to sight the top of the telephone pole above him, he must elevate (raise) the instrument from a horizontal position. The line OT from the eye of the observer, O, to the top of the pole, T, is called the **line of sight**. The angle determined by the horizontal line and the line of sight, $\angle AOT$, is called the **angle of elevation** of the top of the pole, T, from point O.
(The horizontal line and the line of sight must be in the same vertical plane.)

In the figure at the right, if a person using a telescope or some similar instrument wishes to sight the boat below him, he must depress (press down) the instrument from a horizontal position. The line OB from the eye of the observer, O, to the boat, B, is called the line of sight. The angle determined by the horizontal line and the line of sight, $\angle HOB$, is called the **angle of depression** of the boat, B, from point O. (The horizontal line and the line of sight must be in the same vertical plane.)

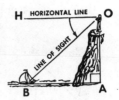

In the preceding figure, if we find the angle of elevation of O from B, $\angle OBA$, and also find the angle of depression of B from O, $\angle HOB$, we discover that both angles contain the same number of degrees. We therefore say that the angle of elevation of O from B is equal to the angle of depression of B from O.

USING THE TANGENT RATIO TO SOLVE PROBLEMS

Procedure. To solve problems by use of the tangent ratio:
1. **Make an approximate scale drawing which contains the line segments and angles given in the problem and those to be found.**
2. **Select a right triangle in which either (*a*) two legs are given (known) and an acute angle is to be found or (*b*) one leg and an acute angle are given (known) and the other leg is to be found.**
3. **Write the formula for the tangent of the acute angle mentioned in step 2, and then substitute in the formula the values given in the problem.**
4. **Solve the resulting equation.**

～～～～～～～ MODEL PROBLEMS ～～～～～～～

1. At a point on the ground 40 feet from the foot of a tree, the angle of elevation of the top of the tree is 42°. Find the height of the tree to the *nearest foot*.

   Solution: Since the segments mentioned in the problem are legs of a right triangle opposite and adjacent to the given acute angle, use the tangent ratio.

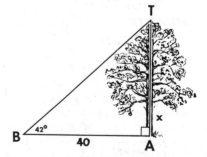

1. $\tan B = \dfrac{\text{length of leg opposite } \angle B}{\text{length of leg adjacent to } \angle B}$

2. $\tan B = \dfrac{AT}{BA}$ Let x = the length of AT.

3. $\tan 42° = \dfrac{x}{40}$ In the table on page 582, $\tan 42° = .9004$.

4. $.9004 = \dfrac{x}{40}$

5. $x = 40(.9004)$ M_{40}

6. $x = 36.016$

Answer: AT, the height of the tree, is equal to 36 feet.

2. A ladder which is leaning against a building makes an angle of 75° with the ground. If the top of the ladder reaches a point which is 20 feet above the ground, find to the *nearest foot* the distance from the foot of the ladder to the foot of the building.

Solution:

Method 1	*Method 2*

Method 1

1. $\tan A = \dfrac{BC}{AC}$

Let x = the length of AC.

2. $\tan 75° = \dfrac{20}{x}$

3. $3.7321 = \dfrac{20}{x}$

4. $3.7321x = 20$ M_x

5. $x = \dfrac{20}{3.7321}$ $D_{3.7321}$

6. $x = 5.3$

Method 2

Find angle B.

1. $\angle B = 90° - 75° = 15°$

2. $\tan B = \dfrac{AC}{BC}$

Let x = the length of AC.

3. $\tan 15° = \dfrac{x}{20}$

4. $.2679 = \dfrac{x}{20}$

5. $x = 20(.2679)$ M_{20}

6. $x = 5.3580$

Answer: 5 feet

[*Note:* In method 1, since the unknown was the leg adjacent to ∠A, the solution required the inconvenient long division $\dfrac{20}{3.7321}$. In method 2, however, when we used the other acute angle, ∠B, the unknown was the leg opposite ∠B; and the solution required the convenient multiplication 20(.2679).]

3. Find to the *nearest degree* the angle of elevation of the sun when a vertical pole 6 feet high casts a shadow 8 feet long.

Solution: The angle of elevation of the sun is the same as ∠A, the angle of elevation of the top of the pole from A. Since the segments mentioned in the problem are legs of a right triangle opposite and adjacent to ∠A, use the tangent ratio.

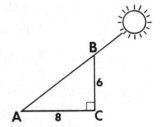

1. $\tan A = \dfrac{\text{length of leg opposite } \angle A}{\text{length of leg adjacent to } \angle A}$

2. $\tan A = \frac{6}{8}$ Express $\frac{6}{8}$ as the decimal .7500.

3. $\tan A = .7500$ In the table on page 582, tan 36° = .7265 and

4. $A = 37°$ tan 37° = .7536. Since .7500 is closer to .7536 than it is to .7265, ∠A is closer to 37°.

Answer: 37°

Exercises

In 1–8, find the line marked x to the *nearest foot* or the angle marked x to the *nearest degree*.

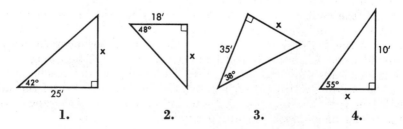

     1.   **2.**   **3.**   **4.**

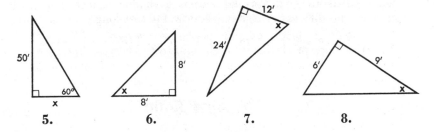

5.   **6.**   **7.**   **8.**

9. At a point on the ground 50 feet from the foot of a tree, the angle of elevation of the top of the tree is 48°. Find the height of the tree to the *nearest foot*.
10. At a point on the ground 250 feet from the base of a tower, the angle of elevation of its top is 32°. Find to the *nearest foot* the height of the tower.
11. A ladder is leaning against a wall. The foot of the ladder is 6.5 feet from the wall. The ladder makes an angle of 74° with the level ground. How high on the wall does the ladder reach? Round off the answer to the *nearest tenth of a foot*.
12. A boy visiting New York City views the Empire State Building from a point on the ground, A, which is 940 feet from the foot, C, of the building. The angle of elevation of the top, B, of the building as seen by the boy is 53°. Find the height of the building to the *nearest foot*.
13. Find to the *nearest foot* the height of a vertical post if its shadow is 18 feet long when the angle of elevation of the sun is 38°.
14. A tree casts a 60-foot shadow at the time when the sun's rays make an angle of 42° with the ground. Find the height of the tree to the *nearest foot*.
15. From the top of a lighthouse 160 feet high, the angle of depression of a boat out at sea is 24°. Find to the *nearest foot* the distance from the boat to the foot of the lighthouse, the foot being at sea level.
16. From the top of a tower 80 feet high, the angle of depression of an object on the ground is 38°. Find to the *nearest foot* the distance from the object to the foot of the tower.
17. Find to the *nearest degree* the angle of elevation of the sun when a boy 5 feet high casts a shadow 5 feet long.
18. Find to the *nearest degree* the angle of elevation of the sun when a vertical post 15 feet high casts a shadow 20 feet long.
19. Find to the *nearest degree* the angle which the sun's rays make with the ground when a flagpole 40 feet high casts a shadow 30 feet long.
20. A ladder leans against a building. The top of the ladder reaches a point on the building which is 18 feet above the ground. The foot of the ladder is 7 feet from the building. Find to the *nearest degree* the angle which the ladder makes with the level ground.

.21. When a yardstick held vertically casts a shadow 7 feet long on level ground, a flagpole nearby casts a shadow 140 feet long.

    a. Find the height of the flagpole to the *nearest foot.*

    b. Find the angle of elevation of the sun to the *nearest degree.*

2. The Sine Ratio

Each of the following triangles represents a right triangle in which an acute angle is 30°. Therefore, the triangles are similar and the ratios of corresponding sides must be equal. In each triangle, let us find the ratio of the length of the leg opposite the 30° angle to the length of the hypotenuse.

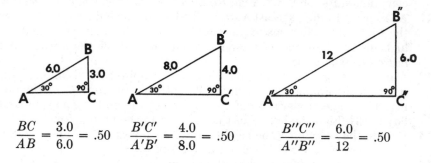

$$\frac{BC}{AB} = \frac{3.0}{6.0} = .50 \qquad \frac{B'C'}{A'B'} = \frac{4.0}{8.0} = .50 \qquad \frac{B''C''}{A''B''} = \frac{6.0}{12} = .50$$

In all three triangles shown, and in any right triangle in which an acute angle is 30°, the ratio $\dfrac{\text{length of the leg opposite the 30° angle}}{\text{length of the hypotenuse}} = .50$, a constant. In right triangles which contain an acute angle other than 30°, this ratio would still be a constant, the value of the constant depending upon the number of degrees in the particular acute angle.

In a right triangle, the ratio of the length of a leg opposite an acute angle to the length of the hypotenuse is called the **sine of the angle.**

In right triangle ABC, with $\angle C = 90°$, the sine of angle A, abbreviated "sin A," is:

$$\sin A = \frac{\text{length of leg opposite } \angle A}{\text{length of hypotenuse}} = \frac{a}{c}$$

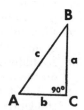

THE TABLE OF SINES

As angle A changes, the sine ratio for angle A also changes. The sine ratio for angle A depends upon the size of angle A, not upon the size of the right triangle which contains angle A. The table containing approximations of sine ratios which mathematicians have constructed for all acute angles between $0°$ and $90°$ is found on page 582 in the second column.

If we use this table as we did when we studied the tangent ratio, we can obtain the following results:

1. $\sin 25° = .4226$.
2. If $\sin x = .7660$, angle $x = 50°$.
3. If $\sin x = .2500$, angle $x = 14°$ to the *nearest degree* because .2500 is closer to .2419, which is $\sin 14°$, than it is to .2588, which is $\sin 15°$.

Exercises

In 1–4, represent the sine of each acute angle.

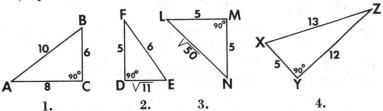

1.   **2.**   **3.**   **4.**

5. In triangle ABC, $\angle C = 90°$, $AC = 4$, and $BC = 3$. Find $\sin A$.
6. In triangle RST, $\angle S = 90°$, $RS = 5$, and $ST = 12$. Find $\sin T$.

In 7–11, use the table on page 582 to find:
7. $\sin 18°$ **8.** $\sin 42°$ **9.** $\sin 58°$ **10.** $\sin 76°$ **11.** $\sin 89°$

In 12–14, use the table on page 582 to find angle x if:
12. $\sin x = .1908$ **13.** $\sin x = .8387$ **14.** $\sin x = .6561$

In 15–17, use the table on page 582 to find angle x to the *nearest degree* if:
15. $\sin x = .1900$ **16.** $\sin x = .8740$ **17.** $\sin x = .1275$

18. *a.* Use the table on page 582 to discover whether $\sin 50°$ is twice $\sin 25°$.
   b. If an angle is doubled, is the sine of the angle also doubled?
19. In triangle ABC, $\angle C = 90°$, $BC = 20$, and $BA = 40$.   (*a*) Find $\sin A$ to the *nearest ten-thousandth*.   (*b*) Find angle A.
20. In triangle ABC, $\angle C = 90°$, $AC = 5$, and $BC = 12$.   (*a*) Find $\sin B$ to the *nearest ten-thousandth*.   (*b*) Find angle B to the *nearest degree*.

USING THE SINE RATIO TO SOLVE PROBLEMS

When the hypotenuse, a leg, and an acute angle of a right triangle are involved in a problem, with any two of these three parts given (known), the use of the sine ratio will help us to find the unknown third part. We proceed as we did when we were using the tangent ratio.

~~~~~~~~~~ **MODEL PROBLEMS** ~~~~~~~~~~

1. A boy who is flying a kite lets out 300 feet of string which makes an angle of 38° with the ground. Assuming that the string is straight, how high above the ground is the kite? [Give the answer correct to the *nearest foot.*]

Solution: Since the segments mentioned in the problem are the leg opposite the acute angle and the hypotenuse of the right triangle, use the sine ratio.

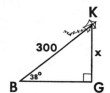

1. $\sin B = \dfrac{\text{length of leg opposite } \angle B}{\text{length of hypotenuse}}$

2. $\sin B = \dfrac{KG}{KB}$ Let x = the length of KG.

3. $\sin 38° = \dfrac{x}{300}$ In the table on page 582, $\sin 38° = .6157$.

4. $.6157 = \dfrac{x}{300}$

5. $x = 300(.6157)$ M_{300}
6. $x = 184.71$

Answer: 185 feet

2. A road is inclined 8° to the horizontal. Find to the *nearest hundred feet* the distance one must drive up this road to increase one's altitude 1000 feet.

Solution: Since the segments mentioned in the problem are the leg opposite the acute angle and the hypotenuse of the right triangle, use the sine ratio.

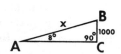

1. $\sin A = \dfrac{\text{length of leg opposite } \angle A}{\text{length of hypotenuse}}$

2. $\sin A = \dfrac{BC}{AB}$ Let x = the length of AB.

3. $\sin 8° = \dfrac{1000}{x}$ In the table on page 582, $\sin 8° = .1392$.

4. $.1392 = \dfrac{1000}{x}$

5. $.1392x = 1000$ M_x

6. $x = \dfrac{1000}{.1392}$ $D_{.1392}$

7. $x = 7184$

Answer: 7200 feet

---

3. A ladder 25 feet long leans against a building and reaches a point 23.5 feet above the ground. Find to the *nearest degree* the angle which the ladder makes with the ground.

Solution: Since the given segments are the hypotenuse and the leg opposite the acute angle to be found, use the sine ratio.

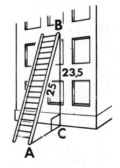

1. $\sin A = \dfrac{\text{length of leg opposite } \angle A}{\text{length of hypotenuse}}$

2. $\sin A = \dfrac{23.5}{25}$ Change $\dfrac{23.5}{25}$ to the decimal .9400.

3. $\sin A = .9400$ In the table on page 582, $\sin 70° = .9397$ and
4. $A = 70°$ $\sin 71° = .9455$. Since .9400 is closer to .9397 than it is to .9455, $\angle A$ is closer to 70°.

Answer: 70°

Exercises

In 1–8, find the line marked x to the *nearest foot* or the angle marked x to the *nearest degree*.

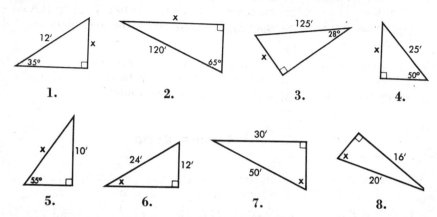

1.   **2.**   **3.**   **4.**

5.   **6.**   **7.**   **8.**

9. A wooden beam 24 feet long leans against a wall and makes an angle of 71° with the ground. Find to the *nearest foot* how high up the wall the beam reaches.

10. A boy who is flying a kite lets out 300 feet of string which makes an angle of 52° with the ground. Assuming that the string is stretched taut, find to the *nearest foot* how high the kite is above the ground.

11. A straight road to the top of a hill is 2500 feet long and makes an angle of 12° with the horizontal. Find the height of the hill to the *nearest hundred feet*.

12. A straight road is inclined at an angle of 10° to the horizontal. If a man drove a distance of 2000 feet up the road, find to the *nearest hundred feet* his increase in altitude.

13. A ladder which leans against a building makes an angle of 75° with the ground and reaches a point on the building 20 feet above the ground. Find to the *nearest foot* the length of the ladder.

14. From an airplane which is flying at an altitude of 3000 feet, the angle of depression of an airport ground signal is 27°. Find to the *nearest hundred feet* the distance between the airplane and the airport signal.

15. An airplane climbs at an angle of 11° with the ground. Find to the *nearest hundred feet* the distance it has traveled when it has attained an altitude of 400 feet.

16. A 20-foot pole which is leaning against a wall reaches a point 18 feet above the ground. Find to the *nearest degree* the angle which the pole makes with the ground.

17. In order to reach the top of a hill which is 250 feet high, one must travel 2000 feet up a straight road which leads to the top. Find to the *nearest degree* the number of degrees in the angle which the road makes with the horizontal.

18. After takeoff, a plane flies in a straight line for a distance of 4000 feet in order to gain an altitude of 800 feet. Find to the *nearest degree* the angle which the rising plane makes with the ground.

3. The Cosine Ratio

Each of the following triangles represents a right triangle in which an acute angle is 53°. Therefore, the triangles are similar and the ratios of corresponding sides must be equal. In each triangle, let us find the ratio of the length of the leg adjacent to the 53° angle to the length of the hypotenuse.

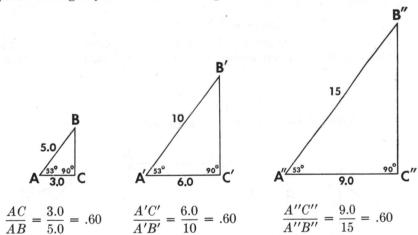

$$\frac{AC}{AB} = \frac{3.0}{5.0} = .60 \qquad \frac{A'C'}{A'B'} = \frac{6.0}{10} = .60 \qquad \frac{A''C''}{A''B''} = \frac{9.0}{15} = .60$$

In all three triangles shown, and in any right triangle in which an acute angle is 53°, the ratio $\dfrac{\text{length of the leg adjacent to the 53° angle}}{\text{length of the hypotenuse}} = .60$, a constant. In right triangles which contain an acute angle other than 53°, this ratio would still be a constant, the value of the constant depending upon the number of degrees in the particular acute angle.

In a right triangle, the ratio of the length of a leg adjacent to an acute angle to the length of the hypotenuse is called the *cosine of the angle.*

In right triangle ABC, with $\angle C = 90°$, the cosine of angle A, abbreviated "cos A," is:

$$\cos A = \frac{\text{length of leg adjacent to } \angle A}{\text{length of hypotenuse}} = \frac{b}{c}$$

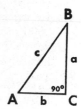

THE TABLE OF COSINES

As angle A changes, the cosine ratio for angle A also changes. The cosine ratio for angle A depends upon the size of angle A, not upon the size of the right triangle which contains angle A. The table containing approximations of cosine ratios which mathematicians have constructed for all acute angles between 0° and 90° is found on page 582 in the third column.

If we use this table as we did when we studied the tangent ratio, we can obtain the following results:

1. $\cos 55° = .5736$.
2. If $\cos x = .9063$, angle $x = 25°$.
3. If $\cos x = .3300$, angle $x = 71°$ to the *nearest degree* because .3300 is closer to .3256, which is cos 71°, than it is to .3420, which is cos 70°.

Exercises

In 1–4, represent the cosine of each acute angle.

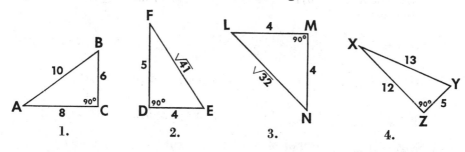

5. In triangle ABC, $\angle C = 90°$, $AC = 4$, and $BC = 3$. Find cos A.
6. In triangle RST, $\angle S = 90°$, $RS = 5$, and $ST = 12$. Find cos T.

In 7–11, use the table on page 582 to find the following:
7. cos 21°   **8.** cos 40°   **9.** cos 67°   **10.** cos 74°   **11.** cos 88°

In 12–14, use the table on page 582 to find angle x if:

12. $\cos x = .9397$ **13.** $\cos x = .3584$ **14.** $\cos x = .0698$

In 15–17, use the table on page 582 to find angle x to the *nearest degree* if:

15. $\cos x = .9750$ **16.** $\cos x = .5934$ **17.** $\cos x = .2968$

18. *a.* Use the table on page 582 to discover whether cos 80° is twice cos 40°.
    b. If an angle is doubled, is the cosine of the angle also doubled?

19. In triangle ABC, $\angle C = 90°$, $AC = 40$, and $AB = 80$.   (*a*) Find cos A to the *nearest ten-thousandth.*   (*b*) Find angle A.

USING THE COSINE RATIO TO SOLVE PROBLEMS

When the leg adjacent to an acute angle in a right triangle and the hypotenuse of the right triangle are involved in a problem, the use of the cosine ratio will help us find the length of one of these sides when the length of the other side and the acute angle are given. We proceed as we did when we were using the tangent ratio or the sine ratio.

～～～～～ MODEL PROBLEMS ～～～～～

1. A plane took off from a field and rose at an angle of 8° with the horizontal ground. Find to the *nearest ten feet* the horizontal distance the plane had covered when it had flown 2000 feet.

Solution: Since the segments mentioned in the problem are the leg adjacent to an acute angle of the right triangle and the hypotenuse of the triangle, use the cosine ratio.

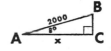

1. $\cos A = \dfrac{\text{length of leg adjacent to } \angle A}{\text{length of hypotenuse}}$

2. $\cos A = \dfrac{AC}{AB}$ Let x = the length of AC.

3. $\cos 8° = \dfrac{x}{2000}$ In the table on page 582, cos 8° = .9903.

4. $.9903 = \dfrac{x}{2000}$

5. $x = 2000(.9903)$ M_{2000}

6. $x = 1980.6$

Answer: 1980 feet

2. A guy wire reaches from the top of a pole to a stake in the ground. The stake is 10 feet from the foot of the pole. The wire makes an angle of 65° with the ground. Find to the *nearest foot* the length of the wire.

Solution: Since the segments mentioned in the problem are the leg adjacent to the acute angle and the hypotenuse of the right triangle, use the cosine ratio.

1. $\cos S = \dfrac{\text{length of leg adjacent to } \angle S}{\text{length of hypotenuse}}$

2. $\cos S = \dfrac{BS}{ST}$ Let x = length of ST.

3. $\cos 65° = \dfrac{10}{x}$ In the table on page 582, cos 65° = .4226.

4. $.4226 = \dfrac{10}{x}$

5. $.4226x = 10$ M_x

6. $x = \dfrac{10}{.4226}$ $D_{.4226}$

7. $x = 23.6$

Answer: 24 feet

~~~~~~

Exercises

In 1–4, find the line marked x to the *nearest foot* or the angle marked x to the *nearest degree*.

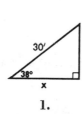
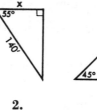
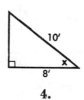

1.   **2.**   **3.**   **4.**

5. A 20-foot ladder leans against a building and makes an angle of 72° with the ground. Find to the *nearest foot* the distance between the foot of the ladder and the building.

6. A man walked 2500 feet along a straight road which is inclined 12° to the horizontal. Find to the *nearest foot* the horizontal distance traveled by the man.

7. A guy wire attached to the top of a pole reaches a stake in the ground 20 feet from the foot of the pole and makes an angle of 58° with the ground. Find to the *nearest foot* the length of the guy wire.

8. An airplane rises at an angle of 14° with the ground. Find to the *nearest 10 feet* the distance it has flown when it has covered a horizontal distance of 1500 feet.

9. Henry is flying a kite. The kite string makes an angle of 43° with the ground. If Henry is standing 100 feet from a point on the ground directly below the kite, find to the *nearest foot* the length of the kite string.

10. A 30-foot steel girder is leaning against a wall. The foot of the girder is 20 feet from the wall. Find to the *nearest degree* the angle which the girder makes with the ground.

11. A plane took off from an airport. When the plane had flown 4000 feet in the direction in which it had taken off, it had covered a horizontal distance of 3900 feet. Find to the *nearest degree* the angle at which the plane rose from the ground.

12. A 40-ft. ladder which is leaning against a wall reaches the wall at a point 36 ft. from the ground. Find to the *nearest degree* the angle which the ladder makes with the wall.

4. Using All Three Trigonometric Ratios

When solving a problem by trigonometry, first make a drawing showing the parts that are given and the part to be found. Then use the proper ratio which relates the part that is to be found and the two parts that are given.

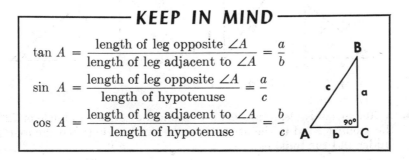

KEEP IN MIND

$$\tan A = \frac{\text{length of leg opposite } \angle A}{\text{length of leg adjacent to } \angle A} = \frac{a}{b}$$

$$\sin A = \frac{\text{length of leg opposite } \angle A}{\text{length of hypotenuse}} = \frac{a}{c}$$

$$\cos A = \frac{\text{length of leg adjacent to } \angle A}{\text{length of hypotenuse}} = \frac{b}{c}$$

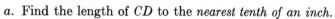

MODEL PROBLEM

In isosceles triangle ABC, $AC = CB = 20$ inches. $\angle A =$ $\angle B = 68°$. CD is perpendicular to AB ($\angle CDB$ is a right angle). $AD = DB$.

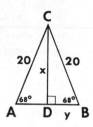

a. Find the length of CD to the *nearest tenth of an inch*.
b. Find the length of AB to the *nearest tenth of an inch*.

Solution:

a. 1. Let $x =$ the length of CD.
   2. In right $\triangle BDC$,
$$\sin B = \frac{CD}{CB}$$
   3. $\sin 68° = \dfrac{x}{20}$

   4. $.9272 = \dfrac{x}{20}$

   5. $x = 20(.9272)$
   6. $x = 18.5440$
   7. $x = 18.5$

Answer: $CD = 18.5$ inches

b. We will find DB in right $\triangle BDC$ and double its length to find AB.
   1. Let $y =$ the length of DB.
   2. In right triangle BDC,
$$\cos B = \frac{DB}{CB}$$
   3. $\cos 68° = \dfrac{y}{20}$

   4. $.3746 = \dfrac{y}{20}$

   5. $y = 20(.3746)$
   6. $y = 7.4920$
   7. $AB = 2y = 2(7.4920) = 14.9840$
   8. $AB = 15.0$

Answer: $AB = 15.0$ inches

Exercises

Exercises 1–7 refer to right $\triangle ABC$. Name the ratio that can be used to find:

1. side a when angle A and side c are given
2. side b when angle A and side c are given
3. side c when side a and angle A are given
4. side b when side a and angle B are given
5. angle A when side a and side b are given
6. angle B when side a and side c are given
7. side a when side b and angle A are given

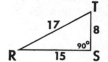

Exercises 8–13 refer to $\triangle RST$. In each exercise, give the value of the ratio as a fraction.

8. sin R **9.** tan T **10.** sin T
11. cos R **12.** cos T **13.** tan R

In 14–25, find the line marked x to the *nearest foot* or the angle marked x to the *nearest degree*.

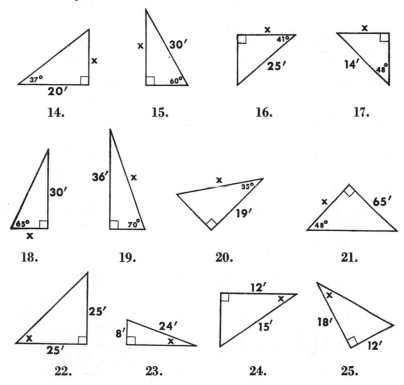

14.   **15.**   **16.**   **17.**

18.   **19.**   **20.**   **21.**

22.   **23.**   **24.**   **25.**

26. A monument stands on level ground. The angle of elevation of the top of the monument, taken at a point 425 feet from the foot of the monument, is 32°. Find the height of the monument to the *nearest foot*.

27. A boy flying a kite lets out 150 feet of string that makes an angle of 64° with the ground. Assuming that the string is straight, find to the *nearest foot* how high the kite is above the ground.

28. A 25-foot guy wire attached to the top of a pole makes an angle of 62° with the ground. Find to the *nearest foot* the distance between the point where the guy wire meets the ground and the foot of the pole.

29. A boy walked 400 feet into a tunnel which slopes downward at an angle of 7° with the horizontal ground. Find to the *nearest ten feet* how far he was beneath the surface.

30. An airplane *A* is 1000 feet above the ground and directly over a church *C*. The angle of elevation of the plane as seen by a boy at a point *B* on the ground some distance from the church is 22°. Find to the *nearest foot:*
  a. how far the boy is from the church
  b. how far the boy is from the plane

31. An observer in a balloon which is 2000 feet above an airport finds that the angle of depression of a steamer out at sea is 21°. Find to the *nearest hundred feet* the distance between the balloon and the steamer.

32. A plane takes off from a field and climbs at an angle of 12°. Find to the *nearest 100 feet* how far the plane must fly to be at an altitude of 1200 feet.

33. Find to the *nearest degree* the angle of elevation of the sun when a tree 24 feet high casts a shadow of 36 feet.

34. A 40-foot ladder is leaning against a building. The foot of the ladder is 32 feet from the building. Find to the *nearest degree* the angle which the ladder makes with the ground.

35. A railroad track slopes upward at an angle of 7° to the horizontal. Find to the *nearest ten feet* the vertical distance it rises in a horizontal distance of 1 mile (5280 feet).

36. From the top of a cliff 450 feet above sea level, the angle of depression of a boat out at sea is 24°. Find to the *nearest foot* the distance through the air from the top of the cliff to the boat.

37. A television tower is 150 feet high and an observer is 120 feet from the base of the tower. Find to the *nearest degree* the angle of elevation of the top of the tower from the point where the observer is standing.

38. The figure at the right represents a view of the roof of a wing of a house. *DB*, the altitude of triangle *ACD*, is 8 feet. Each of the rafters *AD* and *DC* is 15 feet. Find to the *nearest degree* the angle that each rafter makes with *AC*, the base of the triangle.

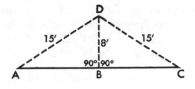

39. In isosceles triangle *ABC*, *AC* and *CB* are each 15 inches. ∠*A* and ∠*B* are each 55°. *AD* = *DB*.

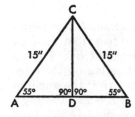

a. Find *CD* to the *nearest tenth of an inch.*
b. Find *AD* to the *nearest tenth of an inch.*
c. Find the area of triangle *ABC* to the *nearest square inch.*

40. In rectangle *ABCD*, diagonal *AC*, which is 20 inches in length, makes an angle of 35° with the base *AB*.

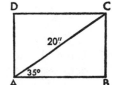

a. Find *AB*, the base of the rectangle, to the *nearest tenth of an inch.*
b. Find *BC*, the altitude of the rectangle, to the *nearest tenth of an inch.*
c. Find the area of the rectangle to the *nearest square inch.*

41. In a rectangle *ABCD*, *AB* = 40 feet and *BC* = 30 feet.

a. Find to the *nearest degree* the angle which diagonal *AC* makes with side *AB*.
b. Find to the *nearest degree* the angle which diagonal *AC* makes with side *AD*.
c. What is a good way to check the answers found in part *a* and part *b*?

42. In a triangle *ABC*, base *BC* = 100 inches, side *AB* = 40 inches, and angle *B* = 62°.

a. Find the altitude to base *BC* to the *nearest tenth of an inch.*
b. Find the area of triangle *ABC* to the *nearest square inch.*

43. In the figure, AB is a chord in circle O. OC is perpendicular to AB at its midpoint C ($\angle OCA = 90°$, $AC = CB$). If radius $OA = 20$ in. and $\angle OAC = 27°$, find:

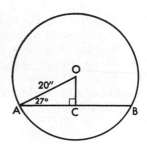

   a. the length of OC to the *nearest tenth of an inch*

   b. the length of AB to the *nearest tenth of an inch*

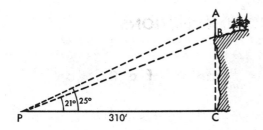

44. In the diagram, P represents a point 310 feet from the foot of a vertical cliff BC. AB is a flagpole standing on the edge of the cliff. At P the angle of elevation of B is 21°; the angle of elevation of A is 25°. Find to the *nearest foot:*

   a. the distance AC

   b. the length of the flagpole AB

45. From the top of a lighthouse 100 feet above sea level, the angles of depression of two boats in line with the foot of the lighthouse are observed to be 18° and 32° respectively. Find to the *nearest foot* the distance between the boats.

CHAPTER XXII

RELATIONS AND FUNCTIONS

1. Understanding the Meaning of a Relation

Consider the following set: All squares, the lengths of whose sides are a whole number of inches less than 4. When we measure the length of a side, S, and the perimeter, P, we find for the squares in this set:

When $S = 1$ in., $P = 4$ in.
When $S = 2$ in., $P = 8$ in.
When $S = 3$ in., $P = 12$ in.

These results can be represented by the set of ordered number pairs $R = \{(1, 4), (2, 8), (3, 12)\}$ in which the first element of each pair represents the number of inches in the length of the square and the second element represents the number of inches in the perimeter of the square.

A set of ordered pairs is called a *relation.*

Observe that in each ordered pair of set R, the second element, P, is 4 times the first element, S. Therefore, the formula $P = 4S$ describes how the elements in each ordered pair are related. This formula is called the *rule of the relation.* The rule of a relation is a rule which can be used to determine the second element that must be paired with the first element of every ordered pair of the relation.

It is not always possible to describe a relation by a rule. For example, there is no rule which describes the relation:

$$R = \{(\text{Helen}, 85), (\text{Sue}, 73), (\text{Ann}, 80), (\text{Iris}, 90)\}$$

In this relation, the first element of each ordered pair of the relation represents the name of a girl and the second element represents the number of pounds she weighs.

In the figure, we see the graph of the relation $R =$ $\{(1, 4), (2, 8), (3, 12)\}$, which consists of three points. These points are also the graph of the formula $P = 4S$ when S is a natural number less than 4.

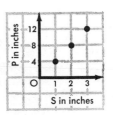

Thus, a relation may be described in one or more ways: (1) by a set of ordered pairs   (2) by a rule stated as a word sentence   (3) by a rule stated as a formula (4) by a graph.

In a relation, the set of numbers from which the first element of each ordered pair is selected is called the **domain** of the relation. The set of second elements of the ordered pairs in the relation is called the **range** of the relation. For example, in the relation $\{(1, 4), (2, 8), (3, 12)\}$, the set of first elements $\{1, 2, 3\}$ is the domain of the relation; the set of second elements $\{4, 8, 12\}$ is the range of the relation.

Now consider the set of squares, the lengths of whose sides are all non-negative numbers of inches. There are an unlimited number of ordered pairs in this relation, some of which are $(4, 16)$, $(10\frac{1}{2}, 42)$, $(11.3, 45.2)$, $(\sqrt{2}, 4\sqrt{2})$, etc. The relation is an infinite set of ordered pairs, and cannot be described by listing its elements. However, the relation can be described by the rule $P = 4S$ because this rule tells us how to assign a second number P to any first number S in every ordered pair of the relation. The domain, or the **domain of definition,** of this relation is the set of non-negative numbers and the range is also the set of non-negative numbers. The graph of this relation is a ray, as shown in the following figure.

We can also use the brace set notation to describe the relation we are discussing. We can write: $\{(S, P) \mid P = 4S\}$, which is read "The set of all ordered pairs (S, P) such that $P = 4S$." (S and P are members of the set of non-negative numbers.)

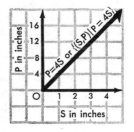

Let us consider the open sentence $y > x + 1$, with the replacement set for both x and y being $\{0, 1, 2, 3, 4\}$. The only ordered number pairs that satisfy $y > x + 1$ are $(0, 2), (0, 3), (0, 4), (1, 3), (1, 4), (2, 4)$. These ordered number pairs are members of a relation. Since each ordered number pair of this relation must satisfy the rule $y > x + 1$, the relation is really the solution set for this rule.

Suppose the sentence $y > x + 1$ has as the replacement set for both x and y the set of real numbers. There are now an infinite number of ordered number pairs in the solution set. This solution set, or relation, which is defined by the rule $y > x + 1$, can be represented in set notation as $\{(x, y) \mid y > x + 1\}$. ($x$ and y are members of the set of real numbers.)

~~~~~~~~~~~~~~~ *MODEL PROBLEMS* ~~~~~~~~~~~~~~~

1. For the relation $\{(0, 0), (1, 1), (2, 4), (3, 9)\}$:

    a. Give the domain of the relation.

    b. Give the range of the relation.

Solution:

    a. Since the domain of this relation is the set whose members are the first elements of the given ordered pairs, the domain of this relation is $\{0, 1, 2, 3\}$.   *Ans.*

    b. Since the range of this relation is the set whose members are the second elements of the given ordered pairs, the range of this relation is $\{0, 1, 4, 9\}$.   *Ans.*

2. If the replacement set for both x and y is $\{1, 2, 3, 4, 5\}$:

    a. List the set of all the ordered pairs in the relation described by the rule $y = 2x + 1$.

    b. State the domain of the relation.

    c. State the range of the relation.

    d. Graph the relation in the Cartesian plane.

Solution:

    a. The rule is $y = 2x + 1$.

        If $x = 1$, then $y = 2 \times 1 + 1$, or 3, which is a member of $\{1, 2, 3, 4, 5\}$.

        If $x = 2$, then $y = 2 \times 2 + 1$, or 5, which is a member of $\{1, 2, 3, 4, 5\}$.

        If $x = 3$, then $y = 2 \times 3 + 1$, or 7, which is not a member of $\{1, 2, 3, 4, 5\}$.

        If $x = 4$, then $y = 2 \times 4 + 1$, or 9, which is not a member of $\{1, 2, 3, 4, 5\}$.

        If $x = 5$, then $y - 2 \times 5 + 1$, or 11, which is not a member of $\{1, 2, 3, 4, 5\}$.

        Therefore, the relation is $\{(1, 3), (2, 5)\}$.   *Ans.*

    b. The domain is $\{1, 2\}$.   *Ans.*

    c. The range is $\{3, 5\}$.   *Ans.*

    d. The graph of the relation $\{(1, 3), (2, 5)\}$ is the set of two points whose coordinates are $(1, 3)$ and $(2, 5)$. Members of the domain are represented by points on the horizontal axis, the x-axis. Members of the range are represented by points on the vertical axis, the y-axis.

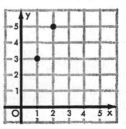

3. *a.* Write the rule for the relation {(1, 6), (2, 12), (3, 18), (4, 24), (5, 30)}, which can also be arranged in tabular form as shown.

x	1	2	3	4	5
y	6	12	18	24	30

    b. Give the domain and range of the relation.

Solution:

    a. Let x represent the first element of each ordered pair; let y represent the second element. Note that the second number of each ordered pair, y, is 6 times the first number of the pair, x. For example, $6 = 6 \times 1$, $12 = 6 \times 2$, $18 = 6 \times 3$, etc. Therefore, the rule for the relation is $y = 6x$.   *Ans.*

    b. The domain is {1, 2, 3, 4, 5}.   *Ans.*
       The range is {6, 12, 18, 24, 30}.   *Ans.*

Exercises

In 1–6:   (*a*) Give the domain of the relation.   (*b*) Give the range of the relation.   (*c*) Graph the relation in the Cartesian plane.

1. {(1, 3), (2, 6), (3, 9), (4, 12)}

2. {(5, 7), (6, 8), (7, 9), (8, 10)}

3. {(20, 15), (15, 10), (10, 5), (5, 0)}

4. {(2, −4), (3, −6), (4, −8), (5, −10)}

5. {(0, 0), (1, 1), (2, 4), (3, 9)}

6. {(0, 3), (4, 0), (−1, −3), (−2, −8)}

In 7–18, using the replacement set {0, 1, 2, 3, 4, 5, 6} for both x and y, list all the ordered pairs in the relation that is defined by the given rule.

7. $y = 2x$ **8.** $y = x + 4$ **9.** $y = 2x - 9$

10. $y = \frac{1}{2}x$ **11.** $y = \frac{1}{4}x + 2$ **12.** $x + y = 10$

13. $2x - y = 8$ **14.** $y = x^2$ **15.** $y = 2x^2$

16. $y = x^2 + 2$ **17.** $y > 4x$ **18.** $y > x^2$

In 19–28, using the set of rational numbers as the replacement set for both x and y:

a. Write an equation which describes the relation.
b. Use set notation to describe the relation.
c. Give four ordered pairs that are members of the relation.

19. y is 5 times x.

20. y is 1 more than twice x.

21. The sum of x and y is 8.

22. x decreased by y is 5.

23. Twice x increased by y is 8.

24. Three times y decreased by x is 6.

25. y is twice the square of x.

26. y is less than one-half of x.

27. y is greater than $3x + 1$.

28. y is less than $2x - 5$.

In 29–34:   (*a*) Give the domain of the relation.   (*b*) Give the range of the relation.   (*c*) Graph the relation in the Cartesian plane.   (*d*) State the rule which defines the relation.

29. $\{(0, 0), (1, 1), (2, 2), (3, 3)\}$

30. $\{(5, 10), (6, 12), (7, 14), (8, 16)\}$

31. $\{(-8, -2), (-4, -1), (0, 0), (4, 1)\}$

32. $\{(1, 0), (2, 2), (3, 4), (4, 6)\}$

33.

x	-1	0	1	2
y	5	4	3	2

34.

x	-4	-3	-2	-1
y	16	9	4	1

In 35–43, using the replacement set $\{-3, -2, -1, 0, 1, 2, 3\}$ for both x and y:

a. List the set of all the ordered pairs in the relation described by the rule.

b. State the domain of the relation.

c. State the range of the relation.

d. Graph the relation in the Cartesian plane.

35. $y = x$ **36.** $y = 3x$ **37.** $y = \frac{1}{2}x$

38. $y = 3x - 2$ **39.** $x + y = 3$ **40.** $x - y = 2$

41. $y = -x$ **42.** $y = x^2$ **43.** $y = |x|$

In 44–52, using the set of real numbers as the replacement sets for both x and y, graph the relation in the Cartesian plane.

44. $\{(x, y) \mid y = x\}$ **45.** $\{(x, y) \mid y = 3x\}$

46. $\{(x, y) \mid y = \frac{1}{2}x\}$ **47.** $\{(x, y) \mid y = 3x - 2\}$

48. $\{(x, y) \mid x + y = 3\}$ **49.** $\{(x, y) \mid x - y = 2\}$

50. $\{(x, y) \mid y = -x\}$ **51.** $\{(x, y) \mid y = x^2\}$

52. $\{(x, y) \mid y = |x|\}$

In 53–56:   (*a*) Write a formula which describes the relation.   (*b*) State whether a point graph or a portion of a line (a line graph) is more appropriate to represent the relation.

53. The number of days, D, in a number of weeks, W, is 7 times W. ($W \geq 1$)

54. At a rate of 40 mph, the distance traveled, D, is 40 times the number of hours traveled, T. ($T \geq 1$)

55. If shirts cost $5 each, the cost, C, of a number of shirts, N, is 5 times N. ($N \geq 1$)

56. The area of a rectangle, A, whose height measures 10 in. and whose base measures b in. is equal to 10 times b sq. in. ($b \geq 1$)

2. Understanding Cartesian Sets

Consider the set $A = \{1, 2\}$ and the set $B = \{1, 2, 3\}$. Using the members of these two sets, let us form in the following way a third set consisting of ordered number pairs: The first number of each ordered pair is an element of set A and the second number is an element of set B. The members of this set are:

$$
\begin{array}{ll}
(1, 1) & (2, 1) \\
(1, 2) & (2, 2) \\
(1, 3) & (2, 3)
\end{array}
$$

This third set $\{(1, 1), (1, 2), (1, 3), (2, 1), (2, 2), (2, 3)\}$ is called the **Cartesian set** of A and B. The set is also called the **Cartesian product** of A and B, written $A \times B$ and read "A cross B." Using the brace set notation, we can define the Cartesian set of set A and set B as follows:

$$A \times B = \{(x, y) \mid x \in A \text{ and } y \in B\}$$

Since $A \times B$ is a set of ordered number pairs, it is an example of a relation. The graph of the relation $A \times B$ is the graph of the number pairs (x, y), with x belonging to A and y belonging to B. The figure, a **lattice of points,** shows the graph of $A \times B$ where $A = \{1, 2\}$ and $B = \{1, 2, 3\}$. Notice that the x-values are 1 and 2, the members of set A; the y-values are 1, 2, and 3, the members of set B.

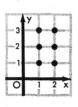

Consider the set of natural numbers less than 4, $U = \{1, 2, 3\}$. Let us form all ordered pairs of numbers which are members of U. They are:

$$
\begin{array}{lll}
(1, 1) & (2, 1) & (3, 1) \\
(1, 2) & (2, 2) & (3, 2) \\
(1, 3) & (2, 3) & (3, 3)
\end{array}
$$

The set whose members are the ordered number pairs we have listed is called the **Cartesian set of U,** written $U \times U$ and read "U cross U." The graph of the relation $U \times U$, as is shown, is the graph of the number pairs (x, y), with x belonging to U ($x \in U$) and y belonging to U ($y \in U$). Notice that the x-values are 1, 2, and 3, the members of set U; the y-values are 1, 2, and 3, the members of set U.

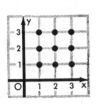

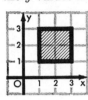

Suppose that the universal set U is the set of all real numbers from 1 to 3, including 1 and 3. Then the Cartesian set of U, the set $U \times U$, has an infinite number of ordered pairs, with the first and second member of each ordered pair belonging to the universal set U. The graph of the relation $U \times U$, as shown, is the graph of all ordered number pairs (x, y) for which x and y are such that $1 \leq x \leq 3$ and $1 \leq y \leq 3$.

MODEL PROBLEM

If $A = \{-2, -1\}$ and $B = \{1, 2, 3\}$, (a) list the members of $A \times B$ and (b) graph the set $A \times B$.

Solution:

(a) $\{(-2, 1), (-1, 1), (-2, 2), (-1, 2), (-2, 3), (-1, 3)\}$

(b) The graph of $A \times B$ is the graph of the ordered pairs listed in answer to part a. Notice that the x-values are -2 and -1, the members of set A; the y-values are 1, 2, and 3, the members of set B.

Exercises

In 1–6:   (a) List the members of the Cartesian set of the two given sets. (b) Graph the Cartesian set as a lattice of points.

1. $A = \{1, 2\}, B = \{2, 3, 4\}$
2. $A = \{1, 2, 3\}, B = \{1, 3\}$
3. $A = \{2, 4, 6\}, B = \{3, 5\}$
4. $A = \{2, 5\}, B = \{2, 3, 6\}$
5. $A = \{3, 5, 7\}, B = \{-3, -2\}$
6. $A = \{-1, 3\}, B = \{2, 3, 6, 8\}$

In 7–11:   (a) List the members of the Cartesian set of the given set U. (b) Graph the Cartesian set of U.

   7. $U = \{1\}$ **8.** $U = \{1, 2\}$ **9.** $U = \{1, 2, 3, 4\}$
10. $U = \{1, 2, 3, 4, 5\}$ **11.** $U = \{1, 2, 3, 4, 5, 6\}$

In 12–18, graph the Cartesian set of U where U is the set of:
12. natural numbers greater than 2 and less than 5
13. integers greater than -2 and less than 4
14. integers greater than or equal to 2 and less than or equal to 6
15. integers greater than or equal to -1 and less than 3
16. real numbers greater than or equal to 1 and less than or equal to 6
17. real numbers greater than or equal to -2 and less than 2
18. real numbers greater than -3 and less than 3

19. If $A = \{1, 3\}$ and $B = \{2, 4\}$:   (a) Find $A \times B$.   (b) Find $B \times A$. (c) Is the set $A \times B$ the same as the set $B \times A$?

20. If set A has x members and set B has y members, represent the number of members in the set (a) $A \times B$ and (b) $B \times A$.

21. If the universal set U has r members, represent the number of members in the Cartesian set of U.

22. If $A = \{1, 3, 5\}$ and $B = \{2, 4, 6\}$:

   a. Write the members of the set $A \times B$.
   b. How many ordered pairs which are members of $A \times B$ have 1 as the first member?
   c. How many ordered pairs in the set $A \times B$ have 7 as the sum of the two numbers of the pair?
   d. How many ordered pairs in the set $A \times B$ have a second number which is twice their first number?
   e. How many of the ordered pairs in the set $A \times B$ have a second number which is 1 more than their first number?
   f. How many of the ordered pairs in the set $A \times B$ have the sum of their two numbers greater than 5?

3. Understanding the Meaning of a Function

There is an important difference between the following two relations:

$$A = \{(-2, 2), (-1, 1), (0, 0), (1, 1), (2, 2)\}$$
$$B = \{(0, 0), (1, 1), (1, -1), (2, 2), (2, -2)\}$$

In relation A, observe that every member of the domain $\{-2, -1, 0, 1, 2\}$ is paired with one and only one member of the range $\{0, 1, 2\}$. For example, the member of the domain, -2, is paired with a unique member of the range, 2.

In relation B, however, some members of the domain $\{0, 1, 2\}$ are paired with two members of the range $\{-2, -1, 0, 1, 2\}$. For example, the member of the domain, 1, is paired with two members of the range, 1 and -1.

A relation such as set A is called a *function.*

A function is a relation (a set of ordered pairs) in which every member of the domain is paired with one and only one member of the range.

A relation such as set B is not a function. Thus, a function is a special kind of relation. Every function is a relation; however, not every relation is a function.

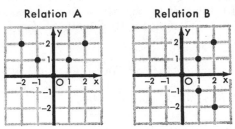

The graph of a relation can help us to determine whether or not that relation is a function.

The graphs of relation A and relation B are shown. The first elements of the ordered pairs are associated with the horizontal axis, or x-axis; the second elements are associated with the vertical axis, or y-axis.

In the graph of relation A, notice that no vertical line passes through more than one point which is the graph of an ordered pair of the relation. That is, to every x-value there corresponds one and only one y-value. Therefore, relation A is a function. From the graph, we see that the domain of this function is $\{-2, -1, 0, 1, 2\}$ and the range is $\{0, 1, 2\}$.

On the other hand, in the graph of relation B, notice that on the vertical line $x = 1$ there are two points which are graphs of ordered pairs of the relation. That is, to the x-value 1 there correspond two y-values, 1 and -1. Similarly, for the x-value 2 there correspond two y-values, 2 and -2. Therefore, relation B is not a function. From the graph we see that the domain of this relation is $\{0, 1, 2\}$ and the range is $\{-2, -1, 0, 1, 2\}$.

In our study of the graphs of relation A and relation B, we used the **vertical line test** for a function. If no vertical line intersects the graph of a relation in more than one point, the relation is a function. If a vertical line does intersect the graph of a relation in more than one point, the relation is not a function.

---------------------- **MODEL PROBLEMS** ----------------------

1. Determine whether the given relation is a function:
   a. $\{(-1, 4), (2, 4), (3, 4), (4, 4)\}$
   b. $\{(2, -1), (2, 0), (2, 1), (2, 2)\}$

   Solution:

   a. The first number of every ordered pair in the relation is associated with a unique second number. Therefore, the relation is a function.
   b. In the ordered pair $(2, -1)$, the first number, 2, is associated with the second number, -1. In the ordered pair $(2, 0)$, the first number, 2, is associated with the second number, 0. In these two ordered pairs, the first number, 2, is associated with different second numbers. Therefore, the relation is not a function.

2. a. Graph the relation defined by the rule $y = 2x - 3$, or by $\{(x, y) \mid y = 2x - 3\}$ if $1 \leq x \leq 4$ and y is a real number.
   b. Tell whether the relation is a function.
   c. State the domain of the relation.
   d. State the range of the relation.

   Solution:

   a. Graph the relation as shown. The endpoints $(1, -1)$ and $(4, 5)$ are part of the graph.
   b. By the vertical line test, we see that the relation is a function.
   c. The domain of the function is the set of x-values such that $1 \leq x \leq 4$, or $\{x \mid 1 \leq x \leq 4\}$.
   d. The range of the function is the set of y-values such that $-1 \leq y \leq 5$, or $\{y \mid -1 \leq y \leq 5\}$.

   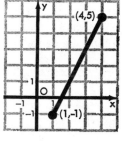

3. For the relation whose graph is shown:
   a. State the domain of the relation.
   b. State the range of the relation.
   c. Tell whether the relation is a function.

   Solution:

   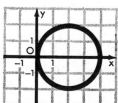

   a. The domain of the relation is the set of x-values such that $0 \leq x \leq 4$, or $\{x \mid 0 \leq x \leq 4\}$.
   b. The range of the relation is the set of y-values such that $-2 \leq y \leq 2$, or $\{y \mid -2 \leq y \leq 2\}$.

c. By the vertical line test, we see that every x-value, other than $x = 0$ and $x = 4$, is paired with two different y-values. Therefore, the relation is not a function.

~~~~~~

Exercises

In 1–8, state whether the relation is a function. Give the reason for your answer.

1. $\{(1, 3), (2, 6), (3, 9), (4, 12)\}$

2. $\{(4, 9), (5, 11), (6, 13), (7, 15)\}$

3. $\{(\frac{1}{4}, \frac{1}{2}), (\frac{1}{4}, -\frac{1}{2}), (49, 7), (49, -7)\}$

4. $\{(2, 5), (3, 10), (4, 17), (5, 26)\}$

5. $\{(-1, 3), (-2, 4), (-1, 2), (-2, 5)\}$

6. $\{(2, 1), (1, 2), (3, 4), (4, 3)\}$

7. $\{(2, 5), (3, 5), (4, 5), (5, 5)\}$

8. $\{(5, 2), (5, 3), (5, 4), (5, 5)\}$

In 9–20, x and y are members of the set of real numbers. (*a*) Graph the relation described by the rule. (*b*) From the graph, determine whether the relation is a function.

9. $y = 2x$, or $\{(x, y) \mid y = 2x\}$ **10.** $y = x + 2$, or $\{(x, y) \mid y = x + 2\}$

11. $y > 2x$, or $\{(x, y) \mid y > 2x\}$ **12.** $y < 2x$, or $\{(x, y) \mid y < 2x\}$

13. $x = -y$, or $\{(x, y) \mid x = -y\}$ **14.** $y > -x$, or $\{(x, y) \mid y > -x\}$

15. $x = 3$, or $\{(x, y) \mid x = 3\}$ **16.** $y = 3$, or $\{(x, y) \mid y = 3\}$

17. $y = 2x^2$, or $\{(x, y) \mid y = 2x^2\}$ **18.** $x = 2y^2$, or $\{(x, y) \mid x = 2y^2\}$

19. $y = |x|$, or $\{(x, y) \mid y = |x|\}$ **20.** $x = |y|$, or $\{(x, y) \mid x = |y|\}$

In 21–24, use a graph to determine the answer to the question. The variables are members of the set of real numbers.

21. Is the set of ordered pairs (s, p), each of whose members makes the sentence $p = 3s$ a true sentence, a function?

22. Is the set of ordered pairs (t, d), each of whose members makes the sentence $d = 40t$ a true sentence, a function?

23. Is the set of ordered pairs (x, y), each of whose members makes the sentence $y = -4$ a true sentence, a function?

24. Is the set of ordered pairs (x, y), each of whose members makes the sentence $x = -4$ a true sentence, a function?

In 25–32, x and y are members of the set of real numbers. In each exercise:

a. Graph the relation described by the rule.

b. State whether the relation is a function.

c. State the domain of the relation.

d. State the range of the relation.

25. $y = x$, or $\{(x, y) \mid y = x\}$ when x is $-3 \le x \le 3$.

26. $y = \frac{1}{2}x$, or $\{(x, y) \mid y = \frac{1}{2}x\}$ when x is $-2 < x \le 4$.

27. $y = 3x + 1$, or $\{(x, y) \mid y = 3x + 1\}$ when x is $-1 < x \le 2$.

28. $y = 3$, or $\{(x, y) \mid y = 3\}$ when the replacement set for x is $\{x \mid x \ge 0\}$.

29. $\{(x, y) \mid x = 2\}$ when the replacement set for x is $\{x \mid x = 2\}$.

30. $y = |x|$, or $\{(x, y) \mid y = |x|\}$ when the replacement set for x is $\{x \mid -4 \le x \le 4\}$.

31. $x = |y|$, or $\{(x, y) \mid x = |y|\}$ when the replacement set for x is $\{x \mid -3 \le x \le 3\}$.

32. $x = y^2$, or $\{(x, y) \mid x = y^2\}$ when the replacement set for x is $\{x \mid 0 \le x \le 9\}$.

In 33–47, each figure is the graph of a relation. The first and second elements of each ordered pair of the relation are members of the set of real numbers. In each exercise:

a. State the domain of the relation.

b. State the range of the relation.

c. Tell whether the relation is a function.

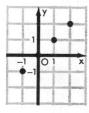

33.

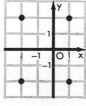

34.

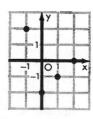

35.

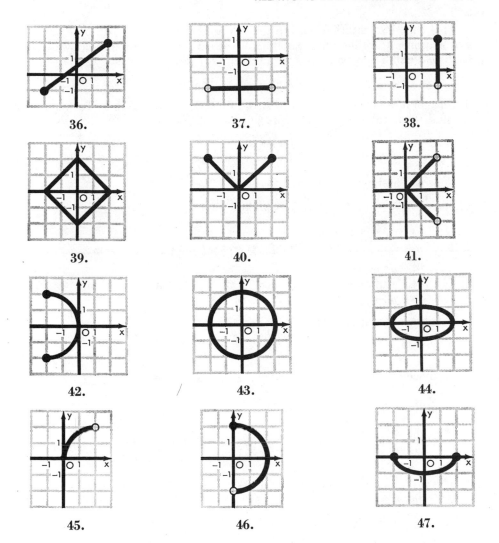

36.   37.   38.

39.   40.   41.

42.   43.   44.

45.   46.   47.

4. Understanding Function Notation

A function may be represented by a letter such as f or g. If f represents a given function and if x is a number in the domain of definition of the function, then we shall designate the number which f assigns to x as $f(x)$, read "f of x." Be careful to note that $f(x)$ *does not* mean f times x. The number $f(x)$ is called the value of f at x.

This function notation can be used to describe the pairings of numbers. For example, the function f which is described by the word statement "with each real number x, pair the real number $4x$," can be written:

$$f(x) = 4x \text{ for each real number } x$$

Then $f(1)$ means the number which the function f pairs with 1. To find $f(1)$, we find the number which $4x$ represents when x is replaced by 1. Thus:

$$f(x) = 4x$$
$$f(1) = 4(1) = 4$$

That is, f assigns to 1 the number 4.

Likewise $f(0) = 4(0)$, or $f(0) = 0$. And $f(\frac{1}{4}) = 4(\frac{1}{4})$, or $f(\frac{1}{4}) = 1$.

~~~~~~~~~~~ **MODEL PROBLEMS** ~~~~~~~~~~~

1. If g is the function defined by $g(x) = 5x + 3$ for each real number x, find:
  (a) $g(-1)$ (b) $g(|-1|)$ (c) $g(2b)$ (d) $g(r + 5)$

Solution: It is given that $g(x) = 5x + 3$ for each real number x.

a. $g(-1) = 5(-1) + 3 = -5 + 3 = -2$

$$g(-1) = -2 \quad Ans.$$

b. Since $|-1| = 1$, $g(|-1|) = 5(1) + 3 = 5 + 3 = 8$

$$g(|-1|) = 8 \quad Ans.$$

c. $g(2b) = 5(2b) + 3 = 10b + 3$

$$g(2b) = 10b + 3 \quad Ans.$$

d. $g(r + 5) = 5(r + 5) + 3 = 5r + 25 + 3 = 5r + 28$

$$g(r + 5) = 5r + 28 \quad Ans.$$

2. If h is the function defined by $h(x) = x^2 - 2$ for each real number x, find:
  (a) $h(2)$ (b) $h(-\frac{1}{2})$ (c) $h(0)$ (d) $h(b - 1)$

Solution: It is given that $h(x) = x^2 - 2$.

a. $h(2) = (2)^2 - 2 = 4 - 2 = 2$

$$h(2) = 2 \quad Ans.$$

b. $h(-\frac{1}{2}) = (-\frac{1}{2})^2 - 2 = \frac{1}{4} - 2 = -1\frac{3}{4}$

$$h(-\frac{1}{2}) = -1\frac{3}{4} \quad Ans.$$

c. $h(0) = (0)^2 - 2 = 0 - 2 = -2$

$$h(0) = -2 \quad Ans.$$

d. $h(b - 1) = (b - 1)^2 - 2 = b^2 - 2b + 1 - 2 = b^2 - 2b - 1$

$$h(b - 1) = b^2 - 2b - 1 \quad Ans.$$

3. If f is the function defined by $f(x) = 2x + 3$ for each real number x, find the solution set of $f(x) = 9$.

Solution: To find the solution set of $f(x) = 9$, we must find the number(s) which can replace x in the open phrase $2x + 3$ and give the result 9. That is, we must find the solution set of the open sentence $2x + 3 = 9$.

$$Check$$

$$
\begin{array}{ll}
2x + 3 = 9 & f(x) = 2x + 3 \\
2x = 6 & f(3) = 2(3) + 3 \\
x = 3 & f(3) = 9 \quad \text{(true)}
\end{array}
$$

Answer: Solution set is $\{3\}$.

Exercises

In 1–12, the variable is a member of the set of real numbers. For the function defined, compute the value at -2, -1, 0, 1, 2, $|-3|$, $\frac{1}{3}$, $\frac{3}{2}$, $\sqrt{3}$.

1. $f(x) = 5x$ **2.** $f(y) = 3y - 1$

3. $f(z) = -z + 2$ **4.** $g(x) = x^2$

5. $h(x) = x^2 - 2x$ **6.** $F(m) = 2m^2 - 4m + 3$

7. $s(x) = -4x^2$ **8.** $f(r) = -r^2 + 8$

9. $t(a) = a^3 + 2a^2 - 5$ **10.** $f(x) = |x|$

11. $g(y) = y^2 - |y|$ **12.** $h(x) = x^2 + x - |x|$

13. For the function f defined by $f(x) = x^2 - 2x + 4$ for each real number x, find:

   a. $f(5)$ *b.* $f(1)$ *c.* $f(\frac{3}{5})$ *d.* $f(0)$

   e. $f(-2)$ *f.* $f(|-4|)$ *g.* $f(\sqrt{2})$ *h.* $2[f(3)]$

   i. $f(b)$ *j.* $f(3a)$ *k.* $f(b + 3)$ *l.* $f(2b - 1)$

14. For the function F defined by $F(x) = x^2 - 2x$ for each x such that $-4 < x < 4$, find the real number represented by:

   a. $F(2)$ *b.* $F(\frac{2}{3})$ *c.* $F(-3)$ *d.* $F(-\frac{1}{2})$

   e. $-[F(-1)]$ *f.* $F(-2) + 3$ *g.* $-[F(|-2|)]$ *h.* $2[F(1)]$

   i. $F(r)$ for any real number r such that $-4 < r < 4$

   j. $F(s - 2)$ for any real number s such that $-2 < s < 6$

   k. $F(m + 1)$ for any real number m such that $-5 < m < 3$

15. If f is the function defined by $f(x) = 3x - 1$ for each real number x, find the solution set of each of the following sentences:

a. $f(x) = 2$	*b.* $f(x) = -4$	*c.* $f(x) = 8$
d. $f(x) = -10$	*e.* $f(x) = 0$	*f.* $f(x) = \frac{1}{2}$
g. $f(x) = -7$	*h.* $f(x) = |-20|$	*i.* $f(x) = 2x$
j. $f(x) > 2$	*k.* $f(x) > -4$	*l.* $f(x) \geq 0$

16. If f is the function defined by $f(x) = x^2 + 2x$ for each real number x, find the solution set of each of the following sentences:

a. $f(x) = 3$ *b.* $f(x) = 8$ *c.* $f(x) = 15$ *d.* $f(x) = 0$ *e.* $f(x) = -1$

5. Graphs of Linear Functions

We have learned that a function may be represented by means of a graph. The graph of the function defined by "$f(x) = x + 1$ for each real number x" is the graph of the solution set of the equation $y = x + 1$ where y equals $f(x)$. Since $y = x + 1$ is of the form $y = Ax + B$, it is a linear equation whose graph is a straight line as shown in figure 1. Observe that the graph is endless, since the function is defined for the entire set of real numbers.

Figure 1

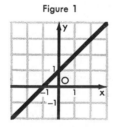

Figure 2

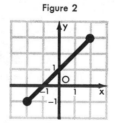

Figure 3

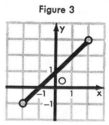

In figure 2, we see the graph of the function defined by "$f(x) = x + 1$ for all x such that $-2 \leq x \leq 2$." Observe that this graph, which is the graph of $y = x + 1$ where $-2 \leq x \leq 2$, differs from the graph in figure 1 in that it is not endless. The graph is a line segment whose endpoints are the points $(-2, -1)$ and $(2, 3)$.

In figure 3, we see the graph of the function defined by "$f(x) = x + 1$ for all x such that $-2 < x < 2$." Observe that this graph, which is the graph of $y = x + 1$ where $-2 < x < 2$, differs from the graph in figure 2 in that the points $(-2, -1)$ and $(2, 3)$ are not included in the graph.

The three functions which we have just discussed are three different functions because their domains of definition are different. However, all of these functions are linear.

A function whose graph is a straight line or part of a straight line is called a *linear function*.

We must be careful not to make the mistake of thinking that every straight line in a Cartesian plane can be considered as the graph of some linear function. The equation of the line whose graph is shown at the right is $x = 3$, and we have learned that such a line does not represent a function. However, it is true that the graphs of all straight lines except those which are described by an equation of the form $x = c$ (for each real number c) are graphs of linear functions.

A linear function f can be defined by $f(x) = Ax + B$ where A and B are real numbers and $A \neq 0$.

Exercises

1. $f(x) = Ax + B$ for each real number x. Draw the graph of $f(x)$ when:

    a. $A = 2, B = 1$ *b.* $A = 1, B = -2$ *c.* $A = \frac{1}{2}, B = 0$

    d. $A = -3, B = 2$ *e.* $A = -1, B = -1$ *f.* $A = \dfrac{-3}{4}, B = 0$

    g. $A = 4, B = 0$ *h.* $A = 0, B = -3$ *i.* $A = 0, B = 0$

2. If f is a linear function such that $f(x) = Ax + B$ for every x in the domain of definition of f:

    a. Determine A and B so that the graph of f, when $x \in \{\text{real numbers}\}$, is the line passing through the points $(1, 3)$ and $(4, 6)$.

    b. State the domain of definition of the function in part *a*.

    c. Determine A and B so that the graph of f, when $x \in \{\text{real numbers}\}$, is the line segment joining the points $(1, 3)$ and $(4, 6)$, and including these points.

    d. State the domain of definition of the function in part *c*.

    e. Determine A and B so that the graph of f, when $x \in \{\text{real numbers}\}$, is the line segment joining the points $(1, 3)$ and $(4, 6)$, but excluding these endpoints.

    f. State the domain of definition of the function in part *e*.

3. If f is a function such that $f(x) = Ax + B$ for every x in the domain of definition of f:

    a. Determine A and B so that the graph of f, when $x \in \{\text{real numbers}\}$, is the line segment joining the points $(-2, 5)$ and $(3, -5)$ and:

        (1) including $(-2, 5)$ and $(3, -5)$

        (2) not including $(-2, 5)$ and $(3, -5)$

        (3) including $(-2, 5)$ and not including $(3, -5)$

        (4) not including $(-2, 5)$ and including $(3, -5)$

    b. State the domain of the function in each of the 4 cases in part *a*.

4. A line L passes through $(-3, -3)$ and $(2, 7)$.

   a. Draw the graph of line L.

   b. Describe the function whose graph consists of the points (x, y) of L such that:

   (1) $-3 \le y \le 7$ (2) $-3 \le y \le 3$ (3) $3 < y < 7$ (4) $-3 < y < 7$

In 5–12, x is a member of the set of real numbers. Tell whether the expression describes a linear function.

5. $x - 4$ **6.** $-(x - 4)$ **7.** $|x - 4|$ **8.** $-|x - 4|$

9. $\dfrac{x - 4}{1}$ **10.** $\dfrac{1}{x - 4}$ **11.** $|x| - 4$ **12.** $x^2 - 4$

13. If f is a function defined by $f(x) = x + 2$ for each real number x and if g is a function defined by $g(x) = 2x - 5$ for each real number x:

   a. Represent $f(x) + g(x)$.

   b. Find: (1) $f(-2) + g(-2)$ (2) $f(0) + g(0)$ (3) $f(2) + g(2)$

   c. Draw the graph of $f(x) + g(x)$ for each real number x.

   d. Draw the graph of $f(x) + g(x)$ for each x such that $-2 \le x \le 2$.

   e. Find the solution set of each sentence:

   (1) $f(x) + g(x) = 0$ (2) $f(x) + g(x) = 12$ (3) $f(x) + g(x) = -9$

6. Graphs of Quadratic Functions

A *quadratic function f* can be defined by $f(x) = Ax^2 + Bx + C$ where A, B, C are real numbers and $A \ne 0$.

If $A = 0$, the function is not a quadratic function. In this unit, we shall assume that $A \ne 0$.

Each of the following examples defines a quadratic function:

$$f(x) = 3x^2 \qquad g(y) = y^2 - 2y \qquad h(t) = t^2 + 2t - 15$$

If f is the function defined by $f(x) = 3x^2$ for each real number x, then let us calculate a few values of $f(x)$:

$$f(-2) = 3(-2)^2 = 12$$
$$f(-1) = 3(-1)^2 = 3$$
$$f(0) = 3(0)^2 = 0$$
$$f(1) = 3(1)^2 = 3$$
$$f(2) = 3(2)^2 = 12$$

Now let us graph the quadratic function defined by $f(x) = 3x^2$ for each integral value of x such that $-2 \le x \le 2$. We do this by graphing the solution set of the equation $y = 3x^2$. When we replace x by each of the elements of the domain, -2, -1, 0, 1, 2 (as we did previously), we find that the solution set consists of the ordered pairs $(-2, 12)$, $(-1, 3)$, $(0, 0)$, $(1, 3)$, $(2, 12)$. The set of points which represents the graphs of these ordered pairs is the graph of the given function, as shown in figure 1.

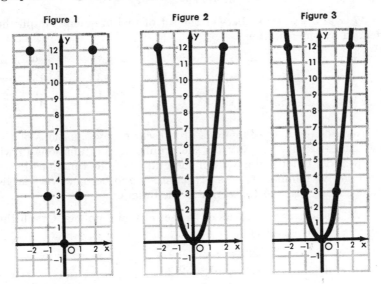

Figure 1   Figure 2   Figure 3

The graph of the quadratic function defined by $f(x) = 3x^2$ for each real number x such that $-2 \leq x \leq 2$ is the graph of an infinite set of ordered pairs (x, y) such that $y = 3x^2$ and $-2 \leq x \leq 2$. These points lie on a curved line, as shown in the graph in figure 2. Notice that the endpoints $(-2, 12)$ and $(2, 12)$ are included in the graph.

The graph of the quadratic function defined by $f(x) = 3x^2$ for each real number x is the graph of an infinite set of ordered pairs (x, y) such that $y = 3x^2$ for each real number x. The graph is shown in figure 3. Notice that the graph is an endless curve that continues to rise both at the right and at the left. This type of curve is called a **parabola**.

Exercises

1. For the quadratic function g defined by $g(t) = 2t^2 + 3t - 4$ for each real number t, find:

   a. $g(-2)$ b. $g(0)$ c. $g(3)$ d. $g(1.5)$ e. $g(\frac{3}{4})$
   f. $g(2)$ g. $g(r)$ h. $g(4s)$ i. $g(a + 1)$ j. $g(2a - 1)$
   k. $g(a^2)$ l. $g(2a)$ m. $2[g(a)]$ n. $g(a) + 2$ o. $g(a + 2)$

In 2–5, the domain of the function is the set of integers such that $-3 \le x \le 3$. Graph the function f which is defined by:

2. $f(x) = 2x^2$ **3.** $f(x) = x^2 - 2$

4. $f(x) = x^2 - 2x$ **5.** $f(x) = x^2 - 2x + 1$

In 6–17, x and y are members of the set of real numbers. Graph the function defined by the equation.

6. $y = x^2$ **7.** $y = 2x^2$ **8.** $y = 3x^2$ **9.** $y = 4x^2$

10. $y = -x^2$ **11.** $y = -2x^2$ **12.** $y = -3x^2$ **13.** $y = -4x^2$

14. $y = \frac{1}{2}x^2$ **15.** $y = \frac{1}{4}x^2$ **16.** $y = \frac{-1}{2}x^2$ **17.** $y = \frac{-1}{4}x^2$

18. In exercises 6–17, the functions are described by equations of the form $y = Ax^2$. (*a*) In what way do the graphs of the functions in which A is a positive number differ from the graphs of the functions in which A is a negative number? (*b*) As $|A|$ increases and becomes very large, what change takes place in the graph of the function?

In 19–23, x and y are members of the set of real numbers. Graph the function defined by the equation:

19. $y = x^2 + 2$ **20.** $y = x^2 + 1$ **21.** $y = x^2$

22. $y = x^2 - 1$ **23.** $y = x^2 - 2$

24. In exercises 19–23, the functions are described by equations of the form $y = x^2 + C$. What change takes place in the graph of the function when C changes from a positive number to zero to a negative number?

In 25–27, the domain of the function is the set of real numbers. Graph the function f defined by:

25. $f(x) = x^2 - 2x - 3$ **26.** $f(x) = x^2 + 2x - 8$ **27.** $f(x) = -x^2 - 2x + 3$

28. f is the quadratic function defined by $f(x) = 2x^2 - 4x - 6$ for each real number x. g is the quadratic function defined by $g(x) = -x^2 + 2x + 3$ for each real number x.

    a. Find the solution set of the sentence $f(x) = 0$.

    b. Draw the graph of $f(x)$.

    c. Find the solution set of the sentence $g(x) = 0$.

    d. Draw the graph of $g(x)$.

    e. Find $f(x) + g(x)$.

    f. Find $f(3) + g(3)$.

    g. Find the solution set of the sentence $f(x) + g(x) = 0$.

    h. Draw the graph of $f(x) + g(x)$.

SQUARES AND SQUARE ROOTS

No.	Square	Square Root	No.	Square	Square Root	No.	Square	Square Root
1	1	1.000	51	2,601	7.141	101	10,201	10.050
2	4	1.414	52	2,704	7.211	102	10,404	10.100
3	9	1.732	53	2,809	7.280	103	10,609	10.149
4	16	2.000	54	2,916	7.348	104	10,816	10.198
5	25	2.236	55	3,025	7.416	105	11,025	10.247
6	36	2.449	56	3,136	7.483	106	11,236	10.296
7	49	2.646	57	3,249	7.550	107	11,449	10.344
8	64	2.828	58	3,364	7.616	108	11,664	10.392
9	81	3.000	59	3,481	7.681	109	11,881	10.440
10	100	3.162	60	3,600	7.746	110	12,100	10.488
11	121	3.317	61	3,721	7.810	111	12,321	10.536
12	144	3.464	62	3,844	7.874	112	12,544	10.583
13	169	3.606	63	3,969	7.937	113	12,769	10.630
14	196	3.742	64	4,096	8.000	114	12,996	10.677
15	225	3.873	65	4,225	8.062	115	13,225	10.724
16	256	4.000	66	4,356	8.124	116	13,456	10.770
17	289	4.123	67	4,489	8.185	117	13,689	10.817
18	324	4.243	68	4,624	8.246	118	13,924	10.863
19	361	4.359	69	4,761	8.307	119	14,161	10.909
20	400	4.472	70	4,900	8.367	120	14,400	10.954
21	441	4.583	71	5,041	8.426	121	14,641	11.000
22	484	4.690	72	5,184	8.485	122	14,884	11.045
23	529	4.796	73	5,329	8.544	123	15,129	11.091
24	576	4.899	74	5,476	8.602	124	15,376	11.136
25	625	5.000	75	5,625	8.660	125	15,625	11.180
26	676	5.099	76	5,776	8.718	126	15,876	11.225
27	729	5.196	77	5,929	8.775	127	16,129	11.269
28	784	5.292	78	6,084	8.832	128	16,384	11.314
29	841	5.385	79	6,241	8.888	129	16,641	11.358
30	900	5.477	80	6,400	8.944	130	16,900	11.402
31	961	5.568	81	6,561	9.000	131	17,161	11.446
32	1,024	5.657	82	6,724	9.055	132	17,424	11.489
33	1,089	5.745	83	6,889	9.110	133	17,689	11.533
34	1,156	5.831	84	7,056	9.165	134	17,956	11.576
35	1,225	5.916	85	7,225	9.220	135	18,225	11.619
36	1,296	6.000	86	7,396	9.274	136	18,496	11.662
37	1,369	6.083	87	7,569	9.327	137	18,769	11.705
38	1,444	6.164	88	7,744	9.381	138	19,044	11.747
39	1,521	6.245	89	7,921	9.434	139	19,321	11.790
40	1,600	6.325	90	8,100	9.487	140	19,600	11.832
41	1,681	6.403	91	8,281	9.539	141	19,881	11.874
42	1,764	6.481	92	8,464	9.592	142	20,164	11.916
43	1,849	6.557	93	8,649	9.644	143	20,449	11.958
44	1,936	6.633	94	8,836	9.695	144	20,736	12.000
45	2,025	6.708	95	9,025	9.747	145	21,025	12.042
46	2,116	6.782	96	9,216	9.798	146	21,316	12.083
47	2,209	6.856	97	9,409	9.849	147	21,609	12.124
48	2,304	6.928	98	9,604	9.899	148	21,904	12.166
49	2,401	7.000	99	9,801	9.950	149	22,201	12.207
50	2,500	7.071	100	10,000	10.000	150	22,500	12.247

VALUES OF THE TRIGONOMETRIC FUNCTIONS

Angle	Sine	Cosine	Tangent	Angle	Sine	Cosine	Tangent
1°	.0175	.9998	.0175	46°	.7193	.6947	1.0355
2°	.0349	.9994	.0349	47°	.7314	.6820	1.0724
3°	.0523	.9986	.0524	48°	.7431	.6691	1.1106
4°	.0698	.9976	.0699	49°	.7547	.6561	1.1504
5°	.0872	.9962	.0875	50°	.7660	.6428	1.1918
6°	.1045	.9945	.1051	51°	.7771	.6293	1.2349
7°	.1219	.9925	.1228	52°	.7880	.6157	1.2799
8°	.1392	.9903	.1405	53°	.7986	.6018	1.3270
9°	.1564	.9877	.1584	54°	.8090	.5878	1.3764
10°	.1736	.9848	.1763	55°	.8192	.5736	1.4281
11°	.1908	.9816	.1944	56°	.8290	.5592	1.4826
12°	.2079	.9781	.2126	57°	.8387	.5446	1.5399
13°	.2250	.9744	.2309	58°	.8480	.5299	1.6003
14°	.2419	.9703	.2493	59°	.8572	.5150	1.6643
15°	.2588	.9659	.2679	60°	.8660	.5000	1.7321
16°	.2756	.9613	.2867	61°	.8746	.4848	1.8040
17°	.2924	.9563	.3057	62°	.8829	.4695	1.8807
18°	.3090	.9511	.3249	63°	.8910	.4540	1.9626
19°	.3256	.9455	.3443	64°	.8988	.4384	2.0503
20°	.3420	.9397	.3640	65°	.9063	.4226	2.1445
21°	.3584	.9336	.3839	66°	.9135	.4067	2.2460
22°	.3746	.9272	.4040	67°	.9205	.3907	2.3559
23°	.3907	.9205	.4245	68°	.9272	.3746	2.4751
24°	.4067	.9135	.4452	69°	.9336	.3584	2.6051
25°	.4226	.9063	.4663	70°	.9397	.3420	2.7475
26°	.4384	.8988	.4877	71°	.9455	.3256	2.9042
27°	.4540	.8910	.5095	72°	.9511	.3090	3.0777
28°	.4695	.8829	.5317	73°	.9563	.2924	3.2709
29°	.4848	.8746	.5543	74°	.9613	.2756	3.4874
30°	.5000	.8660	.5774	75°	.9659	.2588	3.7321
31°	.5150	.8572	.6009	76°	.9703	.2419	4.0108
32°	.5299	.8480	.6249	77°	.9744	.2250	4.3315
33°	.5446	.8387	.6494	78°	.9781	.2079	4.7046
34°	.5592	.8290	.6745	79°	.9816	.1908	5.1446
35°	.5736	.8192	.7002	80°	.9848	.1736	5.6713
36°	.5878	.8090	.7265	81°	.9877	.1564	6.3138
37°	.6018	.7986	.7536	82°	.9903	.1392	7.1154
38°	.6157	.7880	.7813	83°	.9925	.1219	8.1443
39°	.6293	.7771	.8098	84°	.9945	.1045	9.5144
40°	.6428	.7660	.8391	85°	.9962	.0872	11.4301
41°	.6561	.7547	.8693	86°	.9976	.0698	14.3007
42°	.6691	.7431	.9004	87°	.9986	.0523	19.0811
43°	.6820	.7314	.9325	88°	.9994	.0349	28.6363
44°	.6947	.7193	.9657	89°	.9998	.0175	57.2900
45°	.7071	.7071	1.0000	90°	1.0000	.0000	

INDEX

Abscissa, 362
Absolute inequality, 195
Absolute value(s), 113–114
  graph of an open sentence involving, 386
  of numbers, 113–114
  solving equations involving, 187–189
  of zero, 113
Acute angle, 519
Addition
  associative property of, 64–65, 122
  closure property of, 121
  commutative property of, 64, 122
  of fractions with different denominators, 291–294
  of fractions with same denominator, 288–289
  identity element of, 73, 122
  of like monomials, 145
  of polynomials, 155–157
  of radicals, 470–471
  of signed numbers, 118–121
  of signed numbers on a number line, 115–116
Addition property
  of equality, 85
  of inequalities, 192
  of zero, 73–74, 122
Additive
  identity, 122
  identity element, 73
  inverse, 122
Age problems, 240–243
Algebraic
  fraction, 276
  representation, 355
  solution of system of linear equations, 394–397, 399–400
  translating—language into verbal phrases, 45–48
Algebraic expression(s), 45
  evaluating, 54–58, 143
  simplifying, 164
Algorithm, approximating square root by, 461
Angle(s), 517–518
  acute, 519
  base—of isosceles triangle, 528

complementary, 521–522
corresponding—of similar triangles, 531–532
cosine of, 551–554
of depression, 541–542
of elevation, 541–542
initial side of, 518
measure of, 518–519
obtuse, 519
problems, 525–527
right, 519
sides of, 517–518
sine of, 546–549
straight, 519
sum of—of triangle, 525–526
supplementary, 521–522
tangent of, 538–544
terminal side of, 518
vertex of, 517–518
vertex—of isosceles triangle, 528
vertical, 521–522
Annual income, 234
Approximating square root
  by algorithm, 461
  by division, 456–457
  by estimation, 455–456
Area(s)
  formulas, 338–339
  problems, 248–250
  writing formulas for, 357
Arithmetic, numbers of, 4
Arm
  of isosceles triangle, 528
  of right triangle, 500
Ascending powers, 155
Associative property
  of addition, 64–65, 122
  of multiplication, 67–68
Assumption, 60
Average problems, 317–318
Axes, coordinate, 361–362
Axiom, 60

Base, 53, 223
  angle of isosceles triangle, 528
  of isosceles triangle, 528

1